NCERT EXEMPLAR
Problems - Solutions

Mathematics 11th

BEST Solution
Guaranteed •••

NCERT EXEMPLAR

Problems – Solutions

Mathematics 11th

Author

Astha Singhal
Hewanti Kushwaha

ARIHANT PRAKASHAN (Series), MEERUT

卐 **Administrative & Production Offices**

Regd. Office

'Ramchhaya' 4577/15, Agarwal Road, Darya Ganj, New Delhi -110002
Tele: 011- 47630600, 43518550

卐 **Head Office**

Kalindi, TP Nagar, Meerut (UP) - 250002
Tel: 0121-7156203, 7156204

卐 **Sales & Support Offices**

Agra, Ahmedabad, Bengaluru, Bareilly, Chennai, Delhi, Guwahati, Hyderabad, Jaipur, Jhansi, Kolkata, Lucknow, Nagpur & Pune.

卐 **PRICE** ₹275.00

卐 **PO No. :** TXT-59-T071603-6-26

Published by Arihant Publications (India) Ltd.

For further information about the books published by Arihant, log on to www.arihantbooks.com or e-mail at info@arihantbooks.com

Follow us on   

PREFACE

NCERT Exemplar Problems, published by the NCERT, are designed to provide students with a diverse range of quality questions in formats such as Short Answer Type Questions, Long Answer Type Questions and Objective Type Questions catering to varying levels of difficulty.

These problems are essential for success in school and board exams, as well as competitive exams like engineering and medical entrances. Regular practice with these problems prepares students to tackle challenging questions effectively.

This book, **NCERT Exemplar Problems-Solutions Mathematics 11th**, offers precise and detailed solutions to all the questions in the NCERT Exemplar Mathematics textbook. Each solution is complemented by explanatory notes and authentic explanations, enabling students to deepen their conceptual understanding and enhance their analytical skills.

Key features

- **Thinking Process** Provides simple steps to approach and solve the question, clearing up any confusion.
- **Concept Insight** Explains the main ideas and concepts needed to answer the questions correctly.
- **Mistake Alert!** Points out common mistakes students might make and helps them avoid these errors.

We hope this book proves to be a valuable resource, aiding students in their academic journey and leading them to great success.

Authors

CONTENTS

***Note (*)** These Chapters have been deleted from Latest NCERT.*

Chapter

01 Sets

Short Answer Type Questions

Q.1 Write the following sets in the roster form.

(i) $A = \{x : x \in R, 2x + 11 = 15\}$

(ii) $B = \{x \mid x^2 = x, x \in R\}$

(iii) $C = \{x \mid x \text{ is a positive factor of a prime number } p\}$

Thinking Process Solve the equation and get the value of x.

Ans. (i) We have, $A = \{x : x \in R, 2x + 11 = 15\}$

$\therefore \quad 2x + 11 = 15$

$\Rightarrow \quad 2x = 15 - 11$

$\Rightarrow \quad 2x = 4$

$\Rightarrow \quad x = 2$

$\therefore \quad A = \{2\}$

(ii) We have, $B = \{x \mid x^2 = x, x \in R\}$

$\therefore \quad x^2 = x$

$\Rightarrow \quad x^2 - x = 0$

$\Rightarrow \quad x(x - 1) = 0$

$\Rightarrow \quad x = 0, 1$

$\therefore \quad B = \{0, 1\}$

(iii) We have, $C = \{x \mid x$ is a positive factor of a prime number $p\}$.

Since, positive factors of a prime number are 1 and the number itself.

$\therefore \quad C = \{1, p\}$

Q.2 Write the following sets in the roster form.

(i) $D = \{t \mid t^3 = t, t \in R\}$

(ii) $E = \{w \mid \frac{w - 2}{w + 3} = 3, w \in R\}$

(iii) $F = \{x \mid x^4 - 5x^2 + 6 = 0, x \in R\}$

- **Concept Insight** Solve the given equation and get the value of respective variable.

Ans. (i) We have, $D = \{t \mid t^3 = t, t \in R\}$

$\therefore \quad t^3 = t$

$\Rightarrow \quad t^3 - t = 0 \Rightarrow t(t^2 - 1) = 0$

$\Rightarrow \quad t(t-1)(t+1)=0 \Rightarrow t=0,1,-1$

$\therefore \quad D=\{-1,0,1\}$

(ii) We have, $E=\{w \mid \dfrac{w-2}{w+3}=3,\ w \in R\}$

$$\therefore \quad \frac{w-2}{w+3}=3$$

$$\Rightarrow \quad w-2=3w+9 \Rightarrow w-3w=9+2$$

$$\Rightarrow \quad -2w=11 \Rightarrow w=\frac{-11}{2}$$

$$\therefore \quad E=\left\{\frac{-11}{2}\right\}$$

(iii) We have, $F=\{x \mid x^4-5x^2+6=0,\ x \in R\}$

$$\therefore \quad x^4-5x^2+6=0$$

$$\Rightarrow \quad x^4-3x^2-2x^2+6=0$$

$$\Rightarrow \quad x^2(x^2-3)-2(x^2-3)=0 \Rightarrow (x^2-3)(x^2-2)=0$$

$$\Rightarrow \quad x=\pm\sqrt{3}, \pm\sqrt{2}$$

$$\therefore \quad F=\{-\sqrt{3},-\sqrt{2},\sqrt{2},\sqrt{3}\}$$

Note In roster form, the order in which elements are listed in immaterial. Thus, we can also write $F=\{-\sqrt{3},\sqrt{2},-\sqrt{2},\sqrt{3}\}$.

Q.3 If $Y=\{x \mid x$ is a positive factor of the number $2^{p-1}(2^p-1)$, where 2^p-1 is a prime number$\}$. Write Y in the roster form.

Thinking Process First, write all the factors of 2^{p-1} and 2^p-1 and then get Y.

Ans. Given, $Y=\{x \mid x$ is a positive factor of the number $2^{p-1}(2^p-1)$, where 2^p-1 is a prime number$\}$.

Since, the factors of 2^{p-1} are $1, 2, 2^2, 2^3, \ldots, 2^{p-1}$ and factors of 2^p-1 are 1 and 2^p-1.

$$\therefore \quad Y=\{1,2,2^2,2^3,\ldots,2^{p-1},2^p-1,$$
$$2(2^p-1),2^2(2^p-1),\ldots,2^{p-1}(2^p-1)\}$$

Q.4 State which of the following statements are true and which are false. Justify your answer.

(i) $35 \in \{x \mid x$ has exactly four positive factors$\}$.

(ii) $128 \in \{y \mid$ the sum of all the positive factors of y is $2y\}$.

(iii) $3 \notin \{x \mid x^4-5x^3+2x^2-112x+6=0\}$.

(iv) $496 \notin \{y \mid$ the sum of all the positive factors of y is $2y\}$.

Ans. (i) Since, the factors of 35 are 1, 5, 7 and 35. So, statement (i) is true.

(ii) Since, the factors of 128 are 1, 2, 4, 8, 16, 32, 64 and 128.

$\therefore$ Sum of factors $=1+2+4+8+16+32+64+128=255 \neq 2 \times 128$

$\Rightarrow$ Sum of factors of $y \neq 2y$

So, statement (ii) is false.

(iii) We have, $x^4-5x^3+2x^2-112x+6=0$

$\therefore$ For $x=3$,

$$(3)^4 - 5(3)^3 + 2(3)^2 - 112(3) + 6 = 0$$
$$\Rightarrow \quad 81 - 135 + 18 - 336 + 6 = 0$$
$$\Rightarrow \quad -366 = 0$$

Which is not true.

Hence, statement (iii) is true.

(iv) We have, $496 = 2^4 \times 31$

So, the factors of 496 are 1, 2, 4, 8, 16, 31, 62, 124, 248 and 496.

$\therefore$ Sum of factors $= 1 + 2 + 4 + 8 + 16 + 31 + 62 + 124 + 248 + 496$

$= 992 = 2(496)$

So, $496 \in \{y \mid \text{the sum of all the positive factor of } y \text{ is } 2y\}$.

Hence, statement (iv) is false.

Q.5 If $L = \{1, 2, 3, 4\}$, $M = \{3, 4, 5, 6\}$ and $N = \{1, 3, 5\}$, then verify that $L - (M \cup N) = (L - M) \cap (L - N)$.

Ans. Given, $L = \{1, 2, 3, 4\}$, $M = \{3, 4, 5, 6\}$ and $N = \{1, 3, 5\}$

$\therefore$ $M \cup N = \{1, 3, 4, 5, 6\}$

$L - (M \cup N) = \{2\}$

Now, $L - M = \{1, 2\}$, $L - N = \{2, 4\}$

$\therefore$ $(L - M) \cap (L - N) = \{2\}$

Hence, $L - (M \cup N) = (L - M) \cap (L - N)$.

Q.6 If A and B are subsets of the universal set U, then show that

(i) $A \subset A \cup B$

(ii) $A \subset B \Leftrightarrow A \cup B = B$

(iii) $(A \cap B) \subset A$

Ans. (i) We know that, $A \cup B = \{x : x \in A \text{ or } x \in B\}$

Let $x \in A \Rightarrow x \in A \cup B$

Hence, $A \subset A \cup B$

(ii) If $A \subset B$

Let $x \in A \cup B$

$\Rightarrow$ $x \in A$ or $x \in B$

When $x \in A$, then $x \in B$ $[\because A \subset B]$

$\Rightarrow$ $x \in B$

$\therefore$ $A \cup B \subset B$ ...(i)

But $B \subset A \cup B$ ...(ii)

From Eqs. (i) and (ii), we get

$A \cup B = B$

If $A \cup B = B$

Let $y \in A$

$\Rightarrow$ $y \in A \cup B \Rightarrow y \in B$ $[\because A \cup B = B]$

$\Rightarrow$ $A \subset B$

Hence, $A \subset B \Leftrightarrow A \cup B = B$

(iii) Let $x \in A \cap B$

$\Rightarrow$ $x \in A$ and $x \in B$

$\Rightarrow$ $x \in A$

Hence, $A \cap B \subset A$

Q.7 Given that $N = \{1, 2, 3, \dots, 100\}$. Then, write

(i) the subset of N whose elements are even numbers.

(ii) the subset of N whose elements are perfect square numbers.

Ans. We have, $N = \{1, 2, 3, 4, \dots, 100\}$

(i) Required subset whose elements are even numbers $= \{2, 4, 6, 8, \dots, 100\}$

(ii) Required subset whose elements are perfect square numbers

$= \{1, 4, 9, 16, 25, 36, 49, 64, 81, 100\}$

Q.8 If $X = \{1, 2, 3\}$, if n represents any member of X, write the following sets containing all numbers represented by

(i) $4n$ (ii) $n+6$

(iii) $\frac{n}{2}$ (iv) $n-1$

Ans. Given, $X = \{1, 2, 3\}$

(i) $\{4n \mid n \in X\} = \{4, 8, 12\}$ (ii) $\{n+6 \mid n \in X\} = \{7, 8, 9\}$

(iii) $\left\{\frac{n}{2} \mid n \in X\right\} = \left\{\frac{1}{2}, 1, \frac{3}{2}\right\}$ (iv) $\{n-1 \mid n \in X\} = \{0, 1, 2\}$

Q.9 If $Y = \{1, 2, 3, \dots, 10\}$ and a represents any element of Y, write the following sets, containing all the elements satisfying the given conditions.

(i) $a \in Y$ but $a^2 \notin Y$ (ii) $a+1 = 6, a \in Y$

(iii) a is less than 6 and $a \in Y$

Ans. Given, $Y = \{1, 2, 3, \dots, 10\}$

(i) $\{a : a \in Y \text{ and } a^2 \notin Y\} = \{4, 5, 6, 7, 8, 9, 10\}$

[$\because$ For $a = 1, 2, 3$; $1^2 = 1 \in Y$, $2^2 = 4 \in Y$, $3^2 = 9 \in Y$]

(ii) $\{a : a + 1 = 6, a \in Y\} = \{5\}$

(iii) $\{a : a \text{ is less than 6 and } a \in Y\} = \{1, 2, 3, 4, 5\}$

Q.10 A, B and C are subsets of universal set U. If $A = \{2, 4, 6, 8, 12, 20\}$, $B = \{3, 6, 9, 12, 15\}$, $C = \{5, 10, 15, 20\}$ and U is the set of all whole numbers, draw a Venn diagram showing the relation of U, A, B and C.

Ans. Given, $A = \{2, 4, 6, 8, 12, 20\}$, $B = \{3, 6, 9, 12, 15\}$

$C = \{5, 10, 15, 20\}$ and U is the set of whole numbers.

Thus, $A \cap B = \{6, 12\}$, $B \cap C = \{15\}$, $C \cap A = \{20\}$ and $A \cap B \cap C = \phi$

$\therefore$ Venn diagram showing the relation of U, A, B and C is

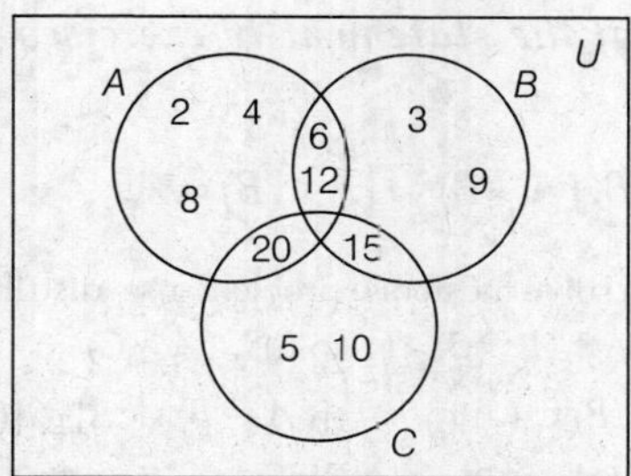

Q.11 Let U be the set of all boys and girls in a school, G be the set of all girls in the school, B be the set of all boys in the school and S be the set of all students in the school who take swimming. Some but not all, students in the school take swimming. Draw a Venn diagram showing one of the possible interrelationship among sets U, G, B and S.

Ans. Venn diagram showing the relation between sets U, G, B and S.

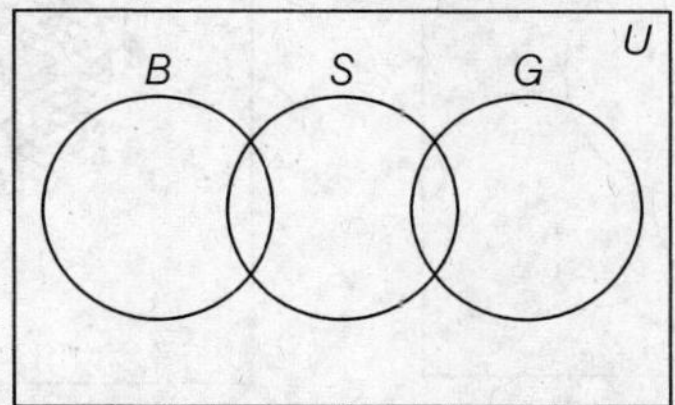

Q.12 For all sets A, B and C, show that $(A - B) \cap (A - C) = A - (B \cup C)$.

Thinking Process To prove this we have to show that $(A - B) \cap (A - C) \subseteq A - (B \cup C)$ and $A - (B \cup C) \subseteq (A - B) \cap (A - C)$.

Ans. Let $x \in (A - B) \cap (A - C)$

$\Rightarrow x \in (A - B)$ and $x \in (A - C)$

$\Rightarrow (x \in A$ and $x \notin B)$ and $(x \in A$ and $x \notin C)$

$\Rightarrow x \in A$ and $(x \notin B$ and $x \notin C)$

$\Rightarrow x \in A$ and $x \notin (B \cup C)$

$\Rightarrow x \in A - (B \cup C)$

$\Rightarrow (A - B) \cap (A - C) \subset A - (B \cup C)$ ... (i)

Now, let $y \in A - (B \cup C)$

$\Rightarrow y \in A$ and $y \notin (B \cup C)$

$\Rightarrow y \in A$ and $(y \notin B$ and $y \notin C)$

$\Rightarrow (y \in A$ and $y \notin B)$ and $(y \in A$ and $y \notin C)$

$\Rightarrow y \in (A - B)$ and $y \in (A - C)$

$\Rightarrow y \in (A - B) \cap (A - C)$

$\Rightarrow A - (B \cup C) \subset (A - B) \cap (A - C)$ ...(ii)

From Eqs. (i) and (ii),

$$A - (B \cup C) = (A - B) \cap (A - C)$$

Determine whether each of the statement in exercises 13 to 17 is True as False. Justify your answer.

Q.13 For all sets A and B, $(A-B)\cup(A\cap B)=A$.

Thinking Process To solve the above problem, use distributive law on sets

i.e., $A\cap(B\cup C)=(A\cap B)\cup(A\cap C)$.

Ans.
$$\text{LHS}=(A-B)\cup(A\cap B)=[(A-B)\cup A]\cap[(A-B)\cup B]$$
$$=A\cap(A\cup B)=A=\text{RHS}$$

Hence, given statement is true.

Q.14 For all sets A, B and C, $A-(B-C)=(A-B)-C$.

Ans. See the Venn diagrams given below, where shaded portions are representing $A-(B-C)$ and $(A-B)-C$ respectively.

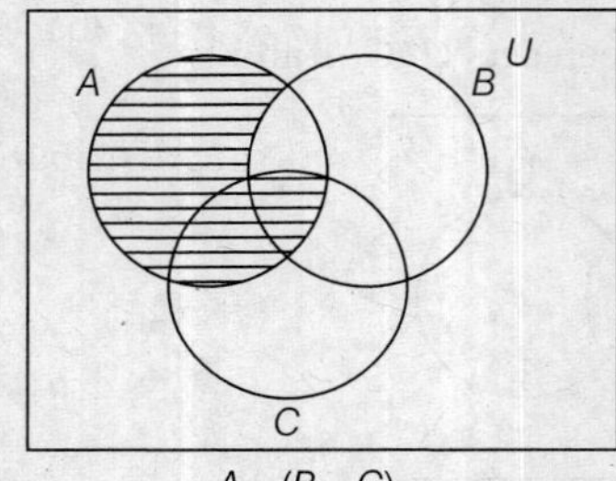

$A-(B-C)$

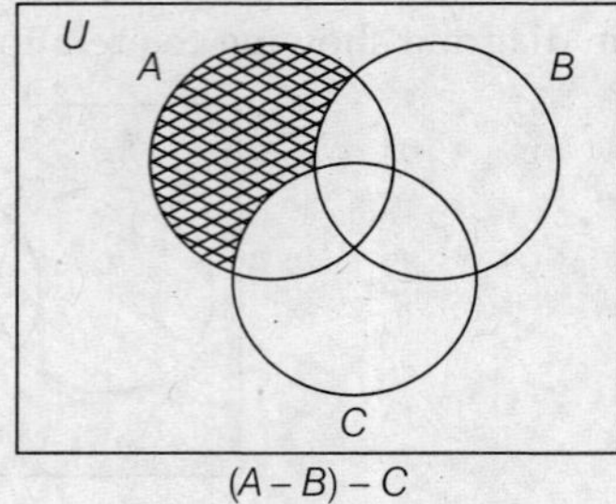

$(A-B)-C$

Clearly, $A-(B-C)\neq(A-B)-C$.

Hence, given statement is false.

Q.15 For all sets A, B and C, if $A\subset B$, then $A\cap C\subset B\cap C$.

Ans. Let $x\in A\cap C$

$\Rightarrow$ $x\in A$ and $x\in C$

$\Rightarrow$ $x\in B$ and $x\in C$ $[\because A\subset B]$

$\Rightarrow$ $x\in(B\cap C)$

$\Rightarrow$ $(A\cap C)\subset(B\cap C)$

Hence, given statement is true.

Q.16 For all sets A, B and C, if $A\subset B$, then $A\cup C\subset B\cup C$.

Ans. Let $x\in A\cup C\Rightarrow x\in A$ or $x\in C$

$\Rightarrow$ $x\in B$ or $x\in C$ $[\because A\subset B]$

$\Rightarrow$ $x\in B\cup C \Rightarrow A\cup C\subset B\cup C$

Hence, given statement is true.

Q.17 For all sets A, B and C, if $A\subset C$ and $B\subset C$, then $A\cup B\subset C$.

Ans. Let $x\in A\cup B\Rightarrow x\in A$ or $x\in B$

$\Rightarrow$ $x\in C$ or $x\in C$ $[\because A\subset C \text{ and } B\subset C]$

$\Rightarrow$ $x\in C \Rightarrow A\cup B\subset C$

Hence, given statement is true.

Using properties of sets prove the statements given in exercies 18 to 21.

Q.18 For all sets A and B, $A \cup (B - A) = A \cup B$.

Thinking Process To solve the above problem, use distributive law *i.e.*, $A \cup (B \cap C) = (A \cup B) \cap (A \cup C)$.

Ans. $\because$

$$\text{LHS} = A \cup (B - A) = A \cup (E \cap A') \quad [\because B - A = B \cap A']$$
$$= (A \cup B) \cap (A \cup A') \quad \text{[using distributive law]}$$
$$= (A \cup B) \cap U \quad [\because A \cup A' = U]$$
$$= A \cup B = \text{RHS} \quad [\because A \cap U = A]$$

Q.19 For all sets A and B, $A - (A - B) = A \cap B$.

Ans.
$$\text{LHS} = A - (A - B) = A - (A \cap B') \quad [\because A - B = A \cap B']$$
$$= A \cap (A \cap B')' = A \cap [A' \cup (B')']$$
$$[\because \text{by De-Morgan's law, } (A \cap B) = A' \cup B']$$
$$= A \cap (A' \cup B) \quad [\because (A')' = A]$$
$$= (A \cap A') \cup (A \cap B) = \phi \cup (A \cap B) \quad \text{[using distributive law]}$$
$$= A \cap B = \text{RHS}$$

Q.20 For all sets A and B, $A - (A \cap B) = A - B$.

Ans.
$$\text{LHS} = A - (A \cap B) = A \cap (A \cap B)' \quad [\because A - B = A \cap B']$$
$$= A \cap (A' \cup B') \quad [\because (A \cap B)' = A' \cup B']$$
$$= (A \cap A') \cup (A \cap B') = \phi \cup (A \cap B') \quad \text{[using distributive law]}$$
$$= A \cap B' \quad [\because \phi \cup A = A]$$
$$= A - B = \text{RHS}$$

Q.21 For all sets A and B, $(A \cup B) - B = A - B$.

Ans.
$$\text{LHS} = (A \cup B) - B = (A \cup B) \cap B' \quad [\because A - B = A \cap B']$$
$$= (A \cap B') \cup (B \cap B') = (A \cap B') \cup \phi \quad [\because B \cap B' = \phi]$$
$$= A \cap B' \quad [\because A \cup \phi = A]$$
$$= A - B = \text{RHS}$$

Q.22 Let $T = \left\{ x \mid \dfrac{x+5}{x-7} - 5 = \dfrac{4x-40}{13-x} \right\}$. Is T an empty set? Justify your answer.

Thinking Process First of all, solve the given equation and get the value of x.

Ans. We have,
$$T = \left\{ x \mid \frac{x+5}{x-7} - 5 = \frac{4x-40}{13-x} \right\}$$
$$\because \quad \frac{x+5}{x-7} - 5 = \frac{4x-40}{13-x}$$
$$\Rightarrow \quad \frac{x+5-5(x-7)}{x-7} = \frac{4x-40}{13-x}$$
$$\Rightarrow \quad \frac{x+5-5x+35}{x-7} = \frac{4x-40}{13-x}$$

$$\Rightarrow \quad \frac{-4x+40}{x-7} = \frac{4x-40}{13-x}$$

$$\Rightarrow \quad -(4x-40)(13-x) = (4x-40)(x-7)$$

$$\Rightarrow \quad (4x-40)(x-7) + (4x-40)(13-x) = 0$$

$$\Rightarrow \quad (4x-40)(x-7+13-x) = 0$$

$$\Rightarrow \quad 4(x-10)6 = 0$$

$$\Rightarrow \quad 24(x-10) = 0$$

$$\Rightarrow \quad x = 10$$

$$\therefore \quad T = \{10\}$$

Hence, T is not an empty set.

Long Answer Type Questions

Q.23 If A, B and C be sets. Then, show that $A \cap (B \cup C) = (A \cap B) \cup (A \cap C)$.

Ans. Let $x \in A \cap (B \cup C)$

$\Rightarrow \quad x \in A$ and $x \in (B \cup C)$

$\Rightarrow \quad x \in A$ and $(x \in B$ or $x \in C)$

$\Rightarrow \quad (x \in A$ and $x \in B)$ or $(x \in A$ and $x \in C)$

$\Rightarrow \quad x \in A \cap B$ or $x \in A \cap C$

i.e., $\quad x \in (A \cap B) \cup (A \cap C)$

$\therefore \quad A \cap (B \cup C) \subset (A \cap B) \cup (A \cap C)$ ...(i)

Again, let $\quad y \in (A \cap B) \cup (A \cap C)$

$\Rightarrow \quad y \in (A \cap B)$ or $y \in (A \cap C)$

$\Rightarrow \quad (y \in A$ and $y \in B)$ or $(y \in A$ and $y \in C)$

$\Rightarrow \quad y \in A$ and $(y \in B$ or $y \in C)$

$\Rightarrow \quad y \in A$ and $y \in B \cup C \Rightarrow y \in A \cap (B \cup C)$

$\Rightarrow \quad (A \cap B) \cup (A \cap C) \subset A \cap (B \cup C)$ ...(ii)

From Eqs. (i) and (ii), we get

$$A \cap (B \cup C) = (A \cap B) \cup (A \cap C)$$

***Q.24** Out of 100 students; 15 passed in English, 12 passed in Mathematics, 8 in Science, 6 in English and Mathematics, 7 in Mathematics and Science, 4 in English and Science, 4 in all the three. Find how many passed

(i) in English and Mathematics but not in Science.

(ii) in Mathematics and Science but not in English.

(iii) in Mathematics only.

(iv) in more than one subject only.

Ans. Let M be the set of students who passed in Mathematics, E be the set of students who passed in English and S be the set of students who passed in Science.

Then, $\quad n(U) = 100, n(E) = 15, n(M) = 12, n(S) = 8, n(E \cap M) = 6,$

$n(M \cap S) = 7, n(E \cap S) = 4$ and $n(E \cap M \cap S) = 4$

(*) Topics related to these question have been removed from latest NCERT.

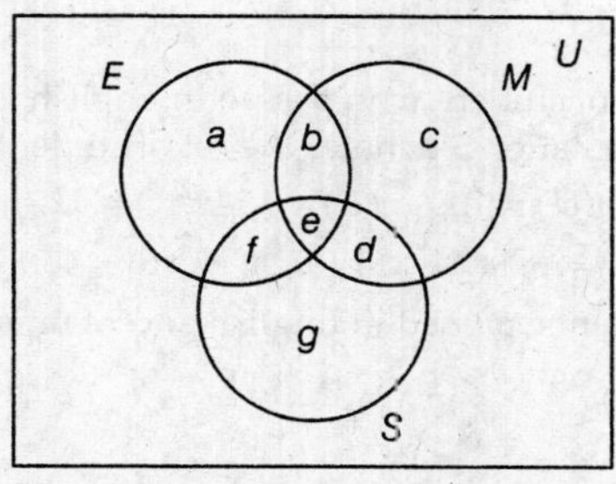

$\because \quad n(E) = 15$

$\Rightarrow \quad a + b + e + f = 15 \quad \text{...(i)}$

and $\quad n(M) = 12$

$\Rightarrow \quad b + c + e + d = 12 \quad \text{...(ii)}$

Also, $\quad n(S) = 8$

$\Rightarrow \quad d + e + f + g = 8 \quad \text{...(iii)}$

$n(E \cap M) = 6$

$\Rightarrow \quad b + e = 6 \quad \text{...(iv)}$

$n(M \cap S) = 7$

$\Rightarrow \quad e + d = 7 \quad \text{... (v)}$

$n(E \cap S) = 4$

$\Rightarrow \quad e + f = 4 \quad \text{... (vi)}$

$n(E \cap M \cap S) = 4$

$\Rightarrow \quad e = 4 \quad \text{... (vii)}$

From Eqs. (vi) and (vii), we get $f = 0$

From Eqs. (v) and (vii), we get $d = 3$

From Eqs. (iv) and (vii), we get $b = 2$

On substituting the values of d, e and f in Eq. (iii), we get

$$3 + 4 + 0 + g = 8$$

$$\Rightarrow \quad g = 1$$

On substituting the value of b, e and d in Eq. (ii), we get

$$2 + c + 4 + 3 = 12 \Rightarrow c = 3$$

On substituting b, e, and f in Eq. (i), we get

$$a + 2 + 4 + 0 = 15 \Rightarrow a = 9$$

(i) Number of students who passed in English and Mathematics but not in Science = $b = 2$

(ii) Number of students who passed in Mathematics and Science but not in English = $d = 3$

(iii) Number of students who passed in Mathematics only = $c = 3$

(iv) Number of students who passed in more than one subject

$$= b + e + d + f = 2 + 4 + 3 + 0 = 9$$

Alternate Method

Let E denotes the set of student who passed in English. M denotes the set of students who passed in Mathematics. S denotes the set of students who passed in Science.

Now, $n(U) = 100,\ n(E) = 15,\ n(m) = 12,\ n(S) = 8,$

$$n(E \cap M) = 6,\ n(M \cap S) = 7,\ n(E \cap S) = 4,\ n(E \cap M \cap S) = 4$$

(i) Number of students passed in English and Mathematics but not in Science

i.e., $n(E \cap M \cap S') = n(E \cap M) - n(E \cap M \cap S)$ $[\because A \cap B' = A - (A \cap B)]$

$= 6 - 4 = 2$

(ii) Number of students passed in Mathematics and Science but not in English.

i.e., $n(M \cap S \cap E') = n(M \cap S) - n(M \cap S \cap E) = 7 - 4 = 3$

(iii) Number of students passed in mathematics only

i.e., $n(M \cap S' \cap E') = n(M) - n(M \cap S) - n(M \cap E) + n(M \cap S \cap E)$

$= 12 - 7 - 6 + 4 = 3$

(iv) Number of students passed in more than one subject only

i.e., $n(E \cap M) + n(M \cap S) + n(E \cap S) - 3\,n(E \cap M \cap S) + n(E \cap M \cap S)$

$= 6 + 7 + 4 - (4 \times 3) + 4 = 17 - 12 + 4 = 5 + 4 = 9$

***Q.25** In a class of 60 students, 25 students play cricket and 20 students play tennis and 10 students play both the games. Find the number of students who play neither.

Thinking process To solve this problem, use the formula

$$n(A \cup B) = n(A) + n(B) - n(A \cap B)$$

Ans. Let C be the set of students who play cricket and T be the set of students who play tennis.

Then, $n(U) = 60,\ n(C) = 25,\ n(T) = 20,$ and $n(C \cap T) = 10$

$\because$ $n(C \cup T) = n(C) + n(T) - n(C \cap T)$

$\Rightarrow$ $n(C \cup T) = 25 + 20 - 10 = 35$

$\therefore$ Number of students who play neither $= n(C' \cap T') = n(U) - n(C \cup T)$

$= 60 - 35 = 25$

***Q.26** In a survey of 200 students of a school, it was found that 120 study Mathematics, 90 study Physics and 70 study Chemistry, 40 study Mathematics and Physics, 30 study Physics and Chemistry, 50 study Chemistry and Mathematics and 20 none of these subjects. Find the number of students who study all the three subjects.

Thinking Process To solve this problem, use the formula for all the three subjects

$$n(A \cup B \cup C) = n(A) + n(B) + n(C) - n(A \cap B) - n(B \cap C) - n(C \cap A) + n(A \cap B \cap C).$$

Ans. Let M be the set of students who study Mathematics, P be the set of students who study Physics and C be the set of students who study Chemistry.

Then, $n(U) = 200,\ n(M) = 120,\ n(P) = 90,$

$n(C) = 70,\ n(M \cap P) = 40,\ n(P \cap C) = 30,$

$n(C \cap M) = 50,\ n(M' \cap P' \cap C') = 20,$

$n(U) - n(M \cup P \cup C) = 20,$

(*) Topics related to these question have been removed from latest NCERT.

$$n(M \cup P \cup C) = 200 - 20 = 180$$

$$\because \quad n(M \cup P \cup C) = n(M) + n(P) + n(C) - n(M \cap P) - n(P \cap C) - n(C \cap M) + n(M \cap P \cap C)$$

$$\Rightarrow \quad 180 = 120 + 90 + 70 - 40 - 30 - 50 + n(M \cap P \cap C)$$

$$\Rightarrow \quad 180 = 160 + n(M \cap P \cap C) \Rightarrow n(M \cap P \cap C) = 180 - 160 = 20$$

So, the number of students who study all the three subjects is 20.

***Q.27** In a town of 10000 families, it was found that 40% families buy newspaper A, 20% families buy newspaper B, 10% families buy newspaper C, 5% families buy A and B, 3% buy B and C and 4% buy A and C. If 2% families buy all the three newspaper. Find

(i) the number of families which buy newspaper A only.

(ii) the number of families which buy none of A, B and C.

Ans. Let A be the set of families which buy newspaper A, B be the set of families which buy newspaper B and C be the set of families which buy newspaper C.

Then, $n(U) = 10000$, $n(A) = 40\%$ of 10000, $n(B) = 20\%$ of 10000 and $n(C) = 10\%$ of 10000

$$n(A \cap B) = 5\% \text{ of } 10000,\ n(B \cap C) = 3\% \text{ of } 10000$$

$$n(A \cap C) = 4\% \text{ of } 10000,\ n(A \cap B \cap C) = 2\% \text{ of } 10000$$

(i) Number of families which buy newspaper A only

$$= n(A) - n(A \cap B) - n(A \cap C) + n(A \cap B \cap C)$$

$$= (40 - 5 - 4 + 2)\% \text{ of } 10000 = 33\% \text{ of } 10000 = 10000 \times \frac{33}{100} = 3300$$

(ii) Number of families which buy none of A, B and C

$$= n(U) - n(A \cup B \cup C)$$

$$= n(U) - [n(A) + n(B) + n(C) - n(A \cap B) - n(B \cap C) - n(A \cap C) + n(A \cap B \cap C)]$$

$$= \{100 - [40 + 20 + 10 - 5 - 3 - 4 + 2]\}\% \text{ of } 10000$$

$$= [100\% - 60\%] \text{ of } 10000 = 40\% \text{ of } 10000 = 10000 \times \frac{40}{100} = 4000$$

***Q.28** In a group of 50 students, the number of students studying French, English, Sanskrit were found to be as follows : French = 17, English = 13, Sanskrit = 15 French and English = 09, English and Sanskrit = 4, French and Sanskrit = 5, English, French and Sanskrit = 3. Find the number of students who study

(i) only French.

(ii) only English.

(iii) only Sanskrit.

(iv) English and Sanskrit but not French.

(v) French and Sanskrit but not English.

(vi) French and English but not Sanskrit.

(vii) atleast one of the three languages.

(viii) none of the three languages.

(*) Topics related to these question have been removed from latest NCERT.

Ans. Let F be the set of students who study French, E be the set of students who study English and S be the set of students who study Sanskrit.

Then, $n(U) = 50,\ n(F) = 17,\ n(E) = 13,$ and $n(S) = 15,$

$n(F \cap E) = 9,\ n(E \cap S) = 4,\ n(F \cap S) = 5,\ n(F \cap E \cap S) = 3$

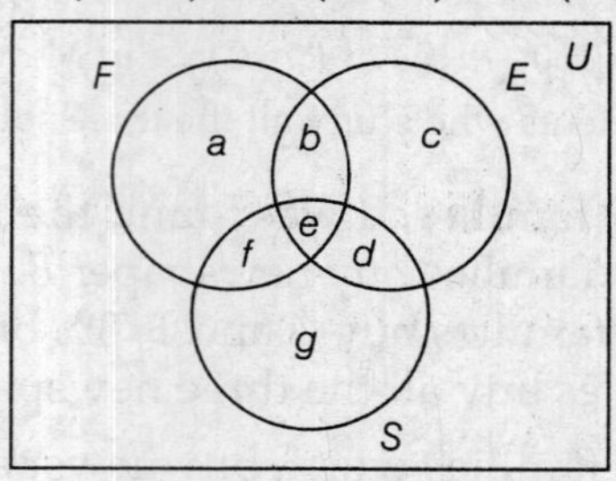

$\because \quad n(F) = 17$

$\Rightarrow \quad a + b + e + f = 17 \quad$ ...(i)

$n(E) = 13$

$\Rightarrow \quad b + c + d + e = 13 \quad$ ...(ii)

$n(S) = 15$

$\Rightarrow \quad d + e + f + g = 15 \quad$ ...(iii)

$n(F \cap E) = 9$

$\Rightarrow \quad b + e = 9 \quad$ ...(iv)

$n(E \cap S) = 4$

$\Rightarrow \quad e + d = 4 \quad$ ...(v)

$n(F \cap S) = 5$

$\Rightarrow \quad f + e = 5 \quad$ ...(vi)

$n(F \cap E \cap S) = 3$

$\Rightarrow \quad e = 3 \quad$ ...(vii)

From Eqs. (vi) and (vii), we get $\quad f = 2$

From Eqs. (v) and (vii), we get $\quad d = 1$

From Eqs. (iv) and (vii), we get $\quad b = 6$

On substituting the values of e, f and d in Eq. (iii), we get

$$1 + 3 + 2 + g = 15 \Rightarrow g = 9$$

On substituting the values of b, d and e in Eq. (ii), we get

$$6 + c + 1 + 3 = 13 \Rightarrow c = 3$$

On substituting the values of b, e and f in Eq. (i), we get

$$a + 6 + 3 + 2 = 17 \Rightarrow a = 6$$

(i) Number of students who study French only, $a = 6$

(ii) Number of students who study English only, $c = 3$

(iii) Number of students who study Sanskrit only, $g = 9$

(iv) Number of students who study English and Sanskrit but not French, $d = 1$

(v) Number of students who study French and Sanskrit but not English, $f = 2$

(vi) Number of students who study French and English but not Sanskrit, $b = 6$

(vii) Number of students who study atleast one of the three languages

$$= a + b + c + d + e + f + g$$
$$= 6 + 6 + 3 + 1 + 3 + 2 + 9 = 30$$

(viii) Number of students who study none of three languages

= Total students – Students who study atleast one of the three languages

$= 50 - 30 = 20$

Objective Type Questions

Choose the correct answers from the given four options in each exercise 29 to 43.

Q.29 Suppose, $A_1, A_2, ..., A_{30}$ are thirty sets each having 5 elements and B_1, B_2, B_n are n sets each with 3 elements, let $\bigcup_{i=1}^{30} A_i = \bigcup_{j=1}^{n} B_j = S$ and each element of S belongs to exactly 10 of the A_i's and exactly 9 of the B_j's. Then, n is equal to

(a) 15 (b) 3 (c) 45 (d) 35

Thinking Process First find the total number of elements for the both sets, then compare them.

Ans. *(c)* If elements are not repeated, then number of elements in

$$A_1 \cup A_2 \cup A_3, \dots \cup A_{30} \text{ is } 30 \times 5.$$

But each element is used 10 times, so number of elements in $S = \frac{30 \times 5}{10} = 15$

If elements in $B_1, B_2, \dots, B_n$ are not repeated, then total number of elements $B_1 \cup B_2 \dots \cup B_n$ is $3n$ but each element is repeated 9 times, so

Number of elements in $S = \frac{3n}{9}$

$\Rightarrow \quad 15 = \frac{3n}{9}$

$\therefore \quad n = 45$

***Q.30** Two finite sets have m and n elements. The number of subsets of the first set is 112 more than that of the second set. The values of m and n are, respectively

(a) 4, 7 (b) 7, 4 (c) 4, 4 (d) 7, 7

- **Concept Insight** if a set A contains n elements, then the number of subsets of A is equal to 2^n.

Ans. *(b)* Since, number of subsets of a set containing m elements is 112 more than the subsets of the set containing n elements.

$\because \quad 2^m - 2^n = 112$

$\Rightarrow \quad 2^n \cdot (2^{m-n} - 1) = 2^4 \cdot 7$

$\Rightarrow \quad 2^n = 2^4 \text{ and } 2^{m-n} - 1 = 7$

(✱) Topics related to these question have been removed from latest NCERT.

$$\Rightarrow \quad n = 4 \text{ and } 2^{m-n} = 8$$
$$\Rightarrow \quad 2^{m-n} = 2^3$$
$$\Rightarrow \quad m - n = 3$$
$$\Rightarrow \quad m - 4 = 3$$
$$\Rightarrow \quad m = 4 + 3 = 7$$
$$\therefore \quad m = 7, n = 4$$

Q.31 The set $(A \cap B')' \cup (B \cap C)$ is equal to

(a) $A' \cup B \cup C$ (b) $A' \cup B$
(c) $A' \cup C'$ (d) $A' \cap B$

Ans. ***(b)*** We know that, $(A \cap B)' = (A' \cup B')$ and $(A')' = A$

$$\therefore \quad (A \cap B')' \cup (B \cap C) = [A' \cup (B')'] \cup (B \cap C) \quad \text{[using De-Morgan's law]}$$
$$= (A' \cup B) \cup (B \cap C) \quad [\because (B')' = B]$$
$$= A' \cup (B \cup (B \cap C))$$
$$= A' \cup B$$

Mistake Alert ! *Do not forget to use De-morgan's law correctly.*

Q.32 Let F_1 be the set of parallelograms, F_2 the set of rectangles, F_3 the set of rhombuses, F_4 the set of squares and F_5 the set of trapeziums in a plane. Then, F_1 may be equal to

(a) $F_2 \cap F_3$ (b) $F_3 \cap F_4$
(c) $F_2 \cup F_5$ (d) $F_2 \cup F_3 \cup F_4 \cup F_1$

Ans. ***(d)*** Every rectangle, rhombus, square in a plane is a parallelogram but every trapezium is not a parallelogram.

So, F_1 is either of F_1, F_2, F_3 and F_4 but not F_5.

$$\therefore \quad F_1 = F_2 \cup F_3 \cup F_4 \cup F_1$$

Q.33 Let S = set of points inside the square, T = set of points inside the triangle and C = set of points inside the circle. If the triangle and circle intersect each other and are contained in a square. Then,

(a) $S \cap T \cap C = \phi$ (b) $S \cup T \cup C = C$ (c) $S \cup T \cup C = S$ (d) $S \cup T = S \cap C$

Ans. ***(c)*** The given sets can be represented in Venn diagram as shown below

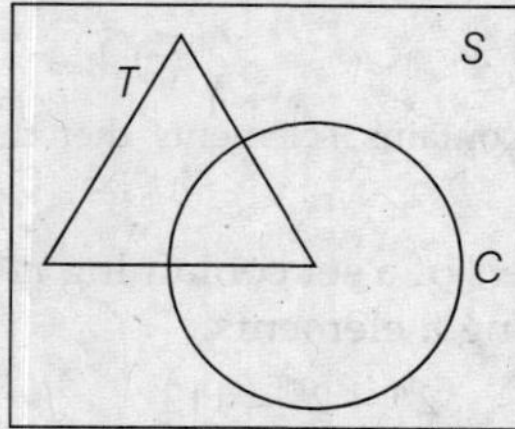

It is clear from the diagram that, $S \cup T \cup C = S$.

Mistake Alert ! *Draw the correct venn diagram carefully for the given conditions.*

Q.34 If R be the set of points inside a rectangle of sides a and $b\,(a, b > 1)$ with two sides along the positive direction of X-axis and Y-axis. Then,

(a) $R = \{(x, y) : 0 \le x \le a, 0 \le y \le b\}$ (b) $R = \{(x, y) : 0 \le x < a, 0 \le y \le b\}$
(c) $R = \{(x, y) : 0 \le x \le a, 0 < y < b\}$ (d) $R = \{(x, y) : 0 < x < a, 0 < y < b\}$

Ans. *(d)* Since, R be the set of points inside the rectangle.

So, $(0, 0)$, $(a, 0)$, $(0, b)$ and (a, b) points are excluded

$\therefore \quad R = \{(x, y) : 0 < x < a \text{ and } 0 < y < b\}$

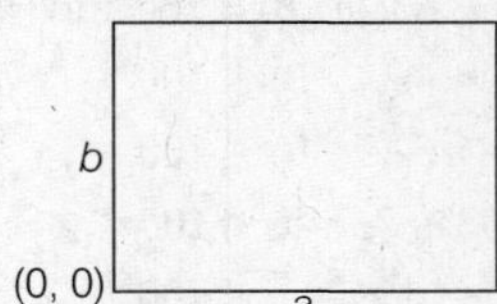

***Q.35** In a class of 60 students, 25 students play cricket 20 students play tennis, and 10 students play both the games. Then the number of students who play neither, is

(a) 0 (b) 25 (c) 35 (d) 45

Ans. *(b)* Let C be the set of students who play cricket and T be the set of students who play tennis and U represent the total students in the calss.

Then, $n(U) = 60,\ n(C) = 25,\ n(T) = 20,\ n(C \cap T) = 10$

Number of students who play neither $= n(C' \cap T')$

$= n(C \cup T)'$ $\quad [\because (A \cup B)' = A' \cup B']$

$= n(U) - [n(C) + n\,CT - n(C \cap T)]$

$= 60 - (25 + 20 - 10) = 60 - 35 = 25$

***Q.36** In a town of 840 persons, 450 persons read Hindi, 300 read English and 200 read both. Then, the number of persons who read neither, is

(a) 210 (b) 290 (c) 180 (d) 260

Ans. *(b)* Let H be the set of persons who read Hindi and E be the set of persons who read English.

Then, $n(U) = 840,\ n(H) = 450,\ n(E) = 300,\ n(H \cap E) = 200$

Number of persons who read neither $= n(H' \cap E') = n(H \cup E)' = n(U) - n(H \cup E)$

$= 840 - [n(H) + n(E) - n(H \cap E)]$

$= 840 - (450 + 300 - 200) = 840 - 550 = 290$

Q.37 If $X = \{8^n - 7n - 1 \mid n \in N\}$ and $Y = \{49n - 49 \mid n \in N\}$. Then,

(a) $X \subset Y$ (b) $Y \subset X$ (c) $X = Y$ (d) $X \cap Y = \phi$

- **Concept Insight** If every element of A is an elements of B, then $A \subseteq B$.

Ans. *(a)* Given, $X = \{8^n - 7n - 1 \mid n \in N\} = \{0, 49, 490, \ldots\}$

and $\quad Y = \{49n - 49 \mid n \in N\} = \{0, 49, 98, 147, \ldots\}$

Clearly, every elements of X is in Y but every element of Y is not in X.

$\therefore \quad X \subset Y$

(*****) Topics related to these question have been removed from latest NCERT.

***Q.38** A survey shows that 63% of the people watch a news channel whereas 76% watch another channel. If x% of the people watch both channel, then

(a) $x = 35$ (b) $x = 63$
(c) $39 \le x \le 63$ (d) $x = 39$

Ans. *(c)* Let A be the set of percentage of those people who watch a news channel and B be the set of percentage of those people who watch another channel.

We have, $n(A) = 63,\ n(B) = 76,$ and $n(A \cap B) = x$

$$\because \quad n(A \cup B) \le 100$$
$$\Rightarrow \quad n(A) + n(B) - n(A \cap B) \le 100$$
$$\Rightarrow \quad 63 + 76 - x \le 100$$
$$\Rightarrow \quad 139 - x \le 100$$
$$\Rightarrow \quad 139 - 100 \le x$$
$$\Rightarrow \quad 39 \le x$$
$$\because \quad n(A) = 63$$
$$\Rightarrow \quad n(A \cap B) \le n(A)$$
$$\Rightarrow \quad x \le 63$$
$$\therefore \quad 39 \le x \le 63$$

Q.39 If sets A and B are defined as

$A = \{(x, y) \mid y = \dfrac{1}{x},\ 0 \ne x \in R\},\ B = \{(x, y) \mid y = -x,\ x \in R,\}$. Then,

(a) $A \cap B = A$ (b) $A \cap B = B$
(c) $A \cap B = \phi$ (d) $A \cup B = A$

Ans. *(c)* Let $x \in R$

We know that, $-x \ne \dfrac{1}{x}$ for any $x \in R$

So, there is no common element in A and B

$$\therefore \quad A \cap B = \phi$$

Q.40 If A and B are two sets, then $A \cap (A \cup B)$ equals to

(a) A (b) B (c) ϕ (d) $A \cap B$

Ans. *(a)* Draw the Venn diagram showing $A \cap (A \cup B)$

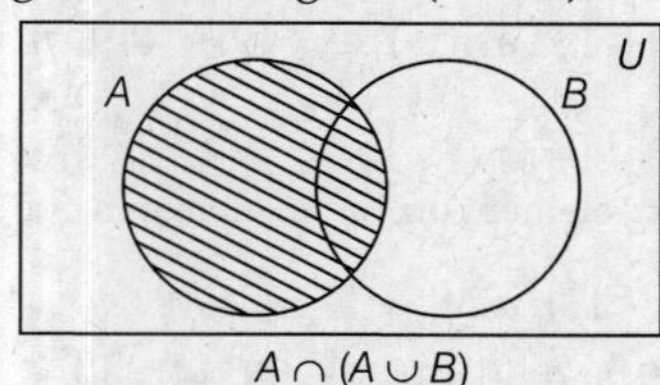

$A \cap (A \cup B)$

So, from the Venn diagram, we get $A \cap (A \cup B) = A$

(*) Topics related to these question have been removed from latest NCERT.

Q.41 If $A = \{1, 3, 5, 7, 9, 11, 13, 15, 17\}$, $B = \{2, 4, \ldots, 18\}$ and N the set of natural numbers is the universal set, then $(A' \cup (A \cup B) \cap B')$ is

(a) ϕ (b) N (c) A (d) B

Thinking Process To solve this problem, use the distributive law i.e., $A \cap (B \cup C) = (A \cap B) \cup (A \cap C)$.

Ans. **(b)** $A' \cup [(A \cup B) \cap B']$

$= A' \cup [(A \cap B') \cup (B \cap B')]$ $[\because A \cap (B \cup C) = (A \cap B) \cup (A \cap C)]$

$= A' \cup [(A \cap B') \cup \phi] = A' \cup (A \cap B')$ $[\because B \cap B' = \phi]$

$= (A' \cup A) \cap (A' \cup B')$

$= N \cap (A' \cup B') = A' \cup B' = (A \cap B)' = \phi' = N$ $[\because A \cap B = \phi]$

Q.42 If $S = \{x \mid x$ is a positive multiple of 3 less than 100$\}$ and $P = \{x \mid x$ is a prime number less than 20$\}$. Then, $n(S) + n(P)$ is equal to

(a) 34 (b) 31 (c) 33 (d) 41

Ans. **(d)** $\because$ $S = \{x \mid x$ is a positive multiple of 3 less than 100$\}$

$= \{3, 6, 9, 12, \ldots\ldots, 99\}$

$\therefore$ $n(S) = 33$

and $P = \{x \mid x$ is a prime number less than 20$\}$

$= \{2, 3, 5, 7, 11, 13, 17, 19\}$

$\therefore$ $n(P) = 8$

$\therefore$ $n(S) + n(P) = 33 + 8 = 41$

Q.43 If X and Y are two sets and X′ denotes the complement of X, then $X \cap (X \cup Y)'$ is equal to

(a) X (b) Y

(c) ϕ (d) $X \cap Y$

Ans. **(c)** $X \cap (X \cup Y)' = X \cap (X' \cap Y')$ [$\because$ De-Morgan's law $(A \cup B)' = A' \cap B'$]

$= (X \cap X') \cap (X \cap Y')$ [using distributive law]

$= \phi \cap (X \cap Y')$ $[\because X \cap X' = \phi]$

$= \phi$

Fill in the blanks in each of exercises of 44-51.

Q.44 The set $\{x \in R : 1 \le x < 2\}$ can be written as ………… .

Ans. The set $\{x \in R : 1 \le x < 2\}$ can be written as $[1, 2)$.

***Q.45** When $A = \phi$, then number of elements in $P(A)$ is ………… .

Ans. $\because$ $A = \phi \Rightarrow n(A) = 0$

We know that, for a set with n elements, there are 2^n elements in its power set.

So, $n\{P(A)\} = 2^{n(A)} = 2^0 = 1$

$\therefore$ number of element in $P(A)$ is 1.

(✱) Topics related to these question have been removed from latest NCERT.

***Q.46** If A and B are finite sets ,such that $A \subset B$, then $n(A \cup B)$ is equal to ....

Ans. If A and B are two finite sets such that $A \subset B$, then $n(A \cup B) = n(B)$.

Q.47 If A and B are any two sets, then $A - B$ is equal to ....

Ans. If A and B are any two sets, then $A - B = A \cap B'$

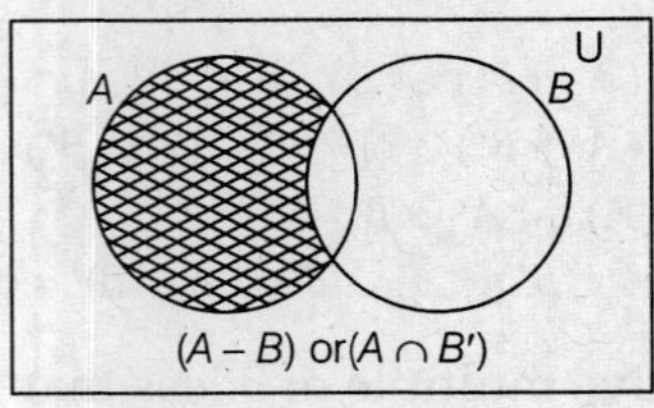

$$\therefore \quad A - B = A \cap B'$$

***Q.48** Power set of the set $A = \{1, 2\}$ is ....

Thinking Process The power set is a collection of all the subsets of a set. To solve this problem, write the all subsets of the given set.

Ans. We have, $A = \{1, 2\}$

So, the subsets of A are $\phi, \{1\}, \{2\}$ and $\{1, 2\}$.

$$\therefore \quad P(A) = \{\phi, \{1\}, \{2\}, \{1, 2\}\}$$

Q.49 If the sets $A = \{1, 3, 5\}$, $B = \{2, 4, 6\}$ and $C = \{0, 2, 4, 6, 8\}$. Then, the universal set of all the three sets A, B and C can be ....

Ans. Universal set for A, B and C is given by $U = \{0, 1, 2, 3, 4, 5, 6, 8\}$

Q.50 If $U = \{1, 2, 3, 4, 5, 6, 7, 8, 9, 10\}$

$A = \{1, 2, 3, 5\}$, $B = \{2, 4, 6, 7\}$ and $C = \{2, 3, 4, 8\}$. Then,

(i) $(B \cup C)'$ is ....

(ii) $(C - A)'$ is ....

Ans. Given, $U = \{1, 2, 3, 4, 5, \ldots, 10\}$,

$A = \{1, 2, 3, 5\}$, $B = \{2, 4, 6, 7\}$

and $C = \{2, 3, 4, 8\}$

$\therefore \quad B \cup C = \{2, 3, 4, 6, 7, 8\}$

(i) $(B \cup C)' = U - (B \cup C) = \{1, 5, 9, 10\}$ $\quad [\because (A \cup B)' = U - (A \cup B)]$

(ii) $C - A = \{4, 8\}$

$\therefore \quad (C - A)' = U - (C - A) = \{1, 2, 3, 5, 6, 7, 9, 10\}$

(✱) Topics related to these question have been removed from latest NCERT.

Q.51 For all sets A and B, $A-(A\cap B)$ is equal to ....

Ans. Venn Diagram for $A-(A\cap B)$ is shown below

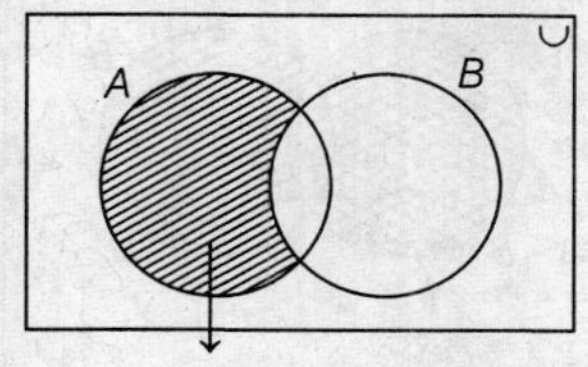

$$A-(A\cap B)=A-B=A\cap B'$$

Q.52 Match the following sets for all sets A, B and C

(i)	$((A'\cup B')-A)'$	(a)	$A-B$
(ii)	$[(B'\cup(B'-A)]'$	(b)	A
(iii)	$(A-B)-(B-C)$	(c)	B
(iv)	$(A-B)\cap(C-B)$	(d)	$(A\times B)\cap(A\times C)$
(v)	$A\times(B\cap C)$	(e)	$(A\times B)\cup(A\times C)$
(vi)	$A\times(B\cup C)$	(f)	$(A\cap C)-B$

Ans. (i) $[(A'\cup B')-A]'=[(A'\cup B')\cap A']'$ $\quad[\because A-B=A\cap B']$

$=[(A\cap B)'\cap A']'$ $\quad[\because$ by De-Morgan's law $(A\cap B)'=A'\cup B']$

$=[(A\cap B)']'\cup(A')'=(A\cap B)\cup A$ $\quad[\because (A')'=A]$

$=A$

(ii) $[B'\cup(B'-A)]'=[B'\cup(B'\cap A')]'$ $\quad[\because A-B=A\cap B']$

$=[B'\cup(B\cup A)']'$ $\quad[\because A'\cap B'=(A\cup B)']$

$=(B')'\cap[(B\cup A)']'$ $\quad[\because (A\cup B)'=A'\cap B']$

$=B\cap(B\cup A)$ $\quad[\because (A')'=A]$

$=B$

(iii) $(A-B)-(B-C)=(A\cap B')-(B\cap C')$ $\quad[\because A-B=A\cap B']$

$=(A\cap B')\cap(B\cap C')'$

$=(A\cap B')\cap[B'\cup(C')']$ $\quad$[using De-Morgan's law]

$=(A\cap B')\cap(B'\cup C)$ $\quad[\because (A')'=A]$

$=[A\cap(B'\cup C)]\cap[B'\cap(B'\cup C)]$ $\quad[\because$ by distributive law$]$

$=[A\cap(B'\cup C)]\cap B'$ $\quad[\because B'\,C\,(B'\cup C)]$

$=(A\cap B')\cap[(B'\cup C)\cap B']$ $\quad[\because$ again, by distributive law$]$

$=(A\cap B')\cap B'$

$=A\cap B'=A-B$

Alternate Method

It is clear from the diagram, $(A-B)-(B-C)=A-B$.

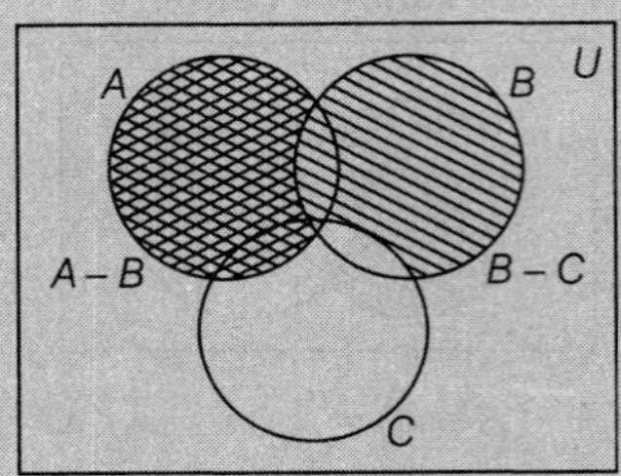

(iv) $(A-B)\cap(C-B)=(A\cap B')\cap(C\cap B')$ [$\because A-B=A\cap B'$]

$=(A\cap C)\cap B'$ [using distributive law]

$=(A\cap C)-B$ [$\because A\cap B'=A-B$]

(v) $A\times(B\cap C)$

Cartesian product of A with the intersection of B and C is $(A\times B)\cap(A\times C)$

$A\times(B\cap C)=(A\times B)\cap(A\times C)$

(vi) $A\times(B\cup C)$

Cartesian product of A with the union of B and C is $(A\times B)\cup(A\times C)$

$A\times(B\cup C)=(A\times B)\cup(A\times C)$

Hence, the correct matches are

(i) ↔ (b), (ii) ↔ (c), (iii) ↔ (a), (iv) ↔ (f), (v) ↔ (d), (vi) ↔ (e)

State True or False for the following statements in each of the exercises from 53 to 58.

Q.53 If A is any set, then $A\subset A$.

Ans. *True*

Since, every set is the subset of itself.

Therefore, for any set A, $A\subset A$.

Q.54 If $M=\{1, 2, 3, 4, 5, 6, 7, 8, 9\}$ and $B=\{1, 2, 3, 4, 5, 6, 7, 8, 9\}$, then $B\not\subset M$.

Ans. *False*

$M=\{1,2,3,4,5,6,7,8,9\}$; $B=\{1,2,3,4,5,6,7,8,9\}$

Since, M contains all the elements of B.

$\therefore$ $B\subset M$

Q.55 The sets {1, 2, 3, 4} and {3, 4, 5, 6} are equal.

Ans. *False*

Since, $2\in\{1, 2, 3, 4\}$

But $2\notin\{3, 4, 5, 6\}$

$\therefore$ $\{1, 2, 3, 4\}\neq\{3, 4, 5, 6\}$

Q.56 $Q \cup Z = Q$, where Q is the set of rational numbers and Z is the set of integers.

Ans. *True*

Since, every integer is also a rational number but every rational number is not an integers. So, $Z \subset Q$

where, Z is the set of integers and Q is the set of rational numbers.

$\therefore \quad Q \cup Z = Q$

Q.57 Let sets R and T be defined as

$$R = \{x \in Z \mid x \text{ is divisible by } 2\}$$
$$T = \{x \in Z \mid x \text{ is divisible by } 6\}. \text{ Then, } T \subset R$$

Ans. *True*

$$R = \{x \in Z \mid x \text{ is divisible by } 2\} = \{\ldots -6, -4, -2, 0, 2, 4, 6, \ldots\}$$
$$T = \{x \in Z \mid x \text{ is divisible by } 6\} = \{\ldots, -12, -6, 0, 6, 12, \ldots\}$$

Thus, R contains all the elements of T.

$\therefore \quad T \subset R$

Q.58 If $A = \{0, 1, 2\}$, $B = \{x \in R \mid 0 \le x \le 2\}$. Then, $A = B$.

Ans. *False*

$$A = \{0, 1, 2\} \text{ and } B = \{x \in R \mid 0 \le x \le 2\}$$

$\Rightarrow \quad n(A) = 3$

So, A is finite.

Since, there are infinite real numbers from 0 to 2. So, B is infinite.

$\therefore \quad A \ne B$

Chapter 02

Relations and Functions

Short Answer Type Questions

Q.1 If $A = \{-1, 2, 3\}$ and $B = \{1, 3\}$, then determine

(i) $A \times B$ (ii) $B \times A$ (iii) $B \times B$ (iv) $A \times A$

Ans. We have, $A = \{-1, 2, 3\}$ and $B = \{1, 3\}$

(i) $A \times B = \{(-1, 1), (-1, 3), (2, 1), (2, 3), (3, 1), (3, 3)\}$

(ii) $B \times A = \{(1, -1), (1, 2), (1, 3), (3, -1), (3, 2), (3, 3)\}$

(iii) $B \times B = \{(1, 1), (1, 3), (3, 1), (3, 3)\}$

(iv) $A \times A = \{(-1, -1), (-1, 2), (-1, 3), (2, -1), (2, 2), (2, 3), (3, -1), (3, 2), (3, 3)\}$

Note In general $A \times B \neq B \times A$

Q.2 If $P = \{x : x < 3, x \in N\}$, $Q = \{x : x \leq 2, x \in W\}$, then find $(P \cup Q) \times (P \cap Q)$, where W is the set of whole numbers.

Ans. We have, $P = \{x : x < 3, x \in N\} = \{1, 2\}$

and $Q = \{x : x \leq 2, x \in W\} = \{0, 1, 2\}$

$\therefore$ $P \cup Q = \{0, 1, 2\}$ and $P \cap Q = \{1, 2\}$

$$(P \cup Q) \times (P \cap Q) = \{0, 1, 2\} \times \{1, 2\}$$
$$= \{(0, 1), (0, 2), (1, 1), (1, 2), (2, 1), (2, 2)\}$$

Mistake Alert! *Do not forget to write the sets accurately in roster form based on the given conditions.*

Q.3 If $A = \{x : x \in W, x < 2\}$, $B = \{x : x \in N, 1 < x < 5\}$ and $C = \{3, 5\}$, then find

(i) $A \times (B \cap C)$ (ii) $A \times (B \cup C)$

Ans. We have, $A = \{x : x \in W, x < 2\} = \{0, 1\}$

and $B = \{x : x \in N, 1 < x < 5\} = \{2, 3, 4\}$ and $C = \{3, 5\}$

(i) $\because$ $B \cap C = \{3\}$

$\therefore$ $A \times (B \cap C) = \{0, 1\} \times \{3\} = \{(0, 3), (1, 3)\}$

(ii) $\because$ $(B \cup C) = \{2, 3, 4, 5\}$

$\therefore$ $A \times (B \cup C) = \{0, 1\} \times \{2, 3, 4, 5\}$

$$= \{(0, 2), (0, 3), (0, 4), (0, 5), (1, 2), (1, 3), (1, 4), (1, 5)\}$$

Mistake Alert! *Be careful with the inequality sign while writing the elements of the respective sets in roaster form.*

Q.4 In each of the following cases, find a and b.

(i) $(2a+b, a-b)=(8, 3)$ (ii) $\left(\frac{a}{4}, a-2b\right)=(0, 6+b)$

Thinking Process Equate the corresponding first and second elements and solve for a and b.

Ans. (i) We have, $(2a+b, a-b)=(8, 3)$

$\Rightarrow$ $2a+b=8$ and $a-b=3$ [since, two ordered pairs are equal, if their corresponding first and second elements are equal]

On substituting, $b=a-3$ in $2a+b=8$, we get

$$2a+a-3=8 \Rightarrow 3a-3=8$$

$$\Rightarrow 3a=11 \Rightarrow a=\frac{11}{3}$$

Again, substituting $a=\frac{11}{3}$ in $b=a-3$, we get

$$b=\frac{11}{3}-3=\frac{11-9}{3}=\frac{2}{3}$$

$$\therefore a=\frac{11}{3} \text{ and } b=\frac{2}{3}$$

(ii) We have, $\left(\frac{a}{4}, a-2b\right)=(0, 6+b)$

$$\Rightarrow \frac{a}{4}=0 \Rightarrow a=0 \text{ and } a-2b=6+b$$

$$\Rightarrow 0-2b=6+b \quad [\because a=0]$$

$$\Rightarrow -3b=6$$

$$\therefore b=-2$$

$$\therefore a=0, b=-2$$

Q.5 $A=\{1, 2, 3, 4, 5\}$, $S=\{(x, y): x \in A, y \in A\}$, then find the ordered pairs which satisfy the conditions given below.

(i) $x+y=5$ (ii) $x+y<5$ (iii) $x+y>8$

Ans. We have, $A=\{1, 2, 3, 4, 5\}$ and $S=\{(x, y): x \in A, y \in A\}$

(i) The set of ordered pairs satisfying $x+y=5$ is, $\{(1, 4), (2, 3), (3, 2), (4, 1)\}$.

(ii) The set of ordered pairs satisfying $x+y<5$ is $\{(1, 1), (1, 2), (1, 3), (2, 1), (2, 2), (3, 1)\}$.

(iii) The set of ordered pairs satisfying $x+y>8$ is $\{(4, 5), (5, 4), (5, 5)\}$.

Q.6 If $R=\{(x, y): x, y \in W, x^2+y^2=25\}$, then find the domain and range of R.

Thinking Process First, write the relation in roster form, then find the domain and range of R.

Ans. We have, $R=\{(x, y): x, y \in W, x^2+y^2=25\}=\{(0, 5), (3, 4), (4, 3), (5, 0)\}$

Domain of $R=$ Set of first elements of ordered pairs in $R=\{0, 3, 4, 5\}$

Range of $R=$ Set of second elements of ordered pairs in $R=\{0, 3, 4, 5\}$

Q.7 If $R_1 = \{(x, y) \mid y = 2x + 7$, where $x \in R$ and $-5 \le x \le 5\}$ is a relation. Then, find the domain and range of R_1.

- **Concept Insight** Domain and range of a relation are the sets of the first and second elements of the ordered pair in a relation, respectively.

Ans. We have, $R_1 = \{x, y) \mid y = 2x + 7$, where $x \in R$ and $-5 \le x \le 5\}$

Domain of $R_1 = \{-5 \le x \le 5, x \in R\} = [-5, 5]$

$\because \quad y = 2x + 7$

When $x = -5$, then $y = 2(-5) + 7 = -3$

When $x = 5$, then $y = 2(5) + 7 = 17$

$\therefore$ Range of $R_1 = \{-3 \le y \le 17, y \in R\} = [-3, 17]$

Q.8 If $R_2 = \{x, y) \mid x$ and y are integers and $x^2 + y^2 = 64\}$ is a relation, then find R_2.

Ans. We have, $R_2 = \{(x, y)\}$ x and y are integers and $x^2 + y^2 = 64\}$

Since, 64 is the sum of squares of 0 and ± 8.

When $x = 0$, then $y^2 = 64 \Rightarrow y = \pm 8$

$x = 8$, then $y^2 = 64 - 8^2 \Rightarrow 64 - 64 = 0$

$x = -8$, then $y^2 = 64 - (-8)^2 = 64 - 64 = 0$

$\therefore \quad R_2 = \{(0, 8), (0, -8), (8, 0), (-8, 0)\}$

Q.9 If $R_3 = \{(x, |x|) \mid x$ is a real number$\}$ is a relation. Then find domain and range of R_3.

Ans. We have, $R_3 = \{(x, |x|) \mid x$ is a real number$\}$

Clearly, domain of $R_3 = R$

Since, image of any real number under R_3 is positive real number or zero.

$\therefore$ Range of $R_3 = R^+ \cup \{0\}$ or $(0, \infty)$

Q.10 Is the given relation a function? Give reason for your answer.

(i) $h = \{(4, 6), (3, 9), (-11, 6), (3, 11)\}$

(ii) $f = \{(x, x) \mid x$ is a real number$\}$

(iii) $g = \left\{\left(n, \frac{1}{n}\right) x \text{ is a positive integer}\right\}$

(iv) $s = \{(n, n^2) \mid n$ is a positive integer$\}$

(v) $t = \{(x, 3) \mid x$ is a real number$\}$

Thinking Process A relation is said to be a function if each element of the domain has only and only one image.

Ans. (i) We have, $h = \{(4, 6), (3, 9), (-11, 6), (3, 11)\}$.

Since, 3 has two images 9 and 11. So, it is not a function.

(ii) We have, $f = \{(x, x) \mid x$ is a real number.

We observe that, every element in the domain has unique image. So, it is a function.

(iii) We have, $g = \left\{\left(n, \frac{1}{n}\right) \middle| x \text{ is a positive integer}\right\}$.

For every positive integer n, $\frac{1}{n}$ is unique and distinct. Therefore, every element in the domain has unique image. So, it is a function.

(iv) We have, $s = \{(n, n^2) \mid n \text{ is a positive integer}\}$.

Since, the square of any positive integer is unique. So, every element in the domain has unique image. Hence, it is a function.

(v) We have, $t = \{(x, 3) \mid x \text{ is a real number}\}$.

Since, every element in the domain has the image 3. So, it is a constant function. Hence, it is a function.

Q.11 **If f and g are real functions defined by $f(x) = x^2 + 7$ and $g(x) = 3x + 5$. Then, find each of the following.**

(a) $f(3) + g(-5)$ **(b) $f\left(\frac{1}{2}\right) \times g(14)$**

(c) $f(-2) + g(-1)$ **(d) $f(t) - f(-2)$**

(e) $\frac{f(t) - f(5)}{t - 5}$, if $t \neq 5$

Ans. Given, f and g are real functions defined by $f(x) = x^2 + 7$ and $g(x) = 3x + 5$.

(a) $f(3) = (3)^2 + 7 = 9 + 7 = 16$ and $g(-5) = 3(-5) + 5 = -15 + 5 = -10$

$\therefore f(3) + g(-5) = 16 - 10 = 6$

(b) $f\left(\frac{1}{2}\right) = \left(\frac{1}{2}\right)^2 + 7 = \frac{1}{4} + 7 = \frac{29}{4}$ and $g(14) = 3(14) + 5 = 42 + 5 = 47$

$\therefore \quad f\left(\frac{1}{2}\right) \times g(14) = \frac{29}{4} \times 47 = \frac{1363}{4}$

(c) $f(-2) = (-2)^2 + 7 = 4 + 7 = 11$ and $g(-1) = 3(-1) + 5 = -3 + 5 = 2$

$\therefore \quad f(-2) + g(-1) = 11 + 2 = 13$

(d) $f(t) = t^2 + 7$ and $f(-2) = (-2)^2 + 7 = 4 + 7 = 11$

$\therefore \quad f(t) - f(-2) = t^2 + 7 - 11 = t^2 - 4$

(e) $f(t) = t^2 + 7$ and $f(5) = 5^2 + 7 = 25 + 7 = 32$

$$\therefore \quad \frac{f(t) - f(5)}{t - 5}, \text{ if } t \neq 5$$

$$= \frac{t^2 + 7 - 32}{t - 5}$$

$$= \frac{t^2 - 25}{t - 5} = \frac{(t - 5)(t + 5)}{(t - 5)} \qquad [\because a^2 - b^2 = (a + b)(a - b)]$$

$$= t + 5 \qquad [\because t \neq 5]$$

Q.12 Let f and g be real functions defined by $f(x) = 2x + 1$ and $g(x) = 4x - 7$.

(a) For what real numbers x, $f(x) = g(x)$?

(b) For what real numbers x, $f(x) < g(x)$?

Ans. We have, $f(x) = 2x + 1$ and $g(x) = 4x - 7$

(a) $\because$ $f(x) = g(x)$

$\therefore$ $2x + 1 = 4x - 7 \Rightarrow 2x = 8$

$\therefore$ $x = 4$

(b) $\because$ $f(x) < g(x)$

$\therefore$ $2x + 1 < 4x - 7 \Rightarrow 2x - 4x + 1 < 4x - 7 - 4x$

$\Rightarrow$ $-2x + 1 < -7 \Rightarrow -2x < -7 - 1$

$\Rightarrow$ $-2x < -8 \Rightarrow \frac{-2x}{-2} > \frac{-8}{-2}$

$\therefore$ $x > 4$

Q.13 If f and g are two real valued functions defined as $f(x) = 2x + 1$ and $g(x) = x^2 + 1$, then find

(i) $f + g$ (ii) $f - g$ (iii) fg (iv) $\frac{f}{g}$

Ans. We have, $f(x) = 2x + 1$ and $g(x) = x^2 + 1$

(i) $(f + g)(x) = f(x) + g(x)$
$= 2x + 1 + x^2 + 1 = x^2 + 2x + 2$

(ii) $(f - g)(x) = f(x) - g(x) = (2x + 1) - (x^2 + 1)$
$= 2x + 1 - x^2 - 1 = 2x - x^2 = x(2 - x)$

(iii) $(fg)(x) = f(x) \cdot g(x) = (2x + 1)(x^2 + 1)$
$= 2x^3 + 2x + x^2 + 1 = 2x^3 + x^2 + 2x + 1$

(iv) $\left(\frac{f}{g}\right)(x) = \frac{f(x)}{g(x)} = \frac{2x + 1}{x^2 + 1}$

Q.14 Express the following functions as set of ordered pairs and determine their range.

$$f : X \to R,\ f(x) = x^3 + 1, \text{ where } X = \{-1, 0, 3, 9, 7\}$$

Ans. We have, $f : X \to R,\ f(x) = x^3 + 1$

Where, $X = \{-1, 0, 3, 9, 7\}$,

When, $x = -1$, then $f(-1) = (-1)^3 + 1 = -1 + 1 = 0$

$x = 0$, then $f(0) = (0)^3 + 1 = 0 + 1 = 1$

$x = 3$, then $f(3) = (3)^3 + 1 = 27 + 1 = 28$

$x = 9$, then $f(9) = (9)^3 + 1 = 729 + 1 = 730$

$x = 7$, then $f(7) = (7)^3 + 1 = 343 + 1 = 344$

$f = \{(-1, 0), (0, 1), (3, 28), (7, 344), (9, 730)\}$

$\therefore$ Range of $f = \{0, 1, 28, 344, 730\}$

Q.15 Find the values of x for which the functions $f(x) = 3x^2 - 1$ and $g(x) = 3 + x$ are equal.

Ans. $\because$ $f(x) = g(x)$

$\therefore$ $3x^2 - 1 = 3 + x$

$\Rightarrow$ $3x^2 - x - 4 = 0$

$\Rightarrow$ $3x^2 - 4x + 3x - 4 = 0$

$\Rightarrow$ $x(3x-4) + 1(3x-4) = 0 \Rightarrow (3x-4)(x+1) = 0$

$\therefore$ $x = -1, \frac{4}{3}$

Long Answer Type Questions

Q.16 Is $g = \{(1,1),(2,3),(3,5),(4,7)\}$ a function, justify. If this is described by the relation, $g(x) = \alpha x + \beta$, then what values should be assigned to α and β?

Thinking Process First, find the two equations by substituting different values of x and $g(x)$.

Ans. We have, $g = \{(1, 1), (2, 3), (3, 5), (4, 7)\}$

Since, every element has unique image under g. So, g is a function.

Now, $g(x) = \alpha x + \beta$

When $x = 1$, then $g(1) = \alpha(1) + \beta$

$\Rightarrow$ $1 = \alpha + \beta$ ...(i)

When $x = 2$, then $g(2) = \alpha(2) + \beta$

$\Rightarrow$ $3 = 2\alpha + \beta$ ...(ii)

On solving Eqs. (i) and (ii), we get $\alpha = 2, \beta = -1$

Q.17 Find the domain of each of the following functions given by

(i) $f(x) = \frac{1}{\sqrt{1 - \cos x}}$

(ii) $f(x) = \frac{1}{\sqrt{x + |x|}}$

(iii) $f(x) = x|x|$

(iv) $f(x) = \frac{x^3 - x + 3}{x^2 - 1}$

(v) $f(x) = \frac{3x}{28 - x}$

Thinking Process To find the domain, determine input values, where the function is defined by checking for restrictions like zero denominators, negative square roots, etc.

Ans. (i) We have, $f(x) = \frac{1}{\sqrt{1 - \cos x}}$

$\because$ $-1 \le \cos x \le 1$

$\Rightarrow$ $-1 \le -\cos x \le 1 \Rightarrow 0 \le 1 - \cos x \le 2$ [adding 1 in each terms]

So, $f(x)$ is defined, if $1 - \cos x \ne 0$

$\Rightarrow$ $\cos x \ne 1$

$\Rightarrow \qquad x \neq 2n\pi, \forall n \in Z$

$\therefore \qquad$ Domain of $f = R - \{2n\pi : n \in Z\}$

(ii) We have, $\qquad f(x) = \dfrac{1}{\sqrt{x + |x|}}$

$$\because \qquad x + |x| = \begin{cases} x - x = 0, & x < 0 \\ x + x = 2x, & x \geq 0 \end{cases}$$

Since, $f(x)$ is defined, if $x > 0$.

$\therefore \qquad$ Domain of $f = R^+$

(iii) We have, $\quad f(x) = x|x|$

Clearly, $f(x)$ is defined for any $x \in R$.

$\therefore \qquad$ Domain of $f = R$

(iv) We have, $\qquad f(x) = \dfrac{x^3 - x + 3}{x^2 - 1}$

$f(x)$ is not defined, if $\qquad x^2 - 1 = 0$

$\Rightarrow \qquad (x - 1)(x + 1) = 0$

$\Rightarrow \qquad x = -1, 1$

$\therefore \qquad$ Domain of $f = R - \{-1, 1\}$

(v) We have, $\qquad f(x) = \dfrac{3x}{28 - x}$

Clearly, $f(x)$ is defined, if $28 - x \neq 0$

$\Rightarrow \qquad x \neq 28$

$\therefore \qquad$ Domain of $f = R - \{28\}$

Q.18 Find the range of the following functions given by

(i) $f(x) = \dfrac{3}{2 - x^2}$ $\qquad$ (ii) $f(x) = 1 - |x - 2|$

(iii) $f(x) = |x - 3|$ $\qquad$ (iv) $f(x) = 1 + 3\cos 2x$

Thinking Process First, find the value of x in terms of y, where $y = f(x)$. Then, find the values of y for which x attains real values.

Ans. (i) We have, $\qquad f(x) = \dfrac{3}{2 - x^2}$

Let $\qquad y = f(x)$

Then, $\qquad y = \dfrac{3}{2 - x^2} \Rightarrow 2 - x^2 = \dfrac{3}{y}$

$\Rightarrow \qquad x^2 = 2 - \dfrac{3}{y} \Rightarrow x = \pm\sqrt{\dfrac{2y - 3}{y}}$

x takes real values, if $2y - 3 \geq 0$ and $y \neq 0$

Now, $\dfrac{2y - 3}{y} \geq 0 \Rightarrow$ either $(2y - 3 \leq 0$ and $y < 0)$ or $(2y - 3 \geq 0$ and $y > 0)$

$\Rightarrow \left(y \leq \dfrac{3}{2} \text{ and } y < 0\right)$ or $\left(y \geq \dfrac{3}{2} \text{ and } y > 0\right)$

$\Rightarrow \qquad (y < 0)$ or $\left(y \geq \dfrac{3}{2}\right)$

$$\Rightarrow \quad y \in (-\infty, 0) \text{ or } y \in \left[\frac{3}{2}, \infty\right)$$

$$\Rightarrow \quad y \in (-\infty, 0) \cup \left[\frac{3}{2}, \infty\right)$$

$$\therefore \quad \text{Range of } f = (-\infty, 0) \cup \left[\frac{3}{2}, \infty\right)$$

(ii) We know that $|x-2| \geq 0 \Rightarrow -|x-2| \leq 0$

$$\Rightarrow \quad 1 - |x-2| \leq 1 \Rightarrow f(x) \leq 1$$

$$\therefore \quad \text{Range of } f = (-\infty, 1]$$

(iii) We know that, $|x-3| \geq 0 \Rightarrow f(x) \geq 0$

$$\therefore \quad \text{Range of } f = [0, \infty)$$

(iv) We know that $-1 \leq \cos 2x \leq 1 \Rightarrow -3 \leq 3\cos 2x \leq 3$

$$\Rightarrow \quad 1-3 \leq 1+3\cos 2x \leq 1+3 \Rightarrow -2 \leq 1+3\cos 2x \leq 1+3$$

$$\Rightarrow \quad -2 \leq f(x) \leq 4$$

$$\therefore \quad \text{Range of } f = [-2, 4]$$

Q.19 Redefine the function $f(x) = |x-2| + |2+x|, -3 \leq x \leq 3$

Thinking Process First, find the interval in which $|x-2|$ and $|2+x|$ is defined, then find the value of $f(x)$ in that interval.

Ans. Since,
$$|x-2| = \begin{cases} -(x-2), & x < 2 \\ x-2, & x \geq 2 \end{cases}$$

and
$$|2+x| = \begin{cases} -(2+x), & x < -2 \\ (2+x), & x \geq -2 \end{cases}$$

$$\therefore \quad f(x) = |x-2| + |2+x|, -3 \leq x \leq 3$$

$$= \begin{cases} -(x-2)-(2+x), & -3 \leq x < -2 \\ -(x-2)+2+x, & -2 \leq x < 2 \\ x-2+2+x, & 2 \leq x \leq 3 \end{cases}$$

$$= \begin{cases} -2x, & -3 \leq x < -2 \\ 4, & -2 \leq x < 2 \\ 2x, & 2 \leq x \leq 3 \end{cases}$$

Q.20 If $f(x) = \dfrac{x-1}{x+1}$, then show that

(i) $f\left(\dfrac{1}{x}\right) = -f(x)$ (ii) $f\left(-\dfrac{1}{x}\right) = \dfrac{-1}{f(x)}$

Ans. We have, $f(x) = \dfrac{x-1}{x+1}$

(i) $$f\left(\frac{1}{x}\right) = \frac{\frac{1}{x}-1}{\frac{1}{x}+1} = \frac{(1-x)/x}{(1+x)/x} = \frac{1-x}{1+x} = \frac{-(x-1)}{x+1} = -f(x)$$

(ii) $f\left(-\dfrac{1}{x}\right)=\dfrac{-\dfrac{1}{x}-1}{-\dfrac{1}{x}+1}=\dfrac{(-1-x)/x}{(-1+x)/x} \Rightarrow f\left(-\dfrac{1}{x}\right)=\dfrac{-(x+1)}{x-1}$

Now, $\dfrac{-1}{f(x)}=\dfrac{-1}{\dfrac{x-1}{x+1}}=\dfrac{-(x+1)}{x-1}$

$\therefore \quad f\left(-\dfrac{1}{x}\right)=-\dfrac{1}{f(x)}$

Q.21 If $f(x)=\sqrt{x}$ and $g(x)=x$ be two functions defined in the domain $R^+ \cup \{0\}$, then find

(i) $(f+g)(x)$ (ii) $(f-g)(x)$

(iii) $(fg)(x)$ (iv) $\left(\dfrac{f}{g}\right)(x)$

Ans. We have, $f(x)=\sqrt{x}$ and $g(x)=x$ be two function defined in the domain $R^+ \cup \{0\}$.

(i) $(f+g)(x)=f(x)+g(x)=\sqrt{x}+x$

(ii) $(f-g)(x)=f(x)-g(x)=\sqrt{x}-x$

(iii) $(fg)(x)=f(x)\cdot g(x)=\sqrt{x}\cdot x=x^{\frac{3}{2}}$

(iv) $\left(\dfrac{f}{g}\right)(x)=\dfrac{f(x)}{g(x)}=\dfrac{\sqrt{x}}{x}=\dfrac{1}{\sqrt{x}}$

Q.22 Find the domain and range of the function $f(x)=\dfrac{1}{\sqrt{x-5}}$

Ans. We have, $f(x)=\dfrac{1}{\sqrt{x-5}}$

$f(x)$ is defined, if $x-5>0 \Rightarrow x>5$

$\therefore$ Domain of $f=(5,\infty)$

Let $f(x)=y$

$\therefore \quad y=\dfrac{1}{\sqrt{x-5}}$

$\Rightarrow \quad \sqrt{x-5}=\dfrac{1}{y} \Rightarrow x-5=\dfrac{1}{y^2}$

$\therefore \quad x=\dfrac{1}{y^2}+5$

$\because \quad x\in(5,\infty)$ if $y\in R^+$

Hence, range of $f=R^+$

Mistake Alert! *Do not forget to exclude values that make the denominator zero and the square root negative while writing the condition for the function to be defined.*

Q.23 If $f(x) = y = \dfrac{ax - b}{cx - a}$, then prove that $f(y) = x$.

Ans. We have, $f(x) = y = \dfrac{ax - b}{cx - a}$

$$\therefore \quad f(y) = \frac{ay - b}{cy - a} = \frac{a\left(\dfrac{ax - b}{cx - a}\right) - b}{c\left(\dfrac{ax - b}{cx - a}\right) - a}$$

$$= \frac{a(ax - b) - b(cx - a)}{c(ax - b) - a(cx - a)} = \frac{a^2x - ab - bcx + ab}{acx - bc - acx + a^2}$$

$$= \frac{a^2x - bcx}{a^2 - bc} = \frac{x(a^2 - bc)}{(a^2 - bc)} = x$$

$\therefore \quad f(y) = x$ **Hence proved.**

Objective Type Questions

Choose the correct answers from the given four options in each exercise 24 to 35.

Q.24 Let $n(A) = m$ and $n(B) = n$. Then, the total number of non-empty relations that can be defined from A to B is

(a) m^n (b) $n^m - 1$ (c) $mn - 1$ (d) $2^{mn} - 1$

Thinking Process First, find the number of element in $A \times B$ and then find the total number of non-empty relations by using $2^{n(A \times B)} - 1$.

Ans. ***(d)*** We have, $n(A) = m$ and $n(B) = n$

$n(A \times B) = n(A) \cdot n(B) = mn$

Total number of non-empty relations from A to $B = 2^{n(A \times B)} - 1 = 2^{mn} - 1$

Q.25 If $[x]^2 - 5[x] + 6 = 0$, where $[\cdot]$ denote the greatest integer function, then

(a) $x \in [3, 4]$ (b) $x \in (2, 3]$ (c) $x \in [2, 3]$ (d) $x \in [2, 4)$

● **Concept Insight** The value of greatest integer function of x is $[x] \in [x, x + 1)$.

Ans. ***(d)*** We have, $[x]^2 - 5[x] + 6 = 0$

$\Rightarrow \quad [x]^2 - 3[x] - 2[x] + 6 = 0$

$\Rightarrow \quad [x]([x] - 3) - 2([x] - 3) = 0$

$\Rightarrow \quad ([x] - 3)([x] - 2) = 0$

$\Rightarrow \quad [x] = 2, 3$

For $[x] = 2$, $\quad x \in [2, 3)$

For $[x] = 3$, $\quad x \in [3, 4)$

$\therefore \quad [x] \in [2, 3) \cup [3, 4) \Rightarrow x \in [2, 4)$

Q.26 Range of $f(x)=\dfrac{1}{1-2\cos x}$ is

(a) $\left[\frac{1}{3}, 1\right]$ (b) $\left[-1, \frac{1}{3}\right]$

(c) $(-\infty, -1] \cup \left[\frac{1}{3}, \infty\right)$ (d) $\left[-\frac{1}{3}, 1\right]$

- **Concept Insight** The value of $\cos x$ lies in the range $[-1, 1]$.

Ans. ***(c)*** We know that, $-1 \le -\cos x \le 1$

$\Rightarrow \quad -2 \le -2\cos x \le 2$

$\Rightarrow \quad 1-2 \le 1-2\cos x \le 1+2 \Rightarrow -1 \le 1-2\cos x \le 3$

But, $\quad 1-2\cos x \ne 0$

$\Rightarrow \quad 1-2\cos x \in [-1,3]-\{0\} \Rightarrow \dfrac{1}{1-2\cos x} \in (-\infty,-1] \cup \left[\frac{1}{3},\infty\right)$

$\therefore$ Range of $f(x)=(-\infty,-1] \cup \left[\frac{1}{3},\infty\right)$

Q.27 Let $f(x)=\sqrt{1+x^2}$, then

(a) $f(xy)=f(x)\cdot f(y)$ (b) $f(xy) \ge f(x)\cdot f(y)$

(c) $f(xy) \le f(x)\cdot f(y)$ (d) None of these

Ans. ***(c)*** We have, $f(x)=\sqrt{1+x^2}$

Now, $f(xy)=\sqrt{1+x^2y^2}$

And $f(x)\cdot f(y)=\sqrt{1+x^2}\cdot\sqrt{1+y^2}$

$=\sqrt{(1+x^2)(1+y^2)}=\sqrt{1+x^2+y^2+x^2y^2}$

$\because \quad \sqrt{1+x^2y^2} \le \sqrt{1+x^2+y^2+x^2y^2}$

$\Rightarrow \quad f(xy) \le f(x)\cdot f(y)$

Q.28 Domain of $\sqrt{a^2-x^2}$ $(a>0)$ is

(a) $(-a, a)$ (b) $[-a, a]$

(c) $[0, a]$ (d) $(-a, 0]$

Ans. ***(b)*** Let $f(x)=\sqrt{a^2-x^2}$

$f(x)$ is defined, if $a^2-x^2 \ge 0$

$\Rightarrow \quad x^2-a^2 \le 0$

$\Rightarrow \quad (x-a)(x+a) \le 0$

$\Rightarrow \quad -a \le x \le a \quad [\because a>0]$

$\therefore$ Domain of $f=[-a, a]$

Mistake Alert! *Do not forget to use the fact that the expression inside the square root function must be non-negative.*

Q.29 If $f(x) = ax + b$, where a and b are integers, $f(-1) = -5$ and $f(3) = 3$, then a and b are equal to

(a) $a = -3$ and $b = -1$
(b) $a = 2$ and $b = -3$
(c) $a = 0$ and $b = 2$
(d) $a = 2$ and $b = 3$

Ans. ***(b)*** We have, $f(x) = ax + b$

Now, $f(-1) = a(-1) + b$

$$-5 = -a + b \quad \ldots(i)$$

and $f(3) = a(3) + b$

$$3 = 3a + b \quad \ldots(ii)$$

On solving Eqs. (i) and (ii), we get, $a = 2$ and $b = -3$

Q.30 The domain of the function f defined by

$$f(x) = \sqrt{4-x} + \frac{1}{\sqrt{x^2-1}} \text{ is equal to}$$

(a) $(-\infty, -1) \cup (1, 4]$
(b) $(-\infty, -1] \cup (1, 4]$
(c) $(-\infty, -1) \cup [1, 4]$
(d) $(-\infty, -1) \cup [1, 4)$

● **Concept Insight** For the square root function to be defined, the expression inside the square root must be non-negative and the denominator of a fraction must not be equal to zero..

Ans. ***(a)*** We have, $f(x) = \sqrt{4-x} + \dfrac{1}{\sqrt{x^2-1}}$

$f(x)$ is defined, if $4 - x \geq 0$ and $x^2 - 1 > 0$

$$x - 4 \leq 0 \text{ and } (x+1)(x-1) > 0$$

$$x \leq 4 \text{ and } x < -1 \text{ or } x > 1$$

$\therefore$ Domain of $f = (-\infty, -1) \cup (1, 4]$

Q.31 The domain and range of the real function f defined by $f(x) = \dfrac{4-x}{x-4}$ is given by

(a) Domain = R, Range = $\{-1, 1\}$
(b) Domain = $R - \{1\}$, Range = R
(c) Domain = $R - \{4\}$, Range $R - \{-1\}$
(d) Domain = $R - \{-4\}$, Range = $\{-1, 1\}$

Thinking Process A function $\dfrac{f(x)}{g(x)}$ is defined, if $g(x) \neq 0$.

Ans. ***(c)*** We have, $f(x) = \dfrac{4-x}{x-4}$

$f(x)$ is defined, if $x - 4 \neq 0$ *i.e.,* $x \neq 4$

$\therefore$ Domain of $f = R - \{4\}$

Let $f(x) = y$

$\therefore$ $y = \dfrac{4-x}{x-4} \Rightarrow xy - 4y = 4 - x$

$\Rightarrow$ $xy + x = 4 + 4y$

$\Rightarrow$ $x(y+1) = 4(1+y)$

$\therefore \quad x = \dfrac{4(1+y)}{(y+1)}$

x takes real values, if $y + 1 \neq 0$ *i.e.*, $y \neq -1$.

$\therefore \quad$ Range of $f = R - \{-1\}$

Q.32 The domain and range of real function f defined by $f(x) = \sqrt{x-1}$ is given by

(a) Domain = $(1, \infty)$, Range = $(0, \infty)$
(b) Domain = $[1, \infty)$, Range = $(0, \infty)$
(c) Domain = $[1, \infty)$, Range = $[0, \infty)$
(d) Domain = $[1, \infty)$, Range = $[0, \infty)$

Thinking Process A function $f(x) = \sqrt{x}$ is defined if $x \geq 0$.

Ans. ***(c)*** We have, $\quad f(x) = \sqrt{x-1}$

$f(x)$ is defined, if $x - 1 \geq 0$

$\Rightarrow \quad x \geq 1$

$\therefore \quad$ Domain of $f = [1, \infty)$

As $\quad x \geq 1$

$\Rightarrow \quad x - 1 \geq 0$

$\Rightarrow \quad \sqrt{x-1} \geq 0$

i.e., $\quad f(x) \geq 0$

$\therefore \quad$ Range of $f = [0, \infty)$

Q.33 The domain of the function f given by $f(x) = \dfrac{x^2 + 2x + 1}{x^2 - x - 6}$.

(a) $R - \{3, -2\}$
(b) $R - \{-3, 2\}$
(c) $R - [3, -2]$
(d) $R - (3, -2)$

Ans. ***(a)*** We have, $f(x) = \dfrac{x^2 + 2x + 1}{x^2 - x - 6}$

$f(x)$ is defined, if $x^2 - x - 6 \neq 0$

$\Rightarrow \quad x^2 - 3x + 2x - 6 \neq 0$

$\Rightarrow \quad x(x-3) + 2(x-3) \neq 0$

$\Rightarrow \quad (x-3)(x+2) \neq 0$

$\therefore \quad x \neq 3, -2$

$\therefore \quad$ Domain of $f = R - \{3, -2\}$

Q.34 The domain and range of the function f given by $f(x) = 2 - |x - 5|$ is

(a) Domain = R^+, Range = $(-\infty, 1]$
(b) Domain = R, Range = $(-\infty, 2]$
(c) Domain = R, Range = $(-\infty, 2)$
(d) Domain = R^+, Range = $(-\infty, 2]$

Ans. ***(b)*** We have, $f(x) = 2 - |x - 5|$

$f(x)$ is defined for all $x \in R$

$\therefore \quad$ Domain of $f = R$

We know that $|x - 5| \geq 0 \Rightarrow -|x - 5| \leq 0 \Rightarrow 2 - |x - 5| \leq 2$

$\therefore \quad f(x) \leq 2$

$\therefore \quad$ Range of $f = (-\infty, 2]$

Q.35 The domain for which the functions defined by $f(x) = 3x^2 - 1$ and $g(x) = 3 + x$ are equal is

(a) $\left\{-1, \frac{4}{3}\right\}$ (b) $\left\{1, \frac{4}{3}\right\}$ (c) $\left\{-1, -\frac{4}{3}\right\}$ (d) $\left\{-2, -\frac{4}{3}\right\}$

Ans. *(a)* We have, $f(x) = 3x^2 - 1$ and $g(x) = 3 + x$

$$f(x) = g(x)$$

$$\Rightarrow \quad 3x^2 - 1 = 3 + x \Rightarrow 3x^2 - x - 4 = 0 \Rightarrow 3x^2 - 4x + 3x - 4 = 0$$

$$\Rightarrow \quad x(3x - 4) + 1(3x - 4) = 0 \quad \Rightarrow \quad (3x - 4)(x + 1) = 0$$

$$\therefore \quad x = -1, \frac{4}{3} \quad \Rightarrow \quad \left\{-1, \frac{4}{3}\right\}$$

So, domain for which $f(x)$ and $g(x)$ are equal is $\left\{-1, \frac{4}{3}\right\}$.

Fill in the blanks :

Q.36 Let f and g be two real functions given by

$$f = \{(0, 1), (2, 0), (3, -4), (4, 2), (5, 1)\}$$

and $\quad g = \{(1, 0), (2, 2), (3, -1), (4, 4), (5, 3)\}$,

then the domain of $f \cdot g$ is given by...........

Thinking Process First find the domain of f and domain of g. Then, domain of $f \cdot g$ = domain of $f \cap$ domain of g.

Ans. We have, $\quad f = \{(0, 1), (2, 0), (3, -4), (4, 2), (5, 1)\}$

and $\quad g = \{(1, 0), (2, 2), (3, -1), (4, 4), (5, 3)\}$

$\therefore \quad$ Domain of $f = \{0, 2, 3, 4, 5\}$

and $\quad$ Domain of $g = \{1, 2, 3, 4, 5\}$

$\therefore$ Domain of $(f \cdot g)$ = Domain of $f \cap$ Domain of $g = \{2, 3, 4, 5\}$

Q.37 Let $f = \{(2, 4), (5, 6), (8, -1), (10, -3)\}$

and $g = \{(2, 5), (7, 1), (8, 4), (10, 13), (11, 5)\}$

be two real functions. Then, match the following:

Column I	Column II
(a) $f - g$	(i) $\left\{\left(2, \frac{4}{5}\right), \left(8, \frac{-1}{4}\right), \left(10, \frac{-3}{13}\right)\right\}$
(b) $f + g$	(ii) $\{(2, 20), (8, -4), (10, -39)\}$
(c) $f \cdot g$	(iii) $\{(2, -1), (8, -5), (10, -16)\}$
(d) $\frac{f}{g}$	(iv) $\{(2, 9), (8, 3), (10, 10)\}$

Thinking Process The domain of $f - g, f + g, f \cdot g$ and $\frac{f}{g}$ is domain of $f \cap$ domain of g with the condition that $g(x) \neq 0$ for $\frac{f}{g}$. Then, find their images.

Ans. We have, $f = \{(2, 4), (5, 6), (8, -1), (10, -3)\}$

and $g = \{(2, 5), (7, 1), (8, 4), (10, 13), (11, 5)\}$

So, $f - g, f + g, f \cdot g, \frac{f}{g}$ are defined in the domain (domain of $f \cap$ domain of g)

i.e., $\{2, 5, 8, 10\} \cap \{2, 7, 8, 10, 11\} \Rightarrow \{2, 8, 10\}$

(a) $(f - g)(2) = f(2) - g(2) = 4 - 5 = -1$

$(f - g)(8) = f(8) - g(8) = -1 - 4 = -5$

$(f - g)(10) = f(10) - g(10) = -3 - 13 = -16$

$\therefore \quad f - g = \{(2, -1), (8, -5), (10, -16)\}$

(b) $(f + g)(2) = f(2) + g(2) = 4 + 5 = 9$

$(f + g)(8) = f(8) + g(8) = -1 + 4 = 3$

$(f + g)(10) = f(10) + g(10) = -3 + 13 = 10$

$\therefore \quad f + g = \{(2, 9), (8, 3), (10, 10)\}$

(c) $(f \cdot g)(2) = f(2) \cdot g(2) = 4 \times 5 = 20$

$(f \cdot g)(8) = f(8) \cdot g(8) = -1 \times 4 = -4$

$(f \cdot g)(10) = f(10) \cdot g(10) = -3 \times 13 = -39$

$\therefore \quad f \cdot g = \{(2, 20), (8, -4), (10, -39)\}$

(d) $\left(\frac{f}{g}\right)(2) = \frac{f(2)}{g(2)} = \frac{4}{5}$

$\left(\frac{f}{g}\right)(8) = \frac{f(8)}{g(8)} = \frac{-1}{4}$

$\left(\frac{f}{g}\right)(10) = \frac{f(10)}{g(10)} = \frac{-3}{13}$

$\therefore \quad \frac{f}{g} = \left\{\left(2, \frac{4}{5}\right), \left(8, -\frac{1}{4}\right), \left(10, \frac{-3}{13}\right)\right\}$

Hence, the correct matches are (a) → (iii), (b) → (iv), (c) → (ii), (d) → (i).

State True or False for the following statements in each of the exercises from 38 to 42.

Q.38 The ordered pair (5, 2) belongs to the relation

$$R = \{(x, y) : y = x - 5, x, y \in Z\}$$

Ans. *False*

We have, $R = \{(x, y) : y = x - 5, x, y \in Z\}$

If $x = 5$, then $y = 5 - 5 = 0$

Hence, (5, 2) does not belong to R.

Q.39 If $P = \{1, 2\}$, then $P \times P \times P = \{(1, 1, 1), (2, 2, 2), (1, 2, 2), (2, 1, 1)\}$.

Ans. *False*

We have, $P = \{1, 2\}$

$P \times P = \{1, 2\} \times \{1, 2\} = \{(1, 1), (1, 2), (2, 1), (2, 2)\}$

$P \times P \times P = \{(1, 1), (1, 2), (2, 1), (2, 1)\} \times \{1, 2\}$

$= \{(1, 1, 1), (1, 2, 1), (2, 1, 1), (2, 2, 1), (1, 1, 2), (1, 2, 2), (2, 1, 2), (2, 2, 2)\}$

Q.40 If $A = \{1, 2, 3\}$, $B = \{3, 4\}$ and $C = \{4, 5, 6\}$, then $(A \times B) \cup (A \times C)$
$= \{(1, 3), (1, 4), (1, 5), (1, 6), (2, 3), (2, 4), (2, 5), (2, 6), (3, 3), (3, 4), (3, 5), (3, 6)\}$.

Thinking Process First, we find $A \times B$ and $A \times C$, then we will find $(A \times B) \cup (A \times C)$.

Ans. *True*

We have, $A = \{1, 2, 3\}$, $B = \{3, 4\}$ and $C = \{4, 5, 6\}$

$$A \times B = \{(1, 3), (1, 4), (2, 3), (2, 4), (3, 3), (3, 4)\}$$

$$A \times C = \{(1, 4), (1, 5), (1, 6), (2, 4), (2, 5), (2, 6), (3, 4), (3, 5), (3, 6)\}$$

$$\therefore \quad (A \times B) \cup (A \times C) = \{(1, 3), (1, 4), (1, 5), (1, 6), (2, 3), (2, 4), (2, 5), (2, 6), (3, 3), (3, 4), (3, 5), (3, 6)\}$$

Q.41 If $(x - 2, y + 5) = \left(-2, \dfrac{1}{3}\right)$ are two equal ordered pairs, then $x = 4$, $y = \dfrac{-14}{3}$.

Thinking Process Equate the corresponding elements of given ordered pairs and solve for x and y.

Ans. *False*

We have, $(x - 2, y + 5) = \left(-2, \dfrac{1}{3}\right)$

$$\Rightarrow \quad x - 2 = -2, \; y + 5 = \frac{1}{3}$$

$$\Rightarrow \quad x = -2 + 2, \; y = \frac{1}{3} - 5$$

$$\therefore \quad x = 0, \quad y = \frac{-14}{3}$$

Q.42 If $A \times B = \{(a, x), (a, y), (b, x), (b, y)\}$, then $A = \{a, b\}$ and $B = \{x, y\}$.

Ans. *True*

We have, $A \times B = \{(a, x), (a, y), (b, x), (b, y)\}$

$A =$ Set of first elements of ordered pairs in $A \times B = \{a, b\}$

And $B =$ Set of second elements of ordered pairs in $A \times B = \{x, y\}$.

Chapter

03

Trigonometric Functions

Short Answer Type Questions

Q.1 Prove that $\dfrac{\tan A+\sec A-1}{\tan A-\sec A+1}=\dfrac{1+\sin A}{\cos A}$.

Thinking Process Here, use the formulae *i.e.*, $\sec^2 A - \tan^2 A = 1$ and $a^2 - b^2 = (a+b)(a-b)$ to solve the above problem.

Ans. LHS $=\dfrac{\tan A+\sec A-1}{\tan A-\sec A+1}$

$$=\frac{\tan A+\sec A-(\sec^2 A-\tan^2 A)}{(\tan A-\sec A+1)} \qquad [\because \sec^2 A-\tan^2 A=1]$$

$$=\frac{(\tan A+\sec A)-(\sec A+\tan A)(\sec A-\tan A)}{(1-\sec A+\tan A)}$$

$$[\because a^2-b^2=(a+b)(a-b)]$$

$$=\frac{(\sec A+\tan A)(1-\sec A+\tan A)}{1-\sec A+\tan A}$$

$$=\sec A+\tan A=\frac{1}{\cos A}+\frac{\sin A}{\cos A}$$

$$=\frac{1+\sin A}{\cos A}=\text{RHS}$$

Hence proved.

Q.2 If $\dfrac{2\sin\alpha}{1+\cos\alpha+\sin\alpha}=y$, then prove that $\dfrac{1-\cos\alpha+\sin\alpha}{1+\sin\alpha}$ is also equal to y.

Ans. Given, $\dfrac{2\sin\alpha}{1+\cos\alpha+\sin\alpha}=y$

Now, $$\frac{1-\cos\alpha+\sin\alpha}{1+\sin\alpha}=\frac{(1-\cos\alpha+\sin\alpha)}{(1+\sin\alpha)}\cdot\frac{(1+\cos\alpha+\sin\alpha)}{(1+\cos\alpha+\sin\alpha)}$$

$$=\frac{\{(1+\sin\alpha)-\cos\alpha\}}{(1+\sin\alpha)}\cdot\frac{\{(1+\sin\alpha)+\cos\alpha\}}{(1+\sin\alpha+\cos\alpha)}$$

$$=\frac{(1+\sin\alpha)^2-\cos^2\alpha}{(1+\sin\alpha)(1+\sin\alpha+\cos\alpha)}$$

$$= \frac{(1+\sin^2\alpha + 2\sin\alpha) - \cos^2\alpha}{(1+\sin\alpha)(1+\sin\alpha+\cos\alpha)}$$

$$= \frac{1+\sin^2\alpha + 2\sin\alpha - 1 + \sin^2\alpha}{(1+\sin\alpha)(1+\sin\alpha+\cos\alpha)} \quad [\because \sin^2\alpha + \cos^2\alpha = 1]$$

$$= \frac{2\sin^2\alpha + 2\sin\alpha}{(1+\sin\alpha)(1+\sin\alpha+\cos\alpha)}$$

$$= \frac{2\sin\alpha(1+\sin\alpha)}{(1+\sin\alpha)(1+\sin\alpha+\cos\alpha)}$$

$$= \frac{2\sin\alpha}{1+\sin\alpha+\cos\alpha} = y \quad \text{[from Eq. (i)]}$$

Hence proved.

Q.3 If $m\sin\theta = n\sin(\theta+2\alpha)$, then prove that $\tan(\theta+\alpha)\cot\alpha = \frac{m+n}{m-n}$.

Thinking Process To simplify the equation use the componendo and dividendo rule *i.e.,* If $\frac{a}{b} = \frac{c}{d}$, then $\frac{a+b}{a-b} = \frac{c+d}{c-d}$.

Ans. Given, $m\sin\theta = n\sin(\theta+2\alpha)$

$$\therefore \quad \frac{\sin(\theta+2\alpha)}{\sin\theta} = \frac{m}{n}$$

Using componendo and dividendo rule, we get

$$\frac{\sin(\theta+2\alpha)+\sin\theta}{\sin(\theta+2\alpha)-\sin\theta} = \frac{m+n}{m-n}$$

$$\Rightarrow \frac{2\sin\left(\frac{\theta+2\alpha+\theta}{2}\right)\cdot\cos\left(\frac{\theta+2\alpha-\theta}{2}\right)}{2\cos\left(\frac{\theta+2\alpha+\theta}{2}\right)\cdot\sin\left(\frac{\theta+2\alpha-\theta}{2}\right)} = \frac{m+n}{m-n}$$

$$\left[\because \sin x + \sin y = 2\sin\frac{x+y}{2}\cdot\cos\frac{x-y}{2} \text{ and } \sin x - \sin y = 2\cos\frac{x+y}{2}\sin\cdot\frac{x-y}{2}\right]$$

$$\Rightarrow \frac{\sin(\theta+\alpha)\cdot\cos\alpha}{\cos(\theta+\alpha)\cdot\sin\alpha} = \frac{m+n}{m-n}$$

$$\Rightarrow \tan(\theta+\alpha)\cdot\cot\alpha = \frac{m+n}{m-n}$$

Hence proved.

Q.4 If $\cos(\alpha+\beta) = \frac{4}{5}$ and $\sin(\alpha-\beta) = \frac{5}{13}$, where α and β lie between 0 and $\frac{\pi}{4}$, then find that value of $\tan 2\alpha$.

Ans. Given, $\cos(\alpha+\beta) = \frac{4}{5}$ and $\sin(\alpha-\beta) = \frac{5}{13}$, where $0 \le \alpha, \beta \le \frac{\pi}{4}$

$\Rightarrow \alpha+\beta$ and $\alpha-\beta$ lie in the first quadrant.

Now, $$\sin(\alpha+\beta) = \sqrt{1-\frac{16}{25}} = \sqrt{\frac{9}{25}} = \pm\frac{3}{5}$$

$$\therefore \quad \sin(\alpha+\beta) = \frac{3}{5} \quad [\because \alpha+\beta \in \text{first quadrant}]$$

and $\cos(\alpha-\beta)=\sqrt{1-\frac{25}{169}}=\sqrt{\frac{144}{169}}=\pm\frac{12}{13}$

$\therefore$ $\cos(\alpha-\beta)=\frac{12}{13}$ [$\because \alpha-\beta \in$ first quadrant]

Now, $\tan(\alpha+\beta)=\frac{\sin(\alpha+\beta)}{\cos(\alpha+\beta)}$

$$=\frac{\frac{3}{5}}{\frac{4}{5}}=\frac{3}{4}$$

and $\tan(\alpha-\beta)=\frac{\sin(\alpha-\beta)}{\cos(\alpha-\beta)}=\frac{\frac{5}{13}}{\frac{12}{13}}=\frac{5}{12}$

$\therefore$ $\tan 2\alpha=\tan(\alpha+\beta+\alpha-\beta)$

$$=\frac{\tan(\alpha+\beta)+\tan(\alpha-\beta)}{1-\tan(\alpha+\beta)\cdot\tan(\alpha-\beta)} \quad \left[\because \tan(x\pm y)=\frac{\tan x\pm\tan y}{1\mp\tan x\cdot\tan y}\right]$$

$$=\frac{\frac{3}{4}+\frac{5}{12}}{1-\frac{3}{4}\cdot\frac{5}{12}}=\frac{\frac{9+5}{12}}{\frac{16-5}{16}}=\frac{14\times16}{12\times11}=\frac{56}{33}$$

Q.5 If $\tan x=\frac{b}{a}$, then find the value of $\sqrt{\frac{a+b}{a-b}}+\sqrt{\frac{a-b}{a+b}}$.

Ans. Given, $\tan x=\frac{b}{a}$

$$\therefore \sqrt{\frac{a+b}{a-b}}+\sqrt{\frac{a-b}{a+b}}=\frac{\sqrt{(a+b)^2}+\sqrt{(a-b)^2}}{\sqrt{(a-b)(a+b)}}$$

$$=\frac{(a+b)+(a-b)}{\sqrt{a^2-b^2}}=\frac{2a}{\sqrt{a^2-b^2}}=\frac{2a}{a\sqrt{1-\left(\frac{b}{a}\right)^2}} \quad \left[\because \frac{b}{a}=\tan x\right]$$

$$=\frac{2}{\sqrt{1-\tan^2 x}}=\frac{2\cos x}{\sqrt{\cos^2 x-\sin^2 x}}=\frac{2\cos x}{\sqrt{\cos 2x}}$$

[$\because \cos 2x=\cos^2 x-\sin^2 x$]

Q.6 Prove that $\cos\theta\cos\frac{\theta}{2}-\cos 3\theta\cos\frac{9\theta}{2}=\sin\frac{7\theta}{2}\sin 4\theta$.

Thinking Process First, we will express it in the form of $2\cos A\cos B$ and then use $2\cos A\cos B=\cos(A+B)+\cos(A-B)$ and then apply

$$\cos A-\cos B=2\sin\left(\frac{A+B}{2}\right)\sin\left(\frac{B-A}{2}\right)$$

Ans. $\text{LHS} = \cos\theta\cos\frac{\theta}{2} - \cos 3\theta\cos\frac{9\theta}{2}$

$$= \frac{1}{2}\left[2\cos\theta\cdot\cos\frac{\theta}{2} - 2\cos 3\theta\cdot\cos\frac{9\theta}{2}\right]$$

$$= \frac{1}{2}\left[\cos\left(\theta+\frac{\theta}{2}\right) + \cos\left(\theta-\frac{\theta}{2}\right) - \cos\left(3\theta+\frac{9\theta}{2}\right) - \cos\left(3\theta-\frac{9\theta}{2}\right)\right]$$

$[\because 2\cos x\cos y = \cos(x+y)+\cos(x-y)]$

$$= \frac{1}{2}\left[\cos\frac{3\theta}{2} + \cos\frac{\theta}{2} - \cos\frac{15\theta}{2} - \cos\frac{3\theta}{2}\right]$$

$$= \frac{1}{2}\left[\cos\frac{\theta}{2} - \cos\frac{15\theta}{2}\right]$$

$$= \frac{1}{2}\left[2\sin\left(\frac{\theta+15\theta}{4}\right)\cdot\sin\left(\frac{15\theta-\theta}{4}\right)\right] \quad \left[\because \cos x - \cos y = 2\sin\frac{x+y}{2}\cdot\sin\frac{y-x}{2}\right]$$

$$= \left(\sin 4\theta\cdot\sin\frac{7\theta}{2}\right) = \text{RHS} \quad [\because \sin^2\theta+\cos^2\theta = 1]$$

$\therefore$ LHS = RHS **Hence proved.**

Q.7 If $a\cos\theta + b\sin\theta = m$ and $a\sin\theta - b\cos\theta = n$, then show that $a^2+b^2 = m^2+n^2$.

Ans. Given, $a\cos\theta + b\sin\theta = m$ ...(i)

and $a\sin\theta - b\cos\theta = n$ ...(ii)

On squaring and adding of Eqs. (i) and (ii), we get

$$m^2+n^2 = (a\cos\theta+b\sin\theta)^2 + (a\sin\theta - b\cos\theta)^2$$

$$= a^2\cos^2\theta + b^2\sin^2\theta + 2ab\sin\theta\cdot\cos\theta + a^2\sin^2\theta + b^2\cos^2\theta - 2ab\sin\theta\cdot\cos\theta$$

$$\Rightarrow m^2+n^2 = a^2(\cos^2\theta+\sin^2\theta) + b^2(\sin^2\theta+\cos^2\theta)$$

$$\Rightarrow m^2+n^2 = a^2+b^2$$

$[\because \sin^2\theta+\cos^2\theta = 1]$ **Hence proved.**

Q.8 Find the value of $\tan 22°30'$.

Ans. Let $\theta = 45° \Rightarrow \frac{\theta}{2} = 22°30'$

We know that $\tan\frac{\theta}{2} = \dfrac{\sin\frac{\theta}{2}}{\cos\frac{\theta}{2}} = \dfrac{2\sin\frac{\theta}{2}\cdot\cos\frac{\theta}{2}}{2\cos^2\frac{\theta}{2}}$

$\left[\because \text{multiply numerator and denominator by } 2\cos\frac{\theta}{2}\right]$

$$\Rightarrow \tan\frac{\theta}{2} = \frac{\sin\theta}{1+\cos\theta}$$

[using the formulae $\sin 2x = 2\sin x\cos x$ and $1+\cos 2x = 2\cos^2 x$]

$$\therefore \tan 22°30' = \frac{\sin 45°}{1+\cos 45°} \quad [\because \theta = 45°]$$

$$= \frac{\frac{1}{\sqrt{2}}}{1+\frac{1}{\sqrt{2}}} = \frac{1}{\sqrt{2}+1}$$

Q.9 Prove that $\sin 4A = 4\sin A\cos^3 A - 4\cos A\sin^3 A$.

Thinking Process Here, apply the formulae $\sin 2x = 2\sin x\cos x$ and $\cos 2x = \cos^2 x - \sin^2 x$.

Ans.
$$\text{LHS} = \sin 4A$$
$$= 2\sin 2A \cdot \cos 2A$$
$$= 2(2\sin A \cdot \cos A)(\cos^2 A - \sin^2 A) \quad \left[\because \cos 2A = \cos^2 A - \sin^2 A \text{ and } \sin 2A = 2\sin A\cdot\cos A\right]$$
$$= 4\sin A\cdot\cos^3 A - 4\cos A\sin^3 A$$
$\therefore$ LHS = RHS **Hence proved.**

Q.10 If $\tan\theta + \sin\theta = m$ and $\tan\theta - \sin\theta = n$, then prove that $m^2 - n^2 = 4\sin\theta\tan\theta$.

Ans. Given, $\tan\theta + \sin\theta = m$ ...(i)

and $\tan\theta - \sin\theta = n$ ...(ii)

Now, $m + n = \tan\theta + \sin\theta + \tan\theta - \sin\theta$

$m + n = 2\tan\theta$ ...(iii)

Also, $m - n = \tan\theta + \sin\theta - \tan\theta + \sin\theta$

$m - n = 2\sin\theta$ ...(iv)

From Eqs. (iii) and (iv), $(m+n)(m-n) = 4\sin\theta\cdot\tan\theta$

$m^2 - n^2 = 4\sin\theta\cdot\tan\theta$ **Hence proved.**

Q.11 If $\tan(A+B) = p$ and $\tan(A-B) = q$, then show that $\tan 2A = \dfrac{p+q}{1-pq}$.

Thinking Process First write $\tan 2A = \tan(A + B + A - B)$, then apply the formula $\tan(x+y) = \dfrac{\tan x + \tan y}{1 - \tan x\tan y}$ by assuming $x = A + B$ and $y = A - B$.

Ans. Given, $\tan(A+B) = p$ ...(i)

And $\tan(A-B) = q$ ...(ii)

$$\therefore \tan 2A = \tan(A + B + A - B)$$
$$= \frac{\tan(A+B) + \tan(A-B)}{1 - \tan(A+B)\tan(A-B)} \quad \left[\because \tan(x+y) = \frac{\tan x + \tan y}{1 - \tan x\tan y}\right]$$
$$= \frac{p+q}{1-pq} \quad \text{[from Eqs. (i) and (ii)]}$$

Q.12 If $\cos\alpha + \cos\beta = 0 = \sin\alpha + \sin\beta$, then prove that $\cos 2\alpha + \cos 2\beta = -2\cos(\alpha+\beta)$.

Ans. Given, $\cos\alpha + \cos\beta = 0 = \sin\alpha + \sin\beta$

$\Rightarrow (\cos\alpha + \cos\beta)^2 - (\sin\alpha + \sin\beta)^2 = 0$

$\Rightarrow \cos^2\alpha + \cos^2\beta + 2\cos\alpha\cos\beta - \sin^2\alpha - \sin^2\beta - 2\sin\alpha\sin\beta = 0$

$\Rightarrow \cos^2\alpha - \sin^2\alpha + \cos^2\beta - \sin^2\beta = 2(\sin\alpha\sin\beta - \cos\alpha\cos\beta)$

$\Rightarrow \cos 2\alpha + \cos 2\beta = -2\cos(\alpha+\beta)$ $[\because \cos 2x = \cos^2 x - \sin^2 x]$ **Hence proved.**

Q.13 If $\dfrac{\sin(x+y)}{\sin(x-y)} = \dfrac{a+b}{a-b}$, then show that $\dfrac{\tan x}{\tan y} = \dfrac{a}{b}$.

Ans. Given, $\dfrac{\sin(x+y)}{\sin(x-y)} = \dfrac{a+b}{a-b}$

Using componendo and dividendo rule, we get

$$\Rightarrow \quad \frac{\sin(x+y)+\sin(x-y)}{\sin(x+y)-\sin(x-y)} = \frac{a+b+a-b}{a+b-a+b}$$

$$\Rightarrow \quad \frac{2\sin\left(\frac{x+y+x-y}{2}\right)\cdot\cos\left(\frac{x+y-x+y}{2}\right)}{2\cos\left(\frac{x+y+x-y}{2}\right)\cdot\sin\left(\frac{x+y-x+y}{2}\right)} = \frac{2a}{2b}$$

$$\left[\because \sin x+\sin y = 2\sin\frac{x+y}{2}\cdot\cos\frac{x-y}{2} \text{ and } \sin x-\sin y = 2\cos\frac{x+y}{2}\cdot\sin\frac{x-y}{2}\right]$$

$$\Rightarrow \quad \frac{\sin x\cdot\cos y}{\cos x\cdot\sin y} = \frac{a}{b}$$

$$\Rightarrow \quad \frac{\tan x}{\tan y} = \frac{a}{b}$$

Hence proved.

Q.14 If $\tan\theta = \dfrac{\sin\alpha - \cos\alpha}{\sin\alpha + \cos\alpha}$, then show that $\sin\alpha + \cos\alpha = \sqrt{2}\cos\theta$.

Ans. Given, $\tan\theta = \dfrac{\sin\alpha - \cos\alpha}{\sin\alpha + \cos\alpha}$

$$\Rightarrow \quad \tan\theta = \frac{\cos\alpha(\tan\alpha - 1)}{\cos\alpha(\tan\alpha + 1)}$$

$$\Rightarrow \quad \tan\theta = \frac{\tan\alpha - \tan\frac{\pi}{4}}{1+\tan\frac{\pi}{4}\cdot\tan\alpha} \qquad \left[\because \tan\frac{\pi}{4} = 1\right]$$

$$\Rightarrow \quad \tan\theta = \tan\left(\alpha - \frac{\pi}{4}\right) \qquad \left[\because \tan(x-y) = \frac{\tan x - \tan y}{1+\tan x\tan y}\right]$$

$$\Rightarrow \quad \theta = \alpha - \frac{\pi}{4}$$

$$\Rightarrow \quad \alpha = \theta + \frac{\pi}{4}$$

$$\text{LHS} = \sin\alpha + \cos\alpha = \sin\left(\theta+\frac{\pi}{4}\right) + \cos\left(\theta+\frac{\pi}{4}\right)$$

$$= \sin\theta\cdot\cos\frac{\pi}{4} + \cos\theta\cdot\sin\frac{\pi}{4} + \cos\theta\cdot\cos\frac{\pi}{4} - \sin\theta\cdot\sin\frac{\pi}{4}$$

$$= \frac{1}{\sqrt{2}}\sin\theta + \frac{1}{\sqrt{2}}\cos\theta + \frac{1}{\sqrt{2}}\cos\theta - \frac{1}{\sqrt{2}}\sin\theta \qquad \left[\because \sin\frac{\pi}{4} = \cos\frac{\pi}{4} = \frac{1}{\sqrt{2}}\right]$$

$$= \frac{2}{\sqrt{2}}\cdot\cos\theta = \sqrt{2}\cos\theta = \text{RHS}$$

Hence proved.

***Q.15** If $\sin\theta + \cos\theta = 1$, then find the general value of θ.

Thinking Process If $\sin\theta = \sin\alpha$, then $\theta = n\pi + (-1)^n \cdot \alpha$, gives general solution of the given equation.

Ans. Given,

$$\sin\theta + \cos\theta = 1$$

$$\Rightarrow \frac{1}{\sqrt{2}}\cdot\sin\theta + \frac{1}{\sqrt{2}}\cdot\cos\theta = \frac{1}{\sqrt{2}}$$

$$\Rightarrow \sin\theta\cdot\cos\frac{\pi}{4} + \cos\theta\cdot\sin\frac{\pi}{4} = \frac{1}{\sqrt{2}} \quad \left[\because \sin\frac{\pi}{4} = \frac{1}{\sqrt{2}} = \cos\frac{\pi}{4}\right]$$

$$\Rightarrow \sin\left(\theta + \frac{\pi}{4}\right) = \sin\frac{\pi}{4} \quad [\because \sin(x+y) = \sin x\cdot\cos y + \cos x\cdot\sin y]$$

$$\Rightarrow \theta + \frac{\pi}{4} = n\pi + (-1)^n\frac{\pi}{4}$$

$$\therefore \theta = n\pi + (-1)^n\frac{\pi}{4} - \frac{\pi}{4}, n \in Z$$

***Q.16** Find the most general value of θ satisfying the equation $\tan\theta = -1$ and $\cos\theta = \frac{1}{\sqrt{2}}$.

Ans. The given equations are

$$\tan\theta = -1 \quad \ldots(i)$$

and

$$\cos\theta = \frac{1}{\sqrt{2}} \quad \ldots(ii)$$

Since, negative tangent and positive cosine are possible together only in IV quadrant.

From Eq. (i), $\tan\theta = -\tan\frac{\pi}{4}$

$$\Rightarrow \tan\theta = \tan\left(2\pi - \frac{\pi}{4}\right) \Rightarrow \tan\theta = \tan\frac{7\pi}{4}$$

$$\therefore \theta = \frac{7\pi}{4} \in \text{IV quadrant}$$

From Eq. (ii), $\cos\theta = \frac{1}{\sqrt{2}} \Rightarrow \cos\theta = \cos\frac{\pi}{4}$

$$\Rightarrow \cos\theta = \cos\left(2\pi - \frac{\pi}{4}\right) \Rightarrow \cos\theta = \cos\frac{7\pi}{4}$$

$$\therefore \theta = \frac{7\pi}{4} \in \text{IV quadrant}$$

Hence, the most general value of θ *i.e.*, $\theta = 2n\pi + \frac{7\pi}{4}; n \in Z$

***Q.17** If $\cot\theta + \tan\theta = 2\operatorname{cosec}\theta$, then find the general value of θ.

Ans. Given,

$$\cot\theta + \tan\theta = 2\operatorname{cosec}\theta$$

$$\Rightarrow \frac{\cos\theta}{\sin\theta} + \frac{\sin\theta}{\cos\theta} = \frac{2}{\sin\theta}$$

(*) Topics related to these question have been removed from latest NCERT.

$$\Rightarrow \quad \frac{\cos^2 + \sin^2\theta}{\sin\theta\cdot\cos\theta} = \frac{2}{\sin\theta} \quad \Rightarrow \quad \frac{1}{\cos\theta} = 2 \qquad [\because \sin\theta \neq 0 \text{ and } \sin^2\theta + \cos^2\theta = 1]$$

$$\Rightarrow \quad \cos\theta = \frac{1}{2} \quad \Rightarrow \quad \cos\theta = \cos\frac{\pi}{3}$$

$$\therefore \quad \theta = 2n\pi \pm \frac{\pi}{3}, n \in Z$$

Q.18 If $2\sin^2\theta = 3\cos\theta$, where $0 \leq \theta \leq 2\pi$, then find the value of θ.

Ans. Given, $2\sin^2\theta = 3\cos\theta$

$$\Rightarrow \quad 2 - 2\cos^2\theta = 3\cos\theta$$

$$\Rightarrow \quad 2\cos^2\theta + 3\cos\theta - 2 = 0 \qquad [\because \sin^2\theta = 1 - \cos^2\theta]$$

$$\Rightarrow \quad 2\cos^2\theta + 4\cos\theta - \cos\theta - 2 = 0$$

$$\Rightarrow \quad 2\cos\theta(\cos\theta + 2) - 1(\cos\theta + 2) = 0$$

$$\Rightarrow \quad (\cos\theta + 2)(2\cos\theta - 1) = 0$$

$$\Rightarrow \quad \cos\theta = -2 \text{ (not possible)} \qquad [\because -1 \leq \cos\theta \leq 1]$$

$$\therefore \quad 2\cos\theta = 1$$

$$\Rightarrow \quad \cos\theta = \frac{1}{2} \Rightarrow \cos\theta = \cos\frac{\pi}{3}$$

$$\therefore \quad \theta = \frac{\pi}{3}$$

Also, $\cos\theta = \cos\left(2\pi - \frac{\pi}{3}\right) \Rightarrow \cos\theta = \cos\frac{5\pi}{3}$ $\qquad [\because 0 \leq \theta \leq 2\pi]$

$$\therefore \quad \theta = \frac{5\pi}{3}$$

So, the values of θ are $\frac{\pi}{3}$ and $\frac{5\pi}{3}$.

Q.19 If $\sec x \cos 5x + 1 = 0$, where $0 < x \leq \frac{\pi}{2}$, then find the value of x.

Ans. Given, $\sec x \cos 5x + 1 = 0$

$$\Rightarrow \quad \frac{\cos 5x}{\cos x} + 1 = 0 \Rightarrow \cos 5x + \cos x = 0$$

$$\Rightarrow \quad 2\cos\left(\frac{5x + x}{2}\right)\cdot\cos\left(\frac{5x - x}{2}\right) = 0 \qquad \left[\because \cos x + \cos y = 2\cos\frac{x+y}{2}\cdot\cos\frac{x-y}{2}\right]$$

$$\Rightarrow \quad 2\cos 3x \cdot \cos 2x = 0$$

$$\Rightarrow \quad \cos 3x = 0 \text{ or } \cos 2x = 0$$

$$\Rightarrow \quad \cos 3x = \cos\frac{\pi}{2} \text{ or } \cos 2x = \cos\frac{\pi}{2}$$

$$\Rightarrow \quad 3x = (2n+1)\frac{\pi}{2}; n \in Z \text{ or } 2x = (2n+1)\frac{\pi}{2}; n \in Z$$

$$\Rightarrow \quad 3x = \frac{\pi}{2}, \frac{3\pi}{2} \text{ or } 2x = \frac{\pi}{2} \Rightarrow x = \frac{\pi}{6}, x = \frac{\pi}{2} \text{ or } x = \frac{\pi}{4} \qquad \left[\because 0 < x \leq \frac{\pi}{2}\right]$$

Hence, the solutions are $\frac{\pi}{2}, \frac{\pi}{4}$ and $\frac{\pi}{6}$.

Long Answer Type Questions

Q.20 If $\sin(\theta+\alpha)=a$ and $\sin(\theta+\beta)=b$, then prove that $\cos 2(\alpha-\beta)-4ab\cos(\alpha-\beta)=1-2a^2-2b^2$.

Thinking Process Express $\cos(\alpha-\beta)=\cos[(\theta+\alpha)-(\theta+\beta)]$, then apply the formulae $\cos(x-y)=\cos x\cos y+\sin x\sin y$ and $\cos 2x=2\cos^2 x-1$

Ans. Given, $\sin(\theta+\alpha)=a$ ...(i)

and $\sin(\theta+\beta)=b$ ...(ii)

$\therefore$ $\cos(\theta+\alpha)=\pm\sqrt{1-a^2}$ and $\cos(\theta+\beta)=\pm\sqrt{1-b^2}$ $[\because \cos^2 x=1-\sin^2 x]$

If we take positive sign, then

$$\cos(\alpha-\beta)=\cos\{\theta+\alpha-(\theta+\beta)\}$$
$$=\cos(\theta+\beta)\cos(\theta+\alpha)+\sin(\theta+\alpha)\sin(\theta+\beta)$$
$$=\sqrt{1-a^2}\sqrt{1-b^2}+a\cdot b=a\cdot b+\sqrt{(1-a^2)(1-b^2)}$$
$$=ab+\sqrt{1-a^2-b^2+a^2b^2}$$

$\therefore$ $\cos(\alpha-\beta)=ab+\sqrt{1-a^2-b^2+a^2b^2}$

Now, $\cos 2(\alpha-\beta)-4ab\cos(\alpha-\beta)$
$$=2\cos^2(\alpha-\beta)-1-4ab\cos(\alpha-\beta)$$
$$=2\cos(\alpha-\beta)(\cos(\alpha-\beta)-2ab)-1$$
$$=2(ab+\sqrt{1-a^2-b^2+a^2b^2})(ab+\sqrt{1-a^2-b^2+a^2b^2}-2ab)-1$$
$$=2[(\sqrt{1-a^2-b^2+a^2b^2}+ab)(\sqrt{1-a^2-b^2+a^2b^2}-ab)-1$$
$$=2[1-a^2-b^2+a^2b^2-a^2b^2]-1$$
$$=2-2a^2-2b^2-1=1-2a^2-2b^2$$

Similarly, if we take (+, –), (–, +) and (–, –) signs for $\cos(\theta+\alpha)$ and $\cos(\theta+\beta)$, then we get the same result. **Hence proved.**

Q.21 If $\cos(\theta+\phi)=m\cos(\theta-\phi)$, then prove that $\tan\theta=\frac{1-m}{1+m}\cot\phi$.

Thinking Process Express $\frac{\cos(\theta-\phi)}{\cos(\phi+\phi)}=\frac{1}{m}$ and apply the componendo and dividends rule.

Ans. Given, $\cos(\theta+\phi)=m\cos(\theta-\phi)\Rightarrow\frac{\cos(\theta-\phi)}{\cos(\theta+\phi)}=\frac{1}{m}$

Using componendo and dividendo rule, $\frac{\cos(\theta-\phi)-\cos(\theta+\phi)}{\cos(\theta-\phi)+\cos(\theta+\phi)}=\frac{1-m}{1+m}$

$$\Rightarrow\quad \frac{-2\sin\left(\frac{\theta-\phi+\theta+\phi}{2}\right)\cdot\sin\left(\frac{\theta-\phi-\theta-\phi}{2}\right)}{2\cos\left(\frac{\theta-\phi+\theta+\phi}{2}\right)\cdot\cos\left(\frac{\theta-\phi-\theta-\phi}{2}\right)}=\frac{1-m}{1+m}$$

$$\left[\begin{array}{l}\because \cos C+\cos D=2\cos\left(\frac{C+D}{2}\right)\cos\left(\frac{C-D}{2}\right)\\ \text{and } \cos C-\cos D=-2\sin\left(\frac{C+D}{2}\right)\sin\left(\frac{C-D}{2}\right)\end{array}\right]$$

$\Rightarrow \quad \dfrac{\sin\theta \cdot \sin\phi}{\cos\theta \cdot \cos\phi} = \dfrac{1-m}{1+m}$ $\left[\because \begin{array}{l} \sin(-\theta) = -\sin\theta \\ \text{and } \cos(-\theta) = \cos\theta \end{array}\right]$

$\Rightarrow \quad \tan\theta \cdot \tan\phi = \dfrac{1-m}{1+m} \Rightarrow \tan\theta = \left(\dfrac{1-m}{1+m}\right)\cot\phi$ **Hence proved.**

Q.22 Find the value of the expression

$$3\left[\sin^4\left(\frac{3\pi}{2}-\alpha\right)+\sin^4(3\pi+\alpha)\right]-2\left[\sin^6\left(\frac{\pi}{2}+\alpha\right)+\sin^6(5\pi-\alpha)\right].$$

Ans. Given expression,

$$3\left[\sin^4\left(\frac{3\pi}{2}-\alpha\right)+\sin^4(3\pi+\alpha)\right]-2\left[\sin^6\left(\frac{\pi}{2}+\alpha\right)+\sin^6(5\pi-\alpha)\right]$$

$$= 3[\cos^4\alpha + \sin^4(\pi+\alpha)] - 2[\cos^6\alpha + \sin^6(\pi-\alpha)]$$

$[\because \sin(2n\pi+\alpha) = \sin\alpha]$

$$= 3[\cos^4\alpha + \sin^4\alpha] - 2[\cos^6\alpha + \sin^6\alpha]$$

$$= 3[(\cos^2\alpha+\sin^2\alpha)^2 - 2\sin^2\alpha\cos^2\alpha] - 2[(\cos^2\alpha+\sin^2\alpha)^3$$

$$(\cos^2\alpha + \sin^2\alpha)]$$

$$= 3[1-2\sin^2\alpha\cos^2\alpha] - 2-[1-3\cos^2\alpha\sin^2\alpha] = 3-2 = 1$$

Q.23 If $a\cos 2\theta + b\sin 2\theta = c$ has α and β as its roots, then prove that $\tan\alpha + \tan\beta = \dfrac{2b}{a+c}$.

Ans. Given, $\quad a\cos 2\theta + b\sin 2\theta = c$

$\Rightarrow \quad a\left(\dfrac{1-\tan^2\theta}{1+\tan^2\theta}\right) + b\left(\dfrac{2\tan\theta}{1+\tan^2\theta}\right) = c$

$\left[\because \sin 2\theta = \dfrac{2\tan\theta}{1+\tan^2\theta} \text{ and } \cos 2\theta = \dfrac{1-\tan^2\theta}{1+\tan^2\theta}\right]$

$\Rightarrow \quad a(1-\tan^2\theta) + 2b\tan\theta = c(1+\tan^2\theta)$

$\Rightarrow \quad a - a\tan^2\theta + 2b\tan\theta = c + c\tan^2\theta$

$\Rightarrow \quad (a+c)\tan^2\theta - 2b\tan\theta + c - a = 0$

Since, this equation has $\tan\alpha$ and $\tan\beta$ as its roots.

$\therefore$ Sum of roots $= \tan\alpha + \tan\beta = \dfrac{-(-2b)}{a+c} = \dfrac{2b}{a+c}$

$\left[\because \text{if } ax^2+bx+c=0 \Rightarrow \text{sum of roots} = -\dfrac{b}{a}\right]$ **Hence Proved.**

Q.24 If $x = \sec\phi - \tan\phi$ and $y = \operatorname{cosec}\phi + \cot\phi$, then show that $xy + x - y + 1 = 0$.

Ans. Given, $\quad x = \sec\phi - \tan\phi \quad$ ...(i)

and $\quad y = \operatorname{cosec}\phi + \cot\phi \quad$ ...(ii)

Now, $\quad xy = (\sec\phi - \tan\phi)(\operatorname{cosec}\phi + \cot\phi)$

$\Rightarrow \quad xy = \sec\phi \cdot \operatorname{cosec}\phi - \operatorname{cosec}\phi \cdot \tan\phi + \sec\phi \cdot \cot\phi - \tan\phi \cdot \cot\phi$

$$\Rightarrow \quad xy = \sec\phi \cdot \operatorname{cosec}\phi - \frac{1}{\cos\phi} + \frac{1}{\sin\phi} - 1$$

$$\Rightarrow \quad 1 + xy = \sec\phi \operatorname{cosec}\phi - \sec\phi + \operatorname{cosec}\phi \quad \text{...(iii)}$$

From Eqs. (i) and (ii), we get

$$x - y = \sec\phi - \tan\phi - \operatorname{cosec}\phi - \cot\phi$$

$$\Rightarrow \quad x - y = \sec\phi - \operatorname{cosec}\phi - \frac{\sin\phi}{\cos\phi} - \frac{\cos\phi}{\sin\phi}$$

$$\Rightarrow \quad x - y = \sec\phi - \operatorname{cosec}\phi - \left(\frac{\sin^2\phi + \cos^2\phi}{\sin\phi \cdot \cos\phi}\right)$$

$$\Rightarrow \quad x - y = \sec\phi - \operatorname{cosec}\phi - \frac{1}{\sin\phi \cdot \cos\phi}$$

$$\Rightarrow \quad x - y = \sec\phi - \operatorname{cosec}\phi - \operatorname{cosec}\phi \cdot \sec\phi$$

$$\Rightarrow \quad x - y = -(\sec\phi \cdot \operatorname{cosec}\phi - \sec\phi + \operatorname{cosec}\phi)$$

$$\Rightarrow \quad x - y = -(xy + 1) \quad \text{[from Eq. (iii)]}$$

$$\Rightarrow \quad xy + x - y + 1 = 0$$

Hence proved.

Q.25 If θ lies in the first quadrant and $\cos\theta = \frac{8}{17}$, then find the value of $\cos(30° + \theta) + \cos(45° - \theta) + \cos(120° - \theta)$.

Ans. Given that, $\cos\theta = \frac{8}{17}$ ...(i)

$$\Rightarrow \quad \sin\theta = \pm\sqrt{1 - \frac{64}{289}} \quad [\because \sin^2 x = 1 - \cos^2 x]$$

$$\Rightarrow \quad \sin\theta = \pm\sqrt{\frac{289 - 64}{289}}$$

$$\Rightarrow \quad \sin\theta = \pm\frac{15}{17}$$

$$\Rightarrow \quad \sin\theta = \frac{15}{17} \quad [\because \theta \text{ lies in the first quadrant}] \text{ ...(ii)}$$

Now, $\cos(30° + \theta) + \cos(45° - \theta) + \cos(120° - \theta)$

$$= \cos(30° + \theta) + \cos(45° - \theta) + \cos(90° + 30° - \theta)$$

$$= \cos(30° + \theta) + \cos(45° - \theta) - \sin(30° - \theta) \quad [\because \cos(90° + \theta) = -\sin\theta]$$

$$= \cos 30° \cos\theta - \sin 30° \sin\theta + \cos 45° \cos\theta + \sin 45° \sin\theta - \sin 30° \cos\theta + \cos 30° \sin\theta$$

$$= \frac{\sqrt{3}}{2}\cos\theta - \frac{1}{2}\sin\theta + \frac{1}{\sqrt{2}}\cos\theta + \frac{1}{\sqrt{2}}\sin\theta - \frac{1}{2}\cos\theta + \frac{\sqrt{3}}{2}\sin\theta$$

$$= \left(\frac{\sqrt{3}}{2} + \frac{1}{\sqrt{2}} - \frac{1}{2}\right)\cos\theta + \left(\frac{1}{\sqrt{2}} - \frac{1}{2} + \frac{\sqrt{3}}{2}\right)\sin\theta$$

$$= \left(\frac{\sqrt{3}}{2} + \frac{1}{\sqrt{2}} - \frac{1}{2}\right)[\cos\theta + \sin\theta] \quad \text{[using Eqs. (i) and (ii)]}$$

$$= \left(\frac{\sqrt{3}}{2} + \frac{1}{\sqrt{2}} - \frac{1}{2}\right)\left(\frac{8}{17} + \frac{15}{17}\right) = \frac{23}{17}\left(\frac{\sqrt{3} - 1}{2} + \frac{1}{\sqrt{2}}\right)$$

Q.26 Find the value of $\cos^4\frac{\pi}{8}+\cos^4\frac{3\pi}{8}+\cos^4\frac{5\pi}{8}+\cos^4\frac{7\pi}{8}$.

Ans. Given expression, $\cos^4\frac{\pi}{8}+\cos^4\frac{3\pi}{8}+\cos^4\frac{5\pi}{8}+\cos^4\frac{7\pi}{8}$

$$=\cos^4\frac{\pi}{8}+\cos^4\frac{3\pi}{8}+\cos^4\left(\pi-\frac{3\pi}{8}\right)+\cos^4\left(\pi-\frac{\pi}{8}\right)$$

$$=\cos^4\frac{\pi}{8}+\cos^4\frac{3\pi}{8}+\left(-\cos\frac{3\pi}{8}\right)^4+\left(-\cos\frac{\pi}{8}\right)^4 \quad [\because \cos(\pi-\theta)=-\cos\theta]$$

$$=2\left[\cos^4\frac{\pi}{8}+\cos^4\frac{3\pi}{8}\right]=2\left[\cos^4\frac{\pi}{8}+\cos^4\left(\frac{\pi}{2}-\frac{\pi}{8}\right)\right]$$

$$=2\left[\cos^4\frac{\pi}{8}+\sin^4\frac{\pi}{8}\right]=2\left[\left(\cos^2\frac{\pi}{8}+\sin^2\frac{\pi}{8}\right)^2-2\cos^2\frac{\pi}{8}\cdot\sin^2\frac{\pi}{8}\right]$$

$$\left[\because \cos\left(\frac{\pi}{2}-\theta\right)=\sin\theta\right]$$

$$=2\left[1-2\cos^2\frac{\pi}{8}\cdot\sin^2\frac{\pi}{8}\right]=2-\left(2\sin\frac{\pi}{8}\cdot\cos\frac{\pi}{8}\right)^2 \quad [\because \cos^2\theta+\sin^2\theta=1]$$

$$=2-\left(\sin\frac{2\pi}{8}\right)^2=2-\sin^2\frac{\pi}{4}=2-\left(\frac{1}{\sqrt{2}}\right)^2=2-\frac{1}{2}=\frac{3}{2} \quad [\because 2\sin\theta\cos\theta=\sin 2\theta]$$

***Q.27** Find the general solution of the equation $5\cos^2\theta+7\sin^2\theta-6=0$.

Ans. Given equation, $5\cos^2\theta+7\sin^2\theta-6=0 \Rightarrow 5\cos^2\theta+7(1-\cos^2\theta)-6=0$

$\Rightarrow \quad 5\cos^2\theta+7-7\cos^2\theta-6=0$

$\Rightarrow \quad -2\cos^2\theta+1=0 \Rightarrow 2\cos^2\theta-1=0$

$\Rightarrow \quad \cos^2\theta=\frac{1}{2} \Rightarrow \cos^2\theta=\cos^2\frac{\pi}{4}$

$\therefore \quad \theta=n\pi\pm\frac{\pi}{4}, n\in Z \quad \left[\begin{array}{l}\because \cos^2\theta=\cos^2\alpha\\ \Rightarrow \theta=n\pi\pm\alpha\end{array}\right]$

***Q.28** Find the general solution of the equation $\sin x-3\sin 2x+\sin 3x = \cos x-3\cos 2x+\cos 3x$.

Ans. Given equation, $\sin x-3\sin 2x+\sin 3x=\cos x-3\cos 2x+\cos 3x$

$\Rightarrow \quad 2\sin\left(\frac{x+3x}{2}\right)\cdot\cos\left(\frac{3x-x}{2}\right)-3\sin 2x=2\cos\left(\frac{3x+x}{2}\right)\cdot\cos\left(\frac{3x-x}{2}\right)-3\cos 2x$

$\left[\because \sin C+\sin D=2\sin\frac{C+D}{2}\cos\frac{C-D}{2} \text{ and } \cos C+\cos D=2\cos\frac{C+D}{2}\cos\frac{C-D}{2}\right]$

$\Rightarrow \quad 2\sin 2x\cos x-3\sin 2x=2\cos 2x\cdot\cos x-3\cos 2x$

$\Rightarrow \quad \sin 2x(2\cos x-3)=\cos 2x(2\cos x-3)$

$\Rightarrow \quad (2\cos x-3)(\sin 2x-\cos 2x)=0$

But $2\cos x-3\neq 0 \quad (\because 1\le\cos 2x\le 1)$

$\therefore \quad \sin 2x-\cos 2x=0$

$\Rightarrow \quad \frac{\sin 2x}{\cos 2x}=1 \Rightarrow \tan 2x=1 \quad \left[\because \cos x\neq\frac{3}{2}\right]$

(✱) Topics related to these question have been removed from latest NCERT.

$$\Rightarrow \quad \tan 2x = \tan\frac{\pi}{4} \Rightarrow 2x = n\pi + \frac{\pi}{4} \quad [\because \tan\theta = \tan\alpha \Rightarrow \theta = n\pi + \alpha]$$

$$\therefore \quad x = \frac{n\pi}{2} + \frac{\pi}{8}, n \in Z$$

***Q.29** Find the general solution of the equation

$(\sqrt{3}-1)\cos\theta + (\sqrt{3}+1)\sin\theta = 2$

Ans. Given equation, $(\sqrt{3}-1)\cos\theta + (\sqrt{3}+1)\sin\theta = 2$ ...(i)

Put $\sqrt{3}-1 = r\sin\alpha$ and $\sqrt{3}+1 = r\cos\alpha$

$$\therefore \quad r^2 = (\sqrt{3}-1)^2 + (\sqrt{3}+1)^2 = 3+1-2\sqrt{3}+3+1+2\sqrt{3}$$

$$\Rightarrow \quad r^2 = 8$$

$$\therefore \quad r = 2\sqrt{2}$$

Now,
$$\tan\alpha = \frac{\sqrt{3}-1}{\sqrt{3}+1} = \frac{\tan\frac{\pi}{3} - \tan\frac{\pi}{4}}{1+\tan\frac{\pi}{3}\cdot\frac{\pi}{4}}$$

$$\Rightarrow \quad \tan\alpha = \tan\left(\frac{\pi}{3} - \frac{\pi}{4}\right) \quad \left[\because \tan(x-y) = \frac{\tan x - \tan y}{1+\tan x \tan y}\right]$$

$$\Rightarrow \quad \tan\alpha = \tan\frac{\pi}{12} \quad \therefore \alpha = \frac{\pi}{12}$$

From Eq. (i), $r\sin\alpha\cos\theta + r\cos\alpha\sin\theta = 2$

$$r[\sin(\theta+\alpha)] = 2 \Rightarrow \sin(\theta+\alpha) = \frac{2}{2\sqrt{2}} \quad [\because r = 2\sqrt{2}]$$

$$\Rightarrow \quad \sin(\theta+\alpha) = \frac{1}{\sqrt{2}} \Rightarrow \sin(\theta+\alpha) = \sin\frac{\pi}{4}$$

$$\Rightarrow \quad \theta+\alpha = n\pi + (-1)^n\frac{\pi}{4} \Rightarrow \theta = n\pi + (-1)^n\cdot\frac{\pi}{4} - \frac{\pi}{12}; n \in Z$$

$$[\because \sin x = \sin y \Rightarrow x = n\pi + (-1)^n y]$$

Alternate Method

Given, $(\sqrt{3}-1)\cos\theta + (\sqrt{3}+1)\sin\theta = 2$ ...(i)

Put $\sqrt{3}-1 = r\cos\alpha$ and $\sqrt{3}+1 = r\sin\alpha$

$$\therefore \quad r = 2\sqrt{2}$$

Now,
$$\tan\alpha = \frac{\sqrt{3}+1}{\sqrt{3}-1} = \frac{1+\frac{1}{\sqrt{3}}}{1-\frac{1}{\sqrt{3}}} \Rightarrow \tan\alpha = \frac{\tan\frac{\pi}{4} + \tan\frac{\pi}{6}}{1-\tan\frac{\pi}{4}\cdot\tan\frac{\pi}{6}}$$

$$\Rightarrow \quad \tan\alpha = \tan\left(\frac{\pi}{4} + \frac{\pi}{6}\right) \Rightarrow \tan\alpha = \tan\frac{5\pi}{12}$$

$$\therefore \quad \alpha = \frac{5\pi}{12}$$

From Eq. (i), $r\cos\alpha\cos\theta + r\sin\alpha\sin\theta = 2$

$$r[\cos(\theta-\alpha)] = 2 \Rightarrow \cos(\theta-\alpha) = \frac{2}{2\sqrt{2}}$$

$$\Rightarrow \quad \cos(\theta-\alpha) = \frac{1}{\sqrt{2}} \Rightarrow \cos(\theta-\alpha) = \cos\frac{\pi}{4}$$

$$\Rightarrow \quad \theta - \alpha = 2n\pi \pm \frac{\pi}{4}$$

$$\therefore \quad \theta = 2n\pi \pm \frac{\pi}{4} + \frac{5\pi}{12}; n \in Z$$

(*) Topics related to these question have been removed from latest NCERT.

Objective Type Questions

Choose the correct answers from the given four options in each exercises 30 to 59.

Q.30 If $\sin\theta + \text{cosec}\theta = 2$, then $\sin^2\theta + \text{cosec}^2\theta$ is equal to

(a) 1 (b) 4 (c) 2 (d) None of these

Ans. *(c)* Given, $\sin\theta + \text{cosec}\,\theta = 2$

On squaring both sides, we get

$\Rightarrow \quad \sin^2\theta + \text{cosec}^2\theta + 2\sin\theta\cdot\text{cosec}\,\theta = 4$

$\Rightarrow \quad \sin^2\theta + \text{cosec}^2\theta = 4 - 2 \Rightarrow \sin^2\theta + \text{cosec}^2\theta = 2$

Q.31 If $f(x) = \cos^2 x + \sec^2 x$, then

(a) $f(x) < 1$ (b) $f(x) = 1$ (c) $2 < f(x) < 1$ (d) $f(x) \geq 2$

● **Concept Insight** For non-negative number $x_1, x_2, \ldots x_n$, $AM \geq GM$

i.e., $\dfrac{x_1 + x_2 + \ldots + x_n}{n} \geq (x_1, x_2 \ldots x_n)^{1/n}$

Ans. *(d)* Given, $f(x) = \cos^2 x + \sec^2 x$

We know that AM ≥ GM

$$\frac{\cos^2 x + \sec^2 x}{2} \geq \sqrt{\cos^2 x\cdot\sec^2 x} \Rightarrow \cos^2 x + \sec^2 x \geq 2 \quad [\because \cos x\cdot\sec x = 1]$$

$\Rightarrow \quad f(x) \geq 2$

Q.32 If $\tan\theta = \frac{1}{2}$ and $\tan\phi = \frac{1}{3}$, then the value of $\theta + \phi$ is

(a) $\frac{\pi}{6}$ (b) π (c) 0 (d) $\frac{\pi}{4}$

Ans. *(d)* Given, $\tan\theta = \frac{1}{2}$ and $\tan\phi = \frac{1}{3}$

Now, $$\tan(\theta + \phi) = \frac{\tan\theta + \tan\phi}{1 - \tan\theta\cdot\tan\phi}$$

$$\Rightarrow \quad \tan(\theta + \phi) = \frac{\frac{1}{2} + \frac{1}{3}}{1 - \frac{1}{2}\cdot\frac{1}{3}} \Rightarrow \tan(\theta + \phi) = \frac{\frac{3+2}{6}}{\frac{6-1}{6}} = 1$$

$$\Rightarrow \quad \tan(\theta + \phi) = \tan\frac{\pi}{4}$$

$$\therefore \quad \theta + \phi = \frac{\pi}{4}$$

Q.33 Which of the following is not correct?

(a) $\sin\theta = -\frac{1}{5}$ (b) $\cos\theta = 1$ (c) $\sec\theta = \frac{1}{2}$ (d) $\tan\theta = 20$

Ans. *(c)* $\because \sin\theta \in [-1, 1]$, $\cos\theta \in [-1, 1]$ and $\tan\theta \in (-\infty, \infty)$

$\therefore$ Option (a), (b) and (d) are correct

We know that the range of $\sec\theta$ is $R - (-1, 1)$.

Hence, $\sec\theta$ cannot be equal to $\frac{1}{2}$. Therefore, option (c) is not correct.

Q.34 The value of $\tan 1° \tan 2° \tan 3° \ldots \tan 89°$ is

(a) 0 (b) 1 (c) $\frac{1}{2}$ (d) Not defined

Ans. *(b)* Given expression, $\tan 1° \tan 2° \tan 3° \ldots \tan 89°$

$= \tan 1° \tan 2° \ldots \tan 45° \cdot \tan(90° - 44°) \tan(90° - 43°) \ldots \tan(90° - 1°)$

$= \tan 1° \cdot \cot 1° \cdot \tan 2° \cdot \cot 2° \ldots \tan 44° \cdot \cot 44° \tan 45°$ $[\because \tan(90° - \theta) = \cot \theta]$

$= 1 \cdot 1 \ldots 1 \cdot 1 = 1$ $[\because \tan \theta \cdot \cot \theta = 1]$

Q.35 The value of $\frac{1 - \tan^2 15°}{1 + \tan^2 15°}$ is

(a) 1 (b) $\sqrt{3}$ (c) $\frac{\sqrt{3}}{2}$ (d) 2

Ans. *(c)* Given expression, $\frac{1 - \tan^2 15°}{1 + \tan^2 15°}$

Let $\theta = 15°$

We know that, $\cos 2\theta = \frac{1 - \tan^2 \theta}{1 + \tan^2 \theta}$

$\therefore \frac{1 - \tan^2 15°}{1 + \tan^2 15°} = \cos 30° = \frac{\sqrt{3}}{2}$ $\left[\because \cos 30° = \frac{\sqrt{3}}{2}\right]$

Q.36 The value of $\cos 1° \cos 2° \cos 3° \ldots \cos 179°$ is

(a) $\frac{1}{\sqrt{2}}$ (b) 0 (c) 1 (d) -1

Ans. *(b)* Given expression, $\cos 1° \cos 2° \cos 3° \ldots \cos 179°$

$= \cos 1° \cos 2° \ldots \cos 90° \ldots \cos 179°$

$= 0$ $[\because \cos 90° = 0]$

Q.37 If $\tan \theta = 3$ and θ lies in third quadrant, then the value of $\sin \theta$ is

(a) $\frac{1}{\sqrt{10}}$ (b) $-\frac{1}{\sqrt{10}}$

(c) $\frac{-3}{\sqrt{10}}$ (d) $\frac{3}{\sqrt{10}}$

Ans. *(c)* Given, $\tan \theta = 3$

$\Rightarrow \sec^2 \theta = 1 + \tan^2 \theta$

$\Rightarrow \sec \theta = \pm \sqrt{1 + 9} = \pm \sqrt{10}$

$\because \sec \theta$ and $\cos \theta$ are negative in third quadrant.

$\therefore \sec \theta = -\sqrt{10} \Rightarrow \cos \theta = -\frac{1}{\sqrt{10}}$

$\Rightarrow \sin \theta = \pm \sqrt{1 - \frac{1}{10}} = \pm \sqrt{\frac{9}{10}} = \pm \frac{3}{\sqrt{10}}$ $[\because \sin^2 \theta = 1 - \cos^2 \theta]$

$\therefore \sin \theta = -\frac{3}{\sqrt{10}}$ [$\because \sin \theta$ is negative in third quadrant]

Q.38 The value of $\tan 75° - \cot 75°$ is equal to

(a) $2\sqrt{3}$ (b) $2+\sqrt{3}$
(c) $2-\sqrt{3}$ (d) 1

Ans. ***(a)*** Given expression, $\tan 75° - \cot 75°$

$$= \frac{\sin 75°}{\cos 75°} - \frac{\cos 75°}{\sin 75°}$$

$$= \frac{\sin^2 75° - \cos^2 75°}{\sin 75° \cdot \cos 75°} = \frac{-(\cos^2 75° - \sin^2 75°)}{\frac{1}{2}\cdot(2\sin 75° \cos 75°)}$$

$$= \frac{-2\cos 150°}{\sin 150°} = \frac{-2\cos(90°+60°)}{\sin(90°+60°)} \quad \left[\begin{array}{l}\because \cos 2\theta = \cos^2\theta - \sin^2\theta \\ \text{and } \sin 2\theta = 2\sin\theta\cos\theta\end{array}\right]$$

$$= \frac{2\sin 60°}{\cos 60°} = \frac{2\cdot\frac{\sqrt{3}}{2}}{\frac{1}{2}} = 2\sqrt{3}$$

Q.39 Which of the following is correct?

(a) $\sin 1° > \sin 1$ (b) $\sin 1° < \sin 1$
(c) $\sin 1° = \sin 1$ (d) $\sin 1° = \frac{\pi}{18°}\sin 1$

Ans. ***(b)*** We know that if θ is increasing from 0° to 90°, then $\sin\theta$ is also increasing.

$$\therefore \quad \sin 1° < \sin 1 \quad [\because 1 \text{ rad} = 57°30']$$

Q.40 If $\tan\alpha = \frac{m}{m+1}$ and $\tan\beta = \frac{1}{2m+1}$, then $\alpha+\beta$ is equal to

(a) $\frac{\pi}{2}$ (b) $\frac{\pi}{3}$
(c) $\frac{\pi}{6}$ (d) $\frac{\pi}{4}$

Ans. ***(d)*** Given, $\tan\alpha = \frac{m}{m+1}$ and $\tan\beta = \frac{1}{2m+1}$

Now, $$\tan(\alpha+\beta) = \frac{\tan\alpha + \tan\beta}{1-\tan\alpha\cdot\tan\beta} = \frac{\frac{m}{m+1}+\frac{1}{2m+1}}{1-\left(\frac{m}{m+1}\right)\left(\frac{1}{2m+1}\right)}$$

$$= \frac{m(2m+1)+m+1}{(m+1)(2m+1)-m}$$

$$= \frac{2m^2+m+m+1}{2m^2+2m+m+1-m}$$

$$\Rightarrow \quad \tan(\alpha+\beta) = \frac{2m^2+2m+1}{2m^2+2m+1}$$

$$\Rightarrow \quad \tan(\alpha+\beta) = 1$$

$$\therefore \quad \alpha+\beta = \frac{\pi}{4}$$

Q.41 The minimum value of $3\cos x + 4\sin x + 8$ is

(a) 5 (b) 9 (c) 7 (d) 3

● **Concept Insight** We know that, $-\sqrt{A^2+B^2} \le A\cos\theta + B\sin\theta \le \sqrt{A^2+B^2}$.

Ans. ***(d)*** Given expression, $3\cos x + 4\sin x + 8$

Let $y = 3\cos x + 4\sin x + 8$

$\Rightarrow y - 8 = 3\cos x + 4\sin x$

$\therefore$ Minimum value of $y - 8 = -\sqrt{9+16}$

$\Rightarrow y - 8 = -5 \Rightarrow y = -5 + 8 = 3$

Hence, the minimum value of $3\cos x + 4\sin x + 8$ is 3.

Q.42 The value of $\tan 3A - \tan 2A - \tan A$ is

(a) $\tan 3A \tan 2A \tan A$

(b) $-\tan 3A \tan 2A \tan A$

(c) $\tan A \tan 2A - \tan 2A \tan 3A - \tan 3A \tan A$

(d) None of the above

Ans. ***(a)*** Let $3A = A + 2A$

$\Rightarrow \tan 3A = \tan(A + 2A)$ [taking tan on both sides]

$\Rightarrow \tan 3A = \dfrac{\tan A + \tan 2A}{1 - \tan A \cdot \tan 2A}$ $\left[\because \tan(x+y) = \dfrac{\tan x + \tan y}{1 - \tan x \tan y}\right]$

$\Rightarrow \tan A + \tan 2A = \tan 3A - \tan 3A \cdot \tan 2A \cdot \tan A$

$\Rightarrow \tan 3A - \tan 2A - \tan A = \tan 3A \cdot \tan 2A \cdot \tan A$

Q.43 The value of $\sin(45° + \theta) - \cos(45° - \theta)$ is

(a) $2\cos\theta$ (b) $2\sin\theta$

(c) 1 (d) 0

Thinking Process Use formule $\sin(A+B) = \sin A\cos B + \cos A\sin B$ and $\cos(A-B) = \cos A\cos B + \sin A\sin B$.

Ans. ***(d)*** Given expression, $\sin(45° + \theta) - \cos(45° - \theta)$

$$= \sin 45° \cdot \cos\theta + \cos 45° \cdot \sin\theta - \cos 45° \cdot \cos\theta - \sin 45° \cdot \sin\theta$$

$$= \frac{1}{\sqrt{2}} \cdot \cos\theta + \frac{1}{\sqrt{2}} \cdot \sin\theta - \frac{1}{\sqrt{2}} \cdot \cos\theta - \frac{1}{\sqrt{2}} \sin\theta = 0$$

Q.44 The value of $\cot\left(\dfrac{\pi}{4} + \theta\right)\cot\left(\dfrac{\pi}{4} - \theta\right)$ is

(a) -1 (b) 0

(c) 1 (d) Not defined

● **Concept Insight** Use formulae $\cot(A+B) = \left(\dfrac{\cot A \cot B - 1}{\cot A + \cot B}\right)$ and

$\cot(A-B) = \left(\dfrac{\cot A \cot B + 1}{\cot B - \cot A}\right)$.

Ans. *(c)* Given expression, $\cot\left(\frac{\pi}{4}+\theta\right)\cot\left(\frac{\pi}{4}-\theta\right)$

$$=\left(\frac{\cot\frac{\pi}{4}\cot\theta-1}{\cot\frac{\pi}{4}+\cot\theta}\right)\cdot\left(\frac{\cot\frac{\pi}{4}\cot\theta+1}{\cot\theta-\cot\frac{\pi}{4}}\right)$$

$$=\left(\frac{\cot\theta-1}{\cot\theta+1}\right)\cdot\left(\frac{\cot\theta+1}{\cot\theta-1}\right)$$

$$=1$$

Q.45 $\cos 2\theta\cos 2\phi+\sin^2(\theta-\phi)-\sin^2(\theta+\phi)$ is equal to

(a) $\sin 2(\theta+\phi)$
(b) $\cos 2(\theta+\phi)$
(c) $\sin 2(\theta-\phi)$
(d) $\cos 2(\theta-\phi)$

Ans. *(b)* Given expression, $\cos 2\theta\cos 2\phi+\sin^2(\theta-\phi)-\sin^2(\theta+\phi)$

$$=\cos 2\theta\cdot\cos 2\phi+\sin(\theta-\phi+\theta+\phi)\cdot\sin(\theta-\phi-\theta-\phi)$$

$$[\because \sin^2 A-\sin^2 B=\sin(A+B)\sin(A-B)]$$

$$=\cos 2\theta\cdot\cos 2\phi-\sin 2\theta\cdot\sin 2\phi \qquad [\because \sin(-x)=-\sin x]$$

$$=\cos(2\theta+2\phi)=\cos 2(\theta+\phi)$$

Q.46 The value of $\cos 12^\circ+\cos 84^\circ+\cos 156^\circ+\cos 132^\circ$ is

(a) $\frac{1}{2}$
(b) 1
(c) $-\frac{1}{2}$
(d) $\frac{1}{8}$

Thinking Process Use the formulae $\cos A+\cos E=2\cos\frac{A+B}{2}\cdot\cos\frac{A-B}{2}$ and $\cos A-\cos B=-2\sin\frac{A+B}{2}\cdot\sin\frac{A-B}{2}$ to solve this problem.

Ans. *(c)* Given expression, $\cos 12^\circ+\cos 84^\circ+\cos 156^\circ+\cos 132^\circ$

$$=\cos 12^\circ+\cos 156^\circ+\cos 84^\circ+\cos 132^\circ$$

$$=2\cos\left(\frac{12^\circ+156^\circ}{2}\right)\cdot\cos\left(\frac{12^\circ-156^\circ}{2}\right)+2\cos\left(\frac{84^\circ+132^\circ}{2}\right)\cdot\cos\left(\frac{84^\circ-132^\circ}{2}\right)$$

$$=2\cos 84^\circ\cos 72^\circ+2\cos 108^\circ\cdot\cos 24^\circ \qquad [\because \cos(-\theta)=\cos\theta]$$

$$=2\cos 84^\circ\cos(90^\circ-18^\circ)+2\cos(90^\circ+18^\circ)\cdot\cos 24^\circ$$

$$=2\cos 84^\circ\sin 18^\circ-2\sin 18^\circ\cdot\cos 24^\circ=2\sin 18^\circ(\cos 84^\circ-\cos 24^\circ)$$

$$=-2\sin 18^\circ\cdot 2\sin\left(\frac{84^\circ+24^\circ}{2}\right)\cdot\sin\left(\frac{84^\circ-24^\circ}{2}\right)=-4\sin 18^\circ\cdot\sin 54^\circ\sin 30^\circ$$

$$=-4\left(\frac{\sqrt{5}-1}{4}\right)\cdot\cos 36^\circ\cdot\frac{1}{2} \qquad [\because \sin\theta=\cos(90^\circ-\theta)]$$

$$=-(\sqrt{5}-1)\left(\frac{\sqrt{5}+1}{4}\right)\cdot\frac{1}{2}=-\left(\frac{5-1}{8}\right)=\frac{1}{2}$$

Q.47 If $\tan A = \frac{1}{2}$ and $\tan B = \frac{1}{3}$, then $\tan(2A + B)$ is equal to

(a) 1 (b) 2 (c) 3 (d) 4

Ans. *(c)* Given, $\tan A = \frac{1}{2}$ and $\tan B = \frac{1}{3}$

Now, $$\tan(2A + B) = \frac{\tan 2A + \tan B}{1 - \tan 2A \cdot \tan B} \quad \text{...(i)}$$

Also, $$\tan 2A = \frac{2\tan A}{1 - \tan^2 A} = \frac{2 \cdot \frac{1}{2}}{1 - \frac{1}{4}} = \frac{4}{3}$$

From Eq. (i), $$\tan(2A + B) = \frac{\frac{4}{3} + \frac{1}{3}}{1 - \frac{4}{3} \cdot \frac{1}{3}} = \frac{\frac{4}{3} + \frac{1}{3}}{\frac{9-4}{9}} = \frac{\frac{5}{3}}{\frac{5}{9}} = 3$$

Q.48 The value of $\sin \frac{\pi}{10} \sin \frac{13\pi}{10}$ is

(a) $\frac{1}{2}$ (b) $-\frac{1}{2}$ (c) $-\frac{1}{4}$ (d) 1

Ans. *(c)* Given expression, $\sin \frac{\pi}{10} \sin \frac{13\pi}{10} = \sin \frac{\pi}{10} \sin \left(\pi + \frac{3\pi}{10}\right)$

$$= -\sin \frac{\pi}{10} \sin \frac{3\pi}{10} = -\sin 18° \cdot \sin 54° \quad [\because \sin(\pi + \theta) = -\sin\theta]$$

$$= -\sin 18° \cdot \cos 36° \quad [\because \sin\theta = \cos(90° - \theta)]$$

$$= -\left(\frac{\sqrt{5} - 1}{4}\right)\left(\frac{\sqrt{5} + 1}{4}\right) \quad [\because \text{put this value here}]$$

$$= -\left(\frac{5 - 1}{16}\right) = -\frac{1}{4}$$

Note $\sin 18° = \frac{\sqrt{5} - 1}{4}$ and $\cos 36° = \frac{\sqrt{5} + 1}{4}$

Q.49 The value of $\sin 50° - \sin 70° + \sin 10°$ is

(a) 1 (b) 0 (c) $\frac{1}{2}$ (d) 2

Thinking Process Here, use the formulae $\sin A - \sin B = 2\cos\left(\frac{A + B}{2}\right) \cdot \sin\left(\frac{A - B}{2}\right)$ and $\sin(-\theta) = -\sin\theta$.

Ans. *(b)* Given expression, $\sin 50° - \sin 70° + \sin 10°$

$$= 2\cos\left(\frac{50° + 70°}{2}\right) \cdot \sin\left(\frac{50° - 70°}{2}\right) + \sin 10°$$

$$= -2\cos 60° \sin 10° + \sin 10°$$

$$= -2 \cdot \frac{1}{2} \sin 10° + \sin 10° = 0$$

Q.50 If $\sin\theta + \cos\theta = 1$, then the value of $\sin 2\theta$ is

(a) 1 (b) $\frac{1}{2}$ (c) 0 (d) −1

Ans. **(c)** Given, $\sin\theta + \cos\theta = 1$

On squaring both sides, we get

$$\sin^2\theta + \cos^2\theta + 2\sin\theta\cdot\cos\theta = 1 \Rightarrow 1 + \sin 2\theta = 1$$

$$\therefore \quad \sin 2\theta = 0$$

Q.51 If $\alpha + \beta = \frac{\pi}{4}$, then the value of $(1 + \tan\alpha)(1 + \tan\beta)$ is

(a) 1 (b) 2 (c) −2 (d) Not defined

Thinking Process formula $\tan(A + B) = \frac{\tan A + \tan B}{1 - \tan A\cdot\tan B}$ to solve this problem.

Ans. **(b)** Given, $\alpha + \beta = \frac{\pi}{4}$

Now, $(1 + \tan\alpha)(1 + \tan\beta) = 1 + \tan\alpha + \tan\beta + \tan\alpha\tan\beta$ ...(i)

We know that $\tan(\alpha + \beta) = \frac{\tan\alpha + \tan\beta}{1 - \tan\alpha\cdot\tan\beta}$

$$\Rightarrow \quad 1 = \frac{\tan\alpha + \tan\beta}{1 - \tan\alpha\cdot\tan\beta} \Rightarrow \tan\alpha + \tan\beta = 1 - \tan\alpha\tan\beta$$

From Eq. (i), $(1 + \tan\alpha)(1 + \tan\beta) = 1 + 1 - \tan\alpha\cdot\tan\beta + \tan\alpha\cdot\tan\beta$

$$= 2$$

Q.52 If $\sin\theta = \frac{-4}{5}$ and θ lies in third quadrant, then the value of $\cos\frac{\theta}{2}$ is

(a) $\frac{1}{5}$ (b) $-\frac{1}{\sqrt{10}}$ (c) $-\frac{1}{\sqrt{5}}$ (d) $\frac{1}{\sqrt{10}}$

● **Concept Insight** Use the formulae $\cos\theta = \pm\sqrt{1 - \sin^2\theta}$ and $\cos\theta = 2\cos^2\frac{\theta}{2} - 1$.

Ans. **(c)** Given that, $\sin\theta = \frac{-4}{5}$

$$\therefore \quad \cos\theta = \pm\sqrt{1 - \frac{16}{25}} = \pm\sqrt{\frac{25 - 16}{25}} = \pm\frac{3}{5}$$

$$\Rightarrow \quad \cos\theta = \frac{-3}{5} \quad [\because \theta \text{ lies in third quadrant}]$$

$$\Rightarrow \quad 2\cos^2\frac{\theta}{2} - 1 = \frac{-3}{5} \Rightarrow 2\cos^2\frac{\theta}{2} = 1 - \frac{3}{5} \Rightarrow 2\cos^2\frac{\theta}{2} = \frac{2}{5}$$

$$\therefore \quad \cos\frac{\theta}{2} = \pm\frac{1}{\sqrt{5}}$$

Since, θ lies in III quadrant.

Therefore, $\frac{\theta}{2}$ lies in II quadrant

$$\therefore \quad \cos\frac{\theta}{2} = -\frac{1}{\sqrt{5}} \quad [\because \cos x \text{ is negative in second quadrant}]$$

Q.53 Number of solutions of equation $\tan x + \sec x = 2\cos x$ lying in the interval $[0, 2\pi]$ is

(a) 0 (b) 1 (c) 2 (d) 3

Ans. *(c)* Given equation, $\tan + \sec x = 2\cos x$

$$\Rightarrow \frac{\sin x}{\cos x} + \frac{1}{\cos x} = 2\cos x$$
$$\Rightarrow 1 + \sin x = 2\cos^2 x$$
$$\Rightarrow 1 + \sin x = 2(1 - \sin^2 x)$$
$$\Rightarrow 1 + \sin x = 2 - 2\sin^2 x$$
$$\Rightarrow 2\sin^2 x + \sin x - 1 = 0$$
$$\Rightarrow 2\sin^2 x + 2\sin x - \sin x - 1 = 0$$
$$\Rightarrow 2\sin x(\sin x + 1) - 1(\sin x + 1) = 0$$
$$\Rightarrow (\sin x + 1)(2\sin x - 1) = 0$$
$$\Rightarrow \sin x + 1 = 0 \text{ or } (2\sin x - 1) = 0$$
$$\Rightarrow \sin x = -1 \text{ or } \sin x = \frac{1}{2}$$
$$\therefore x = \frac{3\pi}{2}, x = \frac{\pi}{6} \qquad [\because x \in [0, 2\pi]]$$

Hence, only two solutions are possible.

Q.54 The value of $\sin\frac{\pi}{18} + \sin\frac{\pi}{9} + \sin\frac{2\pi}{9} + \sin\frac{5\pi}{18}$ is

(a) $\sin\frac{7\pi}{18} + \sin\frac{4\pi}{9}$ (b) 1

(c) $\cos\frac{\pi}{6} + \cos\frac{3\pi}{7}$ (d) $\cos\frac{\pi}{9} + \sin\frac{\pi}{9}$

Ans. *(a)* Given expression, $\sin\frac{\pi}{18} + \sin\frac{\pi}{9} + \sin\frac{2\pi}{9} + \sin\frac{5\pi}{18}$

$$= \sin 10° + \sin 20° + \sin 40° + \sin 50°$$
$$= \sin 50° + \sin 10° + \sin 40° + \sin 20°$$
$$= \sin 130° + \sin 10° + \sin 140° + \sin 20° \qquad [\because \sin x = \sin(\pi - x)]$$
$$= 2\sin 70°\cos 60° + 2\sin 80°\cdot\cos 60° \qquad \left[\because \sin x + \sin y = 2\sin\frac{x+y}{2}\cdot\cos\frac{x-y}{2}\right]$$
$$= 2\cdot\frac{1}{2}\sin 70° + 2\cdot\frac{1}{2}\sin 80° \qquad \left[\because \cos 60° = \frac{1}{2}\right]$$
$$= \sin 70° + \sin 80° = \sin\frac{7\pi}{18} + \sin\frac{4\pi}{9}$$

Q.55 If A lies in the second quadrant and $3\tan A + 4 = 0$, then the value of $2\cot A - 5\cos A + \sin A$ is

(a) $\frac{-53}{10}$ (b) $\frac{23}{10}$ (c) $\frac{37}{10}$ (d) $\frac{7}{10}$

● **Concept Insight** Use the formulae *i.e.*, $\sec A = \pm\sqrt{1 + \tan^2 A}$ and $\sin A = \pm\sqrt{1 - \cos^2 A}$, $\sec A = \frac{1}{\cos A}$ and $\tan A = \frac{1}{\cot A}$.

Ans. ***(b)*** Given equation, $3\tan A + 4 = 0$

$$\Rightarrow \quad 3\tan A = -4$$

$$\Rightarrow \quad \tan A = \frac{-4}{3}$$

$$\Rightarrow \quad \cot A = \frac{-3}{4}$$

$$\Rightarrow \quad \sec A = \pm\sqrt{1+\frac{16}{9}} = \pm\sqrt{\frac{25}{9}} = \pm\frac{5}{3}$$

$$\Rightarrow \quad \sec A = \frac{-5}{3} \quad [\because A \text{ lies in second quadrant}]$$

$$\therefore \quad \cos A = \frac{-3}{5}$$

$$\Rightarrow \quad \sin A = \pm\sqrt{1-\frac{9}{25}} = \pm\frac{\sqrt{25-9}}{25} = \pm\frac{4}{5}$$

$$\Rightarrow \quad \sin A = \frac{4}{5} \quad [\because \text{A lies in second quadrant}]$$

$$\therefore \quad 2\cot A - 5\cos A + \sin A = 2\left(\frac{-3}{4}\right) - 5\left(\frac{-3}{5}\right) + \frac{4}{5}$$

$$= \frac{-6}{4} + 3 + \frac{4}{5}$$

$$= \frac{-30+60+16}{20} = \frac{46}{20} = \frac{23}{10}$$

Q.56 The value of $\cos^2 48° - \sin^2 12°$ is

(a) $\frac{\sqrt{5}+1}{8}$ (b) $\frac{\sqrt{5}-1}{8}$

(c) $\frac{\sqrt{5}+1}{5}$ (d) $\frac{\sqrt{5}+1}{2\sqrt{2}}$

● **Concept Insight** Use the formulae $\cos^2 A - \sin^2 B = \cos(A+B)\cos(A-B)$.

Ans. ***(a)*** Given expression, $\cos^2 48° - \sin^2 12°$

$$= \cos(48° + 12°)\cos(48° - 12°)$$

$$= \cos 60° \cdot \cos 36°$$

$$= \frac{1}{2} \cdot \frac{\sqrt{5}+1}{4} \quad \left[\because \cos 36° = \frac{\sqrt{5}+1}{4}\right]$$

$$= \frac{\sqrt{5}+1}{8}$$

Q.57 If $\tan\alpha = \frac{1}{7}$ and $\tan\beta = \frac{1}{3}$, then $\cos 2\alpha$ is equal to

(a) $\sin 2\beta$ (b) $\sin 4\beta$

(c) $\sin 3\beta$ (d) $\cos 2\beta$

Thinking Process Use the formulae $\cos 2\alpha = \frac{1-\tan^2\alpha}{1+\tan^2\alpha}$ and $\sin 2\alpha = \frac{2\tan\alpha}{1+\tan^2\alpha}$.

Ans. ***(b)*** Given, $\tan\alpha = \frac{1}{7}$ and $\tan\beta = \frac{1}{3}$

Now, $\cos 2\alpha = \frac{1-\tan^2\alpha}{1+\tan^2\alpha} = \frac{1-\frac{1}{49}}{1+\frac{1}{49}} = \frac{\frac{48}{49}}{\frac{50}{49}}$

$$= \frac{48}{50} = \frac{24}{25}$$

$\Rightarrow$ $\cos 2\alpha = \frac{24}{25}$ ...(i)

We know that, $\sin 4\beta = \frac{2\tan 2\beta}{1+\tan^2 2\beta}$ ...(ii)

and $\tan 2\beta = \frac{2\tan\beta}{1-\tan^2\beta} = \frac{2\times\frac{1}{3}}{1-\frac{1}{9}}$

$$= \frac{\frac{2}{3}}{\frac{8}{9}} = \frac{2\times 9}{3\times 8} = \frac{3}{4}$$

From Eq, (ii), $\sin 4\beta = \frac{2\times\frac{3}{4}}{1+\frac{9}{16}} = \frac{\frac{6}{4}}{\frac{25}{16}} = \frac{6\times 16}{4\times 25}$

$\Rightarrow$ $\sin 4\beta = \frac{24}{25}$

$\Rightarrow$ $\sin 4\beta = \cos 2\alpha$ [from Eq. (i)]

$\therefore$ $\cos 2\alpha = \sin 4\beta$

Q.58 If $\tan\theta = \frac{a}{b}$, then $b\cos 2\theta + a\sin 2\theta$ is equal to

(a) a (b) b

(c) $\frac{a}{b}$ (d) None of these

Ans. ***(b)*** Given, $\tan\theta = \frac{a}{b}$

$\therefore$ $b\cos 2\theta + a\sin 2\theta = b\left(\frac{1-\tan^2\theta}{1+\tan^2\theta}\right) + a\left(\frac{2\tan\theta}{1+\tan^2\theta}\right)$

$$= b\left(\frac{1-\frac{a^2}{b^2}}{1+\frac{a^2}{b^2}}\right) + a\left(\frac{\frac{2a}{b}}{1+\frac{a^2}{b^2}}\right) = b\left(\frac{b^2-a^2}{b^2+a^2}\right) + \frac{2a^2b}{a^2+b^2}$$

$$= \frac{b}{a^2+b^2}[b^2-a^2+2a^2] = \frac{(a^2+b^2)b}{(a^2+b^2)} = b$$

Q.59 If for real values of x, $\cos\theta = x + \frac{1}{x}$, then

(a) θ is an acute angle (b) θ is right angle
(c) θ is an obtuse angle (d) No value of θ is possible

Thinking Process The quadratic equation $ax^2 + bx + c = 0$ has real roots, if $b^2 - 4ac \geq 0$, use this condition to solve the above problem.

Ans. *(d)* Here, $\cos\theta = x + \frac{1}{x}$

$\Rightarrow$ $\cos\theta = \frac{x^2+1}{x} \Rightarrow x^2 - x\cos\theta + 1 = 0$

For real values of x, $(-\cos\theta)^2 - 4 \times 1 \times 1 \geq 0$

$\cos^2\theta \geq 4$

Which is not possible. $[\because -1 \leq \cos\theta \leq 1 \Rightarrow 0 \leq \cos^2\theta \leq 1]$

Hence, no value of θ is possible.

Fill in the blanks in exercises 60 to 67.

Q.60 The value of $\frac{\sin 50°}{\sin 130°}$ is ....

Ans. Here, $\frac{\sin 50°}{\sin 130°} = \frac{\sin(180° - 130°)}{\sin 130°} = \frac{\sin 130°}{\sin 130°} = 1$ $[\because \sin(180° - \theta) = \sin\theta]$

Q.61 If $k = \sin\left(\frac{\pi}{18}\right)\sin\left(\frac{5\pi}{18}\right)\sin\left(\frac{7\pi}{18}\right)$, then the numerical value of k is ....

Ans. Here, $k = \sin\left(\frac{\pi}{18}\right)\sin\left(\frac{5\pi}{18}\right)\sin\left(\frac{7\pi}{18}\right)$

$= \sin 10° \sin 50° \sin 70°$

$= \sin 10° \cos 40° \cdot \cos 20°$ $\left[\because \sin\left(\frac{\pi}{2} - x\right) = \cos x\right]$

$= \frac{1}{2}\sin 10°[2\cos 40° \cdot \cos 20°]$

$= \frac{1}{2}\sin 10°[\cos 60° + \cos 20°]$ $[\because 2\cos x \cdot \cos y = \cos(x+y) + \cos(x-y)]$

$= \frac{1}{2}\sin 10°\left(\frac{1}{2}\right) + \frac{1}{2}\sin 10° \cos 20°$

$= \frac{1}{4}\sin 10° + \frac{1}{4}[2\sin 10° \cos 20°]$

$= \frac{1}{4}\sin 10° + \frac{1}{4}[\sin 30° - \sin 10°] = \frac{1}{8}$ $\left[\because \sin 30° = \frac{1}{2}\right]$

$[\because 2\sin A\cos B = \sin(A+B) + \sin(A-B)]$

Q.62 If $\tan A = \frac{1 - \cos B}{\sin B}$, then $\tan 2A =$ ....

Thinking Process Use the formulae $\cos\theta = 1 - 2\sin^2\frac{\theta}{2}$ and $\tan 2\theta = \frac{2\tan\theta}{1 - \tan^2\theta}$.

Ans. Given, $\tan A = \frac{1-\cos B}{\sin B} = \frac{1-1+2\sin^2\frac{B}{2}}{2\sin\frac{B}{2}\cdot\cos\frac{B}{2}} = \tan\frac{B}{2}$ ...(i)

Now, $\tan 2A = \frac{2\tan A}{1-\tan^2 A} \Rightarrow \tan 2A = \frac{2\cdot\tan\frac{B}{2}}{1-\tan^2\frac{B}{2}}$ [from Eq. (i)]

$\Rightarrow$ $\tan 2A = \tan B$

Q.63 If $\sin x + \cos x = a$, then

(i) $\sin^6 x + \cos^6 x =$ .... (ii) $|\sin x - \cos x| =$ ....

Ans. Given, $\sin x + \cos x = a$

On squaring both sides, we get

$$(\sin x + \cos x)^2 = (a)^2$$

$\Rightarrow$ $\sin^2 x + \cos^2 x + 2\sin x\cos x = a^2$

$\Rightarrow$ $\sin x\cdot\cos x = \frac{1}{2}(a^2-1)$ $[\because \sin^2\theta + \cos^2\theta = 1]$

(i) $\sin^6 x + \cos^6 x = (\sin^2 x)^3 + (\cos^2 x)^3$

$= (\sin^2 x + \cos^2 x)(\sin^4 x - \sin^2 x\cos^2 x + \cos^4 x)$ $[a^3+b^3 = (a+b)(a^2-ab+b^2)]$

$= \sin^4 x + \cos^4 x - \frac{1}{4}(a^2-1)^2 = (\sin^2 x + \cos^2 x)^2 - 2\sin^2 x\cos^2 x - \frac{1}{4}(a^2-1)^2$

$= 1 - 2\cdot\frac{1}{4}(a^2-1)^2 - \frac{1}{4}(a^2-1)^2 = \frac{1}{4}[4-3(a^2-1)^2]$

(ii) $|\sin x - \cos x| = \sqrt{(\sin x - \cos x)^2} = \sqrt{\sin^2 x + \cos^2 x - 2\sin x\cos x}$

$= \sqrt{1-2\frac{1}{2}(a^2-1)} = \sqrt{1-a^2+1} = \sqrt{2-a^2}$

Q.64 In a right angle ΔABC with $\angle C = 90°$ the equation whose roots are $\tan A$ and $\tan B$ is ....

● **Concept Insight** The quadratic equation whose roots are α and β can be written as $x^2 - (\alpha+\beta)x + \alpha\beta = 0$.

Ans. Given, in right angled ΔABC, $\angle C = 90°$

A B C

$\Rightarrow$ $\angle A + \angle B = 180° - \angle C = 180° - 90° = 90°$

$\therefore$ $\tan(A+B) = \frac{\tan A + \tan B}{1-\tan A\tan B}$

$\Rightarrow$ $\tan(90°) = \frac{\tan A + \tan B}{1-\tan A\tan B}$

$\Rightarrow$ $\frac{1}{0} = \frac{\tan A + \tan B}{1-\tan A\tan B}$

$\Rightarrow$ $\tan A\tan B = 1$ ...(i)

and $\tan A + \tan B = \frac{\sin A}{\cos A} + \frac{\sin B}{\cos B}$

$$= \frac{\sin A}{\cos A} + \frac{\sin(90° - A)}{\cos(90° - A)} \quad [\because \angle C = 90°, \angle B = 90° - A]$$

$$= \frac{\sin A}{\cos A} + \frac{\cos A}{\sin A} = \frac{\sin^2 A + \cos^2 A}{\sin A \cdot \cos A} = \frac{1}{\sin A \cdot \cos A} = \frac{2}{2 \cdot \sin A \cdot \cos A}$$

$$= \frac{2}{\sin 2A} \quad [\because \sin 2x = 2\sin x \cos x]$$

So, the required equation having roots tan A and tan B is $x^2 - \left(\frac{2}{\sin A}\right)x + 1 = 0.$

Q.65 $3(\sin x - \cos x)^4 + 6(\sin x + \cos x)^2 + 4(\sin^6 x + \cos^6 x) =$ ....

Thinking Process Use the formulae $(a^3 + b^3) = (a + b)(a^2 - ab + b^2)$ and $a^2 + b^2 = (a + b)^2 - 2ab$.

Ans. Given expression, $3(\sin x - \cos x)^4 + 6(\sin x + \cos x)^2 + 4(\sin^6 x + \cos^6 x)$

$= 3[\sin^2 x + \cos^2 x - 2\sin x \cos x]^2 + 6[\sin^2 x + \cos^2 x + 2 \cdot \sin x \cdot \cos x]$
$+ 4[(\sin^2 x)^3 + (\cos^2 x)^3]$

$= 3(1 - \sin 2x)^2 + 6(1 + \sin 2x) + 4[(\sin^2 + \cos^2 x)(\sin^4 x - \sin^2 x \cos^2 x + \cos^4 x)]$

$= 3(1 + \sin^2 2x - 2\sin 2x) + 6 + 6\sin 2x + 4[(\sin^2 x + \cos^2 x)^2 - 3\sin^2 x \cos^2 x]$

$= 3 + 3\sin^2 2x - 6\sin 2x + 6 + 6\sin 2x + 4[1 - 3\sin^2 x \cos^2 x]$

$= 3 + 3 \times 4\sin^2 x \cos^2 x + 6 + 4 - 12\sin^2 x \cos^2 x = 13$

Q.66 Given $x > 0$, the value of $f(x) = -3\cos\sqrt{3 + x + x^2}$ lie in the interval ....

Ans. Given function, $f(x) = -3\cos\sqrt{3 + x + x^2}$

Let $y = \sqrt{3 + x + x^2}$

We know that $-1 \le \cos y \le 1 \Rightarrow -3 \le 3\cos y \le 3 \Rightarrow 3 \ge -3\cos y \ge -3$

So, $-3 \le -3\cos\sqrt{3 + x + x^2} \le 3$

Hence, the value of $f(x)$ lies in $[-3, 3]$.

Q.67 The maximum distance of a point on the graph of the function $y = \sqrt{3}\sin x + \cos x$ from X-axis is ....

Ans. Given, $y = \sqrt{3}\sin x + \cos x$

$$y = 2\left[\frac{\sqrt{3}}{2}\sin x + \frac{1}{2}\cos x\right] = 2\left[\sin x \cdot \cos\frac{\pi}{6} + \cos x \sin\frac{\pi}{6}\right] = 2\sin(x + \pi/6)$$

Graph of $y = 2\sin x$ is shown below

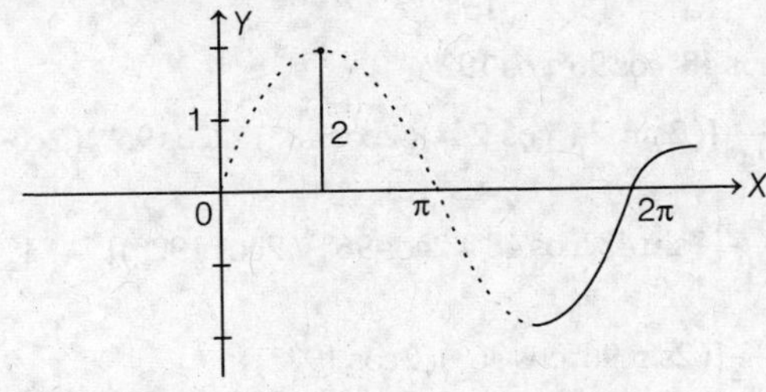

Hence, the maximum distance is 2 units. $[\because -1 \le \sin x \le 1]$

State True or False for the following statements in each of the exercises from 68 to 75. Also give justification.

Q.68 If $\tan A = \dfrac{1-\cos B}{\sin B}$, then $\tan 2A = \tan B$

Ans. *True*

Given, $\tan A = \dfrac{1-\cos B}{\sin B} = \dfrac{1-1+2\sin^2 \dfrac{B}{2}}{2\sin \dfrac{B}{2} \cdot \cos \dfrac{B}{2}} = \tan \dfrac{B}{2}$ ...(i)

Now, $\tan 2A = \dfrac{2\tan A}{1-\tan^2 A}$

$= \dfrac{2 \cdot \tan \dfrac{B}{2}}{1-\tan^2 \dfrac{B}{2}} = \tan B$ [from Eq. (i)]

Q.69 The equality $\sin A + \sin 2A + \sin 3A = 3$ holds for some real value of A.

Ans. *False*

Given, $\sin A + \sin 2A + \sin 3A = 3$

It is possible only if $\sin A$, $\sin 2A$, $\sin 3A$ each has a value 1 because maximum value for sine is 1 for a particular angle. But $\sin A$, $\sin 2A$ and $\sin 3A$ never be equal to 1 simultaneously because angles are different.

Q.70 $\sin 10°$ is greater than $\cos 10°$.

Ans. *False*

We have, $\sin 10° = \sin(90° - 80°) \Rightarrow \sin 10° = \cos 80°$

Since, $\sin x$ is a increasing function in $\left(0, \dfrac{\pi}{2}\right)$ and $\cos x$ is a decreasing function in $\left(0, \dfrac{\pi}{2}\right)$.

$\therefore$ $\cos 80° < \cos 10°$

Hence, $\sin 10° < \cos 10°$

Q.71 $\cos \dfrac{2\pi}{15} \cos \dfrac{4\pi}{15} \cos \dfrac{8\pi}{15} \cos \dfrac{16\pi}{15} = \dfrac{1}{16}$

Ans. *True*

$$\text{LHS} = \cos \frac{2\pi}{15} \cos \frac{4\pi}{15} \cos \frac{8\pi}{15} \cos \frac{16\pi}{15}$$

$$= \cos 24° \cos 48° \cos 96° \cos 192°$$

$$= \frac{1}{16 \sin 24°}[(2\sin 24° \cos 24°)(2\cos 48°)(2\cos 96°)(2\cos 192°)]$$

$$= \frac{1}{16 \sin 24°}[2\sin 48° \cos 48°(2\cos 96°)(2\cos 192°)] \quad [\because \sin 2x = 2\sin x \cos x]$$

$$= \frac{1}{16 \sin 24°}[(2\sin 96° \cos 96°)(2\cos 192°)]$$

$$= \frac{1}{16 \sin 24°}[2 \sin 192° \cos 192°)$$

$$= \frac{1}{16 \sin 24°} \sin 384°$$

$$= \frac{\sin(360° + 24°)}{16 \sin 24°}$$

$$= \frac{1}{16} = \text{RHS} \qquad [\because \sin(360° + \theta) = \sin\theta] \quad \textbf{Hence proved.}$$

Q.72 One value of θ which satisfies the equation $\sin^4\theta - 2\sin^2\theta - 1$ lies between 0 and 2π.

Ans. *False*

Given equation, $\sin^4\theta - 2\sin^2\theta - 1 = 0$

$\Rightarrow \quad \sin^2\theta = \dfrac{2 \pm \sqrt{4+4}}{2}$

$\Rightarrow \quad \sin^2\theta = \dfrac{2 \pm 2\sqrt{2}}{2}$

$\Rightarrow \quad \sin^2\theta = (1+\sqrt{2})$ or $(1-\sqrt{2})$

$\because \quad -1 \le \sin\theta \le 1 \Rightarrow 0 \le \sin^2\theta \le 1$

So, $\quad \sin^2\theta \ne \sqrt{2} + 1$ or $(1-\sqrt{2})$

Hence, no value of θ lies between 0 and 2π.

***Q.73** If $\operatorname{cosec} x = 1 + \cot x$, then $x = 2n\pi, 2n\pi + \dfrac{\pi}{2}$

Ans. *False*

Given, $\quad \operatorname{cosec} x = 1 + \cot x$

$\Rightarrow \quad \dfrac{1}{\sin x} = 1 + \dfrac{\cos x}{\sin x} \Rightarrow \dfrac{1}{\sin x} = \dfrac{\sin x + \cos x}{\sin x}$

$\Rightarrow \quad \sin x + \cos x = 1 \qquad [\because \sin x \ne 0]$

$\Rightarrow \quad \dfrac{1}{\sqrt{2}} \cdot \sin x + \dfrac{1}{\sqrt{2}} \cdot \cos x = \dfrac{1}{\sqrt{2}}$

$\Rightarrow \quad \sin\dfrac{\pi}{4}\sin x + \cos x \cos\dfrac{\pi}{4} = \dfrac{1}{\sqrt{2}} \Rightarrow \cos\left(x - \dfrac{\pi}{4}\right) = \cos\dfrac{\pi}{4}$

$\therefore \quad x - \dfrac{\pi}{4} = 2n\pi \pm \dfrac{\pi}{4} \qquad [\because \cos(A - B) = \cos A \cos B + \sin A \sin B]$

For positive sign, $x = 2n\pi + \dfrac{\pi}{4} + \dfrac{\pi}{4} = 2n\pi + \dfrac{\pi}{2}$

For negative sign, $x = 2n\pi - \dfrac{\pi}{4} + \dfrac{\pi}{4} = 2n\pi$, where $n \in Z$

If we take $x = 2n\pi$, then $\sin x$ becomes 0 but $\sin x \ne 0$

So, $x = 2n\pi + \dfrac{\pi}{2}, n \in Z$

(*) Topics related to these question have been removed from latest NCERT.

***Q.74** If $\tan\theta + \tan 2\theta + \sqrt{3}\tan\theta\tan 2\theta = \sqrt{3}$, then $\theta = \frac{n\pi}{3} + \frac{\pi}{9}$.

Ans. *True*

Given, $\tan\theta + \tan 2\theta + \sqrt{3}\tan\theta\tan 2\theta = \sqrt{3}$

$\Rightarrow \tan\theta + \tan 2\theta = \sqrt{3} - \sqrt{3}\tan\theta\tan 2\theta$

$\Rightarrow \tan\theta + \tan 2\theta = \sqrt{3}(1 - \tan\theta\tan 2\theta)$

$\Rightarrow \frac{\tan\theta + \tan 2\theta}{1 - \tan\theta\tan 2\theta} = \sqrt{3}$

$\Rightarrow \tan(\theta + 2\theta) = \tan\frac{\pi}{3}$ $\left[\because \tan(A+B) = \frac{\tan A + \tan B}{1 - \tan A\tan B}\right]$

$\Rightarrow \tan 3\theta = \tan\frac{\pi}{3}$ $\left[\because \text{if } \tan\theta = \tan\alpha \Rightarrow \theta = n\pi + \alpha, \text{ where } n \in Z\right]$

$\therefore 3\theta = n\pi + \frac{\pi}{3}$

$\theta = \frac{n\pi}{3} + \frac{\pi}{9}, n \in Z$

Q.75 If $\tan(\pi\cos\theta) = \cot(\pi\sin\theta)$, then $\cos\left(\theta - \frac{\pi}{4}\right) = \pm\frac{1}{2\sqrt{2}}$.

Thinking Process Use the formulae $\tan\left(\frac{\pi}{2} - \theta\right) = \cot\theta$ *and* $\tan A = \frac{\sin A}{\cos A}, \cot A = \frac{\cos A}{\sin A}$ *and* $\cos(A \pm B) = \cos A\cos B \mp \sin A\sin B$.

Ans. *True*

We have, $\tan(\pi\cos\theta) = \cot(\pi\sin\theta)$

$\Rightarrow \frac{\sin(\pi\cos\theta)}{\cos(\pi\cos\theta)} = \frac{\cos(\pi\sin\theta)}{\sin(\pi\sin\theta)}$

$\Rightarrow \cos(\pi\cos\theta)\cos(\pi\sin\theta) - \sin(\pi\cos\theta)\sin(\pi\sin\theta) = 0$

$\Rightarrow \cos(\pi\cos\theta + \pi\sin\theta) = 0$

$\Rightarrow \pi\cos\theta + \pi\sin\theta = \pm\frac{\pi}{2}$ $\left[\because \cos\frac{\pi}{2} = 0\right]$

$\Rightarrow \cos\theta + \sin\theta = \pm\frac{1}{2}$

$\Rightarrow \frac{1}{\sqrt{2}}\cdot\sin\theta + \frac{1}{\sqrt{2}}\cdot\cos\theta = \pm\frac{1}{2\sqrt{2}}$

$\Rightarrow \sin\theta\cdot\sin\frac{\pi}{4} + \cos\theta\cdot\cos\frac{\pi}{4} = \pm\frac{1}{2\sqrt{2}}$

$\therefore \cos\left(\theta - \frac{\pi}{4}\right) = \pm\frac{1}{2\sqrt{2}}$

(*) Topics related to these question have been removed from latest NCERT.

Q.76 In the following match each item given under the Column C_1 to its correct answer given under the Column C_2.

Column C_1	Column C_2
(a) $\sin(x+y)\sin(x-y)$	(i) $\cos^2 x - \sin^2 y$
(b) $\cos(x+y)\cos(x-y)$	(ii) $\dfrac{1-\tan\theta}{1+\tan\theta}$
(c) $\cot\left(\dfrac{\pi}{4}+\theta\right)$	(iii) $\dfrac{1+\tan\theta}{1-\tan\theta}$
(d) $\tan\left(\dfrac{\pi}{4}+\theta\right)$	(iv) $\sin^2 x - \sin^2 y$

Ans. (a) $\sin(x+y)\sin(x-y) = \sin^2 x - \sin^2 y$

(b) $\cos(x+y)\cos(x-y) = \cos^2 x - \sin^2 y$

(c) $$\cot\left(\frac{\pi}{4}+\theta\right) = \frac{\cot\frac{\pi}{4}\cot\theta - 1}{\cot\frac{\pi}{4} + \cot\theta} = \frac{-1+\cot\theta}{1+\cot\theta} = \frac{1-\tan\theta}{1+\tan\theta}$$

(d) $$\tan\left(\frac{\pi}{4}+\theta\right) = \frac{\tan\frac{\pi}{4} + \tan\theta}{1-\tan\frac{\pi}{4}\tan\theta} = \frac{1+\tan\theta}{1-\tan\theta}$$

Hence, the correct matches are (a) → (iv), (b) → (i), (c) → (ii), (d) → (iii).

Chapter 04

Principle of Mathematical Induction*

Short Answer Type Questions

Q.1 Give an example of a statement $P(n)$ which is true for all $n \geq 4$ but $P(1)$, $P(2)$ and $P(3)$ are not true. Justify your answer.

Ans. Let the statement $P(n)$: $3n < n!$ where $n! = 1 \times 2 \times 3 \ldots \times n$

For $n = 1$, $3 \times 1 < 1!$ $\Rightarrow$ $3 < 1$ [false]

For $n = 2$, $3 \times 2 < 2!$ $\Rightarrow$ $6 < 2$ [false]

For $n = 3$, $3 \times 3 < 3!$ $\Rightarrow$ $9 < 6$ [false]

For $n = 4$, $3 \times 4 < 4!$ $\Rightarrow$ $12 < 24$ [true]

For $n = 5$, $3 \times 5 < 5!$ $\Rightarrow$ $15 < 120$ [true]

Q.2 Give an example of a statement $P(n)$ which is true for all n. Justify your answer.

Ans. Consider the statement

$$P(n): 1^2 + 2^2 + 3^2 + \ldots + n^2 = \frac{n(n+1)(2n+1)}{6}$$

For $n = 1$, $1 = \frac{1(1+1)(2 \times 1 + 1)}{6}$

$\Rightarrow$ $1 = \frac{2(3)}{6}$

$\Rightarrow$ $1 = 1$, which is true.

For $n = 2$, $1 + 2^2 = \frac{2(2+1)(2 \times 2 + 1)}{6}$

$\Rightarrow$ $5 = \frac{2 \times 3 \times 5}{6} \Rightarrow 5 = 5$, which is true.

For $n = 3$, $1 + 2^2 + 3^2 = \frac{3(3+1)(2 \times 3 + 1)}{6} \Rightarrow 1 + 4 + 9 = \frac{3 \times 4 \times 7}{6}$

$\Rightarrow$ $14 = 14$, which is true.

And so on.

Hence, the given statement is true for all n.

Prove each of the statements in questions 3-16 by the Principle of Mathematical Induction.

(*) This chapter has been deleted from latest NCERT.

Q.3 $4^n - 1$ is divisible by 3, for each natural number n.

Ans. Let $P(n): 4^n - 1$ is divisible by 3 for each natural number n.

***Step* I** Now, we observe that $P(1)$ is true.

$$P(1) = 4^1 - 1 = 3$$

It is clear that 3 is divisible by 3.

Hence, $P(1)$ is true.

***Step* II** Assume that $P(n)$ is true for $n = k$

$P(k): 4^k - 1$ is divisible by 3

i.e., $4^k - 1 = 3q$, where $q \in N$

***Step* III** Now, to prove that $P(k + 1)$ is true.

$$P(k+1): 4^{k+1} - 1$$
$$= 4^k \cdot 4 - 1 = 4^k(3 + 1) - 1$$
$$= 4^k \cdot 3 + 4^k - 1$$
$$= 3 \cdot 4^k + 3q \qquad [\because 4^k - 1 = 3q]$$
$$= 3(4^k + q), \text{ which is divisible by 3.}$$

Thus, $P(k + 1)$ is true whenever $P(k)$ is true.

Hence, by the principle of mathematical induction $P(n)$ is true for each natural number n.

Q.4 $2^{3n} - 1$ is divisible by 7, for all natural numbers n.

Ans. Let $P(n): 2^{3n} - 1$ is divisible by 7, for all natural numbers n.

***Step* I** We observe that $P(1)$ is true.

$$P(1): 2^{3 \times 1} - 1 = 2^3 - 1 = 8 - 1 = 7, \text{ which is divisible by 7.}$$

Hence, $P(1)$ is true.

***Step* II** Now, assume that $P(n)$ is true for $n = k$,

$P(k): 2^{3k} - 1$ is divisible by 7.

$\Rightarrow$ $2^{3k} - 1 = 7q$, where $q \in N$

***Step* III** Now, to prove that $P(k + 1)$ is true.

$$P(k+1): 2^{3(k+1)} - 1$$
$$= 2^{3k} \cdot 2^3 - 1$$
$$= 2^{3k}(7 + 1) - 1$$
$$= 7 \cdot 2^{3k} + 2^{3k} - 1$$
$$= 7 \cdot 2^{3k} + 7q \qquad \text{[from step II]}$$
$$= 7(2^{3k} + q), \text{ which is divisible by 7.}$$

So, $P(k + 1)$ is true whenever $P(k)$ is true.

Hence, by the principle of mathematical induction $P(n)$ is true for all natural numbers n.

Q.5 $n^3 - 7n + 3$ is divisible by 3, for all natural numbers n.

Ans. Let $P(n): n^3 - 7n + 3$ is divisible by 3, for all natural numbers n.

Step I We observe that $P(1)$ is true.

$$P(1) = (1)^3 - 7(1) + 3$$
$$= 1 - 7 + 3$$
$$= -3, \text{ which is divisible by 3.}$$

Hence, $P(1)$ is true.

Step II Now, assume that $P(n)$ is true for $n = k$.

$\therefore \quad P(k) = k^3 - 7k + 3 = 3q$, where $q \in N$

Step III To prove that $P(k+1)$ is true

$$P(k+1): (k+1)^3 - 7(k+1) + 3$$
$$= k^3 + 1 + 3k(k+1) - 7k - 7 + 3$$
$$= k^3 - 7k + 3 + 3k(k+1) - 6$$
$$= 3q + 3[k(k+1) - 2] = 3[q + k(k+1) - 2], \text{ which is divisible by 3}$$

[from step II]

So, $P(k+1)$ is true whenever $P(k)$ is true.

Hence, by the principle of mathematical induction $P(n)$ is true for all natural numbers n.

Q.6 $3^{2n} - 1$ is divisible by 8, for all natural numbers n.

Ans. Let $P(n): 3^{2n} - 1$ is divisible by 8, for all natural numbers n.

Step I We observe that $P(1)$ is true.

$$P(1): 3^{2(1)} - 1 = 3^2 - 1$$
$$= 9 - 1 = 8, \text{ which is divisible by 8.}$$

Hence, $P(1)$ is true.

Step II Now, assume that $P(n)$ is true for $n = k$.

$$P(k): 3^{2k} - 1 = 8q, \text{ where } q \in N$$

Step III Now, to prove that $P(k+1)$ is true.

$$P(k+1): 3^{2(k+1)} - 1$$
$$= 3^{2k} \cdot 3^2 - 1$$
$$= 3^{2k} \cdot (8 + 1) - 1$$
$$= 8 \cdot 3^{2k} + 3^{2k} - 1$$
$$= 8 \cdot 3^{2k} + 8q \quad \text{[from step II]}$$
$$= 8(3^{2k} + q), \text{ which is divisible by 8.}$$

So, $P(k+1)$ is true whenever $P(k)$ is true.

Hence, by the principle of mathematical induction $P(n)$ is true for all natural numbers n.

Q.7 For any natural number n, $7^n - 2^n$ is divisible by 5.

Ans. Consider the given statement is

$P(n): 7^n - 2^n$ is divisible by 5, for any natural number n.

***Step* I** We observe that $P(1)$ is true for $n = 1$

$P(1) = 7^1 - 2^1 = 5$, which is divisible by 5.

Hence, $P(1)$ is true

***Step* II** Now, assume that $P(n)$ is true for $n = k$.

$P(k) = 7^k - 2^k = 5q$, where $q \in N$

***Step* III** Now, to prove that $P(k+1)$ is true.

$$P(k+1): 7^{k+1} - 2^{k+1}.$$
$$= 7^k \cdot 7 - 2^k \cdot 2$$
$$= 7^k \cdot (5+2) - 2^k \cdot 2$$
$$= 7^k \cdot 5 + 2 \cdot 7^k - 2^k \cdot 2$$
$$= 5 \cdot 7^k + 2(7^k - 2^k)$$
$$= 5 \cdot 7^k + 2(5q) \quad \text{[from step II]}$$
$$= 5(7^k + 2q), \text{ which is divisible by 5.}$$

So, $P(k+1)$ is true whenever $P(k)$ is true.

Hence, by the principle of mathematical induction $P(n)$ is true for any natural number n.

Q.8 For any natural number n, $x^n - y^n$ is divisible by $x - y$, where x and y are any integers with $x \neq y$.

Ans. Let $P(n): x^n - y^n$ is divisible by $x - y$, where x and y are any integers with $x \neq y$.

***Step* I** We observe that $P(1)$ is true for $n = 1$.

$P(1): x^1 - y^1 = x - y$, which is divisible by $x - y$.

Hence, $P(1)$ is true

***Step* II** Now, assume that $P(n)$ is true for $n = k$.

$P(k): x^k - y^k$ is divisible by $(x - y)$.

$\therefore \quad x^k - y^k = q(x - y)$, where $q \in N$

***Step* III** Now, to prove that $P(k+1)$ is true.

$$P(k+1): x^{k+1} - y^{k+1}$$
$$= x^k \cdot x - y^k \cdot y$$
$$= x^k \cdot x - x^k \cdot y + x^k \cdot y - y^k \cdot y$$
$$= x^k(x - y) + y(x^k - y^k)$$
$$= x^k(x - y) + yq(x - y) \quad \text{[from step II]}$$
$$= (x - y)[x^k + yq], \text{ which is divisible by } (x - y).$$

So, $P(k+1)$ is true whenever $P(k)$ is true.

Hence, by the principle of mathematical induction $P(n)$ is true for any natural number n.

Q.9 $n^3 - n$ is divisible by 6, for each natural number $n \geq 2$.

Ans. Let $P(n): n^3 - n$ is divisible by 6, for each natural number $n \geq 2$.

***Step* I** We observe that $P(2)$ is true.

$$P(2): (2)^3 - 2 \Rightarrow 8 - 2 = 6, \text{ which is divisible by 6.}$$

Hence, $P(2)$ is true.

***Step* II** Now, assume that $P(n)$ is true for $n = k$.

$P(k): k^3 - k$ is divisible by 6.

$\therefore \quad k^3 - k = 6q$, where $q \in N$

***Step* III** To prove that $P(k+1)$ is true

$$\begin{aligned} P(k+1) &: (k+1)^3 - (k+1). \\ &= k^3 + 1 + 3k(k+1) - (k+1) \\ &= k^3 + 1 + 3k^2 + 3k - k - 1 \\ &= k^3 - k + 3k^2 + 3k \\ &= 6q + 3k(k+1) \end{aligned}$$ [from step II]

We know that the product of two consecutive integers i.e. $K(K+1)$ is always even (divisible by 2).

So, $3k(k+1)$ is divisible by 6 for each $k \in N$.

So, $P(k+1)$ is true whenever $P(K)$ is true. Hence, by the principle of mathematical induction $P(n)$ is true. For each natural number $n \geq 2$.

Mistake Alert! *Student might take $n = 1$ in the step I and get an incorrect conclusion.*

Q.10 $n(n^2 + 5)$ is divisible by 6, for each natural number n.

Sol. Let $P(n): n(n^2 + 5)$ is divisible by 6, for each natural number n.

***Step* I** We observe that $P(1)$ is true.

$$P(1): 1(1^2 + 5) = 6, \text{ which is divisible by 6.}$$

Hence, $P(1)$ is true.

***Step* II** Now, assume that $P(n)$ is true for $n = k$.

$P(k): k(k^2 + 5)$ is divisible by 6.

$\therefore \quad k(k^2 + 5) = 6q, q \in N$

***Step* III** Now, to prove that $P(k+1)$ is true, we have

$$\begin{aligned} P(k+1) &: (k+1)[(k+1)^2 + 5] \\ &= (k+1)[k^2 + 2k + 1 + 5] = (k+1)[k^2 + 2k + 6] \\ &= k^3 + 2k^2 + 6k + k^2 + 2k + 6 = k^3 + 3k^2 + 8k + 6 \\ &= k^3 + 5k + 3k^2 + 3k + 6 = k(k^2 + 5) + 3(k^2 + k + 2) \\ &= (6q) + 3(k^2 + k + 2) \end{aligned}$$ [from step II]

We know that $k^2 + k + 2$ is divisible by 2, where k is a natural number.

Since, $P(k+1): 6q + 3(k^2 + k + 2)$ is divisible by 6. So, $P(k+1)$ is true whenever $P(k)$ is true.

Hence, by the principle of mathematical induction $P(n)$ is true for each natural number n.

Q.11 $n^2 < 2^n$, for all natural numbers $n \geq 5$.

Ans. Consider the given statement

$P(n): n^2 < 2^n$ for all natural numbers $n \geq 5$.

Step I We observe that $P(5)$ is true

$$P(5): 5^2 < 2^5$$

$\Rightarrow$ $25 < 32$, which is true

Hence, $P(5)$ is true.

Step II Now, assume that $P(n)$ is true for $n = k$.

i.e., $P(k) = k^2 < 2^k$

Step III Now, to prove that $P(k+1)$ is true, we have to show that

$$P(k+1): (k+1)^2 < 2^{k+1}$$

Now, $k^2 < 2^k \Rightarrow k^2 + 2k + 1 < 2^k + 2k + 1$ [adding $2k+1$ on both sides]

$\Rightarrow$ $(k+1)^2 < 2^k + 2k + 1$ ...(i)

We know that, $(2k+1) < 2^k$ will be true for each natural number $k \geq 5$

$\Rightarrow$ $2^k + 2k + 1 < 2^k + 2^k$ [adding 2^k on both sides]

$\Rightarrow$ $2^k + 2k + 1 < 2 \cdot 2^k$

$\Rightarrow$ $2^k + 2k + 1 < 2^{k+1}$ ...(ii)

From Eqs. (i) and (ii), we get $(k+1)^2 < 2^{k+1}$

So, $P(k+1)$ is true, whenever $P(k)$ is true. Hence, by the principle of mathematical induction $P(n)$ is true for all natural numbers $n \geq 5$.

Q.12 $2n < (n+2)!$ for all natural numbers n.

Ans. Consider the statement

$P(n): 2n < (n+2)!$ for all natural number n.

Step I We observe that $P(1)$ is true. $P(1): 2(1) < (1+2)!$

$\Rightarrow$ $2 < 3! \Rightarrow 2 < 3 \times 2 \times 1 \Rightarrow 2 < 6$, which is true

Hence, $P(1)$ is true.

Step II Now, assume that $P(n)$ is true for $n = k$,

i.e., $P(k): 2k < (k+2)!$

Step III To prove that $P(k+1)$ is true, we have to show that

$$P(k+1): 2(k+1) < (k+1+2)!$$

Now, take $2k < (k+2)!$

$2k + 2 < (k+2)! + 2$ [adding 2 on both sides]

$2(k+1) < (k+2)! + 2$ ...(i)

Also, we can see that $(k+2)! + 2 < (k+3)!$ will be true for each $k \in N$ ...(ii)

From Eqs. (i) and (ii), we get

$$2(k+1) < (k+1+2)!$$

So, $P(k+1)$ is true whenever $P(k)$ is true.

Hence, by principle of mathematical induction $P(n)$ is true for all natural numbers n.

Q.13 $\sqrt{n} < \frac{1}{\sqrt{1}} + \frac{1}{\sqrt{2}} + \ldots + \frac{1}{\sqrt{n}}$, for all natural numbers $n \geq 2$.

Ans. Consider the statement

$P(n): \sqrt{n} < \frac{1}{\sqrt{1}} + \frac{1}{\sqrt{2}} + \ldots + \frac{1}{\sqrt{n}}$, for all natural numbers $n \geq 2$.

Step I We observe that $P(2)$ is true.

$$P(2): \sqrt{2} < \frac{1}{\sqrt{1}} + \frac{1}{\sqrt{2}}, \text{ which is true.}$$

Hence, $P(2)$ is true

Step II Now, assume that $P(n)$ is true for $n = k$.

i.e., $P(k): \sqrt{k} < \frac{1}{\sqrt{1}} + \frac{1}{\sqrt{2}} + \ldots + \frac{1}{\sqrt{k}}$

Step III To prove that $P(k+1)$ is true, we have to show that

$$P(k+1): \sqrt{k+1} < \frac{1}{\sqrt{1}} + \frac{1}{\sqrt{2}} + \ldots + \frac{1}{\sqrt{k+1}}$$

Now, take $\sqrt{k} < \frac{1}{\sqrt{1}} + \frac{1}{\sqrt{2}} + \ldots + \frac{1}{\sqrt{k}}$ [from step II]

$$\Rightarrow \sqrt{k} + \frac{1}{\sqrt{k+1}} < \frac{1}{\sqrt{1}} + \frac{1}{\sqrt{2}} + \ldots + \frac{1}{\sqrt{k}} + \frac{1}{\sqrt{k+1}}$$

[adding $\frac{1}{\sqrt{k+1}}$ on both sides]

$$\Rightarrow \frac{(\sqrt{k})(\sqrt{k+1}) + 1}{\sqrt{k+1}} < \frac{1}{\sqrt{1}} + \frac{1}{\sqrt{2}} + \ldots + \frac{1}{\sqrt{k}} + \frac{1}{\sqrt{k+1}}$$

$$\frac{\sqrt{k^2+k}+1}{\sqrt{k+1}} < \frac{1}{\sqrt{1}} + \frac{1}{\sqrt{2}} + \ldots. + \frac{1}{\sqrt{k}} + \frac{1}{\sqrt{k+1}}$$

$$\Rightarrow \frac{\sqrt{k^2}+1}{\sqrt{k+1}} < \frac{1}{\sqrt{1}} + \frac{1}{\sqrt{2}} + \ldots. + \frac{1}{\sqrt{k}} + \frac{1}{\sqrt{k+1}} \quad [\because k^2 < k^2 + k]$$

$$\Rightarrow \frac{k+1}{\sqrt{k+1}} < \frac{1}{\sqrt{1}} + \frac{1}{\sqrt{2}} + \ldots + \frac{1}{\sqrt{k}} + \frac{1}{\sqrt{k+1}}$$

$$\Rightarrow \sqrt{k+1} < \frac{1}{\sqrt{1}} + \frac{1}{\sqrt{2}} + \ldots. + \frac{1}{\sqrt{k}} + \frac{1}{\sqrt{k+1}}$$

So, $P(k+1)$ is true whenever $P(k)$ is true. Hence, by principal of mathematical induction $P(n)$ is true. For all natural numbers $n \geq 2$.

Q.14 $2 + 4 + 6 + \ldots + 2n = n^2 + n$, for all natural numbers n.

Ans. Let $P(n): 2 + 4 + 6 + \ldots + 2n = n^2 + n$, For all natural numbers n.

Step I We observe that $P(1)$ is true.

$$P(1): 2(1) = 1^2 + 1 \Rightarrow 2 = 2, \text{ which is true.}$$

Hence, $P(1)$ is true.

Step II Now, assume that $P(n)$ is true for $n = k$.

$\therefore$ $P(k): 2 + 4 + 6 + \ldots + 2k = k^2 + k$

***Step* III** To prove that $P(k+1)$ is true.

$$\begin{aligned} P(k+1): 2+4+6+8+\ldots+2k+2(k+1) &= k^2+k+2(k+1) \quad \text{[from step II]} \\ &= k^2+k+2k+2 \\ &= (k^2+2k+1)+k+1 \\ &= (k+1)^2+k+1 \end{aligned}$$

So, $P(k+1)$ is true, whenever $P(k)$ is true.

Hence, by principal of mathematical induction $P(n)$ is true for all natural numbers n.

Q.15 $1+2+2^2+\ldots+2^n = 2^{n+1}-1$, for all natural numbers n.

Ans. Consider the given statement,

$P(n): 1+2+2^2+\ldots+2^n = 2^{n+1}-1$, for all natural numbers n.

***Step* I** We observe that $P(1)$ is true.

$$P(1): 1+2 = 2^{1+1}-1$$

$$\Rightarrow \quad 3 = 2^2-1$$

$$\Rightarrow \quad 3 = 4-1$$

$$\Rightarrow \quad 3 = 3, \text{ which is true.}$$

Hence, $P(1)$ is true.

***Step* II** Now, assume that $P(n)$ is true for $n=k$.

So, $P(k): 1+2+2^2+\ldots+2^k = 2^{k+1}-1$

***Step* III** Now, to prove that $P(k+1)$ is true.

$$\begin{aligned} P(k+1): 1+2+2^2+\ldots+2^k+2^{k+1} &= 2^{k+1}-1+2^{k+1} \quad \text{[from step II]} \\ &= 2\cdot 2^{k+1}-1 = 2^{k+2}-1 \\ &= 2^{(k+1)+1}-1 \end{aligned}$$

So, $P(k+1)$ is true, whenever $P(k)$ is true.

Hence, by principal of mathematical induction $P(n)$ is true for all natural numbers n.

Q.16 $1+5+9+\ldots+(4n-3) = n(2n-1)$, for all natural numbers n.

Ans. Let $P(n): 1+5+9+\ldots+(4n-3) = n(2n-1)$, for all natural numbers n.

***Step* I** We observe that $P(1)$ is true.

$$P(1): 4(1)-3 = 1(2\times 1-1) \Rightarrow 1 = 1, \text{ which is true.}$$

Hence, $P(1)$ is true.

***Step* II** Now, assume that $P(n)$ is true for $n=k$.

So, $P(k): 1+5+9+\ldots+(4k-3) = k(2k-1)$

***Step* III** Now, to prove that $P(k+1)$ is true.

$$\begin{aligned} P(k+1): 1+5+9+\ldots+(4k-3)+4(k+1)-3 &= k(2k-1)+4(k+1)-3 \quad \text{[from step II]} \\ &= 2k^2-k+4k+4-3 \\ &= 2k^2+3k+1 = 2k^2+2k+k+1 \end{aligned}$$

$= 2k(k + 1) + 1(k + 1) = (k + 1)(2k + 1)$

$= (k + 1)[2k + 2 - 1] = (k + 1)[2(k + 1) - 1]$

So, $P(k + 1)$ is true, whenever $P(k)$ is true. Hence, by principal of mathematical induction $P(n)$ is true for all natural numbers n.

Long Answer Type Questions

Use the Principle of Mathematical Induction in the following questions.

Q.17 A sequence $a_1, a_2, a_3, \ldots$ is defined by letting $a_1 = 3$ and $a_k = 7a_{k-1}$, for all natural numbers $k \geq 2$. Show that $a_n = 3 \cdot 7^{n-1}$ for all natural numbers.

Ans. A sequence $a_1, a_2, a_3, \ldots$ is defined by letting $a_1 = 3$ and $a_k = 7a_{k-1}$, for all natural numbers $k \geq 2$.

Let $P(n): a_n = 3 \cdot 7^{n-1}$ for all natural numbers.

***Step* I** We observe that $P(2)$ is true.

For $n = 2$, $a_2 = 3 \times 7^{2-1} = 3 \cdot 7^1 = 21$ ...(i)

As $a_1 = 3,\ a_k = 7a_{k-1}$

$\Rightarrow a_2 = 7 \cdot a_{2-1} = 7 \cdot a_1$

$\Rightarrow a_2 = 7 \times 3 = 21$, which is true from Eq. (i) $[\because a_1 = 3]$

Hence, $P(2)$ is true.

***Step* II** Now, assume that $P(n)$ is true for $n = k$.

$P(k): a_k = 3 \times 7^{k-1}$

***Step* III** Now, to prove that $P(k + 1)$ is true, we have to show that

$P(k+1): a_{k+1} = 3 \times 7^{(k+1)-1}$

Given that $a_k = 7a_{k-1}$

$\Rightarrow a_{k+1} = 7a_k = 7(3 \times 7^{k-1})$ [from step II]

$= 3 \times 7^{(k+1)} - 1$

So, $P(k + 1)$ is true, whenever $p(k)$ is true. Hence, by principal of mathematical induction $P(n)$ is true for all natural numbers.

Q.18 A sequence $b_0, b_1, b_2, \ldots$ is defined by letting $b_0 = 5$ and $b_k = 4 + b_{k-1}$, for all natural numbers k. Show that $b_n = 5 + 4n$, for all natural number n using mathematical induction.

Ans. Consider the given statement,

$P(n): b_n = 5 + 4n$, for all natural numbers given that $b_0 = 5$ and $b_k = 4 + b_{k-1}$

***Step* I** $P(1)$ is true for $n = 1$.

$P(1): b_1 = 5 + 4 \times 1 = 9$ ...(i)

As $b_0 = 5,\ b_1 = 4 + b_0 = 4 + 5 = 9$, which is true from Eq. (i)

Hence, $P(1)$ is true.

***Step* II** Now, assume that $P(n)$ is true for $n = k$.

$P(k): b_k = 5 + 4k$

***Step* III** Now, to prove that $P(k+1)$ is true, we have to show that

$$P(k+1): b_{k+1} = 5 + 4(k+1)$$

$$\therefore \quad b_{k+1} = 4 + b_{k+1-1} = 4 + b_k$$
$$= 4 + 5 + 4k = 5 + 4(k+1)$$

So, $P(k+1)$ is true whenever $P(k)$ is true. Hence by the principal of mathematical induction $P(n)$ is true for all natural number n.

Q.19 A sequence $d_1, d_2, d_3, \ldots$ is defined by letting $d_1 = 2$ and $d_k = \frac{d_{k-1}}{k}$, for all natural numbers, $k \geq 2$. Show that $d_n = \frac{2}{n!}$, for all $n \in N$.

Ans. Let $P(n): d_n = \frac{2}{n!}, \forall\, n \in N,$

***Step* I** We observe that $P(2): d_2 = \frac{2}{2!} = \frac{2}{2\times 1} = 1$

As, given $\quad d_1 = 2$

and $\quad d_k = \frac{d_{k-1}}{k}$

$\Rightarrow \quad d_2 = \frac{d_1}{2} = \frac{2}{2} = 1$, which is true from Eq. (i)

Hence, $P(2)$ is true.

***Step* II** Now, assume that $P(k)$ is true.

$$P(k): d_k = \frac{2}{k!}$$

***Step* III** Now, to prove that $P(k+1)$ is true, we have to show that

$$P(k+1): d_{k+1} = \frac{2}{(k+1)!}$$

Given that $\quad d_k = \frac{d_{k-1}}{k}$ [from step II]

$$\therefore \quad d_{k+1} = \frac{1}{(k+1)} \cdot d_k = \frac{1}{k+1} \cdot \frac{2}{k!} = \frac{2}{(k+1)!}$$

So, $P(k+1)$ is true. Hence, by principal of mathematical induction $P(n)$ is true for all $n \in N$.

Q.20 Prove that for all $n \in N$

$$\cos\alpha + \cos(\alpha+\beta) + \cos(\alpha+2\beta) + \ldots + \cos[\alpha + (n-1)\beta]$$
$$= \frac{\cos\left[\alpha + \left(\frac{n-1}{2}\right)\beta\right]\sin\left(\frac{n\beta}{2}\right)}{\sin\frac{\beta}{2}}$$

- **Concept Insight** In this question, we will use the formulae $2\cos A \sin B = \sin(A+B) - \sin(A-B)$ and $\sin A - \sin B = 2\cos\left(\frac{A+B}{2}\right)\cdot\sin\left(\frac{A-B}{2}\right)$

Ans. Let $P(n): \cos\alpha + \cos(\alpha+\beta) + \cos(\alpha+2\beta) + \ldots + \cos[\alpha+(n-1)\beta]$

$$= \frac{\cos\left[\alpha + \left(\frac{n-1}{2}\right)\beta\right]\sin\left(\frac{n\beta}{2}\right)}{\sin\frac{\beta}{2}}$$

***Step* I** We observe that $P(1)$ is true.

$$P(1): \cos\alpha = \frac{\cos\left[\alpha + \left(\frac{1-1}{2}\right)\beta\right]\sin\frac{\beta}{2}}{\sin\frac{\beta}{2}} = \frac{\cos(\alpha+0)\sin\frac{\beta}{2}}{\sin\frac{\beta}{2}}$$

$$\Rightarrow \quad \cos\alpha = \cos\alpha$$

Hence, $P(1)$ is true.

***Step* II** Now, assume that $P(n)$ is true for $n = k$.

$$P(k): \cos\alpha + \cos(\alpha+\beta) + \cos(\alpha+2\beta) + \ldots + \cos[\alpha+(k-1)\beta]$$

$$= \frac{\cos\left[\alpha + \left(\frac{k-1}{2}\right)\beta\right]\sin\frac{k\beta}{2}}{\sin\frac{\beta}{2}}$$

***Step* III** Now, to prove that $P(k+1)$ is true, we have to show that

$$P(k+1): \cos\alpha + \cos(\alpha+\beta) + \cos(\alpha+2\beta) + \ldots + \cos[\alpha+(k-1)\beta]$$

$$+ \cos[\alpha+(k+1-1)\beta] = \frac{\cos\left(\alpha + \frac{k\beta}{2}\right)\sin\left[(k+1)\frac{\beta}{2}\right]}{\sin\frac{\beta}{2}}$$

$$\text{LHS} = \cos\alpha + \cos(\alpha+\beta) + \cos(\alpha+2\beta) + \ldots + \cos[\alpha+(k-1)\beta] + \cos(\alpha+k\beta)$$

$$= \frac{\cos\left[\alpha + \left(\frac{k-1}{2}\right)\beta\right]\sin\frac{k\beta}{2}}{\sin\frac{\beta}{2}} + \cos(\alpha+k\beta)$$

$$= \frac{\cos\left[\alpha + \left(\frac{k-1}{2}\right)\beta\right]\sin\frac{k\beta}{2} + \cos(\alpha+k\beta)\sin\frac{\beta}{2}}{\sin\frac{\beta}{2}}$$

$$= \frac{2\cos\left[\alpha + \left(\frac{k-1}{2}\right)\beta\right]\sin\frac{k\beta}{2} + 2\cos(\alpha+k\beta)\sin\frac{\beta}{2}}{2\sin\frac{\beta}{2}}$$

$$= \frac{\sin\left(\alpha + \frac{k\beta}{2} - \frac{\beta}{2} + \frac{k\beta}{2}\right) - \sin\left(\alpha + \frac{k\beta}{2} - \frac{\beta}{2} - \frac{k\beta}{2}\right) + \sin\left(\alpha + k\beta + \frac{\beta}{2}\right) - \sin\left(\alpha + k\beta - \frac{\beta}{2}\right)}{2\sin\frac{\beta}{2}}$$

$$= \frac{\sin\left(\alpha + k\beta + \frac{\beta}{2}\right) - \sin\left(\alpha - \frac{\beta}{2}\right)}{2\sin\frac{\beta}{2}}$$

$$= \frac{2\cos\left[\frac{1}{2}\left(\alpha + \frac{\beta}{2} + k\beta + \alpha - \frac{\beta}{2}\right)\right]\sin\left[\frac{1}{2}\left(\alpha + \frac{\beta}{2} + k\beta - \alpha + \frac{\beta}{2}\right)\right]}{2\sin\frac{\beta}{2}}$$

$$= \frac{\cos\left(\frac{2\alpha + k\beta}{2}\right)\sin\left(\frac{k\beta + \beta}{2}\right)}{\sin\frac{\beta}{2}} = \frac{\cos\left(\alpha + \frac{k\beta}{2}\right)\sin\left[(k+1)\frac{\beta}{2}\right]}{\sin\frac{\beta}{2}} = \text{RHS}$$

So, $P(k+1)$ is true. Hence, $P(n)$ is true for all $n \in N$

Q.21 Prove that $\cos\theta \cos 2\theta \cos 2^2\theta \ldots \cos 2^{n-1}\theta = \dfrac{\sin 2^n\theta}{2^n \sin\theta}, \forall n \in N.$

- **Concept Insight** In this question, we will use the formula $\sin 2\theta = 2\sin\theta\cos\theta$

Ans. Let $P(n): \cos\theta\cos 2\theta \ldots \cos 2^{n-1}\theta = \dfrac{\sin 2^n\theta}{2^n \sin\theta}$

***Step* I** For $n = 1$, $P(1): \cos\theta = \dfrac{\sin 2^1\theta}{2^1\sin\theta} = \dfrac{\sin 2\theta}{2\sin\theta} = \dfrac{2\sin\theta\cos\theta}{2\sin\theta} = \cos\theta$ which is true.

Hence, $P(1)$ is true.

***Step* II** Assume that $P(n)$ is true for $n = k$.

$$P(k): \cos\theta \cdot \cos 2\theta \cdot \cos 2^2\theta \ldots \cos 2^{k-1}\theta = \frac{\sin 2^k\theta}{2^k \sin\theta}$$

***Step* III** To prove that $P(k+1)$ is true.

$$P(k+1): \cos\theta \cdot \cos 2\theta \cdot \cos 2^2\theta \ldots \cos 2^{k-1}\theta \cdot \cos 2^k\theta$$

$$= \frac{\sin 2^k\theta}{2^k\sin\theta} \cdot \cos 2^k\theta = \frac{2\sin 2^k\theta \cdot \cos 2^k\theta}{2 \cdot 2^k \sin\theta} \quad \text{[from Step II]}$$

$$= \frac{\sin(2 \cdot 2^k\theta)}{2^{k+1}\sin\theta} = \frac{\sin[2^{(k+1)}\theta]}{2^{k+1}\sin\theta}$$

which is true.

So, $P(k+1)$ is true. Hence, by principal of mathematical induction $P(n)$ is true.

Q.22 Prove that, $\sin\theta + \sin 2\theta + \sin 3\theta + \ldots + \sin n\theta = \dfrac{\sin\frac{n\theta}{2}\sin\frac{(n+1)}{2}\theta}{\sin\frac{\theta}{2}}$, for all $n \in N$.

Thinking Process Use the formulae of $2\sin A\sin B = \cos(A - B) - \cos(A + B)$ and

$\cos A - \cos B = 2\sin\dfrac{A+B}{2} \cdot \sin\dfrac{B-A}{2}$, also $\cos(-\theta) = \cos\theta$.

Ans. Consider the given statement

$$P(n): \sin\theta + \sin 2\theta + \sin 3\theta + \ldots + \sin n\theta = \frac{\sin\frac{n\theta}{2}\sin\frac{(n+1)\theta}{2}}{\sin\frac{\theta}{2}}, \text{ for all } n \in N$$

***Step* I** We observe that $P(1)$ is true.

$$P(1): \sin\theta = \frac{\sin\frac{\theta}{2}\cdot\sin\frac{(1+1)}{2}\theta}{\sin\frac{\theta}{2}} = \frac{\sin\frac{\theta}{2}\cdot\sin\theta}{\sin\frac{\theta}{2}}$$

$$\Rightarrow \quad \sin\theta = \sin\theta$$

Hence, $P(1)$ is true.

***Step* II** Assume that $P(n)$ is true, for $n = k$.

$$\therefore \quad P(k): \sin\theta + \sin 2\theta + \sin 3\theta + \ldots + \sin k\theta = \frac{\sin\frac{k\theta}{2}\sin\left(\frac{k+1}{2}\right)\theta}{\sin\frac{\theta}{2}}$$

***Step* III** Now, to prove that $P(k+1)$ is true.

$$P(k+1): \sin\theta + \sin 2\theta + \sin 3\theta + \ldots + \sin k\theta + \sin(k+1)\theta = \frac{\sin\frac{(k+1)\theta}{2}\sin\left(\frac{k+1+1}{2}\right)\theta}{\sin\frac{\theta}{2}}$$

$$\text{LHS} = \sin\theta + \sin 2\theta + \sin 3\theta + \ldots + \sin k\theta + \sin(k+1)\theta$$

$$= \frac{\sin\frac{k\theta}{2}\sin\left(\frac{k+1}{2}\right)\theta}{\sin\frac{\theta}{2}} + \sin(k+1)\theta = \frac{\sin\frac{k\theta}{2}\sin\left(\frac{k+1}{2}\right)\theta + \sin(k+1)\theta\cdot\sin\frac{\theta}{2}}{\sin\frac{\theta}{2}}$$

$$= \frac{\cos\left[\frac{k\theta}{2} - \left(\frac{k+1}{2}\right)\theta\right] - \cos\left[\frac{k\theta}{2} + \left(\frac{k+1}{2}\right)\theta\right] + \cos\left[(k+1)\theta - \frac{\theta}{2}\right] - \cos\left[(k+1)\theta + \frac{\theta}{2}\right]}{2\sin\frac{\theta}{2}}$$

$$= \frac{\cos\frac{\theta}{2} - \cos\left(k\theta + \frac{\theta}{2}\right) + \cos\left(k\theta + \frac{\theta}{2}\right) - \cos\left(k\theta + \frac{3\theta}{2}\right)}{2\sin\frac{\theta}{2}} \quad [\because \cos(-x) = \cos x]$$

$$= \frac{\cos\frac{\theta}{2} - \cos\left(k\theta + \frac{3\theta}{2}\right)}{2\sin\frac{\theta}{2}} = \frac{2\sin\frac{1}{2}\left(\frac{\theta}{2} + k\theta + \frac{3\theta}{2}\right)\cdot\sin\frac{1}{2}\left(k\theta + \frac{3\theta}{2} - \frac{\theta}{2}\right)}{2\sin\frac{\theta}{2}}$$

$$= \frac{\sin\left(\frac{k\theta + 2\theta}{2}\right)\cdot\sin\left(\frac{k\theta+\theta}{2}\right)}{\sin\frac{\theta}{2}} = \frac{\sin\frac{(k+1)\theta}{2}\cdot\sin\frac{(k+1+1)\theta}{2}}{\sin\frac{\theta}{2}}$$

So, $P(k+1)$ is true, whenever $P(k)$ is true. Hence, by principal of mathematical induction $P(n)$ is true, for all $n \in N$.

Q.23 Show that $\frac{n^5}{5} + \frac{n^3}{3} + \frac{7n}{15}$ is a natural number, for all $n \in N$.

- **Concept Insight** In this question, we will, use the formula $(a+b)^5 = a^5 + 5ab^4 + 10a^2b^3 + 10a^3b^2 + 5a^4b + b^5$ and $(a+b)^3 = a^3 + b^3 + 3ab(a+b)$

Ans. Consider the given statement

$P(n): \frac{n^5}{5} + \frac{n^3}{3} + \frac{7n}{15}$ is a natural number, for all $n \in N$.

***Step* I** We observe that $P(1)$ is true.

$P(1): \frac{(1)^5}{5} + \frac{1^3}{3} + \frac{7(1)}{15} = \frac{3+5+7}{15} = \frac{15}{15} = 1$, which is a natural number.

Hence, $P(1)$ is true.

***Step* II** Assume that $P(n)$ is true, for $n = k$.

$P(k): \frac{k^5}{5} + \frac{k^3}{3} + \frac{7k}{15}$ is a natural number.

***Step* III** Now, we have to prove that $P(k+1)$ is true.

$$\frac{(k+1)^5}{5} + \frac{(k+1)^3}{3} + \frac{7(k+1)}{15}$$

$$= \frac{k^5 + 5k^4 + 10k^3 + 10k^2 + 5k + 1}{5} + \frac{k^3 + 1 + 3k(k+1)}{3} + \frac{7k+7}{15}$$

$$= \frac{k^5 + 5k^4 + 10k^3 + 10k^2 + 5k + 1}{5} + \frac{k^3 + 1 + 3k^2 + 3k}{3} + \frac{7k+7}{15}$$

$$= \frac{k^5}{5} + \frac{k^3}{3} + \frac{7k}{15} + \frac{5k^4 + 10k^3 + 10k^2 + 5k + 1}{5} + \frac{3k^2 + 3k + 1}{3} + \frac{7}{15}$$

$$= \frac{k^5}{5} + \frac{k^3}{3} + \frac{7k}{15} + k^4 + 2k^3 + 2k^2 + k + k^2 + k + \frac{1}{5} + \frac{1}{3} + \frac{7}{15}$$

$= \frac{k^5}{5} + \frac{k^3}{3} + \frac{7k}{15} + k^4 + 2k^3 + 3k^2 + 2k + 1$, which is a natural number

So, $P(k+1)$ is true, whenever $P(k)$ is true. Hence, $P(n)$ is true.

Q.24 Prove that $\frac{1}{n+1} + \frac{1}{n+2} + \ldots + \frac{1}{2n} > \frac{13}{24}$, for all natural numbers $n > 1$.

Ans. Consider the given statement,

$P(n): \frac{1}{n+1} + \frac{1}{n+2} + \ldots + \frac{1}{2n} > \frac{13}{24}$, for all natural numbers $n > 1$

***Step* I** We observe that, $P(2)$ is true,

$$P(2): \frac{1}{2+1}+\frac{1}{2+2}>\frac{13}{24}.$$

$$\Rightarrow \frac{1}{3}+\frac{1}{4}>\frac{13}{24} \Rightarrow \frac{4+3}{12}>\frac{13}{24}$$

$$\Rightarrow \frac{7}{12}>\frac{13}{24}$$

$$\Rightarrow \frac{14}{24}>\frac{13}{24}, \text{ which is true.}$$

Hence, $P(2)$ is true.

***Step* II** Now, we assume that $P(n)$ is true for $n = k$,

$$P(k): \frac{1}{k+1}+\frac{1}{k+2}+\ldots+\frac{1}{2k}>\frac{13}{24} \quad \ldots(\text{i})$$

***Step* III** Now, to prove $P(k + 1)$ is true, we have to show that

$$P(k+1) = \frac{1}{k+2}+\frac{1}{k+3}+\ldots+\frac{1}{2k}+\frac{1}{2k+1}+\frac{1}{2k+2}>\frac{13}{24}$$

We already know that, $\left(\frac{1}{2k+1}+\frac{1}{2k+2}\right)-\frac{1}{K+1}>0$

Adding this to inequation (i), we get

$$\left(\frac{1}{k+1}+\frac{1}{k+2}+\ldots+\frac{1}{2k}\right)+\left(\frac{1}{2k+1}+\frac{1}{2k+2}-\frac{1}{k+1}\right)>\frac{13}{24}$$

$$\Rightarrow \frac{1}{k+2}+\frac{1}{k+3}+\ldots+\frac{1}{2k}+\frac{1}{2k+1}+\frac{1}{2k+2}>\frac{13}{24}$$

So, $P(k + 1)$ is true, whenever $P(k)$ is true. Hence, by principal of mathematical induction $P(n)$ is true for all natural numbers $n > 1$.

Q.25 Prove that number of subsets of a set containing n distinct elements is 2^n, for all $n \in N$.

Ans. Let $P(n)$: Number of subset of a sets containing n distinct elements is 2^n, for all $n \in N$.

***Step* I** We observe that $P(1)$ is true for $n = 1$.

Number of subsets of a set contain 1 element is $2^1 = 2$, which is true.

Hence, $P(1)$ is true.

***Step* II** Assume that $P(n)$ is true for $n = k$.

$P(k)$: Number of subsets of a set containing k distinct elements is 2^k.

***Step* III** To prove that $P(k + 1)$ is true, we have to show that

$P(k + 1)$: Number of subsets of a set containing $(k + 1)$ distinct elements is 2^{k+1}.

We know that with the addition of one element in the set, the number of subsets becomes double because for each of the subsets of K distint element, we can form a new subset by adding $(k + 1)$th element.

This also gives us 2^k new subsets.

$\therefore$ Number of subsets of a set containing $(k + 1)$ distinct elements $= 2 \times 2^k = 2^{k+1}$.

So, $P(k + 1)$ is true. Hence, by principal of mathematical induction $P(n)$ is true.

Objective Type Questions

Choose the correct answers from the given four options in each exercise 26 to 30.

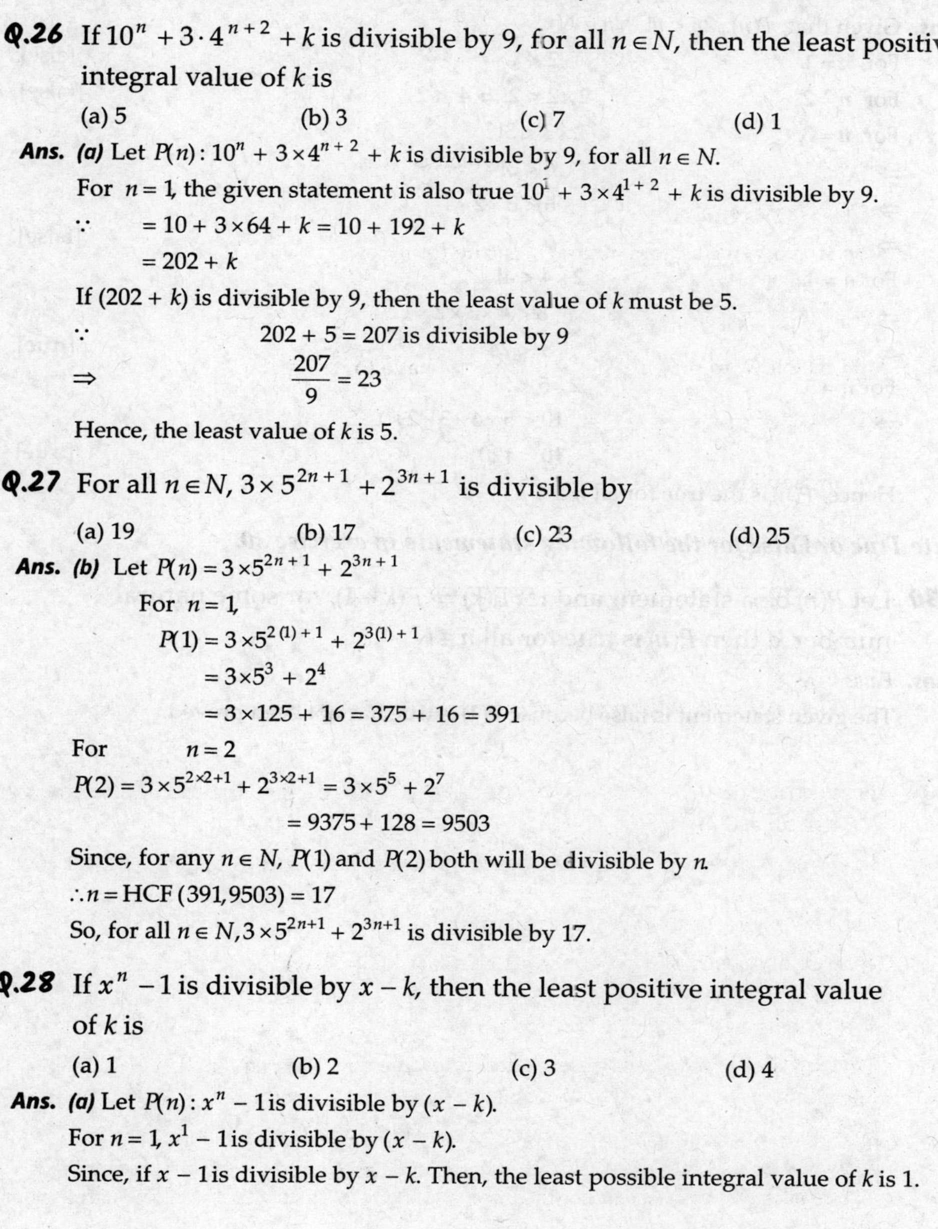

Q.26 If $10^n + 3 \cdot 4^{n+2} + k$ is divisible by 9, for all $n \in N$, then the least positive integral value of k is

(a) 5 (b) 3 (c) 7 (d) 1

Ans. ***(a)*** Let $P(n): 10^n + 3 \times 4^{n+2} + k$ is divisible by 9, for all $n \in N$.

For $n = 1$, the given statement is also true $10^1 + 3 \times 4^{1+2} + k$ is divisible by 9.

$\because \quad = 10 + 3 \times 64 + k = 10 + 192 + k$

$= 202 + k$

If $(202 + k)$ is divisible by 9, then the least value of k must be 5.

$\because \quad 202 + 5 = 207$ is divisible by 9

$\Rightarrow \quad \frac{207}{9} = 23$

Hence, the least value of k is 5.

Q.27 For all $n \in N$, $3 \times 5^{2n+1} + 2^{3n+1}$ is divisible by

(a) 19 (b) 17 (c) 23 (d) 25

Ans. ***(b)*** Let $P(n) = 3 \times 5^{2n+1} + 2^{3n+1}$

For $n = 1$,

$P(1) = 3 \times 5^{2(1)+1} + 2^{3(1)+1}$

$= 3 \times 5^3 + 2^4$

$= 3 \times 125 + 16 = 375 + 16 = 391$

For $\quad n = 2$

$P(2) = 3 \times 5^{2 \times 2+1} + 2^{3 \times 2+1} = 3 \times 5^5 + 2^7$

$= 9375 + 128 = 9503$

Since, for any $n \in N$, $P(1)$ and $P(2)$ both will be divisible by n.

$\therefore n = \text{HCF}(391, 9503) = 17$

So, for all $n \in N, 3 \times 5^{2n+1} + 2^{3n+1}$ is divisible by 17.

Q.28 If $x^n - 1$ is divisible by $x - k$, then the least positive integral value of k is

(a) 1 (b) 2 (c) 3 (d) 4

Ans. ***(a)*** Let $P(n): x^n - 1$ is divisible by $(x - k)$.

For $n = 1$, $x^1 - 1$ is divisible by $(x - k)$.

Since, if $x - 1$ is divisible by $x - k$. Then, the least possible integral value of k is 1.

Fill in the blanks in exercise 29.

Q.29 If $P(n): 2n < n!$, $n \in N$, then $P(n)$ is true for all $n \geq$ ....

Ans. Given that, $P(n): 2n < n!$, $\forall n \in N$

For $n = 1$, $2 < 1$ [false]

For $n = 2$, $2 \times 2 < 2! \Rightarrow 4 < 2$ [false]

For $n = 3$, $2 \times 3 < 3!$

$\Rightarrow 6 < 3!$

$\Rightarrow 6 < 3 \times 2 \times 1$

$\Rightarrow 6 < 6$ [false]

For $n = 4$, $2 \times 4 < 4!$

$\Rightarrow 8 < 4 \times 3 \times 2 \times 1$

$\Rightarrow 8 < 24$ [true]

For $n = 5$, $2 \times 5 < 5!$

$\Rightarrow 10 < 5 \times 4 \times 3 \times 2 \times 1$

$\Rightarrow 10 < 120$ [true]

Hence, $P(n)$ is the true for all $n \geq 4$.

State True or False for the following statements in exercise 30.

Q.30 Let $P(n)$ be a statement and let $P(k) \Rightarrow P(k+1)$, for some natural number k, then $P(n)$ is true for all $n \in N$.

Ans. *False*

The given statement is false because $P(1)$ is true has not been proved.

Chapter

05

Complex Numbers and Quadratic Equations

Short Answer Type Questions

Q.1 For a positive integer n, find the value of $(1-i)^n\left(1-\frac{1}{i}\right)^n$.

Ans. Given expression $=(1-i)^n\left(1-\frac{1}{i}\right)^n$

$$=(1-i)^n\left(1-\frac{1}{i}\times\frac{i}{i}\right)^n$$

$$=(1-i)^n(1-i)^n \qquad [\because i^2=-1]$$

$$=(1-i^2)^n=(1+1)^n=2^n$$

Mistake Alert! *Students should carefully evaluate the integral powers of i (iota).*

Q.2 Evaluate $\sum_{n=1}^{13}(i^n+i^{n+1})$, where $n\in N$.

Thinking Process Use $i^2=-1$, $i^4=(-1)^2=1$, $i^3=-i$, and $i^5=i$ to solve it

Ans. Given that, $\sum_{n=1}^{13}(i^n+i^{n+1}), n\in N$

$$=(i+i^2+i^3+i^4+i^5+i^6+i^7+i^8+i^9+i^{10}+i^{11}+i^{12}+i^{13})$$
$$+(i^2+i^3+i^4+i^5+i^6+i^7+i^8+i^9+i^{10}+i^{11}+i^{12}+i^{13}+i^{14})$$

$$=(i+2i^2+2i^3+2i^4+2i^5+2i^6+2i^7-2i^8$$
$$+2i^9+2i^{10}+2i^{11}+2i^{12}+2i^{13}+i^{14})$$

$$=i-2-2i+2+2i+2(i^4)i^2+2(i)^4i^3+2(i^2)^4+2(i^2)^4i+2(i^2)^5$$
$$+2(i^2)^5\cdot i+2(i^2)^6+2(i^2)^6\cdot i+(i^2)^7$$

$$=i-2-2i+2+2i-2-2i+2+2i-2-2i+2+2i-1=(i-1)$$

Alternate Method

$$\sum_{n=1}^{13}(i^n+i^{n+1}), n\in N=\sum_{n=1}^{13}i^n(1+i)=(1+i)\sum_{n=1}^{13}i^n$$

$$=(1+i)[i+i^2+i^3+i^4+i^5+i^6+i^7+i^8+i^9+i^{10}+i^{11}+i^{12}+i^{13}]$$

$$=(1+i)[i^{13}] \qquad [\because i^n+i^{n+1}+i^{n+2}+i^{n+3}=0, \text{ where } n\in N]$$

where $n\in N$ *i.e.*, $\sum_{n=1}^{12}i^n=0$

$$=(1+i)i \qquad [\because i^{13}=(i^4)^3\cdot i=i]$$

$$=(i^2+i)=i-1 \qquad [\because i^2=-1]$$

Q.3 If $\left(\frac{1+i}{1-i}\right)^3 - \left(\frac{1-i}{1+i}\right)^3 = x + iy$, then find (x, y).

Thinking Process If two complex numbers $z_1 = x_1 + iy_1$ and $z_2 = x_2 + iy_2$ are equal then $x_1 = x_2$ and $y_1 = y_2$.

Ans. Given, $$\left(\frac{1+i}{1-i}\right)^3 - \left(\frac{1-i}{1+i}\right)^3 = x + iy \quad \text{...(i)}$$

$$\therefore \quad \left(\frac{1+i}{1-i}\right)^3 = \left(\frac{1+i}{1-i} \times \frac{1+i}{1+i}\right)^3 = \left(\frac{(1+i)^2}{1-i^2}\right)^3$$

$$= \left(\frac{1+i^2+2i}{2}\right)^3 = i^3$$

$$\Rightarrow \quad \left(\frac{1+i}{1-i}\right)^3 = -i \quad \text{...(ii)}$$

Similarly, $$\left(\frac{1-i}{1+i}\right)^3 = \frac{-1}{i} = \frac{i^2}{i} = i \quad [\because i^2 = -1] \text{...(iii)}$$

Using Eqs. (ii) and (iii) in Eq. (i), we get

$$-i - i = x + iy$$

$$\Rightarrow \quad -2i = x + iy$$

On comparing real and imaginary parts of the above equation, we get

$$x = 0 \text{ and } y = -2$$

So, $$(x, y) = (0, -2)$$

Q.4 If $\frac{(1+i)^2}{2-i} = x + iy$, then find the value of $x + y$.

Ans. Given, $$\frac{(1+i)^2}{2-i} = x + iy$$

$$\Rightarrow \quad \frac{(1+i^2+2i)}{2-i} = x + iy \Rightarrow \frac{2i}{2-i} = x + iy \quad [\because i^2 = -1]$$

$$\Rightarrow \quad \frac{2i(2+i)}{(2-i)(2+i)} = x + iy \Rightarrow \frac{4i+2i^2}{4-i^2} = x + iy$$

$$\Rightarrow \quad \frac{4i-2}{4+1} = x + iy \Rightarrow \frac{-2}{5} + \frac{4i}{5} = x + iy \quad [\because i^2 = -1]$$

On comparing real and imaginary parts both sides, we get

$$x = -\frac{2}{5} \text{ and } y = \frac{4}{5}$$

$$\therefore \quad x + y = \frac{-2}{5} + \frac{4}{5} = \frac{2}{5}$$

Mistake Alert! *Students should carefully rationalise the denominator and then evaluating the powers of iota.*

Q.5 If $\left(\frac{1-i}{1+i}\right)^{100} = a + ib$, then find (a, b).

Ans. Given, $\left(\frac{1-i}{1+i}\right)^{100} = a + ib$

$$\Rightarrow \left[\frac{(1-i)}{(1+i)} \cdot \frac{(1-i)}{(1-i)}\right]^{100} = a + ib$$

$$\Rightarrow \left(\frac{1+i^2-2i}{1-i^2}\right)^{100} = a + ib$$

$$\Rightarrow \left(\frac{-2i}{2}\right)^{100} = a + ib \qquad [\because i^2 = -1]$$

$$\Rightarrow (i^4)^{25} = a + ib \Rightarrow 1 = a + ib \qquad [\because i^4 = 1]$$

Then, $a = 1$ and $b = 0$

$\therefore$ $(a, b) = (1, 0)$

Q.6 If $a = \cos\theta + i\sin\theta$, then find the value of $\frac{1+a}{1-a}$.

Thinking Process To solve the above problem, use the trigonometric formulae $\cos\theta = 2\cos^2\frac{\theta}{2} - 1 = 1 - 2\sin^2\frac{\theta}{2}$ and $\sin\theta = 2\sin\frac{\theta}{2} \cdot \cos\frac{\theta}{2}$.

Ans. Given, $a = \cos\theta + i\sin\theta$

$$\therefore \frac{1+a}{1-a} = \frac{1+\cos\theta + i\sin\theta}{1-\cos\theta - i\sin\theta}$$

$$= \frac{1+2\cos^2\frac{\theta}{2} - 1 + 2i\sin\frac{\theta}{2}\cdot\cos\frac{\theta}{2}}{1-1+2\sin^2\frac{\theta}{2} - 2i\sin\frac{\theta}{2}\cdot\cos\frac{\theta}{2}} = \frac{2\cos\frac{\theta}{2}\left(\cos\frac{\theta}{2} + i\sin\frac{\theta}{2}\right)}{2\sin\frac{\theta}{2}\left(\sin\frac{\theta}{2} - i\cos\frac{\theta}{2}\right)}$$

$$= -\frac{2\cos\frac{\theta}{2}\left(\cos\frac{\theta}{2} + i\sin\frac{\theta}{2}\right)}{2i\sin\frac{\theta}{2}\left(\cos\frac{\theta}{2} + i\sin\frac{\theta}{2}\right)} = -\frac{1}{i}\cot\frac{\theta}{2}$$

$$= i\cot\frac{\theta}{2} \qquad \left[\because \frac{-1}{i} = \frac{i^2}{i} = i\right]$$

Q.7 If $(1+i)z = (1-i)\bar{z}$, then show that $z = -i\bar{z}$.

Ans. We have, $(1+i)z = (1-i)\bar{z} \Rightarrow \frac{z}{\bar{z}} = \frac{(1-i)}{(1+i)}$

$$\Rightarrow \frac{z}{\bar{z}} = \frac{(1-i)(1-i)}{(1+i)(1-i)} \Rightarrow \frac{z}{\bar{z}} = \frac{1+i^2-2i}{1-i^2}$$

$$\Rightarrow \frac{z}{\bar{z}} = \frac{1-1-2i}{2} \Rightarrow \frac{z}{\bar{z}} = -i \qquad [\because i^2 = -1]$$

$\therefore$ $z = -i\bar{z}$ **Hence proved.**

Q.8 If $z = x + iy$, then show that $z\bar{z} + 2(z + \bar{z}) + b = 0$, where $b \in R$, represents a circle.

Ans. Given, $z = x + iy$

Then, $\bar{z} = x - iy$

Now, $z\bar{z} + 2(z + \bar{z}) + b = 0$

$\Rightarrow (x + iy)(x - iy) + 2(x + iy + x - iy) + b = 0$

$\Rightarrow (x^2 - i^2y^2) + 2\cdot(2x) + b = 0$

$\Rightarrow x^2 + y^2 + 4x + b = 0$, which is the equation of a circle.

Q.9 If the real part of $\dfrac{\bar{z}+2}{\bar{z}-1}$ is 4, then show that the locus of the point representing z in the complex plane is a circle.

Ans. Let $z = x + iy \Rightarrow \bar{z} = x - iy$

Now,
$$\frac{\bar{z}+2}{\bar{z}-1} = \frac{x - iy + 2}{x - iy - 1}$$
$$= \frac{[(x+2) - iy][(x-1) + iy]}{[(x-1) - iy][(x-1) + iy]}$$
$$= \frac{(x-1)(x+2) - iy(x-1) + iy(x+2) + y^2}{(x-1)^2 + y^2} \quad [\because i^2 = -1]$$
$$= \frac{(x-1)(x+2) + y^2 + i[(x+2)y - (x-1)y]}{(x-1)^2 + y^2}$$

Since, $\text{Re}\left(\dfrac{\bar{z}+2}{\bar{z}-1}\right) = 4$

$$\therefore \quad \frac{(x-1)(x+2) + y^2}{(x-1)^2 + y^2} = 4$$

$\Rightarrow x^2 - x + 2x - 2 + y^2 = 4(x^2 - 2x + 1 + y^2)$

$\Rightarrow 3x^2 + 3y^2 - 9x + 6 = 0$, which represents a circle.

Hence, z lies on the circle.

Mistake Alert ! *Not using the conjugate correctly in division, which can lead to incorrect simplifications.*

***Q.10** Show that the complex number z, satisfying the condition $\arg\left(\dfrac{z-1}{z+1}\right) = \dfrac{\pi}{4}$ lies on a circle.

Thinking Process First use, $\arg\left(\dfrac{z_1}{z_2}\right) = \arg(z_1) - \arg(z_2)$. Also apply $\arg(z) = \theta = \tan^{-1}\dfrac{y}{x}$, where $z = x + iy$.

Ans. Given that, $\arg\left(\dfrac{z-1}{z+1}\right) = \dfrac{\pi}{4}$

Let $z = x + iy$

(*) Topics related to these question have been removed from latest NCERT.

$$\Rightarrow \quad \arg(z-1)-\arg(z+1)=\frac{\pi}{4}$$

$$\Rightarrow \quad \arg(x+iy-1)-\arg(x+iy+1)=\frac{\pi}{4}$$

$$\Rightarrow \quad \arg(x-1+iy)-\arg(x+1+iy)=\frac{\pi}{4}$$

$$\Rightarrow \quad \arg\tan^{-1}\left(\frac{y}{x-1}\right)-\tan^{-1}\left(\frac{y}{x+1}\right)=\frac{\pi}{4}$$

$$\Rightarrow \quad \tan^{-1}\left[\frac{\frac{y}{x-1}-\frac{y}{x+1}}{1-\left(\frac{y}{x-1}\right)\left(\frac{y}{x+1}\right)}\right]=\frac{\pi}{4}$$

$$\Rightarrow \quad y\frac{\left[\frac{x+1-x+1}{x^2-1}\right]}{\frac{x^2-1+y^2}{x^2-1}}=\tan\frac{\pi}{4}$$

$$\Rightarrow \quad \frac{2y}{x^2+y^2-1}=1$$

$$\Rightarrow \quad x^2+y^2-2y-1=0, \text{ which represents a circle.}$$

Q.11 Solve the equation $|z|=z+1+2i$.

Ans. The given equation is $|z|=z+1+2i$ ...(i)

Let $z=x+iy$

From Eq. (i), $|x+iy|=x+iy+1+2i$

$$\Rightarrow \quad \sqrt{x^2+y^2}=(x+1)+i(y+2) \qquad [\because |z|=\sqrt{x^2+y^2}]$$

On squaring both sides, we get

$$x^2+y^2=(x+1)^2+i^2(y+2)^2+2i(x+1)(y+2)$$

$$\Rightarrow \quad x^2+y^2=x^2+2x+1-y^2-4y-4+2i(x+1)(y+2)$$

On comparing real and imaginary parts both sides, we get

$$x^2+y^2=x^2+2x+1-y^2-4y-4$$

i.e., $2y^2=2x-4y-3$ ...(ii)

and $2(x+1)(y+2)=0$

$$\Rightarrow \quad (x+1)=0 \text{ or } (y+2)=0$$

$$\Rightarrow \quad x=-1 \text{ or } y=-2$$

For $x=-1$, $2y^2=-2-4y-3$ [from Eq. (ii)]

$$2y^2+4y+5=0$$

$$\Rightarrow \quad y=\frac{-4\pm\sqrt{16-4\times2\times5}}{4}$$

$$\Rightarrow \quad y=\frac{-4\pm\sqrt{-24}}{4}\notin R$$

For $y=-2$, $2(-2)^2=2x-4(-2)-3$ [from Eq. (ii)]

$$\Rightarrow \quad 8=2x+8-3$$

$$\Rightarrow \quad 2x=3$$

$\Rightarrow \quad x = \dfrac{3}{2}$

$\therefore \quad z = x + iy = \dfrac{3}{2} - 2i$

Mistake Alert ! *Students should carefully compare the real and imaginary parts to get the correct values of x and y.*

Long Answer Type Questions

Q.12 If $|z+1| = z + 2(1+i)$, then find the value of z.

- **Concept Insight** For an equation involving complex numbers, the real and imaginary parts are equal on both sides of the equation.

Ans. Given, $\quad |z+1| = z + 2(1+i) \quad$ ...(i)

Let $\quad z = x + iy$

Then, $\quad |x + iy + 1| = x + iy + 2(1+i)$

$\Rightarrow \quad \sqrt{(x+1)^2 + y^2} = (x+2) + i(y+2) \quad [\because \sqrt{A^2 + B^2}]$ $|A + iB|$

On squaring both sides, we get

$$(x+1)^2 + y^2 = (x+2)^2 + i^2(y+2)^2 + 2i(x+2)(y+2)$$

$\Rightarrow \quad x^2 + 2x + 1 + y^2 = x^2 + 4x + 4 - y^2 - 4y - 4 + 2i(x+2)(y+2)$

$\Rightarrow \quad x^2 + y^2 + 2x + 1 = x^2 - y^2 + 4x - 4y + 2i(x+2)(y+2)$

On comparing real and imaginary parts both sides, we get

$$x^2 + y^2 + 2x + 1 = x^2 - y^2 + 4x - 4y$$

$\Rightarrow \quad 2y^2 - 2x + 4y + 1 = 0 \quad$ ...(ii)

and $\quad 2(x+2)(y+2) = 0$

$\Rightarrow \quad x + 2 = 0$ or $y + 2 = 0$

$x = -2$ or $y = -2 \quad$ ...(iii)

For $x = -2$, $\quad 2y^2 + 4 + 4y + 1 = 0 \quad$ [from Eq. (ii)]

$\Rightarrow \quad 2y^2 + 4y + 5 = 0$

$\therefore$ Discriminant, $\quad D = b^2 - 4ac$

$\Rightarrow \quad 16 - 4 \times 2 \times 5 < 0$

$\Rightarrow \quad 2y^2 + 4y + 5$ has no real roots.

Thus, for $x = -2$, the value of y is not possible.

For $y = -2$, $2(-2)^2 - 2x + 4(-2) + 1 = 0 \quad$ [from Eq. (ii)]

$\Rightarrow \quad 8 - 2x - 8 + 1 = 0$

$\Rightarrow \quad x = 1/2$

$\therefore \quad z = x + iy = \dfrac{1}{2} - 2i$

***Q.13** If arg $(z-1) = \arg(z+3i)$, then find $x-1 : y$, where $z = x + iy$.

- **Concept Insight** The argument of the complex number is equal to the inverse of the tangent function of the imaginary part divided by real part of the complex numbers *i.e.*, $\theta = \tan^{-1}\left(\frac{y}{x}\right) = \arg(z)$, where $z = x + iy$

Ans. Given, $\arg(z-1) = \arg(z+3i)$

And $z = x + iy$

Now, $\arg(z-1) = \arg(z+3i)$

$\Rightarrow \arg(x+iy-1) = \arg(x+iy+3i)$

$\Rightarrow \arg(x-1+iy) = \arg[x+i(y+3)]$

$\Rightarrow \tan^{-1}\frac{y}{x-1} = \tan^{-1}\frac{y+3}{x}$

$\Rightarrow \frac{y}{x-1} = \frac{y+3}{x} \Rightarrow xy = (x-1)(y+3)$

$\Rightarrow xy = xy - y + 3x - 3$

$\Rightarrow 3x - 3 = y$

$\Rightarrow \frac{3(x-1)}{y} = 1$

$\Rightarrow \frac{x-1}{y} = \frac{1}{3}$

$\therefore (x-1) : y = 1 : 3$

Q.14 Show that $\left|\frac{z-2}{z-3}\right| = 2$ represents a circle. Find its centre and radius.

Thinking Process If $z_1 = x_1 + iy_1$ and $z_2 = x_2 + iy_2$ are two complex numbers, then use the modulus property i.e. $\left|\frac{z_1}{z_2}\right| = \frac{|z_1|}{|z_2|}$, $(z_2 \neq 0)$. Also, we know that general equation of a circle is $x^2 + y^2 + 2gx + 2fy + c = 0$, with centre $(-g, -f)$ and radius $= \sqrt{g^2 + f^2 - c}$.

Ans. Given equation $\left|\frac{z-2}{z-3}\right| = 2$

Let $z = x + iy$

$\Rightarrow \left|\frac{x+iy-2}{x+iy-3}\right| = 2$

$\Rightarrow |x-2+iy| = 2|x-3+iy|$

$\Rightarrow \sqrt{(x-2)^2 + y^2} = 2\sqrt{(x-3)^2 + y^2}$ $\quad [\because |x+iy| = \sqrt{x^2+y^2}]$

On squaring both sides, we get

$$x^2 - 4x + 4 + y^2 = 4(x^2 - 6x + 9 + y^2)$$

$\Rightarrow 3x^2 + 3y^2 - 20x + 32 = 0$ [which represents a circle]

Now, $x^2 + y^2 - \frac{20}{3}x + \frac{32}{3} = 0$ ...(i)

(*) Topics related to these question have been removed from latest NCERT.

On comparing the above equation with $x^2 + y^2 + 2gx + 2fy + c = 0$, we get

$$\Rightarrow \quad 2g = \frac{-20}{3} \Rightarrow g = \frac{-10}{3} \text{ and } 2f = 0 \Rightarrow f = 0 \text{ and } c = \frac{32}{3}$$

$$\therefore \quad \text{Centre} = (-g, -f) = \left(\frac{10}{3}, 0\right)$$

Also, $$\text{radius } (r) = \sqrt{\left(\frac{10}{3}\right)^2 + 0 - \frac{32}{3}} \qquad [\because r = \sqrt{g^2 + f^2 - c}]$$

$$= \frac{1}{3}\sqrt{(100 - 96)} = \frac{2}{3}$$

Q.15 If $\frac{z-1}{z+1}$ is a purely imaginary number $(z \neq -1)$, then find the value of $|z|$.

● **Concept Insight** For purely imaginary number, then real part must be equal to zero.

Ans. Let $$z = x + iy$$

Now, $$\frac{z-1}{z+1} = \frac{x + iy - 1}{x + iy + 1}, z \neq -1$$

$$= \frac{x - 1 + iy}{x + 1 + iy} = \frac{(x - 1 + iy)(x + 1 - iy)}{(x + 1 + iy)(x + 1 - iy)}$$

$$= \frac{(x^2 - 1) + iy(x + 1) - iy(x - 1) - i^2y^2}{(x + 1)^2 - (iy)^2}$$

$$\Rightarrow \quad \frac{z-1}{z+1} = \frac{(x^2 - 1) + y^2 + i[y(x + 1) - y(x - 1)]}{(x + 1)^2 + y^2}$$

Given that $\frac{z-1}{z+1}$ is a purely imaginary number

Then, $$\frac{(x^2 - 1) + y^2}{(x + 1)^2 + y^2} = 0$$

$$\Rightarrow \quad x^2 - 1 + y^2 = 0 \Rightarrow x^2 + y^2 = 1$$

$$\Rightarrow \quad \sqrt{x^2 + y^2} = \sqrt{1} \Rightarrow |z| = 1 \qquad [\because |z| = \sqrt{x^2 + y^2}]$$

***Q.16** z_1 and z_2 are two complex numbers such that $|z_1| = |z_2|$ and $\arg(z_1) + \arg(z_2) = \pi$, then show that $z_1 = -\bar{z}_2$.

Ans. Let $z_1 = r_1(\cos\theta_1 + i\sin\theta_1)$ and $z_2 = r_2(\cos\theta_2 + i\sin\theta_2)$ are two complex numbers. where r_1 and r_2 are respective modulus and θ_1 and θ_2 are their corresponding arguments

Given, $$|z_1| = |z_2|$$

$$\Rightarrow \quad r_1 = r_2 \qquad \ldots(i)$$

And $$\arg(z_1) + \arg(z_2) = \pi$$

$$\Rightarrow \quad \theta_1 + \theta_2 = \pi \Rightarrow \theta_1 = \pi - \theta_2$$

Now, $$z_1 = r_1(\cos\theta_1 + i\sin\theta_1)$$

$$\Rightarrow \quad z_1 = r_2[\cos(\pi - \theta_2) + i\sin(\pi - \theta_2)] \qquad [\because r_1 = r_2 \text{ and } \theta_1 = (\pi - \theta_2)]$$

(*) Topics related to these question have been removed from latest NCERT.

$\Rightarrow \quad z_1 = r_2(-\cos\theta_2 + i\sin\theta_2)$

$\Rightarrow \quad z_1 = -r_2(\cos\theta_2 - i\sin\theta_2)$

$\Rightarrow \quad z_1 = -[r_2(\cos\theta_2 - i\sin\theta_2)]$

$\Rightarrow \quad z_1 = -\bar{z}_2 \qquad [\because \bar{z}_2 = r_2(\cos\theta_2 - i\sin\theta_2)]$ **Hence proved.**

Q.17 If $|z_1| = 1\ (z_1 \neq -1)$ and $z_2 = \dfrac{z_1 - 1}{z_1 + 1}$, then show that the real part of z_2 is zero.

Ans. Let $\quad z_1 = x + iy$

$\Rightarrow \quad |z_1| = \sqrt{x^2 + y^2} = 1 \qquad [\because |z_1| = 1, \text{given}] \qquad \ldots(\text{i})$

Now,

$$z_2 = \frac{z_1 - 1}{z_1 + 1} = \frac{x + iy - 1}{x + iy + 1}$$

$$= \frac{x - 1 + iy}{x + 1 + iy} = \frac{(x - 1 + iy)(x + 1 - iy)}{(x + 1 + iy)(x + 1 - iy)}$$

$$= \frac{x^2 - 1 + iy(x + 1) - iy(x - 1) - i^2y^2}{(x + 1)^2 - i^2y^2}$$

$$= \frac{x^2 - 1 + ixy + iy - ixy + iy + y^2}{(x + 1)^2 + y^2}$$

$$= \frac{x^2 + y^2 - 1 + 2iy}{(x + 1)^2 + y^2} = \frac{1 - 1 + 2iy}{(x + 1)^2 + y^2} \qquad [\because x^2 + y^2 = 1]$$

$$= 0 + \frac{2yi}{(x + 1)^2 + y^2}$$

Hence, the real part of z_2 is zero.

***Q.18** If z_1, z_2 and z_3, z_4 are two pairs of conjugate complex numbers, then find $\arg\left(\dfrac{z_1}{z_4}\right) + \arg\left(\dfrac{z_2}{z_3}\right)$.

Thinking Process First. let $z = r(\cos\theta + i\sin\theta)$, then conjugate of z *i.e.*, $\bar{z} = r(\cos\theta - i\sin\theta)$. Use the property, $\arg\left(\dfrac{z_1}{z_2}\right) = \arg(z_1) - \arg(z_2)$.

Ans. Let $\quad z_1 = r_1(\cos\theta_1 + i\sin\theta_1)$, where θ_1 is the argument

Then, $\quad z_2 = \bar{z}_1 = r_1(\cos\theta_1 - i\sin\theta_1) = r_1[\cos(-\theta_1) + i\sin(-\theta_1)]$

Also, let $\quad z_3 = r_2(\cos\theta_2 + i\sin\theta_2)$, where θ_2 is the argument

Then, $\quad z_4 = \bar{z}_3 = r_2(\cos\theta_2 - i\sin\theta_2) = r_2[\cos(-\theta_2) + i\sin(-\theta_2)]$

$[\because \cos(-\theta) = \cos\theta]$

$$\arg\left(\frac{z_1}{z_4}\right) + \arg\left(\frac{z_2}{z_3}\right) = \arg(z_1) - \arg(z_4) + \arg(z_2) - \arg(z_3)$$

$$= \theta_1 - (-\theta_2) + (-\theta_1) - \theta_2 \qquad [\because \arg(z) = \theta]$$

$$= \theta_1 + \theta_2 - \theta_1 - \theta_2 = 0$$

(*) Topics related to these question have been removed from latest NCERT.

Q.19 If $|z_1| = |z_2| = \cdots = |z_n| = 1$, then show that

$$|z_1 + z_2 + z_3 + \cdots + z_n| = \left|\frac{1}{z_1} + \frac{1}{z_2} + \frac{1}{z_3} + \cdots + \frac{1}{z_n}\right|.$$

Thinking process Use the properties $|z|^2 = z\bar{z}$, $z = \dfrac{1}{\bar{z}}$ and simplify

Ans. Given, $|z_1| = |z_2| = \cdots = |z_n| = 1$

$\Rightarrow$ $|z_1|^2 = |z_2|^2 = \cdots = |z_n|^2 = 1$

$\Rightarrow$ $z_1\bar{z}_1 = z_2\bar{z}_2 = z_3\bar{z}_3 = \cdots = z_n\bar{z}_n = 1$

$\Rightarrow$ $z_1 = \dfrac{1}{\bar{z}_1}, z_2 = \dfrac{1}{\bar{z}_2} = \cdots = z_n = \dfrac{1}{\bar{z}_n}$

Now, $|z_1 + z_2 + z_3 + \ldots + z_n|$

$$= \left|\frac{1}{\bar{z}_1} + \frac{1}{\bar{z}_2} + \frac{1}{\bar{z}_3} + \ldots + \frac{1}{\bar{z}_n}\right|$$

$$= \left|\overline{\frac{1}{z_1} + \frac{1}{z_2} + \frac{1}{z_3} + \ldots + \frac{1}{z_n}}\right|$$

$$= \left|\frac{1}{z_1} + \frac{1}{z_2} + \frac{1}{z_3} + \ldots + \frac{1}{z_n}\right|$$

Hence proved.

***Q.20** If the complex numbers z_1 and z_2, $\arg(z_1) - \arg(z_2) = 0$, then show that $|z_1 - z_2| = |z_1| - |z_2|$.

Ans. Let $z_1 = r_1(\cos\theta_1 + i\sin\theta_1)$

and $z_2 = r_2(\cos\theta_2 + i\sin\theta_2)$

$\Rightarrow$ $\arg(z_1) = \theta_1$ and $\arg(z_2) = \theta_2$

Given, $\arg(z_1) - \arg(z_2) = 0$

$\theta_1 - \theta_2 = 0 \Rightarrow \theta_1 = \theta_2$

Now, $z_2 = r_2(\cos\theta_1 + i\sin\theta_1)$ $[\because \theta_1 = \theta_2]$

Thus, $z_1 - z_2 = (r_1\cos\theta_1 - r_2\cos\theta_1) + i(r_1\sin\theta_1 - r_2\sin\theta_1)$

$\Rightarrow$ $|z_1 - z_2| = \sqrt{(r_1\cos\theta_1 - r_2\cos\theta_1)^2 + (r_1\sin\theta_1 - r_2\sin\theta_1)^2}$

$= \sqrt{r_1^2 + r_2^2 - 2r_1r_2\cos^2\theta_1 - 2r_1r_2\sin^2\theta_1}$

$= \sqrt{r_1^2 + r_2^2 - 2r_1r_2(\sin^2\theta_1 + \cos^2\theta_1)}$

$= \sqrt{r_1^2 + r_2^2 - 2r_1r_2} = \sqrt{(r_1 - r_2)^2}$ $[\because \sin^2\theta + \cos^2\theta = 1]$

$\Rightarrow$ $|z_1 - z_2| = r_1 - r_2$

$= |z_1| - |z_2|$ $[\because r = |z|]$ **Hence proved.**

(*****) Topics related to these question have been removed from latest NCERT.

Q.21 Solve the system of equations $\text{Re}(z^2) = 0, |z| = 2$.

Ans. Given, $\text{Re}(z^2) = 0, |z| = 2$

Let $z = x + iy$ ...(i)

$$|z| = \sqrt{x^2 + y^2}$$

$\because$ $\sqrt{x^2 + y^2} = 2$

On squaring both sides, we get

$\Rightarrow$ $x^2 + y^2 = 4$ ...(ii)

On squaring both sides of Eq. (i), we get

$\Rightarrow$ $z^2 = x^2 + 2ixy - y^2$ $[\because i^2 = -1]$

$\Rightarrow$ $z^2 = (x^2 - y^2) + 2ixy$

$\Rightarrow$ $\text{Re}(z^2) = x^2 - y^2$

$\Rightarrow$ $x^2 - y^2 = 0$ $[\because \text{Re}(z^2) = 0]$ ...(iii)

From Eqs. (ii) and (iii),

$$x^2 + x^2 = 4$$

$\Rightarrow$ $2x^2 = 4 \Rightarrow x^2 = 2$

$\Rightarrow$ $x = \pm\sqrt{2}$

$\therefore$ $y = \pm x \pm \sqrt{2}$ [from Eq. (iii)]

$\because$ $z = x + iy$

$\Rightarrow$ $z = \sqrt{2} \pm i\sqrt{2}, -\sqrt{2} \pm i\sqrt{2}$

Q.22 Find the complex number satisfying the equation $z + \sqrt{2}|(z+1)| + i = 0$.

Thinking Process Firstly, let $z = x + iy$ and substitute the value of z in the given equation, then evaluate its modulus and further equate $\text{Re}(z) = 0$ and $\text{Im}(z) = 0$ to obtain the value of z.

Ans. Given equation is $z + \sqrt{2}|(z + 1)| + i = 0$ ...(i)

Let $z = x + iy$

$\Rightarrow$ $x + iy + \sqrt{2}|x + iy + 1| + i = 0$

$\Rightarrow$ $x + i(1 + y) + \sqrt{2}[\sqrt{(x+1)^2 + y^2}] = 0$

$\Rightarrow$ $x + i(1 + y) + \sqrt{2}\sqrt{(x^2 + 2x + 1 + y^2)} = 0$

On equating real and imaginary parts both sides, we get

$$x + \sqrt{2}\sqrt{x^2 + 2x + 1 + y^2} = 0$$

$\Rightarrow$ $x = -\sqrt{2}\sqrt{x^2 + 2x + 1 + y^2}$

On squaring both sides, we get

$\Rightarrow$ $x^2 = 2(x^2 + 2x + 1 + y^2)$

$\Rightarrow$ $x^2 + 4x + 2y^2 + 2 = 0$ ...(ii)

and $1 + y = 0 \Rightarrow y = -1$

For $y = -1$, $x^2 + 4x + 2 + 2 = 0$ [from Eq. (ii)]

$\Rightarrow$ $x^2 + 4x + 4 = 0 \Rightarrow (x+2)^2 = 0$

$\Rightarrow$ $x + 2 = 0 \Rightarrow x = -2$

$\therefore$ $z = x + iy = -2 - i$

***Q.23** Write the complex number $z = \dfrac{1-i}{\cos\frac{\pi}{3} + i\sin\frac{\pi}{3}}$ in polar form.

Ans. Given,
$$z = \frac{1-i}{\cos\frac{\pi}{3} + i\sin\frac{\pi}{3}} = \frac{-\sqrt{2}\left[\frac{-1}{\sqrt{2}} + i\frac{1}{\sqrt{2}}\right]}{\cos\frac{\pi}{3} + i\sin\frac{\pi}{3}} = \frac{-\sqrt{2}\left[-\cos\frac{\pi}{4} + i\sin\frac{\pi}{4}\right]}{\cos\frac{\pi}{3} + i\sin\frac{\pi}{3}}$$

$$= \frac{-\sqrt{2}\left[\cos\left(\pi - \frac{\pi}{4}\right) + i\sin\left(\pi - \frac{\pi}{4}\right)\right]}{\cos\frac{\pi}{3} + i\sin\frac{\pi}{3}} = \frac{-\sqrt{2}\left[\cos\frac{3\pi}{4} + i\sin\frac{3\pi}{4}\right]}{\cos\frac{\pi}{3} + i\sin\frac{\pi}{3}}$$

$$= -\sqrt{2}\left[\cos\left(\frac{3\pi}{4} - \frac{\pi}{3}\right) + i\sin\left(\frac{3\pi}{4} - \frac{\pi}{3}\right)\right] = -\sqrt{2}\left[\cos\frac{5\pi}{12} + i\sin\frac{5\pi}{12}\right]$$

which is a polar form.

Mistake Alert ! *Students may write wrong sign of angles for cos and sin without writing the expression in the form of $r(\cos\theta + i\sin\theta)$ which can lead to wrong polar form.*

***Q.24** If z and w are two complex numbers such that $|zw| = 1$ and $\arg(z) - \arg(w) = \frac{\pi}{2}$, then show that $\bar{z}\,w = -i$.

Ans. Let $z = r_1(\cos\theta_1 + i\sin\theta_1)$ and $w = r_2(\cos\theta_2 + i\sin\theta_2)$

$\Rightarrow$ $\arg(z) = \theta_1$ and $\arg(w) = \theta_2$

Also, $|zw| = |z||w| = r_1 r_2 = 1$

$\therefore$ $r_1 r_2 = 1$ ...(i)

And $\arg(z) - \arg(w) = \frac{\pi}{2}$

$\Rightarrow$ $\theta_1 - \theta_2 = \frac{\pi}{2}$ ...(ii)

Now, to prove that $\bar{z}w = -i$

$$\text{LHS} = \bar{z}w$$
$$= r_1(\cos\theta_1 - i\sin\theta_1)\, r_2(\cos\theta_2 + i\sin\theta_2)$$
$$= r_1 r_2[\cos(\theta_2 - \theta_1) + i\sin(\theta_2 - \theta_1)]$$
$$= r_1 r_2\left[\cos\left(\frac{-\pi}{2}\right) + i\sin\left(\frac{-\pi}{2}\right)\right] \quad \text{[from Eqs. (i) and (ii)]}$$
$$= 1[0 - i]$$
$$= -i = \text{RHS}$$

Hence proved.

(✱) Topics related to these question have been removed from latest NCERT.

Objective Type Questions

Q.25 Fill in the blanks of the following.

(i) For any two complex numbers z_1, z_2 and any real numbers a, b, $|az_1 - bz_2|^2 + |bz_1 + az_2|^2 = \cdots$

(ii) The value of $\sqrt{-25} \times \sqrt{-9}$ is ...

(iii) The number $\dfrac{(1-i)^3}{1-i^3}$ is equal to ...

(iv) The sum of the series $i + i^2 + i^3 + \cdots$ upto 1000 terms is ...

(v) Multiplicative inverse of $1 + i$ is ...

(vi) If z_1 and z_2 are complex numbers such that $z_1 + z_2$ is a real number, then $z_2 = \cdots$

*(vii) $\arg(z) + \arg \bar{z}$ where, $(\bar{z} \neq 0)$ is ...

(viii) If $|z + 4| \leq 3$, then the greatest and least values of $|z + 1|$ are ... and ...

(ix) If $\left|\dfrac{z-2}{z+2}\right| = \dfrac{\pi}{6}$, then the locus of z is ...

*(x) If $|z| = 4$ and $\arg(z) = \dfrac{5\pi}{6}$, then $z = \cdots$

Ans. (i) $|az_1 - bz_2|^2 + |bz_1 + az_2|^2$

$$= |az_1|^2 + |bz_2|^2 - 2\text{Re}\,(az_1 \cdot b\bar{z}_2) + |bz_1|^2 + |az_2|^2 + 2\text{Re}\,(az_1 \cdot b\bar{z}_2)$$

$[\because |z_1 + z_2|^2 = |z_1|^2 + |z_2|^2 + 2\,\text{Re}\,(z_1 z_2)$ and $|z_1 - z_2|^2 = |z_1|^2 + |z_2|^2 - 2\text{Re}\,(z_1 z_2)\,|]$

$$= (a^2 + b^2)|z_1|^2 + (a^2 + b^2)|z_2|^2 = (a^2 + b^2)(|z_1|^2 + |z_2|^2)$$

(ii) $\sqrt{-25} \times \sqrt{-9} = i\sqrt{25} \times i\sqrt{9} = i^2\,(5 \times 3) = -15$

(iii) $\dfrac{(1-i)^3}{1-i^3} = \dfrac{(1-i)^3}{(1-i)(1+i+i^2)} = \dfrac{(1-i)^2}{i} = \dfrac{1+i^2-2i}{i} = \dfrac{-2i}{i} = -2$ $\qquad [\because i^2 = -1]$

(iv) $i + i^2 + i^3 + \ldots$ upto 1000 terms $= i + i^2 + i^3 + i^4 + \ldots\, i^{1000} = 0$

$$\left[\because i^n + i^{n+1} + i^{n+2} + i^{n+3} = 0, \text{ where } n \in N \text{ i.e., } \sum_{n=1}^{1000} i^n = 0\right]$$

(v) Multiplicative inverse of $1 + i = \dfrac{1}{1+i} = \dfrac{1}{1+i} \times \dfrac{1-i}{1-i} = \dfrac{1-i}{1-i^2} = \dfrac{1}{2}(1-i)$

(vi) Let $z_1 = x_1 + iy_1$ and $z_2 = x_2 + iy_2$

$\Rightarrow \quad z_1 + z_2 = (x_1 + x_2) + i(y_1 + y_2)$

If $\quad z_1 + z_2$ is real, then $y_1 + y_2 = 0$

$\Rightarrow \quad y_2 = -y_1$

$\therefore \quad z_2 = x_2 + iy_2 = x_2 - iy_1$

$\Rightarrow \quad z_2 = \bar{z}_1$ $\qquad$ [when $x_1 = x_2$]

(vii) If $\arg(z) = \theta$, then $\arg(\bar{z}) = -\theta$

$\Rightarrow \quad \arg(z) + \arg(\bar{z}) = \theta + (-\theta) = 0$

(*) Topics related to these question have been removed from latest NCERT.

(viii) Given, $|z+4| \le 3$

For the greatest value of $|z+1|$.

$$|z+1| = |z+4-3| \le |z+4| + |-3| \qquad [\because |z_1 + z_2| \le |z_1| + |z_2|]$$
$$= |z+4-3| \le 3+3$$
$$= |z+4-3| \le 6$$

So, the greatest value of $|z+1| = 6$

Now, for least value of $|z+1|$, we know that the least value of the modulus of a complex number is zero. So, the least value of $|z+1|$ is zero.

(ix) Given, $\left|\dfrac{z-2}{z+2}\right| = \dfrac{\pi}{6}$

Let $z = x + iy$

$$\Rightarrow \frac{|x+iy-2|}{|x+iy+2|} = \frac{\pi}{6} \Rightarrow \frac{|x-2+iy|}{|x+2+iy|} = \frac{\pi}{6}$$

$$\Rightarrow 6|x-2+iy| = \pi|x+2+iy|$$

$$\Rightarrow 6\sqrt{(x-2)^2 + y^2} = \pi\sqrt{(x+2)^2 + y^2}$$

On squaring both sides, we get

$$36[x^2 + 4 - 4x + y^2] = \pi^2 [x^2 + 4x + 4 + y^2]$$

$\Rightarrow (36-\pi^2)x^2 + (36-\pi^2)y^2 - (144 + 4\pi^2)x + 144 - 4\pi^2 = 0$, which is a circle.

(x) Given, $|z| = 4$ and $\arg(z) = \dfrac{5\pi}{6}$

Let $z = x + iy = r(\cos\theta + i\sin\theta)$

$\Rightarrow |z| = r = 4$ and $\arg(z) = \theta$

$\because \theta = \dfrac{5\pi}{6}$

$$\therefore z = 4\left(\cos\frac{5\pi}{6} + i\sin\frac{5\pi}{6}\right) = 4[\cos(\pi - \pi/6) + i\sin(\pi - \pi/6)]$$

$$= 4\left[-\cos\frac{\pi}{6} + i\sin\frac{\pi}{6}\right] \qquad [\because \cos(\pi-\theta) = -\cos\theta \text{ and } \sin(\pi-\theta) = \sin\theta]$$

$$= 4\left[\frac{-\sqrt{3}}{2} + i\frac{1}{2}\right] = -2\sqrt{3} + 2i$$

Q.26 State true or false for the following.

(i) The order relation is defined on the set of complex numbers.

*(ii) Multiplication of a non-zero complex number by $-i$ rotates the point about origin through a right angle in the anti-clockwise direction.

(iii) For any complex number z, the minimum value of $|z| + |z-1|$ is 1.

(iv) The locus represented by $|z-1| = |z-i|$ is a line perpendicular to the join of the points (1, 0) and (0, 1).

(v) If z is a complex number such that $z \ne 0$ and $\text{Re}(z) = 0$, then, $\text{Im}(z^2) = 0$.

(*) Topics related to these question have been removed from latest NCERT.

(vi) The inequality $|z-4|<|z-2|$ represents the region given by $x>3$.

*(vii) Let z_1 and z_2 be two complex numbers such that $|z_1+z_2|=|z_1|+|z_2|$, then $\arg(z_1-z_2)=0$.

(viii) 2 is not a complex number.

Ans. (i) *False*

We can compare two complex numbers when they are purely real. Otherwise comparison of complex number is not possible.

(ii) *False*

Let $z=x+iy$ be a complex number

Now, $iz=-ix-i^{2y}=y-ix$ is a complex number formed in clockwise direction and both are at right angles.

(iii) *True*

Let $z=x+iy$

Then, $z-1=x+iy-1=(x-1)+iy$

$$|z|+|z-1|=\sqrt{x^2+y^2}+\sqrt{(x-1)^2+y^2}$$

If $x=0, y=0$, then the minimum value of $|z|+|z-1|=1$.

(iv) *True*

Given, $|z-1|=|z-i|$

Let $z=x+iy$

Then, $|x-1+iy|=|x-i(1-y)|$

$$(x-1)^2+y^2=x^2+(1-y)^2$$
$$x^2-2x+1+y^2=x^2+1+y^2-2y$$
$$-2x+1=1-2y$$
$$-2x+2y=0$$
$$x-y=0 \Rightarrow y=x$$

$\Rightarrow$ Slope of this line $(m_1)=1$ [$\because y=mx+c$]

$\therefore$ Equation of a line through the points (1, 0) and (0, 1) is

$$y-0=\frac{1-0}{0-1}(x-1)$$

$\Rightarrow$ $y=-(x-1) \Rightarrow x+y=1$

$\Rightarrow$ $y=-x+c$

$\Rightarrow$ Slope of this line $(m_2)=-1$

Since, $m_1m_2=-1$

Hence, line $x-y=0$ is perpendicular to the line $x-y=0$.

(v) *True*

Let $z=x+iy,\ z\neq 0$ and $\text{Re}(z)=0$

i.e., $x=0$

$\therefore$ $z=iy$

$\text{Im}(z^2)=i^2y^2=-y^2$ which is real.

Hence, $\text{Im}(z^2)=0$

(*) Topics related to these question have been removed from latest NCERT.

(vi) *True*

Given inequality is $|z-4|<|z-2|$

Let $z = x + iy$

$\therefore$ $|x-4+iy|<|x-2+iy|$

$\Rightarrow$ $\sqrt{(x-4)^2+y^2}<\sqrt{(x-2)^2+y^2}$

On squaring both sides, we get

$$\Rightarrow \quad (x-4)^2+y^2<(x-2)^2+y^2$$
$$\Rightarrow \quad x^2-8x+16+y^2<x^2-4x+4+y^2$$
$$\Rightarrow \quad -8x+16<-4x+4$$
$$\Rightarrow \quad -8x<-4x-12$$
$$\Rightarrow \quad -4x<-12$$
$$\Rightarrow \quad 4x>12$$
$$\Rightarrow \quad x>3$$

(vii) *False*

Let $z_1 = x_1 + iy_1$ and $z_2 = x_2 + iy_2$

Given, $|z_1+z_2|=|z_1|+|z_2|$

$$|x_1+iy_1+x_2+iy_2|=|x_1+iy_1|+|x_2+iy_2|$$
$$\Rightarrow \quad |(x_1+x_2)+i(y_1+y_2)|=|x_1+iy_1|+|x_2+iy_2|$$
$$\Rightarrow \quad \sqrt{(x_1+x_2)^2+(y_1+y_2)^2}=\sqrt{(x_1^2+y_1^2)}+\sqrt{(x_2^2+y_2^2)}$$

On squaring both sides, we get

$$(x_1+x_2)^2+(y_1+y_2)^2=(x_1^2+y_1^2)+(x_2^2+y_2^2)+2\sqrt{(x_1^2+y_1^2)(x_2^2+y_2^2)}$$
$$\Rightarrow x_1^2+x_2^2+2x_1x_2+y_1^2+y_2^2+2y_1y_2=x_1^2+y_1^2+x_2^2+y_2^2+2\sqrt{(x_1^2+y_1^2)(x_2^2+y_2^2)}$$
$$\Rightarrow \quad 2x_1x_2+2y_1y_2=2\sqrt{(x_1^2+y_1^2)(x_2^2+y_2^2)}$$
$$\Rightarrow \quad x_1x_2+y_1y_2=\sqrt{(x_1^2+y_1^2)(x_2^2+y_2^2)}$$

Again, squaring on both sides, we get

$$x_1^2x_2^2+y_1^2y_2^2+2x_1x_2y_1y_2=x_1^2x_2^2+y_1^2x_2^2+x_1^2y_2^2+y_1^2y_2^2$$
$$\Rightarrow \quad (x_1y_2-x_2y_1)^2=0$$
$$\Rightarrow \quad x_1y_2=x_2y_1$$
$$\Rightarrow \quad \frac{y_1}{x_1}=\frac{y_2}{x_2}$$
$$\Rightarrow \quad \tan^{-1}\left(\frac{y_1}{x_1}\right)=\tan^{-1}\left(\frac{y_2}{x_2}\right)$$
$$\Rightarrow \quad \arg(z_1)=\arg(z_2)$$

(viii) *False*

We know that any real number is also a complex number. As 2 can be written in the form of $2+0i$, which is a complex number, therefore 2 is a complex number.

Q.27 Match the statements of Column A and Column B.

Column A	Column B
*(i) The polar form of $i+\sqrt{3}$ is	(a) Perpendicular bisector of segment joining (–2, 0) and (2, 0).
*(ii) The amplitude of $-1+\sqrt{-3}$ is	(b) On or outside the circle having centre at (0, – 4) and radius 3.
(iii) It $\lvert z+2\rvert = \lvert z-2\rvert$, then locus of z is	(c) $\frac{2\pi}{3}$
(iv) It $\lvert z+2i\rvert = \lvert z-2i\rvert$, then locus of z is	(d) Perpendiculor bisector of segment joining (0, – 2) and (0, 2).
(v) Region represented by $\lvert z+4i\rvert \geq 3$ is	(e) $2\left(\cos\frac{\pi}{6}+i\sin\frac{\pi}{6}\right)$
(vi) Region represented by $\lvert z+4\rvert \leq 3$ is	(f) On or inside the circle having centre (– 4, 0) and radius 3 units.
(vii) Conjugate of $\frac{1+2i}{1-i}$ lies in	(g) First quadrant
(viii) Reciprocal of $1-i$ lies in	(h) Third quadrant

Ans. (i) Given, $z = i+\sqrt{3} = r(\cos\theta + i\sin\theta)$

On equating real and imaginary parts both sides, we get

$$r\cos\theta = \sqrt{3}, r\sin\theta = 1$$

$$\Rightarrow \quad r^2 = (r\cos\theta)^2 + (r\sin\theta)^2 = 1+3 = 4 \Rightarrow r = 2 \quad [\because r > 0]$$

$$\Rightarrow \quad \tan\alpha = \left|\frac{r\sin\theta}{r\cos\theta}\right| = \frac{1}{\sqrt{3}} \quad \left[\because \tan\alpha = \left|\frac{\text{Im}(z)}{\text{Re}(z)}\right|\right]$$

$$\Rightarrow \quad \tan\alpha = \frac{1}{\sqrt{3}} \Rightarrow \alpha = \frac{\pi}{6}$$

$\because \quad x > 0, \; y > 0$

$\therefore$ z lies in Ist quadrant.

Thus, $\arg(z) = \theta = \alpha = \frac{\pi}{6}$

So, the polar form of z is $2\left(\cos\frac{\pi}{6} + i\sin\frac{\pi}{6}\right)$.

(ii) Given, $z = -1+\sqrt{-3} = -1+i\sqrt{3}$

$$\therefore \quad \tan\alpha = \left|\frac{\sqrt{3}}{-1}\right| = \sqrt{3} \Rightarrow \tan\alpha = \tan\frac{\pi}{3} \Rightarrow \alpha = \frac{\pi}{3}$$

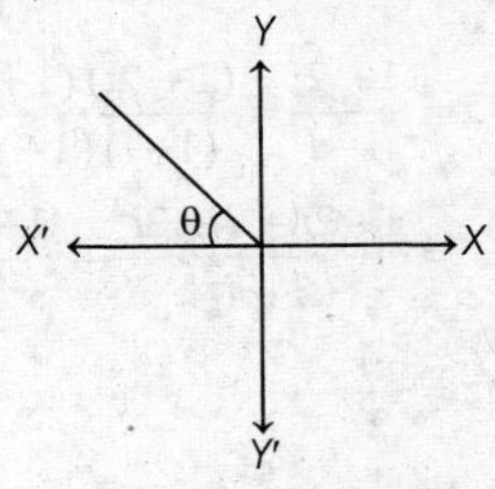

$\because \quad x < 0, \; y > 0$

$\therefore$ z lies in IInd quadrant.

(*) Topics related to these question have been removed from latest NCERT.

$\Rightarrow \quad \theta = \pi - \alpha = \pi - \frac{\pi}{3} = \frac{2\pi}{3}$

(iii) Given, $|z+2| = |z-2|$

Let $z = x + iy$

$\Rightarrow \quad |x+2+iy| = |x-2+iy|$

$\Rightarrow \quad (x+2)^2 + y^2 = (x-2)^2 + y^2$

$\Rightarrow \quad x^2 + 4x + 4 = x^2 - 4x + 4 \quad \Rightarrow \quad 8x = 0$

$\therefore \quad x = 0$

It is a straight line which is a perpendicular bisector of line segment joining the points $(-2, 0)$ and $(2, 0)$.

(iv) Given, $|z+2i| = |z-2i|$

Let $z = x + iy$

$\Rightarrow \quad |x + i(y+2)| = |x + i(y-2)|$

$\Rightarrow \quad x^2 + (y+2)^2 = x^2 + (y-2)^2$

$\Rightarrow \quad 8y = 0 \quad \Rightarrow \quad y = 0$

It is a straight line, which is a perpendicular bisector of line segment joining $(0, -2)$ and $(0, 2)$.

(v) Given, $|z+4i| \geq 3 \quad \Rightarrow \quad |x + iy + 4i| \geq 3$

Let $z = x + iy$

$\Rightarrow \quad |x + i(y+4)| \geq 3 \quad \Rightarrow \quad \sqrt{x^2 + (y+4)^2} \geq 3$

On squaring both sides, we get

$\Rightarrow \quad x^2 + (y+4)^2 \geq 9 \quad \Rightarrow \quad x^2 + y^2 + 8y + 16 \geq 9$

$x^2 + y^2 + 8y + 7 \geq 0$

Which represent a region which lies on or outside the circle having centre $(0, -4)$ and radius 3.

(vi) Given, $|z+4| \leq 3$

$\Rightarrow \quad |x + iy + 4| \leq 3$

$\Rightarrow \quad |x + 4 + iy| \leq 3$

$\Rightarrow \quad \sqrt{(x+4)^2 + y^2} \leq 3$

On squaring both sides, we get

$\Rightarrow \quad (x+4)^2 + y^2 \leq 9 \Rightarrow x^2 + 8x + 16 + y^2 \leq 9$

$\Rightarrow \quad x^2 + y^2 + 8x + 7 \leq 0$

It represent the region which lies on or inside the circle having the centre $(-4, 0)$ and radius 3.

(vii) Given, $z = \frac{1+2i}{1-i} = \frac{(1+2i)(1+i)}{(1-i)(1+i)}$

$= \frac{1+2i+i+2i^2}{1-i^2} = \frac{1-2+3i}{1+1} = \frac{-1+3i}{2}$

$\therefore \quad \bar{z} = \frac{-1}{2} - \frac{3i}{2}$

Since, $x < 0, \; y < 0$

So, $\left(\frac{-1}{2}, \frac{-3}{2}\right)$ lies in third quadrant.

(viii) Given, $z = 1-i$

$\therefore \quad \frac{1}{z} = \frac{1}{1-i} = \frac{1}{1-i} \times \frac{1+i}{1+i} = \frac{1+i}{1-i^2} = \frac{1}{2}(1+i)$

Since, $x < 0, y < 0, y < 0$.

So, $\left(\frac{1}{2}, \frac{1}{2}\right)$ lies in first quadrant.

Hence, the correct matches are (i) → (e), (ii) → (c), (iii) → (a), (iv) → (d), (v) → (b), (vi) → (f), (vii) → (h), (viii) → (g).

Q.28 What is the conjugate of $\frac{2-i}{(1-2i)^2}$?

Thinking process Firstly, rationalise the denominator. Then, use the concept, if $z = a + ib$. $\Rightarrow \bar{z} = a - ib$

Ans. Given,

$$z = \frac{2-i}{(1-2i)^2} = \frac{2-i}{1+4i^2-4i}$$

$$= \frac{2-i}{1-4-4i} = \frac{2-i}{-3-4i} \quad [\because i^2 = -1]$$

$$= \frac{(2-i)}{-(3+4i)} = -\left[\frac{(2-i)(3-4i)}{(3+4i)(3-4i)}\right]$$

$$= -\left(\frac{6-8i-3i+4i^2}{9+16}\right) = -\frac{(-11i+2)}{25} \quad [\because i^2 = -1]$$

$$= \frac{-1}{25}(2-11i) \Rightarrow z = \frac{1}{25}(-2+11i)$$

$$\therefore \quad \bar{z} = \frac{1}{25}(-2-11i) = \frac{-2}{25} - \frac{11}{25}i$$

Q.29 If $|z_1| = |z_2|$, is it necessary that $z_1 = z_2$?

Ans. Given, $|z_1| = |z_2|$

Let $z_1 = x_1 + iy_1$ and $z_2 = x_2 + iy_2$

$\Rightarrow \quad |x_1 + iy_1| = |x_2 + iy_2|$

$\sqrt{x_1^2 + y_1^2} = \sqrt{x_2^2 + y_2^2}$

On squaring both sides, we get

$\Rightarrow \quad x_1^2 + y_1^2 = x_2^2 + y_2^2$

On comparing both sides, we get

$$x_1^2 = x_2^2,\ y_1^2 = y_2^2 \Rightarrow x_1 = \pm x_2,\ y_1 = \pm y_2$$

$$\therefore \quad z_1 = x_1 + iy_1 \text{ or } z_1 = \pm x_2 \pm iy_2$$

Hence, it is not neccessary that $z_1 = z_2$.

Q.30 If $\frac{(a^2+1)^2}{2a-i} = x + iy$, then what is the value of $x^2 + y^2$?

Ans. Given, $\frac{(a^2+1)^2}{2a-i} = x + iy$

$$\Rightarrow \quad \frac{(a^2+1)^2(2a+i)}{(2a-i)(2a+i)} = x + iy$$

$$\Rightarrow \quad \frac{(a^2+1)^2(2a+i)}{4a^2+1} = x + iy \qquad [\because i^2 = -1]$$

$$\Rightarrow \quad \frac{2a(a^2+1)^2}{4a^2+1} + \frac{i(a^2+1)^2}{4a^2+1} = x + iy$$

On equating real and imaginary parts both sides, we get

$$x = \frac{2a(a^2+1)^2}{4a^2+1} \quad \text{and} \quad y = \frac{(a^2+1)^2}{4a^2+1}$$

$$\therefore \quad x^2 + y^2 = 4a^2\left[\frac{(a^2+1)^2}{4a^2+1}\right]^2 + \left[\frac{(a^2+1)^2}{4a^2+1}\right]^2$$

$$= \frac{(4a^2+1)(a^2+1)^4}{(4a^2+1)^2} = \frac{(a^2+1)^4}{(4a^2+1)}$$

***Q.31** Find the value of z, if $|z| = 4$ and $\arg(z) = \frac{5\pi}{6}$.

Ans. Let $\qquad z = r(\cos\theta + i\sin\theta)$

Also, $\qquad |z| = r = 4$ and $\theta = \frac{5\pi}{6} \qquad [\because \arg(z) = \theta]$

$$\therefore \quad z = 4\left[\cos\frac{5\pi}{6} + i\sin\frac{5\pi}{6}\right] \qquad [\because z = r(\cos\theta + i\sin\theta)]$$

$$= 4\left[\cos\left(\pi - \frac{\pi}{6}\right) + i\sin\left(\pi - \frac{\pi}{6}\right)\right]$$

$$[\because \cos(\pi - \theta) = -\cos\theta \text{ and } \sin(\pi - \theta) = \sin\theta]$$

$$= 4\left[-\cos\frac{\pi}{6} + i\sin\frac{\pi}{6}\right] = 4\left[-\frac{\sqrt{3}}{2} + i\frac{1}{2}\right] = -2\sqrt{3} + 2i$$

Q.32 Find the value of $\left|(1+i)\frac{(2+i)}{(3+i)}\right|$.

Thinking Process First, convert the given expression in the form of $a + ib$, then use $|a+ib| = \sqrt{a^2+b^2}$.

Ans. Given,

$$\left|(1+i)\frac{(2+i)}{(3+i)}\right| = \left|\frac{(2+i+2i+i^2)}{(3+i)}\right| = \left|\frac{2+3i-1}{3+i}\right| \qquad [\because i^2 = -1]$$

$$= \left|\frac{1+3i}{3+i}\right| = \left|\frac{(1+3i)(3-i)}{(3+i)(3-i)}\right|$$

$$= \left|\frac{3+9i-i-3i^2}{9-i^2}\right| = \left|\frac{3+8i+3}{9+1}\right| = \left|\frac{6+8i}{10}\right|$$

$$= \sqrt{\frac{6^2}{100} + \frac{8^2}{100}} = \sqrt{\frac{36+64}{100}} = \sqrt{\frac{100}{100}} = 1$$

(*) Topics related to these question have been removed from latest NCERT.

***Q.33** Find the principal argument of $(1+i\sqrt{3})^2$.

Thinking Process Let $z = a + ib$, then the polar form of z is $r(\cos\theta + i\sin\theta)$, where $r = |z| = \sqrt{a^2 + b^2}$ and $\tan\theta = \frac{b}{a}$. Here, θ is argument or amplitude of z *i.e.*, *arg* $(z) = \theta$.

The principal argument is is the angle (θ) from the positive real axis to $z(x, y)$ in the rage $-\pi < \theta \le \pi$.

Ans. Given, $z = (1+i\sqrt{3})^2$

$\Rightarrow z = 1 - 3 + 2i\sqrt{3}$

$\Rightarrow z = -2 + i2\sqrt{3}$

$\Rightarrow \tan\alpha = \left|\frac{2\sqrt{3}}{-2}\right| = |-\sqrt{3}| = \sqrt{3}$ $\left[\because \tan\alpha = \left|\frac{\text{Im}(z)}{\text{Re}(z)}\right|\right]$

$\Rightarrow \tan\alpha = \tan\frac{\pi}{3} \Rightarrow \alpha = \frac{\pi}{3}$

$\because$ $\text{Re}(z) < 0$ and $\text{Im}(z) > 0$

$\therefore$ z lies in IInd quadrant.

$\Rightarrow \arg(z) = \pi - \frac{\pi}{3} \Rightarrow = \frac{2\pi}{3}$

Q.34 Where does z lie, if $\left|\frac{z-5i}{z+5i}\right| = 1$?

Thinking Process If $z_1 = x_1 + iy_1$ and $z_2 = x_2 + iy_2$, then $|z_1| = \sqrt{x_1^2 + y_1^2}$ and $|z_2| = \sqrt{x_2^2 + y_2^2}$.

Also, use the modulus property *i.e.*, $\left|\frac{z_1}{z_2}\right| = \frac{|z_1|}{|z_2|}$.

Ans. Given, $\left|\frac{z-5i}{z+5i}\right| = \left|\frac{x+iy-5i}{x+iy+5i}\right|$

$\Rightarrow \left|\frac{z-5i}{z+5i}\right| = \frac{|x+i(y-5)|}{|x+i(y+5)|}$

$\Rightarrow 1 = \frac{\sqrt{x^2+(y-5)^2}}{\sqrt{x^2+(y+5)^2}}$ $\left[\because \left|\frac{z-5i}{z+5i}\right| = 1\right]$

$\Rightarrow \sqrt{x^2+(y+5)^2} = \sqrt{x^2+(y-5)^2}$

On squaring both sides, we get

$x^2 + (y+5)^2 = x^2 + (y-5)^2$

$\Rightarrow 10y = -10y$

$\Rightarrow 20y = 0$

$\therefore y = 0$

So, z lies on real axis.

(*) Topics related to these question have been removed from latest NCERT.

Choose the correct answers from the given four options in each exercise 35 to 50.

***Q.35** $\sin x + i\cos 2x$ and $\cos x - i\sin 2x$ are conjugate to each other for

(a) $x = n\pi$ (b) $x = \left(n+\frac{1}{2}\right)\frac{\pi}{2}$ (c) $x = 0$ (d) No value of x

Ans.(d) Let $z = \sin x + i\cos 2x$

$\Rightarrow \bar{z} = \sin x - i\cos 2x$ ...(i)

We have, $\bar{z} = \cos x - i\sin 2x$ ...(ii)

From eq (i) and eq (ii), we get

$\therefore \sin x - i\cos 2x = \cos x - i\sin 2x$

On equating real and imaginary parts from both sides, we get

$\Rightarrow \sin x = \cos x$ and $\cos 2x = \sin 2x$

$\Rightarrow \tan x = 1$ and $\tan 2x = 1$

$\Rightarrow \tan x = \tan\frac{\pi}{4}$ and $\tan 2x = \tan\frac{\pi}{4}$

$\Rightarrow x = n\pi + \frac{\pi}{4}$ and $2x = n\pi + \frac{\pi}{4}$

So, $2x = x \Rightarrow 2x - x = 0 \Rightarrow x = 0$ [$\because$ if $\tan\theta = \tan\alpha \Rightarrow \theta = n\pi + \alpha$]

But for $x = 0$, Eqs. (i) and (ii) are not equal

$\therefore$ There exist no value of x

Q.36 The real value of α for which the expression $\frac{1 - i\sin\alpha}{1 + 2i\sin\alpha}$ is purely real is

(a) $(n+1)\frac{\pi}{2}$ (b) $(2n+1)\frac{\pi}{2}$ (c) $n\pi$ (d) None of these

where, $n \in N$

Thinking Process First, convert the given expression into $a + ib$ form and then check whether the complex number $a + ib$ is purely real.

Ans. ***(c)*** Let $z = \frac{1 - i\sin\alpha}{1 + 2i\sin\alpha}$

$$= \frac{(1 - i\sin\alpha)(1 - 2i\sin\alpha)}{(1 + 2i\sin\alpha)(1 - 2i\sin\alpha)} = \frac{1 - i\sin\alpha - 2i\sin\alpha + 2i^2\sin^2\alpha}{1 - 4i^2\sin^2\alpha}$$

[rationalise the denominator]

$$= \frac{1 - 3i\sin\alpha - 2\sin^2\alpha}{1 + 4\sin^2\alpha} = \frac{1 - 2\sin^2\alpha}{1 + 4\sin^2\alpha} - \frac{3i\sin\alpha}{1 + 4\sin^2\alpha}$$

Since, It is given that z is a purely real.

$$\therefore \frac{-3\sin\alpha}{1 + 4\sin^2\alpha} = 0$$

$\Rightarrow -3\sin\alpha = 0 \Rightarrow \sin\alpha = 0$

$\therefore \alpha = n\pi$ [$\because$ if $\sin\theta = \sin\alpha \Rightarrow \theta = n\pi + (-1)^n\alpha$]

(*) Topics related to these question have been removed from latest NCERT.

Q.37 If $z = x + iy$ lies in the third quadrant, then $\frac{\bar{z}}{z}$ also lies in the third quadrant, if

(a) $x > y > 0$ (b) $x < y < 0$ (c) $y < x < 0$ (d) $y > x > 0$

Ans. *(b)* Given, $z = x + iy$ lies in third quadrant. So, $x < 0$ and $y < 0$.

Now, take $\quad \frac{\bar{z}}{z} = \frac{x - iy}{x + iy} = \frac{(x - iy)(x - iy)}{(x + iy)(x - iy)} = \frac{x^2 - y^2 - 2ixy}{x^2 + y^2}$ $\quad [\because i^2 = -1]$

$$\frac{\bar{z}}{z} = \frac{x^2 - y^2}{x^2 + y^2} - \frac{2ixy}{x^2 + y^2}$$

Since, $\frac{\bar{z}}{z}$ also lies in third quadrant.

So, its real and imaginary parts will be less than zero.

$\therefore \quad \frac{x^2 - y^2}{x^2 + y^2} < 0$ and $\frac{-2xy}{x^2 + y^2} < 0$

$\Rightarrow \quad x^2 - y^2 < 0$ and $-2xy < 0$ $\quad [\because x^2 + y^2 > 0]$

$\Rightarrow \quad x^2 < y^2$ and $xy > 0$

So, $\quad x < y < 0$

Mistake Alert! *Do not forget to use correct sign of values for the third quadrant i.e.,* $\text{Re}(z) < 0$ *and* $\text{Im}(z) < 0$.

Q.38 The value of $(z + 3)(\bar{z} + 3)$ is equivalent to

(a) $|z + 3|^2$ (b) $|z - 3|$ (c) $z^2 + 3$ (d) None of these

Ans. *(a)* Given, $(z + 3)(\bar{z} + 3)$

Let $\quad z = x + iy$

$\Rightarrow \quad (z + 3)(\bar{z} + 3) = (x + iy + 3)(x + -iy + 3) = (x + 3 + iy)(x + 3 - iy)$

$= (x + 3)^2 - (iy)^2 = (x + 3)^2 + y^2$

$= |x + 3 + iy|^2 = |z + 3|^2 \quad [\because |a + ib| = \sqrt{a^2 + b^2}]$

Q.39 If $\left(\frac{1 + i}{1 - i}\right)^x = 1$, then

(a) $x = 2n + 1$ (b) $x = 4n$ (c) $x = 2n$ (d) $x = 4n + 1$

where, $n \in N$

Ans. *(b)* Given, $\quad \left(\frac{1 + i}{1 - i}\right)^x = 1$

$\Rightarrow \quad \left[\frac{(1 + i)(1 + i)}{(1 - i)(1 + i)}\right]^x = 1 \Rightarrow \left[\frac{1 + 2i + i^2}{1 - i^2}\right]^x = 1$

$\Rightarrow \quad \left[\frac{2i}{1 + 1}\right]^x = 1 \Rightarrow \left[\frac{2i}{2}\right]^x = 1 \quad [\because i^2 = -1]$

$\Rightarrow \quad i^x = 1 \Rightarrow i^x = (i^{4n}) \quad [\because i^{4n} = 1, n \in N]$

$\Rightarrow \quad x = 4n$, where $n \in N$

Q.40 A real value of x satisfies the equation $\left(\dfrac{3-4ix}{3+4ix}\right)=\alpha-i\beta\,(\alpha,\beta\in R)$, if $\alpha^2+\beta^2$ is equal to

(a) 1 (b) −1 (c) 2 (d) − 2

- **Concept Insight** The product of a complex number and its conjugate is a square of its modulus *i.e.*, $z\bar{z}=|z|^2$

Ans. *(a)* Given equation is $\left(\dfrac{3-4ix}{3+4ix}\right)=\alpha-i\beta,\,(\alpha,\beta\in R)$

$$\Rightarrow\quad (\alpha-i\beta)=\frac{(3-4ix)(3-4ix)}{(3+4ix)(3-4ix)}=\frac{9+16i^2x^2-24ix}{9-16i^2x^2}$$

$$\Rightarrow\quad \alpha-i\beta=\frac{9-16x^2-24ix}{9+16x^2}\qquad [\because i^2=-1]$$

$$\Rightarrow\quad \alpha-i\beta=\frac{9-16x^2}{9+16x^2}-\frac{i24x}{9+16x^2}\qquad ...(i)$$

On taking conjugate both sides, we et

$$\therefore\quad \alpha+i\beta=\frac{9-16x^2}{9+16x^2}+\frac{i24x}{9+16x^2}\qquad [\because \overline{a+ib}=a-ib]\ ...(ii)$$

So,
$$(\alpha-i\beta)(\alpha+i\beta)=\left(\frac{9-16x^2}{9+16x^2}\right)^2-\left(\frac{i24x}{9+16x^2}\right)^2$$

$$\therefore\quad \alpha^2+\beta^2=\frac{81+256x^4-288x^2+576x^2}{(9+16x^2)^2}\qquad [\because i^2=-1]$$

$$=\frac{81+256x^4+288x^2}{(9+16x^2)^2}=\frac{(9+16x^2)^2}{(9+16x^2)^2}=1$$

***Q.41** Which of the following is correct for any two complex numbers z_1 and z_2?

(a) $|z_1z_2|=|z_1||z_2|$ (b) $\arg(z_1z_2)=\arg(z_1)\cdot\arg(z_2)$

(c) $|z_1+z_2|=|z_1|+|z_2|$ (d) $|z_1+z_2|\ge|z_1|-|z_2|$

Ans. *(a)* Let $z_1=r_1(\cos\theta_1+i\sin\theta_1)$

$$\Rightarrow\quad |z_1|=r_1\qquad ...(i)$$

And $z_2=r_2(\cos\theta_2+i\sin\theta_2)$

$$\Rightarrow\quad |z_2|=r_2\qquad ...(ii)$$

Now,
$$z_1z_2=r_1r_2[\cos\theta_1\cos\theta_2+i\sin\theta_1\cos\theta_2+i\cos\theta_1\sin\theta_2+i^2\sin\theta_1\sin\theta_2]$$
$$=r_1r_2[\cos\theta_1\cos\theta_2-\sin\theta_1\sin\theta_2)+i(\sin\theta_1\cos\theta_2+\cos\theta_1\sin\theta_2]$$
$$=r_1r_2[\cos(\theta_1+\theta_2)+i\sin(\theta_1+\theta_2)]$$

$$\Rightarrow\quad |z_1z_2|=r_1r_2$$

$$\therefore\quad |z_1z_2|=|z_1||z_2|\qquad [\text{from Eqs. (i) and (ii)}]$$

(*) Topics related to these question have been removed from latest NCERT.

***Q.42** The point represented by the complex number $(2-i)$ is rotated about origin through an angle $\frac{\pi}{2}$ in the clockwise direction, the new position of point is

(a) $1+2i$ (b) $-1-2i$ (c) $2+i$ (d) $-1+2i$

- **Concept Insight** When a point represented by a complex number z is rotated about the origin by angle θ in the clockwise direction, the new position of the point is given by $z' = ze^{-i\theta}$

Ans. ***(b)*** Given, $z = 2-i$

It is rotated about origin through an angle $\frac{\pi}{2}$ in the clockwise direction

$\therefore$ New position $= ze^{\frac{-i\pi}{2}} = (2-i)\,e^{\frac{-i\pi}{2}}$

$$= (2-i)\left[\cos\left(\frac{-\pi}{2}\right) + i\sin\left(\frac{-\pi}{2}\right)\right] = (2-i)\,[0-i]$$

$$= -2i - 1 = -1 - 2i$$

Q.43 If $x, y \in R$, then $x + iy$ is a non-real complex number, if

(a) $x = 0$ (b) $y = 0$ (c) $x \neq 0$ (d) $y \neq 0$

Ans. ***(d)*** Given that, $x, y \in R$

Then, $x + iy$ is non-real complex number if and only if $y \neq 0$.

Q.44 If $a + ib = c + id$, then

(a) $a^2 + c^2 = 0$ (b) $b^2 + c^2 = 0$

(c) $b^2 + d^2 = 0$ (d) $a^2 + b^2 = c^2 + d^2$

- **Thinking Process** If two complex numbers $z_1 = x_1 + iy_1$ and $z_2 = x_2 + iy_2$ are equal, then $|z_1| = |z_2| \Rightarrow \sqrt{x_1^2 + y_1^2} = \sqrt{x_2^2 + y_2^2}$

Ans. ***(d)*** Given, $a + ib = c + id$

$\Rightarrow$ $|a + ib| = |c + id| \Rightarrow \sqrt{a^2 + b^2} = \sqrt{c^2 + d^2}$

On squaring both sides, we get

$$a^2 + b^2 = c^2 + d^2$$

Q.45 The complex number z which satisfies the condition $\left|\frac{i+z}{i-z}\right| = 1$ lies on

(a) circle $x^2 + y^2 = 1$ (b) the X-axis (c) the Y-axis (d) the line $x + y = 1$

Ans. ***(b)*** Given, $\left|\frac{i+z}{i-z}\right| = 1$

Let $z = x + iy$

$$\therefore \quad \left|\frac{x + i(y+1)}{-x - i(y-1)}\right| = 1 \Rightarrow \frac{x^2 + (y+1)^2}{x^2 + (y-1)^2} = 1$$

(*) Topics related to these question have been removed from latest NCERT.

$\Rightarrow \quad x^2 + (y+1)^2 = x^2 + (y-1)^2$

$\Rightarrow \quad 4y = 0 \Rightarrow y = 0$

So, z lies on X-axis (real axis).

Q.46 If z is a complex number, then

(a) $|z^2| > |z|^2$ (b) $|z^2| = |z|^2$
(c) $|z^2| < |z|^2$ (d) $|z^2| \geq |z|^2$

Ans. ***(b)*** If z is a complex number, then $z = x + iy$

$$|z| = |x + iy| = \sqrt{x^2 + y^2}$$

$$\Rightarrow \quad |z|^2 = x^2 + y^2 \quad \text{...(i)}$$

and $$z^2 = (x+iy)^2 = x^2 + i^2y^2 + i2xy$$

$$z^2 = x^2 - y^2 + i2xy \quad [\because i^2 = -1]$$

$$\Rightarrow \quad |z^2| = \sqrt{(x^2 - y^2)^2 + (2xy)^2}$$

$$\Rightarrow \quad |z^2| = \sqrt{x^4 + y^4 - 2x^2y^2 + 4x^2y^2}$$

$$\Rightarrow \quad |z^2| = \sqrt{x^4 + y^4 + 2x^2y^2} = \sqrt{(x^2 + y^2)^2}$$

$$\Rightarrow \quad |z^2| = x^2 + y^2 \quad \text{...(ii)}$$

From Eqs. (i) and (ii), we get $|z|^2 = |z^2|$

***Q.47** $|z_1 + z_2| = |z_1| + |z_2|$ is possible, if

(a) $z_2 = \bar{z}_1$ (b) $z_2 = \dfrac{1}{z_1}$ (c) $\arg(z_1) = \arg(z_2)$ (d) $|z_1| = |z_2|$

Ans. ***(c)***

Given, $$|z_1 + z_2| = |z_1| + |z_2|$$

Let $z_1 = r_1(\cos\theta_1 + i\sin\theta_1)$ and $z_2 = r_2(\cos\theta_2 + i\sin\theta_2)$

$$\Rightarrow \quad |r_1(\cos\theta_1 + i\sin\theta_1) + r_2(\cos\theta_2 + i\sin\theta_2)| = |r_1(\cos\theta_1 + i\sin\theta_1)| + |r_2(\cos\theta_2 + i\sin\theta_2)|$$

$$\Rightarrow \quad |(r_1\cos\theta_1 + r_2\cos\theta) + i(r_1\sin\theta_1 + r_2\sin\theta_2)| = r_1 + r_2$$

$$\Rightarrow \quad \sqrt{\begin{aligned}&r_1^2\cos^2\theta_1 + r_2^2\cos^2\theta_2 + 2r_1r_2\cos\theta_1\cos\theta_2\\ &+ r_1^2\sin^2\theta_1 + r_2^2\sin^2\theta_2 + 2r_1r_2\sin\theta_1\sin\theta_2\end{aligned}} = r_1 + r_2$$

$$\Rightarrow \quad \sqrt{r_1^2 + r_2^2 + 2r_1r_2[\cos(\theta_1 - \theta_2)]} = r_1 + r_2$$

On squaring both sides, we get

$$r_1^2 + r_2^2 + 2r_1r_2\cos(\theta_1 - \theta_2) = r_1^2 + r_2^2 + 2r_1r_2$$

$$\Rightarrow \quad 2r_1r_2[1 - \cos(\theta_1 - \theta_2)] = 0$$

$$\Rightarrow \quad 1 - \cos(\theta_1 - \theta_2) = 0$$

$$\Rightarrow \quad \cos(\theta_1 - \theta_2) = 1$$

$$\Rightarrow \quad \cos(\theta_1 - \theta_2) = \cos 0°$$

$$\Rightarrow \quad \theta_1 - \theta_2 = 0° \Rightarrow \theta_1 = \theta_2$$

$$\therefore \quad \arg(z_1) = \arg(z_2)$$

(*****) Topics related to these question have been removed from latest NCERT.

***Q.48** The real value of θ for which the expression $\dfrac{1+i\cos\theta}{1-2i\cos\theta}$ is a real number is

(a) $n\pi+\dfrac{\pi}{4}$ (b) $n\pi+(-1)^n\dfrac{\pi}{4}$ (c) $2n\pi\pm\dfrac{\pi}{2}$ (d) None of these

Ans. *(c)* Let $z=\dfrac{1+i\cos\theta}{1-2i\cos\theta}=\dfrac{(1+i\cos\theta)(1+2i\cos\theta)}{(1-2i\cos\theta)(1+2i\cos\theta)}$

$$=\frac{1+i\cos\theta+2i\cos\theta+2i^2\cos^2\theta}{1-4i^2\cos^2\theta}=\frac{1+3i\cos\theta-2\cos^2\theta}{1+4\cos^2\theta} \quad [\because i^2=1]$$

For real value of θ, $\dfrac{3\cos\theta}{1+4\cos^2\theta}=0$ [Since, z is a real number (given)]

$\Rightarrow\quad 3\cos\theta=0\ \Rightarrow\quad \cos\theta=\cos\dfrac{\pi}{2}\quad\Rightarrow\quad\theta=2n\pi\pm\dfrac{\pi}{2}$

***Q.49** The value of arg (x), when $x<0$ is

(a) 0 (b) $\dfrac{\pi}{2}$ (c) π (d) None of these

Ans. *(c)* Let $z=x+0i$ and $x<0$

$$|z|=\sqrt{(-1)^2+(0^2)}=1$$

Since, the point $(x, 0)$ represents $z=x+0i$ lies on the negative side of real axis.

$\therefore$ Principal arg $(z)=\pi$

Q.50 If $f(z)=\dfrac{7-z}{1-z^2}$, where $z=1+2i$, then $|f(z)|$ is

(a) $\dfrac{|z|}{2}$ (b) $|z|$ (c) $2|z|$ (d) None of these

Ans. *(a)* Let $z=1+2i$

$\Rightarrow\quad |z|=\sqrt{1+4}=\sqrt{5}$

Now, $f(z)=\dfrac{7-z}{1-z^2}=\dfrac{7-1-2i}{1-(1+2i)^2}$ [put $z=1+2i$]

$$=\frac{6-2i}{1-1-4i^2-4i}=\frac{6-2i}{4-4i} \quad [\because i^2=-1]$$

$$=\frac{2(3-i)}{2(2-2i)}=\frac{3-i}{2-2i}=\frac{(3-i)(2+2i)}{(2-2i)(2+2i)}$$

$$=\frac{6-2i+6i-2i^2}{4-4i^2}=\frac{6+4i+2}{4+4}=\frac{8+4i}{8}=1+\frac{1}{2}i$$

$$f(z)=1+\frac{1}{2}i$$

$\therefore\quad |f(z)|=\sqrt{1+\dfrac{1}{4}}=\sqrt{\dfrac{4+1}{4}}=\dfrac{\sqrt{5}}{2}=\dfrac{|z|}{2}$ $[\because |z|=\sqrt{5}]$

(✱) Topics related to these question have been removed from latest NCERT.

Chapter

06

Linear Inequalities

Short Answer Type Questions

Solve for x, the inequalities in given exercises 1 to 12.

Q.1 $\frac{4}{x+1} \le 3 \le \frac{6}{x+1}, (x > 0)$

Thinking Process First, solve the first two inequalities, then solve the last two inequalities to get range of x.

Ans. Consider first two inequalities,

$$\frac{4}{x+1} \le 3$$

$\Rightarrow$ $4 \le 3(x+1)$

$\Rightarrow$ $4 \le 3x + 3$

$\Rightarrow$ $1 \le 3x$ [subtracting 3 from both sides]

$\therefore$ $x \ge \frac{1}{3}$ [dividing by 3] ...(i)

Now, consider last two inequalities,

$$3 \le \frac{6}{x+1}$$

$\Rightarrow$ $3(x+1) \le 6$

$\Rightarrow$ $3x + 3 \le 6$

$\Rightarrow$ $3x \le 3$ [subtracting 3 from both sides]

$\therefore$ $x \le 1$ [dividing by 3] ...(ii)

From Eqs. (i) and (ii), we get

$$\frac{1}{3} \le x \le 1$$

i.e., $x \in \left[\frac{1}{3}, 1\right]$

Q.2 $\frac{|x-2|-1}{|x-2|-2} \le 0$

Thinking Process First, let $y = |x-2|$ and then obtained the values of y using the property $|x-a| \ge k \Leftrightarrow x \le a-k$ or $x \ge a+k$ to get the range of x.

Ans. Let $|x-2| = y$

$\therefore \quad \dfrac{y-1}{y-2} \le 0$

$\Rightarrow \quad y-1 \le 0$ and $y-2>0$ or $y-1 \ge 0$ and $y-2<0$

$\Rightarrow \quad y \le 1$ and $y > 2$ or $y \ge 1$ and $y < 2$

$\therefore \quad 1 \le y < 2$

$\Rightarrow \quad 1 \le |x-2| < 2$

$\Rightarrow \quad 1 \le |x-2|$ and $|x-2| < 2$

$\Rightarrow$ either $x-2 \le -1$ or $x-2 \ge 1$

and $\quad -2 < x-2 < 2$

$\Rightarrow \quad x \le 1$ or $x \ge 3$ and $0 < x < 4$

$\Rightarrow \quad x \in (0, 1] \cup [3, 4)$

Q.3 $\dfrac{1}{|x|-3} \le \dfrac{1}{2}$

Ans. Given, $\dfrac{1}{|x|-3} \le \dfrac{1}{2}$

$\Rightarrow$ Either $|x| - 3 \ge 2$ $\quad \left[\because \dfrac{1}{a} < \dfrac{1}{b} \Rightarrow a > b\right]$

$\Rightarrow \quad |x| \ge 5$ [adding 3 to both sides]

$\Rightarrow \quad x \le -5$ or $x \ge 5$ $\quad [\because |x| \ge a \Rightarrow x \le -a\ x \ge a]$

$\Rightarrow \quad x \in (-\infty, -5] \cup [5, \infty)$ ...(i)

or $\quad |x| - 3 < 0$

$\Rightarrow \quad |x| < 3$

$\Rightarrow \quad -3 < x < 3$ $\quad [\because |x| < a \Rightarrow -a < x < a]$ ...(ii)

On combining results of Eqs. (i) and (ii), we get

$$x \in (-\infty, -5] \cup (-3, 3) \cup [5, \infty)$$

Mistake Alert ! *Do not forget to consider all possible solutions, particularly when the inequality is compound (e.g., 'and', 'or' conditions).*

Q.4 $|x-1| \le 5, |x| \ge 2$

Ans. We have, $|x-1| \le 5$

$-5 \le x - 1 \le 5$

$\Rightarrow \quad -4 \le x \le 6$ [adding 1 on each terms]

$\Rightarrow \quad x \in [-4, 6]$ ...(i)

–4 6

and $\quad |x| \ge 2$

$\Rightarrow \quad x \le -2$ or $x \ge 2$

$\Rightarrow \quad x \in (-\infty, -2] \cup [2, \infty)$ ...(ii)

–∞ –2 2 +∞

On combining Eqs. (i) and (ii), we get

$$x \in [-4, -2] \cup [2, 6]$$

Mistake Alert! *Do not misinterpret the solutions on a number line, such as using closed circle brakets for strict inequalities.*

Q.5 $-5 \le \dfrac{2-3x}{4} \le 9$

Ans. We have,
$$-5 \le \frac{2-3x}{4}$$
$\Rightarrow$ $-20 \le 2 - 3x$ [multiplying by 4 on both sides]
$\Rightarrow$ $3x \le 2 + 20$
$\Rightarrow$ $3x \le 22$
$\Rightarrow$ $x \le \dfrac{22}{3}$

and
$$\frac{2-3x}{4} \le 9$$
$\Rightarrow$ $2 - 3x \le 36$
$\Rightarrow$ $-3x \le 34$ [subtracting 2 from both side]
$\Rightarrow$ $3x \ge -34$ [$\because$ multiplying both side by -1]
$\Rightarrow$ $x \ge -\dfrac{34}{3}$ [dividing by 3 on both sides]
$\Rightarrow$ $-\dfrac{34}{3} \le x \le \dfrac{22}{3}$
$\Rightarrow$ $x \in \left[\dfrac{-34}{3}, \dfrac{22}{3}\right]$

Mistake Alert! *Do not forget to reverse the sign of the inequality, while multiplying both side by a negative number.*

Q.6 $4x + 3 \ge 2x + 17,\ 3x - 5 < -2$

Thinking process First, solve the first two inequalities and then solve the last two inequalities to obtain the range of x and then combine the range of x.

Ans. We have,
$$4x + 3 \ge 2x + 17$$
$\Rightarrow$ $4x - 2x \ge 17 - 3 \Rightarrow 2x \ge 14$
$\Rightarrow$ $x \ge \dfrac{14}{2}$ [dividing by 2 on both sides]
$\Rightarrow$ $x \ge 7$ ...(i)

Also, we have
$$3x - 5 < -2$$
$\Rightarrow$ $3x < -2 + 5 \Rightarrow 3x < 3$
$\Rightarrow$ $x < 1$ [dividing by 3 on both sides] ...(ii)

On combining results of Eqs. (i) and (ii), we see that solution is not possible because nothing is common between these two solutions. (*i.e.*, $x < 1$, $x \ge 7$).

Q.7 A company manufactures cassettes. Its cost and revenue functions are $C(x) = 26000 + 30x$ and $R(x) = 43x$, respectively, where x is the number of cassettes produced and sold in a week. How many cassettes must be sold by the company to realise some profit?

Ans. Given, Cost function, $C(x) = 26000 + 30x$

and revenue function, $R(x) = 43x$

For profit, $R(x) > C(x)$

$\Rightarrow \quad 43x > 26000 + 30x$

$\Rightarrow \quad 43x - 30x < 26000$

$\Rightarrow \quad 13x > 26000$

$\Rightarrow \quad x > \dfrac{26000}{13}$ [dividing by 13 on both sides]

$x > 2000$

Hence, more than 2000 cassettes must be produced to get profit.

Q.8 The water acidity in a pool is considered normal when the average pH reading of three daily measurements is between 8.2 and 8.5. If the first two pH readings are 8.48 and 8.35, then find the range of pH value for the third reading that will result in the acidity level being normal.

● **Concept Insight** Average $= \dfrac{\text{Sum of all observations}}{\text{Total number of observations}}$

Ans. Given, first pH value = 8.48

and second pH value = 8.35

Let third pH value be x.

Since, it is given that average pH value lies between 8.2 and 8.5.

$\therefore \quad 8.2 < \dfrac{8.48 + 8.35 + x}{3} < 8.5 \Rightarrow 8.2 < \dfrac{16.83 + x}{3} < 8.5$

$\Rightarrow \quad 3 \times 8.2 < 16.83 + x < 8.5 \times 3$

$\Rightarrow \quad 24.6 < 16.83 + x < 25.5$

$\Rightarrow \quad 24.6 - 16.83 < x < 25.5 - 16.83$ [substracting 16.83 from each terms]

$\Rightarrow \quad 7.77 < x < 8.67$

Thus, third pH value lies between 7.77 and 8.67.

Q.9 A solution of 9% acid is to be diluted by adding 3% acid solution to it. The resulting mixture is to be more than 5% but less than 7% acid. If there is 460 litres of the 9% solution, how many litres of 3% solution will have to be added?

Ans. Let x L of 3% solution be added to 460 L of 9% solution of acid.

Then, total quantity of mixture = $(460 + x)$ L

Total acid content in the $(460 + x)$ L of mixture

$$= \left(460 \times \frac{9}{100} + x \times \frac{3}{100}\right)$$

It is given that acid content in the resulting mixture must be more than 5% but less than 7% acid.

Therefore, $5\% \text{ of } (460 + x) < 460 \times \frac{9}{100} + \frac{3x}{100} < 7\% \text{ of } (460 + x)$

$\Rightarrow \quad \frac{5}{100} \times (460 + x) < 460 \times \frac{9}{100} + \frac{3}{100}x < \frac{7}{100} \times (460 + x)$

$\Rightarrow \quad 5 \times (460 + x) < 460 \times 9 + 3x < 7 \times (460 + x)$

[multiplying each term by 100]

$\Rightarrow \quad 2300 + 5x < 4140 + 3x < 3220 + 7x$

Take first two inequalities, $2300 + 5x < 4140 + 3x$

$\Rightarrow \quad 5x - 3x < 4140 - 2300$

$\Rightarrow \quad 2x < 1840$

$\Rightarrow \quad x < \frac{1840}{2}$ [dividing by 2 on both sides]

$\Rightarrow \quad x < 920$ ...(i)

Take last two inequalities, $4140 + 3x < 3220 + 7x$

$\Rightarrow \quad 3x - 7x < 3220 - 4140$

$\Rightarrow \quad -4x < -920$

$\Rightarrow \quad 4x > 920$

[multiply by −1 so inequality get reversed]

$\Rightarrow \quad x > \frac{920}{4}$

$\Rightarrow \quad x > 230$ ...(ii)

Hence, the number of litres of the 3% solution of acid must be more than 230 L and less than 920 L.

Mistake Alert ! *Do not forget to reverse the sign of the inequality, while multiplying or dividing by a negative number.*

Q.10 A solution is to be kept between 40°C and 45°C. What is the range of temperature in degree fahrenheit, if the conversion formula is $F = \frac{9}{5}C + 32$?

Ans. Let the required temperature be x°F.

Given that, $F = \frac{9}{5}C + 32$

$\Rightarrow \quad 5F = 9C + 32 \times 5$

$\Rightarrow \quad 9C = 5F - 32 \times 5$

$\therefore \quad C = \frac{5F - 160}{9}$

Since, temperature in degree celcius lies between 40°C to 45°C.

Therefore, $40 < \frac{5F - 160}{9} < 45$

$\Rightarrow \quad 40 < \frac{5x - 160}{9} < 45$

$\Rightarrow \quad 360 < 5x - 160 < 405$ [multiplying each term by 9]

$\Rightarrow \quad 360 + 160 < 5x < 405 + 160$ [adding 160 to each term]

$\Rightarrow \quad 520 < 5x < 565$

$\Rightarrow \quad \frac{520}{5} < x < \frac{565}{5}$ [divide each term by 5]

$\Rightarrow \quad 104 < x < 113$

Hence, the range of temperature in degree fahrenheit is 104 °F to 113°F.

Q.11 The longest side of a triangle is twice the shortest side and the third side is 2 cm longer than the shortest side. If the perimeter of the triangle is more than 166 cm, then find the minimum length of the shortest side.

Thinking process First we will consider the shortest side, then remaining side will be calculated easily. Further, use the concept of perimeter to get the required result.

Ans. Let the length of shortest side be x cm.

According to the given information,

Longest side = 2 × Shortest side = $2x$ cm

and third side = 2 + Shortest side = $(2 + x)$ cm

Perimeter of triangle $= x + 2x + (x + 2) = 4x + 2$

According to the question,

Perimeter > 166 cm

$\Rightarrow \quad 4x + 2 > 166 \Rightarrow 4x > 166 - 2$

$\Rightarrow \quad 4x > 164$

$\Rightarrow \quad x > \frac{164}{4}$ [dividing by 4 on both sides]

$\therefore \quad x = 41$ cm

Hence, the minimum length of shortest side be 41cm.

Q.12 In drilling world's deepest hole it was found that the temperature T in degree celcius, x km below the earth's surface was given by $T = 30 + 25(x - 3)$, $3 \le x \le 15$. At what depth will the temperature be between 155°C and 205°C?

Ans. Given, $T = 30 + 25(x - 3)$, $3 \le x \le 15$

According to the question,

$155 < T < 205$

$\Rightarrow \quad 155 < 30 + 25(x - 3) < 205$

$\Rightarrow \quad 155 - 30 < 25(x - 3) < 205 - 30$ [subtracting 30 from each term]

$\Rightarrow \quad 125 < 25(x - 3) < 175$

$\Rightarrow \quad \frac{125}{25} < x - 3 < \frac{175}{25}$ [divide each term by 25]

$\Rightarrow \quad 5 < x - 3 < 7$

$\Rightarrow \quad 5 + 3 < x < 7 + 3$ [adding 3 to each term]

$\Rightarrow \quad 8 < x < 10$

Hence, at the depth 8 km to 10 km temperature lies between 155° to 205°C.

Long Answer Type Questions

Q.13 Solve the following system of inequalities $\frac{2x+1}{7x-1}>5, \frac{x+7}{x-8}>2.$

Ans. The given system of inequalities is

$$\frac{2x+1}{7x-1}>5 \quad \ldots(i)$$

and

$$\frac{x+7}{x-8}>2 \quad \ldots(ii)$$

Now,

$$\frac{2x+1}{7x-1}-5>0$$

$$\Rightarrow \frac{(2x+1)-5(7x-1)}{7x-1}>0 \Rightarrow \frac{2x+1-35x+5}{7x-1}>0$$

$$\Rightarrow \frac{-33x+6}{7x-1}>0 \Rightarrow \frac{33x-6}{7x-1}<0$$

[multiply by -1, so inequality get reversed]

$$\Rightarrow 33x-6<0 \text{ and } 7x-1>0 \text{ or } 33x-6>0 \text{ and } 7x-1<0$$

$$\Rightarrow x<\frac{2}{11} \text{ and } x>\frac{1}{7} \text{ or } x>\frac{2}{11} \text{ and } x<\frac{1}{7}$$

$$\Rightarrow x \in \left(\frac{1}{7}, \frac{2}{11}\right) \quad \ldots(iii)$$

and

$$\frac{x+7}{x-8}>2 \Rightarrow \frac{x+7}{x-8}-2>0 \Rightarrow \frac{x+7-2(x-8)}{x-8}>0 \Rightarrow \frac{x+7-2x+16}{x-8}>0$$

$$\Rightarrow \frac{-x+23}{x-8}>0 \Rightarrow \frac{x-23}{x-8}<0$$

[multiply by -1, so inequality get reversed]

$$\Rightarrow x-23<0 \text{ and } x-8>0 \text{ or } x-23>0 \text{ and } x-8<0$$

$$\Rightarrow x<23 \text{ and } x>8 \text{ or } x>23 \text{ and } x<8$$

$$\Rightarrow x \in (8, 23) \quad \ldots(iv)$$

Since, the intersection of Eqs. (iii) and (iv) is the null set. Hence, the given system of equation has no solution.

***Q.14** Find the linear inequalities for which the shaded region in the given figure is the solution set.

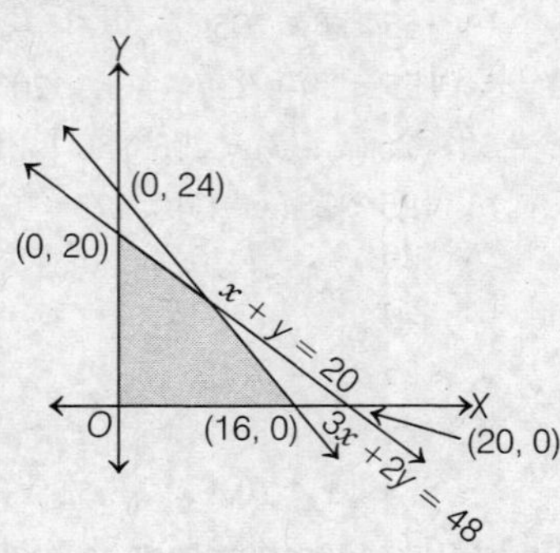

Ans. Consider the line $3x + 2y = 48$, we observe that the shaded region and the origin are on the same side of the line $3x + 2y = 48$ and (0, 0) satisfy the linear constraint $3x + 2y \leq 48$. So, we must have one inequality as $3x + 2y \leq 48$.

Now, consider the line $x + y = 20$. We find that the shaded region and the origin are on the same side of the line $x + y = 20$ and (0, 0) satisfy the constraint $x + y \leq 20$. So, the second inequality is $x + y \leq 20$.

We also notice that the shaded region is above X-axis and is on the right side of Y-axis, so we must have $x \geq 0$, $y \geq 0$.

Thus, the linear inequalities corresponding to the given solution set are $3x + 2y \leq 48, x + y \leq 20$, $x \geq 0$ and $y \geq 0$.

***Q.15** Find the linear inequalities for which the shaded region in the given figure is the solution set.

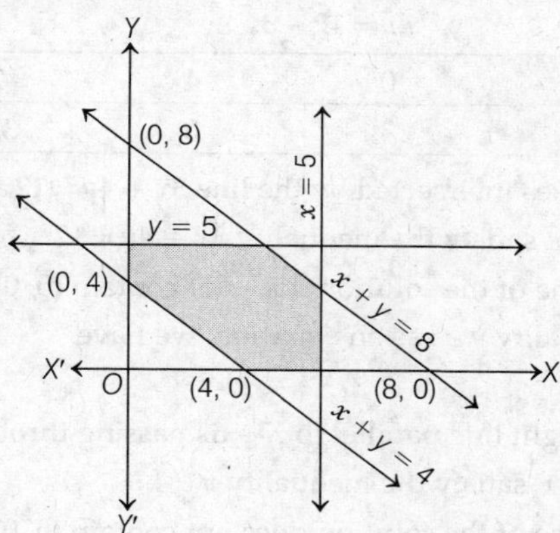

Ans. Consider the line $x + y = 4$, we observe that the shaded region and the origin lie on the opposite side of this line and (0, 0) satisfies $x + y \leq 4$. Therefore, we must have $x + y \geq 4$ as the linear inequality corresponding to the line $x + y = 4$.

Consider the line $x + y = 8$, clearly the shaded region and origin lie on the same side of this line and (0, 0) satisfies the constraint $x + y \leq 8$. Therefore, we must have $x + y \leq 8$, as the linear inequality corresponding to the line $x + y = 8$.

Consider the line $x = 5$. It is clear from the graph that the shaded region and origin are on the left of this line and (0, 0) satisfy the constraint $x \leq 5$.

Hence, $x \leq 5$ is the linear inequality corresponding to $x = 5$.

Consider the line $y = 5$, clearly the shaded region and origin are on the same side (below) of the line and (0, 0) satisfy the constraint $y \leq 5$.

Therefore, $y \leq 5$ is an inequality corresponding to the line $y = 5$.

We also notice that the shaded region is above the X-axis and on the right of the Y-axis *i.e.* shaded region is in first quadrant. So, we must have $x \geq 0$, $y \geq 0$.

Thus, the linear inequalities comprising the given solution set are

$$x + y \geq 4; x + y \leq 8; x \leq 5; y \leq 5; x \geq 0 \text{ and } y \geq 0.$$

(*) Topics related to these question have been removed from latest NCERT.

***Q.16** Show that the following system of linear inequalities has no solution $x+2y \le 3, 3x+4y \ge 12, x \ge 0, y \ge 1$.

Ans. Consider the inequality $x + 2y \le 3$ as an equation, we have

$$x + 2y = 3$$

$$\Rightarrow \quad 2y = 3 - x$$

x	3	1	0
y	0	1	1.5

Now, (0, 0) satisfy the inequality $x + 2y \le 3$.

So, half plane contains (0, 0) as the solution and the line $x + 2y = 3$ intersect the coordinate axes at (3, 0) and (0, 3/2).

Consider the inequality $3x + 4y \ge 12$ as an equation, we have $3x + 4y = 12$

$$\Rightarrow \quad 4y = 12 - 3x$$

x	0	4	2
y	3	0	3/2

Thus, coordinate axes intersected by the line $3x + 4y = 12$ at points (4, 0) and (0, 3).

Now, (0, 0) does not satisfy the inequality $3x + 4y = 12$.

Therefore, half plane of the solution does not contain (0, 0).

Consider the inequality $y \ge 1$ as an equation, we have

$$y = 1.$$

It represents a straight line parallel to X-axis passing through point (0, 1).

Now, (0, 0) does not satisfy the inequality $y \ge 1$.

Therefore, half plane of the solution does not contain (0, 0).

Clearly, $x \ge 0$ represents the region lying on the right side of Y-axis.

The solution set of the given linear constraints will be the intersection of the above region.

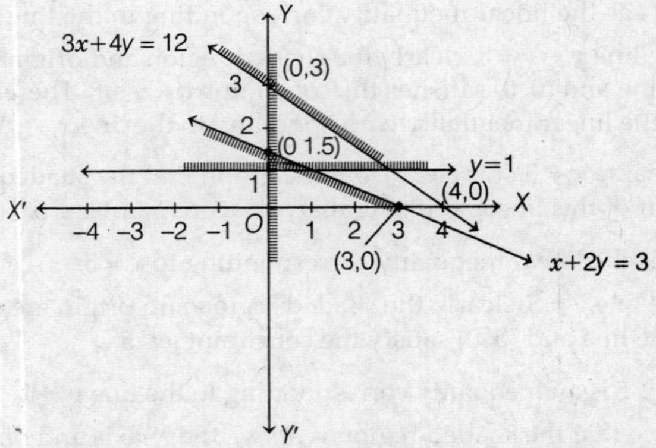

It is clear from the graph that the shaded portions do not have common region.

So, solution set is null set. **Hence proved.**

Mistake Alert! *Misplacing boundary lines or shading the wrong side of the inequalities can lead to inaccurate graphical representations.*

(✱) Topics related to these question have been removed from latest NCERT.

***Q.17** Solve the following system of linear inequalities:
$3x + 2y \geq 24$, $3x + y \leq 15$, $x \geq 4$.

Ans. Consider the inequality $3x + 2y \geq 24$ as an equation, we have $3x + 2y = 24$.

$\Rightarrow \quad 2y = 24 - 3x$

x	0	8	4
y	12	0	6

Hence, line $3x + y = 24$ intersects the coordinate axes at points $(8, 0)$ and $(0, 12)$.
Now, $(0,0)$ does not satisfy the inequality $3x + 2y \geq 24$.
Therefore, half plane of the solution set does not contain $(0,0)$.
Consider the inequality $3x + y \leq 15$ as an equation, we have $3x + y = 15$

$\Rightarrow \quad y = 15 - 3x$

x	0	5	3
y	15	0	6

Line $3x + y = 15$ intersects the coordinate axes at points $(5,0)$ and $(0,15)$.
Now, point $(0,0)$ satisfy the inequality $3x + y \leq 15$.
Therefore, the half plane of the solution contains origin.
Consider the inequality $x \geq 4$ as an equation, we have $x = 4$

It represents a straight line parallel to Y-axis passing through $(4,0)$. Now, point $(0,0)$ does not satisfy the inequality $x \geq 4$.

Therefore, half plane does not contain $(0,0)$.

The graph of the above inequalities is given below.

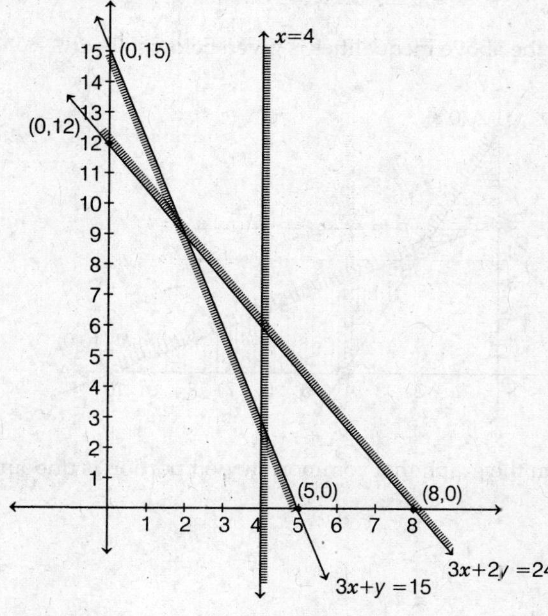

(✱) Topics related to these question have been removed from latest NCERT.

It is clear from the graph that there is no common region corresponding to these inequality.

Hence, the given system of inequalities have no solution.

***Q.18** Show that the solution set of the following system of linear inequalities is an unbounded region $2x+y\geq 8,\ x+2y\geq 10,\ x\geq 0, y\geq 0$

Ans. Consider the inequality $2x + y \geq 8$ as an equation, we have

$$2x + y = 8$$

$$\Rightarrow \quad y = 8 - 2x$$

x	0	4	3
y	8	0	2

The line $2x + y = 8$ intersects the coordinate axes at $(4,0)$ and $(0, 8)$.

Now, point $(0,0)$ does not satisfy the inequality $2x + y \geq 8$.

Therefore, half plane does not contain origin.

Consider the inequality $x + 2y \geq 10$ as an equation, we have

$$x + 2y = 10 \Rightarrow 2y = 10 - x$$

x	10	0	8
y	0	5	1

The line $x + 2y = 10$ intersects the coordinate axes at $(10,0)$ and $(0,5)$.

Now, point $(0,0)$ does not satisfy the inequality $x + 2y \geq 10$.

Therefore, half plane does not contain $(0,0)$.

Consider the inequality $x\geq 0$ and $y\geq 0$. Clearly, it represents the region in first quadrant.

The graph of the above inequalities is given below.

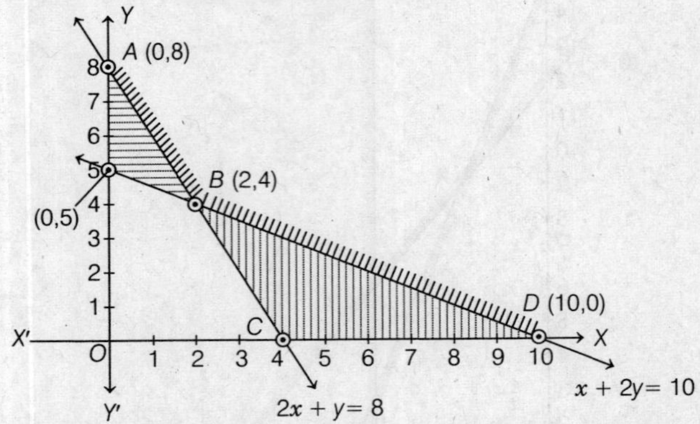

It is clear from the graph that common shaded portion is unbounded.

Hence proved

(*) Topics related to these question have been removed from latest NCERT.

Objective Type Questions

Choose the correct answer from the given four options in each of the exercises 19 to 26.

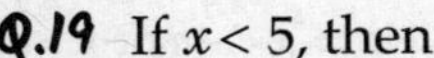

Q.19 If $x < 5$, then

(a) $-x < -5$ (b) $-x \leq -5$

(c) $-x > -5$ (d) $-x \geq -5$

Ans. ***(c)*** If $x < 5$, then $-x > -5$

[if we multiply by a negative number, then the sign of the inequality gets reversed]

Q.20 If x, y and b are real numbers and $x < y$, $b < 0$, then

(a) $\frac{x}{b} < \frac{y}{b}$ (b) $\frac{x}{b} \leq \frac{y}{b}$

(c) $\frac{x}{b} > \frac{y}{b}$ (d) $\frac{x}{b} \geq \frac{y}{b}$

Ans. ***(c)*** It is given that $x < y$, $b < 0$

Since, $b < 0$ the sign of the inequality gets reversed.

$\Rightarrow$ $\frac{x}{b} > \frac{y}{b}$

Q.21 If $-3x + 17 < -13$, then

(a) $x \in (10, \infty)$ (b) $x \in [10, \infty)$

(c) $x \in (-\infty, 10]$ (d) $x \in [-10, 10)$

Ans. ***(a)*** Given, $-3x + 17 < -13$

$\Rightarrow$ $3x - 17 > 13$ [multiplying by -1 on both sides]

$\Rightarrow$ $3x > 30$ [adding 17 on both sides]

$\Rightarrow$ $x > 10$

$\therefore$ $x \in (10, \infty)$

Q.22 If x is a real number and $|x| < 3$, then

(a) $x \geq 3$ (b) $-3 < x < 3$

(c) $x \leq -3$ (d) $-3 \leq x \leq 3$

Ans. ***(b)*** Given, $|x| < 3$

$\Rightarrow$ $-3 < x < 3$ [$\because |x| < a \Rightarrow -a < x < a$]

Q.23 Let x and b are real numbers. If $b > 0$ and $|x| > b$, then

(a) $x \in (-b, \infty)$ (b) $x \in [-\infty, b)$

(c) $x \in (-b, b)$ (d) $x \in (-\infty, -b) \cup (b, \infty)$

Ans. ***(d)*** Given, $|x| > b$ and $b > 0$

$\Rightarrow$ $x < -b$ or $x > b$

$\Rightarrow$ $x \in (-\infty, -b) \cup (b, \infty)$

Q.24 If $|x-1|>5$, then

(a) $x \in (-4, 6)$ (b) $x \in (-4, 6)$
(c) $x \in (-\infty, -4) \cup (6, \infty)$ (d) $x \in [-\infty, -4) \cup [6, \infty)$

Ans. ***(c)*** Given, $|x-1|>5$

$\Rightarrow (x-1) < -5$ or $(x-1) > 5$ $[\because |x| > a \Rightarrow x < -a \text{ or } x > a]$

$\Rightarrow x < -4$ or $x > 6$

$\Rightarrow x \in (-\infty, -4) \cup (6, \infty)$

Q.25 If $|x+2| \le 9$, then

(a) $x \in (-7, 11)$ (b) $x \in [-11, 7]$
(c) $x \in (-\infty, -7) \cup (11, \infty)$ (d) $x \in (-\infty, -7) \cup [11, \infty)$

Ans. ***(b)*** Given, $|x+2| \le 9$,

$\Rightarrow -9 \le x+2 \le 9$ $[\because |x| \le a \Rightarrow -a \le x \le a]$

$\Rightarrow -9-2 \le x \le 9-2$ [subtracting 2 from each term]

$\Rightarrow -11 \le x \le 7 \Rightarrow x \in [-11, 7]$

***Q.26** The inequality representing the following graphs is

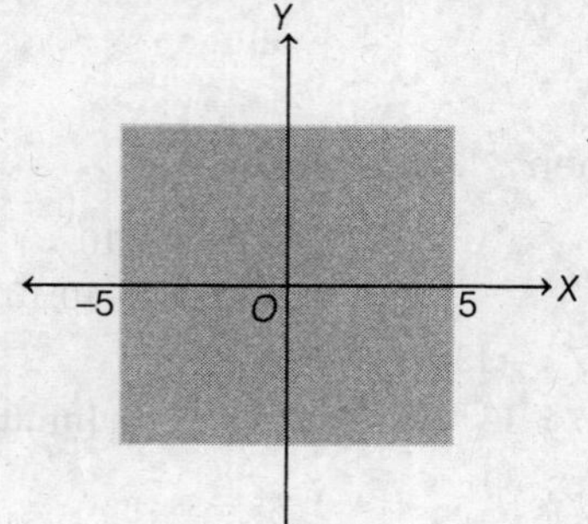

(a) $|x| < 5$ (b) $|x| \le 5$
(c) $|x| > 5$ (d) $|x| \ge 5$

Ans. ***(a)*** The given graph represents $x > -5$ and $x < 5$.

On combining these two results, we get $|x| < 5$.

Solution of a linear inequality in variable x is represented a on number line in exercise 27 to 30. Choose the correct answer.

Q.27

5

(a) $x \in (-\infty, 5)$ (b) $x \in (-\infty, 5]$
(c) $x \in [5, \infty)$ (d) $x \in (5, \infty)$

Ans. ***(d)*** The given graph represents all the values greater than 5, except $x = 5$.

So, $x \in (5, \infty)$.

(*) Topics related to these question have been removed from latest NCERT.

Q.28

(a) $x \in \left(\frac{9}{2}, \infty\right)$
(b) $x \in \left[\frac{9}{2}, \infty\right)$
(c) $x \in -\left[\infty, \frac{9}{2}\right)$
(d) $x \in \left(-\infty, \frac{9}{2}\right]$

Ans. ***(b)*** The given graph represents all the values greater than $\frac{9}{2}$, including $\frac{9}{2}$.

$$\therefore \quad x \in \left[\frac{9}{2}, \infty\right)$$

Q.29

(a) $x \in \left(-\infty, \frac{7}{2}\right)$
(b) $x \in \left(-\infty, \frac{7}{2}\right]$
(c) $x \in \left[\frac{7}{2}, -\infty\right)$
(d) $x \in \left(\frac{7}{2}, \infty\right)$

Ans. ***(a)*** The given graph represents all the values less than $\frac{7}{2}$, excluding $\frac{7}{2}$.

$$\Rightarrow \quad x \in \left(-\infty, \frac{7}{2}\right)$$

Q.30

(a) $x \in (-\infty, -2)$
(b) $x \in (-\infty, -2]$
(c) $x \in (-2, \infty)$
(d) $x \in [-2, \infty)$

Ans. ***(b)*** The given graph represents all values less than -2, including -2.

$$\Rightarrow \quad x \in (-\infty, -2]$$

Q.31 State which of the following statements is True or False.

(i) If $x < y$ and $b < 0$, then $\frac{x}{b} < \frac{y}{b}$.

(ii) If $xy > 0$, then $x > 0$ and $y < 0$

(iii) If $xy > 0$, then $x < 0$ and $y < 0$

(iv) If $xy < 0$, then $x < 0$ and $y < 0$

(v) If $x < -5$ and $x < -2$, then $x \in (-\infty, -5)$

(vi) If $x < -5$ and $x > 2$, then $x \in (-5, 2)$

(vii) If $x > -2$ and $x < 9$, then $x \in (-2, 9)$

(viii) If $|x| > 5$, then $x \in (-\infty, -5) \cup [5, \infty)$

(ix) If $|x| \le 4$, then $x \in [-4, 4]$

*(x) Graph of $x < 3$ is

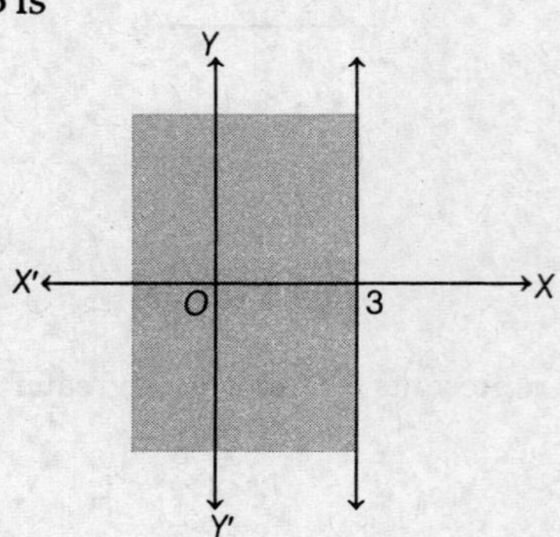

*(xi) Graph of $x \geq 0$ is

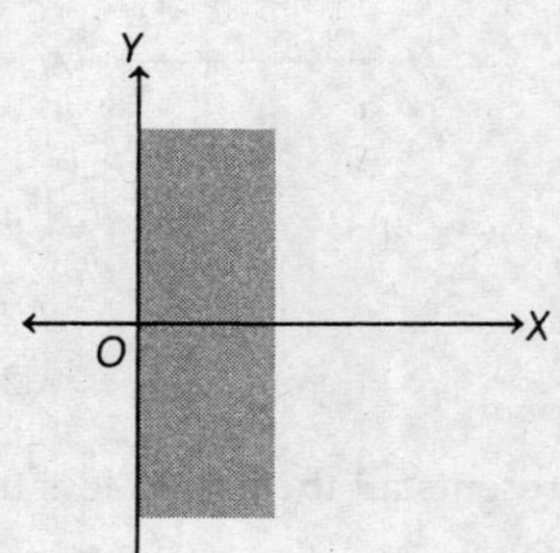

*(xii) Graph of $y \leq 0$ is

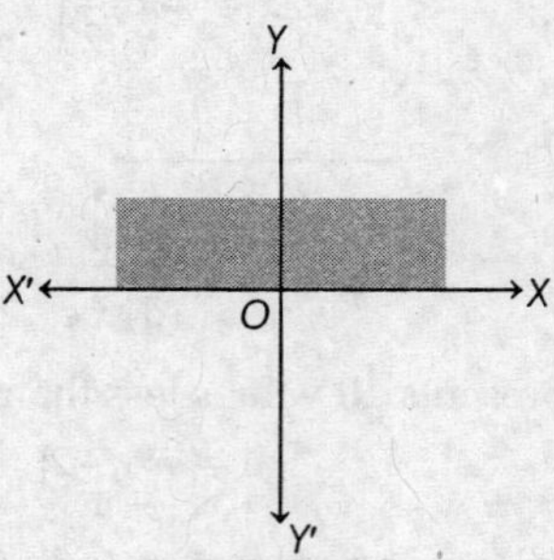

*(xiii) Solution set of $x \geq 0$ and $y \leq 0$ is

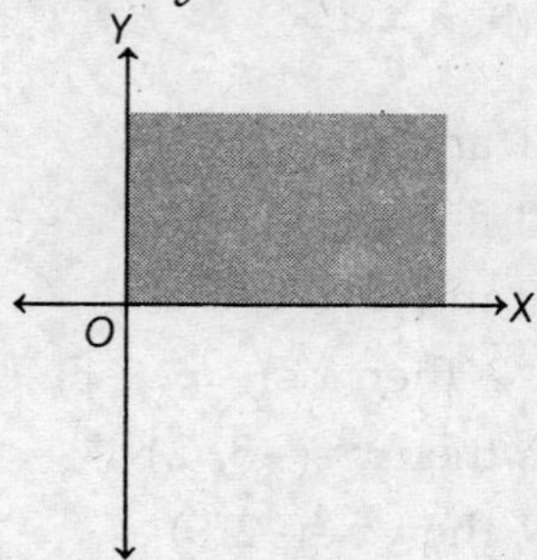

(*) Topics related to these question have been removed from latest NCERT.

*(xiv) Solution set of $x \geq 0$ and $y \leq 1$ is

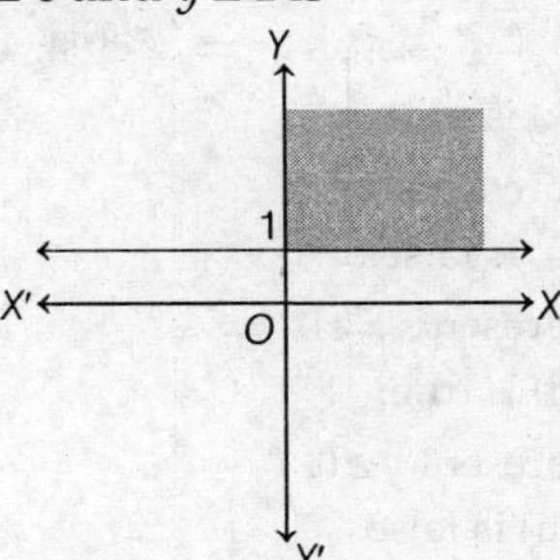

*(xv) Solution set of $x + y \geq 0$ is

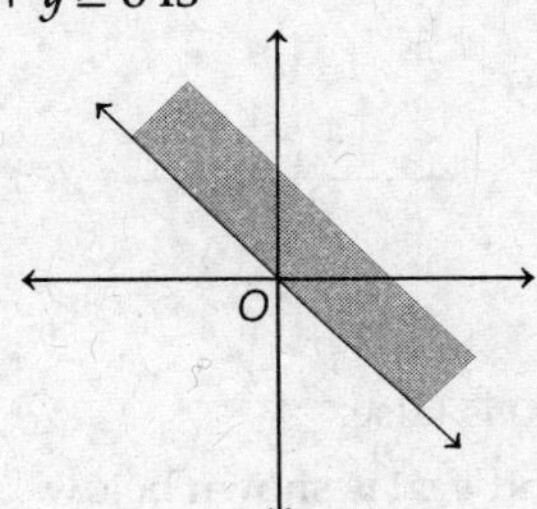

Ans. (i) If $x<y$ and $b<0$

$$\Rightarrow \qquad \frac{x}{b} > \frac{y}{b}$$

[by dividing a negative number, the sign of the inequality gets reversed]

Hence, statement (i) is false.

(ii) If $xy>0$, then, either $x>0, y>0$ or $x<0, y<0$.

Hence, statement (ii) is false

(iii) If $xy>0$, then either $x>0, y>0$ or $x<0, y<0$.

Hence, statement (iii) is true.

(iv) If $xy<0 \Rightarrow$ either $x<0, y>0$ or $x>0, y<0$.

Hence, statement (iv) is false.

(v) If $x<-5$, then $x \in (-\infty, -5)$ ...(i)

If $x<-2$, then $x \in (-\infty, -2)$ ...(ii)

On combining results of Eqs. (i) and (ii), we get $x \in (-\infty, -5)$

Hence, statement (v) is true.

(vi) If $x<-5$ and $x>2$, then x have no value. i.e., $x \in \phi$

Hence, statement (vi) is false.

(vii) If $x>-2$ then $x \in (-2, \infty)$ ...(i)

If $x<9$, then $x \in (-\infty, 9)$ ...(ii)

on combining results of Eqs. (i) and (ii), we get $x \in (-2, 9)$

Hence, statement (vii) is true.

(viii) If $|x|>5$, then either $x<-5$ or $x>5$. $\Rightarrow x \in (-\infty, -5) \cup (5, \infty)$

Hence, statement (viii) is false.

(✱) Topics related to these question have been removed from latest NCERT.

(ix) If $|x| \le 4$, then

$$-4 \le x \le 4 \Rightarrow x \in [-4, 4]$$

Hence, statement (ix) is true.

(x) The given graph represents $x \le 3$.
Hence, statement (x) is false.

(xi) The given graph represents $x \ge 0$.
Hence, statement (xi) is true.

(xii) The given graph represent $y \ge 0$.
Hence, statement (xii) is false.

(xiii) Solution set of $x \ge 0$ and $y \le 0$ lies in IV quadrant as shown in figure

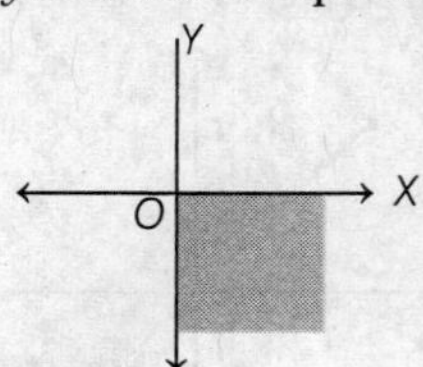

Hence, statement (xiii) is false.

(xiv) Solution set of $x \ge 0$ and $y \le 1$ is shown below

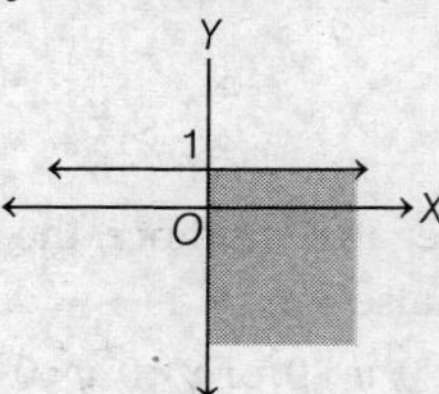

Hence, statement (xiv) is false.

(xv) The given graph represents $x + y \ge 0$.
Hence, statement (xv) is correct.

Q.32 Fill in the blanks of the following.

(i) If $-4x \ge 12$, then $x \ldots -3$.

(ii) If $\frac{-3}{4} x \le -3$, then $x \ldots 4$.

(iii) If $\frac{2}{x+2} > 0$, then $x \ldots -2$.

(iv) If $x > -5$, then $4x \ldots -20$.

(v) If $x > y$ and $z < 0$, then $-xz \ldots -yz$.

(vi) If $p > 0$ and $q < 0$, then $p - q \ldots p$.

(vii) If $|x + 2| > 5$, then $x \ldots -7$ or $x \ldots 3$.

(viii) If $-2x + 1 \ge 9$, then $x \ldots -4$.

Ans. (i) If $-4x \geq 12 \Rightarrow x \leq -3$

[by dividing a negative number, the sign of the inequality gets reversed]

(ii) If $\frac{-3}{4}x \leq -3$

$\Rightarrow \quad x \geq (-3) \times \frac{4}{(-3)} \Rightarrow x \geq 4$

(iii) If $\frac{2}{x+2} > 0$

$\Rightarrow \quad x + 2 > 0$

$\Rightarrow \quad x > -2$

(iv) If $x > -5 \Rightarrow 4x > -20$

(v) If $x > y$ and $z < 0$, then

$xz < yz$ [since, $z < 0$]

$\Rightarrow \quad -xz > -yz$

(vi) If $p > 0$ and $q < 0$,

then $p - q > p$ [$\because q < 0 \Rightarrow -q > 0$]

e.g., consider $2 > 0$ and $-3 < 0$.

$\Rightarrow \quad 2 - (-3) = 2 + 3 = 5 > 2$

(vii) If $|x + 2| > 5$, then

$x + 2 < -5$ or $x + 2 > 5$

$\Rightarrow \quad x < -5 - 2$ or $x > 5 - 2$

$\Rightarrow \quad x < -7$ or $x > 3$

(viii) If $-2x + 1 \geq 9$, then

$-2x \geq 9 - 1 \Rightarrow -2x \geq 8$

$\Rightarrow \quad 2x \leq -8 \Rightarrow x \leq -4$

Chapter

07 Permutations and Combinations

Short Answer Type Questions

Q.1 Eight chairs are numbered 1 to 8. Two women and 3 men wish to occupy one chair each. First the women choose the chairs from amongst the chairs 1 to 4 and then men select from the remaining chairs. Find the total number of possible arrangements.

Thinking process First, think that 2 women occupy the chairs from amongst the chairs 1 to 4 in ${}^4P_2$ ways and 3 men occupy the chairs from the remaining 6 chairs in ${}^6P_3$ ways.

Ans. First, women choose the chairs from amongst the chairs 1 to 4. *i.e.*, total number of chairs is 4.

Since, there are two women, so number of arrangements = ${}^4P_2$ ways.

Now, men have to choose chairs from the remaining 6 chairs.

Since, there are 3 men, so number of arrangements are ${}^6P_3$ ways.

$\therefore$ Total number of possible arrangements = ${}^4P_2 \times {}^6P_3$

$$= \frac{4!}{(4-2)!} \times \frac{6!}{(6-3)!} \left[\because {}^nP_r = \frac{n!}{(n-r)!}\right]$$

$$= \frac{4!}{2!} \times \frac{6!}{3!}$$

$$= \frac{4 \times 3 \times 2!}{2!} \times \frac{6 \times 5 \times 4 \times 3!}{3!}$$

$$= 4 \times 3 \times 6 \times 5 \times 4 = 1440$$

Q.2 If the letters of the word 'RACHIT' are arranged in all possible ways as listed in dictionary. Then, what is the rank of the word 'RACHIT'?

Ans. The letters of the word 'RACHIT' in alphabetical order are A, C, H, I, R and T.

Now, number of words beginning with $A = 5!$

Number of words beginning with $C = 5!$

Numbe of words beginning with $H = 5!$

Number of words beginning with $I = 5!$

Word beginning with R *i.e.*, RACHIT = 1

$\therefore$ Rank of the word 'RACHIT' in dictionary $= 4 \times 5! + 1 = 4 \times 120 + 1$

$$= 480 + 1 = 481$$

Q.3 A candidate is required to answer 7 questions out of 12 questions, which are divided into two groups, each containing 6 questions. He is not permitted to attempt more than 5 questions from either group. Find the number of different ways of doing questions.

Ans. Since, candidate cannot attempt more than 5 questions from either group.
Thus, he is able to attempt minimum two questions from either group.
The number of questions attempted from each group is given in following table

Group I	5	4	3	2
Group II	2	3	4	5

Since, each group has 6 questions and attempted a total of 7 questions.

$\therefore$ Total number of possible ways $= {}^6C_5 \times {}^6C_2 + {}^6C_4 \times {}^6C_3 + {}^6C_3 \times {}^6C_4 + {}^6C_2 \times {}^6C_5$
$= 2[{}^6C_5 \times {}^6C_2 + {}^6C_4 \times {}^6C_3]$
$= 2[6 \times 15 + 15 \times 20]$
$= 2[90 + 300]$
$= 2 \times 390 = 780$

Mistake Alert! *Students might confuse between permutations and combinations, that is permutations are for arrangement while combinations are for selections.*

Q.4 Out of 18 points in a plane, no three are in the same line except five points which are collinear. Find the number of lines that can be formed joining the point.

Thinking Process

(i) First, calculate the total number of lines possible if no points are callinear using the formula = ${}^nC_2$. Then, substract the number of lines formed by the collinear points.

(ii) Finally, add back 1 for the single line formed by those collinear points.

Ans. Total number of points = 18
Out of which 5 points are collinear.
Since, we get a straight line by joining any two points.
$\therefore$ Number of straight lines formed by joining the 18 points taking 2 at a time = ${}^{18}C_2$
and number of straight line formed by joining 5 points taking 2 at a time = ${}^5C_2$
But 5 collinear points, when joined pairwise give only one line.
$\therefore$ Required number of straight lines = ${}^{18}C_2 - {}^5C_2 + 1$
$= 153 - 10 + 1 = 144$

Q.5 We wish to select 6 person from 8 but, if the person A is chosen, then B must be chosen. In how many ways can selections be made?

Ans. Total number of person = 8
Number of person to be selected = 6
It is given that, if A is chosen, then, B must be chosen.
Therefore, following cases arise.

***Case* I** When A is chosen, then B must be chosen.

Number of ways = ${}^{8-2}C_{6-2} = {}^6C_4$

Case **II** When A is not chosen, then, *B* may be chosen.

$\therefore$ Number of ways $= {}^{8-1}C_6 = {}^7C_6$

Hence, required number of ways $= {}^6C_4 + {}^7C_6$

$$= \frac{6 \times 5}{2} + 7 = 15 + 7 = 22$$

Q.6 How many committee of five person with a chairperson can be selected from 12 persons?

Ans. $\because$ Total number of persons = 12

and number of persons to be selected = 5

Out of 12 persons, a chairperson is selected in ${}^{12}C_1$ ways = 12 ways

Now, remaining 4 persons are selected out of 11 persons.

$\therefore$ Number of ways $= {}^{11}C_4 = \frac{11 \times 10 \times 9 \times 8}{4 \times 3 \times 2} = 330$ ways $\left[{}^nC_r = \frac{n!}{r!(n-r)!} \right]$

$\therefore$ Total number of ways to form a committee of 5 persons $= 12 \times 330 = 3960$

Q.7 How many automobile license plates can be made, if each plate contains two different letters followed by three different digits?

- **Concept Insight** A permutations represents an arrangement or order or a sequence of different objects taken some or all at a time. Total permutations of n-different objects taken $r(r \le n)$ at a time is ${}^nP_r = n(n-1)(n-2) \dots (n-r+1) = \frac{n!}{(n-r)!}$

Ans. There are 26 English alphabets and 10 digits (0 to 9).

Since, it is given that each plate contains two different letters followed by three different digits.

$\therefore$Number of arrangements of 26 letters taken 2 at a time

$$= {}^{26}P_2 = \frac{26!}{24!} = 26 \times 25 = 650 \text{ ways}$$

And three-digit number can be formed out of the 10 digits

$\therefore$Number of ways $= {}^{10}P_3 = \frac{10!}{7!} = 10 \times 9 \times 8 = 720$ ways

$\therefore$ Total number of licence plates $= 650 \times 720 = 468000$

Q.8 A bag contains 5 black and 6 red balls, determine the number of ways in which 2 black and 3 red balls can be selected from the lot.

Ans. It is given that bag contains 5 black and 6 red balls.

So, 2 black balls is selected from 5 black balls in ${}^5C_2$ ways.

and 3 red balls are selected from 6 red balls in ${}^6C_3$ ways. $\left[{}^nC_r = \frac{n!}{r!(n-r)!} \right]$

$\therefore$ Total number of ways in which 2 black and 3 red balls are selected $= {}^5C_2 \times {}^6C_3$

$$= \frac{5 \times 4}{2} \times \frac{6 \times 5 \times 4}{3 \times 2} = 10 \times 20 = 200 \text{ ways}$$

Q.9 **Find the number of permutations of n distinct things taken r together, in which 3 particular things must occur together.**

Ans. Total number of things $= n$

We have, to arrange r things out of n in which three things must occur together.

Therefore, combination of n things taken r at a time in which 3 things always occurs

$$= {}^{n-3}C_{r-3}$$

If three things are taken together, then it is considered as 1 group.

Number of arrangement of these three things = 3!

Now, we have to arrange $= r - 3 + 1 = (r - 2)$ objects

$\therefore$ Number of arrangement of $(r - 2)$ objects $= (r - 2)!$

$\therefore$ Total number of arrangements $= {}^{n-3}C_{r-3} \times (r-2)! \times 3!$

Q.10 **Find the number of different words that can be formed from the letters of the word 'TRIANGLE', so that no vowels are together.**

Thinking Process The number of different words means the number of permutation of a letter of the given word i.e. use the concept ${}^nP_r$ for each parts.

Ans. Number of letters in the word 'TRIANGLE' = 8, out of which 5 are consonants and 3 are vowels.

If vowels are not together, then we have following arrangement.

V	C	V	C	V	C	V	C	V	C	V

Consonants can be arranged in = 5! = 120 ways and vowels can occupy 6 places.

The 3 vowels can be arranged at 6 place in ${}^6P_3$ ways $= \dfrac{6!}{(6-3)!} = \dfrac{6!}{3!}$

$$= \frac{6 \times 5 \times 4 \times 3!}{3!} = 120$$

$\therefore$ Total number of words $= 120 \times 120 = 14400$

Q.11 **Find the number of positive integers greater than 6000 and less than 7000 which are divisible by 5, provided that no digit is to be repeated.**

Thinking Process Take the choice only for first three digits because unit digit can be filled only in 2 ways that is 0 or 5 and keep in mind that repetition is not allowed.

Ans. We know that a number is divisible by 5, when at the unit place of the number is 0 or 5.

So, unit digit can be filled in 2 ways.

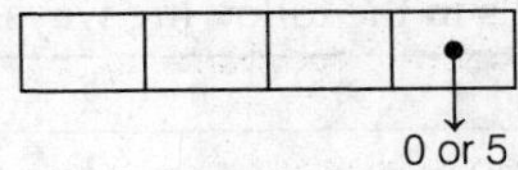

Since, repetition is not allowed. Therefore, tens place can be filled in 7 ways. Similarily hundreds place can be filled in 8 ways.

But, we have to form a number greater than 6000 and less than 7000.

Hence, thousand place can be filled in only 1 ways.

6	8	7	2

$\therefore$ Total number of integers $= 1 \times 8 \times 7 \times 2 = 14 \times 8 = 112$

Q. 12 **There are 10 persons named $P_1, P_2, P_3, \ldots, P_{10}$. Out of 10 persons, 5 persons are to be arranged in a line such that in each arrangement P_1 must occur whereas P_4 and P_5 do not occur. Find the number of such possible arrangements.**

Ans. Given, $P_1, P_2, \ldots, P_{10}$, are 10 persons, out of which 5 persons are to be arranged but P_1 must occur whereas P_4 and P_5 never occur.

$\therefore$ Selection depends on only $10 - 3 = 7$ persons

As, P_1 occurs in each arrangement.

Therefore, we have to select only 4 persons out of 7.

Number of selection $= {}^7C_4 = \dfrac{7!}{4!\,(7-4)!} = \dfrac{7!}{4!\,3!} = \dfrac{5040}{24 \times 6} = 35$

$\therefore$ Required number of arrangements of 5 persons $= 35 \times 5! = 35 \times 120 = 4200$

Q.13 **There are 10 lamps in a hall. Each one of them can be switched on independently. Find the number of ways in which the hall can be illuminated.**

Thinking Process The number of ways, in which the hall can be illuminated is equivalent to the number of selections of one or more things out of n different things is

$${}^nC_1 + {}^nC_2 + {}^nC_3 + \ldots + {}^nC_n = 2^n - 1$$

Ans. Number of lamps = 10

Since, hall can be illuminated by selection of one or more lamps from 10 different lamps.

$\therefore$ Total number of ways $= {}^{10}C_1 + {}^{10}C_2 + {}^{10}C_3 + {}^{10}C_4 + {}^{10}C_5 + {}^{10}C_6 + \ldots + {}^{10}C_{10}$

$= 2^{10} - 1$ $\quad [\because {}^nC_0 + {}^nC_1 + {}^nC_2 + \ldots = 2^n]$

$= 1024 - 1 = 1023$

Q.14 **A box contains two white, three black and four red balls. In how many ways can three balls be drawn from the box, if atleast one black ball is to be included in the draw?**

Ans. There are 2 white, three black and four red balls.

We have to draw 3 balls out of these 9 balls in which atleast one black ball is included.

Hence, we can select the balls in the following ways.

Black balls	1	2	3
Other than black	2	1	0

$\therefore$ Required number of ways $= ({}^3C_1) \times ({}^6C_2) + ({}^3C_2) \times ({}^6C_1) + ({}^3C_3) \times ({}^6C_0)$

$= (3 \times 15) + (3 \times 6) + 1$

$= 45 + 18 + 1 = 64$

Q.15 If ${}^nC_{r-1} = 36$, ${}^nC_r = 84$ and ${}^nC_{r+1} = 126$, then find the value of ${}^rC_2$.

Ans. Given, $${}^nC_{r-1} = 36 \quad \text{...(i)}$$
$${}^nC_r = 84 \quad \text{...(ii)}$$
and $${}^nC_{r+1} = 126 \quad \text{...(iii)}$$
On dividing Eq. (i) by Eq. (ii), we get
$$\frac{{}^nC_{r-1}}{{}^nC_r} = \frac{36}{84} \qquad \left[\because {}^nC_r = \frac{n!}{(n-r)!\,r!)} \text{ and } n! = n\,(n-1)!\right]$$
$$\Rightarrow \frac{n!}{(r-1)!\{n-(r-1)\}!} \cdot \frac{r!\,(n-r)!}{n!} = \frac{3}{7}$$
$$\Rightarrow \frac{1}{(r-1)(n-r+1)!} \cdot \frac{r(r-1)!\,(n-r)!}{1} = \frac{3}{7}$$
$$\Rightarrow \frac{1 \cdot r}{(n-r+1)\,(n-r)!} \cdot (n-r)! = \frac{3}{7} \Rightarrow \frac{r}{n-r+1} = \frac{3}{7}$$
$$\Rightarrow 7r = 3n - 3r + 3$$
$$\Rightarrow 10r - 3n = 3 \quad \text{...(iv)}$$
On dividing Eq. (ii) by Eq. (iii), we get
$$\frac{{}^nC_r}{{}^nC_{r+1}} = \frac{84}{126}$$
$$\Rightarrow \frac{n!}{r!\,(n-r)!} \cdot \frac{(r+1)!\,(n-r-1)!}{n!} = \frac{14}{21}$$
$$\Rightarrow \frac{1}{r!\,(n-r)(n-r-1)!} \cdot \frac{(r+1)\,r!\,(n-r-1)!}{r} = \frac{2}{3} \Rightarrow \frac{r+1}{n-r} = \frac{2}{3}$$
$$\Rightarrow 3r + 3 = 2n - 2r \Rightarrow 2n - 5r = 3 \quad \text{...(v)}$$
On multiplying Eq. (iv) by 2 and Eq. (v) by 3, we get
$$20r - 6n = 6 \quad \text{...(vi)}$$
and $$6n - 15r = 9 \quad \text{...(vii)}$$
On adding Eqs. (vi) and (vii), we get
$$5r = 15 \Rightarrow r = 3$$
On substituting $r = 3$ in E.q. (v), we get $2n = 3 + 15$
$$\Rightarrow 2n = 18$$
$$\Rightarrow n = 9$$
$$\therefore \quad {}^rC_2 = {}^3C_2 = \frac{3!}{2!\,1!} = \frac{3 \times 2!}{2!} = 3$$

Q.16 Find the number of integers greater than 7000 that can be formed with the digits 3, 5, 7, 8 and 9 where no digits are repeated.

Ans. Here, we have to find the number of integers greater than 7000 with the digits 3, 5, 7, 8 and 9. So, with these digits we can make maximum five-digit number because repetition is not allowed.

Now, all the five-digit numbers are greater than 7000.

Number of ways of forming 5-digit number = $5 \times 4 \times 3 \times 2 \times 1 = 120$ and all the four-digit numbers greater than 7000 can be formed in following manner.

Thousand place can be filled in 3 ways. Hundred place can be filled in 4 ways. Tenth place can be filled in 3 ways. Units place can be filled in 2 ways.

Thus, we have total number of 4-digit number = $3 \times 4 \times 3 \times 2 = 72$

$\therefore$ Total number of integers = $120 + 72 = 192$

Note Besides 4 digit integers greater than 7000, five digits integers are always greater than 7000.

Q.17 If 20 lines are drawn in a plane such that no two of them are parallel and no three are concurrent, in how many points will they intersect each other?

Ans. It is given that no two lines are parallel means all line are intersecting and no three lines are concurrent means no three lines intersect at a point.

Since, we know that for one point of intersection, we required two lines.

$\therefore$ Number of point of intersection = ${}^{20}C_2 = \frac{20!}{2!18!} = \frac{20 \times 19 \times 18!}{2 \times 1 \times 18!} \left[{}^{20}C_2 = \frac{20!}{2! \times (20-2)!} \right]$

$= \frac{20 \times 19}{2} = 19 \times 10 = 190$

Q.18 In a certain city, all telephone numbers have six digits, the first two digits always being 41 or 42 or 46 or 62 or 64. How many telephone numbers have all six digits distinct?

Ans. If first two digits are 41, the remaining 4 digits can be arranged in

$= {}^8P_4 = \frac{8!}{(8-4)!} = \frac{8!}{4!}$

$= \frac{8 \times 7 \times 6 \times 5 \times 4!}{4!}$

$= 8 \times 7 \times 6 \times 5 = 1680$

Similarly, if first two digits are 42, 46, 62, or 64, the remaining 4 digits can be arranged in ${}^8P_4$ ways *i.e.*, 1680 ways.

$\therefore$ Total number of telephone numbers have all six digits distinct = $5 \times 1680 = 8400$

Q.19 In an examination, a student has to answer 4 questions out of 5 questions, questions 1 and 2 are however compulsory. Determine the number of ways in which the student can make the choice.

Ans. It is given that 2 questions are compulsory out of 5 questions.

So, these two questions are always included in the selection.

We know that the selection of n distinct objects taken r at a time in which p objects are always included in ${}^{n-p}C_{r-p}$ ways.

$\therefore$ Total number of ways = ${}^{5-2}C_{4-2} = {}^3C_2$

$= \frac{3!}{2!1!} = \frac{3 \times 2!}{2!} = 3$

Q.20 If a convex polygon has 44 diagonals, then find the number of its sides.

Thinking process If a polygon has n sides, then number of diagonals

$$= {}^nC_2 - n = \frac{n!}{2!(n-2)!} - n$$

$$= \frac{n(n-3)}{2}$$

Ans. Let the convex polygon has n sides.

$\therefore$ Number of diagonals $= {}^nC_2 - n$

According to the question, ${}^nC_2 - n = 44$

$$\frac{n!}{2!(n-2)!} - n = 44$$

$$\Rightarrow \frac{n(n-1)}{2} - n = 44$$

$$\Rightarrow n\left[\frac{(n-1)}{2} - 1\right] = 44 \Rightarrow n\left(\frac{n-1-2}{2}\right) = 44$$

$$\Rightarrow n(n-3) = 44 \times 2 \Rightarrow n(n-3) = 88$$

$$\Rightarrow n^2 - 3n - 88 = 0 \Rightarrow (n-11)(n+8) = 0$$

$$\Rightarrow n = 11, -8$$

$$\therefore n = 11 \qquad [\because n \text{ cannot be negative}]$$

Long Answer Type Questions

Q.21 18 mice were placed in two experimental groups and one control group with all groups equally large. In how many ways can the mice be placed into three groups?

Ans. It is given that 18 mice were placed equally in two experimental groups and one control group *i.e.*, three groups.

$$\therefore \text{Required number of arrangements} = \frac{\text{Total arrangement}}{\text{Equally likely arrangement}} = \frac{18!}{6!6!6!} = \frac{18!}{(6!)^3}$$

Q.22 A bag contains six white marbles and five red marbles. Find the number of ways in which four marbles can be drawn from the bag, if (i) they can be of any colour. (ii) two must be white and two red. (iii) they must all be of the same colour.

Ans. Total number of marbles = 6 white + 5 red = 11 marbles

(i) If they can be of any colour means, we have to select 4 marbles out of 11.

$$\therefore \text{Required number of ways} = {}^{11}C_4 = \frac{11}{4!7!} = 330$$

(ii) If two must be white, then selection will be ${}^6C_2$ and two must be red, then selection will be ${}^5C_2$.

$$\therefore \text{Required number of ways} = {}^6C_2 \times {}^5C_2 = \frac{6!}{2!4!} \times \frac{5!}{2!3!} = 15 \times 10 = 150$$

(iii) If they all must be of same colour, then selection of 4 white marbles out of 6 $= {}^6C_4$

And selection of 4 red marble out of 5 $= {}^5C_4$

$\therefore$ Required number of ways $= {}^6C_4 + {}^5C_4 = \frac{6!}{4!2!} + \frac{5!}{4!1!} = 15 + 5 = 20$

Q.23 In how many ways can a football team of 11 players be selected from 16 players? How many of them will

(i) include 2 particular players? (ii) exclude 2 particular players?

Ans. Total number of players = 16

We have to select a team of 11 players

(i) Include 2 particular players $= {}^{16-2}C_{11-2} = {}^{14}C_9 = \frac{14!}{9!5!} = 2002$

[since selection of n objects taken r at a time in which p objects are always included is ${}^{n-p}C_{r-p}$]

(ii) Exclude 2 particular players $= {}^{16-2}C_{11} = {}^{14}C_{11} = \frac{14!}{11!3!} = 364$

[since selection of n objects taken r at a time in which p objects are never included is ${}^{n-p}C_r$]

Q.24 A sports team of 11 students is to be constituted, choosing atleast 5 from class XI and atleast 5 from class XII. If there are 20 students in each of these classes, in how many ways can the team be constituted?

Ans. Total students in each class = 20

We have to select atleast 5 students from each class.

Hence, selection of sports team of 11 students from each class is given in following table

Class XI	5	6
Class XII	6	5

$\therefore$ Total number of ways of selecting a team of 11 players

$= {}^{20}C_5 \times {}^{20}C_6 + {}^{20}C_6 \times {}^{20}C_5 = 2 \times {}^{20}C_5 \times {}^{20}C_6$

Mistake Alert ! *Students should not forget to take the all possible ways of arrangements.*

Q.25 A group consists of 4 girls and 7 boys. In how many ways can a team of 5 members be selected, if the team has

(i) no girls.

(ii) atleast one boy and one girl.

(iii) atleast three girls.

Ans. Number of girls = 4 and Number of boys = 7

We have to select a team of 5 members provided that

(i) team having no girls.

$\therefore$ Required number of ways $= {}^7C_5 = \frac{7!}{5!2!} = \frac{7 \times 6}{2} = 21$

(ii) atleast one boy and one girl

$\therefore$ Required number of ways $= ({}^7C_1 \times {}^4C_4) + ({}^7C_2 \times {}^4C_3) + ({}^7C_3 \times {}^4C_2) + ({}^7C_4 \times {}^4C_1)$

$= (7 \times 1) + (21 \times 4) + (35 \times 6) + (35 \times 4)$

$= 7 + 84 + 210 + 140 = 441$

(iii) when atleast three girls are included $= ({}^4C_3) \times ({}^7C_2) + ({}^4C_4 \times {}^7C_1)$

$\therefore$ Required number of ways $= 4 \times 21 + 7 = 84 + 7 = 91$

Objective Type Questions

Choose the correct answers from the given four options in each exercises 26 to 40.

Q.26 If ${}^nC_{12} = {}^nC_8$, then n is equal to

(a) 20 (b) 12
(c) 6 (d) 30

Ans. (a) Given, ${}^nC_{12} = {}^nC_8$

$\Rightarrow$ ${}^nC_{n-12} = {}^nC_8$ $[\because {}^nC_r = {}^nC_{n-r}]$

$\Rightarrow$ $n - 12 = 8$

$\Rightarrow$ $n = 12 + 8 = 20$

Q.27 The number of possible outcomes when a coin is tossed 6 times is

(a) 36 (b) 64
(c) 12 (d) 32

Ans. (b) Number of outcomes when tossing a coin 1 times = 2 (head or tail)

$\therefore$ Total possible outcomes when a coin is tossed 6 times $= 2^6 = 64$

$[\because 2^n$ for n time tossed coin$]$

Q.28 The number of different four-digit numbers that can be formed with the digits 2, 3, 4, 7 and using each digit only once is

(a) 120 (b) 96 (c) 24 (d) 100

Ans. (c) Given, digits 2, 3, 4 and 7, we have to form four-digit numbers using these digits.

$\therefore$ Required number of ways $= {}^4P_4 = 4! = 4 \times 3 \times 2! = 24$

Q.29 The sum of the digits in unit place of all the numbers formed with the help of 3, 4, 5 and 6 taken all at a time is

(a) 432 (b) 108 (c) 36 (d) 18

Ans. (b) If we fixed 3 at unit place

Total possible number is 3! *i.e.*,6.

Sum of the digits in unit place of all these numbers $= 3! \times 3$

Similarly, if we fixed 4, 5 and 6 at unit place, in each case total possible numbers are 3!.

$\therefore$ Required sum of unit digits of all such numbers $= (3 - 4 + 5 + 6) \times 3!$

$= 18 \times 3! = 18 \times 6 = 108$

Q.30 The total number of words formed by 2 vowels and 3 consonants taken from 4 vowels and 5 consonants is

(a) 60 (b) 120 (c) 7200 (d) 720

Ans. *(c)* Given, total number of vowels = 4

and total number of consonants = 5

Total number of words formed by 2 vowels and 3 consonants

$$= {}^4C_2 \times {}^5C_3 = \frac{4!}{2!2!} \times \frac{5!}{3!2!}$$

$$= \frac{4 \times 3!}{2!2!} \times \frac{5 \times 4 \times 3 \times 2!}{3! \times 2!} = \frac{4 \times 5 \times 4 \times 3}{4}$$

$$= 5 \times 4 \times 3 = 60$$

Permutation of 2 vowel and 3 consonants $= 5! = 5 \times 4 \times 3 \times 2 \times 1 = 120$

So, total number of words $= 60 \times 120 = 7200$

Mistake Alert ! *Please be careful while using either ${}^nC_r$ or ${}^nP_r$. If the things are to be only selected, then use ${}^nC_r$ and if the things are to be arranged, then use ${}^nP_r$.*

Q.31 If a five-digit number divisible by 3 is to be formed using the numbers 0, 1, 2, 3, 4 and 5 without repetitions, then the total number of ways this can be done is

(a) 216 (b) 600 (c) 240 (d) 3125

Ans. *(a)* We know that a number is divisible by 3, when sum of digits in the number must be divisible by 3.

So, if we consider the digits 0, 1, 2, 4, 5, then $0 + 1 + 2 + 4 + 5 = 12$

We see that sum is divisible by 3. Therefore, five-digit numbers using the digits

$$0, 1, 2, 4, 5 = 4 \times 4 \times 3 \times 2 \times 1 = 96$$

4	4	3	2	1

and if we consider the digit 1, 2, 3, 4, 5, then $(1 + 2 + 3 + 4 + 5 = 15)$

This sum is also divisible by 3.

So, five-digit number can be formed using the digits 1, 2, 3, 4, 5 in 5! ways.

$\therefore$ Total number of ways $= 96 + 5! = 96 + 120 = 216$

Q.32 Everybody in a room shakes hands with everybody else. If the total number of hand shakes is 66, then the total number of persons in the room is

(a) 11 (b) 12 (c) 13 (d) 14

Ans. *(b)* Let the total number of persons in the room be n.

We know that two person form 1 hand shake.

$\therefore$ Required number of hand shakes $= {}^nC_2 = \frac{n!}{2!(n-2)!} = \frac{n(n-1)}{2}$ $\left[\because {}^nC_r = \frac{n!}{r!(n-r)!}\right]$

According to the question, $\frac{n(n-1)}{2} = 66$

$\Rightarrow$ $n(n-1) = 132$

$$\Rightarrow \quad n^2 - n - 132 = 0$$
$$\Rightarrow \quad (n-12)(n+11) = 0$$
$$\Rightarrow \quad n = 12, -11$$
$$\therefore \quad n = 12 \qquad [\because n \text{ can't be negative}]$$

Q.33 The number of triangles that are formed by choosing the vertices from a set of 12 points, seven of which lie on the same line is

(a) 105 (b) 15 (c) 175 (d) 185

Ans. *(d)* Total number of triangles formed from 12 points taking 3 at a time = ${}^{12}C_3$

But out of which, 7 points are collinear. So, these 7 points constitute a straight line means no triangle is formed by joining these 7 points.

$\therefore$ Required number of triangles = ${}^{12}C_3 - {}^{7}C_3 = 220 - 35 = 185$

Q.34 The number of parallelograms that can be formed from a set of four parallel lines intersecting another set of three parallel lines is

(a) 6 (b) 18 (c) 12 (d) 9

Ans. *(b)* To form parallelogram we required a pair of line from a set of 4 lines and another pair of line from another set of 3 lines.

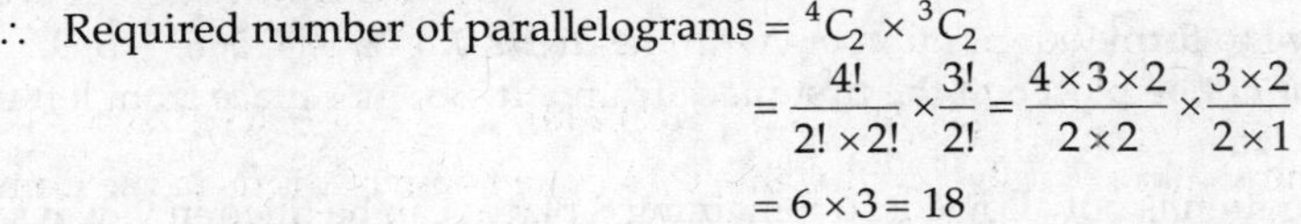

$\therefore$ Required number of parallelograms = ${}^4C_2 \times {}^3C_2$

$$= \frac{4!}{2! \times 2!} \times \frac{3!}{2!} = \frac{4 \times 3 \times 2}{2 \times 2} \times \frac{3 \times 2}{2 \times 1}$$

$$= 6 \times 3 = 18$$

Q.35 The number of ways in which a team of eleven players can be selected from 22 players always including 2 of them and excluding 4 of them is

(a) ${}^{16}C_{11}$ (b) ${}^{16}C_5$ (c) ${}^{16}C_9$ (d) ${}^{20}C_9$

Ans. *(c)* Total number of players = 22

We have to select a team of 11 players. Selection of 11 players when 2 of them is always included and 4 are never included.

Total number of players = 22 – 2 – 4 = 16

$\therefore$ Required number of ways = ${}^{16}C_9$

Q.36 The number of 5-digit telephone numbers having atleast one of their digits repeated is

(a) 90000 (b) 10000

(c) 30240 (d) 69760

Ans. *(d)* If all the digits are repeated, then total number of 5 digit telephone numbers can be formed in 10^5 ways and if no digit is repeated, then 5-digit telephone numbers can be formed in ${}^{10}P_5$ ways.

$\therefore$ Required number of ways = $10^5 - {}^{10}P_5 = 100000 - \frac{10!}{5!}$

$$= 100000 - 10 \times 9 \times 8 \times 7 \times 6$$
$$= 100000 - 30240 = 69760$$

Q.37 The number of ways in which we can choose a committee from four men and six women, so that the committee includes atleast two men and exactly twice as many women as men is

(a) 94 (b) 126 (c) 128 (d) None of these

Ans. ***(a)*** $\because$ Number of men = 4

and number of women = 6

It is given that committee includes two men and exactly twice as many women as men.

Thus, possible selection is given in following table

Men	Women
2	4
3	6

Required number of committee formed $= ({}^4C_2 \times {}^6C_4) + ({}^4C_3 \times {}^6C_6)$

$= (6 \times 15) + (4 \times 1) = 94$

Q.38 The total number of 9-digit numbers which have all different digits is

(a) 10! (b) 9! (c) $9 \times 9!$ (d) $10 \times 10!$

Ans. ***(c)*** We have to form 9-digit numbers with the digits 0, 1, 2, 3, 4, 5, 6, 7, 8, 9. Since, 0 cannot be placed at the first place from left. So, first place from left can be **filled** in 9 ways.

Since, repetition is not allowed, so remaining 8 places can be filled in 9! ways.

$\therefore$ Required number of ways $= 9 \times 9!$

Q.39 The number of words which can be formed out of the letters of the word 'ARTICLE', so that vowels occupy the even place is

(a) 1440 (b) 144 (c) 7! (d) ${}^4C_4 \times {}^3C_3$

Ans. ***(b)*** Total number of letters in the word article is 7, out of which A, E, I are vowels and R, T, C, L are consonants.

Since, it is given that vowels occupy even place, therefore the arrangement of vowels and consonants can be understood with the help of following diagram.

1	2	3	4	5	6	7

Now, vowels can be placed at 2nd, 4th and 6th position.

Therefore, number of arrangements $= {}^3P_3 = 3! = 6$ ways

And consonants can be placed at 1st, 3rd, 5th and 7th position.

Therefore, number of arrangement $= {}^4P_4 = 4! = 24$

$\therefore$ Total number of words $= 6 \times 24 = 144$

Q.40 Given 5 different green dyes, four different blue dyes and three different red dyes, the number of combinations of dyes which can be chosen taking atleast one green and one blue dye is

(a) 3600 (b) 3720

(c) 3800 (d) 3600

Ans. ***(b)*** Possible number of choosing green dyes = 2^5

Possible number of choosing blue dyes = 2^4

Possible number of choosing red dyes = 2^3

If atleast one blue and one green dyes are selected.

Then, total number of combination = $(2^5 - 1)(2^4 - 1) \times 2^3 = 31 \times 15 \times 8 = 3720$

Fill in the blanks in each of exercises of 41-50.

Q.41 If $^nP_r = 840$ and $^nC_r = 35$, then r is equal to ....

Ans. Given, $^nP_r = 840$ and $^nC_r = 35$

$$840 = 35 \times r! \qquad [\because {}^nP_r = {}^nC_r \cdot r!]$$

$$\Rightarrow \quad r! = \frac{840}{35} = 24$$

$$\Rightarrow \quad r! = 4!$$

$$\therefore \quad r = 4$$

Q.42 $^{15}C_8 + {}^{15}C_9 - {}^{15}C_6 - {}^{15}C_7$ is equal to ....

Ans.
$$\begin{aligned} {}^{15}C_8 + {}^{15}C_9 - {}^{15}C_6 - {}^{15}C_7 &= {}^{15}C_{15-8} + {}^{15}C_{15-9} - {}^{15}C_6 - {}^{15}C_7 \qquad [\because {}^nC_r = {}^nC_{n-r}] \\ &= {}^{15}C_7 + {}^{15}C_6 - {}^{15}C_6 - {}^{15}C_7 \\ &= 0 \end{aligned}$$

Q.43 The number of permutations of n different objects, taken r at a time, when repetitions are allowed, is ....

Ans. Number of permutations of n different things taken r at a time when repetition is allowed = $n \times n \times n \ldots r$ times = n^r

Q.44 The number of different words that can be formed from the letters of the word 'INTERMEDIATE' such that two vowels never come together is ....

Thinking process Firstly, we will separate the consonants and vowels and consider each time the set of vowels and consonants as a single letter.

Ans. Total number of letters in the word 'INTERMEDIATE' is 12 out of which 6 are consonants and 6 are vowels. The arrangement of these 12 alphabets in which two vowels never come together can be understood with the help of follow manner.

V	C	V	C	V	C	V	C	V	C	V	C	V

6 consonants out of which 2 are alike can be placed in $\frac{6!}{2!}$ ways and 6 vowels, out of which 3 E's alike and 2 I's are alike can be arranged at seven place in $^7P_6 \times \frac{1}{3!} \times \frac{1}{2!}$ ways.

$$\therefore \text{Total number of words} = \frac{6!}{2!} \times {}^7P_6 \times \frac{1}{3!} \times \frac{1}{2!} = 151200$$

Q.45 Three balls are drawn from a bag containing 5 red, 4 white and 3 black balls. The number of ways in which this can be done, if atleast 2 are red, is ....

Ans. We have 5 red, 4 white and 3 black balls out of which atleast 2 red balls are to be drawn

$\therefore$ Required number of ways $= ({}^5C_2 \times {}^7C_1) + {}^5C_3$

$$= (10 \times 7) + 10$$
$$= 70 + 10 = 80$$

Q.46 The number of six-digit numbers all digits of which are odd, is ....

Ans. Among the digits 0, 1, 2, 3, 4, 5, 6, 7, 8, 9, clearly 1, 3, 5, 7 and 9 are odd.

$\therefore$ Number of six-digit numbers $= 5 \times 5 \times 5 \times 5 \times 5 \times 5 = 5^6$

Q.47 In a football championship, 153 matches were played. Every two teams played one match with each other. The number of teams, participating in the championship is ....

Ans. Let the number of teams participating in championship be n.

Since, it is given that every two teams played one match with each other.

$\therefore$ Total match played $= {}^nC_2$

According to the question,

$${}^nC_2 = 153$$
$$\Rightarrow \quad \frac{n(n-1)}{2} = 153$$
$$\Rightarrow \quad n^2 - n = 306$$
$$\Rightarrow \quad n^2 - n - 306 = 0$$
$$\Rightarrow \quad (n-18)(n+17) = 0$$
$$\Rightarrow \quad n = 18, -17$$
$$n = 18 \quad [\because n \text{ can't be negative}]$$

Hence, the number of teams is 18.

Q.48 The total number of ways in which six '+' and four '–' signs can be arranged in a line such that no two signs '–' occur together, is ....

Ans. The arrangement can be understand with the help of following figure.

–	+	–	+	–	+	–	+	–	+	–	+	–

Thus, '+' sign can be arranged in 1 way because all are identical.

and 4 negative signs can be arranged at 7 places in ${}^7C_4$ ways.

$\therefore$ Total number of ways $= {}^7C_4 \times 1$

$$= \frac{7!}{4!3!} = \frac{7 \times 6 \times 5 \times 4!}{3! \times 4!}$$
$$= \frac{7 \times 6 \times 5}{3 \times 2 \times 1} = 35 \text{ ways}$$

Q.49 **A committee of 6 is to be chosen from 10 men and 7 women, so as to contain atleast 3 men and 2 women. In how many different ways can this be done, if two particular women refuse to serve on the same committee?**

Thinking process (i) First, for at least 3 men and 2 women, the number of ways

$$= {}^{10}C_3 \times {}^7C_3 + {}^{10}C_4 \times {}^7C_2$$

(ii) For 2 particular women to be always there, the number of ways

$$= {}^{10}C_4 \times {}^5C_0 + {}^{10}C_3 \times {}^5C_1$$

(iii) Further, the total number of committee when two particular women are never together = Total number of ways – Number of ways when they are always together.

Ans. $\because$ Total number of men = 10

and total number of women = 7

We have to form a committee containing atleast 3 men and 2 women.

Number of ways $= {}^{10}C_3 \times {}^7C_3 + {}^{10}C_4 \times {}^7C_2$

If two particular women to be always there .

$\therefore$ Number of ways $= {}^{10}C_4 \times {}^5C_0 + {}^{10}C_3 \times {}^5C_1$

Total number of committee when two particular women are never together

= Total number of ways – Number of ways when they are always together.

$= ({}^{10}C_3 \times {}^7C_3 + {}^{10}C_4 \times {}^7C_2) - ({}^{10}C_4 \times {}^5C_0 + {}^{10}C_3 \times {}^5C_1)$

$= (120 \times 35 + 210 \times 21) - (210 + 120 \times 5)$

$= 4200 + 4410 - (210 + 600)$

$= 8610 - 810 = 7800$

Q.50 **A box contains 2 white balls, 3 black balls and 4 red balls. The number of ways three balls be drawn from the box, if atleast one black ball is to be included in the draw is ....**

Ans. Since, there are 2 white, 3 black and 4 red balls. It is given that atleast one black ball is to be included in the draw.

$\therefore$ Required number of ways $= {}^3C_1 \times {}^6C_2 + {}^3C_2 \times {}^6C_1 + {}^3C_3$

$= 3 \times 15 + 3 \times 6 + 1$

$= 45 + 18 + 1 = 64$

State True or False for the following statements in each of the exercises from 51 to 59.

Q.51 **There are 12 points in a plane of which 5 points are collinear, then the number of lines obtained by joining these points in pairs is ${}^{12}C_2 - {}^5C_2$.**

Ans. *False*

Since, 5 points are collinear they will make a line

$\therefore$ Required number of lines $= {}^{12}C_2 - {}^5C_2 + 1$

Q.52 Three letters can be posted in five letter boxes in 3^5 ways.

Ans. *False*

Required number of ways = $5^3 = 125$

(since, to place each letter, there are five boxes.)

Q.53 In the permutations of n things r, taken together, the number of permutations in which m particular things occur together is ${}^{n-m}P_{r-m} \times {}^{r}P_{m}$.

Ans. *False*

Arrangement of n things taken r at a time, in which m things occur together, we considered these m things as 1 group.

Number of object excluding those m objects = $(r - m)$

Now, first, we have to arrange $(r - m + 1)$ objects.

Number of arrangements = $(r - m + 1)!$ and m objects which we consider as 1 group, can be arranged in $m!$ ways.

$\therefore$ Required number of arrangements = $(r - m + 1)! \times m!$

Q.54 In a steamer there are stalls for 12 animals and there are horses, cows and calves (not less than 12 each) ready to be shipped. They can be loaded in 3^{12} ways.

Ans. *True*

There are three types of animals and stalls available for 12 animals.

$\therefore$ Number of ways of loading $= 3^{12}$

Q.55 If some or all of n objects are taken at a time, then the number of combinations is $2^n - 1$.

Ans. *True*

If some or all objects taken at a time, then number of combination will be

$${}^nC_1 + {}^nC_2 + {}^nC_3 + \ldots + {}^nC_n = 2^n - 1 \quad [\because \ {}^nC_0 + {}^nC_1 + {}^nC_2 + \ldots + {}^nC_n = 2^n]$$

Q.56 There will be only 24 selections containing atleast one red ball out of a bag containing 4 red and 5 black balls. It is being given that the balls of the same colour are identical.

Ans. We have 4 red and 5 black balls in a box and atleast one red ball is to be drawn.

$\therefore$ Total number of selection $= [(4 + 1)(5 + 1) - 1] - 5$

$= (5 \times 6 - 1) - 5$

$= (30 - 1) - 5 = 24$

Q.57 Eighteen guests are to be seated, half on each side of a long table. Four particular guests desire to sit on one particular side and three others on other side of the table. The number of ways in which the seating arrangements can be made is $\frac{11!}{5!6!}(9!)(9!)$.

Ans. *True*

After seating 4 on one side and 3 on the other side, we have to select out of 11. Remaining 5 will sit on one side and 6 on the other side out of 11.

Now, number of ways of seating on one half side = $^{(18-4-3)}C_5 \times 9! = {}^{11}C_5 \times 9!$

and the other half side = $^{(11-5)}C_6 \times 9! = {}^6C_6$

$\therefore$ Total arrangements = $^{11}C_5 \times 9! \times {}^6C_6 \times 9!$

$$= \frac{11!}{5!6!} \times 9! \times 1 \times 9!$$

$$= \frac{11!}{5!6!} \times 9! \times 9!$$

Q.58 A candidate is required to answer 7 questions, out of 12 questions which are divided into two groups, each containing 6 questions. He is not permitted to attempt more than 5 questions from either group. He can choose the seven questions in 650 ways.

Ans. *False*

He can attempt questions in following manner

Group (*A*)	2	3	4	5
Group (*B*)	5	4	3	2

Number of ways of attempting 7 questions

$$= {}^6C_2 \times {}^6C_5 + {}^6C_3 \times {}^6C_4 + {}^6C_4 \times {}^6C_3 + {}^6C_5 \times {}^6C_2$$

$$= 2({}^6C_2 \times {}^6C_5 + {}^6C_3 \times {}^6C_4)$$

$$= 2(15 \times 6 + 20 \times 15)$$

$$= 2(90 + 300)$$

$$= 2 \times 390 = 780$$

Q.59 To fill 12 vacancies there are 25 candidates of which 5 are from scheduled castes. If 3 of the vacancies are reserved for scheduled caste candidates while the rest are open to all, the number of ways in which the selection can be made is $^5C_3 \times {}^{20}C_9$.

Ans. *False*

We have to select 3 scheduled caste candidate out of 5 in $^5C_3$ ways.

and we have to select 9 other candidates out of 22 in $^{22}C_9$ ways.

$\therefore$ Total number of ways = $^5C_3 \times {}^{22}C_9$

Match each item given under the column C-I to its correct answer given under the Column C-II.

Q.60 There are 3 books on Mathematics, 4 on Physics and 5 on English. How many different collections can be made such that each collection consists?

Column I	Column II
(i) One book of each subject	(a) 3968
(ii) Atleast one book of each subject	(b) 60
(iii) Atleast one book of English	(c) 3255

Ans. (i) → (b), (ii) → (c), (iii) → (a)

There are three books of Mathematics, 4 of Physics and 5 on English.

(i) One book of each subject $= {}^3C_1 \times {}^4C_1 \times {}^5C_1 = 3 \times 4 \times 5 = 60$

(ii) Atleast one book of each subject $= (2^3 - 1) \times (2^4 - 1) \times (2^5 - 1)$

[∵ if some or all of n object taken at a time, then number of ways $= 2^n - 1$]

$= 7 \times 15 \times 31 = 3255$

(iii) Number of ways of Selection is based on following manner

English book	1	2	3	4	5
Others	11	10	9	8	7

Atleast one book of English $= (2^5 - 1) \times 2^7 = 128 \times 31 = 3968$

Q.61 Five boys and five girls form a line. Find the number of ways of making the seating arrangement under the following condition.

Column I	Column II
(i) Boys and girls alternate	(a) $5! \times 6!$
(ii) No two girls sit together	(b) $10! - 5!\,6!$
(iii) All the girls sit together	(c) $(5!)^2 + (5!)^2$
(iv) All the girls are never together	(d) $2!\,5!\,5!$

Ans. (i) → (c), (ii) → (a), (iii) → (d), (iv) → (b)

(i) Total arrangements when boys and girls sit at alternate positions $= (5!)^2 + (5!)^2$

(ii) Since, no two girls sit together

∴ Arrangement should be

G	B	G	B	G	B	G	B	G	B	G

There are six positions of seating for girls

∴ Required number of ways $= {}^5P_5 \times {}^6P_5 = 5! \times 6!$

(iii) Now, all girls sit together, then they can be consider as one group in which they arrange themselvse in 5! ways and can sit on either side.

$\therefore$ Required number of ways $= 5!\,6!$

(iv) Required number of ways = Total arrangements – number of ways when all the girls sit together

$$= 10! - 5!6!$$

Q.62 There are 10 professors and 20 lecturers, out of whom a committee of 2 professors and 3 lecturers is to be formed. Find

Column I	Column II
(i) in how many ways committee can be formed?	(a) ${}^{10}C_2 \times {}^{19}C_3$
(ii) in how many ways a particular professor is included?	(b) ${}^{10}C_2 \times {}^{19}C_2$
(iii) in how many ways a particular lecturer is included?	(c) ${}^{9}C_1 \times {}^{20}C_3$
(iv) in how many ways a particular lecturer is excluded?	(d) ${}^{10}C_2 \times {}^{20}C_3$

Ans. (i) → (d), (ii) → (c), (iii) → (b), (iv) → (a)

(i) We have is to select 2 professors out of 10 and 3 lecturers out of 20 $= {}^{10}C_2 \times {}^{20}C_3$

(ii) Number of ways when a particular professor is included

$$= {}^{10-1}C_1 \times {}^{20}C_3 = {}^{9}C_1 \times {}^{20}C_3$$

(iii) Number of ways when a particular lecturer is included

$$= {}^{10}C_2 \times {}^{20-1}C_2 = {}^{10}C_2 \times {}^{19}C_2$$

(iv) Number of ways when a particular lecturer is excluded

$$= {}^{10}C_2 \times {}^{20-1}C_3 = {}^{10}C_2 \times {}^{19}C_3$$

Q.63 Using the digits 1, 2, 3, 4, 5, 6, 7, a number of 4 different digits is formed. Find

Column I	Column II
(i) how many numbers are formed?	(a) 840
(ii) how many numbers are exactly divisible by 2?	(b) 200
(iii) how many numbers are exactly divisible by 25?	(c) 360
(iv) how many of these are exactly divisible by 4?	(d) 40

Ans. (i)→ (a), (ii) → (c), (iii)→ (d), (iv) → (b)

(i) Total numbers of 4 digit formed with digits 1, 2, 3, 4, 5, 6, 7 $= {}^{7}P_4$

$$= \frac{7!}{(7-4)!} = \frac{7\times6\times5\times4\times3!}{3!} = 7\times6\times5\times4 = 840$$

(ii) When a number is divisible by 2. At its unit place only even numbers occurs.

$\therefore$ Total numbers $= 4 \times 5 \times 6 \times 3 = 360$

(iii) A number is divisible by 25 if last two digits is divisible by 25

Since, from the given digits only 25 and 75 are divisible by 25.

So,

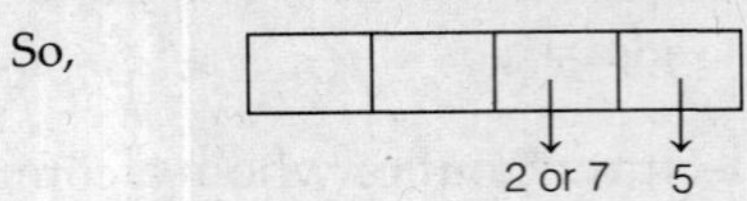

$\therefore$ Total numbers divisible by 25 $= 5 \times 4 \times 2 \times 1 = 40$

$\therefore$ Choice for unit place is only 5 and choice for tens place are 2 and 7.

(iv) A number is divisible by 4, If its last two digit is divisible by 4.

Number of 4-digit number divisible by 4

= Number ending with 12, 16, 24, 32, 36, 64, 72, 76, 52, 56.

Now, number ending with 12

$4 \times 5 \times 1 \times 1 = 20$

Similarly, numbers ending with other numbers (16, 24, 32 .... 56) = 20 (for each)

$\therefore$ Required number $= 10 \times 20 = 200$

Q.64 How many words (with or without dictionary meaning) can be made from the letters of the word MONDAY, assuming that no letter is repeated, if

Column I	Column II
(i) 4 letters are used at a time.	(a) 720
(ii) All letters are used at a time	(b) 240
(iii) All letters are used but the first is a vowel.	(c) 360

Ans. (i)$\rightarrow$ (c), (ii) $\rightarrow$ (a); (iii) $\rightarrow$ (b).

(i) Number of words when 4 letters are used at a time

$$= {}^6P_4 = \frac{6!}{2!} = 6 \times 5 \times 4 \times 3 = 360$$

(ii) Number of words when all letters used at a time

$$= {}^6P_6 = 6! = 6 \times 5 \times 4 \times 3 \times 2 \times 1 = 720$$

(iii) Number of words when all letters used but first is vowel

$$= {}^2P_1 \times 5! = 2 \times 5! = 2 \times 5 \times 4 \times 3 \times 2 \times 1 = 240$$

Chapter

08

Binomial Theorem

Short Answer Type Questions

***Q.1** Find the term independent of x, where $x \neq 0$, in the expansion of $\left(\frac{3x^2}{2} - \frac{1}{3x}\right)^{15}$.

Thinking Process The general term in the expansion of $(x-a)^n$ *i.e.*, $T_{r+1} = {}^nC_r (x)^{n-r}(-a)^r$. For the term independent of x, put $n - r = 0$, then we get the value of r.

Ans. Given expression is $\left(\frac{3x^2}{2} - \frac{1}{3x}\right)^{15}$.

Let T_{r+1} term is the general term.

Then,
$$T_{r+1} = {}^{15}C_r \left(\frac{3x^2}{2}\right)^{15-r} \left(-\frac{1}{3x}\right)^r$$
$$= {}^{15}C_r \, 3^{15-r} \, x^{30-2r} \, 2^{r-15} \, (-1)^r \cdot 3^{-r} \cdot x^{-r}$$
$$= {}^{15}C_r (-1)^r \, 3^{15-2r} 2^{r-15} x^{30-3r}$$

For the term independent of x,
$$30 - 3r = 0$$
$$3r = 30 \Rightarrow r = 10$$

On putting the value of $r = 10$ in the above expansion, we get
$$T_{r+1} = T_{10+1} = 11\text{th term is independent of } x.$$
$$\therefore \quad T_{10+1} = {}^{15}C_{10} (-1)^{10} \, 3^{15-20} \, 2^{10-15}$$
$$= {}^{15}C_{10} \, 3^{-5} \, 2^{-5}$$
$$= {}^{15}C_{10} (6)^{-5} = {}^{15}C_{10} \left(\frac{1}{6}\right)^5$$

***Q.2** If the term free from x in the expansion of $\left(\sqrt{x} - \frac{k}{x^2}\right)^{10}$ is 405, then find the value of k.

Ans. Given expression is $\left(\sqrt{x} - \frac{k}{x^2}\right)^{10}$.

(✱) Topics related to these question have been removed from latest NCERT.

Let T_{r+1} is the general term.

Then, $$T_{r+1} = {}^{10}C_r(\sqrt{x})^{10-r}\left(\frac{-k}{x^2}\right)^r$$

$$= {}^{10}C_r(x)^{\frac{1}{2}(10-r)}(-k)^r \cdot x^{-2r}$$

$$= {}^{10}C_r\, x^{5-\frac{r}{2}}(-k)^r \cdot x^{-2r}$$

$$= {}^{10}C_r\, x^{5-\frac{r}{2}-2r}(-k)^r$$

$$= {}^{10}C_r\, x^{\frac{10-5r}{2}}(-k)^r$$

For the term independent of x, $\frac{10-5r}{2} = 0$

$\Rightarrow$ $10-5r = 0$

$\Rightarrow$ $r = 2$

On puting the value of $r = 2$ in about expansion, we get

Since, $T_{2+1} = T_3$ is independent of x.

$\therefore$ $T_{2+1} = {}^{10}C_2(-k)^2 = 405$

$\Rightarrow$ $\frac{10 \times 9 \times 8!}{2! \times 8!}(-k)^2 = 405$

$\Rightarrow$ $45k^2 = 405$

$\Rightarrow$ $k^2 = \frac{405}{45} = 9$

$\therefore$ $k = \pm 3$

Mistake Alert ! *While solving this question, students may use the wrong formula of general term like* $(a+b)^n = {}^nC_r(b)^{n-r}a^r$ *instead of* ${}^nC_r\, a^{n-r}b^r$.

Q.3 Find the coefficient of x in the expansion of $(1-3x+7x^2)(1-x)^{16}$.

Ans. Given, expression $= (1-3x+7x^2)(1-x)^{16}$.

$$= (1-3x+7x^2)({}^{16}C_0 1^{16} - {}^{16}C_1 1^{15}x^1 + {}^{16}C_2 1^{14}x^2 + \ldots + {}^{16}C_{16}\, x^{16})$$

$$= (1-3x+7x^2)(1-16x+120x^2+\ldots)$$

$\therefore$ Coefficient of $x = -3-16 = -19$

***Q.4** Find the term independent of x in the expansion of $\left(3x - \frac{2}{x^2}\right)^{15}$.

Thinking Process The general term in the expansion of $(x-a)^n$ i.e., $T_{r+1} = {}^nC_r(x)^{n-r}(-a)^r$.

Ans. Given expression is $\left(3x - \frac{2}{x^2}\right)^{15}$.

Let T_{r+1} is the general term.

(*) Topics related to these question have been removed from latest NCERT.

$$\therefore \quad T_{r+1} = {}^{15}C_r(3x)^{15-r}\left(\frac{-2}{x^2}\right)^r = {}^{15}C_r(3x)^{15-r}(-2)^r x^{-2r}$$

$$= {}^{15}C_r 3^{15-r} x^{15-3r}(-2)^r \qquad \text{...(i)}$$

For the term independent of x, $15 - 3r = 0 \Rightarrow r = 5$

On putting $r = 5$ in Eq. (i), we get

$$T_{5+1} = T_6 \text{ is independent of } x.$$

$$\therefore \quad T_{5+1} = {}^{15}C_5\, 3^{15-5}(-2)^5$$

$$= -\frac{15 \times 14 \times 13 \times 12 \times 11 \times 10!}{5 \times 4 \times 3 \times 2 \times 1 \times 10!} \times 3^{10} \times 2^5$$

$$= -3003 \times 3^{10} \times 2^5$$

*** Q.5** Find the middle term (terms) in the expansion of

(i) $\left(\frac{x}{a} - \frac{a}{x}\right)^{10}$ (ii) $\left(3x - \frac{x^3}{6}\right)^9$

- **Concept Insight** In the expansion of $(a + b)^n$, if n is even, then this expansion has only one middle term *i.e.*, $\left(\frac{n}{2} + 1\right)$th term is the middle term and if n is odd, then this expansion has two middle terms *i.e.*, $\left(\frac{n+1}{2}\right)$th and $\left(\frac{n+1}{2} + 1\right)$th are two middle terms.

Ans. (i) Given expression is $\left(\frac{x}{a} - \frac{a}{x}\right)^{10}$.

Here, the power of binomial expression *i.e.*, $n = 10$ is even.

Since, it has one middle term $\left(\frac{10}{2} + 1\right)$th term *i.e.*, 6th term.

$$\therefore \quad T_6 = T_{5+1} = {}^{10}C_5\left(\frac{x}{a}\right)^{10-5}\left(\frac{-a}{x}\right)^5$$

$$= -{}^{10}C_5\left(\frac{x}{a}\right)^5\left(\frac{a}{x}\right)^5$$

$$= -\frac{10 \times 9 \times 8 \times 7 \times 6 \times 5!}{5! \times 5 \times 4 \times 3 \times 2 \times 1}\left(\frac{x}{a}\right)^5\left(\frac{x}{a}\right)^{-5}$$

$$= -9 \times 4 \times 7 = -252$$

(ii) Given expression is $\left(3x - \frac{x^3}{6}\right)^9$.

Here, $n = 9$ is odd.

Since, the Binomial expansion has two middle terms *i.e.*, $\left(\frac{9+1}{2}\right)$th and $\left(\frac{9+1}{2} + 1\right)$th

i.e., 5th term and 6th term.

$$\therefore \quad T_5 = T_{(4+1)} = {}^9C_4(3x)^{9-4}\left(-\frac{x^3}{6}\right)^4$$

(*) Topics related to these question have been removed from latest NCERT.

$$= \frac{9 \times 8 \times 7 \times 6 \times 5!}{4 \times 3 \times 2 \times 1 \times 5!} 3^5 x^5 x^{12} 6^{-4}$$

$$= \frac{7 \times 6 \times 3 \times 3^1}{2^4} x^{17} = \frac{189}{8} x^{17}$$

$$T_6 = T_{5+1} = {}^9C_5 (3x)^{9-5} \left(-\frac{x^3}{6}\right)^5$$

$$\therefore \quad = -\frac{9 \times 8 \times 7 \times 6 \times 5!}{5! \times 4 \times 3 \times 2 \times 1} \cdot 3^4 \cdot x^4 \cdot x^{15} \cdot 6^{-5}$$

$$= \frac{-21 \times 6}{3 \times 2^5} x^{19} = \frac{-21}{16} x^{19}$$

***Q.6** Find the coefficient of x^{15} in the expansion of $(x - x^2)^{10}$.

Ans. Given expression is $(x - x^2)^{10}$.

Let the term T_{r+1} is the general term.

$$\therefore \quad T_{r+1} = {}^{10}C_r x^{10-r} (-x^2)^r$$

$$= (-1)^r \cdot {}^{10}C_r \cdot x^{10-r} \cdot x^{2r}$$

$$= (-1)^r \, {}^{10}C_r \, x^{10+r}$$

For the coefficient of x^{15},

$$10 + r = 15 \Rightarrow r = 5$$

On putting $r = 5$ in Eq. (i), we get

$$T_{5+1} = (-1)^5 \, {}^{10}C_5 \, x^{15}$$

$$\therefore \quad \text{Coefficient of } x^{15} = -\frac{10 \times 9 \times 8 \times 7 \times 6 \times 5!}{5 \times 4 \times 3 \times 2 \times 1 \times 5!}$$

$$= -3 \times 2 \times 7 \times 6 = -252$$

***Q. 7** Find the coefficient of $\frac{1}{x^{17}}$ in the expansion of $\left(x^4 - \frac{1}{x^3}\right)^{15}$.

Thinking Process In this type of questions, first of all find the general term in the expansion $(x - y)^n$ using the formula $T_{r+1} = {}^nC_r x^{n-r} (-y)^r$ and then put $n - r$ equal to the required power of x of which coefficient is to be find out.

Ans. Given expression is $\left(x^4 - \frac{1}{x^3}\right)^{15}$.

Let the term T_{r+1} contains the coefficient of $\frac{1}{x^{17}}$ *i.e.*, x^{-17}.

$$\therefore \quad T_{r+1} = {}^{15}C_r (x^4)^{15-r} \left(-\frac{1}{x^3}\right)^r$$

$$= {}^{15}C_r \, x^{60-4r} (-1)^r x^{-3r}$$

$$= {}^{15}C_r \, x^{60-7r} (-1)^r \quad \text{...(i)}$$

For the coefficient of x^{-17},

$$60 - 7r = -17$$

(*) Topics related to these question have been removed from latest NCERT.

$\Rightarrow \quad 7r = 77 \Rightarrow r = 11$

On putting $r = 11$ in Eq. (i), we get

$$T_{11+1} = {}^{15}C_{11}\, x^{60-77}(-1)^{11} = -{}^{15}C_{11}\, x^{-17}$$

$$\therefore \quad \text{Coefficient of } x^{-17} = -\frac{15!}{11!\,4!} = \frac{-15 \times 14 \times 13 \times 12 \times 11!}{11! \times 4 \times 3 \times 2 \times 1}$$

$$= -15 \times 7 \times 13 = -1365$$

***Q.8** Find the sixth term of the expansion $(y^{1/2} + x^{1/3})^n$, if the Binomial coefficient of the third term from the end is 45.

Thinking process Binomial coefficients of the third term from the end = Binomial coefficients of third term from the beginning = ${}^nC_2$.

Ans. Given expression is $(y^{1/2} + x^{1/3})^n$.

The sixth term of the expansion of $(y^{1/2} + x^{1/3})$ is

$$T_6 = T_{5+1} = {}^nC_5 (y^{1/2})^{n-5} (x^{1/3})^5 \quad \text{...(i)}$$

Now, given that the Binomial coefficient of the third term from the end is 45.

We know that the Binomial coefficient of third term from the end = Binomial coefficient of third term from the begining = ${}^nC_2$

$\because \quad {}^nC_2 = 45$

$\Rightarrow \quad \dfrac{n(n-1)(n-2)!}{2!(n-2)!} = 45$

$\Rightarrow \quad n(n-1) = 90$

$\Rightarrow \quad n^2 - n - 90 = 0$

$\Rightarrow \quad n^2 - 10n + 9n - 90 = 0$

$\Rightarrow \quad n(n-10) + 9(n-10) = 0$

$\Rightarrow \quad (n-10)(n+9) = 0$

$\Rightarrow \quad (n+9) = 0 \text{ or } (n-10) = 0$

$\therefore \quad n = 10 \quad$ [$\because$ n can't be negative]

On putting $n = 10$ in Eq. (i), we get

$$T_6 = {}^{10}C_5\, y^{5/2}\, x^{5/3} = 252 y^{5/2} \cdot x^{5/3}$$

***Q.9** Find the value of r, if the coefficients of $(2r+4)$th and $(r-2)$th terms in the expansion of $(1+x)^{18}$ are equal.

Thinking Process The coefficient of $(r+1)$th term in the expansion of $(1+x)^n$ is ${}^nC_r$. Use this formula to solve the above problem.

Ans. Given expression is $(1+x)^{18}$.

Now, $(2r+4)$th term *i.e.*, T_{2r+3+1}.

$$\therefore \quad T_{2r+3+1} = {}^{18}C_{2r+3}(1)^{18-2r-3}(x)^{2r+3}$$

$$= {}^{18}C_{2r+3}\, x^{2r+3}$$

Now, $(r-2)$th term *i.e.*, T_{r-3+1}.

(*) Topics related to these question have been removed from latest NCERT.

$\therefore \quad T_{r-3+1} = {}^{18}C_{r-3}\, x^{r-3}$

As, $\quad {}^{18}C_{2r+3} = {}^{18}C_{r-3}$

$\Rightarrow \quad 2r + 3 + r - 3 = 18 \quad [\because {}^nC_x = {}^nC_y \Rightarrow x + y = n]$

$\Rightarrow \quad 3r = 18$

$\therefore \quad r = 6$

***Q.10** If the coefficient of second, third and fourth terms in the expansion of $(1+x)^{2n}$ are in AP, then show that $2n^2 - 9n + 7 = 0$.

Thinking Process In the expansion of $(x+y)^n$, the coefficient of $(r+1)$th term is ${}^nC_r$. Use this formula to get the required coefficient. If a, b and c are in AP, then $2b = a + c$.

Ans. Given expression is $(1+x)^{2n}$.

Now, Coefficient of 2nd term $= {}^{2n}C_1$

Coefficient of 3rd term $= {}^{2n}C_2$

Coefficient of 4th term $= {}^{2n}C_3$

Given that ${}^{2n}C_1$, ${}^{2n}C_2$ and ${}^{2n}C_3$ are in AP.

Then, $2 \cdot {}^{2n}C_2 = {}^{2n}C_1 + {}^{2n}C_3$

$$\Rightarrow \quad 2\left[\frac{2n(2n-1)(2n-2)!}{2 \times 1 \times (2n-2)!}\right] = \frac{2n(2n-1)!}{(2n-1)!} + \frac{2n(2n-1)(2n-2)(2n-3)!}{3!(2n-3)!}$$

$$\Rightarrow \quad n(2n-1) = n + \frac{n(2n-1)(2n-2)}{6}$$

$$\Rightarrow \quad n(12n-6) = n(6 + 4n^2 - 4n - 2n + 2)$$

$$\Rightarrow \quad 12n - 6 = (4n^2 - 6n + 8)$$

$$\Rightarrow \quad 6(2n-1) = 2(2n^2 - 3n + 4)$$

$$\Rightarrow \quad 3(2n-1) = 2n^2 - 3n + 4$$

$$\Rightarrow \quad 2n^2 - 3n + 4 - 6n + 3 = 0$$

$$\Rightarrow \quad 2n^2 - 9n + 7 = 0$$

Hence proved.

Q.11 Find the coefficient of x^4 in the expansion of $(1 + x + x^2 + x^3)^{11}$.

Thinking Process First of all, reduce the expansion $(1 + x + x^2 + x^3)^{11}$ into a binomial expression by using factorisation.

Ans. Given, expression $= (1 + x + x^2 + x^3)^{11} = [(1+x) + x^2(1+x)]^{11}$

$= [(1+x)(1+x^2)]^{11} = (1+x)^{11} \cdot (1+x^2)^{11}$

Now, above expression becomes

$= ({}^{11}C_0 + {}^{11}C_1 x + {}^{11}C_2 x^2 + {}^{11}C_3 x^3 + {}^{11}C_4 x^4 + \ldots + {}^{11}C_{11} x^{11})$
$({}^{11}C_0 + {}^{11}C_1 x^2 + {}^{11}C_2 x^4 + \ldots + {}^{11}C_{11} x^{22})$

$= (1 + 11x + 55x^2 + 165x^3 + 330x^4 + \ldots + x^{11})(1 + 11x^2 + 55x^4 + \ldots + x^{22})$

$\therefore$ Coefficient of $x^4 = 55 + 605 + 330 = 990$

(*) Topics related to these question have been removed from latest NCERT.

Long Answer Type Questions

***Q.12** If p is a real number and the middle term in the expansion of $\left(\frac{p}{2}+2\right)^8$ is 1120, find p.

Thinking Process The middle term of the Binomial expression $(x \pm a)^n$ is $\left(\frac{n}{2}+1\right)$th, if n is even and $\left(\frac{n+1}{1}\right)$th and $\left(\frac{n+3}{2}\right)$th if n is odd

Ans. Given expression is $\left(\frac{p}{2}+2\right)^8$.

Here, $n = 8$

Since, this Binomial expansion has only one middle term *i.e.*, $\left(\frac{8}{2}+1\right)$th = 5th term

$$T_5 = T_{4+1} = {}^8C_4\left(\frac{p}{2}\right)^{8-4} \cdot 2^4$$

$$\Rightarrow \quad 1120 = {}^8C_4\, p^4 \cdot 2^{-4}\, 2^4$$

$$\Rightarrow \quad 1120 = \frac{8 \times 7 \times 6 \times 5 \times 4!}{4! \times 4 \times 3 \times 2 \times 1} p^4$$

$$\Rightarrow \quad 1120 = 7 \times 2 \times 5 \times p^4$$

$$\Rightarrow \quad p^4 = \frac{1120}{70} = 16 \Rightarrow p^4 = 2^4$$

$$\Rightarrow \quad p^2 = 4 \Rightarrow p = \pm 2$$

***Q.13** Show that the middle term in the expansion of $\left(x - \frac{1}{x}\right)^{2n}$ is

$$\frac{1 \times 3 \times 5 \times \ldots \times (2n-1)}{n!} \times (-2)^n.$$

Ans. Given expression is $\left(x - \frac{1}{x}\right)^{2n}$. This Binomial expression has even power. So, this has one middle term.

i.e., $\left(\frac{2n}{2}+1\right)$th term $= (n+1)$th term

$$T_{n+1} = {}^{2n}C_n (x)^{2n-n}\left(-\frac{1}{x}\right)^n = {}^{2n}C_n\, x^n (-1)^n x^{-n}$$

$$= {}^{2n}C_n (-1)^n = (-1)^n \frac{(2n)!}{n!\,n!}$$

$$= \frac{1 \cdot 2 \cdot 3 \cdot 4 \cdot 5 \ldots (2n-1)(2n)}{n!\,n!}(-1)^n$$

$$= \frac{1 \cdot 3 \cdot 5 \ldots (2n-1) \cdot 2 \cdot 4 \cdot 6 \ldots (2n)}{1 : 2 \cdot 3 \cdot \ldots n (n!)}(-1)^n$$

(*) Topics related to these question have been removed from latest NCERT.

$$= \frac{1\cdot 3\cdot 5 ...(2n-1) . 2^n (1\cdot 2\cdot 3 ... n)(-1)^n}{(1\cdot 2\cdot 3 ... n)(n!)}$$

$$= \frac{[1\cdot 3\cdot 5 ... (2n-1)]}{n!}(-2)^n$$ **Hence proved.**

Mistake Alert ! When solving this question be careful while using the middle-term. Students may use the formula of middle term of odd number instead of even number.

****Q.14*** Find n in the Binomial $\left(\sqrt[3]{2} + \frac{1}{\sqrt[3]{3}}\right)^n$, if the ratio of 7th term from the beginning to the 7th term from the end is $\frac{1}{6}$.

Ans. Given, the Binomial expression is $\left(\sqrt[3]{2} + \frac{1}{\sqrt[3]{3}}\right)^n$.

Now, 7th term from the beginning $T_7 = T_{6+1} = {}^nC_6(\sqrt[3]{2})^{n-6}\left(\frac{1}{\sqrt[3]{3}}\right)^6$ ...(i)

and 7th term from the end *i.e.*, T_7 from the beginning of $\left(\frac{1}{\sqrt[3]{3}} + \sqrt[3]{2}\right)^n$

i.e., $$T_7' = {}^nC_6\left(\frac{1}{\sqrt[3]{3}}\right)^{n-6}(\sqrt[3]{2})^6$$ ...(ii)

Since, $\frac{T_7}{T_7'} = \frac{1}{6}$

$\therefore$ $$\frac{{}^nC_6(\sqrt[3]{2})^{n-6}\left(\frac{1}{\sqrt[3]{3}}\right)^6}{{}^nC_6\left(\frac{1}{\sqrt[3]{3}}\right)^{n-6}(\sqrt[3]{2})^6} = \frac{1}{6}$$ [from Eqs. (i) and (ii)]

$\Rightarrow$ $$\frac{2^{\frac{n-6}{3}} \cdot 3^{-6/3}}{3^{-\left(\frac{n-6}{3}\right)} . 2^{6/3}} = \frac{1}{6}$$

$\Rightarrow$ $$\left(2^{\frac{n-6}{3}} \cdot 2^{\frac{-6}{3}}\right)\left(3^{\frac{-6}{3}} \cdot 3^{\frac{(n-6)}{3}}\right) = 6^{-1}$$

$\Rightarrow$ $$\left(2^{\frac{n-6}{3} - \frac{6}{3}}\right) . \left(3^{\frac{n-6}{3} - \frac{6}{3}}\right) = 6^{-1} \Rightarrow (2\cdot 3)^{\frac{n}{3} - 4} = 6^{-1}$$

$$(6)^{n/3 - 4} = 6^{-1}$$

$\Rightarrow$ $$\frac{n}{3} - 4 = -1 \Rightarrow \frac{n}{3} = 3$$ [comparing on both sides]

$\therefore$ $$n = 9$$

Q.15 In the expansion of $(x+a)^n$, if the sum of odd terms is denoted by O and the sum of even term by E. Then, prove that

(i) $O^2 - E^2 = (x^2 - a^2)^n$. (ii) $4\,OE = (x+a)^{2n} - (x-a)^{2n}$.

(✱) Topics related to these question have been removed from latest NCERT.

Ans. (i) Given expression is $(x + a)^n$.

$\therefore\ (x + a)^n = {}^nC_0\, x^n a^0 + {}^nC_1 x^{n-1} a^1 + {}^nC_2 x^{n-2} a^2 + {}^nC_3 x^{n-3} a^3 + \dots + {}^nC_n a^n$

Now, sum of odd terms

i.e., $O = {}^nC_0 x^n + {}^nC_2 x^{n-2} a^2 + \dots$

And sum of even terms

i.e., $E = {}^nC_1 x^{n-1} a + {}^nC_3 x^{n-3} a^3 + \dots$

$\because\ (x + a)^n = O + E$ ...(i)

Similarly, $(x - a)^n = O - E$ ...(ii)

$\therefore\ (O + E)(O - E) = (x + a)^n (x - a)^n$ [multiplying Eqs. (i) and (ii)]

$\Rightarrow\ O^2 - E^2 = (x^2 - a^2)^n$

(ii) $4\,OE = (O + E)^2 - (O - E)^2 = [(x + a)^n]^2 - [(x - a)^n]^2$ [from Eqs. (i) and (ii)]

$= (x + a)^{2n} - (x - a)^{2n}$

***Q.16** If x^p occurs in the expansion of $\left(x^2 + \dfrac{1}{x}\right)^{2n}$, then prove that its coefficient is $\dfrac{2n!}{\dfrac{(4n-p)!}{3!}\,\dfrac{(2n+p)!}{3!}}$.

Ans. Given expression is $\left(x^2 + \dfrac{1}{x}\right)^{2n}$.

Let x^p occurs in the expansion of $\left(x^2 + \dfrac{1}{x}\right)^{2n}$.

Now, $T_{r+1} = {}^{2n}C_r (x^2)^{2n-r} \left(\dfrac{1}{x}\right)^r = {}^{2n}C_r\, x^{4n-2r} x^{-r} = {}^{2n}C_r\, x^{4n-3r}$

Let $4n - 3r = p$

$\Rightarrow\ 3r = 4n - p$

$\Rightarrow\ r = \dfrac{4n-p}{3}$

$\therefore$ Coefficient of $x^p = {}^{2n}C_r = \dfrac{(2n)!}{r!\,(2n-r)!} = \dfrac{(2n)!}{\left(\dfrac{4n-p}{3}\right)!\left(2n - \dfrac{4n-p}{3}\right)!}$

$= \dfrac{(2n)!}{\left(\dfrac{4n-p}{3}\right)!\left(\dfrac{6n-4n+p}{3}\right)!} = \dfrac{(2n)!}{\left(\dfrac{4n-p}{3}\right)!\left(\dfrac{2n+p}{3}\right)!}$

Hence proved.

***Q.17** Find the term independent of x in the expansion of

$$(1 + x + 2x^3)\left(\frac{3}{2}x^2 - \frac{1}{3x}\right)^9.$$

Ans. Given expression is $(1 + x + 2x^3)\left(\dfrac{3}{2}x^2 - \dfrac{1}{3x}\right)^9$.

(*) Topics related to these question have been removed from latest NCERT.

Now, consider $\left(\frac{3}{2}x^2 - \frac{1}{3x}\right)^9$

$$T_{r+1} = {}^9C_r\left(\frac{3}{2}x^2\right)^{9-r}\left(-\frac{1}{3x}\right)^r$$

$$= {}^9C_r\left(\frac{3}{2}\right)^{9-r} x^{18-2r}\left(-\frac{1}{3}\right)^r x^{-r} = {}^9C_r\left(\frac{3}{2}\right)^{9-r}\left(-\frac{1}{3}\right)^r x^{18-3r}$$

Hence, the general term in the expansion of $(1 + x + 2x^3)\left(\frac{3}{2}x^2 - \frac{1}{3x}\right)^9$

$$= {}^9C_r\left(\frac{3}{2}\right)^{9-r}\left(-\frac{1}{3}\right)^r x^{18-3r} + {}^9C_r\left(\frac{3}{2}\right)^{9-r}\left(-\frac{1}{3}\right)^r x^{19-3r} + 2\cdot\left[{}^9C_r\left(\frac{3}{2}\right)^{9-r}\left(-\frac{1}{3}\right)^r x^{21-3r}\right]$$

For term independent of x, putting $18 - 3r = 0$, $19 - 3r = 0$ and $21 - 3r = 0$, we get

$$r = 6,\ r = 19/3,\ r = 7$$

So, the possible value of r are 6 and 7. [$\because r$ can't be fraction]

$\therefore$ The term independent of x is ${}^9C_6\left(\frac{3}{2}\right)^{9-6}\left(-\frac{1}{3}\right)^6 + 2\cdot{}^9C_7\frac{3^{9-7}}{2}\left(-\frac{1}{3}\right)^7$

$$= \frac{9\times8\times7\times6!}{6!\times3\times2}\cdot\frac{3^3}{2^3}\cdot\frac{1}{3^6} - 2\cdot\frac{9\times8\times7!}{7!\times2\times1}\cdot\frac{3^2}{2^2}\cdot\frac{1}{3^7}$$

$$= \frac{84}{8}\cdot\frac{1}{3^3} - \frac{36}{4}\cdot\frac{2}{3^5} = \frac{7}{18} - \frac{2}{27} = \frac{21-4}{54} = \frac{17}{54}$$

Choose the correct answers from the given four options in each exercise 18 to 24 question.

Q.18 The total number of terms in the expansion of $(x + a)^{100} + (x - a)^{100}$ after simplification is

(a) 50 (b) 202 (c) 51 (d) None of these

Ans. ***(c)*** We have, $(x + a)^{100} + (x - a)^{100}$

Number of terms in the expansion of $(x + a)^{100} = 101$

Number of terms in the expansion of $(x - a)^{100} = 101$

Now, 50 terms of $(x + a)^{100}$ cancel out negative 50 terms of $(x - a)^{100}$.

So, the remaining 51 terms of $(x + a)^{100}$ get added to the 51 terms of $(x - a)^{100}$.

***Q.19** If the integers $r > 1$, $n > 2$; and coefficients of $(3r)^{\text{th}}$ and $(r + 2)$nd terms in the Binomial expansion of $(1 + x)^{2n}$ are equal, then

(a) $n = 2r$ (b) $n = 3r$ (c) $n = 2r + 1$ (d) None of these

Thinking Process In the expansion of $(x + y)^n$, the coefficient of $(r + 1)$th term is ${}^nC_r$.

Ans. ***(a)*** Given that $r > 1$, $n > 2$ and the coefficients of $(3r)$th and $(r + 2)$nd term are equal in the expansion of $(1 + x)^{2n}$.

Then, $$T_{3r} = T_{3r-1+1} = {}^{2n}C_{3r-1}\, x^{3r-1}$$

and $$T_{r+2} = T_{r+1+1} = {}^{2n}C_{r+1}\, x^{r+1}$$

(*) Topics related to these question have been removed from latest NCERT.

Given, $^{2n}C_{3r-1} = {}^{2n}C_{r+1}$

$\Rightarrow$ $3r - 1 + r + 1 = 2n$ $[\because {}^nC_x = {}^nC_y \Rightarrow x + y = n]$

$\Rightarrow$ $4r = 2n$

$\Rightarrow$ $n = \frac{4r}{2}$

$\therefore$ $n = 2r$

***Q.20** The two successive terms in the expansion of $(1 + x)^{24}$ whose coefficients are in the ratio 1 : 4 are

(a) 3rd and 4th (b) 4th and 5th (c) 5th and 6th (d) 6th and 7th

Ans. ***(c)*** Let two successive terms in the expansion of $(1 + x)^{24}$ be $(r + 1)$th and $(r + 2)$th terms.

$\therefore$ $T_{r+1} = {}^{24}C_r\, x^r$

and $T_{r+2} = {}^{24}C_{r+1}\, x^{r+1}$

Given, $\frac{^{24}C_r}{^{24}C_{r+1}} = \frac{1}{4}$

$$\Rightarrow \frac{\frac{(24)!}{r!(24-r)!}}{\frac{(24)!}{(r+1)!(24-r-1)!}} = \frac{1}{4}$$

$$\Rightarrow \frac{(r+1)\,r!\,(23-r)!}{r!(24-r)\,(23-r)!} = \frac{1}{4}$$

$$\Rightarrow \frac{r+1}{24-r} = \frac{1}{4} \Rightarrow 4r + 4 = 24 - r$$

$$\Rightarrow 5r = 20 \Rightarrow r = 4$$

$$\therefore T_{4+1} = T_5 \text{ and } T_{4+2} = T_6$$

Hence, the two successive terms are 5th and 6th terms.

***Q.21** The coefficient of x^n in the expansion of $(1 + x)^{2n}$ and $(1 + x)^{2n-1}$ are in the ratio

(a) 1 : 2 (b) 1 : 3

(c) 3 : 1 (d) 2 : 1

Ans. ***(d)*** Since, Coefficient of x^n in the expansion of $(1 + x)^{2n} = {}^{2n}C_n$ and coefficient of x^n in the expansion of $(1 + x)^{2n-1} = {}^{2n-1}C_n$

$$\because \frac{^{2n}C_n}{^{2n-1}C_n} = \frac{\frac{(2n)!}{n!\,n!}}{\frac{(2n-1)!}{n!(n-1)!}} = \frac{(2n)!\,n!\,(n-1)!}{n!\,n!\,(2n-1)!}$$

$$= \frac{2n\,(2n-1)!\,n!\,(n-1)!}{n!\,n\,(n-1)!\,(2n-1)!}$$

$$= \frac{2n}{n} = \frac{2}{1} = 2:1$$

(✱) Topics related to these question have been removed from latest NCERT.

Q.22 If the coefficients of 2nd, 3rd and the 4th terms in the expansion of $(1+x)^n$ are in AP, then the value of n is

(a) 2 (b) 7
(c) 11 (d) 14

Ans. ***(b)*** Since, the expansion of $(1+x)^n$ is ${}^nC_0 + {}^nC_1x + {}^nC_2x^2 + {}^nC_3x^3 + \ldots + {}^nC_nx^n$

$\therefore$ Coefficient of 2nd term $= {}^nC_1$,

Coefficient of 3rd term $= {}^nC_2$,

and coefficient of 4th term $= {}^nC_3$.

Given that ${}^nC_1$, ${}^nC_2$ and ${}^nC_3$ are in AP.

$$\therefore \quad 2\,{}^nC_2 = {}^nC_1 + {}^nC_3$$

$$\Rightarrow \quad 2\left[\frac{(n)!}{(n-2)!\,2!}\right] = \frac{(n)!}{(n-1)!} + \frac{(n)!}{3!(n-3)!}$$

$$\Rightarrow \quad \frac{2\cdot n(n-1)(n-2)!}{(n-2)!\,2!} = \frac{n(n-1)!}{(n-1)!} + \frac{n(n-1)(n-2)(n-3)!}{3\cdot 2\cdot 1(n-3)!}$$

$$\Rightarrow \quad n(n-1) = n + \frac{n(n-1)(n-2)}{6}$$

$$\Rightarrow \quad 6n - 6 = 6 + n^2 - 3n + 2$$

$$\Rightarrow \quad n^2 - 9n + 14 = 0$$

$$\Rightarrow \quad n^2 - 7n - 2n + 14 = 0$$

$$\Rightarrow \quad n(n-7) - 2(n-7) = 0$$

$$\Rightarrow \quad (n-7)(n-2) = 0$$

$$\therefore \quad n = 2 \text{ or } n = 7$$

Since, $n = 2$ is not possible.

$$\therefore \quad n = 7$$

***Q.23** If A and B are coefficient of x^n in the expansion of $(1+x)^{2n}$ and $(1+x)^{2n-1}$ respectively, then $\frac{A}{B}$ equals to

(a) 1 (b) 2
(c) $\frac{1}{2}$ (d) $\frac{1}{n}$

Ans. ***(b)*** Since, the coefficient of x^n in the expansion of $(1+x)^{2n}$ is ${}^{2n}C_n$.

$$\therefore \quad A = {}^{2n}C_n$$

Now, the coefficient of x^n in the expansion of $(1+x)^{2n-1}$ is ${}^{2n-1}C_n$.

$$\therefore \quad B = {}^{2n-1}C_n$$

Now, $$\frac{A}{B} = \frac{{}^{2n}C_n}{{}^{2n-1}C_n} = \frac{2}{1} = 2$$

Same as solution number 21.

(*) Topics related to these question have been removed from latest NCERT.

***Q.24** If the middle term of $\left(\frac{1}{x}+x\sin x\right)^{10}$ is equal to $7\frac{7}{8}$, then the value of x is

(a) $2n\pi+\frac{\pi}{6}$ (b) $n\pi+\frac{\pi}{6}$

(c) $n\pi+(-1)^n\frac{\pi}{6}$ (d) $n\pi+(-1)^n\frac{\pi}{3}$

Ans. **(c)** Given expression is $\left(\frac{1}{x}+x\sin x\right)^{10}$.

Since, $n=10$ is even, so this expression has only one middle term *i.e.*, 6th term.

$$\therefore \quad T_6=T_{5+1}={}^{10}C_5\left(\frac{1}{x}\right)^{10-5}(x\sin x)^5$$

$$\Rightarrow \quad \frac{63}{8}={}^{10}C_5\,x^{-5}x^5\sin^5 x$$

$$\Rightarrow \quad \frac{63}{8}=\frac{10\cdot9\cdot8\cdot7\cdot6\cdot5!}{5\cdot4\cdot3\cdot2\cdot1\cdot5!}\sin^5 x$$

$$\Rightarrow \quad \frac{63}{8}=2\cdot9\cdot2\cdot7\cdot\sin^5 x$$

$$\Rightarrow \quad \sin^5 x=\frac{1}{32}$$

$$\Rightarrow \quad \sin^5 x=\left(\frac{1}{2}\right)^5 \Rightarrow \sin x=\frac{1}{2}$$

$$\therefore \quad x=n\pi+(-1)^n\,\pi/6$$

Fill in the blanks in each of exercises of 25-33.

***Q.25** The largest coefficient in the expansion of $(1+x)^{30}$ is ....

Thinking Process In the expansion of $(1+x)^n$, the largest coefficient is ${}^nC_{n/2}$ (when n is even).

Ans. The largest coefficient in the expansion of $(1+x)^{30}={}^{30}C_{30/2}={}^{30}C_{15}$

Q.26 The number of terms in the expansion of $(x+y+z)^n$ ....

Ans. Given expression is $(x+y+z)^n=[x+(y+z)]^n$.

$[x+(y+z)]^n={}^nC_0x^n+{}^nC_1x^{n-1}(y+z)+{}^nC_2x^{n-2}(y+z)^2+\ldots+{}^nC_n(y+z)^n$

$\therefore$ Number of terms $=1+2+3+\ldots+n+(n+1)=\frac{(n+1)(n+2)}{2}$

Alternate Method

$$(x+a)^{100}+(x-a)^{100}={}^{100}C_0\,x^{100}+{}^{100}C_1\,x^{99}a+\ldots+{}^{100}C_{100}\,a^{100}$$
$$+{}^{100}C_0\,x^{100}-{}^{100}C_1\,x^{99}a+\ldots+{}^{100}C_{100}\,a^{100}$$
$$=2\,[\underbrace{{}^{100}C_0\,x^{100}+{}^{100}C_2\,x^{98}a^2+\ldots+{}^{100}C_{100}\,a^{100}}_{51\text{ terms}}]$$

$\therefore$ Number of terms = 51

(*) Topics related to these question have been removed from latest NCERT.

***Q.27** In the expansion of $\left(x^2 - \frac{1}{x^2}\right)^{16}$, the value of constant term is ....

Ans. Let general term be T_{r+1}.

$$\therefore \quad T_{r+1} = {}^{16}C_r (x^2)^{16-r}\left(-\frac{1}{x^2}\right)^r$$

$$= {}^{16}C_r\, x^{32-2r}(-1)^r x^{-2r} = {}^{16}C_r\, x^{32-4r}(-1)^r$$

For constant term, $32 - 4r = 0 \Rightarrow r = 8$

$\therefore$ Constant term $= T_{8+1} = {}^{16}C_8$

***Q.28** If the seventh term from the beginning and the end in the expansion of $\left(\sqrt[3]{2} + \frac{1}{\sqrt[3]{3}}\right)^n$ are equal, then n equals to ....

Ans. Given expression is $\left(\sqrt[3]{2} + \frac{1}{\sqrt[3]{3}}\right)^n$.

$\therefore$ Seventh term from beginning $= T_7 = T_{6+1} = {}^nC_6(\sqrt[3]{2})^{n-6}\left(\frac{1}{\sqrt[3]{3}}\right)^6$ ...(i)

Since, T_7 from the end is same as the T_7 from the beginning of $\left(\frac{1}{\sqrt[3]{3}} + \sqrt[3]{2}\right)^n$.

Then, $$T_7 = {}^nC_6\left(\frac{1}{\sqrt[3]{3}}\right)^{n-6}(\sqrt[3]{2})^6 \quad \text{...(ii)}$$

$$\therefore \quad {}^nC_6(2)^{\frac{n-6}{3}}(3)^{-6/3} = {}^nC_6(3)^{-\frac{(n-6)}{3}}\,2^{6/3} \quad \text{[from Eqs. (i) and (ii)]}$$

$$\Rightarrow \quad (2)^{\frac{n-12}{3}} = \left(\frac{1}{3^{1/3}}\right)^{n-12}$$

$$(2)^{\left(\frac{n-12}{3}\right)}.(3)^{\left(\frac{n-12}{3}\right)} = 1 \Rightarrow (6)^{\left(\frac{n-12}{3}\right)} = 6^0$$

which is true, when $\frac{n-12}{3} = 0.$

$$\Rightarrow \quad n - 12 = 0 \Rightarrow n = 12$$

***Q.29** The coefficient of $a^{-6}b^4$ in the expansion of $\left(\frac{1}{a} - \frac{2b}{3}\right)^{10}$ is ....

- **Concept Insight** In the expansion of $(x-a)^n$, $T_{r+1} = {}^nC_r\, x^{n-r}(-a)^r$

Ans. Given expression is $\left(\frac{1}{a} - \frac{2b}{3}\right)^{10}$.

Let T_{r+1} has the coefficient of $a^{-6}b^4$.

$$\therefore \quad T_{r+1} = {}^{10}C_r\left(\frac{1}{a}\right)^{10-r}\left(-\frac{2b}{3}\right)^r$$

For coefficient of $a^{-6}b^4$, $\quad 10 - r = 6 \Rightarrow r = 4$

Coefficient of $a^{-6}b^4 = {}^{10}C_4(-2/3)^4$

$$\therefore \quad = \frac{10\cdot 9\cdot 8\cdot 7\cdot 6!}{6!\cdot 4\cdot 3\cdot 2\cdot 1}\cdot\frac{2^4}{3^4} = \frac{1120}{27}$$

(*) Topics related to these question have been removed from latest NCERT.

***Q.30** Middle term in the expansion of $(a^3 + ba)^{28}$ is ....

Ans. Given expression is $(a^3 + ba)^{28}$.

$\because$ $n = 28$ [even]

$\therefore$ Middle term $= \left(\frac{28}{2} + 1\right)$th term = 15th term

$$\therefore \quad T_{15} = T_{14+1}$$
$$= {}^{28}C_{14}(a^3)^{28-14}(ba)^{14}$$
$$= {}^{28}C_{14}\, a^{42} b^{14} a^{14}$$
$$= {}^{28}C_{14}\, a^{56} b^{14}$$

***Q.31** The ratio of the coefficients of x^p and x^q in the expansion of $(1+x)^{p+q}$ is ....

Ans. Given expression is $(1+x)^{p+q}$.

$\therefore$ Coefficient of $x^p = {}^{p+q}C_p$

and coefficient of $x^q = {}^{p+q}C_q$

$$\therefore \quad \frac{{}^{p+q}C_p}{{}^{p+q}C_q} = \frac{{}^{p+q}C_p}{{}^{p+q}C_p} = 1:1 \qquad [\because {}^nC_r = {}^nC_{n-r}]$$

***Q.32** The position of the term independent of x in the expansion of $\left(\sqrt{\frac{x}{3}} + \frac{3}{2x^2}\right)^{10}$ is ....

Ans. Given expression is $\left(\sqrt{\frac{x}{3}} + \frac{3}{2x^2}\right)^{10}$.

Let the general term be T_{r+1}.

Then, $$T_{r+1} = {}^{10}C_r\left(\sqrt{\frac{x}{3}}\right)^{10-r}\left(\frac{3}{2x^2}\right)^r$$
$$= {}^{10}C_r \cdot x^{\frac{10-r}{2}} \cdot 3^{\frac{-10+r}{2}} \cdot 3^r \cdot 2^{-r} \cdot x^{-2r} = {}^{10}C_r\, x^{\frac{10-5r}{2}}\, 3^{\frac{-10+3r}{2}}\, 2^{-r}$$

For constant term, $10 - 5r = 0 \Rightarrow r = 2$

Hence, third term is independent of x.

Q.33 If 25^{15} is divided by 13, then the remainder is ....

Ans. Let $$25^{15} = (26-1)^{15}$$
$$= {}^{15}C_0\, 26^{15} - {}^{15}C_1 26^{14} + \ldots - {}^{15}C_{15}$$
$$= {}^{15}C_0 26^{15} - {}^{15}C_1 26^{14} + \ldots - 1 - 13 + 13$$
[adding and subtracting 13]
$$= {}^{15}C_0\, 26^{15} - {}^{15}C_1\, 26^{14} + \ldots - 13 + 12$$
$$= 13k + 12, \text{ where } k \in N$$

It is clear that, when 25^{15} is devided by 13, then remainder will be 12.

(*) Topics related to these question have been removed from latest NCERT.

State True or False for the following statements in each of the exercises from 34 to 40.

Q.34 The sum of the series $\sum_{r=0}^{10} {}^{20}C_r$ is $2^{19} + \frac{{}^{20}C_{10}}{2}$.

Ans. *False*

Given series, $\sum_{r=0}^{10} {}^{20}C_r = {}^{20}C_0 + {}^{20}C_1 + {}^{20}C_2 + \dots + {}^{20}C_{10}$

$= {}^{20}C_0 + {}^{20}C_1 + \dots + {}^{20}C_{10} + {}^{20}C_{11} + \dots {}^{20}C_{20} - ({}^{20}C_{11} + \dots + {}^{20}C_{20})$

$= 2^{20} - ({}^{20}C_{11} + \dots + {}^{20}C_{20})$ $\quad [\because {}^nC_0 + {}^nC_1 + \dots + {}^nC_n = 2^n]$

Hence, the given statement is false.

Q.35 The expression $7^9 + 9^7$ is divisible by 64.

Ans. *True*

Given expression $= 7^9 + 9^7 = (1+8)^7 - (1-8)^9$

$= ({}^7C_0 + {}^7C_1 8 + {}^7C_2 8^2 + \dots + {}^7C_7 8^7) - ({}^9C_0 - {}^9C_1 8 + {}^9C_2 8^2 \dots - {}^9C_9 8^9)$

$= (1 + 7 \times 8 + 21 \times 8^2 + \dots) - (1 - 9 \times 8 + 36 \times 8^2 + \dots - 8^9)$

$= (7 \times 8 + 9 \times 8) + (21 \times 8^2 - 36 \times 8^2) + \dots$

$= 2 \times 64 + (21 - 36)64 + \dots$

which is divisible by 64.

Hence, the statement is true.

Q.36 The number of terms in the expansion of $[(2x + y^3)^4]^7$ is 8.

Ans. *False*

Given expression is $[(2x + y^3)^4]^7 = (2x + y^3)^{28}$.

Here, $n = 28$

$\therefore$ The number of terms in this expression is $(n + 1)$.

i.e., $28 + 1 = 29$

So, the given statement is false.

*** Q.37** The sum of coefficients of the two middle terms in the expansion of $(1+x)^{2n-1}$ is equal to ${}^{2n-1}C_n$.

Ans. False

We have, the Binomial expression is $(1+x)^{2n-1}$.

Since, this expression has two middle terms *i.e.,* $\left(\frac{2n-1+1}{2}\right)$th term and $\left(\frac{2n-1+1}{2} + 1\right)$th term *i.e.,* nth term and $(n+1)$th term.

$\therefore$ Coefficient of nth term $= {}^{2n-1}C_{n-1}$

Coefficient of $(n+1)$th term $= {}^{2n-1}C_n$

Sum of coefficients $= {}^{2n-1}C_{n-1} + {}^{2n-1}C_n$

$= {}^{2n-1+1}C_n = {}^{2n}C_n$ $\quad [\because {}^nC_r + {}^nC_{r-1} = {}^{n+1}C_r]$

(*) Topics related to these question have been removed from latest NCERT.

Q.38 The last two digits of the numbers 3^{400} are 01.

Ans. *True*

Given, $3^{400} = 9^{200} = (10 - 1)^{200}$

$\Rightarrow \quad (10 - 1)^{200} = {}^{200}C_0 10^{200} - {}^{200}C_1 10^{199} + \ldots - {}^{200}C_{199} 10^1 + {}^{200}C_{200} 1^{200}$

$\Rightarrow \quad (10 - 1)^{200} = 10^{200} - 200 \times 10^{199} + \ldots - 10 \times 200 + 1$

So, it is clear that the last two digits are 01.

* **Q.39** If the expansion of $\left(x - \frac{1}{x^2}\right)^{2n}$ contains a term independent of x, then n is a multiple of 2.

Ans. *False*

Given Binomial expression is $\left(x - \frac{1}{x^2}\right)^{2n}$.

Let T_{r+1} term be independent of x.

Then, $T_{r+1} = {}^{2n}C_r (x)^{2n-r} \left(-\frac{1}{x^2}\right)^r$

$= {}^{2n}C_r \, x^{2n-r} (-1)^r x^{-2r} = {}^{2n}C_r \, x^{2n-3r} (-1)^r$

To find a term independent of x,

$$2n - 3r = 0$$

$$\therefore \quad r = \frac{2n}{3}$$

which is not a integer for all n that are multiples of 2.

So, the given expression is not possible to true.

Q.40 The number of terms in the expansion of $(a + b)^n$, where $n \in N$, is one less than the power n.

Ans. *False*

We know that the number of terms in the expansion of $(a + b)^n$, where $n \in N$, is one more than the power n. i.e. $n + l$.

(*) Topics related to these question have been removed from latest NCERT.

Chapter

09

Sequence and Series

Short Answer Type Questions

***Q.1** The first term of an AP is a and the sum of the first p terms is zero, show that the sum of its next q terms is $\dfrac{-a(p+q)q}{p-1}$.

● **Concept Insight** Use the formula ; $S_n = \dfrac{n}{2}\{2a+(n-1)d\}$ and $a_n = s_n - s_{n-1}$.

Ans. Let the common difference of an AP is d.

According to the question,

$$S_p = 0$$

$$\Rightarrow \quad \frac{p}{2}[2a+(p-1)d] = 0 \qquad \left[\because S_n = \frac{n}{2}\{2a+(n-1)d\}\right]$$

$$\Rightarrow \quad 2a+(p-1)d = 0$$

$$\therefore \quad d = \frac{-2a}{p-1}$$

Now, sum of next q terms $= S_{p+q} - S_p = S_{p+q} - 0$

$$= \frac{p+q}{2}[2a+(p+q-1)d]$$

$$= \frac{p+q}{2}[2a+(p-1)d+qd]$$

$$= \frac{p+q}{2}\left[2a+(p-1)\cdot\frac{-2a}{p-1}+\frac{q(-2a)}{p-1}\right]$$

$$= \frac{p+q}{2}\left[2a+(-2a)-\frac{2aq}{p-1}\right]$$

$$= \frac{p+q}{2}\left[\frac{-2aq}{p-1}\right]$$

$$= \frac{-a(p+q)q}{(p-1)}$$

Hence proved.

(✱) Topics related to these question have been removed from latest NCERT.

***Q.2** A man saved ₹ 66000 in 20 yr. In each succeeding year after the first year, he saved ₹ 200 more than what he saved in the previous year. How much did he save in the first year?

Ans. Let man saved in first year ₹a. Since, an increment of ₹ 200 is made in each succeding year.

So,it forms an AP whose first term = a, common difference $(d) = 200$ and $n = 20$

$$\therefore \quad S_{20} = \frac{20}{2}[2a + (20-1)d] \quad \left[\because S_n = \frac{n}{2}\{2a + (n-1)d\}\right]$$

$$\Rightarrow \quad 66000 = 10[2a + 19d]$$

$$\Rightarrow \quad 66000 = 20a + 190d$$

$$\Rightarrow \quad 66000 = 20a + 190 \times 200$$

$$\Rightarrow \quad 20a = 66000 - 38000$$

$$\Rightarrow \quad 20a = 28000$$

$$\therefore \quad a = \frac{28000}{20} = 1400$$

Hence, he saved ₹ 1400 in the first year.

***Q.3** A man accepts a position with an initial salary of ₹ 5200 per month. It is understood that he will receive an automatic increase of ₹ 320 in the very next month and each month thereafter.

(i) Find his salary for the tenth month.

(ii) What is his total earnings during the first year?

Thinking process Firstly, use the nth term of the AP. *i.e.*, $a_n = a + (n-1)d$ and secondly, sum of nth term of the AP i.e., $S_n = \frac{n}{2}[2a + (n-1)d]$

Sol. Since, the man get a fixed increment of ₹ 320 each month.

Therefore, this forms an AP whose first term = 5200 and common difference $(d) = 320$

(i) Salary for tenth month *i.e.*, for $n = 10$,

$$a_{10} = a + (n-1)d$$

$$\Rightarrow \quad a_{10} = 5200 + (10-1) \times 320$$

$$\Rightarrow \quad a_{10} = 5200 + 9 \times 320$$

$$\Rightarrow \quad a_{10} = 5200 + 2880$$

$$\Rightarrow \quad a_{10} = 8080$$

Hence, salary for the tenth month is ₹ 8080.

(ii) In a year there are 12 month *i.e.*, $n = 12$,

$$\text{Total earning during the first year} = S_{12} = \frac{12}{2}[2 \times 5200 + (12-1)320]$$

$$= 6[10400 + 11 \times 320]$$

$$= 6[10400 + 3520] = 6 \times 13920 = 83520$$

Hence, his total earning during the first year is ₹ 83520.

(*) Topics related to these question have been removed from latest NCERT.

Q.4 If the pth and qth terms of a GP are q and p respectively, show that its $(p+q)$th term is $\left(\dfrac{q^p}{p^q}\right)^{\frac{1}{p-q}}$.

Ans. Let the first term and common ratio of GP be a and r, respectively.

According to the question, pth term $= q$

$$\Rightarrow \quad ar^{p-1} = q \quad \text{...(i)}$$

and $\quad q$th term $= p$

$$\Rightarrow \quad ar^{q-1} = p \quad \text{...(ii)}$$

On dividing Eq. (i) by Eq. (ii), we get

$$\frac{ar^{p-1}}{ar^{q-1}} = \frac{q}{p}$$

$$\Rightarrow \quad r^{p-1-q+1} = \frac{q}{p}$$

$$\Rightarrow \quad r^{p-q} = \frac{q}{p} \Rightarrow r = \left(\frac{q}{p}\right)^{\frac{1}{p-q}}$$

On substituting the value of r in Eq. (i), we get

$$a\left(\frac{q}{p}\right)^{\frac{p-1}{p-q}} = q \Rightarrow a = \frac{q}{\left(\frac{q}{p}\right)^{\frac{p-1}{p-q}}} = q\cdot\left(\frac{p}{q}\right)^{\frac{p-1}{p-q}}$$

$$\therefore \quad (p+q)\text{th term, } T_{p+q} = a\cdot r^{p+q-1} = q\cdot\left(\frac{p}{q}\right)^{\frac{p-1}{p-q}}.(r)^{p+q-1}$$

$$= q.\left(\frac{p}{q}\right)^{\frac{p-1}{p-q}}\left[\left(\frac{q}{p}\right)^{\frac{1}{p-q}}\right]^{p+q-1} = q.\left(\frac{p}{q}\right)^{\frac{p-1}{p-q}}\left(\frac{q}{p}\right)^{\frac{p+q-1}{p-q}}$$

$$= q\cdot\left(\frac{p}{q}\right)^{\frac{p-1}{p-q}}\left(\frac{p}{q}\right)^{\frac{-(p+q-1)}{p-q}} = q.\left(\frac{p}{q}\right)^{\frac{p-1}{p-q}-\frac{(p+q-1)}{p-q}}$$

$$= q.\left(\frac{p}{q}\right)^{\frac{p-1-p-q+1}{p-q}} = q.\left(\frac{p}{q}\right)^{\frac{-q}{p-q}}$$

$$= q\cdot\left(\frac{q}{p}\right)^{\frac{q}{p-q}}$$

$$= \frac{q^{\left(\frac{q}{p-q}+1\right)}}{p^{\left(\frac{q}{p-q}\right)}} = \frac{q^{\left(\frac{p}{p-q}\right)}}{p^{\left(\frac{q}{p-q}\right)}} = \left[\frac{q^p}{p^q}\right]^{\frac{1}{p-q}}$$

Hence proved.

Mistake Alert ! *Students might get confused between common ratio and common difference. So, be careful.*

***Q.5** A carpenter was hired to build 192 window frames. The first day he made five frames and each day, thereafter he made two more frames than he made the day before. How many days did it take him to finish the job?

Ans. We have, $a = 5$ and $d = 2$

Let he finished the job in n days.

Then, according to the question

$$S_n = 192$$

$$\Rightarrow \quad 192 = \frac{n}{2}[2 \times 5 + (n-1)\,2] \qquad \left[\because S_n = \frac{n}{2}[2a + (n-1)\,d]\right]$$

$$\Rightarrow \quad 192 = \frac{n}{2}[10 + 2n - 2]$$

$$\Rightarrow \quad 192 = \frac{n}{2}[8 + 2n]$$

$$\Rightarrow \quad 192 = 4n + n^2$$

$$\Rightarrow \quad n^2 + 4n - 192 = 0$$

$$\Rightarrow \quad (n-12)(n+16) = 0$$

$$\Rightarrow \quad n = 12, -16$$

$$\therefore \quad n = 12 \qquad [n \text{ can't be negative}]$$

Hence, the carpenter will finish the job in 12 days.

***Q.6** We know the sum of the interior angles of a triangle is 180°. Show that the sums of the interior angles of polygons with 3, 4, 5, 6, ... sides form an arithmetic progression. Find the sum of the interior angles for a 21 sided polygon.

Ans. We know that sum of interior angles of a polygon of side $n = (2n-4) \times 90°$
$= (n-2) \times 180°$

Sum of interior angles of a polygon with 3 sides is 180°.

Sum of interior angles of polygon with 4 side $= (4-2) \times 180° = 360°$

Similarly, sum of interior angles of polygon with 5, 6, 7... sides are 540°, 720°, 900°,...

The series will be 180°, 360° 540°, 720°, 900°,...

Here, $a = 180°$

and $d = 360° - 180° = 180°$

Since, common difference is same between two consecutive terms of the series.

So, it form an AP.

We have to find the sum of interior angles of a 21 sides polygon.

It means, we have to find the 19th term of the above series.

$$\therefore \quad a_{19} = a + (19-1)\,d$$

$$= 180° + 18 \times 180° = 3420°$$

(✱) Topics related to these question have been removed from latest NCERT.

Q.7 A side of an equilateral triangle is 20 cm long. A second equilateral triangle is inscribed in it by joining the mid-points of the sides of the first triangle. The process is continued as shown in the accompanying diagram. Find the perimeter of the sixth inscribed equilateral triangle.

Ans. Side of equilateral $\Delta ABC = 20$ cm. By joining the mid-points of this triangle, we get another equilateral triangle of side equal to half of the length of side of ΔABC.

Continuing in this way, we get a set of equilateral triangles with side equal to half of the side of the previous triangle.

$\therefore$ Perimeter of first triangle $= 20 \times 3 = 60$ cm

Perimeter of second triangle $= 10 \times 3 = 30$ cm

Perimeter of third triangle $= 5 \times 3 = 15$ cm

Now, the series will be 60, 30, 15,...

Here, $a = 60$

$\therefore$ $r = \frac{30}{60} = \frac{1}{2}$ $\left[\because \frac{\text{second term}}{\text{first term}} = r\right]$

Since, the perimeter of sixth inscribed triangle is the sixth term of the series.

$\therefore$ $a_6 = ar^{6-1}$ $[\because a_n = ar^{n-1}]$

$= 60 \times \left(\frac{1}{2}\right)^5 = \frac{60}{32} = \frac{15}{8}$ cm

***Q.8** In a potato race 20 potatoes are placed in a line at intervals of 4 m with the first potato 24 m from the starting point. A contestant is required to bring the potatoes back to the starting place one at a time. How far would he run in bringing back all the potatoes?

Ans. According to the given information, we have following diagram.

24 m 4 m 4 m 4 m
1 2 3 4 19 20

Distance travelled to bring first potato $= 24 + 24 = 2 \times 24 = 48$ m

Distance travelled to bring second potato $= 2(24 + 4) = 2 \times 28 = 56$ m

Distance travelled to bring third potato $= 2(24 + 4 + 4) = 2 \times 32 = 64$ m

Then, the series of distances are 48, 56, 64,...

Here, $a = 48$,

$d = 56 - 48 = 8$

and $n = 20$

To find the total distance that he run in bringing back all potatoes, we have to find the sum of 20 terms of the above series.

$\therefore$ $S_{20} = \frac{20}{2}[2 \times 48 + 19 \times 8]$ $\left[\because S_n = \frac{n}{2}\{2a + (n-1)d\}\right]$

$= 10[96 + 152]$

$= 10 \times 248 = 2480$ m

(*) Topics related to these question have been removed from latest NCERT.

***Q.9** In a cricket tournament 16 school teams participated. A sum of ₹ 8000 is to be awarded among themselves as prize money. If the last placed team is awarded ₹ 275 in prize money and the award increases by the same amount for successive finishing places, how much amount will the first place team receive?

Ans. Let the first place team got ₹ a.

Since, award money increases by the same amount for successive finishing places. Therefore series is an AP.

Let the constant amount be d.

Here, $l = 275, n = 16$ and $S_{16} = 8000$

$\therefore \quad l = a + (n-1)\,d$

$\Rightarrow \quad l = a + (16-1)(-d)$

[take common difference negative because series is decreasing]

$\Rightarrow \quad 275 = a - 15\,d \qquad \text{...(i)}$

and $\quad S_{16} = \dfrac{16}{2}[2a + (n-1)\cdot(-d)]$

$\Rightarrow \quad 8000 = 8\,[2a - 15d]$

$\Rightarrow \quad 1000 = 2a - 15d \qquad \text{...(ii)}$

On subtracting Eq. (i) from Eq. (ii), we get

$(2a - 15\,d) - (a - 15\,d) = 1000 - 275$

$\Rightarrow \quad 2a - 15\,d - a + 15\,d = 725$

$\therefore \quad a = 725$

Hence, first place team receive ₹ 725.

***Q.10** If $a_1, a_2, a_3, \ldots, a_n$ are in AP, where $a_i > 0$ for all i, show that

$$\frac{1}{\sqrt{a_1}+\sqrt{a_2}} + \frac{1}{\sqrt{a_2}+\sqrt{a_3}} + \ldots + \frac{1}{\sqrt{a_{n-1}}+\sqrt{a_n}} = \frac{n-1}{\sqrt{a_1}+\sqrt{a_n}}$$

Ans. Since, $a_1, a_2, a_3, \ldots, a_n$ are in AP.

$\Rightarrow \quad a_2 - a_1 = a_3 - a_2 = \ldots = a_n - a_{n-1} = d$ [common difference]

If $\quad a_2 - a_1 = d$, then $(\sqrt{a_2})^2 - (\sqrt{a_1})^2 = d$

$\Rightarrow \quad (\sqrt{a_2} - \sqrt{a_1})(\sqrt{a_2} + \sqrt{a_1}) = d$

$$\Rightarrow \quad \frac{1}{\sqrt{a_1}+\sqrt{a_2}} = \frac{\sqrt{a_2}-\sqrt{a_1}}{d}$$

Similarly,

$$\frac{1}{\sqrt{a_2}+\sqrt{a_3}} = \frac{\sqrt{a_3}-\sqrt{a_2}}{d}$$

... ...

... ...

... ...

$$\frac{1}{\sqrt{a_{n-1}}+\sqrt{a_n}} = \frac{\sqrt{a_n}-\sqrt{a_{n-1}}}{d}$$

(*) Topics related to these question have been removed from latest NCERT.

On adding these terms, we get

$$\frac{1}{\sqrt{a_1}+\sqrt{a_2}}+\frac{1}{\sqrt{a_2}+\sqrt{a_3}}+\ldots+\frac{1}{\sqrt{a_{n-1}}+\sqrt{a_n}}$$

$$=\frac{1}{d}[\sqrt{a_2}-\sqrt{a_1}+\sqrt{a_3}-\sqrt{a_2}+\ldots+\sqrt{a_n}-\sqrt{a_{n-1}}] \quad \text{[using above relations]}$$

$$=\frac{1}{d}[\sqrt{a_n}-\sqrt{a_1}] \quad \ldots(i)$$

Again, $a_n = a_1 + (n-1)\,d$ $\quad [\because T_n = a+(n-1)\,d]$

$\Rightarrow$ $a_n - a_1 = (n-1)\,d$

$\Rightarrow$ $(\sqrt{a_n})^2 - (\sqrt{a_1})^2 = (n-1)\,d$

$\Rightarrow$ $(\sqrt{a_n}-\sqrt{a_1})(\sqrt{a_n}+\sqrt{a_1}) = (n-1)\,d \Rightarrow \sqrt{a_n}-\sqrt{a_1} = \dfrac{(n-1)\,d}{\sqrt{a_n}+\sqrt{a_1}}$

On putting this value in Eq. (i), we get

$$\frac{1}{\sqrt{a_1}+\sqrt{a_2}}+\frac{1}{\sqrt{a_2}+\sqrt{a_3}}+\ldots+\frac{1}{\sqrt{a_{n-1}}+\sqrt{a_n}}$$

$$=\frac{(n-1)\,d}{d\,(\sqrt{a_n}+\sqrt{a_1})}=\frac{n-1}{\sqrt{a_n}+\sqrt{a_1}}$$

Hence proved.

***Q.11** Find the sum of the series $(3^3-2^3)+(5^3-4^3)+(7^3-6^3)+\ldots$ to (i) n terms. (ii) 10 terms.

Ans. Given series, $(3^3-2^3)+(5^3-4^3)+(7^3-6^3)+$ $\quad \ldots(i)$

$$=(3^3+5^3+7^3+\ldots)-(2^3+4^3+6^3+\ldots)$$

Let T_n be the nth term of the series (i)

Then, T_n = (nth term of $3^3, 5^3, 7^3, \ldots$) – (nth term of $2^3, 4^3, 6^3, \ldots$) $=(2n+1)^3-(2n)^3$

$$=(2n+1-2n)[(2n+1)^2+(2n+1)\,2n+(2n)^2][\because a^3-b^3=(a-b)(a^2+ab+b^2)]$$

$$=[4n^2+1+4n+4n^2+2n+4n^2]=12n^2+6n+1$$

(i) Let S_n denote the sum of n term of series (i).

Then, $S_n = \Sigma\, T_n = \Sigma\,[12n^2+6n+1]$

$$=12\Sigma n^2+6\Sigma n+\Sigma(1)$$

$$=12\cdot\frac{n(n+1)(2n+1)}{6}+\frac{6n(n+1)}{2}+n$$

$$=2n(n+1)(2n+1)+3n(n+1)+n$$

$$=(2n^2+2n)(2n+1)+3n^2+3n+n$$

$$=4n^3+2n^2+4n^2+2n+3n^2+3n+n=4n^3+9n^2+6n$$

(ii) Sum of 10 terms, $S_{10}=4\times(10)^3+9\times(10)^2+6\times 10$

$$=4\times 1000+9\times 100+60$$

$$=4000+900+60=4960$$

(*) Topics related to these question have been removed from latest NCERT.

***Q.12** Find the rth term of an AP sum of whose first n terms is $2n+3n^2$.

Ans. Given, sum of n terms of an AP,

$$S_n = 2n + 3n^2$$

We know that

$$\begin{aligned} T_n &= S_n - S_{n-1} \\ &= (2n + 3n^2) - [2(n-1) + 3(n-1)^2] \\ &= (2n + 3n^2) - [2n - 2 + 3(n^2 - 1 - 2n)] \\ &= (2n + 3n^2) - (2n - 2 + 3n^2 + 3 - 6n) \\ &= 2n + 3n^2 - 2n + 2 - 3n^2 - 3 + 6n = 6n - 1 \end{aligned}$$

$\therefore$ rth term, $T_r = 6r - 1$

Long Answer Type Questions

Q.13 If A is the arithmetic mean and G_1, G_2 be two geometric mean between any two numbers, then prove that $2A = \frac{G_1^2}{G_2} + \frac{G_2^2}{G_1}$.

Ans. Let the numbers be a and b.

Then, $A = \frac{a+b}{2} \Rightarrow 2A = a + b$ ... (i)

And G_1, G_2 be geometric mean between a and b, then a, G_1, G_2, b are in GP.

Let r be the common ratio.

Then, $b = ar^{4-1}$ $[\because a_n = ar^{n-1}]$

$\Rightarrow$ $b = ar^3 \Rightarrow \frac{b}{a} = r^3$

$\therefore$ $r = \left(\frac{b}{a}\right)^{1/3}$

Now, $G_1 = ar = a\left(\frac{b}{a}\right)^{1/3}$ $\left[\because r = \left(\frac{b}{a}\right)^{1/3}\right]$

and $G_2 = ar^2 = a\left(\frac{b}{a}\right)^{2/3}$

$$\text{RHS} = \frac{G_1^2}{G_2} + \frac{G_2^2}{G_1} = \frac{\left[a\left(\frac{b}{a}\right)^{1/3}\right]^2}{a\left(\frac{b}{a}\right)^{2/3}} + \frac{\left[a\left(\frac{b}{a}\right)^{2/3}\right]^2}{a\left(\frac{b}{a}\right)^{1/3}}$$

$$= \frac{a^2\left(\frac{b}{a}\right)^{2/3}}{a\left(\frac{b}{a}\right)^{2/3}} + \frac{a^2\left(\frac{b}{a}\right)^{4/3}}{a\left(\frac{b}{a}\right)^{1/3}}$$

$= a + a\left(\frac{b}{a}\right) = a + b = 2A =$ LHS [from Eq. (i)] **Hence proved.**

(*) Topics related to these question have been removed from latest NCERT.

***Q.14** If $\theta_1, \theta_2, \theta_3, \ldots, \theta_n$ are in AP, whose common difference is d, show that $\sec\theta_1 \sec\theta_2 + \sec\theta_2 \sec\theta_3 + \ldots + \sec\theta_{n-1} \sec\theta_n = \dfrac{\tan\theta_n - \tan\theta_1}{\sin d}$.

Ans. Since, $\theta_1, \theta_2, \theta_3, \ldots, \theta_n$ are in AP.

$$\Rightarrow \qquad \theta_2 - \theta_1 = \theta_3 - \theta_2 = \cdots = \theta_n - \theta_{n-1} = d \qquad \ldots\text{(i)}$$

Now, we have to prove

$$\sec\theta_1 \sec\theta_2 + \sec\theta_2 \sec\theta_3 + \ldots + \sec\theta_{n-1} \sec\theta_n = \frac{\tan\theta_n - \tan\theta_1}{\sin d}$$

or it can be written as

$$\sin d\,[\sec\theta_1 \sec\theta_2 + \sec\theta_2 \sec\theta_3 + \cdots + \sec\theta_{n-1} \sec\theta_n] = \tan\theta_n - \tan\theta_1$$

Now, take only first term of LHS

$$\sin d \sec\theta_1 \sec\theta_2 = \frac{\sin d}{\cos\theta_1 \cos\theta_2} = \frac{\sin(\theta_2 - \theta_1)}{\cos\theta_1 \cos\theta_2} \qquad \text{[from Eq. (i)]}$$

$$= \frac{\sin\theta_2 \cos\theta_1 - \cos\theta_2 \sin\theta_1}{\cos\theta_1 \cos\theta_2}$$

$$[\because \sin(A - B) = \sin A \cdot \cos B - \cos A \cdot \sin B]$$

$$= \frac{\sin\theta_2 \cos\theta_1}{\cos\theta_1 \cos\theta_2} - \frac{\cos\theta_2 \sin\theta_1}{\cos\theta_1 \cos\theta_2} = \tan\theta_2 - \tan\theta_1$$

Similarly, we can solve other terms which will be $\tan\theta_3 - \tan\theta_2, \tan\theta_4 - \tan\theta_3, \cdots$

$$\therefore \qquad \text{LHS} = \tan\theta_2 - \tan\theta_1 + \tan\theta_3 - \tan\theta_2 + \cdots + \tan\theta_n - \tan\theta_{n-1}$$

$$= -\tan\theta_1 + \tan\theta_n = \tan\theta_n - \tan\theta_1$$

$$= \text{RHS}$$

Hence proved.

***Q.15** If the sum of p terms of an AP is q and the sum of q terms is p, show that the sum of $p+q$ terms is $-(p+q)$. Also, find the sum of first $p-q$ terms (where, $p > q$).

Ans. Let first term and common difference of the AP be a and d, respectively.

Then,
$$S_p = q$$

$$\Rightarrow \qquad \frac{p}{2}[2a + (p-1)d] = q$$

$$2a + (p-1)d = \frac{2q}{p} \qquad \ldots\text{(i)}$$

And
$$S_q = p$$

$$\Rightarrow \qquad \frac{q}{2}[2a + (q-1)d] = p$$

$$\Rightarrow \qquad 2a + (q-1)d = \frac{2p}{q} \qquad \ldots\text{(ii)}$$

On subtracting Eq. (ii) from Eq. (i), we get

$$2a + (p-1)d - 2a - (q-1)d = \frac{2q}{p} - \frac{2p}{q}$$

(✱) Topics related to these question have been removed from latest NCERT.

$$\Rightarrow \quad [(p-1)-(q-1)]\ d = \frac{2q^2 - 2p^2}{pq}$$

$$\Rightarrow \quad [p-1-q+1]\ d = \frac{2(q^2 - p^2)}{pq}$$

$$\Rightarrow \quad (p-q)\ d = \frac{2(q^2 - p^2)}{pq}$$

$$\therefore \quad d = \frac{-2(p+q)}{pq} \quad \text{...(iii)}$$

On substituting the value of d in Eq. (i), we get

$$2a + (p-1)\left(\frac{-2(p+q)}{pq}\right) = \frac{2q}{p}$$

$$\Rightarrow \quad 2a = \frac{2q}{p} + \frac{2(p+q)(p-1)}{pq}$$

$$\Rightarrow \quad a = \left[\frac{q}{p} + \frac{(p+q)(p-1)}{pq}\right] \quad \text{...(iv)}$$

Now, $S_{p+q} = \frac{p+q}{2}[2a + (p+q-1)\,d]$

$$= \frac{p+q}{2}\left[\frac{2q}{p} + \frac{2(p+q)(p-1)}{pq} - \frac{(p+q-1)2(p+q)}{pq}\right]$$

[from Eqs. (iii) and (iv)]

$$= (p+q)\left[\frac{q}{p} + \frac{(p+q)(p-1)-(p+q-1)(p+q)}{pq}\right]$$

$$= (p+q)\left[\frac{q}{p} + \frac{(p+q)(p-1-p-q+1)}{pq}\right]$$

$$= (p+q)\left[\frac{q}{p} - \frac{p+q}{p}\right] = (p+q)\left[\frac{q-p-q}{p}\right]$$

$$S_{p+q} = -(p+q)$$

Now, $S_{p-q} = \frac{p-q}{2}[2a + (p-q-1)\,d]$

$$= \frac{p-q}{2}\left[\frac{2q}{p} + \frac{2(p+q)(p-1)}{pq} - \frac{(p-q-1)2\,(p+q)}{pq}\right]$$

[from Eqs. (iii) and (iv)]

$$= (p-q)\left[\frac{q}{p} + \frac{(p+q)(p-1-p+q+1)}{pq}\right]$$

$$= (p-q)\left[\frac{q}{p} + \frac{(p+q)q}{pq}\right]$$

$$= (p-q)\left[\frac{q}{p} + \frac{p+q}{p}\right]$$

$$= (p-q)\frac{(p+2q)}{p}$$

Hence proved

Q.16 If pth, qth and rth terms of an AP and GP are a, b, and c respectively, show that $a^{b-c} \cdot b^{c-a} \cdot c^{a-b} = 1$.

Ans. Let A, d are the first term and common difference of AP and x, R are the first term and common ratio of GP, respectively.

According to the given condition,

$$A + (p-1)\,d = a \quad \text{...(i)}$$

$$A + (q-1)\,d = b \quad \text{...(ii)}$$

$$A + (r-1)\,d = c \quad \text{...(iii)}$$

and

$$a = xR^{p-1} \quad \text{...(iv)}$$

$$b = xR^{q-1} \quad \text{...(v)}$$

$$c = xR^{r-1} \quad \text{...(vi)}$$

On subtracting Eq. (ii) from Eq. (i), we get

$$d(p-1-q+1) = a-b$$

$$\Rightarrow \quad a-b = d(p-q) \quad \text{...(vii)}$$

On subtracting Eq. (iii) from Eq. (ii), we get

$$d(q-1-r+1) = b-c$$

$$\Rightarrow \quad b-c = d\,(q-r) \quad \text{...(viii)}$$

On subtracting Eq. (i) from Eq. (iii), we get

$$d(r-1-p+1) = c-a$$

$$\Rightarrow \quad c-a = d\,(r-p) \quad \text{...(ix)}$$

Now, we have to prove that $a^{b-c}\, b^{c-a}\, c^{a-b} = 1$

Taking LHS $= a^{b-c}\, b^{c-a}\, c^{a-b}$

Using Eqs. (iv), (v), (vi) and (vii), (viii), (ix), we get

$$\text{LHS} = (x\,R^{p-1})^{d(q-r)}\,(x\,R^{q-1})^{d(r-p)}\,(xR^{r-1})^{d\,(p-q)}$$

$$= x^{d(q-r)+d(r-p)+d(p-q)}\,R^{(p-1)\,d(q-r)+(q-1)\,d\,(r-p)+(r-1)\,d(p-q)}$$

$$= x^{d(q-r+r-p+p-q)}\,R^{d\,(pq-pr-q+r+qr-pq-r+p+rp-rq-p+q)} = x^0\,R^0 = 1$$

$= \text{RHS}$ **Hence proved.**

Objective Type Questions

Choose the correct answers from the given four options in each exercise 17 to 26.

***Q.17** If the sum of n terms of an AP is given by $S_n = 3n + 2n^2$, then the common difference of the AP is

(a) 3 (b) 2 (c) 6 (d) 4

Ans. ***(d)*** Given, $S_n = 3n + 2n^2$

First term of the AP,

$$\therefore \quad T_1 = S_1 = 3\times 1 + 2\,(1)^2 = 3 + 2 = 5$$

and

$$T_2 = S_2 - S_1 = [3\times 2 + 2\times(2)^2] - [3\times 1 + 2\times(1)^2] = 14 - 5 = 9$$

$\therefore$ Common difference $(d) = T_2 - T_1 = 9 - 5 = 4$

(*) Topics related to these question have been removed from latest NCERT.

Q.18 The third term of GP is 4. The product of its first 5 terms is

(a) 4^3 (b) 4^4 (c) 4^5 (d) None of these

Ans. ***(c)*** Given, $T_3 = 4$

Let a and r be the first term and common ratio, respectively.

Then, $ar^2 = 4$ ...(i)

Product of first 5 terms $= a \cdot ar \cdot ar^2 \cdot ar^3 \cdot ar^4$

$= a^5 r^{10} = (ar^2)^5 = (4)^5$ [from Eq. (i)]

***Q.19** If 9 times the 9th term of an AP is equal to 13 times the 13th term, then the 22nd term of the AP is

(a) 0 (b) 22 (c) 220 (d) 198

Ans. ***(a)*** Let the first term be a and common difference be d.

According to the question, $9 \cdot T_9 = 13 \cdot T_{13}$

$\Rightarrow 9(a + 8d) = 13(a + 12d)$

$\Rightarrow 9a + 72d = 13a + 156d$

$\Rightarrow (9a - 13a) = 156d - 72d$

$\Rightarrow -4a = 84d$

$\Rightarrow a = -21d$

$\Rightarrow a + 21d = 0$ ...(i)

$\therefore$ 22nd term *i.e.*, $T_{22} = [a + 21d]$

$T_{22} = 0$ [from Eq. (i)]

Q.20 If x, $2y$ and $3z$ are in AP, where the distinct numbers x, y, z are in GP, then the common ratio of the GP is

(a) 3 (b) $\frac{1}{3}$ (c) 2 (d) $\frac{1}{2}$

Ans. ***(b)*** Given, $x, 2y$ and $3z$ are in AP.

Then, $2y = \frac{x + 3z}{2}$

$\Rightarrow 4y = x + 3z$ ...(i)

And x, y, z are in GP.

Then, $\frac{y}{x} = \frac{z}{y} = \lambda$

$\Rightarrow y = x\lambda$ and $z = \lambda y = \lambda^2 x$

On substituting these values in Eq. (i), we get

$4(x\lambda) = x + 3(\lambda^2 x)$

$\Rightarrow 4\lambda x = x + 3\lambda^2 x \Rightarrow 4\lambda = 1 + 3\lambda^2$

$\Rightarrow 3\lambda^2 - 4\lambda + 1 = 0 \Rightarrow (3\lambda - 1)(\lambda - 1) = 0$

$\therefore \lambda = \frac{1}{3}$ or $\lambda = 1$

(*) Topics related to these question have been removed from latest NCERT.

***Q.21** If in an AP, $S_n = qn^2$ and $S_m = qm^2$, where S_r denotes the sum of r terms of the AP, then S_q equals to

(a) $\frac{q^3}{2}$ (b) mnq (c) q^3 (d) $(m+n)q^2$

Thinking Process Firstly, use the concept $T_n = S_n - S_{n-1}$ and then $S_n = \frac{n}{2}[2a+(n-1)d]$ and simplify it.

Ans. *(c)* Given, $S_n = qn^2$ and $S_m = qm^2$

$\therefore$ $S_1 = q,\ S_2 = 4q,\ S_3 = 9q$ and $S_4 = 16q$

Now, $T_1 = q$

$\therefore$ $T_2 = S_2 - S_1 = 4q - q = 3q$

$T_3 = S_3 - S_2 = 9q - 4q = 5q$

$T_4 = S_4 - S_3 = 16q - 9q = 7q$

So, the series is $q, 3q, 5q, 7q, \ldots$

Here, $a = q$ and $d = 3q - q = 2q$

$\therefore$ $S_q = \frac{q}{2}[2\times q + (q-1)2q]$

$= \frac{q}{2}\times[2q + 2q^2 - 2q] = \frac{q}{2}\times 2q^2 = q^3$

Alternate Method

Given, $S_n = qn^2$ and $S_m = qm^2$

$\therefore$ $S_q = q(q)^2 = q^3$

***Q.22** Let S_n denote the sum of the first n terms of an AP. If $S_{2n} = 3S_n$ then $S_{3n} : S_n$ is equal to

(a) 4 (b) 6 (c) 8 (d) 10

Ans. *(b)* Let first term be a and common difference be d.

Then, $S_n = \frac{n}{2}[2a + (n-1)d]$ ...(i)

$\therefore$ $S_{2n} = \frac{2n}{2}[2a + (2n-1)d]$

$\Rightarrow$ $S_{2n} = n[2a + (2n-1)d]$ ...(ii)

and $S_{3n} = \frac{3n}{2}[2a + (3n-1)d]$ ...(iii)

According to the question, $S_{2n} = 3S_n$

$\Rightarrow$ $n[2a + (2n-1)d] = 3\frac{n}{2}[2a + (n-1)d]$

$\Rightarrow$ $4a + (4n-2)d = 6a + (3n-3)d$

$\Rightarrow$ $-2a + (4n - 2 - 3n + 3)d = 0$

$\Rightarrow$ $-2a + (n+1)d = 0$

$\Rightarrow$ $d = \frac{2a}{n+1}$ ...(iv)

(✱) Topics related to these question have been removed from latest NCERT.

Now, $$\frac{S_{3n}}{S_n} = \frac{\frac{3n}{2}[2a + (3n-1)d]}{\frac{n}{2}[2a + (n-1)d]} = \frac{6a + (9n-3)\frac{2a}{n+1}}{2a + (n-1)\frac{2a}{n+1}}$$

$$= \frac{6an + 6a + 18an - 6a}{2an + 2a + 2an - 2a}$$

$$= \frac{24an}{4an} = 6$$

Q.23 The minimum value of $4^x + 4^{1-x}$, $x \in R$ is

(a) 2 (b) 4 (c) 1 (d) 0

Ans. ***(b)*** We know that, AM ≥ GM

$$\Rightarrow \frac{4^x + 4^{1-x}}{2} \geq \sqrt{4^x \cdot 4^{1-x}}$$

$$\Rightarrow 4^x + 4^{1-x} \geq 2\sqrt{4}$$

$$\Rightarrow 4^x + 4^{1-x} \geq 2 \cdot 2$$

$$\Rightarrow 4^x + 4^{1-x} \geq 4$$

***Q.24** Let S_n denote the sum of the cubes of the first n natural numbers and s_n denote the sum of the first n natural numbers, then $\sum_{r=1}^{n} \frac{S_r}{s_r}$ equals to

(a) $\frac{n(n+1)(n+2)}{6}$ (b) $\frac{n(n+1)}{2}$ (c) $\frac{n^2 + 3n + 2}{2}$ (d) None of these

Ans. ***(a)*** We have, $\sum_{r=1}^{n} \frac{S_r}{s_r} = \frac{S_1}{s_1} + \frac{S_2}{s_2} + \frac{S_3}{s_3} + \dots + \frac{S_n}{s_n}$

Let T_n be the nth term of the above series.

$$\therefore \quad T_n = \frac{S_n}{s_n} = \frac{\left[\frac{n(n+1)}{2}\right]^2}{\frac{n(n+1)}{2}} \quad [\because S_n = \Sigma n^3, s_n = \Sigma n]$$

$$= \frac{n(n+1)}{2} = \frac{1}{2}[n^2 + n]$$

$$\therefore \text{Sum of the above series} = \Sigma T_n = \frac{1}{2}[\Sigma n^2 + \Sigma n]$$

$$= \frac{1}{2}\left[\frac{n(n+1)(2n+1)}{6} + \frac{n(n+1)}{2}\right] = \frac{1}{2} \cdot \frac{n(n+1)}{2}\left[\frac{(2n+1)}{3} + 1\right]$$

$$= \frac{1}{4}n(n+1)\left[\frac{2n+1+3}{3}\right] = \frac{1}{4 \times 3}n(n+1)(2n+4)$$

$$= \frac{1}{12}n(n+1)(2n+4) = \frac{1}{6}n(n+1)(n+2)$$

(✱) Topics related to these question have been removed from latest NCERT.

***Q.25** If t_n denotes the nth term of the series $2+3+6+11+18+\dots$, then t_{50} is

(a) $49^2 - 1$ (b) 49^2 (c) $50^2 + 1$ (d) $49^2 + 2$

Ans. ***(d)*** Let S_n be sum of the series $2 + 3 + 6 + 11 + 18 + \dots + t_{50}$.

$$\therefore \quad S_n = 2 + 3 + 6 + 11 + 18 + \dots + t_{50} \quad \text{...(i)}$$

$$\text{and} \quad S_n = 0 + 2 + 3 + 6 + 11 + 18 + \dots + t_{49} + t_{50} \quad \text{...(ii)}$$

On subtracting Eq. (ii) from Eq. (i), we get

$$0 = 2 + 1 + 3 + 5 + 7 + \cdots - t_{50}$$

$$\Rightarrow \quad t_{50} = 2 + 1 + 3 + 5 + 7 + \cdots \text{ upto 49 terms}$$

$$\therefore \quad t_{50} = 2 + [1 + 3 + 5 + 7 + \cdots \text{ upto 49 terms}]$$

$$= 2 + \frac{49}{2}[2 \times 1 + 48 \times 2]$$

$$= 2 + \frac{49}{2} \times [2 + 96] = 2 + 49(1 + 48)$$

$$= 2 + 49 \times 49 = 2 + (49)^2$$

Alternate Method

General term of the series can be written as $t_n = 2 + (n-1)^2$

$\therefore$ 50th term is $t_{50} = 2 + (50-1)^2 = 2 + (49)^2 = 49^2 + 2$

Q.26 The lengths of three unequal edges of a rectangular solid block are in GP. The volume of the block is 216 cm^3 and the total surface area is 252 cm^2. The length of the longest edge is

(a) 12 cm (b) 6 cm (c) 18 cm (d) 3 cm

Ans. ***(a)*** Let the length, breadth and height of rectangular solid block be $\frac{a}{r}$, a and ar, respectively.

$$\therefore \quad \text{Volume} = \frac{a}{r} \times a \times ar = 216 \text{ cm}^3$$

$$\Rightarrow \quad a^3 = 216 \Rightarrow a^3 = 6^3$$

$$\therefore \quad a = 6 \quad \text{...(i)}$$

$$\text{Now,} \quad \text{Surface area} = 2\left(\frac{a^2}{r} + a^2 r + a^2\right) = 252$$

$$\Rightarrow \quad 2a^2\left(\frac{1}{r} + r + 1\right) = 252$$

$$\Rightarrow \quad 2 \times 36\left(\frac{1 + r^2 + r}{r}\right) = 252 \quad \text{[from Eq. (i)]}$$

$$\Rightarrow \quad \frac{1 + r^2 + r}{r} = \frac{252}{2 \times 36} \Rightarrow 1 + r^2 + r = \frac{7}{2}r$$

$$\Rightarrow \quad 2r^2 + 2r + 2 = 7r$$

$$\Rightarrow \quad 2r^2 - 5r + 2 = 0 \Rightarrow (2r-1)(r-2) = 0$$

$$\therefore \quad r = \frac{1}{2}, 2$$

(*) Topics related to these question have been removed from latest NCERT.

For $r = \frac{1}{2}$: Length $= \frac{a}{r} = \frac{6 \times 2}{1} = 12$

Breadth $= a = 6$

Height $= ar = 6 \times \frac{1}{2} = 3$

For $r = 2$: Length $= \frac{a}{r} = \frac{6}{2} = 3$

Breadth $= a = 6$

Height $= ar = 6 \times 2 = 12$

Hence, the length of the longest edge is 12 cm.

Fill in the blanks in each of exercises of 27-29.

Q.27 For *a, b, c* to be in G.P. the value of $\frac{a-b}{b-c}$ is equal to ....

Ans. Given that *a, b* and *c* are in GP.

Then, $\frac{b}{a} = \frac{c}{b} = r$ [constant]

$\Rightarrow$ $b = ar \Rightarrow c = br$

Now, $\frac{a-b}{b-c} = \frac{a-ar}{ar-br} = \frac{a(1-r)}{r(a-b)} = \frac{a(1-r)}{r(a-ar)} = \frac{a(1-r)}{ar(1-r)} = \frac{1}{r}$

$\therefore$ $\frac{a-b}{b-c} = \frac{1}{r} = \frac{a}{b}$ or $\frac{b}{c}$

Alternate Method

Given that *a, b* and *c* are in G.P.

Then, $a, b = ar, c = ar^2$

Now, $\frac{a-b}{b-c} = \frac{a-ar}{ar-ar^2} = \frac{(a-ar)}{(a-ar)r} = \frac{1}{r}$ or $\frac{a}{b}$ or $\frac{b}{c}$

***Q.28** The sum of terms equidistant from the beginning and end in an AP is equal to ....

Ans. Let AP be $a, a+d, a+2d \cdots a+(n-1)d$

$\therefore$ $a_1 + a_n = a + a + (n-1)d$

$= 2a + (n-1)d$ ...(i)

Now, $a_2 + a_{n-1} = (a+d) + [a + (n-2)d]$

$= 2a + (n-1)d$

$\Rightarrow$ $a_2 + a_{n-1} = a_1 + a_n$ [from Eq. (i)]

and $a_3 + a_{n-2} = (a+2d) + [a+(n-3)d]$

$= 2a + (n-1)d$

$= a_1 + a_n$ [from Eq. (i)]

To follow this pattern, we can see that the sum of terms equidistant from the beginning and end in an AP is equal to [first term + last term].

(*) Topics related to these question have been removed from latest NCERT.

Q.29 The third term of a GP is 4, the product of the first five terms is .....

Sol. Given, $T_3 = 4$

Let a and r be the first term and common ratio, respectively.

Then, $$ar^2 = 4 \quad \text{...(i)}$$

Product of first 5 terms $= a \cdot ar \cdot ar^2 \cdot ar^3 \cdot ar^4$

$$= a^5 r^{10} = (ar^2)^5 = (4)^5 \quad \text{[using Eq. (i)]}$$

State True or False for the following statements in each of the exercises from 30 to 34.

Q.30 Two sequences cannot be in both AP and GP together.

Ans. *False*

Consider an AP $a, a + d, a + 2d, \ldots$

Now, $$\frac{a_2}{a_1} = \frac{a + d}{a} \neq \frac{a + 2d}{a + d} \Rightarrow \frac{a_2}{a_1} \neq \frac{a_3}{a_2}$$

Thus, AP is not a GP unless all the terms are equal.

***Q.31** Every progression is a sequence but the converse *i.e.*, every sequence is also a progression need not necessarily be true.

Ans. *True*

Consider the progression $a, a + d, a + 2d, \ldots$

and sequence of prime number be 2, 3, 5, 7, 11,...

Clearly, progression is a sequence but sequence is not progression because it does not follow a specific pattern.

***Q.32** Any term of an AP (except first) is equal to half the sum of terms which are equidistant from it.

Ans. *True*

Consider an AP $a, a + d, a + 2d, \ldots$

Now, $$a_2 + a_4 = a + d + a + 3d$$

$$= 2a + 4d = 2a_3$$

$$\Rightarrow \quad a_3 = \frac{a_2 + a_4}{2}$$

Again, $$\frac{a_3 + a_5}{2} = \frac{a + 2d + a + 4d}{2}$$

$$= \frac{2a + 6d}{2}$$

$$= a + 3d = a_4$$

$$\Rightarrow \quad a_4 = \frac{a_3 + a_5}{2}$$

Hence, the statement is true.

(*) Topics related to these question have been removed from latest NCERT.

Q.33 The sum or difference of two GPs, is again a GP.

● **Concept Insight** Use the formula : n^{th} term of G.P is $a_n = ar^{n-1}$

Ans. *False*

Let two GPs are $a, ar_1, ar_1^2, ar_1^3, \ldots$ and $b, br_2, br_2^2, br_2^3, \ldots$

Now, sum of two GPs is $a + b, (ar_1 + br_2), (ar_1^2 + br_2^2), \ldots$

Now, $\frac{T_2}{T_1} = \frac{ar_1 + br_2}{a + b}$ and $\frac{T_3}{T_2} = \frac{ar_1^2 + br_2^2}{ar_1 + br_2}$

$\therefore$ $\frac{T_2}{T_1} \neq \frac{T_3}{T_2}$

Again, difference of two GPs is $a - b, ar_1 - br_2, ar_1^2 - br_2^2, \ldots$

Now, $\frac{T_2}{T_1} = \frac{ar_1 - br_2}{a - b}$ and $\frac{T_3}{T_2} = \frac{ar_1^2 - br_2^2}{ar_1 - br_2}$

$\therefore$ $\frac{T_2}{T_1} \neq \frac{T_3}{T_2}$

So, the sum or difference of two GPs is not a GP. Hence, the statement is false.

***Q.34** If the sum of n terms of a sequence is quadratic expression, then it always represents an AP.

Ans. *False*

Let $S_n = an^2 + bn + c \Rightarrow S_1 = a + b + c$

$a_1 = a + b + c \Rightarrow S_2 = 4a + 2b + c$ $[\because S_1 = a_1]$

$\therefore$ $a_2 = S_2 - S_1$

$= 4a + 2b + c - (a + b + c) = 3a + b$

$S_3 = 9a + 3b + c$

$\therefore$ $a_3 = S_3 - S_2 = 5a + b$

Now, $a_2 - a_1 = (3a + b) - (a + b + c) = 2a - c$

$a_3 - a_2 = (5a + b) - (3a + b) = 2a$

Now, $a_2 - a_1 \neq a_3 - a_2$

Hence, the statement is false.

Match the question given under column I with their appropriate answer given under the column II.

Q.35 Match the following.

Column I	Column II
(a) $4, 1, \frac{1}{4}, \frac{1}{16}$	(i) AP
(b) 2, 3, 5, 7	(ii) Sequence
(c) 13, 8, 3, – 2, – 7	(iii) GP

(*) Topics related to these question have been removed from latest NCERT.

Ans. (a) $4, 1, \frac{1}{4}, \frac{1}{16}$

Here, $\frac{T_2}{T_1} = \frac{1}{4}, \frac{T_3}{T_2} = \frac{1}{4}$ and $\frac{T_4}{T_3} = \frac{1/16}{1/4} = \frac{1}{4}$

Hence, it is a GP.

$\therefore$ (a) $\leftrightarrow$ (iii)

(b) 2, 3, 5, 7

Here, $T_2 - T_1 = 3 - 2 = 1$

and $T_3 - T_2 = 5 - 3 = 2$

$\because$ $T_2 - T_1 \neq T_3 - T_2$

Hence, it is not an AP.

Again, $\frac{T_2}{T_1} = 3/2$ and $\frac{T_3}{T_2} = 5/3$

$\because$ $\frac{T_2}{T_1} \neq \frac{T_3}{T_2}$

It is not a GP.

Hence, it is a sequence.

$\therefore$ (b) $\leftrightarrow$ (ii)

(c) 13, 8, 3, – 2, – 7

$T_2 - T_1 = 8 - 13 = -5$ and $T_3 - T_2 = 3 - 8 = -5$

$\because$ $T_2 - T_1 = T_3 - T_2$

Hence, it is an AP.

$\therefore$ (c) $\leftrightarrow$ (i)

****Q.36*** Match the following.

Column I	Column II
(a) $1^2 + 2^2 + 3^2 + \cdots + n^2$	(i) $\left[\frac{n(n+1)}{2}\right]^2$
(b) $1^3 + 2^3 + 3^3 + \cdots + n^3$	(ii) $n(n+1)$
(c) $2 + 4 + 6 + \cdots + 2n$	(iii) $\frac{n(n+1)(2n+1)}{6}$
(d) $1 + 2 + 3 + \cdots + n$	(iv) $\frac{n(n+1)}{2}$

Ans. (a) $1^2 + 2^2 + 3^2 + \cdots + n^2$

Consider the identity, $(k+1)^3 - k^3 = 3k^2 + 3k + 1$

On putting $k = 1, 2, 3, \ldots, (n-1), n$ successively, we get

$$2^3 - 1^3 = 3\cdot 1^2 + 3\cdot 1 + 1$$
$$3^3 - 2^3 = 3\cdot 2^2 + 3\cdot 2 + 1$$
$$4^3 - 3^3 = 3\cdot 3^2 + 3\cdot 3 + 1$$
$$\ldots\ldots \quad \ldots\ldots \quad \ldots\ldots$$
$$\ldots\ldots \quad \ldots\ldots \quad \ldots\ldots$$
$$n^3 - (n-1)^3 = 3\cdot(n-1)^2 + 3\cdot(n-1) + 1$$
$$(n+1)^3 - n^3 = 3\cdot n^2 + 3\cdot n + 1$$

(✱) Topics related to these question have been removed from latest NCERT.

Adding columnwise, we get

$$(n+1)^3 - 1^3 = n^3 + 3n^2 + 3n = 3\left(\sum_{r=1}^{n} r^2\right) + 3\frac{n(n+1)}{2} + n \qquad \left[\because \sum_{r=1}^{n} r = \frac{n(n+1)}{2}\right]$$

$$\Rightarrow \quad 3\left(\sum_{r=1}^{n} r^2\right) = n^3 + 3n^2 + 3n - \frac{3n(n+1)}{2} - n$$

$$\Rightarrow \quad 3\left(\sum_{r=1}^{n} r^2\right) = \frac{2n^3 + 3n^2 + n}{2} = \frac{n(n+1)(2n+1)}{2}$$

$$\Rightarrow \quad \sum_{r=1}^{n} r^2 = \frac{n(n+1)(2n+1)}{6}$$

Therefore, $\sum_{r=1}^{n} r^2 = 1^2 + 2^2 + \ldots + n^2 = \frac{n(n+1)(2n+1)}{6}$

Hence, (a) $\leftrightarrow$ (iii)

(b) $1^3 + 2^3 + 3^3 + \cdots + n^3$

Consider the identity $(k+1)^4 - k^4 = 4k^3 + 6k^2 + 4k + 1$

On putting $k = 1, 2, 3, \cdots (n-1), n$ successively, we get

$$\begin{aligned}
2^4 - 1^4 &= 4\cdot 1^3 + 6\cdot 1^2 + 4\cdot 1 + 1\\
3^4 - 2^4 &= 4\cdot 2^3 + 6\cdot 2^2 + 4\cdot 2 + 1\\
4^4 - 3^4 &= 4\cdot 3^3 + 6\cdot 3^2 + 4\cdot 3 + 1\\
&\cdots\cdots \quad \cdots\cdots \quad \cdots\cdots\\
&\cdots\cdots \quad \cdots\cdots \quad \cdots\cdots\\
n^4 - (n-1)^4 &= 4(n-1)^3 + 6(n-1)^2 + 4(n-1) + 1\\
(n+1)^4 - n^4 &= 4\cdot n^3 + 6\cdot n^2 + 4\cdot n + 1
\end{aligned}$$

Adding columnwise, we get

$$(n+1)^4 - 1^4 = 4\cdot(1^3 + 2^3 + \cdots + n^3) + 6(1^2 + 2^2 + 3^2 + \cdots + n^2)$$
$$+ 4(1 + 2 + 3 + \cdots + n) + (1 + 1 + \cdots + 1)\, n \text{ terms}$$

$$\Rightarrow \quad n^4 + 4n^3 + 6n^2 + 4n = 4\left(\sum_{r=1}^{n} r^3\right) + 6\left(\sum_{r=1}^{n} r^2\right) + 4\left(\sum_{r=1}^{n} r\right) + n$$

$$\Rightarrow \quad n^4 + 4n^3 + 6n^2 + 4n = 4\left(\sum_{r=1}^{n} r^3\right) + 6\left[\frac{n(n+1)(2n+1)}{6}\right] + 4\left[\frac{n(n+1)}{2}\right] + n$$

On solving, we get

$$\Rightarrow \quad \sum_{r=1}^{n} r^3 = \frac{n^2(n+1)^2}{4} \Rightarrow \sum_{r=1}^{n} r^3 = \left[\frac{n(n+1)}{2}\right]^2 = \left(\sum_{r=1}^{n} r\right)^2$$

Therefore, $\sum_{r=1}^{n} r^3 = 1^3 + 2^3 + \cdots + n^3 = \left[\frac{n(n+1)}{2}\right]^2 = \left(\sum_{r=1}^{n} r\right)^2$

Hence, (b) $\leftrightarrow$ (i)

(c) $2 + 4 + 6 + \cdots + 2n = 2[1 + 2 + 3 + \cdots + n] = 2 \times \frac{n(n+1)}{2} = n(n+1)$

Hence, (C) $\leftrightarrow$ (ii)

(d) Let $\qquad S_n = 1 + 2 + 3 + \cdots + n$

Clearly, it is an arithmetic series with first term, $a = 1$,

common difference, $\quad d = 1$

$$S_n = \frac{n}{2}[2(1) + (n-1)1] = \frac{n(n+1)}{2} \qquad \left[\because S_n = \frac{n}{2}[2a + (n-1)d]\right]$$

$$\therefore \quad 1 + 2 + 3 + \cdots + n = \frac{n(n+1)}{2}.$$

Hence, (d) $\leftrightarrow$ (iv)

Chapter

10

Straight Lines

Short Answer Type Questions

Q.1 Find the equation of the straight line which passes through the point (1 – 2) and cuts off equal intercepts from axes.

Ans. Let the intercepts along the X and Y-axes both be a.

$\therefore$ Equation of the line is $\frac{x}{a} + \frac{y}{a} = 1$ (intercept form of straight line). ...(i)

Since, the point (1, –2) lies on the line,

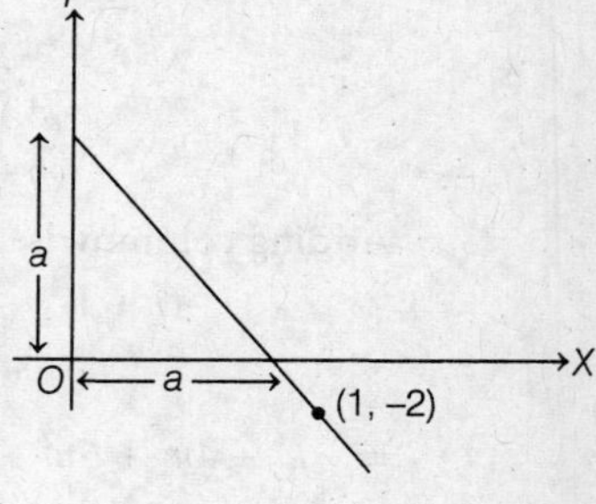

$$\therefore \quad \frac{1}{a} - \frac{2}{a} = 1$$

$$\Rightarrow \quad \frac{1-2}{a} = 1$$

$$\Rightarrow \quad a = -1$$

On putting $a = -1$ in Eq. (i), we get

$$\frac{x}{-1} + \frac{y}{-1} = 1$$

$$\Rightarrow \quad x + y = -1$$

$$\Rightarrow \quad x + y + 1 = 0$$

Q.2 Find the equation of the line passing through the point (5, 2) and perpendicular to the line joining the points (2, 3) and (3, –1).

Thinking Process First of all find the slope, using the formula = $\frac{y_2 - y_1}{x_2 - x_1}$. Then, the slope of perpendicular line is $-\frac{1}{m}$.

Ans. Consider the given points $A(5, 2)$, $B(2, 3)$ and $C(3, -1)$.

Slope of the line passing through the points B and C,

$$m_{BC} = \frac{-1-3}{3-2} = -4$$

Since, the required line is perpendicular to the line joining the points B and C.

So, the slope of required line is $-\frac{1}{m_1} = \frac{1}{4}$. [$\because$ for perpendicular lines, $m_1 m_2 = -1$]

Since, the equation of a line passing through the point $A(5, 2)$ and having slope $\frac{1}{4}$ is

$$y - 2 = \frac{1}{4}(x - 5).$$

$$\Rightarrow \quad 4y - 8 = x - 5$$

$$\Rightarrow \quad x - 4y + 3 = 0$$

Q.3 Find the angle between the lines $y = (2 - \sqrt{3})(x + 5)$ and $y = (2 + \sqrt{3})(x - 7)$.

Thinking Process If the angle between the lines having the slope m_1 and m_2 is θ, then $\tan\theta = \left|\frac{m_1 - m_2}{1 + m_1 m_2}\right|$. Use this formula to solve the above problem.

Ans. Given lines, $\quad y = (2 - \sqrt{3})(x + 5) \quad$ ...(i)

Slope of this line, $\quad m_1 = (2 - \sqrt{3}) \quad [\because y = mx + C]$

and $\quad y = (2 + \sqrt{3})(x - 7) \quad$ ...(ii)

Slope of this line, $\quad m_2 = (2 + \sqrt{3})$

Let θ be the angle between lines (i) and (ii), then

$$\tan\theta = \left|\frac{m_1 - m_2}{1 + m_1 m_2}\right|$$

$$\Rightarrow \quad \tan\theta = \left|\frac{(2 - \sqrt{3}) - (2 + \sqrt{3})}{1 + (2 - \sqrt{3})(2 + \sqrt{3})}\right| \Rightarrow \tan\theta = \left|\frac{-2\sqrt{3}}{1 + 4 - 3}\right|$$

$$\Rightarrow \quad \tan\theta = \sqrt{3}$$

$$\Rightarrow \quad \tan\theta = \tan\frac{\pi}{3}$$

$$\therefore \quad \theta = \frac{\pi}{3} = 60^\circ$$

For obtuse angle $= \pi - \frac{\pi}{3} = \frac{2\pi}{3} = 120^\circ$

Hence, the angle between the lines are 60° or 120°.

Q.4 Find the equation of the lines which passes through the point (3, 4) and cuts off intercepts from the coordinate axes such that their sum is 14.

Ans.

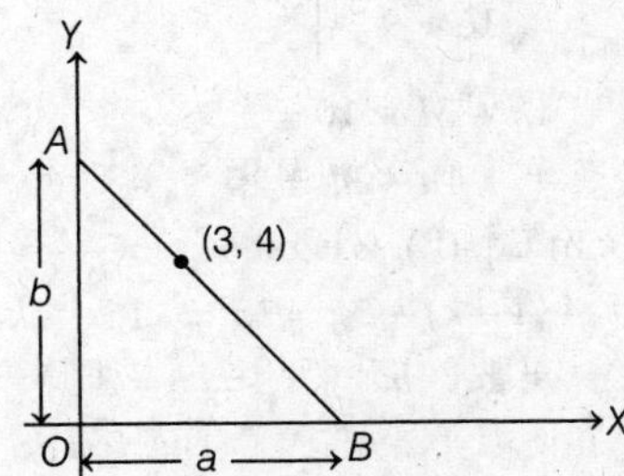

Let the intercepts along the X and Y-axes be a and b, respectively

Given, $\quad a + b = 14 \Rightarrow b = 14 - a$

(✱) Topics related to these question have been removed from latest NCERT.

Now, the equation of line is $\frac{x}{a}+\frac{y}{b}=1$ ...(i)

$\Rightarrow \quad \frac{x}{a}+\frac{y}{14-a}=1$

Since, the point (3, 4) lies on the line.

$\therefore \quad \frac{3}{a}+\frac{4}{14-a}=1$

$\Rightarrow \quad \frac{42-3a+4a}{a(14-a)}=1 \Rightarrow 42+a=14a-a^2$

$\Rightarrow \quad a^2-13a+42=0 \Rightarrow a^2-7a-6a+42=0$

$\Rightarrow \quad a(a-7)-6(a-7)=0 \Rightarrow (a-7)(a-6)=0$

$\Rightarrow \quad a-7=0 \text{ or } a-6=0$

$\therefore \quad a=7 \text{ or } a=6$

When $a=7$, then $b=7$

When $a=6$, then $b=8$

$\therefore$ The equation of line, when $a=7$ and $b=7$ is

$$\frac{x}{7}+\frac{y}{7}=1 \Rightarrow x+y=7$$

And, the equation of line, when $a=6$ and $b=8$ is $\frac{x}{6}+\frac{y}{8}=1$

i.e., $\quad 4x+3y=24$

Q.5 Find the points on the line $x+y=4$ which lie at a unit distance from the line $4x+3y=10$.

Thinking Process The perpendicular distance of a point (x_1, y_1) from the line $Ax+By+C=0$ is d, where $d=\left|\frac{Ax_1+By_1+C}{\sqrt{A^2+B^2}}\right|$.

Ans. Let the required point be (h, k) and point (h, k) lies on the line $x+y=4$

i.e., $\quad h+k=4$ ...(i)

The distance of the point (h, k) from the line $4x+3y=10$ is

$$\left|\frac{4h+3k-10}{\sqrt{16+9}}\right|=1$$

$$4h+3k-10=\pm 5$$

Taking positive sign, $\quad 4h+3k=15$ ...(ii)

From Eq. (i), put $h=4-k$ in Eq. (ii), we get

$$4(4-k)+3k=15 \Rightarrow 16-4k+3k=15 \Rightarrow k=1$$

On putting $k=1$ in Eq. (i), we get $h+1=4 \Rightarrow h=3$

So, the point is (3,1).

Taking negative sign, $\quad 4h+3k-10=-5$

$\Rightarrow \quad 4(4-k)+3k=5$ [put $h=4-k$]

$\Rightarrow \quad 16-4k+3k=5 \Rightarrow -k=5-16=-11$

$\therefore \quad k=11$

On putting $k = 11$ in Eq. (i), we get

$$h + 11 = 4 \Rightarrow h = -7$$

So, the point is $(-7, 11)$

Hence, the required points are $(3, 1)$ and $(-7, 11)$.

*** Q.6** Show that the tangent of an angle between the lines $\frac{x}{a} + \frac{y}{b} = 1$ and $\frac{x}{a} - \frac{y}{b} = 1$ is $\frac{2ab}{a^2 - b^2}$.

Ans. Given, equation of lines are

$$\frac{x}{a} + \frac{y}{b} = 1 \quad \text{...(i)}$$

$$\Rightarrow \quad y = -\frac{b}{a} x + b$$

$$\therefore \quad \text{Slope, } m_1 = -\frac{b}{a} \quad [\because y = mx + c]$$

and

$$\frac{x}{a} - \frac{y}{b} = 1 \quad \text{...(ii)}$$

$$\Rightarrow \quad y = \frac{b}{a} x - b$$

$$\therefore \quad \text{Slope, } m_2 = \frac{b}{a}$$

Let θ be the angle between the given lines, then

$$\tan\theta = \left|\frac{m_1 - m_2}{1 + m_1 m_2}\right| \Rightarrow \tan\theta = \left|\frac{-\frac{b}{a} - \frac{b}{a}}{1 + \left(\frac{-b}{a}\right)\left(\frac{b}{a}\right)}\right|$$

$$\Rightarrow \quad \tan\theta = \left|\frac{\frac{-2b}{a}}{\frac{a^2 - b^2}{a^2}}\right| \Rightarrow \tan\theta = \frac{2ab}{a^2 - b^2}$$

Hence proved.

Q.7 Find the equation of lines passing through (1, 2) and making angle 30° with Y-axis.

- **Concept Insight** Equation of a line passing through the point (x_1, y_1) and having slope m is $y - y_1 = m(x - x_1)$.

Ans. Given that, angle with Y-axis = 30°
and angle with X-axis = 60°

$\therefore$ Slope of the line, $m = \tan 60° = \sqrt{3}$

So, the equation of a line passing through (1, 2) and having slope $\sqrt{3}$, is

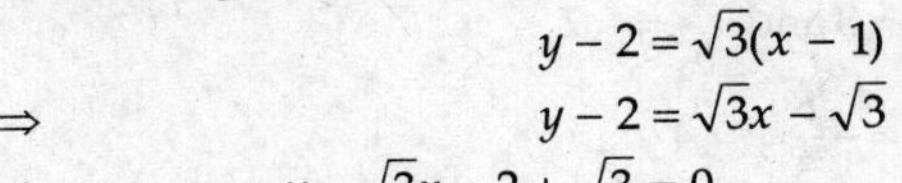

$$y - 2 = \sqrt{3}(x - 1)$$

$$\Rightarrow \quad y - 2 = \sqrt{3}x - \sqrt{3}$$

$$\Rightarrow \quad y - \sqrt{3}x - 2 + \sqrt{3} = 0$$

(✱) Topics related to these question have been removed from latest NCERT.

*** Q.8** Find the equation of the line passing through the point of intersection of $2x + y = 5$ and $x + 3y + 8 = 0$ and parallel to the line $3x + 4y = 7$.

Thinking Process First of all, solve the given equation of lines to get the point of intersection. Then, if a line having slope m_1 is parallel to another line having slope m_2, then $m_1 = m_2$. Now, use the formula *i.e.*, equation of a line passing through the point (x_1, y_1) with slope m is $y - y_1 = m(x - x_1)$.

Ans. Given, equation of lines $\quad 2x + y = 5 \quad$ ...(i)

and $\quad x + 3y = -8 \quad$ ...(ii)

From Eq. (i), $\quad y = 5 - 2x$

Now, put the value of y in Eq. (ii), we get

$$x + 3(5 - 2x) = -8$$

$$\Rightarrow \quad x + 15 - 6x = -8 \Rightarrow -5x = -23 \Rightarrow x = \frac{23}{5}$$

Now, put $x = \frac{23}{5}$ in Eq. (i), we get

$$y = 5 - \frac{46}{5} = \frac{25 - 46}{5} = \frac{-21}{5}$$

Since, the required line is parallel to the line $3x + 4y = 7$.

So, slope of the line is $m = \frac{-3}{4}$.

Now, the equation of the line passing through the point $\left(\frac{23}{5}, \frac{-21}{5}\right)$ having slope $\frac{-3}{4}$ is

$$y + \frac{21}{5} = \frac{-3}{4}\left(x - \frac{23}{5}\right) \Rightarrow 4y + \frac{84}{5} = -3x + \frac{69}{5} \quad [\because y - y_1 = m(x - x_1)]$$

$$\Rightarrow \quad 3x + 4y + \frac{84 - 69}{5} \Rightarrow 3x + 4y + \frac{15}{5} = 0 \Rightarrow 3x + 4y + 3 = 0$$

*** Q.9** For what values of a and b the intercepts cut off on the coordinate axes by the line $ax + by + 8 = 0$ are equal in length but opposite in signs to those cut off by the line $2x - 3y + 6 = 0$ on the axes?

Ans. Given, equation of lines $\quad ax + by + 8 = 0$

$$\Rightarrow \quad \frac{x}{\frac{-8}{a}} + \frac{y}{\frac{-8}{b}} = 1$$

So, the intercepts are $\frac{-8}{a}$ and $\frac{-8}{b}$ and $2x - 3y + 6 = 0$.

$$\Rightarrow \quad \frac{x}{-3} + \frac{y}{2} = 1$$

So, the intercepts are -3 and 2.

According to the question, $\quad \frac{-8}{a} = 3$ and $\frac{-8}{b} = -2$

$$\therefore \quad a = -\frac{8}{3}, b = 4$$

(✱) Topics related to these question have been removed from latest NCERT.

Q.10 If the intercept of a line between the coordinate axes is divided by the point $(-5, 4)$ in the ratio $1:2$, then find the equation of the line.

- **Concept Insight** The coordinates of a point which divide the line joining two points (x_1, y_1) and (x_2, y_2) in the ratio $m_1 : m_2$ internally is $\left(\frac{m_1 x_2 + m_2 x_1}{m_1 + m_2}, \frac{m_1 y_2 + m_2 y_1}{m_1 + m_2}\right)$.

Ans. Let the intercepts along the X and Y-axes are h and k, respectively.

The coordinates of A and B are $(h, 0)$ and $(0, k)$ respectively.

$$-5 = \frac{1 \times 0 + 2 \times h}{1 + 2}$$

$\therefore$ $$-5 = \frac{2h}{3} \Rightarrow h = -\frac{15}{2}$$

and $$4 = \frac{1 \times k + 0 \times 2}{1 + 2}$$

$\Rightarrow$ $$k = 12$$

$\therefore$ $$A = \left(-\frac{15}{2}, 0\right) \text{ and } B = (0, 12)$$

Hence, the equation of a line passing through two points (x_1, y_1) and (x_2, y_2) is given by

$$y - y_1 = \frac{y_2 - y_1}{x_2 - x_1}(x - x_1) \Rightarrow y - 0 = \frac{12 - 0}{0 + 15/2}\left(x + \frac{15}{2}\right)$$

$\Rightarrow$ $$y = \frac{12 \times 2}{15}\left(x + \frac{15}{2}\right) \Rightarrow 5y = 8x + 60 \Rightarrow 8x - 5y + 60 = 0$$

* **Q.11** Find the equation of a straight line on which length of perpendicular from the origin is four units and the line makes an angle of 120° with the positive direction of X-axis.

Thinking Process The equation of the line having normal distance P from the origin and angle α which the normal makes with the positive direction of X-axis is $x\cos\alpha + y\sin\alpha = p$. Use this formula to solve the above problem.

Ans. Given that, $OC = P = 4$ units

$\angle BAX = 120°$

Let $\angle COA = \alpha$, $\angle OCA = 90°$

$\because$ $\angle BAX = \angle COA + \angle OCA$ [exterior angle property]

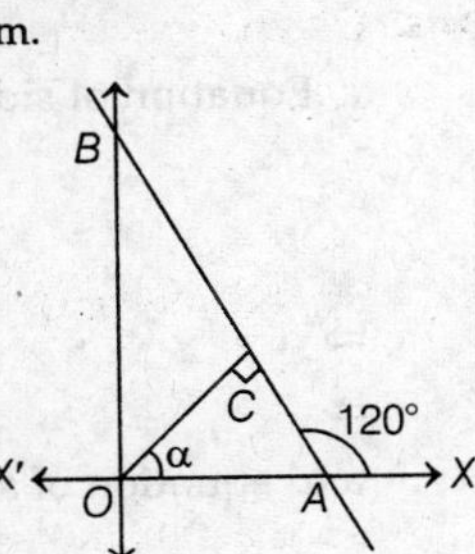

$\Rightarrow$ $120° = \alpha + 90°$

$\therefore$ $\alpha = 30°$

Now, the equation of required line is

$$x\cos 30° + y\sin 30° = 4$$

$\Rightarrow$ $$x \cdot \frac{\sqrt{3}}{2} + y \cdot \frac{1}{2} = 4 \Rightarrow \sqrt{3}x + y = 8$$

(*) Topics related to these question have been removed from latest NCERT.

***Q.12** Find the equation of one of the sides of an isosceles right angled triangle whose hypotenuse is given by $3x + 4y = 4$ and the opposite vertex of the hypotenuse is (2, 2).

- **Concept Insight** An acute angle (say θ) between two lines with slope m_1 and m_2 is given by $\tan\theta = \left|\dfrac{m_2 - m_1}{1 + m_1 m_2}\right|$

Ans. Let slope of line AC be m and slope of line BC is $\dfrac{-3}{4}$ and let angle between line AC and BC be θ.

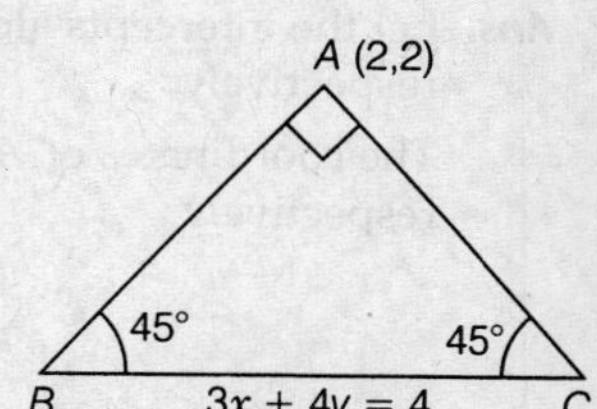

$$\therefore \quad \tan\theta = \left|\frac{m + \frac{3}{4}}{1 - \frac{3m}{4}}\right| \Rightarrow \tan 45° = \pm\left[\frac{m + \frac{3}{4}}{1 - \frac{3m}{4}}\right]$$

Taking positive sign,
$$1 = \frac{m + \frac{3}{4}}{1 - \frac{3m}{4}}$$

$$\Rightarrow \quad m + \frac{3}{4} = 1 - \frac{3m}{4}$$

$$\Rightarrow \quad m + \frac{3m}{4} = 1 - \frac{3}{4}$$

$$\Rightarrow \quad \frac{7m}{4} = \frac{1}{4} \Rightarrow m = \frac{1}{7}$$

Taking negative sign,
$$1 = -\left(\frac{m + \frac{3}{4}}{1 - \frac{3m}{4}}\right) \Rightarrow 1 - \frac{3m}{4} = -m - \frac{3}{4}$$

$$\Rightarrow \quad m - \frac{3m}{4} = -1 - \frac{3}{4}$$

$$\Rightarrow \quad \frac{m}{4} = \frac{-7}{4} \Rightarrow m = -7$$

$\therefore$ Equation of side AC passing through (2, 2) and having slope $\left(\dfrac{1}{7}\right)$ is
$$y - 2 = \frac{1}{7}(x - 2)$$
$$\Rightarrow \quad 7y - 14 = x - 2$$
$$\Rightarrow \quad x - 7y + 12 = 0$$

and equation of side AB passing through (2, 2) and having slope (– 7) is
$$y - 2 = -7(x - 2)$$
$$\Rightarrow \quad y - 2 = -7x + 14$$
$$\Rightarrow \quad 7x + y - 16 = 0$$

(✱) Topics related to these question have been removed from latest NCERT.

Long Answer Type Questions

Q.13 If the equation of the base of an equilateral triangle is $x+y=2$ and the vertex is (2, –1), then find the length of the side of the triangle.

Ans. Given that equilateral ΔABC having equation of base is $x+y=2$.

In ΔABD,
$$\sin 60^\circ = \frac{AD}{AB}$$

$$\Rightarrow \quad AD = AB\sin 60^\circ = AB\frac{\sqrt{3}}{2}$$

$$\therefore \quad AD = AB\frac{\sqrt{3}}{2} \quad \ldots\text{(i)}$$

Now, the length of perpendicular from (2, –1) to the line $x+y=2$ is given by

$$AD = \left|\frac{2+(-1)-2}{\sqrt{1^2+1^2}}\right| = \frac{1}{\sqrt{2}}$$

From Eq. (i),
$$\frac{1}{\sqrt{2}} = AB\frac{\sqrt{3}}{2}$$

$$AB = \sqrt{\frac{2}{3}}$$

Q.14 A variable line passes through a fixed point P. The algebraic sum of the perpendiculars drawn from the points (2, 0), (0, 2) and (1, 1) on the line is zero. Find the coordinates of the point P.

Thinking Process Let the slope of the line be m. Then, the equation of the line passing through the fixed point $P(x_1, y_1)$ is $y - y_1 = m(x - x_1)$. According to the given condition, take the algebraic sum of perpendicular distances equal to zero, we get $y_1 - 1 = m(x_1 - 1)$. Thus, (x_1, y_1) is (1, 1).

Ans. Let slope of the line be m and the coordinates of fixed point P are (x_1, y_1).

$\therefore$ Equation of line is $y - y_1 = m(x - x_1)$ ...(i)

Since, the given points are $A(2, 0)$, $B(0, 2)$ and $C(1, 1)$.

Now, perpendicular distance from A is

$$\frac{0 - y_1 - m(2 - x_1)}{\sqrt{1+m^2}} \quad \ldots\text{(ii)}$$

Perpendicular distance from B is

$$\frac{2 - y_1 - m(0 - x_1)}{\sqrt{1+m^2}} \quad \ldots\text{(iii)}$$

and perpendicular distance from C is

$$\frac{1 - y_1 - m(1 - x_1)}{\sqrt{1+m^2}} \quad \ldots\text{(iv)}$$

Now, on adding Eqs. (ii), (iii) and (iv), we get

$$\frac{-y_1 - 2m + mx_1 + 2 - y_1 + mx_1 + 1 - y_1 - m + mx_1}{\sqrt{1+m^2}} = 0$$

$$\Rightarrow \quad -3y_1 - 3m + 3mx_1 + 3 = 0$$

$$\Rightarrow \quad -y_1 - m + mx_1 + 1 = 0$$

Since, (1, 1) lies on this line. So, the point P is (1, 1).

Q.15 In what direction should a line be drawn through the point (1, 2), so that its point of intersection with the line $x + y = 4$ is at a distance $\frac{\sqrt{6}}{3}$ from the given point?

Ans. Let slope of the line be m. As, the line passes through the point $A(1, 2)$.

$\therefore$ Equation of line, $y - 2 = m(x - 1)$

$$mx - y + 2 - m = 0 \quad \text{...(i)}$$

and

$$x + y - 4 = 0 \quad \text{...(ii)}$$

$$\frac{x}{(4 - 2 + m)} = \frac{y}{2 - m + 4m} = \frac{1}{1 + m}$$

$$\Rightarrow \quad \frac{x}{2 + m} = \frac{y}{3m + 2} = \frac{1}{1 + m} \Rightarrow x = \frac{2 + m}{1 + m}$$

and

$$y = \frac{3m + 2}{1 + m}$$

So, the point of intersection is $B\left(\frac{m+2}{m+1}, \frac{3m+2}{m+1}\right)$.

Now,

$$(AB)^2 = \left(\frac{m+2}{m+1} - 1\right)^2 + \left(\frac{3m+2}{m+1} - 2\right)^2$$

$$\because \quad AB = \frac{\sqrt{6}}{3} \quad \text{[given]}$$

$$\therefore \quad \left(\frac{m + 2 - m - 1}{m+1}\right)^2 + \left(\frac{3m + 2 - 2m - 2}{m+1}\right)^2 = \frac{6}{9}$$

$$\Rightarrow \quad \left(\frac{1}{m+1}\right)^2 + \left(\frac{m}{m+1}\right)^2 = \frac{6}{9} \Rightarrow \frac{1 + m^2}{(1+m)^2} = \frac{6}{9}$$

$$\Rightarrow \quad \frac{1 + m^2}{1 + m^2 + 2m} = \frac{6}{9}$$

$$\Rightarrow \quad 9 + 9m^2 = 6 + 6m^2 + 12m$$

$$\Rightarrow \quad 3m^2 - 12m + 3 = 0$$

$$\Rightarrow \quad m^2 - 4m + 1 = 0$$

$$\Rightarrow \quad m = \frac{4 \pm \sqrt{16 - 4}}{2} = 2 \pm \sqrt{3}$$

$$= 2 + \sqrt{3} \text{ or } 2 - \sqrt{3}$$

$$\therefore \quad \theta = 75° \text{ or } 15°$$

Q.16 A straight line moves so that the sum of the reciprocals of its intercepts made on axes is constant. Show that the line passes through a fixed point.

Ans. Since, the intercept form of a line is $\frac{x}{a}+\frac{y}{b}=1$

Given, $$\frac{1}{a}+\frac{1}{b}=\text{constant}=\frac{1}{k}\text{ (say)}$$

$$\because \quad \frac{1}{a}+\frac{1}{b}=\frac{1}{k}$$

$$\Rightarrow \quad \frac{k}{a}+\frac{k}{b}=1$$

So, (k, k) lies on $\frac{x}{a}+\frac{y}{b}=1$.

Hence, the line passes through the fixed point.

Q.17 Find the equation of the line which passes through the point $(-4, 3)$ and the portion of the line intercepted between the axes is divided internally in the ratio 5 : 3 by this point.

- **Concept Insight** If the point (h, k) divides the join of $A(x_1, y_1)$ and $B(x_2, y_2)$ internally, in the ratio $m_1 : m_2$. Then, first of all, find the coordinates of A and B using section formula for internal division *i.e.*, $h=\frac{m_1x_2+m_2x_1}{m_1+m_2}$, $k=\frac{m_1y_2+m_2y_1}{m_1+m_2}$. Then, find the equation of required line.

Ans. Since, the line intersects X and Y-axes respectively at $A(x, 0)$ and $B(0, y)$.

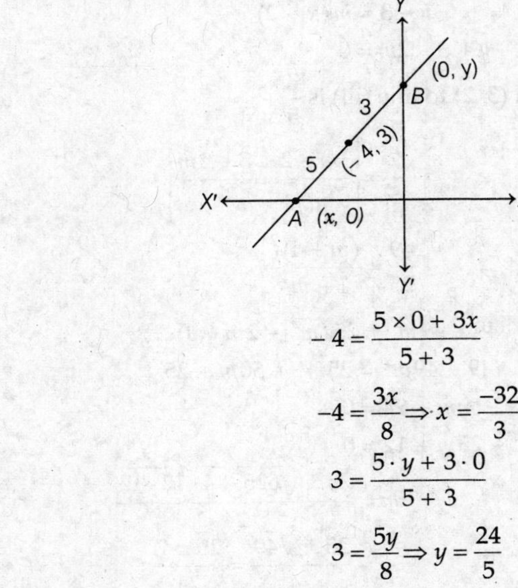

$$-4=\frac{5\times 0+3x}{5+3}$$

$$\Rightarrow \quad -4=\frac{3x}{8}\Rightarrow x=\frac{-32}{3}$$

and $$3=\frac{5\cdot y+3\cdot 0}{5+3}$$

$$\Rightarrow \quad 3=\frac{5y}{8}\Rightarrow y=\frac{24}{5}$$

Since, the intercept along the X and Y-axes both are $a=\frac{-32}{3}$ and $b=\frac{24}{5}$, respectively.

(✱) Topics related to these question have been removed from latest NCERT.

$\therefore$ The required equation of line is

$$\frac{x}{-32/3}+\frac{y}{24/5}=1$$

$$\Rightarrow \quad \frac{-3x}{32}+\frac{5y}{24}=1$$

$$\Rightarrow \quad -9x+20y=96$$

$$\Rightarrow \quad 9x-20y+96=0$$

***Q.18** Find the equations of the lines through the point of intersection of the lines $x-y+1=0$ and $2x-3y+5=0$ and whose distance from the point (3, 2) is $\frac{7}{5}$.

Ans. Given, equation of line are $x-y+1=0$ ...(i)

and $2x-3y+5=0$ ...(ii)

From Eq. (i), $x=y-1$

Now, put the value of x in Eq. (ii), we get

$$2(y-1)-3y+5=0$$

$$\Rightarrow \quad 2y-2-3y+5=0$$

$$\Rightarrow \quad 3-y=0 \Rightarrow y=3$$

On putting $y=3$ in Eq. (i), we get

$$x=2$$

So, the point of intersection is (2, 3).

Let slope of the required line be m.

$\therefore$ Equation of line is $y-3=m(x-2)$

$\Rightarrow \quad mx-y+3-2m=0$ ...(iii)

Since, the distance from (3, 2) to line (iii) is $\frac{7}{5}$.

$$\therefore \quad \frac{7}{5}=\left|\frac{3m-2+3-2m}{\sqrt{1+m^2}}\right|$$

$$\Rightarrow \quad \frac{49}{25}=\frac{(m+1)^2}{1+m^2}$$

$$\Rightarrow \quad 49+49m^2=25(m^2+2m+1)$$

$$\Rightarrow \quad 49+49m^2=25m^2+50m+25$$

$$\Rightarrow \quad 24m^2-50m+24=0$$

$$\Rightarrow \quad 12m^2-25m+12=0$$

$$\therefore \quad m=\frac{25\pm\sqrt{625-4\cdot 12\cdot 12}}{24}$$

$$=\frac{25\pm\sqrt{49}}{24}=\frac{25\pm 7}{24}$$

$$=\frac{32}{24} \text{ or } \frac{18}{24}=\frac{4}{3} \text{ or } \frac{3}{4}$$

(*) Topics related to these question have been removed from latest NCERT.

Thus, the first equation of a line is $y - 3 = \frac{4}{3}(x - 2)$

$$\Rightarrow \quad 3y - 9 = 4x - 8$$

$$\Rightarrow \quad 4x - 3y + 1 = 0$$

and second equation of line is $y - 3 = \frac{3}{4}(x - 2)$

$$\Rightarrow \quad 4y - 12 = 3x - 6$$

$$\Rightarrow \quad 3x - 4y + 6 = 0$$

Q.19 If the sum of the distances of a moving point in a plane from the axes is 1, then find the locus of the point.

Thinking Process Given that $|x| + |y| = 1$, which gives us locus of the point which is square.

Ans. Let the coordinates of moving point P be (x, y).

Given that, the sum of distances of this point in a plane from the axes is 1.

$$\therefore \quad |x| + |y| = 1$$

$$\Rightarrow \quad \pm x \pm y = 1$$

$$\Rightarrow \quad x + y = 1,$$

$$-x - y = 1,$$

$$-x + y = 1,$$

and $$x - y = 1$$

So, these equations give us locus of the point P which is a square.

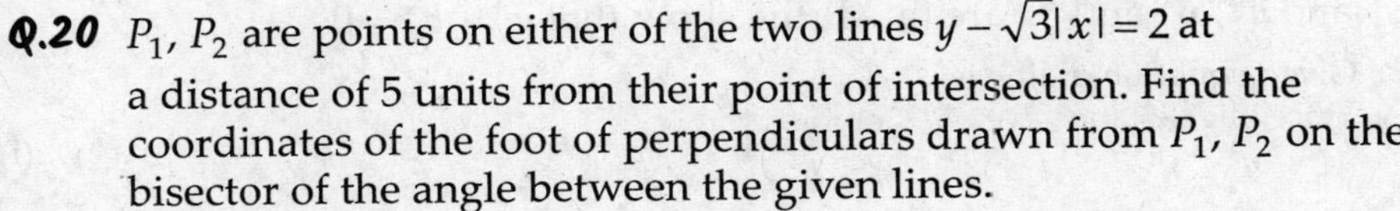

Q.20 P_1, P_2 are points on either of the two lines $y - \sqrt{3}|x| = 2$ at a distance of 5 units from their point of intersection. Find the coordinates of the foot of perpendiculars drawn from P_1, P_2 on the bisector of the angle between the given lines.

Thinking Process Lines are $y = \sqrt{3}x + 2$ and $y = -\sqrt{3}x + 2$ according as $x \geq 0$ or $x < 0$. Y-axis is the bisector of the angles between the lines. P_1, P_2 are the points on these lines at a distance of 5 units from the point of intersection of these lines which have a point on Y-axis as common foot of perpendiculars drawn from these points. Then, the y-coordinate of the foot of the perpendiculars is given by $2 + 5\cos 30°$.

Ans. Given equation of lines are $y - \sqrt{3}x = 2$ $\quad [\because x \geq 0]$

and $y + \sqrt{3}x = 2$ $\quad [\because x < 0]$

$$\Rightarrow \quad y = \sqrt{3}x + 2 \quad \ldots\text{(i)}$$

and $$y = -\sqrt{3}x + 2 \quad \ldots\text{(ii)}$$

On solving Eqs. (i) and (ii), we get point of intersection.

$$\sqrt{3}x + 2 = -\sqrt{3}x + 2$$

$$\Rightarrow \quad 2\sqrt{3}x = 0 \Rightarrow x = 0$$

On putting $x = 0$ in Eq. (i), we get

$$y = 2$$

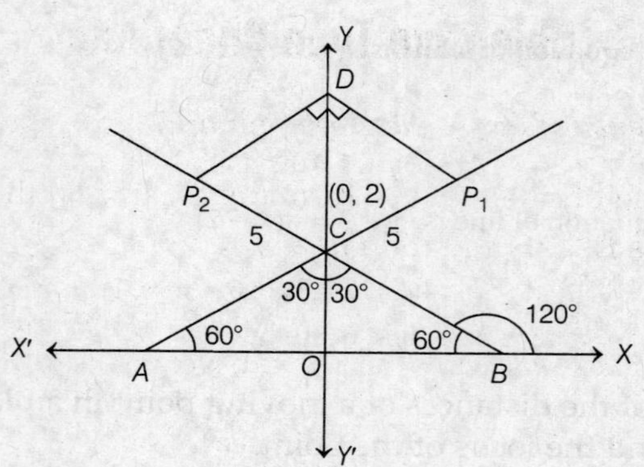

So, the point of intersection of lines (i) and (ii) is (0, 2).

Here, $$OC = 2$$

In ΔDP_1C, $$\frac{CD}{CP_1} = \cos 30°$$

$\therefore$ $$CD = 5\cos 30° = 5\cdot\frac{\sqrt{3}}{2}$$

$\Rightarrow$ $$OD = OC + CD = 2 + 5\frac{\sqrt{3}}{2}$$

So, the coordinates of the foot of perpendiculars are $\left(0, 2 + \frac{5\sqrt{3}}{2}\right)$.

Q.21 If p is the length of perpendicular from the origin on the line $\frac{x}{a} + \frac{y}{b} = 1$ and a^2, p^2 and b^2 are in AP, the show that $a^4 + b^4 = 0$.

Ans. Given equation of line is,

$$\frac{x}{a} + \frac{y}{b} = 1 \quad \ldots\text{(i)}$$

Perpendicular length from the origin on the line (i) is given by p

i.e., $$p = \frac{1}{\sqrt{\frac{1}{a^2} + \frac{1}{b^2}}} = \frac{ab}{\sqrt{a^2 + b^2}}$$

$\therefore$ $$p^2 = \frac{a^2b^2}{a^2 + b^2}$$

Given that, a^2, p^2 and b^2 are in AP.

$\therefore$ $$2p^2 = a^2 + b^2$$

$\Rightarrow$ $$\frac{2a^2b^2}{a^2 + b^2} = a^2 + b^2$$

$\Rightarrow$ $$2a^2b^2 = (a^2 + b^2)^2$$

$\Rightarrow$ $$2a^2b^2 = a^4 + b^4 + 2a^2b^2$$

$\Rightarrow$ $$a^4 + b^4 = 0$$

Objective Type Questions

Choose the correct answers from the given four options in each exercise 22 to 41.

Q.22 A line cutting off intercept -3 from the Y-axis and the tangent at angle to the X-axis is $\frac{3}{5}$, its equation is

(a) $5y - 3x + 15 = 0$ (b) $3y - 5x + 15 = 0$
(c) $5y - 3x - 15 = 0$ (d) None of these

Ans. ***(a)*** Given, $c = -3$ and $m = \frac{3}{5}$

$\therefore$ Equation of the line is $y = mx + c$

$$y = \frac{3}{5}x - 3$$

$\Rightarrow$ $5y = 3x - 15$

$\Rightarrow$ $5y - 3x + 15 = 0$

***Q.23** Slope of a line which cuts off intercepts of equal lengths on the axes is

(a) -1 (b) 0
(c) 2 (d) $\sqrt{3}$

Ans. ***(a)*** Let equation of line be $\frac{x}{a} + \frac{y}{a} = 1$

$\Rightarrow$ $x + y = a$

$\Rightarrow$ $y = -x + a$

On comparing with $y = mx + c$, we get $m = -1$

$\therefore$ Required slope $= -1$

***Q.24** The equation of the straight line passing through the point (3, 2) and perpendicular to the line $y = x$ is

(a) $x - y = 5$ (b) $x + y = 5$
(c) $x + y = 1$ (d) $x - y = 1$

Ans. ***(b)*** Given, line passes through the point (3, 2) and perpendicular to the line $y = x$.

$\because$ The slope of perpendicular line $(m) = -1$ $\left[\because m_2 = -\frac{1}{m_1}\right]$

Now, equation of line which passes through (3, 2) is

$$y - 2 = -1(x - 3)$$

$\Rightarrow$ $y - 2 = -x + 3 \Rightarrow x + y = 5$

***Q.25** The equation of the line passing through the point (1, 2) and perpendicular to the line $x + y + 1 = 0$ is

(a) $y - x + 1 = 0$ (b) $y - x - 1 = 0$
(c) $y - x + 2 = 0$ (d) $y - x - 2 = 0$

(*) Topics related to these question have been removed from latest NCERT.

Ans. ***(b)*** Given point is (1, 2) and equation of line is

$$x + y + 1 = 0$$

$$\Rightarrow \quad y = -x - 1$$

So, slope of given line is −1.

$\therefore$ Slope of the perpendicular line $= \dfrac{-1}{-1} = 1$

So, the required equation of line passing through the point (1, 2) is

$$y - 2 = 1(x - 1)$$

$$\Rightarrow \quad y - 2 = x - 1$$

$$\Rightarrow \quad y - x - 1 = 0$$

****Q.26** The tangent of angle between the lines whose intercepts on the axes are $a, -b$ and $b, -a$ respectively, is

(a) $\dfrac{a^2 - b^2}{ab}$ (b) $\dfrac{b^2 - a^2}{2}$ (c) $\dfrac{b^2 - a^2}{2ab}$ (d) None of these

Ans. ***(c)*** Since, intercepts on the axes are $a, -b$ then equation of the line is $\dfrac{x}{a} - \dfrac{y}{b} = 1$.

$$\Rightarrow \quad \frac{y}{b} = \frac{x}{a} - 1$$

$$\Rightarrow \quad y = \frac{bx}{a} - b$$

So, the slope of this line *i.e.*, $m_1 = \dfrac{b}{a}$.

Also, for intercepts on the axes as $b, -a$ then equation of the line is

$$\frac{x}{b} - \frac{y}{a} = 1$$

$$\Rightarrow \quad \frac{y}{a} = \frac{x}{b} - 1 \Rightarrow y = \frac{a}{b}x - a$$

So, slope of this line *i.e.*, $m_2 = \dfrac{a}{b}$

Now, $$\tan\theta = \frac{\frac{b}{a} - \frac{a}{b}}{1 + \frac{a}{b}\cdot\frac{b}{a}} = \frac{\frac{b^2 - a^2}{ab}}{2} = \frac{b^2 - a^2}{2ab} \qquad \left[\because \tan = \left|\frac{m_1 - m_2}{1 + m_1 m_2}\right|\right]$$

Q.27 If the line $\dfrac{x}{a} + \dfrac{y}{b} = 1$ passes through the points (2, −3) and (4, −5), then (a, b) is

(a) (1, 1) (b) (−1, 1) (c) (1, −1) (d) (−1, −1)

Ans. ***(d)*** Given, line is $\dfrac{x}{a} + \dfrac{y}{b} = 1$ ...(i)

Since, the points (2, −3) and (4, −5) lies on this line.

$$\therefore \quad \frac{2}{a} - \frac{3}{b} = 1 \qquad \text{...(ii)}$$

(*) Topics related to these question have been removed from latest NCERT.

and $$\frac{4}{a}-\frac{5}{b}=1 \quad \text{...(iii)}$$

On multiplying by 2 in Eq. (ii) and then subtracting Eq. (iii) from Eq. (ii), we get

$$-\frac{6}{b}+\frac{5}{b}=1 \Rightarrow \frac{-1}{b}=1$$

$\therefore$ $$b=-1$$

On putting $b=-1$ in Eq. (ii), we get

$$\frac{2}{a}+3=1 \Rightarrow \frac{2}{a}=-2 \Rightarrow a=-1$$

$\therefore$ $$(a, b)=(-1,-1)$$

Q.28 The distance of the point of intersection of the lines $2x-3y+5=0$ and $3x+4y=0$ from the line $5x-2y=0$ is

(a) $\frac{130}{17\sqrt{29}}$ (b) $\frac{13}{7\sqrt{29}}$ (c) $\frac{130}{7}$ (d) None of these

Thinking Process First of all, find the point of intersection of the given first two lines, then get the perpendicular distance from this point to the third line. Using formula *i.e.*, distance of a point (x_1, y_1), from the line $ax+by+c=0$ is $d=\frac{|ax_1+by_1+c|}{\sqrt{a^2+b^2}}$.

Ans. ***(a)*** Given, equation of lines are

$$2x-3y+5=0 \quad \text{...(i)}$$

and $$3x+4y=0 \quad \text{...(ii)}$$

From Eq. (ii), put the value of $x=\frac{-4y}{3}$ in Eq. (i), we get

$$2\left(\frac{-4y}{3}\right)-3y+5=0 \Rightarrow -8y-9y+15=0$$

$$\Rightarrow \quad y=\frac{15}{17}$$

From Eq. (ii), $$3x+4\cdot\frac{15}{17}=0$$

$$\Rightarrow \quad x=\frac{-60}{17\cdot 3}=\frac{-20}{17}$$

So, the point of intersection is $\left(\frac{-20}{17}, \frac{15}{17}\right)$.

$\therefore$ Required distance from the line $5x-2y=0$ is,

$$d=\frac{\left|5\times\frac{-20}{17}-2\left(\frac{15}{17}\right)\right|}{\sqrt{25+4}}=\frac{\left|\frac{-100}{17}-\frac{30}{17}\right|}{\sqrt{29}}=\frac{130}{17\sqrt{29}}$$

$\left[\because \text{ distance of a point } p(x_1, y_1) \text{ from the line } ax+by+c=0 \text{ is } d=\frac{|ax_1+by_1+c|}{\sqrt{a^2+b^2}}\right]$

***Q.29** The equation of the lines which pass through the point (3, –2) and are inclined at 60° to the line $\sqrt{3}x + y = 1$ is

(a) $y + 2 = 0, \sqrt{3}x - y - 2 - 3\sqrt{3} = 0$
(b) $x - 2 = 0, \sqrt{3}x - y + 2 + 3\sqrt{3} = 0$
(c) $\sqrt{3}x - y - 2 - 3\sqrt{3} = 0$
(d) None of the above

Ans. ***(a)*** Given point A is (3, –2) and the equation of line $\sqrt{3}x + y = 1$

$$\Rightarrow \quad y = -\sqrt{3}\,x + 1$$

$$\therefore \quad \text{Slope, } m_1 = -\sqrt{3}$$

Let slope of the required line be m_2.

$$\text{then,} \quad \tan\theta = \left|\frac{-\sqrt{3} - m_2}{1 - \sqrt{3}\,m_2}\right| \quad \left[\because \tan\theta = \left|\frac{m_1 - m_2}{1 + m_1 m_2}\right|\right]$$

$$\Rightarrow \quad \tan 60° = \pm\left(\frac{-\sqrt{3} - m_2}{1 - \sqrt{3}\,m_2}\right) \quad \ldots\text{(i)}$$

$$\Rightarrow \quad \sqrt{3} = \left(\frac{-\sqrt{3} - m_2}{1 - \sqrt{3}\,m_2}\right) \quad \text{[take positive sign]}$$

$$\Rightarrow \quad \sqrt{3} - 3m_2 = -\sqrt{3} - m_2$$

$$\Rightarrow \quad 2\sqrt{3} = 2m_2 \quad \Rightarrow m_2 = \sqrt{3}$$

$\therefore$ Equation of line passing through (3, – 2) and having slope $\sqrt{3}$ is

$$y + 2 = \sqrt{3}(x - 3)$$

$$y - \sqrt{3}x + 2 + 3\sqrt{3} = 0$$

$$\Rightarrow \quad \sqrt{3}x - y - 2 - 3\sqrt{3} = 0 \quad \text{[take negative sign in Eq. (i)]}$$

$$\Rightarrow \quad \sqrt{3} - 3m_2 = \sqrt{3} + m_2$$

$$\Rightarrow \quad m_2 = 0$$

$\therefore$ The equation of line is $\quad y + 2 = 0\,(x - 3)$

$$\Rightarrow \quad y + 2 = 0 \quad \ldots\text{(ii)}$$

So, the required equation of lines are $\sqrt{3}\,x - y - 2 - 3\sqrt{3} = 0$ and $y + 2 = 0$.

Q.30 The equations of the lines passing through the point (1, 0) and at a distance $\frac{\sqrt{3}}{2}$ from the origin, are

(a) $\sqrt{3}x + y - \sqrt{3} = 0, \sqrt{3}x - y - \sqrt{3} = 0$
(b) $\sqrt{3}x + y + \sqrt{3} = 0, \sqrt{3}x - y + \sqrt{3} = 0$
(c) $x + \sqrt{3}y - \sqrt{3} = 0, x - \sqrt{3}y - \sqrt{3} = 0$
(d) None of the above

Ans. ***(a)*** Let slope of the line be m.

$\because$ Equation of line passing through (1, 0) is

$$y - 0 = m\,(x - 1)$$

$$\Rightarrow \quad y - mx + m = 0 \quad \ldots\text{(i)}$$

(✱) Topics related to these question have been removed from latest NCERT.

Since, the distance of Eq. (i) from origin is $\frac{\sqrt{3}}{2}$.

Then, $$\frac{\sqrt{3}}{2} = \frac{0-0+m}{\sqrt{1+m^2}}$$

$$\Rightarrow \quad \frac{\sqrt{3}}{2} = \frac{m}{\sqrt{1+m^2}}$$

$$\Rightarrow \quad \frac{3}{4} = \frac{m^2}{1+m^2} \Rightarrow 3 + 3m^2 = 4m^2$$

$$\Rightarrow \quad m^2 = 3 \quad \Rightarrow m = \pm\sqrt{3}$$

So, the first equation of line is

$$y = \sqrt{3}(x-1)$$

$$\Rightarrow \quad \sqrt{3}x - y - \sqrt{3} = 0$$

and the second equation of line is

$$y = -\sqrt{3}(x-1) \Rightarrow \sqrt{3}x + y - \sqrt{3} = 0$$

Q.31 The distance between the lines $y = mx + c_1$ and $y = mx + c_2$ is

(a) $\frac{c_1 - c_2}{\sqrt{m^2+1}}$ (b) $\frac{|c_1 - c_2|}{\sqrt{1+m^2}}$ (c) $\frac{c_2 - c_1}{\sqrt{1+m^2}}$ (d) 0

Ans. (b) Given, equation of the lines are

$$y = mx + c_1 \quad \text{...(i)}$$

and $$y = mx + c_2 \quad \text{...(ii)}$$

$\therefore$ Distance between Eqs. (i) and (ii) is given by $d = \frac{|c_1 - c_2|}{\sqrt{1+m^2}}$

***Q.32** The coordinates of the foot of perpendiculars from the point (2, 3) on the line $y = 3x + 4$ is given by

(a) $\left(\frac{37}{10}, \frac{-1}{10}\right)$ (b) $\left(-\frac{1}{10}, \frac{37}{10}\right)$ (c) $\left(\frac{10}{37}, -10\right)$ (d) $\left(\frac{2}{3}, -\frac{1}{3}\right)$

Ans. (b) Given, equation of the line is

$$y = 3x + 4 \quad \text{...(i)}$$

$\therefore$ Slope of this line, $m_1 = 3$

So, the slope of perpendicular line OP is $-\frac{1}{3}$.

[$\because OP \perp AB$ and slope of perpendicular line is given by $m_2 = -\frac{1}{m_1}$]

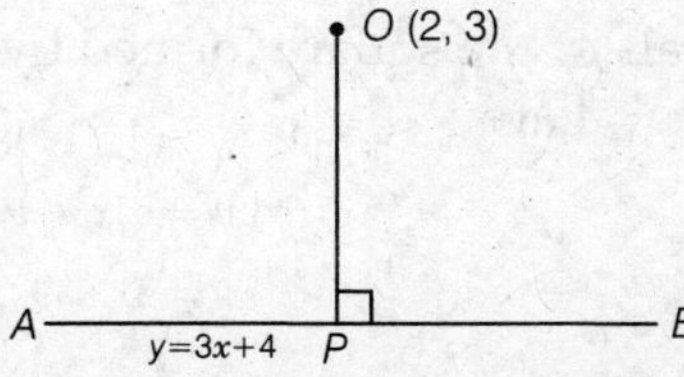

(✱) Topics related to these question have been removed from latest NCERT.

$\therefore$ Equation of line OP is $y-3=-\frac{1}{3}(x-2)$

$\Rightarrow \quad 3y-9=-x+2$

$\Rightarrow \quad x+3y-11=0 \quad \ldots$(ii)

On putting the value of y from Eq. (i) in Eq. (ii), we get

$$x+3(3x+4)-11=0$$

$\Rightarrow \quad x+9x+12-11=0$

$\Rightarrow \quad 10x+1=0$

$\Rightarrow \quad x=-\frac{1}{10}$

On putting $x=\frac{-1}{10}$ in Eq. (i), we get $y=\frac{-3}{10}+4=\frac{-3+40}{10}=\frac{37}{10}$

So, the foot of perpendicular is $\left(-\frac{1}{10}, \frac{37}{10}\right)$.

Mistake Alert! *Students might get confused in two equations whether the given slope is of line AB or perpendicular line OP. So, be careful in these two equations of slope.*

Q.33 If the coordinates of the middle point of the portion of a line intercepted between the coordinate axes is (3, 2), then the equation of the line will be

(a) $2x+3y=12$ (b) $3x+2y=12$ (c) $4x-3y=6$ (d) $5x-2y=10$

Ans. ***(a)*** Since, the coordinates of the middle point are P(3, 2).

$\therefore \quad 3=\frac{0+a}{2}$

$\Rightarrow \quad 3=\frac{a}{2} \Rightarrow a=6$

Similarly, $b=4$

$\therefore$ Equation of the line is $\frac{x}{6}+\frac{y}{4}=1$

$\Rightarrow \quad 2x+3y=12$

***Q.34** Equation of the line passing through (1, 2) and parallel to the line $y=3x-1$ is

(a) $y+2=x+1$ (b) $y+2=3(x+1)$ (c) $y-2=3(x-1)$ (d) $y-2=x-1$

Ans. ***(c)*** Since, the line passes through (1, 2) and parallel to the line $y=3x-1$.

So, slope of the required line $m=3$. [$\because$ slope of $y=3x-1$ is 3]

Hence, the equation of line passing through (1, 2) and having slope is

$y-2=3(x-1)$

Q.35 Equations of diagonals of the square formed by the lines $x=0$, $y=0$, $x=1$ and $y=1$ are

(a) $y=x$, $y+x=1$ (b) $y=x$, $x+y=2$

(c) $2y=x$, $y+x=\frac{1}{3}$ (d) $y=2x$, $y+2x=1$

(*) Topics related to these question have been removed from latest NCERT.

Ans. ***(a)*** Equation of OB passing through the points (0, 0) and (1, 1) is

$$y - 0 = \frac{1-0}{1-0}(x - 0)$$

$$\Rightarrow \qquad y = x$$

and equation of AC passing through the points (1, 0) and (0, 1) is

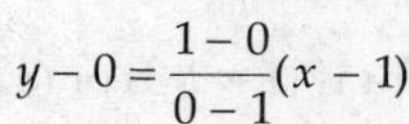

$$y - 0 = \frac{1-0}{0-1}(x - 1)$$

$$\Rightarrow \qquad y = -x + 1$$

$$\Rightarrow \qquad x + y - 1 = 0$$

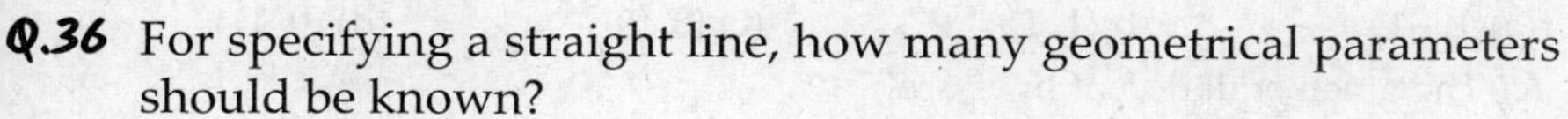

Q.36 For specifying a straight line, how many geometrical parameters should be known?

(a) 1 (b) 2
(c) 4 (d) 3

Ans. ***(b)*** Equation of straight lines are

$$y = mx + c, \text{ parameter} = 2 \qquad \ldots\text{(i)}$$

$$\frac{x}{a} + \frac{y}{b} = 1, \text{ parameter} = 2 \qquad \ldots\text{(ii)}$$

$$y - y_1 = m(x - x_1), \text{ parameter} = 2 \qquad \ldots\text{(iii)}$$

and $$x\cos w + y\sin w = p, \text{ parameter} = 2 \qquad \ldots\text{(iv)}$$

It is clear that from Eqs. (i), (ii), (iii) and (iv), for specifying a straight line, clearly two parameters should be known.

***Q.37** The point (4, 1) undergoes the following two successive transformations

(i) Reflection about the line $y = x$

(ii) Translation through a distance 2 units along the positive X-axis.

Then, the final coordinates of the point are

(a) (4, 3) (b) (3, 4) (c) (1, 4) (d) $\left(\frac{7}{2}, \frac{7}{2}\right)$

Ans. ***(b)*** Let the reflection of $A(4, 1)$ in $y = x$ be $B(h, k)$.

Now, mid-point of AB is $\left(\frac{4+h}{2}, \frac{1+k}{2}\right)$ which lies on $y = x$.

i.e., $$\frac{4+h}{2} = \frac{1+k}{2} \Rightarrow h - k = -3 \qquad \ldots\text{(i)}$$

So, the slope of line $y = x$ is 1.

$$\therefore \qquad \text{Slope of } AB = \frac{k-1}{h-4}$$

$$\Rightarrow \qquad 1 \cdot \left(\frac{k-1}{h-4}\right) = -1$$

(✱) Topics related to these question have been removed from latest NCERT.

$$\Rightarrow \quad h - 4 = 1 - k$$

$$\Rightarrow \quad h + k = 5 \quad \ldots\text{(ii)}$$

and $\quad h - k = -3$

$$2h = 2 \Rightarrow h = 1$$

On putting $h = 1$ in Eq. (ii), we get

$$k = 4$$

So, the point is (1, 4).

Hence, after translation the point is $(1 + 2, 4)$ or $(3, 4)$.

Q.38 A point equidistant from the lines $4x + 3y + 10 = 0$, $5x - 12y + 26 = 0$ and $7x + 24y - 50 = 0$ is

(a) $(1, -1)$ (b) $(1, 1)$ (c) $(0, 0)$ (d) $(0, 1)$

Ans. *(c)* The given equation of lines are

$$4x + 3y + 10 = 0 \quad \ldots\text{(i)}$$

$$\Rightarrow \quad 5x - 12y + 26 = 0 \quad \ldots\text{(ii)}$$

$$\Rightarrow \quad 7x + 24y - 50 = 0 \quad \ldots\text{(iii)}$$

Let the point (h, k) which is equidistant from these lines.

Distance of a point (h, k) from line (i) $= \dfrac{|4h + 3k + 10|}{\sqrt{16 + 9}}$

Distance of a point (h, k) from line (ii) $= \dfrac{|5h - 12k + 26|}{\sqrt{25 + 144}}$

Distance from the line (iii) $= \dfrac{|7h + 24k - 50|}{\sqrt{7^2 + 24^2}}$

So, the point (h, k) is equidistant from lines (i), (ii) and (iii).

$$\therefore \quad \frac{|4h + 3k + 10|}{\sqrt{16 + 9}} = \frac{|5h - 12k + 26|}{\sqrt{25 + 144}} = \frac{|7h + 24k - 50|}{\sqrt{49 + 576}}$$

$$\Rightarrow \quad \frac{|4h + 3k + 10|}{5} = \frac{|5h - 12k + 26|}{13} = \frac{|7h + 24k - 50|}{25}$$

Clearly, if $h = 0$, $k = 0$, then $\dfrac{10}{5} = \dfrac{26}{13} = \dfrac{50}{25} = 2$

Hence, the required point is (0, 0).

***Q.39** A line passes through (2, 2) and is perpendicular to the line $3x + y = 3$. Its y-intercept is

(a) $\dfrac{1}{3}$ (b) $\dfrac{2}{3}$ (c) 1 (d) $\dfrac{4}{3}$

Thinking Process First of all, find the required equation of line using the formulae. *i.e.*, $y - y_1 = m(x - x_1)$ and then put $x = 0$ to get y-intercept.

(*) Topics related to these question have been removed from latest NCERT.

Ans. ***(d)*** Given line is $y = 3 - 3x$.

Then, slope of the required line $= \frac{1}{3}$

$\because$ Equation of the required line passing through (2, 2) is

$$y - 2 = \frac{1}{3}(x - 2) \Rightarrow 3y - 6 = x - 2$$

$$\Rightarrow \quad x - 3y + 4 = 0$$

For y-intercept, put $\quad x = 0,\ 0 - 3y + 4 = 0$

$$\Rightarrow \quad y = \frac{4}{3}$$

Q.40 The ratio in which the line $3x + 4y + 2 = 0$ divides the distance between the lines $3x + 4y + 5 = 0$ and $3x + 4y - 5 = 0$ is

(a) 1 : 2 (b) 3 : 7 (c) 2 : 3 (d) 2 : 5

Ans. ***(b)*** Let point $A(x_1, y_1)$ lies on the line $3x + 4y + 5 = 0$, then $3x_1 + 4y_1 + 5 = 0$

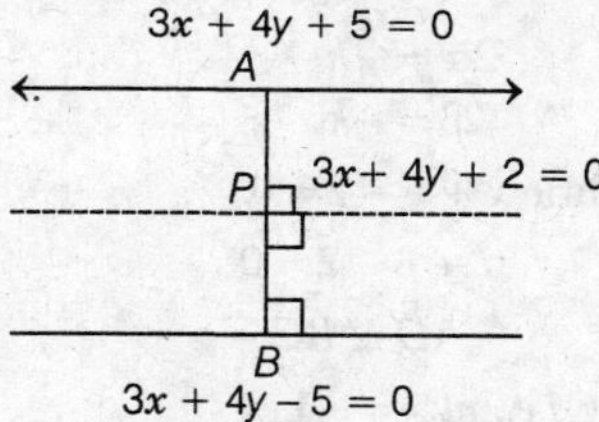

Now, perpendicular distance from A to the line

$$3x + 4y + 2 = 0$$

$$\Rightarrow \quad \frac{|3x_1 + 4y_1 + 2|}{\sqrt{9 + 16}} = \frac{|-5 + 2|}{\sqrt{9 + 16}} = \frac{3}{5}$$

Let point $B(x_2, y_2)$ lies on the line $3x + 4y - 5 = 0$ *i.e.*, $3x_2 + 4y_2 - 5 = 0$.

Now, perpendicular distance from B to the line $3x + 4y + 2 = 0$,

$$\frac{|3x_2 + 4y_2 + 2|}{\sqrt{9 + 16}} = \frac{|5 + 2|}{\sqrt{9 + 16}} = \frac{7}{5}$$

Hence, the required ratio is $\frac{3}{5} : \frac{7}{5}$ *i.e.*, 3 : 7.

Mistake Alert ! *While solving this question, students be careful while putting the coordinates in the distance formula.*

Q.41 One vertex of the equilateral triangle with centroid at the origin and one side as $x + y - 2 = 0$ is

(a) (−1, −1) (b) (2, 2) (c) (−2, −2) (d) (2, −2)

Thinking Process Let ABC be the equilateral triangle with vertex $A(h, k)$ and the point $D(\alpha, \beta)$ on BC. Then, apply the theorem, centroid G divides the median in 2 : 1 and use section formula. Further, use the condition of two perpendicular lines i.e. $m_1 m_2 = -1$.

Also, $\alpha + \beta - 2 = 0$ and $\left(\frac{k - 0}{h - 0}\right) \cdot (-1) = -1$.

(✱) Topics related to these question have been removed from latest NCERT.

Ans. *(c)* Let ABC be the equilateral triangle with vertex $A(h, k)$.

Let the coordinates of D are (α, β).

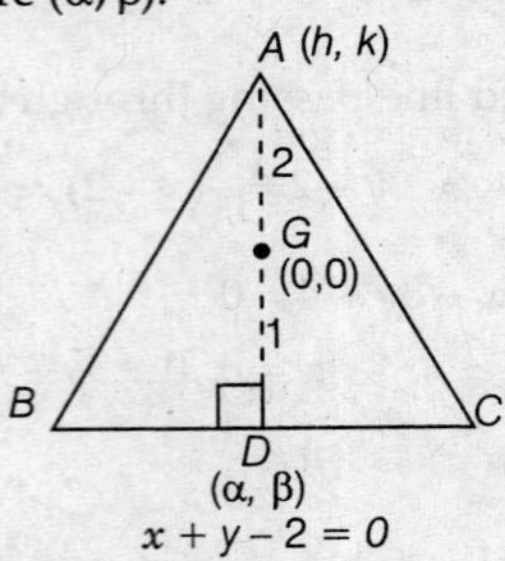

We know that $AG : GD = 2 : 1$ from the vertex A.

$$\therefore \quad 0 = \frac{2\alpha + h}{3}$$

$$\text{and} \quad 0 = \frac{2\beta + k}{3}$$

$$\Rightarrow \quad 2\alpha = -h$$

$$\text{and} \quad 2\beta = -k \quad \ldots\text{(i)}$$

Also, $D(\alpha, \beta)$ lies on the line $x + y - 2 = 0$.

$$\therefore \quad \alpha + \beta - 2 = 0 \quad \ldots\text{(ii)}$$

$$AD \perp BC$$

Since, the slope of line BC *i.e.*, $m_{BC} = -1$

and slope of the line AG *i.e.*, $m_{AG} = \frac{k - 0}{h - 0} = \frac{k}{h}$

$$\Rightarrow \quad (-1) \cdot \left(\frac{k}{h}\right) = -1$$

$$\Rightarrow \quad h = k \quad \ldots\text{(iii)}$$

From Eqs. (i) and (iii), we get

$$2\alpha = -h \text{ and } 2\beta = -h$$

$$\therefore \quad \alpha = \beta$$

From Eq. (ii), we get $\quad 2\alpha - 2 = 0$

$$\Rightarrow \quad \alpha = 1$$

If $\quad \alpha = 1$, then $\beta = 1$

From Eq. (i), $\quad h = -2, k = -2$

So, the vertex A is $(-2, -2)$.

Fill in the blanks in each of exercises of 42-47.

Q.42 If a, b and c are in AP, then the straight lines $ax + by + c = 0$ will always pass through ....

Thinking Process If a, b and c are in AP, then $2b = a + c$. Use this property to solve the above problem.

Ans. Given line is $\quad ax + by + c = 0 \quad \ldots$(i

Since, a, b and c are in AP, then

$$b = \frac{a+c}{2}$$

$$\Rightarrow \qquad a - 2b + c = 0 \qquad \text{...(ii)}$$

On comparing Eqs.(i) and (ii), we get

$$x = 1, y - 2 \qquad \text{[use the value of } b \text{ in Eq. (i)]}$$

So, (1, – 2) lies on the line.

Q.43 **The line which cuts off equal intercept from the axes and pass through the point (1, –2) is ....**

Ans. Let equation of line is

$$\frac{x}{a} + \frac{y}{a} = 1 \Rightarrow x + y = a \qquad \text{...(i)}$$

Since, this line passes through (1, –2).

$$\frac{1}{a} - \frac{2}{a} = 1$$

$$\Rightarrow \qquad 1 - 2 = a \Rightarrow a = -1$$

∴ Required equation of the line is

$$-x - y = 1$$

$$\Rightarrow \qquad x + y + 1 = 0$$

***Q.44** **Equation of the line through the point (3, 2) and making an angle of 45° with the line $x - 2y = 3$ are ....**

Ans. Given the point $P(3, 2)$ and equation of the line is $x - 2y = 3$.

$$y = \frac{x}{2} - \frac{3}{2} \qquad \text{...(i)}$$

∴ Slope of this line is $m_1 = \frac{1}{2}$

Let the slope of the required line is m.

Then, $$\tan\theta = \left|\frac{m - \frac{1}{2}}{1 + \frac{1}{2}m}\right|$$

$$\Rightarrow \qquad 1 = \pm\left(\frac{m - \frac{1}{2}}{1 + \frac{m}{2}}\right) \qquad [\because \tan 45° = 1] \text{ ... (i)}$$

Take positive sign,

$$1 + \frac{m}{2} = m - \frac{1}{2}$$

$$\Rightarrow \qquad m - \frac{m}{2} = 1 + \frac{1}{2}$$

$$\Rightarrow \qquad \frac{m}{2} = \frac{3}{2} \Rightarrow m = 3$$

(*) Topics related to these question have been removed from latest NCERT.

Taking negative sign,

$$1 = -\left(\frac{m - \frac{1}{2}}{1 + \frac{m}{2}}\right)$$

$$\Rightarrow \quad 1 + \frac{m}{2} = -m + \frac{1}{2}$$

$$\Rightarrow \quad m + \frac{m}{2} = \frac{1}{2} - 1$$

$$\Rightarrow \quad \frac{3m}{2} = \frac{-1}{2} \Rightarrow m = \frac{-1}{3}$$

$\therefore$ First equation of the line is

$$y - 2 = 3(x - 3)$$

$$\Rightarrow \quad 3x - y - 7 = 0$$

and second equation of the line is

$$y - 2 = -\frac{1}{3}(x - 3)$$

$$\Rightarrow \quad 3y - 6 = -x + 3$$

$$\Rightarrow \quad x + 3y - 9 = 0$$

Q.45 The points (3, 4) and (2, –6) are situated on the .... of the line $3x - 4y - 8 = 0$.

Ans. Given line is $\quad 3x - 4y - 8 = 0 \quad$ ...(i)

For point (3, 4),

$$= 9 - 4 \times 4 - 8$$

$$= 9 - 16 - 8$$

$$= 9 - 24$$

$$= -15 < 0 \quad \text{...(i}$$

For point (2, –6),

$$= 6 + 24 - 8 = 0$$

$$= 22 > 0 \quad \text{...(ii}$$

Since, the values are of opposite sign.

Hence, the points (3, 4) and (2, –6) lies on opposite side to the line.

Q.46 A point moves so that square of its distance from the point (3, –2) is numerically equal to its distance from the line $5x - 12y = 3$. The equation of its locus is ....

Ans. Let the coordinates of the point are (h, k),

$\therefore$ Distance between (3, – 2) and (h, k),

$$d_1^2 = (3 - h)^2 + (-2 - k)^2 \quad \text{...(i}$$

Now, distance of the point (h, k) from the line $5x - 12y = 3$ is,

$$d_2 = \left|\frac{5h - 12k - 3}{\sqrt{25 + 144}}\right| = \left|\frac{5h - 12k - 3}{13}\right| \quad \text{...(ii}$$

We have, $\quad d_1^2 = d_2$

$$\Rightarrow \quad (3-h)^2+(2+k)^2=\frac{5h-12k-3}{13} \quad \text{[from Eqs. (i) and (ii)]}$$

$$\Rightarrow \quad 9-6h+h^2+4+4k+k^2=\frac{5h-12k-3}{13}$$

$$\Rightarrow \quad h^2+k^2-6h+4k+13=\frac{5h-12k-3}{13}$$

$$\Rightarrow \quad 13h^2+13k^2-78h+52k+169=5h-12k-3$$

$$\Rightarrow \quad 13h^2+13k^2-83h+64k+172=0$$

$\therefore$ Locus of this point is

$$13x^2+13y^2-83x+64y+172=0$$

Q.47 Locus of the mid-points of the portion of the line $x\sin\theta+y\cos\theta=p$ intercepted between the axes is ....

Ans. Given, equation of the line is

$$x\sin\theta+y\cos\theta=p \quad \text{...(i)}$$

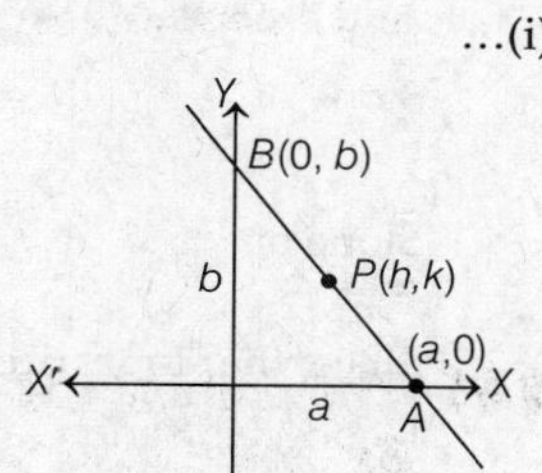

Let the mid-point of AB is $p(h,k)$.

So, the mid-point of AB are $\left(\frac{a}{2},\frac{b}{2}\right)$.

Since, the point $(a, 0)$ lies on the line (i), then

$$a\sin\theta+0=p$$

$$\Rightarrow \quad a\sin\theta=p \Rightarrow a=\frac{p}{\sin\theta}$$

and the point $(0, b)$ also lies on the line, then

$$0+b\cos\theta=p$$

$$\Rightarrow \quad b\cos\theta=p \Rightarrow b=\frac{p}{\cos\theta}$$

Now, $\quad$ mid-point of $AB=\left(\frac{a}{2},\frac{b}{2}\right)$ or $\left(\frac{p}{2\sin\theta},\frac{p}{2\cos\theta}\right)$

$$\because \quad \frac{p}{2\sin\theta}=h \Rightarrow \sin\theta=\frac{p}{2h}$$

and $$\frac{p}{2\cos\theta}=k \Rightarrow \cos\theta=\frac{p}{2k}$$

$$\therefore \quad \sin^2\theta+\cos^2\theta=\frac{p^2}{4h^2}+\frac{p^2}{4k^2}$$

$$\Rightarrow \quad 1=\frac{p^2}{4}\left(\frac{1}{h^2}+\frac{1}{k^2}\right)$$

So, locus of the mid-point $P(h,k)$ is

$$4=p^2\left(\frac{1}{x^2}+\frac{1}{y^2}\right)$$

$$\Rightarrow \quad 4x^2y^2=p^2(x^2+y^2)$$

State True or False for the following statements in each of the exercises from 48 to 56.

Q.48 If the vertices of a triangle have integral coordinates, then the triangle cannot be equilateral.

Ans. *True*

We know that, if the vertices of a triangle have integral coordinates, then the triangle cannot be equilateral. Hence, the given statement is true.

Since, in equilateral triangle, we get $\tan 60° = \sqrt{3}$ = Slope of the line, so with integral coordinates as vertices, the triangle cannot be equilateral.

***Q.49** The points $A(-2, 1)$, $B(0, 5)$ and $C(-1, 2)$ are collinear.

Ans. *False*

Given points are $A(-2, 1)$, $B(0, 5)$ and $C(-1, 2)$.

Now, slope of $AB = \dfrac{5-1}{0+2} = 2$

Slope of $BC = \dfrac{2-5}{-1-0} = 3$

Slope of $AC = \dfrac{2-1}{-1+2} = 1$

Since, the slopes are different.

Hence, A, B and C are not collinear. So, statement is false.

***Q.50** Equation of the line passing through the point $(a\cos^3\theta, a\sin^3\theta)$ and perpendicular to the line $x\sec\theta + y\,\text{cosec}\,\theta = a$ is $x\cos\theta - y\sin\theta = a\sin 2\theta$.

Ans. *False*

Given point $p\,(a\cos^3\theta, a\sin^3\theta)$ and the line is $x\sec\theta + y\,\text{cosec}\,\theta = a$

$\because$ Slope of this line $= \dfrac{-\sec\theta}{\text{cosec}\,\theta} = -\tan\theta$ and slope of required line $= \dfrac{1}{\tan\theta} = \cot\theta$

$\therefore$ Equation of the required line passing through $(a\cos^3\theta, b\sin^3\theta)$ is

$$y - a\sin^3\theta = \cot\theta\,(x - a\cos^3\theta)$$

$$\Rightarrow \quad y\sin\theta - a\sin^4\theta = x\cos\theta - a\cos^4\theta$$

$$\Rightarrow \quad x\cos\theta - y\sin\theta = a\cos^4\theta - a\sin^4\theta$$

$$\Rightarrow \quad x\cos\theta - y\sin\theta = a[(\cos^2\theta + \sin^2\theta)(\cos^2\theta - \sin^2\theta)]$$

$$\Rightarrow \quad x\cos\theta - y\sin\theta = a\cos 2\theta \qquad [\because \cos 2A = \cos^2 A - \sin^2 A$$

Hence, the given statement is false.

Q.51 The straight line $5x + 4y = 0$ passes through the point of intersection of the straight lines $x + 2y - 10 = 0$ and $2x + y + 5 = 0$.

Ans. *True*

Given that, $x + 2y - 10 = 0$ ...(i

and $2x + y + 5 = 0$ ...(ii

(*) Topics related to these question have been removed from latest NCERT.

From Eq. (i), put the value of $x = 10 - 2y$ in Eq. (ii), we get

$$20 - 4y + y + 5 = 0$$

$$\Rightarrow \quad 20 - 3y + 5 = 0$$

$$\Rightarrow \quad y = \frac{25}{3}$$

$$\therefore \quad x + \frac{50}{3} - 10 = 0 \quad \text{[from Eq. (i)]}$$

$$\Rightarrow \quad x + \frac{20}{3} = 0$$

$$\Rightarrow \quad x = \frac{-20}{3}$$

So, the point of intersection is $\left(-\frac{20}{3}, \frac{25}{3}\right)$.

If the line $5x + 4y = 0$ passes through the point $\left(-\frac{20}{3}, \frac{25}{3}\right)$, then this point should lie on this line.

$$\because \quad 5\left(\frac{-20}{3}\right) + \frac{4(25)}{3} = \frac{-100}{3} + \frac{100}{3} = 0$$

So, this point lies on the given line.

Hence, the statement is true.

Q.52 The vertex of an equilateral triangle is (2, 3) and the equation of the opposite side is $x + y = 2$. Then, the other two sides are $y - 3 = (2 \pm \sqrt{3})(x - 2)$.

Ans. *True*

Let ABC be an equilateral triangle with vertex $A(2, 3)$, and equation of BC is $x + y = 2$ *i.e.*, slope $= -1$.

Let slope of line AB is m.

Since, the angle between line AB and BC is 60°.

$$\therefore \quad \tan 60° = \left|\frac{m+1}{1-m}\right|$$

$$\Rightarrow \quad \sqrt{3} = \pm\left(\frac{m+1}{1-m}\right) \quad \text{[take positive sign]}$$

$$\Rightarrow \quad \sqrt{3} - \sqrt{3}\,m = m + 1$$

$$\Rightarrow \quad \sqrt{3} - 1 = m(1 + \sqrt{3})$$

$$\Rightarrow \quad m = \frac{(\sqrt{3}-1)(\sqrt{3}-1)}{(\sqrt{3}+1)(\sqrt{3}-1)} = \frac{3 + 1 - 2\sqrt{3}}{3 - 1} = \frac{4 - 2\sqrt{3}}{2} = 2 - \sqrt{3}$$

Similarly, slope of $AC = 2 + \sqrt{3}$ [take negative sign]

$\therefore$ Equation of other two sides are $y - 3 = (2 \pm \sqrt{3})(x - 2)$

Hence, the statement is true.

(✱) Topics related to these question have been removed from latest NCERT.

***Q.53** The equation of the line joining the point (3, 5) to the point of intersection of the lines $4x+y-1=0$ and $7x-3y-35=0$ is equidistant from the points (0, 0) and (8, 34).

- **Concept Insight** Equation of a line passing through the points (x_1, y_1) and (x_2, y_2) is $y-y_1=\frac{y_2-y_1}{x_2-x_1}(x-x_1)$.

Ans. *True*

Given equation of lines are

$$4x+y-1=0 \quad \ldots(i)$$

and

$$7x-3y-35=0 \quad \ldots(ii)$$

From Eq. (i), on putting $y=1-4x$ in Eq. (ii), we get

$$7x-3+12x-35=0$$

$$\Rightarrow \quad 19x-38=0 \Rightarrow x=2$$

On putting $x=2$ in Eq. (i), we get

$$8+y-1=0 \Rightarrow y=-7$$

Now, the equation of a line passing through (3, 5) and (2, –7) is

$$y-5=\frac{-7-5}{2-3}(x-3)$$

$$\Rightarrow \quad y-5=12(x-3)$$

$$\Rightarrow \quad 12x-y-31=0 \quad \ldots(iii)$$

Distance from (0, 0) to the line (iii), we get

$$d_1=\frac{|-31|}{\sqrt{144+1}}=\frac{31}{\sqrt{145}}$$

$\therefore$ Distance from (8, 34) to the line (iii), we get

$$d_2=\frac{|96-34-31|}{\sqrt{145}}=\frac{31}{\sqrt{145}}$$

$$\because \quad d_1=d_2$$

Hence, the statement is true.

***Q.54** The line $\frac{x}{a}+\frac{y}{b}=1$ moves in such a way that $\frac{1}{a^2}+\frac{1}{b^2}=\frac{1}{c^2}$, where c is a constant. The locus of the foot of the perpendicular from the origin on the given line is $x^2+y^2=c^2$.

Ans. *True*

Given that equation of line is

$$\frac{x}{a}+\frac{y}{b}=1 \quad \left[\text{here, slope } m_1=-\frac{b}{a}\right] \ldots(i)$$

Equation of line passing through origin and perpendicular to line (i) is

$$\frac{x}{b}-\frac{y}{a}=0 \quad \left[\text{here, slope } m_2=\frac{a}{b}\right]$$

$$[\because m_1 \cdot m_2=-1, \text{ for perpendicular lines}] \ldots(ii)$$

(*) Topics related to these question have been removed from latest NCERT.

Now, foot of perpendicular is the point of intersection of lines (i) and (ii).
To find its locus we have to eliminate the variable a and b.
On squaring and adding Eqs. (i) and (ii), we get

$$\frac{x^2}{a^2}+\frac{y^2}{b^2}+\frac{2xy}{ab}+\frac{x^2}{b^2}+\frac{y^2}{a^2}-\frac{2xy}{ab}=1$$

$$\Rightarrow \quad x^2\left(\frac{1}{a^2}+\frac{1}{b^2}\right)+y^2\left(\frac{1}{a^2}+\frac{1}{b^2}\right)=1$$

$$\Rightarrow \quad \frac{x^2}{c^2}+\frac{y^2}{c^2}=1$$

$$\Rightarrow \quad x^2+y^2=c^2 \qquad \left[\because \frac{1}{a^2}+\frac{1}{b^2}=\frac{1}{c^2}\right]$$

Hence, the statement is true.

Q.55 The lines $ax+2y+1=0$, $bx+3y+1=0$ and $cx+4y+1=0$ are concurrent, if a, b and c are in GP.

Thinking Process First of all find the intersection point of first two line. Then, if the lines are concurrent then this point should lies on the third line.

Ans. *False*

Given lines are

$$ax+2y+1=0 \quad \text{...(i)}$$
$$bx+3y+1=0 \quad \text{...(ii)}$$
and
$$cx+4y+1=0 \quad \text{...(iii)}$$

From Eq. (i), on putting $y=\frac{-ax-1}{2}$ in Eq. (ii), we get

$$bx-\frac{3}{2}(ax+1)+1=0$$

$$\Rightarrow \quad 2bx-3ax-3+2=0 \Rightarrow x(2b-3a)=1 \Rightarrow x=\frac{1}{2b-3a}$$

Now, putting $x=\frac{1}{2b-3a}$ in Eq. (i), we get

$$\frac{a}{2b-3a}+2y+1=0$$

$$\Rightarrow \quad 2y=-\left[\frac{a+2b-3a}{2b-3a}\right] \Rightarrow 2y=\frac{-(2b-2a)}{2b-3a}$$

$$\Rightarrow \quad y=\frac{(a-b)}{2b-3a}$$

So, the point of intersection is $\left(\frac{1}{2b-3a}, \frac{a-b}{2b-3a}\right)$.

Since, this point lies on $cx+4y+1=0$, then

$$\frac{c}{2b-3a}+\frac{4(a-b)}{2b-3a}+1=0$$

(✱) Topics related to these question have been removed from latest NCERT.

$\Rightarrow \quad c + 4a - 4b + 2b - 3a = 0 \Rightarrow -2b + a + c = 0 \Rightarrow 2b = a + c$

So, a, b, c are in AP.

Hence, the given statement is false.

Q.56 Line joining the points (3, –4) and (–2, 6) is perpendicular to the line joining the points (–3, 6) and (9, –18).

Ans. *False*

Given points are $A(3, -4)$, $B(-2, 6)$, $P(-3, 6)$ and $Q(9, -18)$.

Now, slope of $AB = \dfrac{6+4}{-2-3} = -2$ and slope of $PQ = \dfrac{-18-6}{9+3} = -2$

Since, slope of AB = slope of PQ.

So, line AB is parallel to line PQ.

Match the questions given under Column I_1 with their appropriate answers given under the Column II_2

Q.57 Match the following.

Column I	Column II
(i) The coordinates of the points P and Q on the line $x + 5y = 13$ which are at a distance of 2 units from the line $12x - 5y + 26 = 0$ are	(a) (3, 1), (–7, 11)
(ii) The coordinates of the point on the line $x + y = 4$, which are at a unit distance from the line $4x + 3y - 10 = 0$ are	(b) $\left(-\frac{1}{3}, \frac{11}{3}\right), \left(\frac{4}{3}, \frac{7}{3}\right)$
(iii) The coordinates of the point on the line joining $A(-2, 5)$ and $B(3, 1)$ such that $AP = PQ = QB$ are	(c) $\left(1, \frac{12}{5}\right), \left(-3, \frac{16}{5}\right)$

Ans. (i) Let the coordinate of point $P(x_1, y_1)$ on the line $x + 5y = 13$ *i.e.*,

$$P(13 - 5y_1, y_1).$$

$\therefore$ Distance of P from the line $12x - 5y + 26 = 0$,

$$2 = \left|\frac{12(13 - 5y_1) - 5y_1 + 26}{\sqrt{144 + 25}}\right|$$

$\Rightarrow \quad 2 = \pm \dfrac{156 - 60y_1 - 5y_1 + 26}{13}$

$\Rightarrow \quad -65y_1 = -156$ [take positive sign]

$\Rightarrow \quad y_1 = \dfrac{156}{65} = \dfrac{12}{5}$

$\because \quad x_1 = 13 - 5y_1 = 13 - 12 = 1$

So, the coordinates of is $P\left(1, \dfrac{12}{5}\right)$.

Similarly, the coordinates of Q are $\left(-3, \dfrac{16}{5}\right)$. [take negative sign]

(ii) Let coordinates of the point on the line $x + y = 4$ be $(4 - y_1, y_1)$.
Distance from the line $4x + 3y - 10 = 0$.

$$1 = \left| \frac{4(4 - y_1) + 3y_1 - 10}{\sqrt{16 + 9}} \right|$$

$$\Rightarrow \quad 1 = \pm \frac{16 - 4y_1 + 3y_1 - 10}{5} \quad \text{[take negative sign]}$$

$$\Rightarrow \quad 5 = 6 - y_1$$

$$\Rightarrow \quad y_1 = 1$$

If $\quad y_1 = 1$, then $x_1 = 4 - y_1 = 4 - 1 = 3$

So, the point is (3, 1).
Similarly, on taking negative sign, the point is (–7, 11).

(iii) Given point $A(-2, 5)$ and $B(3, 1)$.

A (–2, 5) ——— P (x_1, y_1) ——— Q (x_2, y_2) ——— B (3, 1)

Now, the point P divides line joining the point A and B in 1 : 2.

$$\because \quad x_1 = \frac{1 \cdot 3 + 2(-2)}{1 + 2} = \frac{3 - 4}{3} = \frac{-1}{3}$$

and
$$y_1 = \frac{1 \cdot 1 + 2 \cdot 5}{1 + 2} = \frac{11}{3}$$

So, the coordinates of P are $\left(\frac{-1}{3}, \frac{11}{3}\right)$.

Thus, the point Q divided the line joining A to B in 2 : 1.

$$\because \quad x_2 = \frac{2 \cdot 3 + 1(-2)}{2 + 1} = \frac{4}{3}$$

and
$$y_2 = \frac{2 \cdot 1 + 1 \cdot 5}{2 + 1} = \frac{7}{3}$$

Hence, the coordinates of Q are $\left(\frac{4}{3}, \frac{7}{3}\right)$.

Hence, the correct matches are (i) → (c), (ii) → (a), (iii) → (b).

Q.58 The value of the λ, if the lines $(2x + 3y + 4) + \lambda(6x - y + 12) = 0$ are

Column I	Column II
*(i) parallel to Y-axis is	(a) $\lambda = -\frac{3}{4}$
*(ii) perpendicular to $7x + y - 4 = 0$ is	(b) $\lambda = -\frac{1}{3}$
(iii) passes through (1, 2) is	(c) $\lambda = -\frac{17}{41}$
*(iv) parallel to X-axis is	(d) $\lambda = 3$

(*) Topics related to these question have been removed from latest NCERT.

Ans. (i) Given equation of the line is

$(2x + 3y + 4) + \lambda (6x - y + 12) = 0$ ...(i)

If line is parallel to Y-axis *i.e.*, it is perpendicular to X-axis

$\therefore$ Slope $= m = \tan 90° = \infty$

From line (i), $x(2 + 6\lambda) + y(3 - \lambda) + 4 + 12\lambda = 0$

and slope of this line $= \dfrac{-(2 + 6\lambda)}{3 - \lambda}$

$$\Rightarrow \quad \frac{-2 - 6\lambda}{3 - \lambda} = \infty$$

$$\Rightarrow \quad \frac{-2 - 6\lambda}{3 - \lambda} = \frac{1}{0}$$

$$\Rightarrow \quad 3 - \lambda = 0$$

$$\Rightarrow \quad \lambda = 3$$

(ii) If the line (i) is perpendicular to the line $7x + y - 4 = 0$ or $y = -7x + 4$, then

$$\therefore \quad \frac{-(2 + 6\lambda)}{(3 - \lambda)}(-7) = -1 \qquad [\because \text{for perpendicular lines } m_1m_2 = -1]$$

$$\Rightarrow \quad 14 + 42\lambda = -3 + \lambda$$

$$\Rightarrow \quad 41\lambda = -17$$

$$\Rightarrow \quad \lambda = -\frac{17}{41}$$

(iii) If the line (i) passes through the point (1, 2).

Then, $(2 + 6 + 4) + \lambda(6 - 2 + 12) = 0$

$$\Rightarrow \quad 12 + 16\lambda = 0 \Rightarrow \lambda = -\frac{3}{4}$$

(iv) If the line is parallel to X-axis, then the slope = 0.

$$\text{Thus,} \quad \frac{-(2 + 6\lambda)}{3 - \lambda} = 0$$

$$\Rightarrow \quad -(2 + 6\lambda) = 0 \Rightarrow \lambda = -\frac{1}{3}$$

So, the correct matches are (i) → (d), (ii) → (c), (iii) → (a), (iv) → (b).

***Q.59** The equation of the line through the intersection of the lines $2x - 3y = 0$ and $4x - 5y = 2$ and

Column I	Column II
(i) through the point (2, 1) is	(a) $2x - y = 4$
(ii) perpendicular to the line $x + 2y + 1 = 0$	(b) $x + y - 5 = 0$
(iii) parallel to the line $3x - 4y + 5 = 0$ is	(c) $x - y - 1 = 0$
(iv) equally inclined to the axes is	(d) $3x - 4y - 1 = 0$

(*) Topics related to these question have been removed from latest NCERT.

Ans. Given equation of the lines are

$$2x - 3y = 0 \quad \ldots\text{(i)}$$

and $$4x - 5y = 2 \quad \ldots\text{(ii)}$$

From Eq. (i), put $x = \frac{3y}{2}$ in Eq. (ii), we get

$$4 \cdot \frac{(3y)}{2} - 5y = 2$$

$\Rightarrow$ $$6y - 5y = 2 \Rightarrow \quad y = 2$$

Now, put $y = 2$ in Eq. (i), we get

$$x = 3$$

So, the intersection point is (3, 2).

(i) The equation of the line passes through the point (3, 2) and (2, 1), is

$$y - 2 = \frac{1-2}{2-3}(x - 3)$$

$\Rightarrow$ $$y - 2 = (x - 3) \quad \Rightarrow x - y - 1 = 0$$

(ii) If the required line is perpendicular to the line $x + 2y + 1 = 0$

$\because$ Slope of the required line = 2

$\therefore$ Equation of the line is

$$y - 2 = 2(x - 3)$$

$\Rightarrow$ $$2x - y - 4 = 0$$

(iii) If the required line is parallel to the line $3x - 4y + 5 = 0$, then the slope of the required line = $\frac{3}{4}$.

$\therefore$ Equation of the required line is

$$y - 2 = \frac{3}{4}(x - 3)$$

$\Rightarrow$ $$4y - 8 = 3x - 9 \Rightarrow \quad 3x - 4y - 1 = 0$$

(iv) If the line is equally inclined to the axes, then

$$m = \pm \tan 45° = \pm 1$$

$\therefore$ Equation of the line is

$$y - 2 = -1(x - 3) \quad \text{[take negative value]}$$

$\Rightarrow$ $$y - 2 = -x + 3$$

$\Rightarrow$ $$x + y - 5 = 0$$

So, the correct matches are (i) $\rightarrow$ (c), (ii) $\rightarrow$ (a), (iii) $\rightarrow$ (d), (iv) $\rightarrow$ (b).

Chapter

11

Conic Sections

Short Answer Type Questions

Q.1 Find the equation of the circle which touches both the axes in first quadrant and whose radius is *a*.

- **Concept Insight** The equation of circle is $(x-h)^2+(y-x)^2=r^2$, where (h, k) is centre and '*r*' is the radius.

Ans. Given that radius of the circle is a, since, the circle touches both axes. So centere of the circle is *(h,k) i.e., (a, a)*

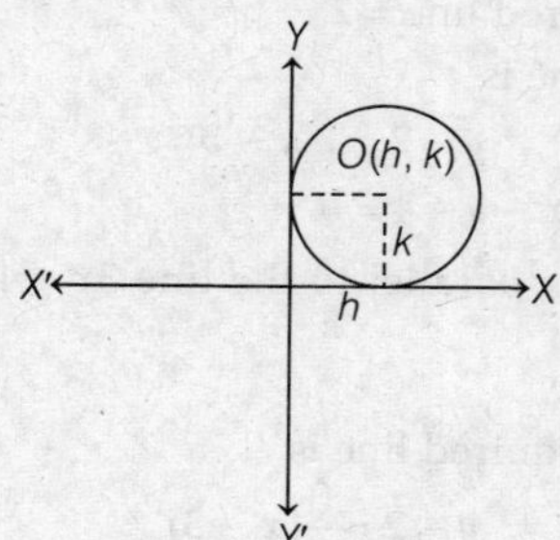

So, the required equation of circle is

$$(x-a)^2+(y-a)^2=a^2 \Rightarrow x^2-2ax+a^2+y^2-2ay+a^2=a^2$$

$$\Rightarrow \quad x^2+y^2-2ax-2ay+a^2=0$$

Q.2 Show that the point (x, y) given by $x=\dfrac{2at}{1+t^2}$ and $y=\dfrac{a(1-t^2)}{1+t^2}$ lies on a circle.

Ans. Given points are $\quad x=\dfrac{2at}{1+t^2}$ and $y=\dfrac{a(1-t^2)}{1+t^2}$.

$$\because \quad x^2+y^2=\frac{4a^2t^2}{(1+t^2)^2}+\frac{a^2(1-t^2)^2}{(1+t^2)^2}$$

$$\Rightarrow \quad \frac{1}{a^2}(x^2+y^2)=\frac{4t^2+1+t^4-2t^2}{(1+t^2)^2}$$

$$\Rightarrow \quad \frac{1}{a^2}(x^2+y^2)=\frac{t^4+2t^2+1}{(1+t^2)^2}$$

$$\Rightarrow \quad \frac{1}{a^2}(x^2+y^2)=\frac{(1+t^2)^2}{(1+t^2)^2}$$

$\Rightarrow \quad x^2 + y^2 = a^2$, which is a required equation of circle.

Hence, the given point lies on the circle.

Mistake Alert! *Carefully expand and simplify both x^2 and y^2 to ensure terms can be combined.*

Q.3 If a circle passes through the points (0, 0), $(a, 0)$ and $(0, b)$, then find the coordinates of its centre.

- **Concept Insight** General equation of the circle is $x^2 + y^2 + 2gx + 2fy + c = 0$. Now, satisfy the given points to get the values of g and f. The centre of the circle is $(-g, -f)$.

Ans. Let the equation of circle is

$$x^2 + y^2 + 2gx + 2fy + c = 0 \quad \text{...(i)}$$

Since, it passes through (0, 0).

So, $\quad 0 + c = 0 \Rightarrow c = 0$

Now, equation (i) becomes $x^2 + y^2 + 2gx + 2fy = 0$

Since, this circle passes through the points, $A(a, 0)$ and $B(0, b)$.

$$\therefore \quad a^2 + 2ag = 0 \quad \text{...(ii)}$$

$$\text{and} \quad b^2 + 2bf = 0 \quad \text{... (iii)}$$

From Eq. (ii), we get $\quad a + 2g = 0 \Rightarrow g = -a/2$

From Eq. (iii), we get $\quad b + 2f = 0 \Rightarrow f = -b/2$

Hence, the coordinates of centre of the circle are $\left(\frac{a}{2}, \frac{b}{2}\right)$.

Q.4 Find the equation of the circle which touches X-axis and whose centre is (1, 2).

Ans. Given that centre of the circle is (1, 2) and radius is equal to ordinate of the centre as it touches the X-axis, then $r = 2$

So, the equation of circle is $(x-h)^2 + (y-k)^2 = r^2$, where (h, k) is centre and 'r' is the radius.

Then, $\quad (x-1)^2 + (y-2)^2 = 2^2$

$\Rightarrow \quad x^2 - 2x + 1 + y^2 - 4y + 4 = 4$

$\Rightarrow \quad x^2 + y^2 - 2x - 4y + 1 = 0$

Q.5 If the lines $3x - 4y + 4 = 0$ and $6x - 8y - 7 = 0$ are tangents to a circle, then find the radius of the circle.

Thinking Process The distance between two parallel lines $ax + by + c_1 = 0$ and $ax + by + c_2 = 0$ is given by $d = \left|\frac{c_1 - c_2}{\sqrt{a^2 + b^2}}\right|$. Use this formula to solve the above problem.

Ans. Given equation of lines are

$$3x - 4y + 4 = 0 \quad \text{...(i)}$$

$$6x - 8y - 7 = 0$$

$$\text{or} \quad 3x - 4y - 7/2 = 0 \quad \text{...(ii)}$$

It is clear that lines (i) and (ii) are parallel and $c_1 = 4$, $c_2 = \frac{-7}{2}$

Now, distance between them *i.e.*, $a = 3$ and $b = -4$

$$d = \left|\frac{4 + 7/2}{\sqrt{9+16}}\right| = \left|\frac{\frac{8+7}{2}}{5}\right| = 3/2$$

∴ Distance between these parallel tangents = Diameter of these circle

∴ Diameter of the circle = 3/2

Hence, radius of the circle = 3/4

Q.6 Find the equation of a circle which touches both the axes and the line $3x - 4y + 8 = 0$ and lies in the third quadrant.

Ans.

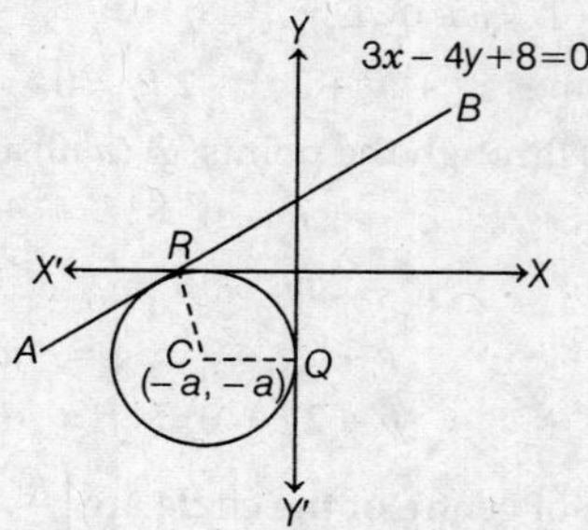

Let a be the radius of the circle. Then, the coordinates of the center are $(-a, -a)$.
Now, perpendicular distance from C to the line AB = Radius of the circle

$$d = \left|\frac{-3a + 4a + 8}{\sqrt{9+16}}\right| = \left|\frac{a+8}{5}\right|$$

∵ $$a = \pm\left(\frac{a+8}{5}\right)$$

Taking positive sign, $$a = \frac{a+8}{5}$$

⇒ $$5a = a + 8 \Rightarrow 4a = 8 \Rightarrow a = 2$$

Taking negative sign, $$a = \frac{-a-8}{5}$$

⇒ $$5a = -a - 8$$

⇒ $$6a = -8 \Rightarrow a = -4/3$$

But $a \neq -4/3$ [∵ distance can't be negative]

∴ $a = 2$

So, the required equation of circle is

$$(x+2)^2 + (y+2)^2 = 2^2 \quad [\because a = 2]$$

⇒ $$x^2 + 4x + 4 + y^2 + 4y + 4 = 4$$

⇒ $$x^2 + y^2 + 4x + 4y + 4 = 0$$

Mistake Alert! *Carefully calculate the distance from the centre to the line* $3x - 4y + 8 = 0$

Q.7 If one end of a diameter of the circle $x^2 + y^2 - 4x - 6y + 11 = 0$ is (3, 4), then find the coordinates of the other end of the diameter.

Thinking Process First of all, the centre of the circle from the given equation, then find the mid-point of the diameter of the circle.

Ans. Given equation of the circle is

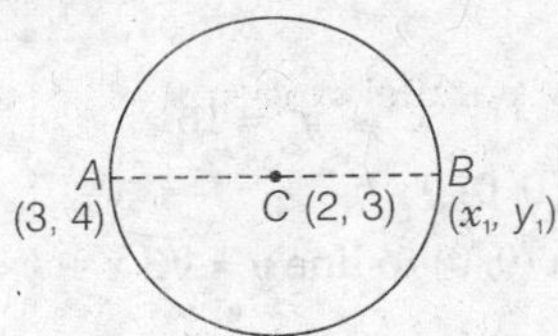

$$x^2 + y^2 - 4x - 6y + 11 = 0.$$

On comparing with the general equation of the circle

$$x^2 + y^2 + 2gx + 2fy + c = 0, \text{ we get}$$

or $$2g = -4 \text{ and } 2f = -6$$

So, the centre of the circle is $(-g, -f)$ *i.e.*, (2, 3).

Since, the mid-point of diameter AB is (2, 3).

Then, $$2 = \frac{3 + x_1}{2} \quad \text{[by mid-point formula]}$$

$$\Rightarrow \quad 4 = 3 + x_1$$

$$\therefore \quad x_1 = 1$$

And $$3 = \frac{4 + y_1}{2}$$

$$\Rightarrow \quad 6 = 4 + y_1 \Rightarrow y_1 = 2$$

So, the coordinates of other end of the diameter will be (1, 2).

Q.8 Find the equation of the circle having (1, – 2) as its centre and passing through $3x + y = 14$, $2x + 5y = 18$.

Ans. Given, centre of the circle is (1, – 2) and the circle passing through the lines

$$3x + y = 14 \quad \text{...(i)}$$

and $$2x + 5y = 18 \quad \text{...(ii)}$$

From Eq. (i), put $y = 14 - 3x$ in Eq. (ii), we get

$$2x + 70 - 15x = 18$$

$$\Rightarrow \quad -13x = -52 \Rightarrow x = 4$$

Now, put $x = 4$ in Eq. (i), we get

$$12 + y = 14 \Rightarrow y = 2$$

Since, point (4, 2) lie on these lines also lies on the circle.

$\therefore$ Radius of the circle $= \sqrt{(4-1)^2 + (2+2)^2} = \sqrt{9 + 16} = 5$

Now, the required equation of the circle is

$$(x - 1)^2 + (y + 2)^2 = 5^2$$

$$\Rightarrow \quad x^2 - 2x + 1 + y^2 + 4y + 4 = 25$$

$$\Rightarrow \quad x^2 + y^2 - 2x + 4y - 20 = 0$$

Q.9 If the line $y = \sqrt{3}x + k$ touches the circle $x^2 + y^2 = 16$, then find the value of k.

- **Concept Insight** The distances from the point (m, n) to the line $Ax + By + C = 0$ is $d = \left|\frac{Am + Bn + C}{\sqrt{A^2 + B^2}}\right|$

Ans. Given equation of circle,

$$x^2 + y^2 = 16$$

$\therefore$ Radius $= 4$ and centre $= (0, 0)$

Now, perpendicular from (0, 0) to line $y = \sqrt{3}\,x + k =$ Radius of the circle

$$\left|\frac{0 - 0 + k}{\sqrt{3 + 1}}\right| = 4$$

$\left[\because\right.$ the distance from the point (m, n) to the line $\left. Ax + By + C = 0 \text{ is } d = \left|\frac{Am + Bn + C}{\sqrt{A^2 + B^2}}\right|\right]$

$\Rightarrow$ $$\pm\frac{k}{2} = 4$$

$\therefore$ $$k = \pm 8$$

Q.10 Find the equation of a circle concentric with the circle $x^2 + y^2 - 6x + 12y + 15 = 0$ and has double of its area.

- **Concept Insight** Concentric circles have the same centre.

Ans. Given equation of the circle is

$$x^2 + y^2 - 6x + 12y + 15 = 0 \quad \text{...(i)}$$

On comparing with the general equation of circle, $x^2 + y^2 + 2gx + 2hy + c = 0$, we get

$\therefore$ $$2g = -6 \Rightarrow g = -3$$

$$2f = 12 \Rightarrow f = 6$$

and $$c = 15$$

$\therefore$ $$\text{Centre} = (-g, -f) = (3, -6)$$

So, the centre of the required circle will be (3, – 6). [since, the circles are concentric]

Radius of the given circle $= \sqrt{g^2 + f^2 - c} = \sqrt{9 + 36 - 15} = \sqrt{30}$

Let radius of the required circle $= r_1$

$\therefore$ $$2 \times \text{Area of the given circle} = \text{Area of the required circle}$$

$\Rightarrow$ $$2[\pi(\sqrt{30})^2] = \pi r_1^2$$

$\Rightarrow$ $$60 = r_1^2$$

$\Rightarrow$ $$r_1 = \sqrt{60}$$

$\therefore$ $$\sqrt{g^2 + f^2 - c} = \sqrt{60}$$

$\Rightarrow$ $$9 + 36 - c = 60$$

$\Rightarrow$ $$c = -15$$

So, the required equation of circle is $x^2 + y^2 - 6x + 12y - 15 = 0$.

Q.11 If the latusrectum of an ellipse is equal to half of minor axis, then find its eccentricity.

Ans. Consider the equation of the ellipse is $\frac{x^2}{a^2} + \frac{y^2}{b^2} = 1$.

$\therefore$ Length of major axis $= 2a$

Length of minor axis $= 2b$

and length of latusrectum $= \frac{2b^2}{a}$

Given, $\frac{2b^2}{a} = \frac{2b}{2}$

$\Rightarrow$ $a = 2b \Rightarrow b = \frac{a}{2}$

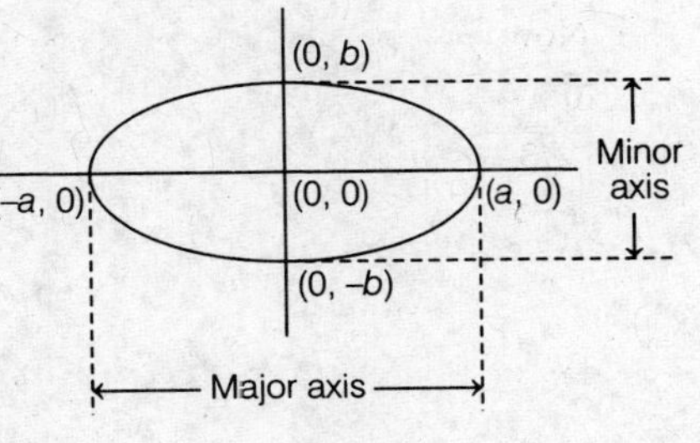

We know that $b^2 = a^2(1-e^2)$

$\Rightarrow$ $\left(\frac{a}{2}\right)^2 = a^2(1-e^2)$

$\Rightarrow$ $\frac{a^2}{4} = a^2(1-e^2)$

$\Rightarrow$ $1 - e^2 = \frac{1}{4}$

$\Rightarrow$ $e^2 = 1 - \frac{1}{4}$

$\therefore$ $e = \sqrt{\frac{3}{4}} = \frac{\sqrt{3}}{2}$

Q.12 Given the ellipse with equation $9x^2 + 25y^2 = 225$, find the eccentricity and foci.

Thinking Process Find the values of a and b by the given equation of ellipse, then use the formula $b^2 = a^2(1-e^2)$ to get the value of e.

Ans. Given equation of ellipse, $9x^2 + 25y^2 = 225$

$\Rightarrow$ $\frac{x^2}{25} + \frac{y^2}{9} = 1$

On comparing with $\frac{x^2}{a^2} + \frac{y^2}{b^2} = 1$, we get

$\Rightarrow$ $a = 5, b = 3$

We know that $b^2 = a^2(1-e^2)$

$\Rightarrow$ $9 = 25(1-e^2)$

$\Rightarrow$ $\frac{9}{25} = 1 - e^2$

$\Rightarrow$ $e^2 = 1 - \frac{9}{25}$

$\therefore$ $e = \sqrt{1 - \frac{9}{25}} = \sqrt{\frac{25-9}{25}} = \sqrt{\frac{16}{25}} = \frac{4}{5}$

Now, foci $= (\pm\, ae, 0) = \left(\pm\, 5 \times \frac{4}{5}, 0\right) = (\pm\, 4, 0)$

Q.13 If the eccentricity of an ellipse is $\frac{5}{8}$ and the distance between its foci is 10, then find latus rectum of the ellipse.

Ans. Given that eccentricity $= \frac{5}{8}$ *i.e.*, $e = \frac{5}{8}$

Let equation of the ellipse be $\frac{x^2}{a^2} + \frac{y^2}{b^2} = 1$,

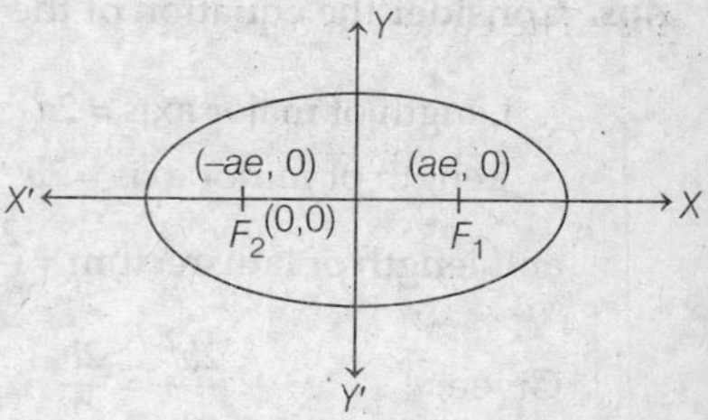

Since, the foci of this ellipse is $(\pm ae, 0)$.

$\therefore$ Distance between foci $= 2ae = 10$

$$\Rightarrow \quad 2a \times \frac{5}{8} = 10$$

$$\therefore \quad a = 8$$

We know that

$$\Rightarrow \quad b^2 = a^2(1 - e^2)$$

$$\Rightarrow \quad b^2 = 64\left(1 - \frac{25}{64}\right)$$

$$\Rightarrow \quad b^2 = 64\left(\frac{64 - 25}{64}\right)$$

$$b^2 = 39$$

$\therefore$ Length of latus rectum of ellipse $= \frac{2b^2}{a} = 2\left(\frac{39}{8}\right) = \frac{39}{4}$

Q.14 Find the equation of ellipse whose eccentricity is $\frac{2}{3}$, latus rectum is 5 and the centre is (0, 0).

Thinking Process First of all, find the values of a and b using the formula $b^2 = a^2(1 - e^2)$, then get the equation of the ellipse.

Ans. Given, $e = \frac{2}{3}$ and latus rectum $= 5$

i.e., $$\frac{2b^2}{a} = 5 \Rightarrow b^2 = \frac{5a}{2} \quad \ldots(i)$$

We know that $$b^2 = a^2(1 - e^2)$$

$$\Rightarrow \quad \frac{5a}{2} = a^2\left(1 - \frac{4}{9}\right)$$

$$\Rightarrow \quad \frac{5}{2} = \frac{5a}{9} \Rightarrow a = 9/2$$

$$\Rightarrow \quad a^2 = \frac{81}{4}$$

$$\Rightarrow \quad b^2 = \frac{5 \times 9}{2 \times 2} = \frac{45}{4} \quad \text{[from Eq. (i)]}$$

Hence, the required equation of the ellipse is $\frac{4x^2}{81} + \frac{4y^2}{45} = 1$.

Q.15 Find the distance between the directrices of ellipse $\frac{x^2}{36}+\frac{y^2}{20}=1.$

Ans. The equation of ellipse is $\frac{x^2}{36}+\frac{y^2}{20}=1$

On comparing this equation with $\frac{x^2}{a^2}+\frac{y^2}{b^2}=1$, we get

$$a=6,\ b=2\sqrt{5}$$

We know that $b^2=a^2(1-e^2)$

$\Rightarrow$ $20=36(1-e^2)$

$\Rightarrow$ $\frac{20}{36}=1-e^2$

$\therefore$ $e=\sqrt{1-\frac{20}{36}}=\sqrt{\frac{16}{36}}$

$$e=\frac{4}{6}=\frac{2}{3}$$

$\therefore$ Distance between the directrices $=\frac{2a}{e}$

$$=\frac{2\times 6}{\left(\frac{2}{3}\right)}=18$$

Q.16 Find the coordinates of a point on the parabola $y^2=8x$ whose focal distance is 4.

Thinking Process The distance of *a* point $P(h, k)$ on parabola from the focus F is called the focal distance.

Ans. Given parabola is $y^2=8x$ ...(i)

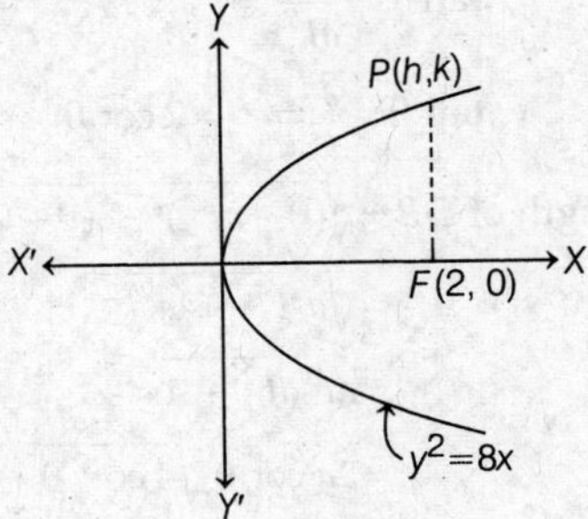

On comparing with $y^2=4ax$, we get

$$8x=4ax \Rightarrow a=2$$

The point (h,k) lies on parabola $y^2=8x$

$$k^2=8h \quad \text{...(ii)}$$

Given, focal distance $PF=4$

$\Rightarrow$ $PF^2=16$

$$(h-2)^2+(k-0)^2=16$$
$$h^2-4h+4+k^2=16$$
$$h^2-4h+4+8h-16=0$$
$$h^2+4h-12=0$$
$$(h+6)(h-2)=0$$

i.e., $h=-6, 2$

But $h=-6$ is not acceptable as (h,k) lies in 1st and 4th quadrent only where abscissa is + ve

So, $h=2$

$$K^2=16 \Rightarrow K=\pm 4$$

Hence, the required points are (2, 4) and (2, – 4)

***Q.17** Find the length of the line segment joining the vertex of the parabola $y^2=4ax$ and a point on the parabola, where the line segment makes an angle θ to the X-axis.

Ans. Given equation of the parabola is $y^2=4ax$

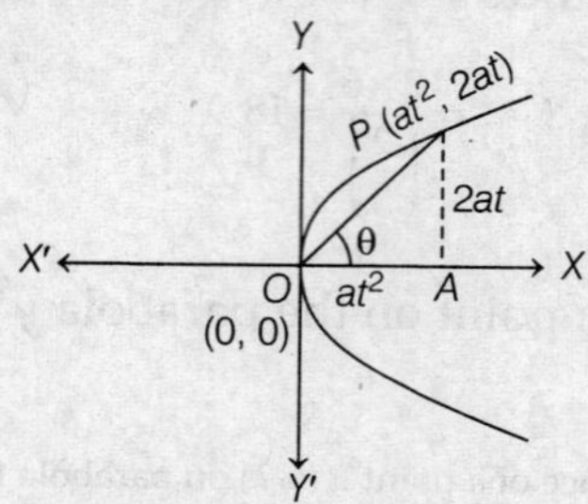

Let the coordinates of any point P on the parabola be $(at^2, 2at)$.

In ΔPOA, $\tan\theta=\frac{2\,at}{at^2}=\frac{2}{t}$.

$\Rightarrow$ $\tan\theta=\frac{2}{t}\Rightarrow t=2\cot\theta$ ...(i)

$\therefore$ length of $OP=\sqrt{(0-at^2)^2+(0-2at)^2}$

$$=\sqrt{a^2t^4+4a^2t^2}$$
$$=at\sqrt{t^2+4}$$
$$=2a\cot\theta\sqrt{4\cot^2\theta+4} \quad \text{[from Eq. (i)]}$$
$$=4a\cot\theta\sqrt{1+\cot^2\theta}$$
$$=4a\cot\theta\cdot\operatorname{cosec}\theta$$
$$=\frac{4a\cos\theta}{\sin\theta}\cdot\frac{1}{\sin\theta}$$
$$=\frac{4a\cos\theta}{\sin^2\theta}$$

(✱) Topics related to these question have been removed from latest NCERT.

***Q.18** **If the points (0, 4) and (0, 2) are respectively the vertex and focus of a parabola, then find the equation of the parabola.**

Ans. Given, vertex of the parabola (0, 4) and focus of the parabola (0, 2).

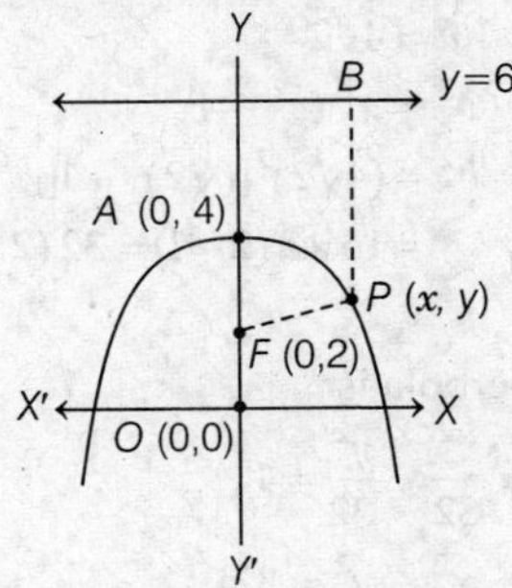

By definition of the parabola, $PB = PF$

$$\Rightarrow \left|\frac{0 + y - 6}{\sqrt{0 + 1}}\right| = \sqrt{(x - 0)^2 + (y - 2)^2}$$

$$\Rightarrow |y - 6| = \sqrt{x^2 + y^2 - 4y + 4}$$

$$\Rightarrow x^2 + y^2 - 4y + 4 = y^2 + 36 - 12y$$

$$\Rightarrow x^2 + 8y = 32$$

which is the required equation of parabola.

***Q.19** **If the line $y = mx + 1$ is tangent to the parabola $y^2 = 4x$, then find the value of m.**

Ans. Given that, line $y = mx + 1$ is tangent to the parabola $y^2 = 4x$.

$$\therefore \quad y = mx + 1 \quad \text{...(i)}$$

$$\text{and} \quad y^2 = 4x \quad \text{...(ii)}$$

From Eqs. (i) and (ii),

$$\Rightarrow (mx + 1)^2 = 4x$$

$$m^2x^2 + 2mx + 1 = 4x$$

$$\Rightarrow m^2x^2 + 2mx - 4x + 1 = 0$$

$$\Rightarrow m^2x^2 + x(2m - 4) + 1 = 0$$

It will be a tangent to the parabola, if its discriminant must be zero

$$\Rightarrow (2m - 4)^2 - 4m^2 \times 1 = 0$$

$$\Rightarrow 4m^2 + 16 - 16m - 4m^2 = 0 \Rightarrow 16m = 16$$

$$\therefore m = 1$$

Q.20 **If the distance between the foci of a hyperbola is 16 and its eccentricity is $\sqrt{2}$, then obtain the equation of the hyperbola.**

Thinking Process First of all, find the values of a and b using the given condition, then put them in $\frac{x^2}{a^2} - \frac{y^2}{b^2} = 1$ to get the required equation of the hyperbola.

(*) Topics related to these question have been removed from latest NCERT.

Ans. Distance between the foci i.e. $2ae = 16 \Rightarrow ae = 8$

and $e = \sqrt{2}$

$\therefore$ $a\sqrt{2} = 8$

$$a = 4\sqrt{2} \quad \ldots\text{(i)}$$

We know that $b^2 = a^2 (e^2 - 1)$

$\Rightarrow$ $b^2 = (4\sqrt{2})^2[(\sqrt{2})^2 - 1]$

$= 16 \times 2 (2-1) = 32 (2-1)$

$\Rightarrow$ $b^2 = 32 \quad \ldots\text{(ii)}$

Hence, the equation of hyperbola is

$$\frac{x^2}{32} - \frac{y^2}{32} = 1 \quad \text{[from Eqs. (i) and (ii)]}$$

$\Rightarrow$ $x^2 - y^2 = 32$

Q.21 Find the eccentricity of the hyperbola $9y^2 - 4x^2 = 36$.

Ans. Given, equation of the hyperbola is

$$9y^2 - 4x^2 = 36$$

$\Rightarrow$ $\frac{9y^2}{36} - \frac{4x^2}{36} = \frac{36}{36}$

$\Rightarrow$ $\frac{y^2}{4} - \frac{x^2}{9} = 1 \Rightarrow -\frac{x^2}{9} + \frac{y^2}{4} = 1$

Since, this equation in form of $-\frac{x^2}{a} + \frac{y^2}{b^2} = 1$, where $a = 3$ and $b = 2$

$\therefore$ $e = \sqrt{1 + \left(\frac{a}{b}\right)^2}$

$$= \sqrt{1 + \frac{9}{4}} = \frac{\sqrt{13}}{2}$$

Q.22 Find the equation of the hyperbola with eccentricity $\frac{3}{2}$ and foci at $(\pm 2, 0)$.

Ans. Given that eccentricity *i.e.*, $e = \frac{3}{2}$ and $(\pm ae, 0) = (\pm 2, 0)$

$\therefore$ $ae = 2 \Rightarrow a \cdot \frac{3}{2} = 2 \Rightarrow a = \frac{4}{3} \quad \ldots\text{(i)}$

$\because$ $b^2 = a^2 (e^2 - 1)$

$\Rightarrow$ $b^2 = \frac{16}{9}\left(\frac{9}{4} - 1\right)$

$\Rightarrow$ $b^2 = \frac{16}{9}\left(\frac{5}{4}\right) = \frac{20}{9} \quad \ldots\text{(ii)}$

So, the equation of hyperbola is $\frac{x^2}{\frac{16}{9}} - \frac{y^2}{\frac{20}{9}} = 1$ [from Eqs. (i) and (ii)]

$\Rightarrow$ $\frac{x^2}{4} - \frac{y^2}{5} = \frac{4}{9}$

Long Answer Type Questions

Q.23 If the lines $2x - 3y = 5$ and $3x - 4y = 7$ are the diameters of a circle of area 154 square units, then obtain the equation of the circle.

Thinking Process First of all, find the intersection point of the given lines, then get radius of circle from given area. Now, use formula equation of circle with centre (h, k) and radius a is $(x - h)^2 + (y - k)^2 = a^2$.

Ans. Given lines are $2x - 3y - 5 = 0$ ... (i)

and $3x - 4y - 7 = 0$

From Eqs. (i) and (ii), we get $\dfrac{x}{21 - 20} = \dfrac{y}{-15 + 14} = \dfrac{1}{-8 + 9}$

$\Rightarrow \dfrac{x}{1} = \dfrac{y}{-1} = \dfrac{1}{1}$

$\Rightarrow x = 1, y = -1$

Since, the intersection point of these lines will be coordinates of the centre *i.e.*, coordinates of the centre as $(1, -1)$.

Let the radius of the circle is r.

Then, $\pi r^2 = 154$

$\Rightarrow \dfrac{22}{7} \times r^2 = 154$

$\Rightarrow r^2 = \dfrac{154 \times 7}{22}$

$\Rightarrow r^2 = 49$

So, the equation of circle is

$$(x - 1)^2 + (y + 1)^2 = 49$$

$$\Rightarrow x^2 - 2x + 1 + y^2 + 2y + 1 = 49$$

$$\Rightarrow x^2 + y^2 - 2x + 2y = 47$$

Q.24 Find the equation of the circle which passes through the points (2, 3) and (4, 5) and the centre lies on the straight line $y - 4x + 3 = 0$.

Ans. Let the general equation of the circle is

$$x^2 + y^2 + 2gx + 2fy + c = 0 \quad \text{...(i)}$$

Since, this circle passes through the points (2, 3) and (4, 5).

$\therefore 4 + 9 + 4g + 6f + c = 0$

$\Rightarrow 4g + 6f + c = -13$ ...(ii)

and $16 + 25 + 8g + 10f + c = 0$

$\Rightarrow 8g + 10f + c = -41$ ...(iii)

Since, the centre of the circle $(-g, -f)$ lies on the straight line $y - 4x + 3 = 0$

i.e. $4g - f + 3 = 0$ ...(iv)

From Eq. (iv), we get $4g = f - 3$

On putting $4g = f - 3$ in Eq. (ii), we get

$$f - 3 + 6f + c = -13$$

$$\Rightarrow \quad 7f + c = -10 \quad \text{...(v)}$$

From Eqs. (ii) and (iii), we get

$$\begin{array}{r} 8g + 12f + 2c = -26 \\ 8g + 10f + c = -41 \\ - \quad - \quad - \qquad + \\ \hline 2f + c = 15 \end{array} \quad \text{...(vi)}$$

From Eqs. (v) and (vi), we get

$$\begin{array}{r} 7f + c = -10 \\ 2f + c = 15 \\ - \quad - \quad - \\ \hline 5f = -25 \end{array}$$

$$\therefore \quad f = -5$$

Now, from Eq. (vi), we get $c = 10 + 15 = 25$

From Eq. (iv), we get $4g + 5 + 3 = 0$

$$\Rightarrow \quad g = -2$$

From Eq. (i), equation of the circle is $x^2 + y^2 - 4x - 10y + 25 = 0$.

Q.25 Find the equation of a circle whose centre is (3, – 1) and which cuts off a chord of length 6 units on the line $2x - 5y + 18 = 0$.

Ans. Given centre of the circle is (3, – 1) and the equation of a chord is $2x - 5y + 18 = 0$

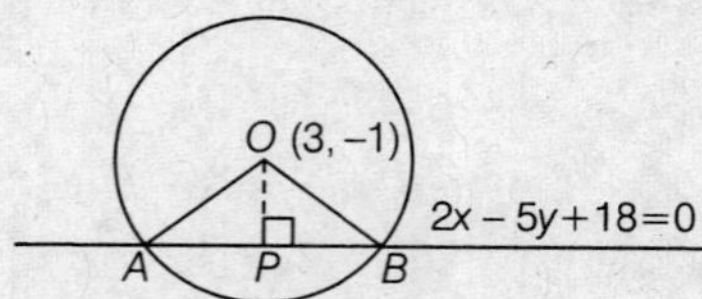

Now, perpendicular distance, $OP = \left|\dfrac{6 + 5 + 18}{\sqrt{4 + 25}}\right| = \dfrac{29}{\sqrt{29}} = \sqrt{29}$

In ΔOPB, $\quad OB^2 = OP^2 + PB^2 \quad [\because AB = 6 \Rightarrow PB = 3]$

$$\Rightarrow \quad OB^2 = 29 + 9$$

$$\Rightarrow \quad OB^2 = 38$$

So, the radius of the circle is $\sqrt{38}$,

$\therefore$ Equation of the circle with radius $r = \sqrt{38}$ and centre $(3, -1)$ is

$$(x - 3)^2 + (y + 1)^2 = 38$$

$$\Rightarrow \quad x^2 - 6x + 9 + y^2 + 2y + 1 = 38$$

$$x^2 + y^2 - 6x + 2y = 28$$

Q.26 Find the equation of a circle of radius 5 which is touching another circle $x^2 + y^2 - 2x - 4y - 20 = 0$ at (5, 5).

Ans.

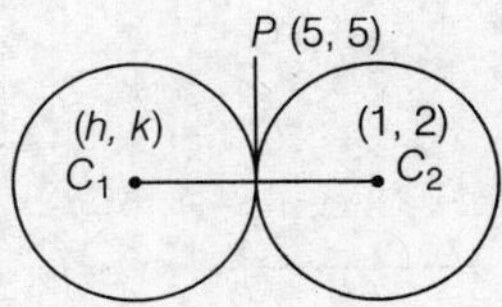

Given equation of the circle is $x^2 + y^2 - 2x - 4y - 20$, centre (1, 2).

Radius $= \sqrt{1 + 4 + 20} = 5$ $\quad [\because r = \sqrt{g^2 + f^2 - c}]$

Let the coordinates of centre of the required circle are (h, k)

So, it is clear that P is the mid-point of C_1C_2.

$$\therefore \quad 5 = \frac{1+h}{2} \Rightarrow h = 9 \text{ and } 5 = \frac{2+k}{2} \Rightarrow k = 8$$

So, the required equation of the circle is

$$(x - 9)^2 + (y - 8)^2 = 25$$

$$\Rightarrow \quad x^2 - 18x + 81 + y^2 - 16y + 64 = 25$$

$$\Rightarrow \quad x^2 + y^2 - 18x - 16y + 120 = 0$$

Q.27 Find the equation of a circle passing through the point (7, 3) having radius 3 units and whose centre lies on the line $y = x - 1$.

Thinking Process First of all let the equation of a circle with centre (h, k) and radius r is $(x - h)^2 + (y - k)^2 = r^2$, then the point satisfies the equation of line and the equation of circle. Thus, we get the values of (h, k) and then find the required equation of the circle.

Ans. Let equation of circle be

$$(x - h)^2 + (y - k)^2 = r^2$$

$$\Rightarrow \quad (x - h)^2 + (y - k)^2 = 9 \quad [\because r = 3, \text{ given}] \ldots\text{(i)}$$

Given, centre (h, k) lies on the line

$$y = x - 1$$

i.e. $$k = h - 1 \quad \ldots\text{(ii)}$$

Now, the circle passes through the point (7, 3).

$$\therefore \quad (7 - h)^2 + (3 - k)^3 = 9$$

$$\Rightarrow \quad 49 - 14h + h^2 + 9 - 6k + k^2 = 9$$

$$\Rightarrow \quad h^2 + k^2 - 14h - 6k + 49 = 0 \quad \ldots\text{(iii)}$$

On putting $k = h - 1$ in Eq. (iii), we get

$$h^2 + (h - 1)^2 - 14h - 6(h - 1) + 49 = 0$$

$$\Rightarrow \quad h^2 + h^2 - 2h + 1 - 14h - 6h + 6 + 49 = 0$$

$$\Rightarrow \quad 2h^2 - 22h + 56 = 0$$

$$\Rightarrow \quad h^2 - 11h + 28 = 0$$

$$\Rightarrow \quad h^2 - 7h - 4h + 28 = 0$$

$$\Rightarrow \quad h(h - 7) - 4(h - 7) = 0$$

$$\Rightarrow \quad (h - 7)(h - 4) = 0$$

$\therefore$ $$h = 4, 7$$

When $h = 7$, then $k = 7 - 1 = 6$ [from Eq. (ii)]

$\therefore$ Centre (7, 6)

When $h = 4$, then $k = 3$

$\therefore$ Centre = (4, 3)

So, the equation of circle with centre (7, 6), is

$$(x - 7)^2 + (y - 6)^2 = 9$$

$$\Rightarrow \quad x^2 - 14x + 49 + y^2 - 12y + 36 = 9$$

$$\Rightarrow \quad x^2 + y^2 - 14x - 12y + 76 = 0$$

And the equation of the circle with centre (4, 3) is

$$(x - 4)^2 + (y - 3)^2 = 9$$

$$\Rightarrow \quad x^2 - 8x + 16 + y^2 - 6y + 9 = 9$$

$$\Rightarrow \quad x^2 + y^2 - 8x - 6y + 16 = 0$$

***Q.28** Find the equation of each of the following parabolas

(i) Directrix $x = 0$, focus at (6, 0)

(ii) vertex at (0, 4), focus at (0, 2)

(iii) focus at $(-1, -2)$, directrix $x - 2y + 3 = 0$

Ans. (i) Given, directrix $x = 0$ and focus = (6, 0)

So, the equation of the parabola

$$(x - 6)^2 + y^2 = x^2 \quad [\because PS = PM]$$

$$\Rightarrow \quad x^2 + 36 - 12x + y^2 = x^2$$

$$\Rightarrow \quad y^2 - 12x + 36 = 0$$

(ii) Given, vertex = (0, 4) and focus = (0, 2)

So, the equation of parabola is

$$\sqrt{(x - 0)^2 + (y - 2)^2} = |y - 6|$$

$$\Rightarrow \quad x^2 + y^2 - 4y + 4 = y^2 - 12y + 36$$

$$\Rightarrow \quad x^2 - 4y + 12y - 32 = 0$$

$$\Rightarrow \quad x^2 + 8y - 32 = 0$$

$$\Rightarrow \quad x^2 = 32 - 8y$$

(iii) Given, focus at $(-1, -2)$ and directrix $x - 2y + 3 = 0$

So, the equation of parabola is $\sqrt{(x + 1)^2 + (y + 2)^2} = \left|\dfrac{x - 2y + 3}{\sqrt{1 + 4}}\right|$

$$\Rightarrow \quad x^2 + 2x + 1 + y^2 + 4y + 4 = \frac{1}{5}[x^2 + 4y^2 + 9 - 4xy - 12y + 6x]$$

$$\Rightarrow 4x^2 + 4xy + y^2 + 4x + 32y + 16 = 0$$

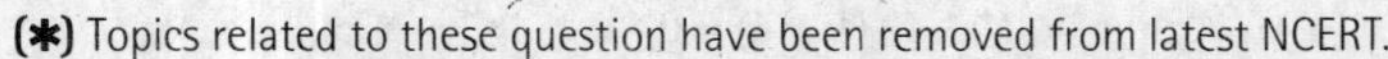
(*) Topics related to these question have been removed from latest NCERT.

***Q.29** Find the equation of the set of all points the sum of whose distances from the points (3, 0), (9, 0) is 12.

Ans. Let the coordinates of the point be (x, y), then according to the question,

P(x, y)

A(3, 0) B(9, 0)

Given, $PA + PB = 12$

i.e., $\sqrt{(x-3)^2 + y^2} + \sqrt{(x-9)^2 + y^2} = 12$

$\Rightarrow \quad \sqrt{(x-3)^2 + y^2} = 12 - \sqrt{(x-9)^2 + y^2}$

On squaring both sides, we get

$$x^2 - 6x + 9 + y^2 = 144 + (x^2 - 18x + 81 + y^2) - 24\sqrt{(x-9)^2 + y^2}$$

$\Rightarrow \quad 12x - 216 = -24\sqrt{(x-9)^2 + y^2}$

$\Rightarrow \quad x - 18 = -2\sqrt{(x-9)^2 + y^2}$

$\Rightarrow \quad x^2 - 36x + 324 = 4(x^2 - 18x + 81 + y^2)$

$\Rightarrow \quad 3x^2 + 4y^2 - 36x = 0$

Q.30 Find the equation of the set of all points whose distance from (0, 4) are $\frac{2}{3}$ of their distance from the line $y = 9$.

Thinking Process Consider the point (x, y), and apply the given condition, then get the equation of set of all points.

Ans. Let the point be $P(x, y)$.

$\therefore$ Distance of P from (0, 4) $= \sqrt{x^2 + (y-4)^2}$

So, the distance from the line $y = 9$ is $\left|\frac{y-9}{\sqrt{1}}\right|$

$\therefore \quad \sqrt{x^2 + (y-4)^2} = \frac{2}{3}\left|\frac{y-9}{1}\right|$

$\Rightarrow \quad x^2 + y^2 - 8y + 16 = \frac{4}{9}(y^2 - 18y + 81)$

$\Rightarrow \quad 9x^2 + 9y^2 - 72y + 144 = 4y^2 - 72y + 324$

$\Rightarrow \quad 9x^2 + 5y^2 = 180$

Q.31 Show that the set of all points such that the difference of their distances from (4, 0) and (– 4, 0) is always equal to 2 represent a hyperbola.

Ans. Let the point be $P(x, y)$.

$\therefore$ Distance of P from (4, 0) is $\sqrt{(x-4)^2 + y^2}$ ... (i)

and the distance of P from (– 4, 0) $\sqrt{(x+4)^2 + y^2}$ ... (ii)

Now, $\sqrt{(x+4)^2 + y^2} - \sqrt{(x-4)^2 + y^2} = 2$

$\Rightarrow \quad \sqrt{(x+4)^2 + y^2} = 2 + \sqrt{(x-4)^2 + y^2}$

(*) Topics related to these question have been removed from latest NCERT.

On squaring both sides, we get

$$x^2 + 8x + 16 + y^2 = 4 + x^2 - 8x + 16 + y^2 + 4\sqrt{(x-4)^2 + y^2}$$

$\Rightarrow \quad 16x - 4 = 4\sqrt{(x-4)^2 + y^2}$

$\Rightarrow \quad 4(4x - 1) = 4\sqrt{(x-4)^2 + y^2}$

$\Rightarrow \quad 16x^2 - 8x + 1 = x^2 + 16 - 8x + y^2$

$\Rightarrow \quad 15x^2 - y^2 = 15$, which is a hyperbola.

Q.32 Find the equation of the hyperbola with

(i) Vertices $(\pm 5, 0)$, foci $(\pm 7, 0)$

*(ii) Vertices $(0, \pm 7)$, $e = \frac{4}{3}$.

(iii) Foci $(0, \pm\sqrt{10})$, passing through $(2, 3)$.

Ans. (i) Given vertices $= (\pm 5, 0)$, foci $= (\pm 7, 0)$ and $a = \pm 5$

$\therefore \quad (\pm ae, 0) = (\pm 7, 0)$

Now $\quad ae = 7 \Rightarrow 5e = 7$

$\Rightarrow \quad e = \frac{7}{5}$

$\because \quad b^2 = a^2(e^2 - 1)$

$\Rightarrow \quad b^2 = 25\left(\frac{49}{25} - 1\right)$

$\Rightarrow \quad b^2 = 25\left(\frac{49 - 25}{25}\right)$

$\Rightarrow \quad b^2 = 24$

So, the equation of hyperbola is

$$\frac{x^2}{25} - \frac{y^2}{24} = 1 \qquad [\because a^2 = 25 \text{ and } b^2 = 24]$$

(ii) Given, vertices $= (0, \pm 7)$, $e = \frac{4}{3}$

$\therefore \quad b = 7, e = \frac{4}{3}$

$\because \quad e^2 = 1 + \frac{a^2}{b^2} \qquad \left[\because e = \sqrt{1 + \frac{a^2}{b^2}}\right]$

$\Rightarrow \quad \frac{16}{9} - 1 = \frac{a^2}{49}$

$\Rightarrow \quad \frac{7}{9} = \frac{a^2}{49} \Rightarrow a^2 = \frac{343}{9}$

So, the equation of hyperbola is

$$-\frac{x^2 \times 9}{343} + \frac{y^2}{49} = 1$$

$\Rightarrow \quad -\frac{9x^2}{7} + y^2 = 49 \Rightarrow 9x^2 - 7y^2 + 343 = 0$

(*) Topics related to these question have been removed from latest NCERT.

(iii) Given, foci $=(0, \pm \sqrt{10})$

$\because$ $$be = \sqrt{10}$$

$$b^2e^2 = 10 \qquad \left[\because e = \sqrt{1+\frac{a^2}{b^2}}\right]$$

$$b^2\left(1+\frac{a^2}{b^2}\right) = 10$$

$\Rightarrow$ $$a^2 + b^2 = 10$$

$\Rightarrow$ $$a^2 = 10 - b^2 \qquad \ldots(i)$$

$\therefore$ Equation of the hyperbola is

$$-\frac{x^2}{a^2}+\frac{y^2}{b^2}=1 \qquad \ldots(i)$$

Since, hyperbola passes through the point (2, 3).

$\therefore$ $$-\frac{4}{a^2}+\frac{9}{b^2}=1$$

$\Rightarrow$ $$\frac{-4}{10-b^2}+\frac{9}{b^2}=1 \qquad \text{[from Eq. (i)]}$$

$\Rightarrow$ $$\frac{-4b^2+90-9b^2}{b^2(10-b^2)}=1$$

$\Rightarrow$ $$-13b^2+90 = 10b^2 - b^4$$

$\Rightarrow$ $$b^4 - 23b^2 + 90 = 0 \Rightarrow b^4 - 18b^2 - 5b^2 + 90 = 0$$

$\Rightarrow$ $$b^2(b^2-18) - 5(b^2-18) = 0 \Rightarrow (b^2-18)(b^2-5) = 0$$

$\Rightarrow$ $$b^2 = 18 \Rightarrow b = \pm 3\sqrt{2}$$

or $$b^2 = 5 \Rightarrow b = \pm\sqrt{5}$$

$\therefore$ $$b^2 = 18 \text{ then } a^2 = -8 \qquad \text{[not possible]}$$

When $$b^2 = 5, \text{ then } a^2 = 5$$

So, the equation of hyperbola is $-\frac{x^2}{5}+\frac{y^2}{5}=1 \Rightarrow y^2 - x^2 = 5$

Objective Type Questions

State True or False for the following statements in each of the exercises from 33 to 40.

Q.33 The line $x + 3y = 0$ is a diameter of the circle $x^2 + y^2 + 6x + 2y = 0$.

- **Concept Insight** If a line is the diameter of circle, then the centre of the circle should lie on line. Use this property to solve the given problem.

Ans. *False*

Given equation of the circle is $x^2 + y^2 + 6x + 2y = 0$

On comparing with $x^2 + y^2 + 2gx + 2fy + c = 0$, we get

Centre $= (-3, -1)$

Since, given line is $x + 3y = 0 \Rightarrow -3 - 3 = -6 \neq 0$

So, centre does not passes through the given line.

Hence, this line is not diameter of the circle.

Q.34 The shortest distance from the point (2, – 7) to the circle $x^2 + y^2 - 14x - 10y - 151 = 0$ is equal to 5.

Ans. *False*

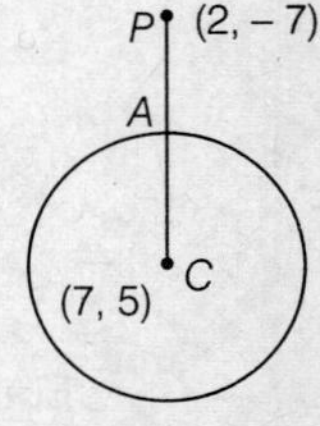

Given circle is $x^2 + y^2 - 14x - 10y - 151 = 0$.

$\therefore$ Centre = (7, 5)

and Radius $= \sqrt{49 + 25 + 151} = \sqrt{225} = 15$

So, the distance between the point (2,–7) and centre of the circle is given by

$$d_1 = \sqrt{(2-7)^2 + (-7-5)^2} = \sqrt{25 + 144} = \sqrt{169} = 13$$

$\therefore$ Shortest distance, $d = |PC - AC| = |PC - r| = |13 - 15| = 2$

Q.35 If the line $lx + my = 1$ is a tangent to the circle $x^2 + y^2 = a^2$, then the point (l, m) lies on a circle.

Thinking process Use that the distance from the centre of the circle to the given line is radius of the circle.

Ans. *False*

Given circle is $x^2 + y^2 = a^2$ ...(i)

$\therefore$ Radius of circle = a and centre = (0, 0)

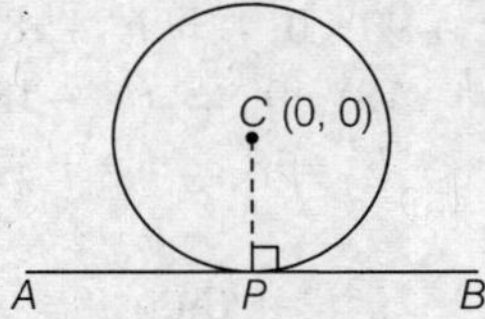

Since, the line $lx + my = 1$ is a tangent to the circle $x^2 + y^2 = a^2$

$\therefore$ Perpendicular distance from centre

= Radius of circle

$$\Rightarrow \left| \frac{-1}{\sqrt{l^2 + m^2}} \right| = a$$

$$\Rightarrow \frac{1}{l^2 + m^2} = a^2$$

$$\Rightarrow l^2 + m^2 = \frac{1}{a^2}$$

So, point (l, m) does not lie on the circle. $[\because l^2 + m^2 \neq a^2]$

Q.36 The point (1, 2) lies inside the circle $x^2 + y^2 - 2x + 6y + 1 = 0$.

- **Concept Insight** If the point (x_1, y_1) lies inside the circle $S \equiv x^2 + y^2 + 2gx + 2fy + c = 0$, then $x_1^2 + y_1^2 + 2gx_1 + 2fy_1 + c < 0$ and if $S_1 > 0$, then the point lies outside the circle.

Ans. *False*

Given circle is $S \equiv x^2 + y^2 - 2x + 6y + 1 = 0$.

Since, the point is (1, 2).

Now, $S_1 \equiv 1 + 4 - 2 + 12 + 1 = 16 > 0$

$\Rightarrow \qquad S_1 > 0$

So, the point (1, 2) lies outside the circle.

***Q.37** The line $lx + my + n = 0$ will touch the parabola $y^2 = 4ax$, if $ln = am^2$.

Ans. *True*

Given equation of a line is

$$lx + my + n = 0 \quad \text{...(i)}$$

and parabola $y^2 = 4ax$ ...(ii)

From Eq. (i), put $x = -\left(\dfrac{my + n}{l}\right)$ in Eq. (ii), we get

$$y^2 = -\frac{4a(my + n)}{l}$$

$$\Rightarrow \quad ly^2 = -4a\,my - 4\,an$$

$$\Rightarrow \quad ly^2 + 4\,amy + 4an = 0$$

For tangent, $D = 0$

$$\Rightarrow \quad 16\,a^2m^2 - 4l \times 4\,an = 0$$

$$\Rightarrow \quad 16\,a^2m^2 = 16\,anl$$

$$\Rightarrow \quad am^2 = nl$$

Q.38 If P is a point on the ellipse $\dfrac{x^2}{16} + \dfrac{y^2}{25} = 1$ whose foci are S and S', then PS + PS′ = 8.

Ans. *False*

Given equation of the ellipse is $\dfrac{x^2}{16} + \dfrac{y^2}{25} = 1$

Here, $a = 4, b = 5$

which is in form of $\dfrac{x^2}{a^2} + \dfrac{y^2}{b^2} = 1$, where $b > a$

$$\therefore \quad \text{Foci, } S = (0, be), S'(0, -be)$$

$$\therefore \quad e = \sqrt{1 - \frac{a^2}{b^2}} = \sqrt{\frac{25 - 16}{25}} = 3/5$$

$$\text{Foci, } S = \left(0, \frac{3 \times 5}{5}\right), S' = \left(0, -\frac{3 \times 5}{5}\right) \textit{ i.e., } S = (0, 3), S' = (0, -3)$$

Let the coordinates of point P be (x, y), then $PS + PS' = 2b = 2 \times 5 = 10$

***Q.39** The line $2x + 3y = 12$ touches the ellipse $\dfrac{x^2}{9} + \dfrac{y^2}{4} = 2$ at the point (3,2).

Ans. *True*

Given equation of the line is $2x + 3y = 12$ ...(i)

and equation of the ellipse is $\dfrac{x^2}{9} + \dfrac{y^2}{4} = 2$ ...(ii)

(*) Topics related to these question have been removed from latest NCERT.

Since, the equation of tangent at the point (x_1, y_1) is $\frac{xx_1}{9}+\frac{yy_1}{4}=2$

$\therefore$ Tangent at the point (3, 2),

$$\frac{3x}{9}+\frac{2y}{4}=2$$

$$\Rightarrow \quad \frac{x}{3}+\frac{y}{2}=2$$

$\Rightarrow \quad 2x+3y=12$, which is the given line.

Hence, the statement is true.

Q.40 The locus of the point of intersection of lines $\sqrt{3}x-y-4\sqrt{3}k=0$ and $\sqrt{3}kx+ky-4\sqrt{3}=0$ for different value of k is a hyperbola whose eccentricity is 2.

Thinking Process First of all, eliminate k from the given equations of line, then get the equation of hyperbola.

Ans. *True*

Given equations of line are

$$\sqrt{3}x-y-4\sqrt{3}k=0 \quad \text{...(i)}$$

and $$\sqrt{3}kx+ky-4\sqrt{3}=0 \quad \text{...(ii)}$$

From Eq. (i), we get

$$4\sqrt{3}\,k=\sqrt{3}\,x-y$$

$$\Rightarrow \quad k=\frac{\sqrt{3}x-y}{4\sqrt{3}}$$

Substitute the value of k in Eq. (ii), we get

$$\sqrt{3}x\left(\frac{\sqrt{3}x-y}{4\sqrt{3}}\right)+\left(\frac{\sqrt{3}x-y}{4\sqrt{3}}\right)y-4\sqrt{3}=0$$

$$\Rightarrow \quad \frac{1}{4}(\sqrt{3}x^2-xy)+\frac{1}{4}\left(xy-\frac{y^2}{\sqrt{3}}\right)-4\sqrt{3}=0$$

$$\Rightarrow \quad \frac{\sqrt{3}}{4}x^2-\frac{y^2}{4\sqrt{3}}-4\sqrt{3}=0$$

$$\Rightarrow \quad 3x^2-y^2-48=0$$

$\Rightarrow 3x^2-y^2=48$, which represents hyperbola with $a^2=16$

$$\Rightarrow \quad a=4$$

and $$b^2=48$$

$$\Rightarrow \quad b=4\sqrt{3}$$

Now, for eccentricity of the hyperbola $e^2=1+\frac{b^2}{a^2}$

$$=1+\frac{48}{16}=1+3=4$$

$$\Rightarrow \quad e=2$$

Fill in the blanks in exercises from 41 to 46.

Q.41 The equation of the circle having centre at (3, – 4) and touching the line $5x + 12y - 12 = 0$ is ....

- **Concept Insight** Perpendicular distance from the centre to the tangent line = radius of the circle.

Ans. The perpendicular distance from centre (3, – 4) to the line is, $d = \left|\frac{15 - 48 - 12}{\sqrt{25 + 144}}\right| = \frac{45}{13}$

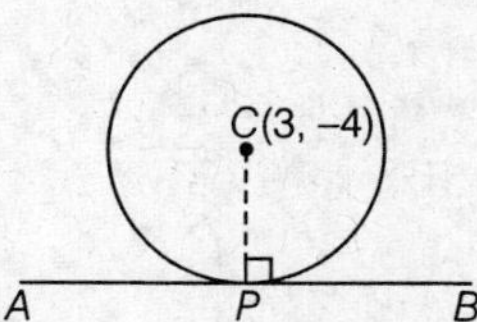

So, the required equations of the circle is $(x - 3)^2 + (y + 4)^2 = \left(\frac{45}{13}\right)^2$.

***Q.42** The equation of the circle circumscribing the triangle whose sides are the lines $y = x + 2$, $3y = 4x$, $2y = 3x$ is ....

Ans. Given equations of lines are

$$y = x + 2 \quad \text{...(i)}$$

$$3y = 4x \quad \text{...(ii)}$$

and $$2y = 3x \quad \text{...(iii)}$$

From Eqs. (i) and (ii), we get

$$\frac{4x}{3} = x + 2$$

$\Rightarrow$ $$4x = 3x + 6 \Rightarrow x = 6$$

On putting $x = 6$ in Eq. (i), we get

$$y = 8$$

$\therefore$ Point $A = (6, 8)$

From Eqs. (i) and (iii), we get

$$\frac{3x}{2} = x + 2$$

$\Rightarrow$ $$3x = 2x + 4 \Rightarrow x = 4$$

When $x = 4$, then $y = 6$

$\therefore$ Point, $B = (4, 6)$

From Eqs. (ii) and (iii), we get $x = 0, y = 0$

Now, $C = (0, 0)$

Let the equation of circle is

$$x^2 + y^2 + 2gx + 2fy + c = 0$$

Since, the points A (6, 8), B (4, 6) and C (0, 0) lie on this circle.

$$36 + 64 + 12g + 16f + c = 0$$

(*) Topics related to these question have been removed from latest NCERT.

$\Rightarrow \quad 12g + 16f + c = -100 \quad \ldots(iv)$

and $\quad 16 + 36 + 8g + 12f + c = 0$

$\Rightarrow \quad 8g + 12f + c = -52 \quad \ldots(v)$

$\Rightarrow \quad c = 0 \quad \ldots(vi)$

From Eqs. (iv), (v) and (vi), we get

$$12g + 16f = -100$$

$\Rightarrow \quad 3g + 4f + 25 = 0$

$\Rightarrow \quad 2g + 3f + 13 = 0$ [dividing by 4 both sides]

From above two equations, we get

$$\frac{g}{+52-75} = \frac{f}{50-39} = \frac{1}{9-8}$$

$$\Rightarrow \quad \frac{g}{-23} = \frac{f}{11} = \frac{1}{1}$$

$$\Rightarrow \quad g = -23,\ f = 11$$

So, the equation of circle is

$$x^2 + y^2 - 46x + 22y + 0 = 0$$

$$\Rightarrow \quad x^2 + y^2 - 46x + 22y = 0$$

Q.43 An ellipse is described by using an endless string which is passed over two pins. If the axes are 6 cm and 4 cm, the length of the string and distance between the pins are ....

Ans. Let equation of the ellipse be $\frac{x^2}{a^2} + \frac{y^2}{b^2} = 1$.

$\therefore$ major axis, $\quad 2a = 6$ and $2b = 4$

$\Rightarrow$ minor axis, $\quad 2b = 4 \Rightarrow a = 2$ and $b = 3$

We know that

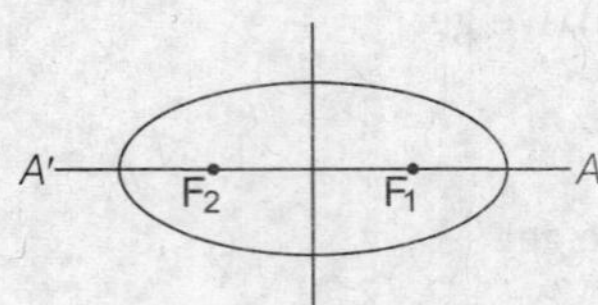

$$c^2 = a^2 - b^2 = (3)^2 - (2)^2 = 9 - 4 = 5 \Rightarrow c = \sqrt{5}$$

The two fixed pins are the focus whose coordinates are (ae, o) and $(-ae, o)$.

$\therefore$ Distances between the pins = $F_1F_2 = 2\sqrt{5} = cc'$

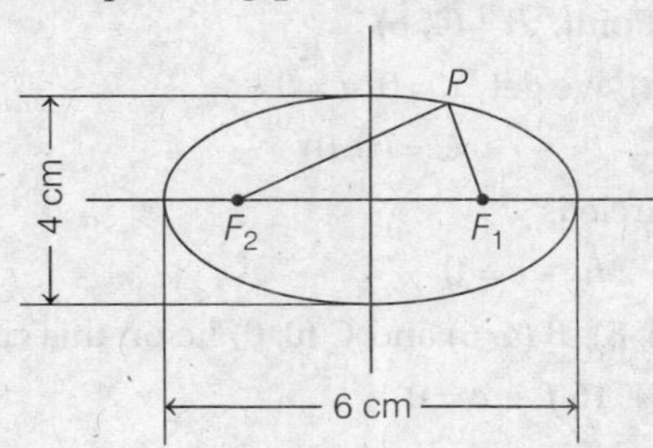

By the definition of the ellipse, length of Major axis = $Pf_1 + Pf_2 = 2a = 6$ cm

$\therefore$ Length of the string = $PF_1 + PF_2 + F_1F_2$

$$= (6 + 2\sqrt{5}) \text{ cm}$$

Q.44 The equation of the ellipse having foci (0, 1), (0, – 1) and minor axis of length 1 is ....

Ans. We know that foci of the ellipse are $(0, \pm be)$.

$$\because \quad be \equiv 1$$

$\therefore$ Length of minor axis, $2a = 1 \Rightarrow a = \frac{1}{2}$

$$e^2 = 1 - \frac{a^2}{b^2}$$

$$\Rightarrow \quad (be)^2 = b^2 - a^2 \Rightarrow 1 = b^2 - \frac{1}{4}$$

$$\Rightarrow \quad 1 + \frac{1}{4} = b^2 \Rightarrow \frac{5}{4} = b^2$$

So, the required equation of ellipse is

$$\frac{x^2}{\frac{1}{4}} + \frac{y^2}{\frac{5}{4}} = 1$$

$$\Rightarrow \quad \frac{4x^2}{1} + \frac{4y^2}{5} = 1$$

***Q.45** The equation of the parabola having focus at (– 1, – 2) and directrix is $x - 2y + 3 = 0$, is ....

Ans. Given, focus at $F(-1, -2)$ and directrix is $x - 2y + 3 = 0$

Let any point on the parabola be $P(x, y)$ i.e. $PF = PM$

$$PF^2 = PM^2$$

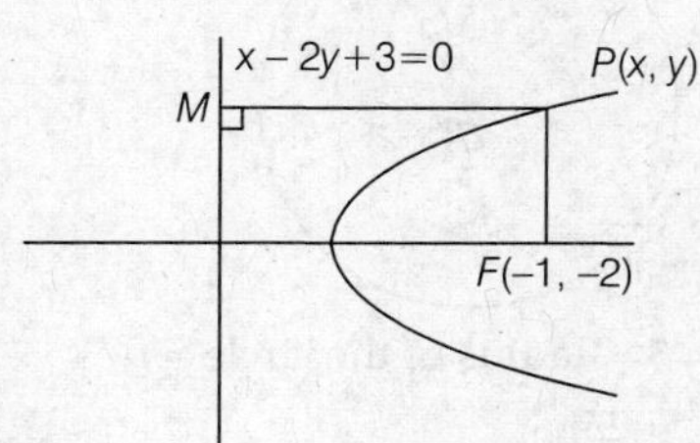

$$\therefore \quad PF = \left| \frac{x - 2y + 3}{\sqrt{1 + 4}} \right|$$

$$\Rightarrow \quad (x + 1)^2 + (y + 2)^2 = \frac{(x - 2y + 3)^2}{5}$$

$$\Rightarrow \quad 5[x^2 + 2x + 1 + y^2 + 4y + 4] = x^2 + 4y^2 + 9 - 4xy - 12y + 6x$$

$$\Rightarrow \quad 4x^2 + y^2 + 4x + 32y + 4xy + 16 = 0$$

(*) Topics related to these question have been removed from latest NCERT.

Q.46 The equation of the hyperbola with vertices at $(0, \pm 6)$ and eccentricity $\frac{5}{3}$ is .... and its foci are ....

Ans. Let the equation of the hyperbola be $-\frac{x^2}{a^2}+\frac{y^2}{b^2}=1$.

Then, $\quad$ vertices $=(0, \pm b)=(0, \pm 6)$

$$\therefore \quad b=6 \text{ and } e=\frac{5}{3}$$

$$\because \quad e=\sqrt{1+\frac{a^2}{b^2}} \Rightarrow \frac{25}{9}=1+\frac{a^2}{36}$$

$$\Rightarrow \quad \frac{25-9}{9}=\frac{a^2}{36} \Rightarrow 16=\frac{a^2}{4} \Rightarrow a^2=64$$

So, the equation of hyperbola is

$$\frac{-x^2}{64}+\frac{y^2}{36}=1 \Rightarrow \frac{y^2}{36}-\frac{x^2}{64}=1$$

$$\because \quad \text{Foci}=(0, \pm be)=\left(0, \pm \frac{5}{3} \times 6\right)=(0, \pm 10)$$

Choose the correct answers from the given four options in each exercise 47 to 59.

Q.47 The area of the circle centred at (1, 2) and passing through the point(4, 6) is

(a) 5π $\quad$ (b) 10π

(c) 25π $\quad$ (d) None of these

Ans. *(c)* Given, centre of the circle is (1, 2) and point on the circle is $P(4, 6)$

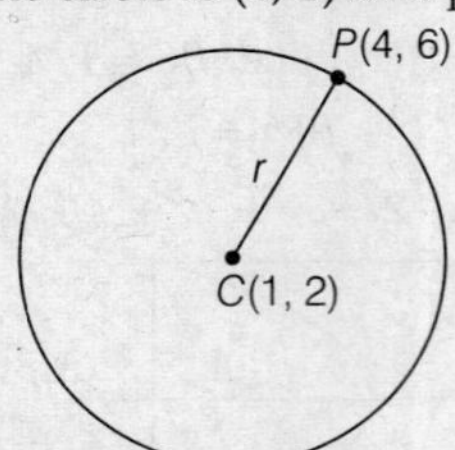

Now, $CP=\sqrt{9+16}=5=$ Radius of the circle $=r$

$\therefore$ Required area $=\pi r^2=25\pi$

Q.48 Equation of a circle which passes through (3, 6) and touches the axes is

(a) $x^2+y^2+6x+6y+3=0$

(b) $x^2+y^2-6x-6y-9=0$

(c) $x^2+y^2-6x-6y+9=0$

(d) None of these

Ans. *(c)* Let the centre of the circle be (a, a), then equation of the circle is $(x-a)^2 + (y-a)^2 = a^2$.

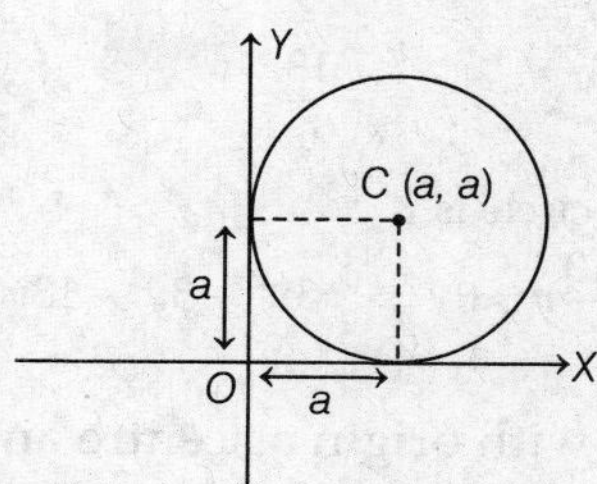

Since, the point (3, 6) lies on this circle, then

$$(3-a)^2 + (6-a)^2 = a^2$$

$$\Rightarrow \quad a^2 + 9 - 6a + 36 - 12a + a^2 = a^2$$

$$\Rightarrow \quad a^2 - 18a + 45 = 0$$

$$\Rightarrow \quad a^2 - 15a - 3a + 45 = 0$$

$$\Rightarrow \quad a(a-15) - 3(a-15) = 0$$

$$\Rightarrow \quad (a-3)(a-15) = 0$$

$$\Rightarrow \quad a = 3, a = 15$$

So, the required equation of circle is

$$(x-3)^2 + (y-3)^2 = 9$$

$$\Rightarrow \quad x^2 - 6x + 9 + y^2 - 6y + 9 = 9$$

$$\Rightarrow \quad x^2 + y^2 - 6x - 6y + 9 = 0$$

Q. 49 Equation of the circle with centre on the *Y*-axis and passing through the origin and the point (2, 3) is

(a) $x^2 + y^2 + 13y = 0$
(b) $3x^2 + 3y^2 + 13x + 3 = 0$
(c) $3x^2 + 3y^2 - 13y = 0$
(d) $x^2 + y^2 + 13x + 3 = 0$

Ans. *(c)* Let general equation of the circle is $x^2 + y^2 + 2gx + 2fy + c = 0$.

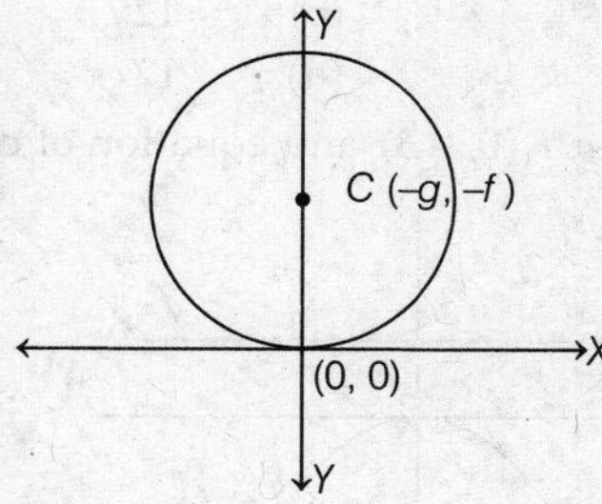

Since the point (0, 0) lies on it $\Rightarrow c = 0$.

And the point (2, 3) lies on it

$$\Rightarrow \quad 4 + 9 + 4g + 6f = 0$$

$$\Rightarrow \quad 2g + 3f = -\frac{13}{2}$$

Since, the centre lie on Y-axis, then $g = 0$.

$$\therefore \quad 3f = -\frac{13}{2}$$

$$\Rightarrow \quad f = -\frac{13}{6}$$

So, the required equation of circle is

$$x^2 + y^2 - 2\times\frac{13}{6}y = 0 \Rightarrow 3x^2 + 3y^2 - 13y = 0$$

Q.50 The equation of a circle with origin as centre and passing through the vertices of an equilateral triangle whose median is of length $3a$ is

(a) $x^2 + y^2 = 9a^2$
(b) $x^2 + y^2 = 16a^2$
(c) $x^2 + y^2 = 4a^2$
(d) $x^2 + y^2 = a^2$

- **Concept insight** Centroid of the triangle coincides with the centre of the the circle and the radius of the circle is $\frac{2}{3}$ of the length of the median.

Ans. *(c)* Given, length of the median $AD = 3a$

$\because$ Radius of the circle $= \frac{2}{3} \times$ Length of median $= \frac{2}{3} \times 3a = 2a$

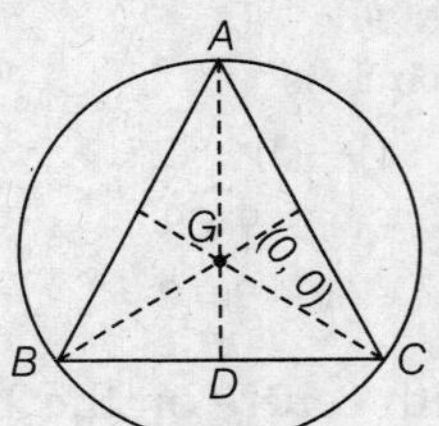

So, the equation of the circle is $x^2 + y^2 = 4a^2$.

Q.51 If the focus of a parabola is $(0, -3)$ and its directrix is $y = 3$, then its equation is

(a) $x^2 = -12y$
(b) $x^2 = 12y$
(c) $y^2 = -12x$
(d) $y^2 = 12x$

Ans. *(a)* Given, focus of parabola at $F(0, -3)$ and equation of directrix is $y = 3$.

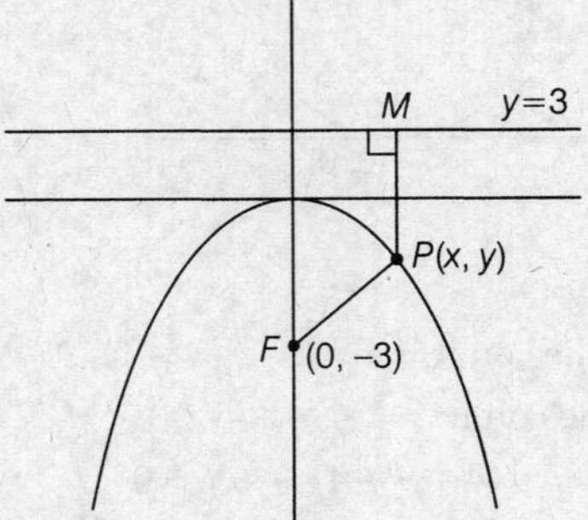

Let any point on the parabola is $P(x, y)$.

Then, $\quad PM = |y - 3|$

For Parabola $PF = PM$

$\Rightarrow \quad \sqrt{(x-0)^2 + (y+3)^2} = |y-3|$

$\Rightarrow \quad x^2 + y^2 + 6y + 9 = y^2 - 6y + 9$

$\Rightarrow \quad x^2 + 12y = 0$

$\Rightarrow \quad x^2 = -12y$

Q.52 If the parabola $y^2 = 4ax$ passes through the point (3, 2), then the length of its latus rectum is

(a) $\frac{2}{3}$ (b) $\frac{4}{3}$ (c) $\frac{1}{3}$ (d) 4

Ans. ***(b)*** Given, parabola is

$$y^2 = 4ax \quad \text{... (i)}$$

$\therefore$ Length of latus rectum $= 4a$

Since, the parabola passes through the point (3, 2).

Then, $4 = 4a\,(3) \Rightarrow a = -\frac{1}{3}$

$\therefore$ Length of latus rectum $4a = -\frac{4}{3}$

***Q.53** If the vertex of the parabola is the point (– 3, 0) and the directrix is the line $x + 5 = 0$, then its equation is

(a) $y^2 = 8(x+3)$ (b) $x^2 = 8(y+3)$

(c) $y^2 = -8(x+3)$ (d) $y^2 = 8(x+5)$

Ans. ***(a)*** Here, vertex $= (-3, 0)$

$\therefore \quad a = -3$ and directrix, $x + 5 = 0$

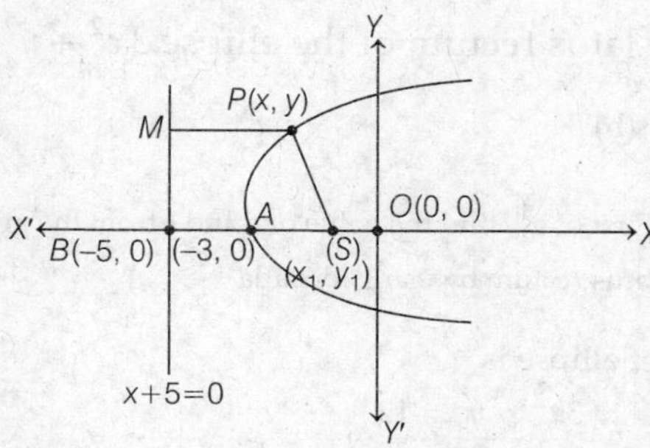

Since, axis of the parabola is a line perpendicular to directrix and A is the mid-point of BS.

Then, $-3 = \frac{x_1 - 5}{2}$ [by mid-point formula]

$\Rightarrow \quad -6 = x_1 - 5 \Rightarrow x_1 = -1,$

Also, $0 = \frac{0 + y_1}{2} \Rightarrow y_1 = 0$

$\therefore \quad S = (-1, 0)$

(✱) Topics related to these question have been removed from latest NCERT.

$\because$ for parabola, $PM = PS$

$\Rightarrow \quad |x + 5| = \sqrt{(x + 1)^2 + y^2}$

$\Rightarrow \quad x^2 + 2x + 1 + y^2 = x^2 + 10x + 25$

$\Rightarrow \quad y^2 = 8x + 24$

$\Rightarrow \quad y^2 = 8(x + 3)$

***Q.54** The equation of the ellipse whose focus is $(1, -1)$, directrix the line $x - y - 3 = 0$ and eccentricity $\frac{1}{2}$ is

(a) $7x^2 + 2xy + 7y^2 - 10x + 10y + 7 = 0$ (b) $7x^2 + 2xy + 7y^2 + 7 = 0$

(c) $7x^2 + 2xy + 7y^2 + 10x - 10y - 7 = 0$ (d) None of these

Ans. ***(a)*** Given that focus of the ellipse is $(1, -1)$ and the equation of directrix is $x - y - 3 = 0$ and $e = \frac{1}{2}$

Let $P(x, y)$ be any point on the ellipse and focus be $F(1, -1)$.

$\therefore \quad \dfrac{PF}{\text{Distance of } P \text{ from } (x - y - 3 = 0)} = \dfrac{1}{2}$

$\Rightarrow \quad \dfrac{\sqrt{(x - 1)^2 + (y + 1)^2}}{\dfrac{|x - y - 3|}{\sqrt{2}}} = \dfrac{1}{2}$

$\Rightarrow \quad \dfrac{2[x^2 - 2x + 1 + y^2 + 2y + 1]}{(x - y - 3)^2} = \dfrac{1}{4}$

$\Rightarrow \quad 8x^2 - 16x + 16 + 8y^2 + 16y = x^2 + y^2 + 9 - 2xy + 6y - 6x$

$\Rightarrow \quad 7x^2 + 7y^2 + 2xy - 10x + 10y + 7 = 0$

Q.55 The length of the latus rectum of the ellipse $3x^2 + y^2 = 12$ is

(a) 4 (b) 3 (c) 8 (d) $\frac{4}{\sqrt{3}}$

Thinking Process First of all, find the value of a and b from the given equation, after that get length of latus rectum by using formula $\frac{2a^2}{b}$.

Ans. ***(d)*** Given equation of ellipse is

$$3x^2 + y^2 = 12$$

$\Rightarrow \quad \dfrac{x^2}{4} + \dfrac{y^2}{12} = 1$

$\therefore \quad a^2 = 4 \Rightarrow a = 2$

and $\quad b^2 = 12 \Rightarrow b = 2\sqrt{3}$

$\because \quad b > a$

$\therefore \quad$ Length of latus rectum $= \dfrac{2a^2}{b} = \dfrac{2 \times 4}{2\sqrt{3}} = \dfrac{4}{\sqrt{3}}$

(*) Topics related to these question have been removed from latest NCERT.

Q.56 If e is eccentricity of the ellipse $\frac{x^2}{a^2}+\frac{y^2}{b^2}=1$ (where, $a< b$), then

(a) $b^2 = a^2(1-e^2)$
(b) $a^2 = b^2(1-e^2)$
(c) $a^2 = b^2(e^2-1)$
(d) $b^2 = a^2(e^2-1)$

Ans. *(b)* Given, $\frac{x^2}{a^2}+\frac{y^2}{b^2}=1,\ a<b$

We know that, $e=\sqrt{1-\frac{a^2}{b^2}} \Rightarrow e^2=\frac{(b^2-a^2)}{b^2}$

$\Rightarrow \quad b^2e^2 = b^2 - a^2$

$\Rightarrow \quad a^2 = b^2(1-e^2)$

Q.57 The eccentricity of the hyperbola whose latus rectum is 8 and conjugate axis is equal to half of the distance between the foci is

(a) $\frac{4}{3}$
(b) $\frac{4}{\sqrt{3}}$
(c) $\frac{2}{\sqrt{3}}$
(d) None of these

Ans. *(c)* Length of latus rectum of the hyperbola *i.e.*,

$$8=\frac{2b^2}{a} \Rightarrow b^2 = 4a \quad \text{...(i)}$$

$\therefore$ Distance between the foci = $2ae$

Since, transverse axis be a and conjugate axis be b. $\therefore$

$$\frac{1}{2}(2ae) = 2b$$

$\Rightarrow \quad ae = 2b$ ...(ii)

$\Rightarrow \quad b^2 = a^2(e^2-1)$ ...(iii)

From Eqs. (i) and (ii), we get

$$4a = \frac{a^2e^2}{4} \quad \text{[from Eqs. (i) and (iii)]}$$

$\Rightarrow \quad 16a = a^2e^2$

$\Rightarrow \quad 16 = ae^2 \Rightarrow a = \frac{16}{e^2}$ ...(iv)

$\because \quad 4a = a^2(e^2-1)$ [from Eqs. (i) and (iii)]

$\Rightarrow \quad \frac{4}{a} = e^2 - 1$

$\Rightarrow \quad \frac{4e^2}{16} = e^2 - 1$

$\Rightarrow \quad e^2\left(1-\frac{4}{16}\right) = 1$

$\Rightarrow \quad e^2\left(\frac{12}{16}\right) = 1 \Rightarrow e^2 = \left(\frac{16}{12}\right)$

$\Rightarrow \quad e^2 = \frac{4}{3} \Rightarrow e = \frac{2}{\sqrt{3}}$

Q.58 The distance between the foci of a hyperbola is 16 and its eccentricity is $\sqrt{2}$. Its equation is

(a) $x^2 - y^2 = 32$ (b) $\frac{x^2}{4} - \frac{y^2}{9} = 1$ (c) $2x - 3y^2 = 7$ (d) None of these

Thinking Process The distance between the foci of hyperbola is $2ae$ and. Use the relation, $b^2 = a^2(e^2 - 1)$ to set the value of a and b.

Ans. *(a)* Given that, distance between the foci of hyperbola

i.e., $2ae = 16 \Rightarrow ae = 8$ ...(i)

and $e = \sqrt{2}$ ...(ii)

Now, $\sqrt{2}\,a = 8$

$\Rightarrow a = 4\sqrt{2}$

$\because b^2 = a^2(e^2 - 1)$

$\Rightarrow b^2 = 32(2 - 1)$

$\Rightarrow b^2 = 32$

$\therefore \frac{x^2}{32} - \frac{y^2}{32} = 1$

$\Rightarrow x^2 - y^2 = 32$

Q.59 Equation of the hyperbola with eccentricity $\frac{3}{2}$ and foci at $(\pm 2, 0)$ is

(a) $\frac{x^2}{4} - \frac{y^2}{5} = \frac{4}{9}$ (b) $\frac{x^2}{9} - \frac{y^2}{9} = \frac{4}{9}$ (c) $\frac{x^2}{4} - \frac{y^2}{9} = 1$ (d) None of these

Ans. *(a)* Given, eccentricity of the hyperbola, $e = 3/2$

and foci $= (\pm 2, 0), = (\pm ae, 0)$

$\because ae = 2$

$\Rightarrow a \times \frac{3}{2} = 2 \Rightarrow a = \frac{4}{3}$

$\because b^2 = a^2(e^2 - 1)$

$\Rightarrow b^2 = \frac{16}{9}\left(\frac{9}{4} - 1\right) \Rightarrow b^2 = \frac{16}{9}\left(\frac{5}{4}\right)$

$\Rightarrow b^2 = \frac{20}{9}$

So, the equation of the hyperbola is

$$\frac{x^2}{\frac{16}{9}} - \frac{y^2}{\frac{20}{9}} = 1$$

$$\Rightarrow \frac{x^2}{4} - \frac{y^2}{5} = \frac{4}{9}$$

Chapter

12

Introduction to Three Dimensional Geometry

Short Answer Type Questions

Q.1 Locate the following points

(i) $(1, -1, 3)$ (ii) $(-1, 2, 4)$

(iii) $(-2, -4, -7)$ (iv) $(-4, 2, -5)$

Ans. Given, coordinates are

(i) $(1, -1, 3)$ lies in IV octant (ii) B $(-1, 2, 4)$ lies in II octant

(iii) C $(-2, -4, -7)$ lies in VII octant (iv) D $(-4, 2, -5)$ lies in VI octant

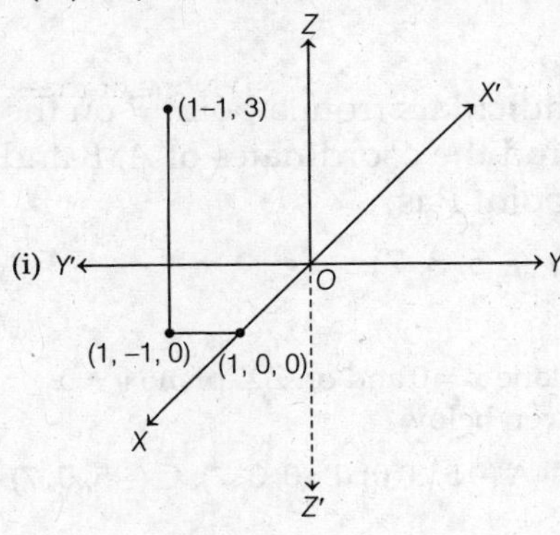

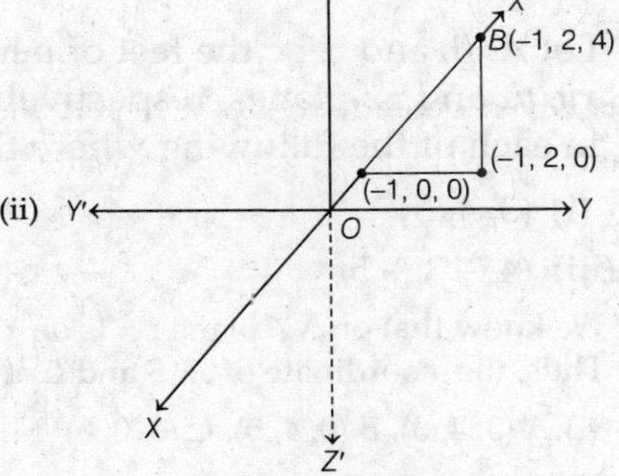

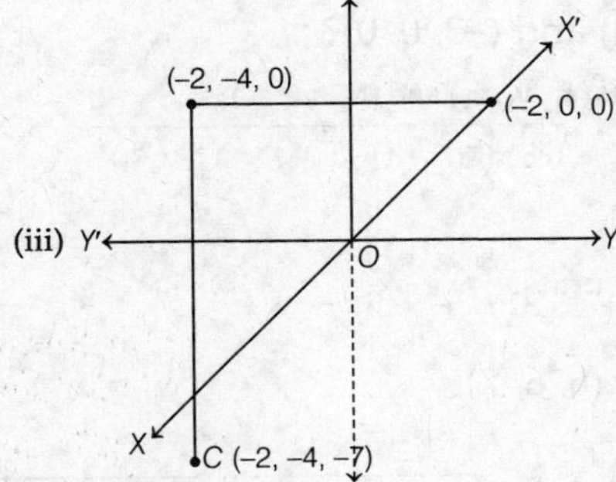

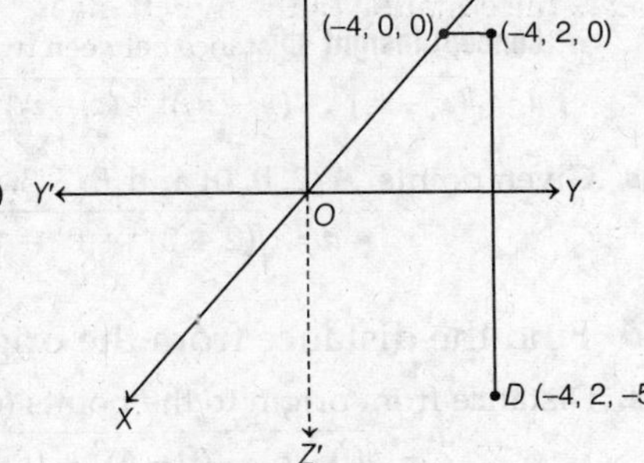

Q.2 Name the octant in which each of the following points lies.

(i) (1, 2, 3) (ii) (4,– 2, 3)

(iii) (4,– 2, – 5) (iv) (4, 2,– 5)

(v) (– 4, 2, 5) (vi) (– 3, – 1, 6)

(vii) (2,– 4, – 7) (viii) (– 4, 2, – 5).

Ans. (i) Point (1, 2 ,3) lies in first octant. (ii) (4, – 2, 3) lies in fourth octant.

(iii) (4, – 2, – 5) lies in eighth octant. (iv) (4, 2, – 5) lies in fifth octant.

(v) (– 4, 2, 5) lies in second octant. (vi) (– 3, – 1, 6) lies in third octant.

(vii) (2,– 4, – 7) lies in eighth octant. (viii) (– 4, 2, – 5) lies in sixth octant.

Q.3 Let *A*, *B*, *C* be the feet of perpendiculars from a point *P* on the *x*, *y* and *z*-axes respectively. Find the coordinates of *A*, *B* and *C* in each of the following where the point *P* is

(i) (3, 4, 2) (ii) (– 5, 3, 7)

(iii) (4, – 3, – 5)

Ans. The coordinates of *A*, *B* and *C* are given below

(i) A (3, 0, 0), B (0,4, 0), C (0,0, 2) (ii) A (– 5, 0, 0), B (0, 3, 0), C (0,0, 7)

(iii) A (4, 0, 0), B (0, – 3, 0), C (0,0,– 5)

Q.4 Let *A*, *B*, and *C* be the feet of perpendiculars from a point *P* on the *xy*, *yz* and *zx*-planes, respectively. Find the coordinates of *A*, *B* and *C* in each of the following where the point *P* is

(i) (3, 4, 5) (ii) (– 5, 3, 7)

(iii) (4, – 3, – 5)

Ans. We know that on *XY*-plane $z = 0$, on *YZ*-plane $x = 0$ and on *ZX*-plane $y = 0$. Thus, the coordinate of *A*, *B* and *C* are given below

(i) A (3, 4, 0), B (0, 4, 5), C (3, 0, 5) (ii) A (– 5, 3, 0), B (0, 3, 7), C (– 5, 0, 7)

(iii) A (4,– 3, 0), B (0, – 3, – 5), C (4, 0,– 5)

Q.5 How far apart are the points (2, 0, 0) and (–3, 0, 0)?

- **Concept Insight** Distance between two points (x_1, y_1, z_1) and (x_2, y_2, z_2) is,
$d = \sqrt{(x_1 - x_2)^2 + (y_1 - y_2)^2 + (z_1 - z_2)^2}$ or $d = \sqrt{(x_2 - x_1)^2 + (y_2 - y_1)^2 + (z_2 - z_1)^2}$.

Ans. Given points, *A* (2, 0, 0) and *B* (– 3, 0, 0)

$$d = \sqrt{(2 + 3)^2 + 0^2 + 0^2} = 5 \text{ units.}$$

Q.6 Find the distance from the origin to (6, 6, 7).

Ans. Distance from origin to the points (6, 6,7)

$$= \sqrt{(0 - 6)^2 + (0 - 6)^2 + (0 - 7)^2} \quad [\because d = \sqrt{(x_1 - x_2)^2 + (y_1 - y_2)^2 + (z_1 - z_2)^2}]$$

$$= \sqrt{36 + 36 + 49}$$

$$= \sqrt{121} = 11 \text{ units.}$$

Q.7 Show that, if $x^2 + y^2 = 1$, then the point $(x, y, \sqrt{1 - x^2 - y^2})$ is at a distance 1 unit from the origin.

Ans. Given, $x^2 + y^2 = 1$

$\therefore$ Distance of the point $(x, y, \sqrt{1 - x^2 - y^2})$ from origin is given by

$$d = \left| \sqrt{x^2 + y^2 + (\sqrt{1 - x^2 - y^2})^2} \right|$$

$$= \left| \sqrt{x^2 + y^2 + 1 - x^2 - y^2} \right| = 1 \text{unit}$$

Hence proved.

Q.8 Show that the point $A(1, -1, 3)$, $B(2, -4, 5)$ and $C(5, -13, 11)$ are collinear.

- **Concept Insight** If the three points A, B, and C are collinear, then $AB + BC = AC$.

Ans. Given points, $A(1, -1, 3)$, $B(2, -4, 5)$ and $C(5, -13, 11)$.

$$AB = \sqrt{(1-2)^2 + (-1+4)^2 + (3-5)^2}$$

$$= \sqrt{1 + 9 + 4} = \sqrt{14} \text{ units}$$

$$BC = \sqrt{(2-5)^2 + (-4+13)^2 + (5-11)^2}$$

$$= \sqrt{9 + 81 + 36} = \sqrt{126} = 3\sqrt{14} \text{ units}$$

$$AC = \sqrt{(1-5)^2 + (-1+13)^2 + (3-11)^2}$$

$$= \sqrt{16 + 144 + 64} = \sqrt{224} = 4\sqrt{14} \text{ units}$$

$$\because \quad AB + BC = = \sqrt{14} + 3\sqrt{14} = 4\sqrt{14} = AC$$

So, the points A, B and C are collinear.

***Q.9** Three consecutive vertices of a parallelogram $ABCD$ are $A(6, -2, 4)$, $B(2, 4, -8)$ and $C(-2, 2, 4)$. Find the coordinates of the fourth vertex.

Ans. Let the coordinates of the fourth vertex be $D(x, y, z)$.

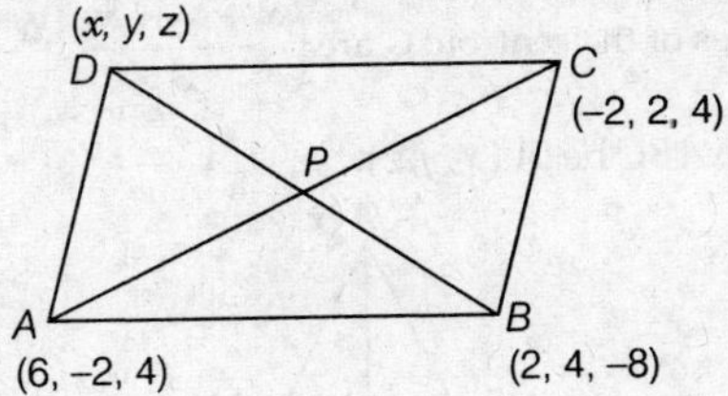

Mid-points of diagonal AC,

$$x = \frac{x_1 + x_2}{2}, \; y = \frac{y_1 + y_2}{2}, \; z = \frac{z_1 + z_2}{2}$$

$$\Rightarrow \quad x = \frac{6 - 2}{2} = 2, \; y = \frac{-2 + 2}{2} = 0, \; z = \frac{4 + 4}{2} = 4$$

Since, the mid-point of AC are $(2, 0, 4)$.

(*) Topics related to these question have been removed from latest NCERT.

Now, mid-point of BD, $2 = \frac{x+2}{2} \Rightarrow x + 2 = 4 \Rightarrow x = 2$

$$\Rightarrow \quad 0 = \frac{y+4}{2} \Rightarrow y = -4$$

$$\Rightarrow \quad 4 = \frac{z-8}{2} \Rightarrow z - 8 = 8 \Rightarrow z = 16$$

So, the coordinates of fourth vertex D are $(2, -4, 16)$.

Q.10 Show that the triangle ABC with vertices $A(0, 4, 1)$, $B(2, 3, -1)$ and $C(4, 5, 0)$ is right angled.

Thinking Process In a right angled triangle, sum of the square of two sides is equal to square of third side.

Ans. Given, the vertices of the ΔABC are $A(0, 4, 1)$, $B(2, 3, -1)$ and $C(4, 5, 0)$.

Now,
$$AB = \sqrt{(0-2)^2 + (4-3)^3 + (1+1)^2}$$
$$= \sqrt{4+1+4} = \sqrt{9} = 3 \text{ units}$$
$$BC = \sqrt{(2-4)^2 + (3-5)^2 + (-1-0)^2}$$
$$= \sqrt{4+4+1} = \sqrt{9} = 3 \text{ units}$$
$$AC = \sqrt{(0-4)^2 + (4-5)^2 + (1-0)^2}$$
$$= \sqrt{16+1+1} = \sqrt{18} \text{ units}$$

$$\because \quad AC^2 = AB^2 + BC^2$$
$$\Rightarrow \quad 18 = 9 + 9$$

Hence, ΔABC is a right angled triangle.

***Q.11** Find the third vertex of triangle whose centroid is origin and two vertices are $(2, 4, 6)$ and $(0, -2, -5)$.

- **Concept Insight** If the vertices of the ΔABC are $A(x_1, y_1, z_1)$, $B(x_2, y_2, z_2)$ and $C(x_3, y_3, z_3)$, then the coordinates of the centroid G are $\left(\frac{x_1+x_2+x_3}{3}, \frac{y_1+y_2+y_3}{3}, \frac{z_1+z_2+z_3}{3}\right)$.

Ans. Let third vertex of ΔABC be $A(x, y, z)$.

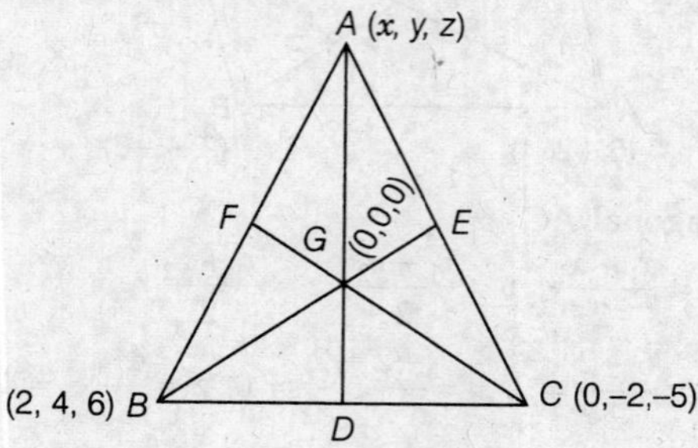

Given, the coordinate of centroid G are $(0, 0, 0)$.

$$\because \quad 0 = \frac{x+2+0}{3} \Rightarrow x + 2 = 0 \Rightarrow x = -2$$

(*) Topics related to these question have been removed from latest NCERT.

$$0=\frac{y+4-2}{3} \Rightarrow y+2=0 \Rightarrow y=-2$$

$$0=\frac{z+6-5}{2} \Rightarrow z+1=0 \Rightarrow z=-1$$

Hence, the third vertex of the triangle is (– 2, – 2, –1).

***Q.12** Find the centroid of a triangle, the mid-point of whose sides are $D(1, 2, -3)$, $E(3, 0, 1)$ and $F(-1, 1, -4)$.

- **Concept Insight** Mid-point of two points (x_1, y_1, z_1) and (x_2, y_2, z_2) is $\left(\frac{x_1+y_1+z_1}{2}, \frac{x_2+y_2+z_2}{2}\right)$.

Ans. Given, mid-points of sides are $D(1, 2, -3)$, $E(3, 0, 1)$ and $F(-1, 1, -4)$.

Let the vertices of the ΔABC are $A(x_1, y_1, z_1)$, $B(x_2, y_2, z_3)$ and $C(x_3, y_3, z_3)$.

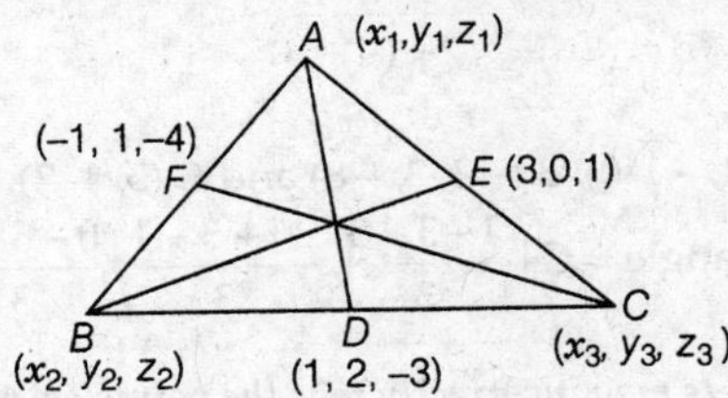

Then, mid-point of BC are (1, 2, – 3).

$$\therefore \quad 1=\frac{x_2+x_3}{2} \Rightarrow x_2+x_3=2; \quad \text{...(i)}$$

$$2=\frac{y_2+y_3}{2} \Rightarrow y_2+y_3=4 \quad \text{...(ii)}$$

$$\text{and} \quad -3=\frac{z_2+z_3}{2} \Rightarrow z_2+z_3=-6 \quad \text{...(iii)}$$

Similarly, for the sides AB and AC,

$$-1=\frac{x_1+x_2}{2} \Rightarrow x_1+x_2=-2; \quad \text{...(iv)}$$

$$1=\frac{y_1+y_2}{2} \Rightarrow y_1+y_2=2; \quad \text{...(v)}$$

$$-4=\frac{z_1+z_2}{2} \Rightarrow z_1+z_2=-8; \quad \text{...(vi)}$$

$$3=\frac{x_1+x_3}{2} \Rightarrow x_1+x_3=6; \quad \text{...(vii)}$$

$$0=\frac{y_1+y_3}{2} \Rightarrow y_1+y_3=0 \quad \text{...(viii)}$$

$$\text{and} \quad 1=\frac{z_1+z_3}{2} \Rightarrow z_1+z_3=2 \quad \text{...(ix)}$$

On adding Eqs. (i) and (iv), we get

$$x_1+2x_2+x_3=0 \quad \text{...(x)}$$

On adding Eqs. (ii) and (v), we get

$$y_1+2y_2+y_3=6 \quad \text{...(xi)}$$

(✱) Topics related to these question have been removed from latest NCERT.

On adding Eqs. (iii) and (vi), we get

$$z_1 + 2z_2 + z_3 = -14 \quad \text{...(xii)}$$

From Eqs. (vii) and (x), we get,

$$2x_2 = -6 \Rightarrow x_2 = -3$$

If $x_2 = -3$, then $x_3 = 5$

If $x_3 = 5$, then $x_1 = 1$

From Eqs. (xi) and (viii), we get

$$2y_2 = 6 \Rightarrow y_2 = 3$$

If $y_2 = 3$, then $y_1 = -1$

If $y_1 = -1$, then $y_3 = 1$

From Eqs. (xii) and (ix), we get

$$2z_2 = -16 \Rightarrow z_2 = -8$$

If $z_2 = -8$, then $z_1 = 0$

If $z_1 = 0$, then $z_3 = 2$

So, the points are $A(1, -1, 0)$, $B(-3, 3, -8)$ and $C(5, 1, 2)$.

$\therefore$ Centroid of the triangle $= G\left(\frac{1-3+5}{3}, \frac{-1+3+1}{3}, \frac{0-8+2}{3}\right)$ *i.e.*, $G(1, 1, -2)$

Mistake Alert! *Students may incorrectly take the points as* $A(1, -3, 5)$ $B(-1, 3, 1)$ *and* $C(0, -8, 2)$ *instead of* $A(1, -1, 0)$, $B(-3, 3, -8)$ *and* $C(5, 1, 2)$.

***Q.13** The mid-points of the sides of a triangle are (5, 7, 11), (0, 8, 5) and (2, 3, – 1). Find its vertices.

Ans. Let vertices of the ΔABC are $A(x_1, y_1, z_1)$, $B(x_2, y_2, z_2)$ and $C(x_3, y_3, z_3)$ and the mid-points of sides AB, BC and AC are $F(2, 3, -1)$, $D(5, 7, 11)$ and $E(0, 8, 5)$, respectively.

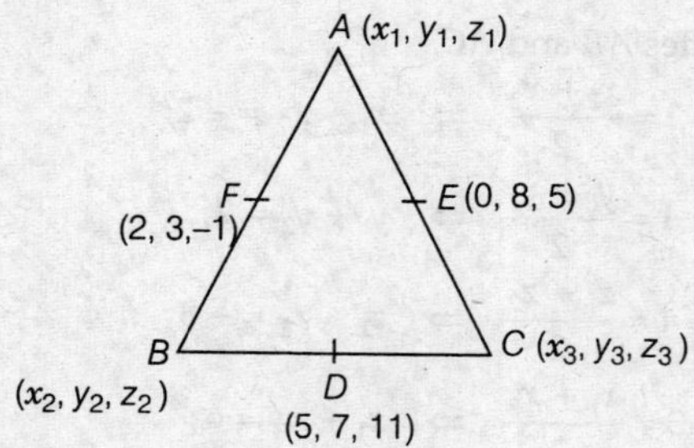

$\therefore$ Mid-point of side BC,

$$5 = \frac{x_2 + x_3}{2} \Rightarrow x_2 + x_3 = 10 \quad \text{...(i)}$$

$$7 = \frac{y_2 + y_3}{2} \Rightarrow y_2 + y_3 = 14 \quad \text{...(ii)}$$

$$11 = \frac{z_2 + z_3}{2} \Rightarrow z_2 + z_3 = 22 \quad \text{...(iii)}$$

(*) Topics related to these question have been removed from latest NCERT.

Similarly, for the sides AB and AC,

$$2 = \frac{x_1 + x_2}{2} \Rightarrow x_1 + x_2 = 4 \quad \text{...(iv)}$$

$$3 = \frac{y_1 + y_2}{2} \Rightarrow y_1 + y_2 = 6 \quad \text{...(v)}$$

$$-1 = \frac{z_1 + z_2}{2} \Rightarrow z_1 + z_2 = -2 \quad \text{...(vi)}$$

and

$$0 = \frac{x_1 + x_3}{2} \Rightarrow x_1 + x_3 = 0 \quad \text{...(vii)}$$

$$8 = \frac{y_1 + y_3}{2} \Rightarrow y_1 + y_3 = 16 \quad \text{...(viii)}$$

$$5 = \frac{z_1 + z_3}{2} \Rightarrow z_1 + z_3 = 10 \quad \text{...(ix)}$$

From Eqs. (i) and (iv), we get

$$x_1 + 2x_2 + x_3 = 14 \quad \text{...(x)}$$

From Eqs. (ii) and (v), we get

$$y_1 + 2y_2 + y_3 = 20 \quad \text{...(xi)}$$

From Eqs. (iii) and (vi), we get

$$z_1 + 2z_2 + z_3 = 20 \quad \text{...(xii)}$$

From Eqs. (vii) and (x), we get

$$2x_2 = 14 \Rightarrow x_2 = 7$$

If $x_2 = 7$, then $x_3 = 10 - 7 = 3$

If $x_3 = 3$, then $x_1 = -3$

$\therefore\ x_1 = -3, x_2 = 7, x_3 = 3$

From Eqs. (viii) and (xi), we get

$$2y_2 = 4 \Rightarrow y_2 = 2$$

If $y_2 = 2$, then $y_1 = 4$

If $y_1 = 4$, then $y_3 = 12$

$\therefore\ y_1 = 4, y_2 = 2, y_3 = 12$

From Eqs. (ix) and (xii), we get

$$2z_2 = 10 \Rightarrow z_2 = 5$$

If $z_2 = 5$, then $z_1 = -7$

If $z_1 = -7$, then $z_3 = 17$

$\therefore\ z_1 = -7, z_2 = 5, z_3 = 17$

So, the vertices are $A(-3, 4, -7)$, $B(7, 2, 5)$ and $C(3, 12, 17)$.

***Q.14** The vertices of a parallelogram $ABCD$ are $A(1, 2, 3)$, $B(-1, -2, -1)$ and $C(2, 3, 2)$. Find the fourth vertex D.

Thinking Process The diagonals of a parallelogram bisect each other at the same vertex. Use this property to solve the problem.

(*) Topics related to these question have been removed from latest NCERT.

Ans. Let the fourth vertex of the parallelogram $ABCD$ be $D(x, y, z)$.

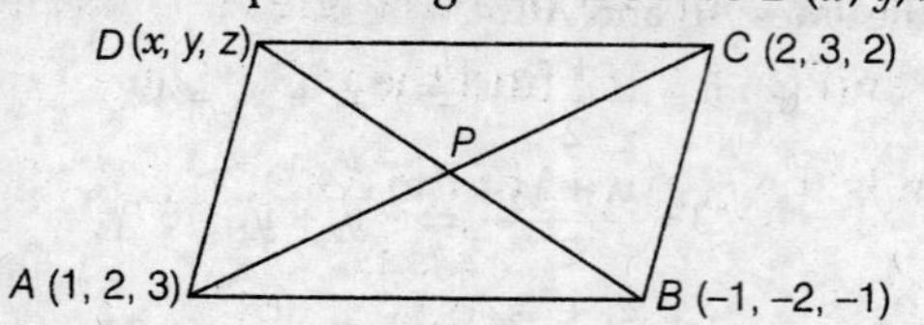

Then, the mid-point of AC is

$$P\left(\frac{1+2}{2}, \frac{2+3}{2}, \frac{3+2}{2}\right) \text{ i.e., } P\left(\frac{3}{2}, \frac{5}{2}, \frac{5}{2}\right).$$

Now, mid-point of BD,

$$\frac{3}{2} = \frac{-1+x}{2} \Rightarrow 3 = -1+x \Rightarrow x = 4$$

$$\frac{5}{2} = \frac{-2+y}{2} \Rightarrow 5 = -2+y \Rightarrow y = 7$$

$$\frac{5}{2} = \frac{-1+z}{2} \Rightarrow 5 = -1+z \Rightarrow z = 6$$

So, the coordinates of fourth vertex are (4, 7, 6).

***Q.15** Find the coordinate of the points which trisect the line segment joining the points $A(2, 1, -3)$ and $B(5, -8, 3)$

- **Concept Insight** If point P divided line segment joining the points $A(x_1, y_1, z_1)$ and $B(x_2, y_2, z_2)$ in $m_1 : m_2$ internally, then the coordinates of P are $\left(\frac{m_1 x_2 + m_2 x_1}{m_1 + m_2}, \frac{m_1 y_2 + m_2 y_1}{m_1 + m_2}, \frac{m_1 z_2 + m_2 z_1}{m_1 + m_2}\right)$.

Ans. Let the $P(x_1, y_1, z_1)$ and $Q(x_2, y_2, z_2)$ trisect the line segment AB. *i.e.*, $AP = PQ = QB$

A (2, 1, –3) — P (x_1, y_1, z_1) — Q (x_2, y_2, z_2) — B (5, –8, 3)

Since, the point P divided line AB in 1 : 2 internally, then

$$x_1 = \frac{2\times 2 + 1\times 5}{1+2} = \frac{4+5}{3} = \frac{9}{3} = 3$$

$$y_1 = \frac{2\times 1 + 1\times(-8)}{3} = \frac{2-8}{3} = \frac{-6}{3} = -2$$

$$z_1 = \frac{2\times(-3) + 1\times 3}{3} = \frac{-6+3}{3} = \frac{-3}{3} = -1$$

Since, the point Q divide the line segment AB in 2 : 1 internally, then

$$x_2 = \frac{1\times 2 + 2\times 5}{3} = \frac{12}{3} = 4$$

$$y_2 = \frac{1\times 1 + (-8)\times 2}{3} = \frac{1-16}{3} = \frac{-15}{3} = -5$$

$$z_2 = \frac{1\times(-3) + 2\times 3}{3} = \frac{-3+6}{3} = \frac{3}{3} = 1$$

So, the coordinates of P are (3, – 2, – 1) and the coordinates of Q are (4, – 5, 1).

(✱) Topics related to these question have been removed from latest NCERT.

***Q.16** If the origin is the centroid of a triangle ABC having vertices $A(a, 1, 3)$, $B(-2, b, -5)$ and $C(4, 7, c)$, find the values of a, b, c.

Ans. Given, origin is the centroid of the ΔABC *i.e.* $G(0, 0, 0)$.

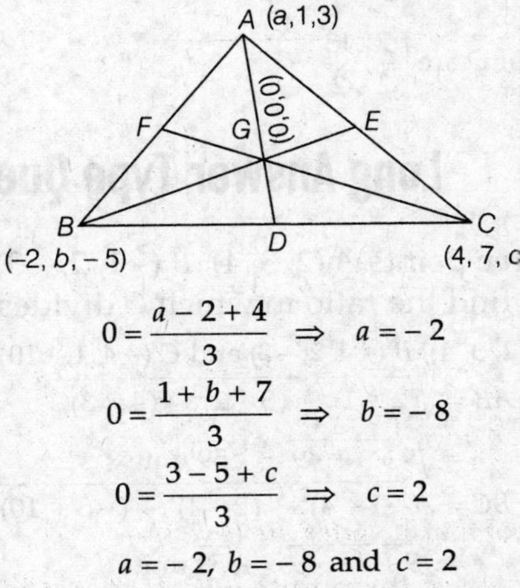

$$\because \quad 0 = \frac{a - 2 + 4}{3} \Rightarrow a = -2$$

$$0 = \frac{1 + b + 7}{3} \Rightarrow b = -8$$

$$0 = \frac{3 - 5 + c}{3} \Rightarrow c = 2$$

$$\therefore \quad a = -2,\ b = -8 \text{ and } c = 2$$

Mistake Alert ! *Students may get confused in applying the centroid formula as* $\left(\frac{x_1 + y_1 + z_1}{2}, \frac{x_2 + y_2 + z_2}{2}\right)$ *instead of* $\left(\frac{x_1 + x_2 + x_3}{3}, \frac{y_1 + y_2 + y_3}{3}, \frac{z_1 + z_2 + z_3}{3}\right)$.

***Q.17** Let $A(2, 2, -3)$, $B(5, 6, 9)$ and $C(2, 7, 9)$ be the vertices of a triangle. The internal bisector of the angle A meets BC at the point D. Find the coordinates of D.

Ans. Let the coordinates of D are (x, y, z).

A (2, 2,–3)
B (5, 6, 9) D (x, y, z) C (2, 7, 9)

$$AB = \sqrt{(5-2)^2 + (6-2)^2 + (9+3)^2} = \sqrt{9 + 16 + 144} = \sqrt{169} = 13 \text{ units}$$

$$AC = \sqrt{(2-2)^2 + (7-2)^2 + (9+3)^2} = \sqrt{0 + 25 + 144} = \sqrt{169} = 13$$

$$\Rightarrow \quad \frac{AB}{AC} = \frac{13}{13}$$

$$\Rightarrow \quad AB = AC$$

Since, AD is the internal bisector of the angle A.

$$\text{So,} \quad \frac{BD}{DC} = \frac{1}{1}$$

$$\Rightarrow \quad BD = DC$$

(*) Topics related to these question have been removed from latest NCERT.

Since, D divides the line BC in two equal parts. So, D is the mid-point of BC.

$\therefore \quad x = \dfrac{5+2}{2} = \dfrac{7}{2}$ [by mid-point formula]

$y = \dfrac{6+7}{2} = \dfrac{13}{2}$ and $z = \dfrac{9+9}{2} = 9$

So, the coordinates of D are $\left(\dfrac{7}{2}, \dfrac{13}{2}, 9\right)$.

Long Answer Type Questions

Q.18 Show that the three points $A(2, 3, 4)$, $B(-1, 2, -3)$ and $C(-4, 1, -10)$ are collinear and find the ratio in which C divides AB.

Ans. Given points are $A(2, 3, 4)$, $B(-1, 2, -3)$ and $C(-4, 1, -10)$.

$$\therefore \quad AB = \sqrt{(2+1)^2 + (3-2)^2 + (4+3)^2}$$

$$= \sqrt{9+1+49} = \sqrt{59} \text{ units}$$

$$BC = \sqrt{(-1+4)^2 + (2-1)^2 + (-3+10)^2}$$

$$= \sqrt{9+1+49} = \sqrt{59} \text{ units}$$

$$AC = \sqrt{(2+4)^2 + (3-1)^2 + (4+10)^2}$$

$$= \sqrt{36+4+196} = \sqrt{236} = 2\sqrt{59} \text{ units}$$

Now, $AB + BC = \sqrt{59} + \sqrt{59} = 2\sqrt{59}$ units

$\because \quad AB + BC = AC$

Hence, the points A, B and C are collinear.

Now, $AC : BC = 2\sqrt{59} : \sqrt{59} = 2 : 1$

So, C divides AB in 2 :1 externally.

***Q.19** The mid-point of the sides of a triangle are $(1, 5, -1)$, $(0, 4, -2)$ and $(2, 3, 4)$. Find its vertices and also find the centroid of the triangle.

Thinking Process Firstly, find the vertices of the triangle using the mid-point formula, then find the centroid of the triangle by using the formula following $\left(\dfrac{x_1+y_1+z_1}{3}, \dfrac{x_2+y_2+z_2}{3}, \dfrac{x_3+y_3+z_3}{3}\right)$.

Ans. Let the vertices of ΔABC are $A(x_1, y_1, z_1)$, $B(x_2, y_2, z_2)$ and $C(x_3, y_3, z_3)$.

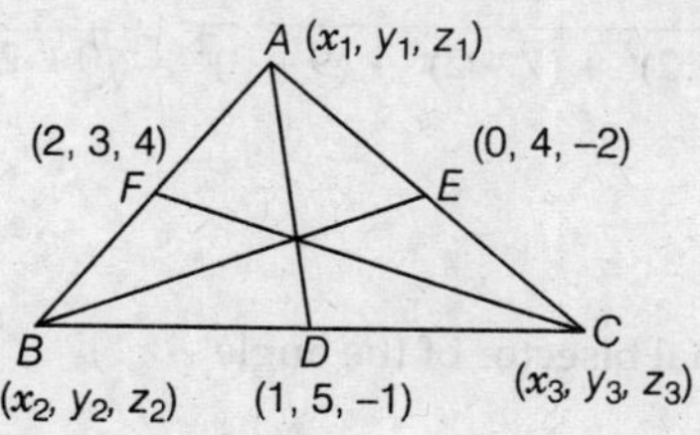

Since, the mid-point of side BC is $D(1, 5, -1)$.

(*) Topics related to these question have been removed from latest NCERT.

Then, $\frac{x_2 + x_3}{2} = 1 \Rightarrow x_2 + x_3 = 2$ ...(i)

$\frac{y_2 + y_3}{2} = 5 \Rightarrow y_2 + y_3 = 10$ ...(ii)

$\frac{z_2 + z_3}{2} = -1 \Rightarrow z_2 + z_3 = -2$ ...(iii)

Similarly, the mid-points of AB and AC are $F(2, 3, 4)$ and $E(0, 4, -2)$, respectively.

Then $\frac{x_1 + x_2}{2} = 2 \Rightarrow x_1 + x_2 = 4$ ...(iv)

$\frac{y_1 + y_2}{2} = 3 \Rightarrow y_1 + y_2 = 6$ ...(v)

$\frac{z_1 + z_2}{2} = 4 \Rightarrow z_1 + z_2 = 8$ ...(vi)

and $\frac{x_1 + x_3}{2} = 0 \Rightarrow x_1 + x_3 = 0$ ...(vii)

$\frac{y_1 + y_3}{2} = 4 \Rightarrow y_1 + y_3 = 8$ ...(viii)

$\frac{z_1 + z_3}{2} = -2 \Rightarrow z_1 + z_3 = -4$ ...(ix)

From Eqs. (i) and (iv), we get

$x_1 + 2x_2 + x_3 = 6$ ...(x)

From Eqs. (ii) and (v), wer get

$y_1 + 2y_2 + y_3 = 16$ ...(xi)

From Eqs. (iii) and (vi), we get

$z_1 + 2z_2 + z_3 = 6$ ...(xii)

From Eqs. (vii) and (x), we get

$$2x_2 = 6 \Rightarrow x_2 = 3$$

If $x_2 = 3$, then $x_3 = -1$
If $x_3 = -1$, then $x_1 = 1$

$\therefore$ $x_1 = 1,\ x_2 = 3,\ x_3 = -1$

From Eqs. (viii) and (xi), we get

$$2y_2 = 8 \Rightarrow y_2 = 4$$

If $y_2 = 4$, then $y_1 = 2$
If $y_1 = 2$, then $y_3 = 6$

$\Rightarrow$ $y_1 = 2,\ y_2 = 4,\ y_3 = 6$

From Eqs. (ix) and (xii), we get

$$2z_2 = 10 \Rightarrow z_2 = 5$$

If $z_2 = 5$, then $z_1 = 3$
If $z_1 = 3$, then $z_3 = -7$

$\Rightarrow$ $z_1 = 3,\ z_2 = 5,\ z_3 = -7$

So, the vertices of the triangle are $A(1, 2, 3)$, $B(3, 4, 5)$ and $C(-1, 6, -7)$.

Hence, centroid of the triangle $= G\left(\frac{1+3-1}{3}, \frac{2+4+6}{3}, \frac{3+5-7}{3}\right)$ *i.e.* $G(1, 4, 1/3)$.

Q.20 Prove that the points (0, –1, – 7),(2, 1, – 9) and (6, 5, – 13) are collinear. Find the ratio in which the first point divides the join of the other two.

Ans. Let the given points be $A(0, -1, -7)$, $B(2, 1, -9)$ and $C(6, 5, -13)$

$$AB = \sqrt{(0-2)^2 + (-1-1)^2 + (-7+9)^2} = \sqrt{4+4+4} = \sqrt{12} = 2\sqrt{3} \text{ units}$$

$$BC = \sqrt{(2-6)^2 + (1-5)^2 + (-9+13)^2} = \sqrt{16+16+16} = \sqrt{48} = 4\sqrt{3} \text{ units}$$

$$AC = \sqrt{(0-6)^2 + (-1-5)^2 + (-7+13)^2} = \sqrt{36+36+36} = \sqrt{108} = 6\sqrt{3} \text{ units}$$

$\because$ $AB + BC = 2\sqrt{3} + 4\sqrt{3} = 6\sqrt{3}$ units

So, $AB + BC = AC$

Hence, the points A, B and C are collinear.

A B C

$$AB : AC = 2\sqrt{3} : 6\sqrt{3} = 1 : 3$$

So, point A divides B and C in 1 : 3 externally.

Q.21 What are the coordinates of the vertices of a cube whose edge is 2 units, one of whose vertices coincides with the origin and the three edges passing through the origin, coincides with the positive direction of the axes through the origin?

Ans. The coordinates of the cube whose edge is 2 units, are (2, 0, 0), (2, 2, 0), (0, 2, 0), (0, 2, 2),(0, 0, 2), (2, 0, 2), (0, 0, 0) and (2, 2, 2).

Objective Type Questions

Choose the correct answer from the given four options indicated against each of the exercises from 22 to 34.

Q.22 The distance of point $P(3, 4, 5)$ from the YZ-plane is

(a) 3 units (b) 4 units

(c) 5 units (d) 550 units

Ans. ***(a)*** Given, point is $P(3, 4, 5)$.

Distance of P from YZ-plane,

$$d = \sqrt{(0-3)^2 + (4-4)^2 + (5-5)^2} = 3 \text{ units} \quad [\because \text{On } YZ\text{-plane, } x = 0]$$

Q.23 What is the length of foot of perpendicular drawn from the point $P(3, 4, 5)$ on Y-axis?

(a) $\sqrt{41}$ (b) $\sqrt{34}$

(c) 5 (d) None of these

Ans. ***(b)*** We know that on the Y-axis, $x = 0$ and $z = 0$.

$\therefore$ Let the point on Y-axis be $A(0, 4, 0)$.

$$PA = \sqrt{(0-3)^2 + (4-4)^2 + (0-5)^2}$$

$$= \sqrt{9 + 0 + 25} = \sqrt{34} \text{ units}$$

Q.24 Distance of the point (3, 4, 5) from the origin (0, 0, 0) is

(a) $\sqrt{50}$ (b) 3 (c) 4 (d) 5

Ans. **(a)** Let the given points are P (3, 4, 5) and O (0, 0, 0),

$$PO = \sqrt{(0-3)^2 + (0-4)^2 + (0-5)^2}$$
$$= \sqrt{9 + 16 + 25} = \sqrt{50} \text{ units}$$

Q.25 If the distance between the points (a, 0, 1) and (0, 1, 2) is $\sqrt{27}$, then the value of a is

(a) 5 (b) ± 5
(c) – 5 (d) None of these

Ans. **(b)** Let the given points are A (a, 0, 1) and B (0, 1, 2).

$\therefore \quad AB = \sqrt{(a-0)^2 + (0-1)^2 + (1-2)^2} \quad [\because d = \sqrt{(x_2^2 - x_1)^2 + (y_2 - y_1)^2 + (z_2 - z_1)^2}]$

$\Rightarrow \quad \sqrt{27} = \sqrt{a^2 + 1 + 1} \Rightarrow 27 = a^2 + 2$ [squaring on both sides]

$\Rightarrow \quad a^2 = 25 \Rightarrow a = \pm 5$

Q.26 X-axis is the intersection of two planes

(a) XY and XZ (b) YZ and ZX
(c) XY and YZ (d) None of these

Ans. **(a)** We know that on the XY and XZ-planes, the line of intersection is X-axis.

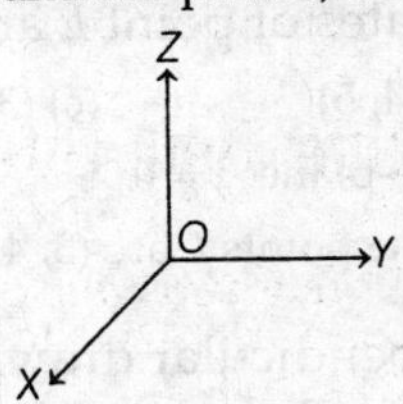

Q.27 Equation of Y-axis is considered as

(a) $x = 0, y = 0$ (b) $y = 0, z = 0$
(c) $z = 0, x = 0$ (d) None of these

Ans. **(c)** On Y-axis, coordinates of x and z are zero.

So, equation of Y-axis is $x = 0$ and $z = 0$.

Q.28 The point (– 2, –3, – 4) lies in the

(a) first octant (b) seventh octant
(c) second octant (d) eight octant

Ans. **(b)** The point (– 2, – 3, – 4) lies in seventh octant.

Mistakes Alert ! *Misinterpreting the signs of the x, y and z coordinates can lead to incorrect octant identification.*

Q.29 A plane is parallel to YZ-plane, so it is perpendicular to

(a) X-axis (b) Y-axis (c) Z-axis (d) None of these

Ans. **(a)** A plane is parallel to YZ-plane, so it is perpendicular to X-axis.

Q.30 The locus of a point for which $y = 0$ and $z = 0$, is

(a) equation of X-axis (b) equation of Y-axis
(c) equation at Z-axis (d) None of these

Ans. *(a)* We know that equation on the X-axis, $y = 0$, $z = 0$.

So, the locus of the point for which $y = 0$ and $z = 0$ is equation of X-axis.

Q.31 The locus of a point for which $x = 0$ is

(a) XY-plane (b) YZ-plane
(c) ZX-plane (d) None of these

Ans. *(b)* On the YZ-plane, $x = 0$, hence the locus of the point is YZ-plane.

Q.32 If a parallelopiped is formed by planes drawn through the points (5, 8, 10) and (3, 6, 8) parallel to the coordinate planes, then the length of diagonal of the parallelopiped is

(a) $2\sqrt{3}$ (b) $3\sqrt{2}$ (c) $\sqrt{2}$ (d) $\sqrt{3}$

Ans. *(a)* Let the given points of the parallelopiped are A (5, 8, 10) and B (3, 6, 8).

$\therefore$ Length of diagonal, $AB = \sqrt{(5-3)^2 + (8-6)^2 + (10-8)^2}$

$= \sqrt{4+4+4} = \sqrt{12} = 2\sqrt{3}$ units

Q.33 L is the foot of the perpendicular drawn from a point P (3, 4, 5) on the XY-plane. The coordinates of point L are

(a) (3, 0, 0) (b) (0, 4, 5) (c) (3, 0, 5) (d) None of these

Ans. *(d)* We know that on the XY-plane, $z = 0$.

Hence, the coordinates of the points L are (3, 4, 0).

Q.34 L is the foot of the perpendicular drawn from a point (3, 4, 5) on X-axis. The coordinates of L are

(a) (3, 0, 0) (b) (0, 4, 0)
(c) (0, 0, 5) (d) None of these

Ans. *(a)* On the X-axis, $y = 0$ and $z = 0$

Hence, the required coordinates of L are (3, 0, 0).

Fill in the blanks in exercises from 35 to 49.

Q.35 The three axes OX, OY and OZ determine ....

Ans. The three axes OX, OY and OZ determine three coordinates planes.

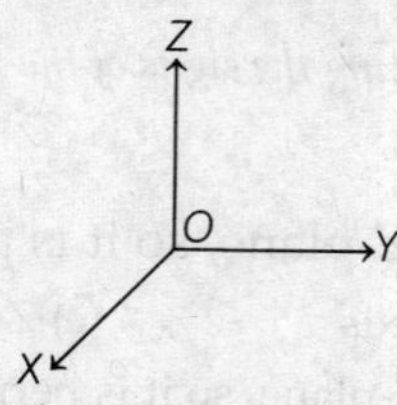

Q.36 The three planes determine a rectangular parallelopiped which has .... of rectangular faces.

Ans. Three points

Q.37 The coordinates of a point are the perpendicular distance from the .... on the respectives axes.

Ans. Given points

Q.38 The three coordinate planes divide the space into .... parts.

Ans. Eight

Q.39 If a point P lies in YZ-plane, then the coordinates of a point on YZ-plane is of the form ....

Ans. We know that on YZ-plane, $x = 0$. So, the coordinates of the required point is $(0, y, z)$.

Q.40 The equation of YZ-plane is ....

Ans. The equation of YZ-plane is $x = 0$.

Q.41 If the point P lies on Z-axis, then coordinates of P are of the form ....

Ans. On the Z-axis, $x = 0$ and $y = 0$. So, the required coordinates of P are $(0, 0, z)$.

Q.42 The equation of Z-axis, are ....

Ans. The equation of Z-axis are $x = 0$ and $y = 0$.

Q.43 A line is parallel to XY-plane if all the points on the line have equal... .

Ans. z-coordinates.

Q.44 A line is parallel to X-axis, if all the points on the line have equal...... .

Ans. y and z-coordinates.

Q.45 $x = a$ represent a plane parallel to ....

Ans. $x = a$ represent a plane parallel to YZ-plane.

Q.46 The plane parallel to YZ-plane is perpendicular to ....

Ans. The plane parallel to YZ-plane is perpendicular to X-axis.

Q.47 The length of the longest piece of a string that can be stretched straight in a rectangular room whose dimensions are 10, 13 and 8 units are ....

Ans. Given dimensions are $a = 10$, $b = 13$ and $c = 8$.

$$\therefore \text{ Required length} = \sqrt{a^2 + b^2 + c^2}$$

$$= \sqrt{10^2 + 13^2 + 8^2}$$

$$= \sqrt{100 + 169 + 64} = \sqrt{333} \text{ units}$$

Q.48 If the distance between the points $(a, 2, 1)$ and $(1, -1, 1)$ is 5, then $a =$ ....

Ans. Given points are $(a, 2, 1)$ and $(1, -1, 1)$.

$\therefore \quad \sqrt{(a-1)^2 + (2+1)^2 + (1-1)^2} = 5 \quad [\because d = \sqrt{(x_2 - x_1)^2 + (y_2 - y_1)^2 + (z_2 - z_1)^2}]$

On squaring both sides, we get

$\Rightarrow \quad (a-1)^2 + 9 + 0 = 25$

$\Rightarrow \quad a^2 - 2a + 1 + 9 = 25$

$\Rightarrow \quad a^2 - 2a - 15 = 0$

$\Rightarrow \quad a^2 - 5a + 3a - 15 = 0$

$\Rightarrow \quad a(a-5) + 3(a-5) = 0$

$\Rightarrow \quad (a-5)(a+3) = 0$

$\Rightarrow \quad a - 5 = 0 \text{ or } a + 3 = 0$

$\therefore \quad a = 5 \text{ or } -3$

***Q.49** If the mid-points of the sides of a triangle AB, BC and CA are $D(1, 2, -3)$, $E(3, 0, 1)$ and $F(-1, 1, -4)$, then the centroid of the ΔABC is ....

Ans. Let the vertices of ΔABC are $A(x_1, y_1, z_1)$, $B(x_2, y_2, z_2)$ and $C(x_3, y_3, z_3)$.

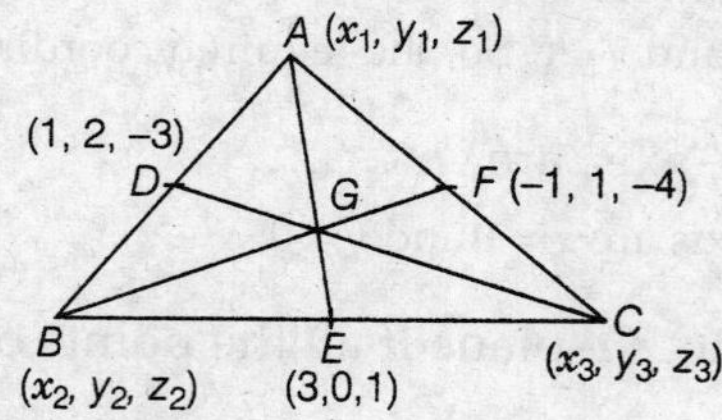

Since, D is the mid-point of AB, then

$$\frac{x_1 + x_2}{2} = 1 \Rightarrow x_1 + x_2 = 2 \quad \text{...(i)}$$

$$\frac{y_1 + y_2}{2} = 2 \Rightarrow y_1 + y_2 = 4 \quad \text{...(ii)}$$

$$\frac{z_1 + z_2}{2} = -3 \Rightarrow z_1 + z_2 = -6 \quad \text{...(iii)}$$

Similarly, E and F are the mid-points of sides BC and AC, respectively.

$$\frac{x_2 + x_3}{2} = 3 \Rightarrow x_2 + x_3 = 6 \quad \text{...(iv)}$$

$$\frac{y_2 + y_3}{2} = 0 \Rightarrow y_2 + y_3 = 0 \quad \text{...(v)}$$

$$\frac{z_2 + z_3}{2} = 1 \Rightarrow z_2 + z_3 = 2 \quad \text{...(vi)}$$

and

$$\frac{x_1 + x_3}{2} = -1 \Rightarrow x_1 + x_3 = -2 \quad \text{...(vii)}$$

$$\frac{y_1 + y_3}{2} = 1 \Rightarrow y_1 + y_3 = 2 \quad \text{...(viii)}$$

(*) Topics related to these question have been removed from latest NCERT.

$$\frac{z_1 + z_3}{2} = -4 \Rightarrow z_1 + z_3 = -8 \quad \text{...(ix)}$$

From Eqs. (i) and (iv), we get

$$x_1 + 2x_2 + x_3 = 8 \quad \text{...(x)}$$

From Eqs. (ii) and (v), we get

$$y_1 + 2y_2 + y_3 = 4 \quad \text{...(xi)}$$

From Eqs. (iii) and (vi), we get

$$z_1 + 2z_2 + z_3 = -4 \quad \text{...(xii)}$$

From Eqs. (vii) and (x), we get

$$2x_2 = 10 \Rightarrow x_2 = 5$$

If $x_2 = 5$, then $x_3 = 1$

If $x_3 = 1$, then $x_1 = -3$

$$\because \quad x_1 = -3, \; x_2 = 5, \; x_3 = 1$$

From Eqs. (viii) and (xi), we get

$$2y_2 = 2 \Rightarrow y_2 = 1$$

If $y_2 = 1$, then $y_3 = -1$

If $y_3 = -1$, then $y_1 = 3$

$$\because \quad y_1 = 3, \; y_2 = 1, \; y_3 = -1$$

From Eqs. (ix) and (xii), we get

$$2z_2 = 4 \Rightarrow z_2 = 2$$

If $z_2 = 2$, then $z_3 = 0$

If $z_3 = 0$, then $z_1 = -8$

$$\because \quad z_1 = -8, \; z_2 = 2, \; z_3 = 0$$

So, the vertices of ΔABC are $A(-3, 3, -8)$, $B(5, 1, 2)$ and $C(1, -1, 0)$.

Hence, coordinates of centroid of $\Delta ABC = G\left(\frac{-3+5+1}{3}, \frac{3+1-1}{3}, \frac{-8+2+0}{3}\right)$

i.e., $G(1, 1, -2)$.

Q.50 Match each item given under the Column C_1 to its correct answer given under Column C_2.

Column C_1	Column C_2
(a) In XY-plane	(i) I[st] octant
(b) Point (2, 3, 4) lies in the	(ii) YZ-plane
(c) Locus of the points having X coordinate 0 is	(iii) Z-coordinate is zero
(d) A line is parallel to X-axis if and only	(iv) Z-axis
(e) If $X = 0$, $Y = 0$ taken together will represent the	(v) plane parallel to XY-plane
(f) $Z = C$ represent the plane	(vi) if all the points on the line have equal Y and Z-coordinates
(g) Planes $X = A$, $Y = B$ represent the line	(vii) from the point on the respective

Column C_1	Column C_2
(h) Coordinates of a point are the distances from the origin to the feet of perpendiculars	(viii) parallel to Z-axis
(i) A ball is the solid region in the space enclosed by a	(ix) disc
(j) Region in the plane enclosed by a circle is known as a	(x) sphere

Ans. (a) In XY-plane, z-coordinates is zero. Hence, (a) $\leftrightarrow$ (iii)

(b) The point (2, 3, 4) lies in the I octant. Hence, (b) $\leftrightarrow$ (i)

(c) Locus of the points having x-coordinate is zero is YZ-plane. Hence, (c) $\leftrightarrow$ (ii)

(d) A line is parallel to X-axis if and only if all the points on the line have equal y and z -coordinates. Hence, (d) $\leftrightarrow$ (vi)

(e) $x = 0$, $y = 0$ represent Z-axis. Hence, (e) $\leftrightarrow$ (iv)

(f) $z = c$ represent the plane parallel to XY-plane. Hence, (f) $\leftrightarrow$ (v)

(g) The planes $x = a$, $y = b$ represent the line parallel to Z-axis. Hence, (g) $\leftrightarrow$ (viii)

(h) Coordinates of a point are the distances from the origin to the feet of perpendicular from the point on the respective. Hence, (h) $\leftrightarrow$ (vii)

(i) A ball is the solid region in the space enclosed by a sphere. Hence, (i) $\leftrightarrow$ (x)

(j) The region in the plane enclosed by a circle is known as a disc. Hence, (j) $\leftrightarrow$ (ix)

Chapter 13

Limits and Derivatives

Short Answer Type Questions

Q.1 Evaluate $\lim_{x \to 3} \dfrac{x^2-9}{x-3}$.

Thinking Process First, rearrange the function in the form of $(a^2-b^2)=(a+b)(a-b)$. After that, apply the given limit

Ans. Given, $\lim_{x \to 3} \dfrac{x^2-9}{x-3} = \lim_{x \to 3} \dfrac{x^2-(3)^2}{x-3}$

$$= \lim_{x \to 3} \frac{(x+3)(x-3)}{(x-3)} = \lim_{x \to 3}(x+3) \qquad [\because a^2-b^2=(a+b)(a-b)]$$

$$= 3+3=6$$

Q.2 Evaluate $\lim_{x \to 1/2} \dfrac{4x^2-1}{2x-1}$.

Ans. Given,

$$\lim_{x \to 1/2} \frac{4x^2-1}{2x-1} = \lim_{x \to 1/2} \frac{(2x)^2-(1)^2}{2x-1}$$

$$= \lim_{x \to 1/2} \frac{(2x+1)(2x-1)}{(2x-1)}$$

$$= \lim_{x \to 1/2} (2x+1) \qquad [\because a^2-b^2=(a+b)(a-b)]$$

$$= 2 \times \frac{1}{2} + 1 = 1+1 = 2$$

Q.3 Evaluate $\lim_{h \to 0} \dfrac{\sqrt{x+h}-\sqrt{x}}{h}$.

Ans. Given,

$$\lim_{h \to 0} \frac{\sqrt{x+h}-\sqrt{x}}{h} = \lim_{h \to 0} \frac{(x+h)^{1/2}-(x)^{1/2}}{x+h-x} \qquad \left[\frac{0}{0} \text{ form}\right]$$

Put $x+h=y$,

If $h \to 0 \Rightarrow y \to x$

$$\therefore \quad \lim_{h \to 0} \frac{\sqrt{x+h}-\sqrt{x}}{h} = \lim_{y \to x} \frac{y^{\frac{1}{2}}-x^{\frac{1}{2}}}{y-x} \qquad \left[\because \lim_{x \to a} \frac{x^n-a^n}{x-a} = na^{n-1}\right]$$

$$= \frac{1}{2} x^{\frac{1}{2}-1} = \frac{1}{2\sqrt{x}}$$

Q.4 Evaluate $\lim_{x \to 0} \frac{(x+2)^{1/3} - 2^{1/3}}{x}$.

Ans. Given, $\lim_{x\to 0} \frac{(x+2)^{1/3} - 2^{1/3}}{x} = \lim_{x\to 0} \frac{(x+2)^{1/3} - 2^{1/3}}{(x+2) - 2}$ $\left[\frac{0}{0}\text{ form}\right]$

Put $x + 2 = h$,

if $x \to 0 \Rightarrow h \to 2$

$$= \lim_{h\to 2} \frac{h^{\frac{1}{3}} - 2^{\frac{1}{3}}}{h-2}$$

$$= \frac{1}{3} \times 2^{\frac{1}{3}-1} \qquad \left[\because \lim_{x\to a} \frac{x^n - a^n}{x-a} = na^{n-1}\right]$$

$$= \frac{1}{3} \times (2)^{-2/3}$$

$$= \frac{1}{3(2)^{2/3}}$$

Q.5 Evaluate $\lim_{x \to 0} \frac{(1+x)^6 - 1}{(1+x)^2 - 1}$.

Ans. Given, $\lim_{x\to 0} \frac{(1+x)^6 - 1}{(1+x)^2 - 1} = \lim_{x\to 0} \frac{\frac{(1+x)^6 - 1}{x}}{\frac{(1+x)^2 - 1}{x}}$

[dividing numerator and denominator by x]

$$= \lim_{x\to 0} \frac{\frac{(1+x)^6 - 1}{(1+x) - 1}}{\frac{(1+x)^2 - 1}{(1+x) - 1}}$$

$$= \frac{\lim_{x\to 0} \frac{(1+x)^6 - (1)^6}{(1+x) - 1}}{\lim_{x\to 0} \frac{(1+x)^2 - (1)^2}{(1+x) - 1}} \qquad \left[\because \lim_{x\to a} \frac{f(x)}{g(x)} = \frac{\lim_{x\to a} f(x)}{\lim_{x\to a} g(x)}\right]$$

Put $1 + x = h$,

if $x \to 0 \Rightarrow h \to 1$

$$= \lim_{h\to 1} \frac{\frac{(h)^6 - (1)^6}{h-1}}{\frac{(h)^2 - (1)^2}{h-1}}$$

$$= \frac{6(1)^{6-1}}{2(1)^{2-1}} \qquad \left[\therefore \lim_{x\to a} \frac{x^n - a^n}{x-a} = na^{n-1}\right]$$

$$= \frac{6\times 1}{2\times 1} = \frac{6}{2} = 3$$

Q.6 Evaluate $\lim_{x \to a} \dfrac{(2+x)^{5/2} - (a+2)^{5/2}}{x-a}$.

Ans. Given, $\lim_{x \to a} \dfrac{(2+x)^{5/2} - (a+2)^{5/2}}{x-a} = \lim_{x \to a} \dfrac{(2+x)^{5/2} - (a+2)^{5/2}}{(2+x)-(a+2)}$

Put $2+x=h$,

if $x \to a \Rightarrow h \to 2+a$

$$= \lim_{h \to 2+a} \frac{h^{\frac{5}{2}} - (a+2)^{\frac{5}{2}}}{h-(a+2)}$$

$$= \frac{5}{2}(a+2)^{\frac{5}{2}-1} \qquad \left[\because \lim_{x \to a} \frac{x^n - a^n}{x-a} = na^{n-1}\right]$$

$$= \frac{5}{2}(a+2)^{3/2} \qquad [\because x \to a \Rightarrow x+2 \to a+2]$$

Mistake Alert! *Students may forget to change the limit while changing the variable in these similar type of questions.*

Q.7 Evaluate $\lim_{x \to 1} \dfrac{x^4 - \sqrt{x}}{\sqrt{x}-1}$.

Ans. Given, $\lim_{x \to 1} \dfrac{x^4 - \sqrt{x}}{\sqrt{x}-1} = \lim_{x \to 1} \dfrac{\sqrt{x}[(x)^{7/2} - 1]}{\sqrt{x}-1}$

$$= \lim_{x \to 1} \frac{(x)^{7/2} - 1}{\sqrt{x}-1} \cdot \lim_{x \to 1} \sqrt{x}$$

$$\left[\because \lim_{x \to a} f(x) \cdot g(x) = \lim_{x \to a} f(x) \cdot \lim_{x \to a} g(x)\right]$$

$$= \lim_{x \to 1} \frac{\dfrac{x^{\frac{7}{2}} - 1}{x-1}}{\dfrac{(x)^{\frac{1}{2}} - 1}{x-1}} \cdot 1$$

$$= \frac{\lim_{x \to 1} \dfrac{x^{7/2} - 1}{x-1}}{\lim_{x \to 1} \dfrac{x^{\frac{1}{2}} - 1}{x-1}} \qquad \left[\because \lim_{x \to a} \frac{f(x)}{g(x)} = \frac{\lim_{x \to a} f(x)}{\lim_{x \to a} g(x)}\right]$$

$$= \frac{\frac{7}{2}(1)^{\frac{7}{2}-1}}{\frac{1}{2}(1)^{\frac{1}{2}-1}} = \frac{\frac{7}{2}}{\frac{1}{2}} = 7$$

Q.8 Evaluate $\lim_{x \to 2} \dfrac{x^2 - 4}{\sqrt{3x-2} - \sqrt{x+2}}$.

Thinking Process First, rationalise the denominator to simplify the equation. After that, apply the given limit.

Ans. Given, $\lim_{x \to 2} \dfrac{x^2 - 4}{\sqrt{3x-2} - \sqrt{x+2}} = \lim_{x \to 2} \dfrac{(x^2-4)(\sqrt{3x-2} + \sqrt{x+2})}{(\sqrt{3x-2} - \sqrt{x+2})(\sqrt{3x-2} + \sqrt{x+2})}$

$$= \lim_{x \to 2} \frac{(x^2-4)(\sqrt{3x-2} + \sqrt{x+2})}{(\sqrt{3x-2})^2 - (\sqrt{x+2})^2} \qquad [\because (a+b)(a-b) = a^2 - b^2]$$

$$= \lim_{x \to 2} \frac{(x^2-4)(\sqrt{3x-2} + \sqrt{x+2})}{(3x-2) - (x+2)}$$

$$= \lim_{x \to 2} \frac{(x^2-4)(\sqrt{3x-2} + \sqrt{x+2})}{3x - 2 - x - 2}$$

$$= \lim_{x \to 2} \frac{(x^2-4)(\sqrt{3x-2} + \sqrt{x+2})}{2x - 4}$$

$$= \lim_{x \to 2} \frac{(x+2)(x-2)(\sqrt{3x-2} + \sqrt{x+2})}{2(x-2)}$$

$$= \lim_{x \to 2} \frac{(x+2)(\sqrt{3x-2} + \sqrt{x+2})}{2}$$

$$= \frac{(2+2)(\sqrt{6-2} + \sqrt{2+2})}{2} = \frac{4(2+2)}{2} = 8$$

Q.9 Evaluate $\lim_{x \to \sqrt{2}} \dfrac{x^4 - 4}{x^2 + 3\sqrt{2}x - 8}$.

Thinking process It is not directly solvable by putting the value of $x = \sqrt{2}$. Firstly, factorise the numerator and denominator by splitting the middle term and cancel the common factor and then, put the value of x.

Ans. Given, $\lim_{x \to \sqrt{2}} \dfrac{x^4 - 4}{x^2 + 3\sqrt{2}x - 8} = \lim_{x \to \sqrt{2}} \dfrac{(x^2)^2 - (2)^2}{x^2 + 3\sqrt{2}x - 8}$

$$= \lim_{x \to \sqrt{2}} \frac{(x^2-2)(x^2+2)}{x^2 + 4\sqrt{2}x - \sqrt{2}x - 8} \qquad [a^2 - b^2 = (a+b)(a-b)]$$

$$= \lim_{x \to \sqrt{2}} \frac{(x-\sqrt{2})(x+\sqrt{2})(x^2+2)}{x(x+4\sqrt{2}) - \sqrt{2}(x+4\sqrt{2})}$$

$$= \lim_{x \to \sqrt{2}} \frac{(x-\sqrt{2})(x+\sqrt{2})(x^2+2)}{(x-\sqrt{2})(x+4\sqrt{2})}$$

$$= \lim_{x \to \sqrt{2}} \frac{(x+\sqrt{2})(x^2+2)}{(x+4\sqrt{2})}$$

$$= \frac{(\sqrt{2}+\sqrt{2})[(\sqrt{2})^2+2]}{(\sqrt{2}+4\sqrt{2})} = \frac{2\sqrt{2}(2+2)}{5\sqrt{2}} = \frac{8}{5}$$

Q.10 Evaluate $\lim\limits_{x \to 1} \dfrac{x^7 - 2x^5 + 1}{x^3 - 3x^2 + 2}$.

Ans. Given, $\lim\limits_{x \to 1} \dfrac{x^7 - 2x^5 + 1}{x^3 - 3x^2 + 2}$ $\left[\dfrac{0}{0} \text{ form}\right]$

$$= \lim_{x \to 1} \frac{x^7 - x^5 - x^5 + 1}{x^3 - x^2 - 2x^2 + 2}$$

$$= \lim_{x \to 1} \frac{x^5(x^2 - 1) - 1(x^5 - 1)}{x^2(x - 1) - 2(x^2 - 1)}$$

On dividing numerator and denominator by $(x - 1)$, then

$$= \lim_{x \to 1} \frac{\dfrac{x^5(x^2 - 1)}{(x - 1)} - \dfrac{1(x^5 - 1)}{(x - 1)}}{\dfrac{x^2(x - 1)}{(x - 1)} - \dfrac{2(x^2 - 1)}{(x - 1)}}$$

$$= \frac{\lim\limits_{x \to 1} x^5(x + 1) - \lim\limits_{x \to 1} \left(\dfrac{x^5 - 1}{x - 1}\right)}{\lim\limits_{x \to 1} x^2 - 2 \lim\limits_{x \to 1} (x + 1)}$$

$$\left[\because \lim_{x \to a} \frac{f(x)}{g(x)} = \frac{\lim\limits_{x \to a} f(x)}{\lim\limits_{x \to a} g(x)} \text{ and } \lim_{x \to a} [f(x) - g(x)] = \lim_{x \to a} f(x) - \lim_{x \to a} g(x)\right]$$

$$= \frac{1 \times 2 - 5 \times (1)^4}{1 - 2 \times 2} = \frac{2 - 5}{1 - 4}$$

$$= \frac{-3}{-3} = 1$$

Q.11 Evaluate $\lim\limits_{x \to 0} \dfrac{\sqrt{1 + x^3} - \sqrt{1 - x^3}}{x^2}$.

Ans. Given, $\lim\limits_{x \to 0} \dfrac{\sqrt{1 + x^3} - \sqrt{1 - x^3}}{x^2} = \lim\limits_{x \to 0} \dfrac{\sqrt{1 + x^3} - \sqrt{1 - x^3}}{x^2} \cdot \dfrac{\sqrt{1 + x^3} + \sqrt{1 - x^3}}{\sqrt{1 + x^3} + \sqrt{1 - x^3}}$

[rationalise the numerator]

$$= \lim_{x \to 0} \frac{(1 + x^3) - (1 - x^3)}{x^2(\sqrt{1 + x^3} + \sqrt{1 - x^3})} \qquad [\because (a - b)(a + b) = a^2 - b^2]$$

$$= \lim_{x \to 0} \frac{1 + x^3 - 1 + x^3}{x^2(\sqrt{1 + x^3} + \sqrt{1 - x^3})}$$

$$= \lim_{x \to 0} \frac{2x^3}{x^2(\sqrt{1 + x^3} + \sqrt{1 - x^3})}$$

$$= \lim_{x \to 0} \frac{2x}{(\sqrt{1 + x^3} + \sqrt{1 - x^3})}$$

$$= 0$$

Q.12 Evaluate $\lim_{x \to -3} \dfrac{x^3 + 27}{x^5 + 243}$.

Ans. Given, $\lim_{x \to -3} \dfrac{x^3 + 27}{x^5 + 243} = \lim_{x \to -3} \dfrac{\dfrac{x^3 + 27}{x + 3}}{\dfrac{x^5 + 243}{x + 3}}$

[∵ dividing numerator and denominator by $x + 3$]

$$= \lim_{x \to -3} \frac{\dfrac{x^3 - (-3)^3}{x - (-3)}}{\dfrac{x^5 - (-3)^5}{x - (-3)}} = \frac{\lim\limits_{x \to -3} \dfrac{x^3 - (-3)^3}{x - (-3)}}{\lim\limits_{x \to -3} \dfrac{x^5 - (-3)^5}{x - (-3)}} \quad \left[\because \lim_{x \to a} \frac{f(x)}{g(x)} = \frac{\lim\limits_{x \to a} f(x)}{\lim\limits_{x \to a} g(x)}\right]$$

$$= \frac{3(-3)^{3-1}}{5(-3)^{5-1}} = \frac{3(-3)^2}{5(-3)^4} \quad \left[\because \lim_{x \to a} \frac{x^n - a^n}{x - a} = na^{n-1}\right]$$

$$= \frac{3}{5(-3)^2} = \frac{3}{45} = \frac{1}{15}$$

Q.13 Evaluate $\lim_{x \to 1/2} \left(\dfrac{8x - 3}{2x - 1} - \dfrac{4x^2 + 1}{4x^2 - 1}\right)$.

Ans. Given, $\lim_{x \to 1/2} \left(\dfrac{8x - 3}{2x - 1} - \dfrac{4x^2 + 1}{4x^2 - 1}\right) = \lim_{x \to 1/2} \left[\dfrac{(8x - 3)(2x + 1) - (4x^2 + 1)}{(4x^2 - 1)}\right]$

$$= \lim_{x \to 1/2} \left[\frac{16x^2 + 8x - 6x - 3 - 4x^2 - 1}{4x^2 - 1}\right]$$

$$= \lim_{x \to 1/2} \left[\frac{12x^2 + 2x - 4}{4x^2 - 1}\right]$$

$$= \lim_{x \to 1/2} \frac{2(6x^2 + x - 2)}{4x^2 - 1}$$

$$= \lim_{x \to 1/2} \frac{2(6x^2 + 4x - 3x - 2)}{4x^2 - 1}$$

$$= \lim_{x \to 1/2} \frac{2[2x(3x + 2) - 1(3x + 2)]}{4x^2 - 1}$$

$$= \lim_{x \to 1/2} \frac{2[(3x + 2)(2x - 1)]}{(2x)^2 - (1)^2}$$

$$= \lim_{x \to 1/2} \frac{2(3x + 2)(2x - 1)}{(2x - 1)(2x + 1)} \quad [\because a^2 - b^2 = (a - b)(a + b)]$$

$$= \lim_{x \to 1/2} \frac{2(3x + 2)}{2x + 1} = \frac{2\left(3 \times \frac{1}{2} + 2\right)}{2 \times \frac{1}{2} + 1} = \frac{3}{2} + 2 = \frac{7}{2}$$

Note The common factors will be cancelled only in the limit. But in a function, you do not cancelled directly until it is in an indeterminate form.

Q.14 Find the value of n, if $\lim_{x \to 2} \frac{x^n - 2^n}{x - 2} = 80, n \in N$.

Ans. Given,
$$\lim_{x \to 2} \frac{x^n - 2^n}{x - 2} = 80$$

$$\Rightarrow \quad n(2)^{n-1} = 80 \qquad \left[\because \lim_{x \to a} \frac{x^n - a^n}{x - a} = na^{n-1}\right]$$

$$\Rightarrow \quad n(2)^{n-1} = 5 \times 16$$

$$\Rightarrow \quad n \times 2^{n-1} = 5 \times (2)^4$$

$$\Rightarrow \quad n \times 2^{n-1} = 5 \times (2)^{5-1}$$

On comparing both sides, we get

$$n = 5$$

Q.15 Evaluate $\lim_{x \to 0} \frac{\sin 3x}{\sin 7x}$.

Thinking process Here, we will convert given limit into a standard form and use the result $\lim_{x \to 0} \frac{\sin x}{x}$ or $\lim_{x \to 0} \frac{x}{\sin x} = 1$

Ans. Given, $\lim_{x \to 0} \frac{\sin 3x}{\sin + 7x} = \lim_{x \to 0} \frac{\frac{\sin 3x}{3x} \cdot 3x}{\frac{\sin 7x}{7x} \cdot 7x}$

$$= \frac{3}{7} \cdot \frac{\lim_{x \to 0} \frac{\sin 3x}{3x}}{\lim_{x \to 0} \frac{\sin 7x}{7x}}$$

$$= \frac{3}{7} \qquad \left[\because \lim_{x \to 0} \frac{\sin x}{x} = 1 \text{ and as } x \to 0 \Rightarrow kx \to 0\right]$$

Q.16 Evaluate $\lim_{x \to 0} \frac{\sin^2 2x}{\sin^2 4x}$.

Ans. Given, $\lim_{x \to 0} \frac{\sin^2 2x}{\sin^2 4x} = \lim_{x \to 0} \frac{\sin 2x \cdot \sin 2x}{\sin 4x \cdot \sin 4x}$

$$= \lim_{x \to 0} \frac{\frac{\sin 2x}{2x} \cdot 2x \frac{\sin 2x}{2x} \cdot 2x}{\frac{\sin 4x}{4x} \cdot 4x \cdot \frac{\sin 4x}{4x} \cdot 4x}$$

$$= \frac{\lim_{x \to 0} \frac{\sin 2x}{2x} \cdot \lim_{x \to 0} \frac{\sin 2x}{2x}}{4 \lim_{x \to 0} \frac{\sin 4x}{4x} \cdot \lim_{x \to 0} \frac{\sin 4x}{4x}}$$

$$= \frac{1}{4} \qquad \left[\because \lim_{x \to 0} \frac{\sin x}{x} = 1\right]$$

Alternate Method

Given $\lim_{x\to 0}\dfrac{\sin^2 2x}{\sin^2 4x} = \lim_{x\to 0}\dfrac{\sin^2 2x}{4\sin^2 2x\cos^2 2x}$ $[\because \sin 2\theta = 2\sin\theta\cos\theta]$

$$= \lim_{x\to 0}\frac{1}{4\cos^2 2x} = \frac{1}{4(1)} = \frac{1}{4}$$

Q.17 Evaluate $\lim_{x\to 0}\dfrac{1-\cos 2x}{x^2}$.

Ans. Given, $\lim_{x\to 0}\dfrac{1-\cos 2x}{x^2} = \lim_{x\to 0}\dfrac{1-1+2\sin^2 x}{x^2}$ $[\because \cos 2x = 1-2\sin^2 x]$

$$= \lim_{x\to 0}\frac{2\sin^2 x}{x^2}$$

$$= 2\lim_{x\to 0}\frac{\sin^2 x}{x^2}$$

$$= 2\lim_{x\to 0}\left(\frac{\sin x}{x}\right)^2$$

$$= 2\times 1 = 2$$ $\left[\because \lim_{x\to 0}\dfrac{\sin x}{x} = 1\right]$

Q.18 Evaluate $\lim_{x\to 0}\dfrac{2\sin x - \sin 2x}{x^3}$.

Ans. Given, $\lim_{x\to 0}\dfrac{2\sin x - \sin 2x}{x^3} = \lim_{x\to 0}\dfrac{2\sin x - 2\sin x\cos x}{x^3}$ $[\because \sin 2x = 2\sin x\cos x]$

$$= \lim_{x\to 0}\frac{2\sin x(1-\cos x)}{x^3}$$

$$= 2\lim_{x\to 0}\frac{\sin x}{x}\cdot\lim_{x\to 0}\left(\frac{1-\cos x}{x^2}\right)$$

$$= 2\cdot 1\lim_{x\to 0}\frac{1-\cos x}{x^2}$$ $\left[\because \lim_{x\to 0}\dfrac{\sin x}{x} = 1\right]$

$$= 2\lim_{x\to 0}\frac{1-1+2\sin^2\frac{x}{2}}{x^2} = 2\lim_{x\to 0}\frac{2\sin^2\frac{x}{2}}{4\times\frac{x^2}{4}}$$ $\left[\cos x = 1-2\sin^2\dfrac{x}{2}\right]$

$$= \frac{2\cdot 2}{4}\lim_{x\to 0}\left(\frac{\sin\frac{x}{2}}{\frac{x}{2}}\right)^2 = \lim_{x\to 0}\left(\frac{\sin\frac{x}{2}}{\frac{x}{2}}\right)^2 = 1$$

Q.19 Evaluate $\lim_{x\to 0}\dfrac{1-\cos mx}{1-\cos nx}$.

Ans. Given, $\lim_{x\to 0}\dfrac{1-\cos mx}{1-\cos nx} = \lim_{x\to 0}\dfrac{1-1+2\sin^2\frac{mx}{2}}{1-1+2\sin^2\frac{nx}{2}}$ $\left[\because \cos mx = 1-2\sin^2\dfrac{mx}{2} \text{ and } \cos nx = 1-2\sin^2\dfrac{nx}{2}\right]$

$$= \lim_{x \to 0} \frac{\sin^2 \frac{mx}{2}}{\sin^2 \frac{nx}{2}} = \lim_{x \to 0} \frac{\frac{\sin^2 \frac{mx}{2}}{\left(\frac{mx}{2}\right)^2} \cdot \left(\frac{mx}{2}\right)^2}{\frac{\sin^2 \frac{nx}{2}}{\left(\frac{nx}{2}\right)^2} \cdot \left(\frac{nx}{2}\right)^2} = \frac{\lim_{x \to 0} \left(\frac{\sin \frac{mx}{2}}{\frac{mx}{2}}\right)^2}{\lim_{x \to 0} \left(\frac{\sin \frac{nx}{2}}{\frac{nx}{2}}\right)^2} \cdot \frac{m^2 \frac{x^2}{4}}{n^2 \frac{x^2}{4}}$$

$$= \frac{m^2}{n^2} \cdot \frac{\lim_{x \to 0} \left(\frac{\sin \frac{mx}{2}}{\frac{mx}{2}}\right)^2}{\lim_{x \to 0} \left(\frac{\sin \frac{nx}{2}}{\frac{nx}{2}}\right)^2} = \frac{m^2}{n^2} \left[\because \lim_{x \to 0} \frac{\sin x}{x} = 1 \text{ and as } x \to 0 \Rightarrow kx \to 0\right]$$

Q.20 Evaluate $\lim_{x \to \pi/3} \frac{\sqrt{1 - \cos 6x}}{\sqrt{2}\left(\frac{\pi}{3} - x\right)}$.

Ans. Given, $\lim_{x \to \pi/3} \frac{\sqrt{1 - \cos 6x}}{\sqrt{2}\left(\frac{\pi}{3} - x\right)} = \lim_{x \to \pi/3} \frac{\sqrt{1 - \cos 2(3x)}}{\sqrt{2}\left(\frac{\pi}{3} - x\right)}$

$$= \lim_{x \to \pi/3} \frac{\sqrt{1 - 1 + 2\sin^2 3x}}{\sqrt{2}\left(\frac{\pi}{3} - x\right)} \qquad [\because \cos 2x = 1 - 2\sin^2 x]$$

$$= \lim_{x \to \pi/3} \frac{\sqrt{2} \sin 3x}{\sqrt{2}\left(\frac{\pi}{3} - x\right)} = \lim_{x \to \pi/3} \frac{\sin 3x}{\frac{\pi}{3} - x}$$

$$= \lim_{x \to \pi/3} \frac{\sin(\pi - 3x)}{\frac{\pi - 3x}{3}} \qquad [\because \sin(\pi - \theta) = \sin \theta]$$

$$= 3 \lim_{x \to \pi/3} \frac{\sin(\pi - 3x)}{(\pi - 3x)} = 3 \times 1 \qquad \left[\because \lim_{x \to 0} \frac{\sin x}{x} = 1\right]$$

$$= 3 \qquad \left[\because \text{as } x \to \frac{\pi}{3} \Rightarrow \left(\frac{\pi}{3} - x\right) \to 0 \Rightarrow (\pi - 3x) \to 0\right]$$

Q.21 Evaluate $\lim_{x \to \frac{\pi}{4}} \frac{\sin x - \cos x}{x - \frac{\pi}{4}}$.

Thinking Process First, multiply and divide by $\sqrt{2}$ in numerator to form the formula of $\sin(a - b)$. After that, use the result $\lim_{x \to 0} \frac{\sin x}{x} = 1$

Ans. Given, $\lim_{x \to \pi/4} \frac{\sqrt{2}\left(\sin x \cdot \frac{1}{\sqrt{2}} - \cos x \cdot \frac{1}{\sqrt{2}}\right)}{\left(x - \frac{\pi}{4}\right)}$

$$= \lim_{x \to \pi/4} \frac{\sqrt{2}\left(\sin x \cos \frac{\pi}{4} - \cos x \cdot \sin \frac{\pi}{4}\right)}{\left(x - \frac{\pi}{4}\right)}$$

$$\left[\because \cos \frac{\pi}{4} = \frac{1}{\sqrt{2}} \text{ and } \sin \frac{\pi}{4} = \frac{1}{\sqrt{2}}\right]$$

$$= \lim_{x \to \pi/4} \frac{\sqrt{2}\left\{\sin\left(x - \frac{\pi}{4}\right)\right\}}{\left(x - \frac{\pi}{4}\right)} \quad [\because \sin(a-b) = \sin a \cos b - \cos a \sin b]$$

$$= \sqrt{2} \lim_{x \to \pi/4} \frac{\sin\left(x - \frac{\pi}{4}\right)}{\left(x - \frac{\pi}{4}\right)} = \sqrt{2} \quad \left[\because \lim_{x \to 0} \frac{\sin x}{x} = 1\right]$$

$$\left[\because \text{as } x \to \frac{\pi}{4} \Rightarrow \left(x - \frac{\pi}{4}\right) \to 0\right]$$

Q.22 Evaluate $\lim_{x \to \pi/6} \frac{\sqrt{3} \sin x - \cos x}{x - \frac{\pi}{6}}$.

Ans. Given, $\lim_{x \to \pi/6} \frac{\sqrt{3} \sin x - \cos x}{x - \frac{\pi}{6}} = \lim_{x \to \pi/6} \frac{2\left(\frac{\sqrt{3}}{2} \sin x - \frac{1}{2} \cos x\right)}{\left(x - \frac{\pi}{6}\right)}$

$$= \lim_{x \to \pi/6} \frac{2\left(\sin x \cos \frac{\pi}{6} - \cos x \sin \frac{\pi}{6}\right)}{\left(x - \frac{\pi}{6}\right)} = 2 \lim_{x \to \pi/6} \frac{\sin\left(x - \frac{\pi}{6}\right)}{\left(x - \frac{\pi}{6}\right)} \quad \left[\because \cos \frac{\pi}{6} = \frac{\sqrt{3}}{2}, \sin \frac{\pi}{6} = \frac{1}{2}\right]$$

$$[\because \sin A \cos B - \cos A \sin B = \sin (A - B)]$$

$$= 2 \quad \left[\because \lim_{x \to 0} \frac{\sin x}{x} = 1\right]$$

$$\left[\because \text{as } x \to \frac{\pi}{6} \Rightarrow \left(x - \frac{\pi}{6}\right) \to 0\right]$$

Q.23 Evaluate $\lim_{x \to 0} \frac{\sin 2x + 3x}{2x + \tan 3x}$.

Thinking Process First, multiply and divide by $2x$ and $3x$ in numerator and denominator, respectively. After that, use the result $\lim_{x \to 0} \frac{\sin x}{x} = 1$ and $\lim_{x \to 0} \frac{\tan x}{x} = 1$

Ans. Given, $\lim_{x \to 0} \frac{\sin 2x + 3x}{2x + \tan 3x} = \lim_{x \to 0} \frac{\frac{\sin 2x + 3x}{2x} \cdot 2x}{\frac{2x + \tan 3x}{3x} \cdot 3x}$

$$= \lim_{x \to 0} \frac{\left(\frac{\sin 2x}{2x} + \frac{3x}{2x}\right) 2x}{\left(\frac{2x}{3x} + \frac{\tan 3x}{3x}\right) 3x} = \lim_{x \to 0} \frac{\frac{\sin 2x}{2x} + \frac{3}{2}}{\frac{2}{3} + \frac{\tan 3x}{3x}} \cdot \frac{2}{3}$$

$$= \frac{2}{3} \lim_{x \to 0} \frac{\frac{\sin 2x}{2x} + \frac{3}{2}}{\frac{2}{3} + \lim_{x \to 0} \frac{\tan 3x}{3x}}$$

$$= \frac{2}{3}\left(\frac{1+\frac{3}{2}}{\frac{2}{3}+1}\right) \qquad \left[\because \lim_{x \to 0} \frac{\sin x}{x} = 1 \text{ and } \lim_{x \to 0} \frac{\tan x}{x} = 1\right]$$

$$= \frac{2}{3} \times \frac{\frac{5}{2}}{\frac{5}{3}} = \frac{2}{3} \times \frac{5}{2} \times \frac{3}{5} = 1$$

Q.24 Evaluate $\lim_{x \to a} \frac{\sin x - \sin a}{\sqrt{x} - \sqrt{a}}$.

Ans. Given, $\lim_{x \to a} \frac{\sin x - \sin a}{\sqrt{x} - \sqrt{a}} = \lim_{x \to 0} \frac{2\cos\left(\frac{x+a}{2}\right)\sin\left(\frac{x-a}{2}\right)}{\sqrt{x} - \sqrt{a}}$

$$\left[\because \sin C - \sin D = 2\cos\frac{C+D}{2}.\sin\frac{C-D}{2}\right]$$

$$= \lim_{x \to a} \frac{2\cos\left(\frac{x+a}{2}\right)\sin\left(\frac{x-a}{2}\right)(\sqrt{x}+\sqrt{a})}{(\sqrt{x}-\sqrt{a})(\sqrt{x}+\sqrt{a})}$$

$$= \lim_{x \to a} \frac{2\cos\left(\frac{x+a}{2}\right)\sin\left(\frac{x-a}{2}\right)(\sqrt{x}+\sqrt{a})}{x-a}$$

$$= 2\lim_{x \to a} \cos\left(\frac{x+a}{2}\right) \lim_{x \to a} (\sqrt{x}+\sqrt{a}) \lim_{x \to a} \frac{\sin\left(\frac{x-a}{2}\right)}{2\left(\frac{x-a}{2}\right)}$$

Put $\frac{x-a}{2} = h,$

if $x \to a \Rightarrow h \to 0$

$$= 2\cos a \cdot 2\sqrt{a} \cdot \left[\frac{1}{2} \lim_{h \to 0} \frac{\sin(h)}{(h)}\right]$$

$$= 2\cos a \cdot 2\sqrt{a} \cdot \frac{1}{2} \qquad \left[\because \lim_{h \to 0} \frac{\sin x}{x} = 1\right]$$

$$= 2\sqrt{a}\cos a$$

Q.25 Evaluate $\lim_{x \to \pi/6} \frac{\cot^2 x - 3}{\operatorname{cosec} x - 2}$.

Ans. Given $\lim_{x \to \pi/6} \frac{\cot^2 x - 3}{\operatorname{cosec} x - 2} = \lim_{x \to \pi/6} \frac{\operatorname{cosec}^2 x - 1 - 3}{\operatorname{cosec} x - 2}$ $\quad [\because \operatorname{cosec}^2 x = 1 + \cot^2 x]$

$$= \lim_{x \to \pi/6} \frac{\operatorname{cosec}^2 x - 4}{\operatorname{cosec} x - 2} = \lim_{x \to \pi/6} \frac{(\operatorname{cosec} x)^2 - (2)^2}{\operatorname{cosec} x - 2}$$

$$= \lim_{x \to \pi/6} \frac{(\text{cosec}\, x + 2)(\text{cosec}\, x - 2)}{(\text{cosec}\, x - 2)} = \lim_{x \to \pi/6} (\text{cosec}\, x + 2)$$

$[\because a^2 - b^2 = (a+b)(a-b)]$

$$= \text{cosec}\frac{\pi}{6} + 2 = 2 + 2 = 4$$

Q.26 Evaluate $\lim_{x \to 0} \dfrac{\sqrt{2} - \sqrt{1 + \cos x}}{\sin^2 x}$.

Ans. Given, $\lim_{x \to 0} \dfrac{\sqrt{2} - \sqrt{1 + \cos x}}{\sin^2 x}$

$$= \lim_{x \to 0} \frac{\sqrt{2} - \sqrt{2\cos^2 \frac{x}{2}}}{\sin^2 x} \qquad \left[\because \cos x = 2\cos^2 \frac{x}{2} - 1\right]$$

$$= \lim_{x \to 0} \frac{\sqrt{2}\left(1 - \cos \frac{x}{2}\right)}{\sin^2 x}$$

$$= \lim_{x \to 0} \frac{\sqrt{2}\left(2\sin^2 \frac{x}{4}\right)}{\sin^2 x} = \lim_{x \to 0} 2\sqrt{2} \frac{\sin^2 \frac{x}{4}}{\left(\frac{x}{4}\right)^2} \cdot \frac{\left(\frac{x}{4}\right)^2}{\sin^2 x} \qquad \left[\because \cos x = 1 - 2\sin^2 \frac{x}{2}\right]$$

$$= 2\sqrt{2} \lim_{x \to 0} \left(\frac{\sin \frac{x}{4}}{\frac{x}{4}}\right)^2 \cdot \lim_{x \to 0} \left(\frac{x}{\sin x}\right)^2 \cdot \frac{1}{16}$$

$$= 2\sqrt{2} \cdot 1 \cdot 1 \cdot \frac{1}{16} = \frac{1}{4\sqrt{2}} \qquad \left[\because \lim_{x \to 0} \frac{\sin x}{x} = \frac{x}{\sin x} = 1\right]$$

Q.27 Evaluate $\lim_{x \to 0} \dfrac{\sin x - 2\sin 3x + \sin 5x}{x}$.

Ans. Given, $\lim_{x \to 0} \dfrac{\sin x - 2\sin 3x + \sin 5x}{x} = \lim_{x \to 0} \dfrac{\sin 5x + \sin x - 2\sin 3x}{x}$

$$= \lim_{x \to 0} \frac{2\sin 3x \cos 2x - 2\sin 3x}{x} = \lim_{x \to 0} \frac{2\sin 3x(\cos 2x - 1)}{x}$$

$$\left[\because \sin a + \sin b = 2\sin \frac{a+b}{2} \cos \frac{a-b}{2}\right]$$

$$= \lim_{x \to 0} \frac{2\sin 3x}{\frac{1}{3} \times 3x}(\cos 2x - 1) = 6 \lim_{x \to 0} \frac{\sin 3x}{3x}(\cos 2x - 1)$$

$$= 6 \lim_{x \to 0} \frac{\sin 3x}{3x} \cdot \lim_{x \to 0} (\cos 2x - 1) = 6 \times 1 \times 0 = 0 \qquad [\because \cos 0 = 1]$$

$$\left[\lim_{x \to 0} \frac{\sin x}{x} = 1\right]$$

Alternate Method

we have, $\lim_{x\to 0}\frac{\sin x}{x} - 2\lim_{x\to 0}\frac{\sin 3x}{3x}\cdot 3 + \lim_{x\to 0}\frac{\sin 5x}{5x}\cdot 5$

$\Rightarrow \quad 1-2\times 3+5$

$\Rightarrow \quad 1-6+5$

$\Rightarrow \quad 0$

Mistake Alert ! *In most of the times, when we put the limit, it becomes an indeterminate form. Firstly simplify the function by using the formulae and remove the causes.*

Q.28 If $\lim_{x\to 1}\frac{x^4-1}{x-1} = \lim_{x\to k}\frac{x^3-k^3}{x^2-k^2}$, then find the value of k.

Ans. Given, $\lim_{x\to 1}\frac{x^4-1}{x-1} = \lim_{x\to k}\frac{x^3-k^3}{x^2-k^2}$

$$\Rightarrow \quad 4(1)^{4-1} = \lim_{x\to k}\frac{\frac{x^3-k^3}{x-k}}{\frac{x^2-k^2}{x-k}} \qquad \left[\because \lim_{x\to a}\frac{x^n-a^n}{x-a} = na^{n-1}\right]$$

$$\Rightarrow \quad 4 = \frac{\lim_{x\to k}\frac{x^3-k^3}{x-k}}{\lim_{x\to k}\frac{x^2-k^2}{x-k}} \qquad \left[\because \lim_{x\to a}\frac{f(x)}{g(x)} = \frac{\lim_{x\to a} f(x)}{\lim_{x\to a} g(x)}\right]$$

$$\Rightarrow \quad 4 = \frac{3k^2}{2k} \Rightarrow 4 = \frac{3}{2}k \qquad \left[\because \lim_{x\to a}\frac{x^n-a^n}{x-a} = na^{n-1}\right]$$

$$\therefore \quad k = \frac{4\times 2}{3} = \frac{8}{3}$$

Differentiate each of the functions w.r.t. x in exercises 29 to 42.

Q.29 $\dfrac{x^4+x^3+x^2+1}{x}$

Concept Insight To differentiate $h(x) = f(x) + g(x)$. w.r.t. x, use sum rule, $\frac{d}{dx}[h(x)] = \frac{d}{dx}[f(x)] + [g(x)] = \frac{d}{dx}f(x) + \frac{d}{dx}g(x)$ and also use $\frac{d}{dx}(x^n) = nx^{n-1}$.

Ans. $$\frac{d}{dx}\left(\frac{x^4+x^3+x^2+1}{x}\right) = \frac{d}{dx}\left(x^3+x^2+x+\frac{1}{x}\right)$$

$$= \frac{d}{dx}x^3 + \frac{d}{dx}x^2 + \frac{d}{dx}x + \frac{d}{dx}\left(\frac{1}{x}\right)$$

$$= 3x^2 + 2x + 1 - \frac{1}{x^2} \qquad \left[\because \frac{d}{dx}x^n = nx^{n-1}\right]$$

$$= \frac{3x^4+2x^3+x^2-1}{x^2}$$

Q.30 $\left(x+\frac{1}{x}\right)^3$

Thinking Process We have the function of a function as $y = f\{g(x)\}$. Here, f is a function of g and g is a function of x. The derivative of such functions are given as $\frac{dy}{dx} = f'\{g(x)\}.g'(x)$

Ans. Let $y = \left(x+\frac{1}{x}\right)^3$

$$\therefore \quad \frac{dy}{dx} = \frac{d}{dx}\left(x+\frac{1}{x}\right)^3$$

$$= 3\left(x+\frac{1}{x}\right)^{3-1}\frac{d}{dx}\left(x+\frac{1}{x}\right) \qquad \text{[by chain rule]}$$

$$= 3\left(x+\frac{1}{x}\right)^2\left(1-\frac{1}{x^2}\right)$$

$$= 3\left(x^2+\frac{1}{x^2}+2\right)\left(1-\frac{1}{x^2}\right)$$

$$= \left(3x^2+\frac{3}{x^2}+6\right)\left(1-\frac{1}{x^2}\right)$$

$$= 3x^2-3+\frac{3}{x^2}-\frac{3}{x^4}+6-\frac{6}{x^2}$$

$$= 3x^2-\frac{3}{x^2}-\frac{3}{x^4}+3$$

Q.31 $(3x+5)(1+\tan x)$

Ans. Let $y = (3x+5)(1+\tan x)$

$$\therefore \quad \frac{dy}{dx} = \frac{d}{dx}[(3x+5)(1+\tan x)]$$

$$= (3x+5)\frac{d}{dx}(1+\tan x) + (1+\tan x)\frac{d}{dx}(3x+5)$$

$$\left[\because \frac{d}{dx}[f(x)g(x)] = f(x)g'(x)+g(x)f'(x)\right]$$

$$= (3x+5)(\sec^2 x) + (1+\tan x)\cdot 3$$

$$= 3x\sec^2 x + 5\sec^2 x + 3\tan x + 3$$

Q.32 $(\sec x-1)(\sec x+1)$

Ans. Let $y = (\sec x-1)(\sec x+1)$

$$\Rightarrow \quad y = (\sec^2 - 1) \qquad [\because (a+b)(a-b) = a^2-b^2]$$

$$= \tan^2 x \qquad [\because \sec^2 x = 1+\tan^2 x]$$

$$\therefore \quad \frac{dy}{dx} = 2\tan x\cdot\frac{d}{dx}\tan x \qquad \text{[by chain rule]}$$

$$= 2\tan x\cdot\sec^2 x$$

Q.33 $\dfrac{3x+4}{5x^2-7x+9}$

Ans. Let $\quad y=\dfrac{3x+4}{5x^2-7x+9}$

$$\therefore \quad \frac{dy}{dx}=\frac{(5x^2-7x+9)\frac{d}{dx}(3x+4)-(3x+4)\frac{d}{dx}(5x^2-7x+9)}{(5x^2-7x+9)^2}$$

$$\left[\because \left(\frac{d}{dx}\right)\frac{f(x)}{g(x)}=\frac{g(x)f'(x)-f(x).g'(x)}{[g(x)]^2}\right]$$

$$=\frac{(5x^2-7x+9)\cdot 3-(3x+4)(10x-7)}{(5x^2-7x+9)^2}$$

$$=\frac{15x^2-21x+27-30x^2+21x-40x+28}{(5x^2-7x+9)^2}$$

$$=\frac{-15x^2-40x+55}{(5x^2-7x+9)^2}$$

$$=\frac{55-40x-15x^2}{(5x^2-7x+9)^2}$$

Q.34 $\dfrac{x^5-\cos x}{\sin x}$

Ans. Let $\quad y=\dfrac{x^5-\cos x}{\sin x}$

$$\therefore \quad \frac{dy}{dx}=\frac{\sin x\frac{d}{dx}(x^5-\cos x)-(x^5-\cos x)\frac{d}{dx}\sin x}{(\sin x)^2} \qquad \text{[by quotient rule]}$$

$$=\frac{\sin x(5x^4+\sin x)-(x^5-\cos x)\cos x}{\sin^2 x} \qquad \left[\therefore \frac{d}{dx}(\sin x)=\cos x, \frac{d}{dx}\cos(x)=-\sin x\right]$$

$$=\frac{5x^4\sin x+\sin^2 x-x^5\cos x+\cos^2 x}{\sin^2 x}$$

$$=\frac{5x^4\sin x-x^5\cos x+\sin^2 x+\cos^2 x}{\sin^2 x}$$

$$=\frac{5x^4\sin x-x^5\cos x+1}{\sin^2 x} \qquad [\because \sin^2 x+\cos^2 x=1]$$

Q.35 $\dfrac{x^2\cos\frac{\pi}{4}}{\sin x}$

Ans. Let $\quad y=\dfrac{x^2\cos\frac{\pi}{4}}{\sin x}=\dfrac{\frac{x^2}{\sqrt{2}}}{\sin x} \qquad \left[\because \cos\frac{\pi}{4}=\frac{1}{\sqrt{2}}\right]$

$$\Rightarrow \quad y=\frac{1}{\sqrt{2}}\cdot\frac{x^2}{\sin x}$$

$$\therefore \quad \frac{dy}{dx} = \frac{1}{\sqrt{2}}\left[\frac{\sin x \cdot \frac{d}{dx}(x^2) - x^2 \frac{d}{dx}(\sin x)}{\sin^2 x}\right] \quad \text{[by quotient rule]}$$

$$= \frac{1}{\sqrt{2}}\left[\frac{\sin x \cdot (2x) - x^2 \cdot \cos x}{\sin^2 x}\right]$$

$$= \frac{x}{\sqrt{2}} \cdot \left[\frac{2\sin x - x\cos x}{\sin^2 x}\right]$$

$$= \frac{x}{\sqrt{2}}[2\text{cosec } x - x\cot x \,\text{cosec}\, x] \quad \left[\because \frac{1}{\sin x} = \text{cosec}\, x \text{ and } \frac{\cos x}{\sin x} = \cot x\right]$$

$$= \frac{x}{\sqrt{2}}\text{cosec } x[2 - x\cot x]$$

Q.36 $(ax^2 + \cot x)(p + q\cos x)$

Ans. Let $y = (ax^2 + \cot x)(p + q\cos x)$

$$\therefore \frac{dy}{dx} = (ax^2 + \cot x)\frac{d}{dx}(p + q\cos x) + (p + q\cos x)\frac{d}{dx}(ax^2 + \cot x) \quad \text{[by product rule]}$$

$$= (ax^2 + \cot x)(-q\sin x) + (p + q\cos x)(2ax - \text{cosec}^2 x) \quad \left[\because \frac{d}{dx}\cot x = -\text{cosec}^2 x\right]$$

$$= -q\sin x(ax^2 + \cot x) + (p + q\cos x)(2ax - \text{cosec}^2 x)$$

Q.37 $\dfrac{a + b\sin x}{c + d\cos x}$

Ans. Let $y = \dfrac{a + b\sin x}{c + d\cos x}$

$$\therefore \frac{dy}{dx} = \frac{(c + d\cos x)\frac{d}{dx}(a + b\sin x) - (a + b\sin x)\frac{d}{dx}(c + d\cos x)}{(c + d\cos x)^2} \quad \text{[by quotient rule]}$$

$$= \frac{(c + d\cos x)(b\cos x) - (a + b\sin x)(-d\sin x)}{(c + d\cos x)^2}$$

$$= \frac{bc\cos x + bd\cos^2 x + ad\sin x + bd\sin^2 x}{(c + d\cos x)^2}$$

$$= \frac{bc\cos x + ad\sin x + bd(\cos^2 x + \sin^2 x)}{(c + d\cos x)^2} = \frac{bc\cos x + ad\sin x + bd}{(c + d\cos x)^2}$$

Q.38 $(\sin x + \cos x)^2$

Ans. Let $y = (\sin x + \cos x)^2$

$$\therefore \quad \frac{dy}{dx} = 2(\sin x + \cos x)\frac{d}{dx}(\sin x + \cos x) \quad \text{[by chain rule]}$$

$$= 2(\sin x + \cos x)(\cos x - \sin x)$$

$$= 2(\cos^2 x - \sin^2 x) = 2\cos 2x \quad [\because \cos 2x = \cos^2 x - \sin^2 x]$$

Alternate Method

Let $y = \sin^2 x + \cos^2 x + 2\sin x \cos x$

$\Rightarrow$ $y = 1 + \sin 2x$ [$\because \sin^2\theta + \cos^2\theta = 1$ and $\sin 2\theta = 2\sin\theta\cos\theta$]

$\therefore$ $\frac{dy}{dx} = \frac{d}{dx}(1) + \frac{d}{dx}(\sin 2x)$

$\frac{dy}{dx} = 0 + 2\cos 2x = 2\cos 2x$ [by chain rule]

Q.39 $(2x-7)^2(3x+5)^3$

Ans. Let $y = (2x-7)^2(3x+5)^3$

$\therefore$ $\frac{dy}{dx} = (2x-7)^2\frac{d}{dx}(3x+5)^3 + (3x+5)^3\frac{d}{dx}(2x-7)^2$ [by product rule]

$= (2x-7)^2(3)(3x+5)^2(3) + (3x+5)^3 2(2x-7)(2)$ [by chain rule]

$= 9(2x-7)^2(3x+5)^2 + 4(3x+5)^3(2x-7)$

$= (2x-7)(3x+5)^2[9(2x-7) + 4(3x+5)]$

$= (2x-7)(3x+5)^2(18x - 63 + 12x + 20)$

$= (2x-7)(3x+5)^2(30x-43)$

Alternate Method

Let $y = (2x-7)^3(3x+5)^3$

On taking log both sides, we get

$\log y = \log(2x-7)^2(3x+5)^3$

$= \log(2x-7)^2 + \log(3x+5)^3$ [$\because \log(ab) = \log a + \log b$]

$\Rightarrow$ $\log y = 2\log(2x-7) + 3\log(3x+5)$ [$\because \log a^b = b\log a$]

On differentiating both sides w.r.t x, we get

$\frac{1}{y}\cdot\frac{dy}{dx} = 2\cdot\frac{1}{2x-7}\cdot 2 + 3\cdot\frac{1}{3x+5}\cdot 3$ $\left[\because \frac{d}{dx}[\log_e x] = \frac{1}{x}\right]$

$\Rightarrow$ $\frac{1}{y}\frac{dy}{dx} = \frac{4}{2x-7} + \frac{9}{3x+5}$

$\Rightarrow$ $\frac{dy}{dx} = y\left[\frac{4}{2x-7} + \frac{9}{3x+5}\right]$

$= (2x-7)^2(3x+5)^3\left[\frac{4}{2x-7} + \frac{9}{3x+5}\right]$

$= (2x-7)^2(3x-5)^3\left[\frac{12x + 20 + 18x - 63}{(2x-7)(3x+5)}\right]$

$= (2x-7)(3x-5)^2(30x-43)$

Q.40 $x^2\sin x + \cos 2x$

Ans. Let $y = x^2\sin x + \cos 2x$

$\therefore$ $\frac{dy}{dx} = \frac{d}{dx}(x^2\sin x) + \frac{d}{dx}\cos 2x$

$= x^2\cdot\cos x + \sin x\,(2x) + (-\sin 2x)\cdot 2$ [by product rule and chain rule]

$= x^2\cos x + 2x\sin x - 2\sin 2x$

Q.41 $\sin^3 x \cos^3 x$

Ans. Let $y = \sin^3 x \cos^3 x$

$\therefore \quad \dfrac{dy}{dx} = \sin^3 x \cdot \dfrac{d}{dx}\cos^3 x + \cos^3 x \dfrac{d}{dx}\sin^3 x$ [by product rule]

$= \sin^3 x \cdot 3\cos^2 x(-\sin x) + \cos^3 x \cdot 3\sin^2 x \cos x$ [by chain rule]

$= -3\cos^2 x \sin^4 x + 3\sin^2 x \cos^4 x$

$= 3\sin^2 x \cos^2 x(\cos^2 x - \sin^2 x) = 3\sin^2 x \cos^2 x \cos 2x$

$[\because \cos 2x = \cos^2 x - \sin^2 x]$

$= \dfrac{3}{4}(2\sin x \cos x)^2 \cos 2x = \dfrac{3}{4}\sin^2 2x \cos 2x$ $[\because \sin 2x = 2\sin x \cos x]$

Q.42 $\dfrac{1}{ax^2 + bx + c}$

Ans. Let $y = \dfrac{1}{ax^2 + bx + c} = (ax^2 + bx + c)^{-1}$

$\therefore \quad \dfrac{dy}{dx} = -(ax^2 + bx + c)^{-2}(2ax + b)$ [by chain rule]

$= \dfrac{-(2ax + b)}{(ax^2 + bx + c)^2}$

Long Answer Type Questions

Differentiate each of the functions with respect to x in exercises 43 to 46 using first principle.

Q.43 $\cos(x^2 + 1)$

Concept Insight The first principle of derivative is defined as $f'(x) = \lim_{h \to 0} \dfrac{f(x+h) - f(x)}{h}$.

Ans. Let $f(x) = \cos(x^2 + 1)$ and $f(x+h) = \cos\{(x+h)^2 + 1\}$

$\therefore \quad \dfrac{d}{dx} f(x) = \lim_{h \to 0} \dfrac{f(x+h) - f(x)}{h}$

$= \lim_{h \to 0} \dfrac{\cos\{(x+h)^2 + 1\} - \cos(x^2 + 1)}{h}$

$= \lim_{h \to 0} \dfrac{-2\sin\left\{\dfrac{(x+h)^2 + 1 + x^2 + 1}{2}\right\}\sin\left\{\dfrac{(x+h)^2 + 1 - x^2 - 1}{2}\right\}}{h}$

$\left[\because \cos C - \cos D = -2\sin\dfrac{C+D}{2} \cdot \sin\dfrac{C-D}{2}\right]$

$= \lim_{h \to 0} \dfrac{1}{h}\left[-2\sin\left\{\dfrac{(x+h)^2 + x^2 + 2}{2}\right\}\sin\left\{\dfrac{(x+h)^2 - x^2}{2}\right\}\right]$

$= \lim_{h \to 0} \dfrac{1}{h}\left[-2\sin\left\{\dfrac{(x+h)^2 + x^2 + 2}{2}\right\}\sin\left\{\dfrac{x^2 + h^2 + 2xh - x^2}{2}\right\}\right]$

$$= \lim_{h \to 0} \frac{1}{h}\left[-2\sin\left\{\frac{(x+h)^2+x^2+2}{2}\right\}\sin\left\{\frac{h^2+2hx}{2}\right\}\right]$$

$$= -2\lim_{h \to 0}\sin\left\{\frac{(x+h)^2+x^2+2}{2}\right\}\lim_{h \to 0}\left\{\frac{\sin h\left(\frac{h+2x}{2}\right)}{h\left(\frac{h+2x}{2}\right)}\right\}\times\left(\frac{h+2x}{2}\right)$$

$$= -2\lim_{h \to 0}\sin\left\{\frac{(x+h)^2+x^2+2}{2}\right\}\lim_{h \to 0}\left(\frac{h+2x}{2}\right) \qquad \left[\because \lim_{x \to 0}\frac{\sin x}{x}=1\right]$$

$$= -2x\sin(x^2+1) \qquad [\because \text{as } x \to 0 \Rightarrow kx \to 0]$$

Q.44 $\dfrac{ax+b}{cx+d}$

Ans. Let $$f(x) = \frac{ax+b}{cx+d}$$

Then, $$f(x+h) = \frac{a(x+h)+b}{c(x+h)+d}$$

$\therefore$ $$\frac{d}{dx}f(x) = \lim_{h \to 0}\frac{1}{h}[f(x+h)-f(x)]$$

$$= \lim_{h \to 0}\frac{1}{h}\left[\frac{a(x+h)+b}{c(x+h)+d}-\frac{ax+b}{cx+d}\right]$$

$$= \lim_{h \to 0}\frac{1}{h}\left[\frac{ax+b+ah}{c(x+h)+d}-\frac{ax+b}{cx+d}\right]$$

$$= \lim_{h \to 0}\frac{1}{h}\left[\frac{(ax+ah+b)(cx+d)-(ax+b)\{c(x+h)+d\}}{\{c(x+h)+d\}(cx+d)}\right]$$

$$= \lim_{h \to 0}\frac{1}{h}\left[\frac{(ax+ah+b)(cx+d)-(ax+b)(cx+ch+d)}{\{c(x+h)+d)\}(cx+d)}\right]$$

$$= \lim_{h \to 0}\frac{1}{h}\left[\frac{acx^2+achx+bcx+adx+adh+bd-\{acx^2+achx+adx+bcx+bch+bd\}}{\{c(x+h)+d\}(cx+d)}\right]$$

$$= \lim_{h \to 0}\frac{1}{h}\left[\frac{acx^2+achx+bcx+adx+adh+bd-acx^2-achx-adx-bcx-bch-bd\}}{\{c(x+h)+d\}(cx+d)}\right]$$

$$= \lim_{h \to 0}\frac{1}{h}\left[\frac{adh-bch}{\{c(x+h)+d\}(cx+d)}\right]$$

$$= \lim_{h \to 0}\frac{ad-bc}{\{c(x+h)+d\}(cx+d)} = \frac{ad-bc}{(cx+d)^2}$$

Q.45 $x^{2/3}$

Ans. Let
$$f(x) = x^{2/3}$$
$$f(x+h) = (x+h)^{2/3}$$
Now,
$$\frac{d}{dx} f(x) = \lim_{h \to 0} \frac{f(x+h) - f(x)}{h}$$
$$= \lim_{h \to 0} \frac{1}{h}[(x+h)^{2/3} - x^{2/3}]$$
$$= \lim_{h \to 0} \frac{1}{h}\left[x^{2/3}\left(1+\frac{h}{x}\right)^{2/3} - x^{2/3}\right]$$
$$= \lim_{h \to 0} \frac{1}{h}\left[\left(x^{2/3}\left(1+\frac{h}{x}\cdot\frac{2}{3}+\frac{1}{2}\times\frac{2}{3}\left(\frac{2}{3}-1\right)\frac{h^2}{x^2}+\cdots\right)-1\right)\right]$$
$$\left[\because (1+x)^n = 1 + nx + \frac{n(n-1)}{2!}x^2 + \cdots\right]$$
$$= \lim_{h \to 0} \frac{1}{h}\left[x^{2/3}\left(\frac{2}{3}\cdot\frac{h}{x} - \frac{2}{18}\cdot\frac{h^2}{x^2}+\cdots\right)\right]$$
$$= \lim_{h \to 0} \frac{x^{2/3}}{h}\cdot\frac{2}{3}\frac{h}{x}\left(1-\frac{1}{6}\cdot\frac{h}{x}+\cdots\right)$$
$$= \frac{2}{3}x^{(2/3)-1} = \frac{2}{3}x^{-1/3}$$

Alternate Method

Let
$$f(x) = x^{2/3}$$
Then,
$$f(x+h) = (x+h)^{2/3}$$
$\therefore$
$$\frac{d}{dx} f(x) = \lim_{h \to 0} \frac{f(x+h) - f(x)}{h}$$
$$= \lim_{h \to 0}\left[\frac{(x+h)^{2/3} - x^{2/3}}{h}\right] = \lim_{(x+h)\to x}\left[\frac{(x+h)^{2/3} - x^{2/3}}{(x+h)-x}\right]$$
$$= \frac{2}{3}x^{(2/3)-1} \qquad \left[\because \lim_{x \to a}\frac{x^n - a^n}{x-a} = na^{n-1}\right]$$
$$= \frac{2}{3}x^{-1/3}$$

Q.46 $x \cos x$

Ans. Let
$$f(x) = x\cos x$$
Then,
$$f(x+h) = (x+h)\cos(x+h)$$
$\therefore$
$$\frac{d}{dx} f(x) = \lim_{h \to 0} \frac{f(x+h) - f(x)}{h}$$
$$= \lim_{h \to 0} \frac{1}{h}[(x+h)\cos(x+h) - x\cos x]$$
$$= \lim_{h \to 0} \frac{1}{h}[x\cos(x+h) + h\cos(x+h) - x\cos x]$$
$$= \lim_{h \to 0} \frac{1}{h}[x\{\cos(x+h) - \cos x\} + h\cos(x+h)]$$

$$= \lim_{h \to 0} \frac{1}{h}\left[x\left\{- 2\sin\left(\frac{2x+h}{2}\right)\sin\frac{h}{2}\right\} + h\cos(x+h)\right]$$

$$\left[\cos a - \cos b = -2\sin\left(\frac{a+b}{2}\right)\sin\left(\frac{a-b}{2}\right)\right]$$

$$= \lim_{h \to 0}\left[-2x\sin\left(x+\frac{h}{2}\right)\frac{\sin\frac{h}{2}}{h} + \cos(x+h)\right]$$

$$= -2\lim_{h \to 0} x\sin\left(x+\frac{h}{2}\right)\lim_{h \to 0}\frac{\sin\frac{h}{2}}{\frac{h}{2}}\cdot\frac{1}{2} + \lim_{h \to 0}\cos(x+h)$$

$$= -2\cdot x\sin x\cdot(1)\cdot\frac{1}{2} + \cos x$$

$$\left[\because \lim_{x \to a}[f(x)+g(x)] = \lim_{x \to a} f(x) + \lim_{x \to a} g(x) \text{ and } \lim_{x \to a} g(x) = \lim_{x \to a} f(x)\cdot\lim_{x \to a} g(x)\right]$$

$$= \cos x - x\sin x$$

Evaluate each of the following limits in exercises 47 to 53.

Q.47 $\lim_{y \to 0}\frac{(x+y)\sec(x+y) - x\sec x}{y}$

Ans. Given, $\lim_{y \to 0}\frac{(x+y)\sec(x+y) - x\sec x}{y}$

$$= \lim_{y \to 0}\frac{\frac{x+y}{\cos(x+y)} - \frac{x}{\cos x}}{y} \qquad \left[\because \sec x = \frac{1}{\cos x}\right]$$

$$= \lim_{y \to 0}\frac{(x+y)\cos x - x\cos(x+y)}{y\cos x\cos(x+y)}$$

$$= \lim_{y \to 0}\left[\frac{x\cos x + y\cos x - x\cos(x+y)}{y\cos x\cos(x+y)}\right]$$

$$= \lim_{y \to 0}\frac{x\{\cos x - \cos(x+y)\} + y\cos x}{y\cos x\cos(x+y)}$$

$$= \lim_{y \to 0}\frac{x\left[-2\sin\left(x+\frac{y}{2}\right)\sin\left(\frac{-y}{2}\right)\right] + y\cos x}{y\cos x\cos(x+y)}$$

$$\left[\because \cos C - \cos D = -2\sin\frac{C+D}{2}\cdot\sin\frac{C-D}{2}\right]$$

$$= \lim_{y \to 0}\left[\frac{x\left\{2\sin\left(x+\frac{y}{2}\right)\sin\frac{y}{2}\right\} + y\cos x}{y\cos x\cos(x+y)}\right] \qquad [\because \sin(-x) = -\sin x]$$

$$= \lim_{y \to 0} \frac{2x \sin\left(x + \frac{y}{2}\right)}{\cos x \cos(x+y)} \cdot \lim_{y \to 0} \frac{\sin \frac{y}{2}}{\frac{y}{2}} \cdot \frac{1}{2} + \lim_{y \to 0} \sec(x+y)$$

$$= \lim_{y \to 0} \frac{2x \sin\left(x + \frac{y}{2}\right)}{\cos x \cos(x+y)} \cdot \frac{1}{2} + \lim_{y \to 0} \sec(x+y)$$

$$\left[\because \lim_{x \to 0} \frac{\sin x}{x} = 1 \text{ and as } x \to 0 \Rightarrow kx \to 0\right]$$

$$= \frac{2x \sin x}{\cos x \cos x} \cdot \frac{1}{2} + \sec x$$

$$= x \tan x \sec x + \sec x$$

$$= \sec x\,(x \tan x + 1)$$

Q.48 $\lim_{x \to 0} \dfrac{\sin(\alpha+\beta)x + \sin(\alpha-\beta)x + \sin 2\alpha x}{\cos 2\beta x - \cos 2\alpha x} \cdot x$

Ans. Given, $\lim_{x \to 0} \dfrac{[\sin(\alpha+\beta)x + \sin(\alpha-\beta)x + \sin 2\alpha x]}{\cos 2\beta x - \cos 2\alpha x} \cdot x$

$$= \lim_{x \to 0} \frac{[2\sin \alpha x \cdot \cos \beta x + \sin 2\alpha x]}{\cos 2\beta x - \cos 2\alpha x} \cdot x \qquad \left[\because \sin C + \sin D = 2\sin \frac{C+D}{2} \cos \frac{C-D}{2}\right]$$

$$= \lim_{x \to 0} \frac{[2\sin \alpha x \cos \beta x + \sin 2\alpha x]x}{2\sin(\alpha+\beta)x \sin(\alpha-\beta)x} \qquad \left[\because \cos C - \cos D = 2\sin \frac{C+D}{2} \cdot \sin \frac{D-C}{2}\right]$$

$$= \lim_{x \to 0} \frac{[2\sin \alpha x \cos \beta x + 2\sin \alpha x \cos \alpha x]x}{2\sin(\alpha+\beta)x \sin(\alpha-\beta)x} \qquad [\sin 2x = 2\sin x \cdot \cos x]$$

$$= \lim_{x \to 0} \frac{2\sin \alpha x[\cos \beta x + \cos \alpha x]x}{2\sin(\alpha+\beta)x \sin(\alpha-\beta)x}$$

$$= \lim_{x \to 0} \frac{\sin \alpha x \left[2\cos\left(\frac{\alpha+\beta}{2}\right)x \cos\left(\frac{\alpha-\beta}{2}\right)x\right]x}{2\sin\left(\frac{\alpha+\beta}{2}\right)x \cos\left(\frac{\alpha+\beta}{2}\right)x \cdot 2\sin\left(\frac{\alpha-\beta}{2}\right)x \cos\left(\frac{\alpha-\beta}{2}\right)x}$$

$$\left[\because \cos C + \cos D = 2\cos \frac{C+D}{2} \cos \frac{C-D}{2} \text{ and } \sin 2\theta = 2\sin\theta\cos\theta\right]$$

$$= \lim_{x \to 0} \frac{\sin \alpha x \cdot x}{2\sin\left(\frac{\alpha+\beta}{2}\right)x \sin\left(\frac{\alpha-\beta}{2}\right)x}$$

$$= \frac{1}{2} \lim_{x \to 0} \frac{\frac{\sin \alpha x}{\alpha x} \cdot x \cdot (\alpha x)}{\frac{\sin\left(\frac{\alpha+\beta}{2}\right)x}{\left(\frac{\alpha+\beta}{2}\right)x} \cdot \frac{\sin\left(\frac{\alpha-\beta}{2}\right)x}{\left(\frac{\alpha-\beta}{2}\right)x} \cdot \left(\frac{\alpha+\beta}{2}\right)x \cdot \left(\frac{\alpha-\beta}{2}\right)x}$$

$$= \frac{\frac{1}{2}\lim_{x \to 0} \frac{\sin \alpha x}{\alpha x} \cdot \alpha x^2}{\lim_{x \to 0} \frac{\sin\left(\frac{\alpha+\beta}{2}\right)x}{\left(\frac{\alpha+\beta}{2}\right)x} \lim_{x \to 0} \frac{\sin\left(\frac{\alpha-\beta}{2}\right)x}{\left(\frac{\alpha-\beta}{2}\right)x} \cdot \left(\frac{\alpha^2-\beta^2}{4}\right)x^2}$$

$$= \frac{1}{2} \cdot \frac{\alpha \cdot 4}{\alpha^2 - \beta^2} \left[\frac{\lim_{x \to 0} \frac{\sin \alpha x}{\alpha x}}{\lim_{x \to 0} \frac{\sin\left(\frac{\alpha+\beta}{2}\right)x}{\left(\frac{\alpha+\beta}{2}\right)x} \lim_{x \to 0} \frac{\sin\left(\frac{\alpha-\beta}{2}\right)x}{\left(\frac{\alpha-\beta}{2}\right)x}} \right] = \frac{1}{2} \cdot \frac{4\alpha}{\alpha^2 - \beta^2} = \frac{2\alpha}{\alpha^2 - \beta^2}$$

$$\left[\because \lim_{x \to 0} \frac{\sin x}{x} = 1 \text{ and as } x \to 0 \Rightarrow kx \to 0\right]$$

Q.49 $\lim_{x \to \pi/4} \frac{\tan^3 x - \tan x}{\cos\left(x + \frac{\pi}{4}\right)}$

Ans. Given, $\lim_{x \to \pi/4} \frac{\tan^3 x - \tan x}{\cos\left(x + \frac{\pi}{4}\right)}$ $\left[\frac{0}{0} \text{ form}\right]$

$$= \lim_{x \to \pi/4} \frac{\tan x\,(\tan^2 x - 1)}{\cos\left(x + \frac{\pi}{4}\right)} = -\lim_{x \to \pi/4} \tan x \cdot \lim_{x \to \pi/4} \left(\frac{1 - \tan^2 x}{\cos\left(x + \frac{\pi}{4}\right)}\right)$$

$$= -1 \times \lim_{x \to \pi/4} \frac{(1 + \tan x)(1 - \tan x)}{\cos\left(x + \frac{\pi}{4}\right)} \qquad [\because a^2 - b^2 = (a+b)(a-b)]$$

$$= -\lim_{x \to \pi/4} (1 + \tan x) \lim_{x \to \pi/4} \left[\frac{\cos x - \sin x}{\cos x \cdot \cos\left(x + \frac{\pi}{4}\right)}\right]$$

$$= -(1+1) \times \lim_{x \to \pi/4} \frac{\sqrt{2}\left[\frac{1}{\sqrt{2}} \cdot \cos x - \frac{1}{\sqrt{2}} \cdot \sin x\right]}{\cos x \cdot \cos\left(x + \frac{\pi}{4}\right)} = -2\sqrt{2} \lim_{x \to \pi/4} \left[\frac{\cos\frac{\pi}{4} \cdot \cos x - \sin\frac{\pi}{4} \cdot \sin x}{\cos x \cdot \cos\left(x + \frac{\pi}{4}\right)}\right]$$

$$= -2\sqrt{2} \lim_{x \to \pi/4} \frac{\cos\left(x + \frac{\pi}{4}\right)}{\cos x \cdot \cos\left(x + \frac{\pi}{4}\right)} \qquad [\because \cos A \cdot \cos B - \sin A \sin B = \cos(A + B)]$$

$$= -2\sqrt{2} \times \frac{1}{\frac{1}{\sqrt{2}}} = -2\sqrt{2} \times \sqrt{2} = -4$$

Q.50 $\lim_{x \to \pi} \dfrac{1 - \sin\frac{x}{2}}{\cos\frac{x}{2}\left(\cos\frac{x}{4} - \sin\frac{x}{4}\right)}$

Ans. Given, $\lim_{x \to \pi} \dfrac{1 - \sin\frac{x}{2}}{\cos\frac{x}{2}\left(\cos\frac{x}{4} - \sin\frac{x}{4}\right)}$

$$= \lim_{x\to\pi} \frac{\cos^2\frac{x}{4} + \sin^2\frac{x}{4} - 2\cdot\sin\frac{x}{4}\cdot\cos\frac{x}{4}}{\cos\frac{x}{2}.(\cos\frac{x}{4} - \sin\frac{x}{4})} \quad [\because \sin^2\theta + \cos^2\theta = 1, \sin 2\theta = 2\sin\theta\cos\theta]$$

$$= \lim_{x\to\pi} \frac{\left(\cos\frac{x}{4} - \sin\frac{x}{4}\right)^2}{\left(\cos^2\frac{x}{4} - \sin^2\frac{x}{4}\right)\left(\cos\frac{x}{4} - \sin\frac{x}{4}\right)} \quad [\because \cos 2\theta = \cos^2\theta - \sin^2\theta]$$

$$= \lim_{x\to\pi} \frac{\left(\cos\frac{x}{4} - \sin\frac{x}{4}\right)}{\left(\cos\frac{x}{4} + \sin\frac{x}{4}\right)\left(\cos\frac{x}{4} - \sin\frac{x}{4}\right)} \quad [\because a^2 - b^2 = (a+b)(a-b)]$$

$$= \lim_{x\to\pi} \frac{1}{\cos\frac{x}{4} + \sin\frac{x}{4}} = \frac{1}{\frac{1}{\sqrt{2}} + \frac{1}{\sqrt{2}}} = \frac{\sqrt{2}}{2} = \frac{1}{\sqrt{2}}$$

Q.51 Show that $\lim_{x \to 4} \dfrac{|x-4|}{x-4}$ does not exist,

Ans. Given, $\lim_{x \to 4} \dfrac{|x-4|}{x-4}$

Now, $\text{LHL} = \lim_{x\to 4^-} \dfrac{-(x-4)}{x-4}$ $\quad [\because |x-4| = -(x-4), x < 4]$

$= -1$

$\text{RHL} = \lim_{x\to 4^+} \dfrac{(x-4)}{x-4} = 1$ $\quad [\because |x-4| = (x-4), x > 4]$

$\therefore$ LHL $\neq$ RHL

So at $x = 4$ limit does not exist.

Mistake Alert ! *In an absolute function, sometimes it may be possible that* LHL $\neq$ RHL *Please be careful about it.*

Q.52 If $f(x)=\begin{cases}\dfrac{k\cos x}{\pi-2x}, & \text{when } x\neq\dfrac{\pi}{2}\\ 3, & \text{when } x=\dfrac{\pi}{2}\end{cases}$ and $\lim\limits_{x\to\pi/2} f(x)=f\left(\dfrac{\pi}{2}\right)$, then find the value of k.

Ans. Given, $f(x)=\begin{cases}\dfrac{k\cos x}{\pi-2x}, & x\neq\dfrac{\pi}{2}\\ 3, & x=\dfrac{\pi}{2}\end{cases}$

$\therefore$ $\quad$ LHL $=\lim\limits_{x\to\frac{\pi^-}{2}}\dfrac{k\cos x}{\pi-2x}=\lim\limits_{h\to0}\dfrac{k\cos\left(\dfrac{\pi}{2}-h\right)}{\pi-2\left(\dfrac{\pi}{2}-h\right)}$ $\quad\left[\text{Put } x=\dfrac{\pi}{2}-h, \text{ if } x\to\dfrac{\pi}{2}\Rightarrow h\to0\right]$

$$=\lim_{h\to0}\frac{k\sin h}{\pi-\pi+2h}=\lim_{h\to0}\frac{k\sin h}{2h}$$

$$=\frac{k}{2}\lim_{h\to0}\frac{\sin h}{h}=\frac{k}{2}\cdot1=\frac{k}{2}\qquad\left[\because \lim_{h\to0}\frac{\sin x}{x}=1\right]$$

RHL $=\lim\limits_{x\to\frac{\pi^+}{2}}\dfrac{k\cos x}{\pi-2x}=\lim\limits_{h\to0}\dfrac{k\cos\left(\dfrac{\pi}{2}+h\right)}{\pi-2\left(\dfrac{\pi}{2}+h\right)}$ $\quad\left[\text{Put } x=\dfrac{\pi}{2}+h, \text{ if } x\to\dfrac{\pi}{2}\Rightarrow h\to0\right]$

$$=\lim_{h\to0}\frac{-k\sin h}{\pi-\pi-2h}=\lim_{h\to0}\frac{k\sin h}{2h}=\frac{k}{2}\lim_{h\to0}\frac{\sin h}{h}=\frac{k}{2}\qquad[\because \cos(90^\circ+\theta)=-\sin\theta]$$

It is given that, $\lim\limits_{x\to\pi/2} f(x)=f\left(\dfrac{\pi}{2}\right)\Rightarrow\dfrac{k}{2}=3$

$\therefore$ $\quad k=6$

Q.53 If $f(x)=\begin{cases}x+2, & x\le-1\\ cx^2, & x>-1\end{cases}$, then find c when $\lim\limits_{x\to-1} f(x)$ exists.

Thinking Process First, find the limit LHL and RHL and put them equal to each other because if $\lim\limits_{x\to0} f(x)$ exist, then LHL=RHL.

Ans. Given, $\quad f(x)=\begin{cases}x+2, & x\le-1\\ cx^2, & x>-1\end{cases}$

LHL $=\lim\limits_{x\to-1^-} f(x)=\lim\limits_{x\to-1^-}(x+2)$

$=\lim\limits_{h\to0}(-1-h+2)=\lim\limits_{h\to0}(1-h)=1$ $\quad$ [put $x=-1-h$, if $x\to-1\Rightarrow h\to0$]

RHL $=\lim\limits_{x\to-1^+} f(x)=\lim\limits_{x\to-1^+} cx^2=\lim\limits_{h\to0} c(-1+h)^2=c$

Since, $\lim\limits_{x\to-1} f(x)$ exist.

So, $\quad$ LHL = RHL $\quad$ [put $x=-1+h$, if $x\to-1\Rightarrow h\to0$]

$\therefore$ $\quad c=1$

Objective Type Questions

Choose the correct answers from the given four options in each exercise 54 to 76.

Q.54 $\lim\limits_{x \to \pi} \dfrac{\sin x}{x - \pi}$ is equal to

(a) 1 (b) 2 (c) −1 (d) −2

Ans. ***(c)*** Given, $\lim\limits_{x \to \pi} \dfrac{\sin x}{x - \pi} = \lim\limits_{x \to \pi} \dfrac{\sin(\pi - x)}{-(\pi - x)}$ $[\because \sin\theta = \sin(\pi - \theta)]$

$$= -\lim_{x \to \pi} \frac{\sin(\pi - x)}{(\pi - x)} = -1 \quad \left[\because \lim_{x \to 0} \frac{\sin x}{x} = 1 \text{ and as } x \to 0 \Rightarrow \pi - x = 0\right]$$

Q.55 $\lim\limits_{x \to 0} \dfrac{x^2 \cos x}{1 - \cos x}$ is equal to

(a) 2 (b) $\dfrac{3}{2}$ (c) $\dfrac{-3}{2}$ (d) 1

Ans. ***(a)*** Given, $\lim\limits_{x \to 0} \dfrac{x^2 \cos x}{1 - \cos x} = \lim\limits_{x \to 0} \dfrac{x^2 \cos x}{2\sin^2 \dfrac{x}{2}}$ $\left[\because 1 - \cos x = 2\sin^2 \dfrac{x}{2}\right]$

$$= 2\lim_{x \to 0} \frac{\left(\dfrac{x}{2}\right)^2}{\sin^2 \dfrac{x}{2}} \cdot \lim_{x \to 0} \cos x = 2 \cdot 1 = 2$$

Q.56 $\lim\limits_{x \to 0} \dfrac{(1 + x)^n - 1}{x}$ is equal to

(a) n (b) 1

(c) $-n$ (d) 0

Ans. ***(a)*** Given, $\lim\limits_{x \to 0} \dfrac{(1 + x)^n - 1}{x} = \lim\limits_{x \to 0} \dfrac{(1 + x)^n - 1}{(1 + x) - 1}$

$$= \lim_{x \to 0} \frac{(1 + x)^n - 1^n}{(1 + x) - 1} = \lim_{(1 + x) \to 1} \frac{(1 + x)^n - 1^n}{(1 + x) - 1}$$

$$= n \cdot (1)^{n-1} = n \quad \left[\because \lim_{x \to a} \frac{x^n - a^n}{x - a} = na^{n-1}\right]$$

$[\because \text{as } x \to \Rightarrow 1 + x \to 1]$

Q.57 $\lim\limits_{x \to 1} \dfrac{x^m - 1}{x^n - 1}$ is equal to

(a) 1 (b) $\dfrac{m}{n}$

(c) $-\dfrac{m}{n}$ (d) $\dfrac{m^2}{n^2}$

Ans. ***(b)*** Given, $\lim\limits_{x \to 1} \dfrac{x^m - 1}{x^n - 1} = \lim\limits_{x \to 1} \dfrac{\dfrac{x^m - 1}{x - 1}}{\dfrac{x^n - 1}{x - 1}} = \dfrac{\lim\limits_{x \to 1} \dfrac{x^m - 1^m}{x - 1}}{\lim\limits_{x \to 1} \dfrac{x^n - 1^n}{x - 1}}$

$$= \frac{m(1)^{m-1}}{n(1)^{n-1}} = \frac{m}{n} \qquad \left[\because \lim_{x \to a} \frac{x^n - a^n}{x - a} = na^{n-1}\right]$$

Q.58 $\lim\limits_{\theta \to 0} \dfrac{1 - \cos 4\theta}{1 - \cos 6\theta}$ is equal to

(a) $\dfrac{4}{9}$ (b) $\dfrac{1}{2}$ (c) $\dfrac{-1}{2}$ (d) -1

Ans. ***(a)*** Given, $\lim\limits_{\theta \to 0} \dfrac{1 - \cos 4\theta}{1 - \cos 6\theta} = \lim\limits_{\theta \to 0} \dfrac{2\sin^2 2\theta}{2\sin^2 3\theta}$ $[\because 1 - \cos 2\theta = 2\sin^2 \theta]$

$$= \frac{\lim\limits_{\theta \to 0} \dfrac{\sin^2 2\theta}{(2\theta)^2} \cdot (2\theta)^2}{\lim\limits_{\theta \to 0} \dfrac{\sin^2 3\theta}{(3\theta)^2} \cdot (3\theta)^2} = \frac{4}{9} \cdot \frac{\lim\limits_{\theta \to 0} \left(\dfrac{\sin 2\theta}{2\theta}\right)^2}{\lim\limits_{\theta \to 0} \left(\dfrac{\sin 3\theta}{3\theta}\right)^2}$$

$$= \frac{4}{9} \qquad \left[\because \lim_{x \to 0} \frac{\sin x}{x} = 1 \text{ and as } x \to 0 \Rightarrow kx \to 0\right]$$

Q.59 $\lim\limits_{x \to 0} \dfrac{\operatorname{cosec} x - \cot x}{x}$ is equal to

(a) $\dfrac{-1}{2}$ (b) 1 (c) $\dfrac{1}{2}$ (d) 1

Ans. ***(c)*** Given, $\lim\limits_{x \to 0} \dfrac{\operatorname{cosec} x - \cot x}{x}$

$$= \lim_{x \to 0} \frac{\dfrac{1}{\sin x} - \dfrac{\cos x}{\sin x}}{x} = \lim_{x \to 0} \frac{1 - \cos x}{x \cdot \sin x}$$

$$= \lim_{x \to 0} \frac{2\sin^2 \dfrac{x}{2}}{x \cdot 2\sin \dfrac{x}{2} \cos \dfrac{x}{2}} = \lim_{x \to 0} \frac{\tan \dfrac{x}{2}}{x} = \lim_{x \to 0} \frac{\tan \dfrac{x}{2}}{\dfrac{x}{2}} \cdot \frac{1}{2} = \frac{1}{2} \qquad \left[\because \lim_{\theta \to 0} \frac{\tan \theta}{\theta} = 1\right]$$

Q.60 $\lim\limits_{x \to 0} \dfrac{\sin x}{\sqrt{x+1} - \sqrt{1-x}}$ is equal to

(a) 2 (b) 0 (c) 1 (d) -1

Thinking Process When we put the limit, then we get an indeterminate form. So, firstly rationalize the function, simplify it and then put the limit.

Ans. ***(c)*** Given, $\lim\limits_{x \to 0} \dfrac{\sin x}{\sqrt{x + 1} - \sqrt{1 - x}}$

$$= \lim_{x \to 0} \frac{\sin x}{\sqrt{x + 1} - \sqrt{1 - x}} \cdot \frac{\sqrt{x + 1} + \sqrt{1 - x}}{\sqrt{x + 1} + \sqrt{1 - x}}$$

$$= \lim_{x \to 0} \frac{\sin x(\sqrt{x+1} + \sqrt{1-x})}{(x+1)-(1-x)} = \lim_{x \to 0} \frac{\sin x(\sqrt{x+1} + \sqrt{1-x})}{x+1-1+x}$$

$$= \frac{1}{2} \lim_{x \to 0} \frac{\sin x}{x} \lim_{x \to 0} (\sqrt{x+1} + \sqrt{1-x}) = \frac{1}{2} \cdot 1 \cdot 2 = 1 \qquad \left[\because \lim_{x \to 0} \frac{\sin x}{x} = 1\right]$$

Q.61 $\lim_{x \to \pi/4} \frac{\sec^2 x - 2}{\tan x - 1}$ is

(a) 3 (b) 1 (c) 0 (d) 2

Ans. (d) Given, $\lim_{x \to \pi/4} \frac{\sec^2 x - 2}{\tan x - 1}$

$$= \lim_{x \to \pi/4} \frac{1 + \tan^2 x - 2}{\tan x - 1} = \lim_{x \to \pi/4} \frac{\tan^2 x - 1}{\tan x - 1} \qquad [\because \sec^2 x = 1 + \tan^2 x]$$

$$= \lim_{x \to \pi/4} \frac{(\tan x + 1)(\tan x - 1)}{(\tan x - 1)} = \lim_{x \to \pi/4} (\tan x + 1)$$

$$= \tan \frac{\pi}{4} + 1 = 2$$

Q.62 $\lim_{x \to 1} \frac{(\sqrt{x} - 1)(2x - 3)}{2x^2 + x - 3}$ is equal to

(a) $\frac{1}{10}$ (b) $\frac{-1}{10}$ (c) 1 (d) None of these

Ans. (b) Given, $\lim_{x \to 1} \frac{(\sqrt{x} - 1)(2x - 3)}{2x^2 + x - 3} = \lim_{x \to 1} \frac{(\sqrt{x} - 1)(2x - 3)}{(2x + 3)(x - 1)}$

$$= \lim_{x \to 1} \frac{(\sqrt{x} - 1)(2x - 3)}{(2x + 3)(\sqrt{x} - 1)(\sqrt{x} + 1)}$$

$$= \lim_{x \to 1} \frac{2x - 3}{(2x + 3)(\sqrt{x} + 1)}$$

$$= \frac{\lim_{x \to 1} (2x - 3)}{\lim_{x \to 1} (2x + 3)(\sqrt{x} + 1)} = \frac{-1}{5 \times 2} = \frac{-1}{10}$$

Q.63 If $f(x) = \begin{cases} \frac{\sin[x]}{[x]}, & [x] \neq 0 \\ 0, & [x] = 0 \end{cases}$, where $[\cdot]$ denotes the greatest integer function, then $\lim_{x \to 0} f(x)$ is equal to

(a) 1 (b) 0 (c) -1 (d) Does not exist

Ans. (d) Given, $f(x) = \begin{cases} \frac{\sin[x]}{[x]}, & [x] \neq 0 \\ 0, & [x] = 0 \end{cases} = \begin{bmatrix} \frac{\sin[x]}{[x]}, x \in R - [0, 1) \\ 0, 0 \leq x < 1 \end{bmatrix}$

$\therefore$ LHL $= \lim_{x \to 0^-} f(x)$

$$= \lim_{h \to 0} f(0-h) = \lim_{h \to 0} \frac{\sin[0-h]}{[0-h]} = \lim_{h \to 0} \frac{\sin[-h]}{[-h]} = \lim_{h \to 0} \frac{\sin(-1)}{-1} = \sin 1$$

$$\text{RHL} = \lim_{x \to 0^+} f(x) = \lim_{h \to 0} f(0+h) = 0 \qquad [\because f(x) = 0, 0 \le x < 1]$$

$\because$ LHL $\neq$ RHL

So, limit does not exist.

Q.64 $\lim_{x \to 0} \frac{|\sin x|}{x}$ is equal to

(a) 1 (b) $= -1$
(c) Does not exist (d) None of these

Ans. ***(c)*** Given, limit $= \lim_{x \to 0} \frac{|\sin x|}{x}$

$$\because \quad |\sin x| = \begin{cases} \sin x, & x \ge 0 \\ -\sin x, & x < 0 \end{cases}$$

$$\therefore \quad \text{LHL} = \lim_{x \to 0^-} \left(\frac{-\sin x}{x}\right) = -\lim_{x \to 0^-} \frac{\sin x}{x} = -1$$

$$\text{RHL} = \lim_{x \to 0^+} \frac{\sin x}{x} = 1$$

$\because$ LHL $\neq$ RHL

So, limit does not exist.

Q.65 If $f(x) = \begin{cases} x^2 - 1, & 0 < x < 2 \\ 2x + 3, & 2 \le x < 3 \end{cases}$, then the quadratic equation whose roots are $\lim_{x \to 2^-} f(x)$ and $\lim_{x \to 2^+} f(x)$ is

(a) $x^2 - 6x + 9 = 0$ (b) $x^2 - 7x + 8 = 0$
(c) $x^2 - 14x + 49 = 0$ (d) $x^2 - 10x + 21 = 0$

Ans. (d) Given, $f(x) = \begin{cases} x^2 - 1, & 0 < x < 2 \\ 2x + 3, & 2 \le x < 3 \end{cases}$

$$\therefore \quad \lim_{x \to 2^-} f(x) = \lim_{x \to 2^-} (x^2 - 1)$$

$$= \lim_{h \to 0} [(2-h)^2 - 1] = \lim_{h \to 0} (4 + h^2 - 4h - 1)$$

[Put $x = 2 - h$, if $x \to 2 \Rightarrow h \to 0$]

$$= \lim_{h \to 0} (h^2 - 4h + 3) = 3$$

and
$$\lim_{x \to 2^+} f(x) = \lim_{x \to 2^+} (2x + 3)$$

$$= \lim_{h \to 0} [2(2+h) + 3] \qquad [\text{Put } x = 2 + h, \text{ if } y \to 2 \Rightarrow h \to 0]$$

$$= \lim_{h \to 0} (4 + 2h + 3) = 7$$

So, the quadratic equation whose roots are 3 and 7 is $x^2 - (3+7)x + 3 \times 7 = 0$ *i.e.*, $x^2 - 10x + 21 = 0$.

Q.66 $\lim_{x \to 0} \dfrac{\tan 2x - x}{3x - \sin x}$ is equal to

(a) 2 (b) $\dfrac{1}{2}$ (c) $\dfrac{-1}{2}$ (d) $\dfrac{1}{4}$

Ans. (b) Given, $\lim_{x \to 0} \dfrac{\tan 2x - x}{3x - \sin x} = \lim_{x \to 0} \dfrac{x\left[\dfrac{\tan 2x}{x} - 1\right]}{x\left[3 - \dfrac{\sin x}{x}\right]}$

$$= \frac{\lim_{x \to 0}\left(2 \times \dfrac{\tan 2x}{2x}\right) - 1}{3 - \lim_{x \to 0} \dfrac{\sin x}{x}} = \frac{2-1}{3-1} = \frac{1}{2}$$

Q.67 If $f(x) = x - [x]$, $\in R$, then $f'\left(\dfrac{1}{2}\right)$ is equal to

(a) $\dfrac{3}{2}$ (b) 1 (c) 0 (d) -1

Ans. (b) Given, $f(x) = x - [x]$

Now, first we have to check the differentiability of $f(x)$ at $x = \dfrac{1}{2}$.

$$\therefore \quad Lf'\left(\frac{1}{2}\right) = \text{LHD} = \lim_{h \to 0} \frac{f\left(\dfrac{1}{2} - h\right) - f\left(\dfrac{1}{2}\right)}{-h}$$

$$= \lim_{h \to 0} \frac{\left(\dfrac{1}{2} - h\right) - \left[\dfrac{1}{2} - h\right] - \dfrac{1}{2} + \left[\dfrac{1}{2}\right]}{-h} = \lim_{h \to 0} \frac{\dfrac{1}{2} - h - 0 - \dfrac{1}{2} + 0}{-h} = 1$$

and
$$Rf'\left(\frac{1}{2}\right) = \text{RHD} = \lim_{h \to 0} \frac{f\left(\dfrac{1}{2} + h\right) - f\left(\dfrac{1}{2}\right)}{h}$$

$$= \lim_{h \to 0} \frac{\left(\dfrac{1}{2} + h\right) - \left[\dfrac{1}{2} + h\right] - \dfrac{1}{2} + \left[\dfrac{1}{2}\right]}{h} = \lim_{h \to 0} \frac{\dfrac{1}{2} + h - 0 - \dfrac{1}{2} + 0}{h} = 1$$

$$\because \quad \text{LHL} = \text{RHD} \Rightarrow f'\left(\frac{1}{2}\right) = 1$$

Q.68 If $y = \sqrt{x} + \dfrac{1}{\sqrt{x}}$, then $\dfrac{dy}{dx}$ at $x = 1$ is equal to

(a) 1 (b) $\dfrac{1}{2}$ (c) $\dfrac{1}{\sqrt{2}}$ (d) 0

Ans. (d) Given, $y = \sqrt{x} + \dfrac{1}{\sqrt{x}}$

Now, $\dfrac{dy}{dx} = \dfrac{1}{2\sqrt{x}} - \dfrac{1}{2x^{3/2}}$

$$\therefore \quad \left(\frac{dy}{dx}\right)_{x=1} = \frac{1}{2} - \frac{1}{2} = 0$$

Q.69 If $f(x) = \dfrac{x-4}{2\sqrt{x}}$, then $f'(1)$ is equal to

(a) $\dfrac{5}{4}$ (b) $\dfrac{4}{5}$ (c) 1 (d) 0

Ans. *(a)* Given, $f(x) = \dfrac{x-4}{2\sqrt{x}}$

Now, $f'(x) = \dfrac{2\sqrt{x} - (x-4)\cdot 2\cdot \dfrac{1}{2\sqrt{x}}}{4x}$ [by quotient rule]

$= \dfrac{2x-(x-4)}{4x^{3/2}} = \dfrac{2x - x + 4}{4x^{3/2}}$

$= \dfrac{x+4}{4x^{3/2}}$

$\therefore$ $f'(1) = \dfrac{1+4}{4\times(1)^{3/2}} = \dfrac{5}{4}$

Q.70 If $y = \dfrac{1+\dfrac{1}{x^2}}{1-\dfrac{1}{x^2}}$, then $\dfrac{dy}{dx}$ is equal to

(a) $\dfrac{-4x}{(x^2-1)^2}$ (b) $\dfrac{-4x}{x^2-1}$ (c) $\dfrac{1-x^2}{4x}$ (d) $\dfrac{4x}{x^2-1}$

Ans. *(a)* Given, $y = \dfrac{1+\dfrac{1}{x^2}}{1-\dfrac{1}{x^2}} \Rightarrow y = \dfrac{x^2+1}{x^2-1}$

$\therefore$ $\dfrac{dy}{dx} = \dfrac{(x^2-1)\,2x - (x^2+1)(2x)}{(x^2-1)^2}$ [by quotient rule]

$\dfrac{dy}{dx} = \dfrac{2x(x^2-1-x^2-1)}{(x^2-1)^2}$

$= \dfrac{2x\,(-2)}{(x^2-1)^2} = \dfrac{-4x}{(x^2-1)^2}$

Q.71 If $y = \dfrac{\sin x + \cos x}{\sin x - \cos x}$, then $\dfrac{dy}{dx}$ at $x = 0$ is equal to

(a) -2 (b) 0 (c) $\dfrac{1}{2}$ (d) Does not exist

Ans. *(a)* Given, $y = \dfrac{\sin x + \cos x}{\sin x - \cos x}$

$\therefore$ $\dfrac{dy}{dx} = \dfrac{(\sin x - \cos x)(\cos x - \sin x) - (\sin x + \cos x)(\cos x + \sin x)}{(\sin x - \cos x)^2}$ [by quotient rule]

$= \dfrac{-(\sin x - \cos x)^2 - (\sin x + \cos x)^2}{(\sin x - \cos x)^2}$

$$= \frac{-[(\sin x - \cos x)^2 + (\sin x + \cos x)^2]}{(\sin x - \cos x)^2}$$

$$= \frac{-[\sin^2 x + \cos^2 x - 2\sin x \cos x + \sin^2 x + \cos^2 x + 2\sin x \cos x]}{(\sin x - \cos x)^2}$$

$$= \frac{-2}{(\sin x - \cos x)^2} \qquad [\because \sin^2 x + \cos^2 x = 1]$$

$$\therefore \left(\frac{dy}{dx}\right)_{x=0} = -2$$

Alternate Method

Let $y = \frac{\sin x + \cos x}{\sin x - \cos x}$

On dividing numerator and denominator by $\cos x$, we get

$$y = \frac{\frac{\sin x}{\cos x} + \frac{\cos x}{\cos x}}{\frac{\sin x}{\cos x} - \frac{\cos x}{\cos x}}$$

$$\Rightarrow \quad y = \frac{\tan x + 1}{\tan x - 1}$$

$$y = -\left[\frac{\tan\frac{\pi}{4} + \tan x}{1 - \tan\frac{\pi}{4} \cdot \tan x}\right]$$

$$\Rightarrow \quad y = -\tan\left(\frac{\pi}{4} + x\right)$$

On differentiating w.r.t 'x', we get

$$\frac{dy}{dx} = -\sec^2\left(\frac{\pi}{4} + x\right) \cdot \frac{d}{dx}\left(\frac{\pi}{4} + x\right)$$

$$= -\sec^2\left(\frac{\pi}{4} + x\right)$$

$$\therefore \quad \left(\frac{dy}{dx}\right)_{x=0} = -\sec^2 \frac{\pi}{4}$$

$$= -(\sqrt{2})^2 = -2$$

Q.72 If $y = \frac{\sin(x+9)}{\cos x}$, then $\frac{dy}{dx}$ at $x = 0$ is equal to

(a) $\cos 9$ (b) $\sin 9$ (c) 0 (d) 1

Ans. (a) Given, $y = \frac{\sin(x+9)}{\cos x}$

$$\therefore \quad \frac{dy}{dx} = \frac{\cos x \cos(x+9) - \sin(x+9)(-\sin x)}{(\cos x)^2} \qquad \text{[by quotient rule]}$$

$$= \frac{\cos x \cos(x+9) + \sin x \sin(x+9)}{\cos^2 x}$$

$$\therefore \quad \left(\frac{dy}{dx}\right)_{x=0} = \frac{1 \cdot \cos 9 + 0}{(1)^2}$$

$$= \cos 9$$

Q.73 If $f(x)=1+x+\frac{x^2}{2}+\ldots+\frac{x^{100}}{100}$, then $f'(1)$ is equal to

(a) $\frac{1}{100}$ (b) 100 (c) 0 (d) Does not exist

Ans. *(b)* Given, $f(x)=1+x+\frac{x^2}{2}+\ldots+\frac{x^{100}}{100}$

$\therefore$ $f'(x)=0+1+2\times\frac{x}{2}+\ldots+100\frac{x^{99}}{100}$

$\Rightarrow$ $f'(x)=1+x+x^2+\ldots+x^{99}$

Now, $f'(1)=1+1+1+\ldots+1(100 \text{ times})$

$=100$

Q.74 If $f(x)=\frac{x^n-a^n}{x-a}$ for some constant a, then $f'(a)$ is equal to

(a) 1 (b) 0 (c) $\frac{1}{2}$ (d) Does not exist

Ans. *(d)* Given, $f(x)=\frac{x^n-a^n}{x-a}$

$\therefore$ $f'(x)=\frac{(x-a)nx^{n-1}-(x^n-a^n)(1)}{(x-a)^2}$ [by quotient rule]

$\Rightarrow$ $f'(x)=\frac{nx^{n-1}(x-a)-x^n+a^n}{(x-a)^2}$

Now, $f'(a)=\frac{na^{n-1}(0)-a^n+a^n}{(a-a)^2}$

$\Rightarrow$ $f'(a)=\frac{0}{0}$

Since, $f'(x)$ is not defined at $x=a$.

So, $f'(a)$ does not exist.

Q.75 If $f(x)=x^{100}+x^{99}+\ldots+x+1$, then $f'(1)$ is equal to

(a) 5050 (b) 5049 (c) 5051 (d) 50051

Ans. *(a)* Given, $f(x)=x^{100}+x^{99}+\ldots+x+1$

$\therefore$ $f'(x)=100x^{99}+99x^{98}+\ldots+1+0$

$=100x^{99}+99x^{98}+\ldots+1$

Now, $f'(1)=100+99+\ldots+1$

$=\frac{100}{2}[2\times100+(100-1)(-1)]$

$\left[\because \text{In A.P. series, sum of first } n \text{ terms } S_n=\frac{n}{2}\{2a+(n-1)d\}, \text{ where } a=\text{first term and } d=\text{common difference}\right]$

$=50[200-99]=50\times101$

$=5050$

Q.76 If $f(x) = 1 - x + x^2 - x^3 + \dots - x^{99} + x^{100}$, then $f'(1)$ is equal to

(a) 150 (b) −50 (c) −150 (d) 50

Ans. ***(d)*** Given, $f(x) = 1 - x + x^2 - x^3 + \dots - x^{99} + x^{100}$

$$\therefore \quad f'(x) = 0 - 1 + 2x - 3x^2 + \dots - 99x^{98} + 100x^{99}$$
$$= -1 + 2x - 3x^2 + \dots - 99x^{98} + 100x^{99}$$
$$\therefore \quad f'(1) = -1 + 2 - 3 + \dots - 99 + 100$$
$$= (-1 - 3 - 5 - \dots - 99) + (2 + 4 + \dots + 100)$$
$$= -\frac{50}{2}[2 \times 1 + (50 - 1)\, 2] + \frac{50}{2}[2 \times 2 + (50 - 1) 2]$$
$$= -25\,[2 + 49 \times 2] + 25[4 + 49 \times 2]$$
$$= -25\,(2 + 98) + 25\,(4 + 98)$$
$$= -25 \times 100 + 25 \times 102$$
$$= -2500 + 2550 = 50$$

Fill in the blanks in exercises 77 to 80.

Q.77 If $f(x) = \dfrac{\tan x}{x - \pi}$ then $\lim\limits_{x \to \pi} f(x) =$ ....

Ans. Given, $f(x) = \dfrac{\tan x}{x - \pi}$

Now, $\lim\limits_{x \to \pi} f(x) = \lim\limits_{x \to \pi} \dfrac{\tan x}{x - \pi}$ [Put $x = \pi + h$, if $x \to \pi \Rightarrow h \to 0$]

$$= \lim_{h \to 0} \frac{\tan(\pi + h)}{\pi + h - \pi} = \lim_{h \to 0} \frac{\tan h}{h} = 1 \qquad \left[\because \lim_{x \to 0} \frac{\tan x}{x} = 1\right]$$

Q.78 $\lim\limits_{x \to 0} \left(\sin mx \cot \dfrac{x}{\sqrt{3}} \right) = 2$, then $m =$ ......

Ans. Given,
$$\lim_{x \to 0} \left(\sin mx \cot \frac{x}{\sqrt{3}} \right) = 2$$
$$\Rightarrow \quad \lim_{x \to 0} \left(\frac{\sin mx}{mx} \cdot mx \cdot \frac{1}{\tan \frac{x}{\sqrt{3}}} \right) = 2$$
$$\Rightarrow \quad \lim_{x \to 0} \left(\frac{\sin mx}{mx} \cdot mx \cdot \frac{\frac{x}{\sqrt{3}}}{\tan \frac{x}{\sqrt{3}}} \cdot \frac{1}{\frac{x}{\sqrt{3}}} \right) = 2$$
$$\Rightarrow \quad \lim_{x \to 0} \frac{\sin mx}{mx} \cdot \lim_{x \to 0} \frac{\frac{x}{\sqrt{3}}}{\tan \frac{x}{\sqrt{3}}} \cdot \lim_{x \to 0} \frac{mx}{\frac{x}{\sqrt{3}}} = 2$$
$$\Rightarrow \quad (1) \cdot (1) (\sqrt{3}m) = 2$$
$$\therefore \quad m = \frac{2}{\sqrt{3}} = \frac{2\sqrt{3}}{3} = \frac{2}{\sqrt{3}}$$

Q.79 If $y = 1 + \frac{x}{1!} + \frac{x^2}{2!} + \frac{x^3}{3!} + \ldots$, then $\frac{dy}{dx} = \ldots\ldots$

Ans. Given,
$$y = 1 + \frac{x}{1!} + \frac{x^2}{2!} + \frac{x^3}{3!} + \frac{x^4}{4!} + \ldots$$

$\therefore$
$$\frac{dy}{dx} = 0 + 1 + \frac{2x}{2} + \frac{3x^2}{6} + \frac{4x^3}{24} \quad [\because n! = 1 \times 2 \times 3 \ldots \times n]$$
$$= 1 + x + \frac{x^2}{2} + \frac{x^3}{6} + \ldots$$
$$= 1 + \frac{x}{1!} + \frac{x^2}{2!} + \frac{x^3}{3!} + \ldots$$
$$= y$$

Alternate Method

Given,
$$y = 1 + \frac{x}{1!} + \frac{x^2}{2!} + \frac{x^3}{3!} + \ldots\ldots$$

$\Rightarrow$
$$y = e^x$$

$\therefore$
$$\frac{dy}{dx} = e^x = y$$

Q.80 $\lim_{x \to 3^+} \frac{x}{[x]} = \ldots$

Ans. Given,
$$\lim_{x \to 3^+} \frac{x}{[x]} = \lim_{h \to 0} \frac{(3+h)}{[3+h]} \quad [\text{put } x = 3 + h, \text{ if } x \to 3 \Rightarrow h \to 0]$$
$$= \lim_{h \to 0} \frac{(3+h)}{3} = 1$$

Chapter

14 Mathematical Reasoning*

Short Answer Type Questions

Q.1 Which of the following sentences are statements? Justify

(i) A triangle has three sides.

(ii) 0 is a complex number.

(iii) Sky is red.

(iv) Every set is an infinite set.

(v) $15+8>23$.

(vi) $y+9=7$

(vii) Where is your bag?

(viii) Every square is a rectangle.

(ix) Sum of opposite angles of a cyclic quadrilateral is 180°.

(x) $\sin^2 x+\cos^2 x=0$

- **Concept Insight** A statement always has a value that is either true or false and never changes from one thing (or person) to other thing (or person).

Ans. As we know, a statement is a sentence which is either true or false but not both simultaneously.

(i) It is true statement. → Triangle is a closed polygon of three sides

(ii) It is true statement. → As $0+0i$

(iii) It is false statement. → As sky is blue.

(iv) It is false statement. → No every set is not an infinite set.

(v) It is false statement. → $15+8=23 \not> 23$

(vi) $y+9=7$

It is not considered as a statement, since the value of y is not given.

(vii) It is a question, so it is not a statement.

(viii) It is a true statement. → square is a rectangle whose all sides are equal

(ix) It is true statement.

(x) It is false statement. → $[\sin^2 x+\cos^2 x=1]$

(*) This chapter has been deleted from latest NCERT.

Q.2 Find the component statements of the following compound statements.

(i) Number 7 is prime and odd.

(ii) Chennai is in India and is the capital of Tamil Nadu.

(iii) The number 100 is divisible by 3, 11 and 5.

(iv) Chandigarh is the capital of Haryana and UP.

(v) $\sqrt{7}$ is a rational number or an irrational number.

(vi) 0 is less than every positive integer and every negative integer.

(vii) Plants use sunlight, water and carbon dioxide for photosynthesis.

(viii) Two lines in a plane either intersect at one point or they are parallel.

(ix) A rectangle is a quadrilateral or a 5 sided polygon.

Thinking process The connecting words are 'and', 'or'. On that basis, break it into component statements.

Ans. (i) p: Number 7 is prime.

q: Number 7 is odd.

(ii) P: Chennai is in India.

q: Chennai is capital of Tamil Nadu.

(iii) p: 100 is divisible by 3.

q: 100 is divisible by 11.

r: 100 is divisible by 5.

(iv) p: Chandigarh is the capital of Haryana.

q: Chandigarh is the capital of UP.

(v) p: $\sqrt{7}$ is a rational number.

q: $\sqrt{7}$ is an irrational number.

(vi) p: 0 is less than every positive integer.

q: 0 is less than every negative integer.

(vii) p: Plants use sunlight for photosynthesis.

q: Plants use water for photosynthesis.

r: Plants use carbon dioxide for photosynthesis.

(viii) p: Two lines in a plane intersect at one point.

q: Two lines in a plane are parallel.

(ix) p: A rectangle is a quadrilateral.

q: A rectangle is a 5-sided polygon.

Q. 3 Write the component statements of the following compound statements and check whether the compound statement is true or false.

(i) 57 is divisible by 2 or 3.

(ii) 24 is a multiple of 4 and 6.

(iii) All living things have two eyes and two legs.

(iv) 2 is an even number and a prime number.

Thinking process Firstly, separate the given compound statement into component statements. After that check whether they are true on false.

Ans. (i) Given compound statement is of the form '$p \vee q$'. Since, the statement '$p \vee q$' has the truth value T whenever either p or q or both have the truth value T.

Its component statements are

p : 57 is divisible by 2. [false]

q : 57 is divisible by 3. [true]

So, it is true statement.

(ii) Given compound statement is of the form '$p \wedge q$'. Since, the statement '$p \wedge q$' have the truth value T whenever both p and q have the truth value T.

Its component statements are

p : 24 is multiple of 4 [true]

q : 24 is multiple of 6. [true]

So, it is a true statement.

(iii) Since, '$p \wedge q$' has the truth value F whenever either p or q or both have the truth value F.

Its component statements are

p : All living things have two eyes. [false]

q : All living things have two legs. [false]

It is a false statement.

(iv) Its component statements are

p : 2 is an even number. [true]

q : 2 is a prime number. [true]

So, It is a true statement.

Q.4 Write the negation on the following simple statements.

(i) The number 17 is prime.

(ii) $2+7=6$.

(iii) Violets are blue.

(iv) $\sqrt{5}$ is a rational number.

(v) 2 is not a prime number.

(vi) Every real number is an irrational number.

(vii) Cow has four legs.

(viii) A leap year has 366 days.

(ix) All similar triangles are not congruent.

(x) Area of a circle is same as the perimeter of the circle.

Thinking Process : In negative statement, if word 'not' is not given in the statement, then insert word 'not' in the statement. If word 'not' is given in the statement then remove word 'not' from the statement.

Ans. (i) The number 17 is not prime.

(ii) $2 + 7 \neq 6$.

(iii) Violets are not blue.

(iv) $\sqrt{5}$ is not a rational number.

(v) 2 is a prime number.

(vi) There exists a real number which is not an irrational number.

(vii) Cow does not have four legs.

(viii) A leap year does not have 366 days.

(ix) There exist similar triangles are not congruent.

(x) Area of a circle is not same as the perimeter of the circle.

Q.5 Translate the following statements into symbolic form

(i) Rahul passed in Hindi and English.

(ii) x and y are even integers.

(iii) 2, 3 and 6 are factors of 12.

(iv) Either x or $x+1$ is an odd integer.

(v) A number is either divisible by 2 or 3.

(vi) Either $x = 2$ or $x = 3$ is a root of $3x^2 - x - 10 = 0$.

(vii) Students can take Hindi or English as an optional paper.

Thinking process Write statement with ^ symbol on with ^ symbol.

Ans. (i) p : Rahul passed in Hindi.

q : Rahul passed in English.

$p \wedge q$: Rahul passed in Hindi and English.

(ii) p : x is an even integers.

q : y is an even integers.

$p \wedge q$: x and y are even integers.

(iii) p : 2 is factor of 12.

q : 3 is factor of 12.

r : 6 is factor of 12.

$p \wedge q \wedge r$: 2, 3 and 6 are factor of 12.

(iv) $p : x$ is an odd integer.

$q : (x + 1)$ is an odd integer.

$p \vee q$: Either x or $(x + 1)$ is an odd integer.

(v) p : A number is divisible by 2.

q : A number is divisible by 3.

$p \vee q$: A number is either divisible by 2 or 3.

(vi) $p : x = 2$ is a root of $3x^2 - x - 10 = 0$.

$q : x = 3$ is a root of $3x^2 - x - 10 = 0$.

$p \vee q$: Either $x = 2$ or $x = 3$ is a root of $3x^2 - x - 10 = 0$.

(vii) p : Students can take Hindi as an optional paper.

q : Students can take English as an optional subject.

$p \vee q$: Students can take Hindi or English as an optional paper.

Q.6 Write down the negation of following compound statements.

(i) All rational numbers are real and complex.

(ii) All real numbers are rationals or irrationals.

(iii) $x = 2$ and $x = 3$ are roots of the quadratic equation $x^2 - 5x + 6 = 0$.

(iv) A triangle has either 3-sides or 4-sides.

(v) 35 is a prime number or a composite number.

(vi) All prime integers are either even or odd.

(vii) $|x|$ is equal to either x or $-x$.

(viii) 6 is divisible by 2 and 3.

Thinking Process

Use (i) $\sim(p \wedge q) = \sim p \vee \sim q$

(ii) $\sim(p \vee q) = \sim p \wedge \sim q$

Ans. (i) Let p : All rational numbers are real.

q : All rational numbers are complex.

$\sim p$: All rational number are not real.

$\sim q$: All rational numbers are not complex.

$\sim(p \wedge q)$: There exists a rational number which is not real or not complex.

$[\because \sim(p \wedge q) = \sim p \vee \sim q]$

(ii) Let p : All real numbers are rationals.

q : All real numbers are irrational.

Then, the negation of the given statement is given by

$\sim(p \vee q)$: There exists a real number that is neither rational nor irrational

$[\because \sim(p \vee q) = \sim p \wedge \sim q]$

(iii) Let $p : x = 2$ is a root of quadratic equation $x^2 - 5x + 6 = 0$.

$q : x = 3$ is a root of quadratic equation $x^2 - 5x + 6 = 0$.

Then, the negation of conjunction of above statement is given by

$\sim(p \wedge q)$: $x = 2$ is not a root of quadratic equation $x^2 - 5x + 6 = 0$ or $x = 3$ is not a root of the quadratic equation $x^2 - 5x + 6 = 0$.

(iv) Let p : A triangle has 3-sides.

q : A triangle has 4-sides.

Then, negation of disjunction of the above statement is given by

$\sim(p \vee q)$: A triangle has neither 3-sides nor 4-sides.

(v) Let p : 35 is a prime number.

q : 35 is a composite number.

Then, negation of disjunction of the above statement is given by

$\sim(p \vee q)$: 35 is not a prime number and it is not a composite number.

(vi) Let p : All prime integers are even.

q : All prime integers are odd.

Then negation of disjunction of the above statement is given by

$\sim(p \vee q)$: All prime integers are not even and all prime integers are not odd.

(vii) Let p : $|x|$ is equal to x.

q : $|x|$ is equal to $-x$.

Then, negation of disjunction of the above statement is given by

$\sim(p \vee q)$: $|x|$ is not equal to x and it is not equal to $-x$.

(viii) Let p : 6 is divisible by 2.

q : 6 is divisible by 3.

Then, negation of conjunction of above statement is given by

$\sim(p \wedge q)$: 6 is not divisible by 2 or it is not divisible by 3

Q.7 Rewrite each of the following statements in the form of conditional statements.

(i) The square of an odd number is odd.

(ii) You will get a sweet dish after the dinner.

(iii) You will fail, if you will not study.

(iv) The unit digit of an integer is 0 or 5, if it is divisible by 5.

(v) The square of a prime number is not prime.

(vi) $2b = a + c$, if a, b and c are in AP.

Ans. We know that some of the common expressions of conditional statement $p \rightarrow q$ are

(i) if p, then q (ii) q if p

(iii) p only if q (iv) p is sufficient for q

(v) q is necesary for p (vi) $\sim q$ implies $\sim p$

So, use above information to get the answer

(i) If the number is odd number, then its square is odd number.
(ii) If you take the dinner, then you will get sweet dish.
(iii) If you will not study, then you will fail.
(iv) If an integer is divisible by 5, then its unit digits are 0 or 5.
(v) If the number is prime, then its square is not prime.
(vi) If a, b and c are in AP, then $2b = a + c$.

Q.8 Form the biconditional statement $p \leftrightarrow q$, where

(i) p : The unit digits of an integer is zero.
q : It is divisible by 5.
(ii) p : A natural number n is odd.
q : Natural number n is not divisible by 2.
(iii) p : A triangle is an equilateral triangle.
q : All three sides of a triangle are equal.

Thinking process In a biconditional statement, two statements are connected by 'if and only if'.

Ans. (i) $p \leftrightarrow q$: The unit digit of an integer is zero, if and only if it is divisible by 5.
(ii) $p \leftrightarrow q$: A natural number n is odd if and only if it is not divisible by 2.
(iii) $p \leftrightarrow q$: A triangle is an equilateral triangle if and only if all three sides of triangle are equal.

Q.9 Write down the contrapositive of the following statements.

(i) If $x = y$ and $y = 3$, then $x = 3$.
(ii) If n is a natural number, then n is an integer.
(iii) If all three sides of a triangle are equal, then the triangle is equilateral.
(iv) If x and y are negative integers, then xy is positive.
(v) If natural number n is divisible by 6, then n is divisible by 2 and 3.
(vi) If it snows, then the weather will be cold.
(vii) If x is a real number such that $0 < x < 1$, then $x^2 < 1$.

Thinking Process We know that, the statement $(\sim q) \rightarrow (\sim p)$ is called contrapositive of the statement $p \rightarrow q$.

Ans. (i) If $x \neq 3$, then $x \neq y$ or $y \neq 3$.
(ii) If n is not an integer, then it is not a natural number.
(iii) If the triangle is not equilateral, then all three sides of the triangle are not equal.
(iv) If xy is not positive integer, then either x or y is not negative integer.
(v) If natural number n is not divisible by 2 or 3, then n is not divisible by 6.
(vi) The weather will not be cold, if it does not snow.
(vii) If $x^2 \nless 1$, then x is not a real number such that $0 < x < 1$.

Q.10 Write down the converse of following statements.

(i) If a rectangle 'R' is a square, then R is a rhombus.

(ii) If today is Monday, then tomorrow is Tuesday.

(iii) If you go to Agra, then you must visit Taj Mahal.

(iv) If sum of squares of two sides of a triangle is equal to the square of third side of a triangle, then the triangle is right angled.

(v) If all three angles of a triangle are equal, then the triangle is equilateral.

(vi) If $x:y=3:2$, then $2x=3y$.

(vii) If S is a cyclic quadrilateral, then the opposite angles of S are supplementary.

(viii) If x is zero, then x is neither positive nor negative.

(ix) If two triangles are similar, then the ratio of their corresponding sides are equal.

Thinking Process We know that, the converse of the statement "$p \to q$" is "$q \to p$".

Ans. (i) If a rectangle 'R' is rhombus, then it is square.

(ii) If tomorrow is Tuesday, then today is Monday.

(iii) If you must visit Taj Mahal, then you go to Agra.

(iv) If the triangle is right angle, then sum of squares of two sides of a triangle is equal to the square of third side.

(v) If the triangle is equilateral, then all three angles of triangle are equal.

(vi) If $2x=3y$, then $x:y=3:2$

(vii) If the opposite angles of quadrilateral are supplementary, then S is cyclic quadrilateral.

(viii) If x is neither positive nor negative, then x is 0.

(ix) If the ratio of corresponding sides of two triangles are equal, then triangles are similar.

Q.11 Identify the quantifiers in the following statements.

(i) There exists a triangle which is not equilateral.

(ii) For all real numbers x and y, $xy=yx$.

(iii) There exists a real number which is not a rational number.

(iv) For every natural number x, $x+1$ is also a natural number.

(v) For all real numbers x with $x>3$, x^2 is greater than 9.

(vi) There exists a triangle which is not an isosceles triangle.

(vii) For all negative integers x, x^3 is also a negative integers.

(viii) There exists a statement in above statements which is not true.

(ix) There exists an even prime number other than 2.

(x) There exists a real number x such that $x^2+1=0$.

Ans. Quantifier are the phrases like 'There exists' and 'For every', 'For all' etc.

(i) There exists (ii) For all

(iii) There exists (iv) For every

(v) For all (vi) There exists

(vii) For all (viii) There exists

(ix) There exists (x) There exists

Q.12 Prove by direct method that for any integer 'n', $n^3 - n$ is always even.

Thinking Process We know that in direct method to show a statement, if p then q is true, we assume p is true and show q is true i.e., $p \to q$.

Ans. Here, two cases arise

***Case* I** When n is even,

Let $n = 2K,\ K \in Z$

$\Rightarrow$ $n^3 - n = (2K)^3 - (2K) = 2K(4K^2 - 1)$

$= 2\lambda$, where $\lambda = K(4K^2 - 1)$

Thus, $(n^3 - n)$ is even, when n is even.

***Case* II** When n is odd,

Let $n = 2K + 1,\ K \in Z$

$$\Rightarrow n^3 - n = (2K+1)^3 - (2K+1)$$
$$= (2K+1)[(2K+1)^2 - 1]$$
$$= (2K+1)[4K^2 + 1 + 4K - 1]$$
$$= (2K+1)(4K^2 + 4K)$$
$$= 4K(2K+1)(K+1)$$
$$= 2\mu, \text{ when } \mu = 2K(K+1)(2K+1)$$

Then, $n^3 - n$ is even when n is odd.

So, $n^3 - n$ is always even.

Q.13 Check validity of the following statement.

(i) p : 125 is divisible by 5 and 7.

(ii) q : 131 is a multiple of 3 or 11.

Ans. (i) p : 125 is divisible by 5 and 7.

Let q : 125 is divisible by 5.

r : 125 is divisible by 7.

q is true, r is false.

$\Rightarrow$ $q \wedge r$ is false.

[since, $p \wedge q$ has the truth value F (false) whenever either p or q or both have the truth value F.]

Hence, p is not valid.

(ii) q : 131 is a multiple of 3 or 11.

Let p : 131 is multiple of 3.

r : 131 is a multiple of 11.

p is false, r is false.

$\Rightarrow \quad p \vee r$ is false.

Hence, q is not valid.

Q.14 Prove the following statement by contradiction method

p : The sum of an irrational number and a rational number is irrational.

Ans. Let p is false i.e., sum of an irrational and a rational number is rational.

Let $\sqrt{m}$ is irrational and n is rational number.

$\Rightarrow \quad \sqrt{m} + n = r \quad$ [rational]

$\Rightarrow \quad \sqrt{m} = r - n$

$\sqrt{m}$ is irrational, where as $(r - n)$ is rational. This is contradiction.

Then, our supposition is wrong.

Hence, p is true.

Q.15 Prove by direct method that for any real number x, y if $x = y$, then $x^2 = y^2$.

Thinking Process In direct method, assume p is true and show q is true i.e., $p \Rightarrow q$.

Ans. Let $p : x = y, \quad x, y \in R$

On squaring both sides, we get

$x^2 = y^2 : q$ [say]

$p \Rightarrow q$

Hence, we have the result.

Q.16 Using contrapositive method prove that, if n^2 is an even integer, then n is also an even integer.

Thinking Process In contrapositive method, assume $\sim q$ is true and show $\sim p$ is true *i.e.*, $\sim q \Rightarrow \sim p$ that means $p \Rightarrow q$.

Ans. Let $p : n^2$ is an even integer.

$q : n$ is also an even integer.

Let $\sim q$ is true *i.e.*, n is not an even integer.

$\Rightarrow n^2$ is not an even integer. [since, square of an odd integer is odd]

$\Rightarrow \quad \sim p$ is true.

$\therefore \quad p$ is true

$\Rightarrow \quad q$ is true

Hence proved.

Objective Type Questions

Choose the correct answers from the given four options in each exercise 17 to 36.

Q.17 Which of the following is a statement?

(a) x is a real number (b) Switch off the fan

(c) 6 is a natural number (d) Let me go

Ans. ***(c)*** As we know, a statement is a sentence which is either true or false.

So, 6 is a natural number, which is true.

Hence, it is a statement.

Q.18 Which of the following is not a statement.

(a) Smoking is injurious to health (b) $2 + 2 = 4$

(c) 2 is the only even prime number (d) Come here

Ans. ***(d)*** 'Come here' is not a statement. Since, no sentence can be called a statement, if it is an order.

Q.19 The connective in the statement '$2+7>9$ or $2+7<9$' is

(a) and (b)or (c) > (d)<

Ans. ***(b)***

In '$2 + 7 > 9$ or $2 + 7 < 9$', or is the connective.

Q. 20 The connective in the statement "Earth revolves round the Sun and Moon is a satellite of earth" is

(a) or (b) Earth (c) Sun (d) and

Ans. ***(d)*** Connective word is 'and'.

Q.21 The negation of the statement "A circle is an ellipse" is

(a) An ellipse is a circle (b) An ellipse is not a circle

(c) A circle is not an ellipse (d) A circle is an ellipse

Ans. ***(c)*** Let p: A circle is an ellipse.

$\sim p$: A circle is not an ellipse.

Q.22 The negation of the statement "7 is greater than 8" is

(a) 7 is equal to 8 (b) 7 is not greater than 8

(c) 8 is less than 7 (d) None of these

Ans. ***(b)*** Let p: 7 is greater than 8.

$\sim p$: 7 is not greater than 8.

Q.23 The negation of the statement "72 is divisible by 2 and 3" is

(a) 72 is not divisible by 2 or 72 is not divisible by 3

(b) 72 is not divisible by 2 and 72 is not divisible by 3

(c) 72 is divisible by 2 and 72 is not divisible by 3

(d) 72 is not divisible by 2 and 72 is divisible by 3

Ans. ***(b)*** Let p : 72 is divisible by 2 and 3.

Let q : 72 is divisible by 2.

r : 72 is divisible by 3.

$\sim q$: 72 is not divisible by 2.

$\sim r$: 72 is not divisible by 3.

$\sim(q \wedge r) : \sim q \vee \sim r$

$\Rightarrow$ 72 is not divisible by 2 or 72 is not divisible by 3.

Q.24 The negation of the statement "Plants take in CO_2 and give out O_2" is

(a) Plants do not take in CO_2 and do not give out O_2

(b) Plants do not take in CO_2 or do not give out O_2

(c) Plants take is CO_2 and do not give out O_2

(d) Plants take in CO_2 or do not give out O_2

Ans. ***(b)*** Let p : Plants take in CO_2 and give out O_2.

Let q : Plants take in CO_2.

r : Plants give out O_2.

$\sim q$: Plants do not take in CO_2.

$\sim r$: Plants do not give out O_2.

$\sim(q \wedge r)$: Plants do not take in CO_2 or do not give out O_2.

Q.25 The negative of the statement "Rajesh or Rajni lived in Bangalore" is

(a) Rajesh did not live in Bangalore or Rajni lives in Bangalore

(b) Rajesh lives in Bangalore and Rajni did not live in Bangalore

(c) Rajesh did not live in Bangalore and Rajni did not live in Bangalore

(d) Rajesh did not live in Bangalore or Rajni did not live in Bangalore

Ans. ***(c)*** Let p : Rajesh or Rajni lived in Bangalore.

Let q : Rajesh lived in Bangalore.

r : Rajni lived in Bangalore.

$\sim q$: Rajesh did not live in Bangalore.

$\sim r$: Rajni did not live in Bangalore.

$\sim(q \vee r)$: Rajesh did not live in Bangalore and Rajni did not live in Bangalore.

Q.26 The negation of the statement "101 is not a multiple of 3" is

(a) 101 is a multiple of 3

(b) 101 is a multiple of 2

(c) 101 is an odd number

(d) 101 is an even number

Ans. ***(a)*** Let p : 101 is not a multiple of 3.

$\sim p$: 101 is a multiple of 3.

Q.27 The contrapositive of the statement
"If 7 is greater than 5, then 8 is greater than 6" is

(a) If 8 is greater than 6, then 7 is greater than 5.

(b) If 8 is not greater than 6, then 7 is greater than 5.

(c) If 8 is not greater than 6, then 7 is not greater than 5.

(d) If 8 is greater than 6, then 7 is not greater than 5.

Ans. ***(c)*** Let $p: 7$ is greater than 5.

$q: 8$ is greater than 6.

$\therefore p \rightarrow q$

$\sim p: 7$ is not greater than 5.

$\sim q: 8$ is not greater than 6.

$(\sim q) \rightarrow (\sim p)$ *i.e.*, If 8 is not greater than 6, then 7 is not greater than 5.

Q.28 The converse of the statement "If $x > y$, then $x + a > y + a$" is

(a) If $x < y$, then $x + a < y + a$
(b) If $x + a > y + a$, then $x > y$
(c) If $x < y$, then $x + a < y + a$
(d) If $x > y$, then $x + a < y + a$

Ans. ***(b)***

Let

$$p: x > y$$
$$q: x + a > y + a$$
$$p \rightarrow q$$

Converse of the above statement is

$$q \rightarrow p$$

i.e., If $x + a > y + a$, then $x > y$.

Q.29 The converse of the statement "If sun is not shining, then sky is filled with clouds" is

(a) If sky is filled with clouds, then the sun is not shining
(b) If sun is shining, then sky is filled with clouds
(c) If sky is clear, then sun is shining
(d) If sun is not shining, then sky is not filled with clouds

Ans. ***(a)*** Let p : Sun is not shining.

q : Sky is filled with clouds.

Converse of the above statement $p \rightarrow q$ is $q \rightarrow p$.

If sky is filled with clouds, then the Sun is not shining.

Q.30 The contrapositive of the statement "If p, then q", is

(a) if q, then p
(b) if p, then $\sim q$
(c) if $\sim q$, then $\sim p$
(d) if $\sim p$, then $\sim q$

Ans. ***(c)*** $p \rightarrow q$

If p, then q

Contrapositive of the statement $p \rightarrow q$ is $(\sim q) \rightarrow (\sim p)$.

If $\sim q$, then $\sim p$.

Q.31 The statement "If x^2 is not even, then x is not even" is converse of the statement

(a) If x^2 is odd, then x is even
(b) If x is not even, then x^2 is not even
(c) If x is even, then x^2 is even
(d) If x is odd, then x^2 is even

Ans. *(b)* Let $p: x^2$ is not even.

$q: x$ is not even.

Converse of the statement $p \rightarrow q$ is $q \rightarrow p$.

i.e., If x is not even, then x^2 is not even.

Q.32 The contrapositive of statement 'If Chandigarh is capital of Punjab, then Chandigarh is in India' is

(a) if Chandigarh is not in India, then Chandigarh is not the capital of Punjab
(b) if Chandigarh is in India, then Chandigarh is Capital of Punjab
(c) if Chandigarh is not capital of Punjab, then Chandigarh is not capital of India
(d) if Chandigarh is capital of Punjab, then Chandigarh is not is India

Ans. *(a)* Let p: Chandigarh is capital of Punjab.

q: Chandigarh is in India.

$\sim p$: Chandigarh is not capital of Punjab.

$\sim q$: Chandigarh is not in India.

Contrapositive of the statement $p \rightarrow q$ is $(\sim q) \rightarrow (\sim p)$

If $(\sim q)$, then $(\sim p)$.

If Chandigarh is not in India, then Chandigarh is not the capital of Punjab.

Q.33 Which of the following is the conditional $p \rightarrow q$?

(a) q is sufficient for p
(b) p is necessary for q
(c) p only if q
(d) if q then p

Ans. *(c)* '$p \rightarrow q$' is same as 'p only if q'.

Q.34 The negation of the statement "The product of 3 and 4 is 9" is

(a) it is false that the product of 3 and 4 is 9
(b) the product of 3 and 4 is 12
(c) the product of 3 and 4 is not 12
(d) it is false that the product of 3 and 4 is not 9

Ans. *(a)* The negation of the above statement is 'It is false that the product of 3 and 4 is 9'.

Q.35 Which of the following is not a negation of "A natural number is greater than zero"

(a) A natural number is not greater than zero
(b) It is false that a natural number is greater than zero
(c) It is false that a natural number is not greater than zero
(d) None of the above

Ans. *(c)* The false negation of the given statement is "It is false that a natural number is not greater than zero".

Q.36 Which of the following statement is a conjunction?

(a) Ram and Shyam are friends

(b) Both Ram and Shyam are tall

(c) Both Ram and Shyam are enemies

(d) None of the above

Ans. *(d)* If two simple statements p and q are connected by the word 'and', then the resulting compound statement p and q is called a conjuction of p and q.

Here, none of the given statement is conjunction.

Q.37 State whether the following sentences are statements or not

(i) The angles opposite to equal sides of a triangle are equal.

(ii) The moon is a satellite of Earth.

(iii) May God bless you.

(iv) Asia is a continent.

(v) How are you?

Ans. (i) It is a statement.

(ii) It is a statement.

(iii) It is not a statement, since it is an exclamation.

(iv) It is a statement.

(v) It is not a statement, since it is a question.

Chapter

15

Statistics

Short Answer Type Questions

Q.1 Find the mean deviation about the mean of the distribution.

Size	20	21	22	23	24
Frequency	6	4	5	1	4

- **Concept Insight** First of all use the mean formula $\bar{x} = \frac{\Sigma f_i x_i}{\Sigma f_i}$ and then calculate the mean deviation or MD about mean $= \frac{\Sigma f_i |x_i - \bar{x}|}{\Sigma f_i}$.

Ans.

Size (x_i)	Frequency (f_i)	$f_i\, x_i$	$\lvert x_i - \bar{x} \rvert$	$f_i \lvert x_i - \bar{x} \rvert$
20	6	120	1.65	9.90
21	4	84	0.65	2.60
22	5	110	0.35	1.75
23	1	23	1.35	1.35
24	4	96	2.35	9.40
Total	20	433		25

Now, $\text{Mean } (\bar{x}) = \frac{\Sigma f_i x_i}{\Sigma f_i} = \frac{433}{20} = 21.65$

$\therefore$ $\text{MD about mean} = \frac{\Sigma f_i \lvert x_i - \bar{x} \rvert}{\Sigma f_i} = \frac{25}{20} = 1.25$

Q.2 Find the mean deviation about the median of the following distribution.

Marks obtained	10	11	12	14	15
Number of students	2	3	8	3	4

Ans.

Marks obtained	f_i	cf	$d_i = \lvert x_i - M \rvert$	$f_i\, d_i$
10	2	2	2	4
11	3	5	1	3
12	8	13	0	0

Marks obtained	f_i	cf	$d_i = \lvert x_i - M \rvert$	$f_i d_i$
14	3	16	2	6
15	4	20	3	12
Total	$\Sigma f_i = 20$			$\Sigma f_i d_i = 25$

Here, $N = 20$ [even]

So, median is equal to the mean of two marks corresponds to *cf* just greater than or equal to $\frac{N}{2} = 10$ and $\left(\frac{N}{2} + 1\right) = 11$

$$\therefore \quad \text{Median}\,(M) = \frac{12 + 12}{2} = 12$$

$$\therefore \quad \text{MD about median} = \frac{\Sigma f_i d_i}{\Sigma f_i} = \frac{25}{20} = 1.25$$

Q.3 Calculate the mean deviation about the mean of the set of first n natural numbers when n is an odd number.

Ans. Consider first natural number when n is an odd *i.e.,* 1, 2, 3, 4, ...n (odd).

$$\text{Mean } \bar{x} = \frac{1 + 2 + 3 + \ldots + n}{n} = \frac{n(n+1)}{2n} = \frac{n+1}{2}$$

$$\therefore \quad \text{MD} = \frac{\left|1 - \frac{n+1}{2}\right| + \left|2 - \frac{n+1}{2}\right| + \left|3 - \frac{n+1}{2}\right| + \ldots + \left|n - \frac{n+1}{2}\right|}{n}$$

$$= \frac{1}{n}\left[\left|1 - \frac{n+1}{2}\right| + \left|2 - \frac{n+1}{2}\right| + \ldots + \left|\frac{n-1}{2} - \frac{n+1}{2}\right| + \left|\frac{n+1}{2} - \frac{n+1}{2}\right| + \left|\frac{n+3}{2} - \frac{n+1}{2}\right| + \ldots + \left|\frac{2n-2}{2} - \frac{n+1}{2}\right| + \left|n - \frac{n+1}{2}\right|\right]$$

$$= \frac{2}{n}\left[1 + 2 + \ldots + \frac{n-3}{2} + \frac{n-1}{2}\right] \qquad \left[\text{Here, } \left(\frac{n-1}{2}\right) \text{ terms}\right]$$

$$= \frac{2}{n}\left[\frac{\left(\frac{n-1}{2}\right)\left(\frac{n-1}{2} + 1\right)}{2}\right] \qquad \left[\because \text{ sum of first } n \text{ natural numbers} = \frac{n(n+1)}{2}\right]$$

$$= \frac{2}{n} \cdot \frac{1}{2}\left[\left(\frac{n-1}{2}\right)\left(\frac{n+1}{2}\right)\right] = \frac{1}{n}\left(\frac{n^2 - 1}{4}\right) = \frac{n^2 - 1}{4n}$$

Q.4 Calculate the mean deviation about the mean of the set of first n natural numbers when n is an even number.

Ans. Consider first n natural number, when n is even *i.e.,* 1, 2, 3, 4, ...n (even)

$$\therefore \quad \text{Mean } \bar{x} = \frac{1 + 2 + 3 + \ldots + n}{n} = \frac{n(n+1)}{2n} = \frac{n+1}{2}$$

$$\text{MD} = \frac{1}{n}\left[\left|1 - \frac{n+1}{2}\right| + \left|2 - \frac{n+1}{2}\right| + \left|3 - \frac{n+1}{2}\right| + \ldots + \left|\frac{n-2}{2} - \frac{n+1}{2}\right| + \left|\frac{n}{2} - \frac{n+1}{2}\right| + \left|\frac{n+2}{2} - \frac{n+1}{2}\right| + \ldots + \left|n - \frac{n+1}{2}\right|\right]$$

$$= \frac{1}{n}\left[\left|\frac{1-n}{2}\right| + \left|\frac{3-n}{2}\right| + \left|\frac{5-n}{2}\right| + ... + \left|\frac{-3}{2}\right| + \left|\frac{-1}{2}\right| + \left|\frac{1}{2}\right| + ... + \left|\frac{n-1}{2}\right|\right]$$

$$= \frac{2}{n}\left[\frac{1}{2} + \frac{3}{2} + ... + \frac{n-1}{2}\right] = \frac{1}{n}[1 + 3 + ... + (n-1)] \qquad \left[\text{Here, } \frac{n}{2} \text{ term}\right]$$

$$= \frac{1}{n} \cdot \left(\frac{n}{2}\right)^2 \qquad [\because \text{sum of first } n \text{ odd numbers } = n^2]$$

$$= \frac{1}{n} \cdot \frac{n^2}{4} = \frac{n}{4}$$

Q.5 Find the standard deviation of first n natural numbers.

Ans.

x_i	1	2	3	4	5	...	...	n
x_i^2	1	4	9	16	25	...	...	n^2

Now, $\Sigma x_i = 1 + 2 + 3 + 4 + ... + n = \frac{n(n+1)}{2}$

And $\Sigma x_i^2 = 1^2 + 2^2 + 3^2 + ... + n^2 = \frac{n(n+1)(2n+1)}{6}$

$\therefore$ Standard deviation

$$\sigma = \sqrt{\frac{\Sigma x_i^2}{N} - \left(\frac{\Sigma x_i}{N}\right)^2} = \sqrt{\frac{n(n+1)(2n+1)}{6n} - \frac{n^2(n+1)^2}{4n^2}}$$

$$= \sqrt{\frac{(n+1)(2n+1)}{6} - \frac{(n+1)^2}{4}}$$

$$= \sqrt{\frac{2(2n^2 + 3n + 1) - 3(n^2 + 2n + 1)}{12}}$$

$$= \sqrt{\frac{4n^2 + 6n + 2 - 3n^2 - 6n - 3}{12}} = \sqrt{\frac{n^2 - 1}{12}}$$

Mistake Alert! *Students may forget to take the square root of the variance to find the standard deviation*

Q.6 The mean and standard deviation of some data for the time taken to complete a test are calculated with the following results

Number of observation = 25, mean = 18.2 seconds, standard deviation = 3.25 seconds

Further, another set of 15 observations $x_1, x_2, ... x_{15}$, also in seconds, is now available and we have $\sum_{i=1}^{15} x_i = 279$ and $\sum_{i=1}^{15} x_i^2 = 5524$. Calculate the standard deviation based on all 40 observations.

Ans. Given, $n_1 = 25, \bar{x}_1 = 18.2, \sigma_1 = 3.25,$

$n_2 = 15, \sum_{i=1}^{15} x_i = 279$ and $\sum_{i=1}^{15} x_i^2 = 5524$

For first set, $\Sigma x_i = 25 \times 18.2 = 455$

$$\therefore \quad \sigma_1^2 = \frac{\Sigma x_i^2}{25} - (18.2)^2$$

$$\Rightarrow \quad (3.25)^2 = \frac{\Sigma x_i^2}{25} - 331.24$$

$$\Rightarrow \quad 10.5625 + 331.24 = \frac{\Sigma x_i^2}{25}$$

$$\Rightarrow \quad \Sigma x_i^2 = 25 \times (10.5625 + 331.24)$$

$$= 25 \times 341.8025$$

$$= 8545.0625$$

For combined SD of the 40 observations, $n = 40$ we get

Now, $\Sigma x_i^2 = 5524 + 8545.0625 = 14069.0625$

And $\Sigma x_i = 455 + 279 = 734$

$$\therefore \quad \text{SD} = \sqrt{\frac{14069.0625}{40} - \left(\frac{734}{40}\right)^2}$$

$$= \sqrt{351.726 - (18.35)^2} = \sqrt{351.726 - 336.7225}$$

$$= \sqrt{15.0035} = 3.87 \text{ (approx)}$$

Q.7 The mean and standard deviation of a set of n_1 observations are $\bar{x}_1$ and s_1, respectively while the mean and standard deviation of another set of n_2 observations are $\bar{x}_2$ and s_2, respectively. Show that the standard deviation of the combined set of $(n_1 + n_2)$ observations is given by

$$\text{SD} = \sqrt{\frac{n_1(s_1)^2 + n_2(s_2)^2}{n_1 + n_2} + \frac{n_1 n_2(\bar{x}_1 - \bar{x}_2)^2}{(n_1 + n_2)^2}}.$$

Ans. Let x_i and y_j be the two sets of observations, where $i = 1, 2, 3 \ldots, n_1$ and $j = 1, 2, 3, \ldots, n_2$

$$\therefore \quad \bar{x}_1 = \frac{1}{n_1}\sum_{i=1}^{n_1} x_i \text{ and } \bar{x}_2 = \frac{1}{n_2}\sum_{j=1}^{n_2} y_j$$

$$\Rightarrow \quad s_1^2 = \frac{1}{n_1}\sum_{i=1}^{n_1}(x_i - \bar{x}_1)^2$$

$$\text{and} \quad s_2^2 = \frac{1}{n_2}\sum_{j=1}^{n_2}(y_j - \bar{x}_2)^2$$

Now, mean $\bar{x}$ of the combined series is given by

$$\bar{x} = \frac{1}{n_1 + n_2}\left[\sum_{i=1}^{n_1} x_i + \sum_{j=1}^{n_2} y_j\right] = \frac{n_1 \bar{x}_1 + n_2 \bar{x}_2}{n_1 + n_2}$$

The variance σ^2 of the combined series is given by

$$\sigma^2 = \frac{1}{n_1 + n_2}\left[\sum_{i=1}^{n_1}(x_i - \bar{x})^2 + \sum_{j=1}^{n_2}(y_j - \bar{x})^2\right]$$

Now, $$\sum_{i=1}^{n_1}(x_i-\bar{x})^2=\sum_{i=1}^{n_1}(x_i-\bar{x}_1+\bar{x}_1-\bar{x})^2$$

$$=\sum_{i=1}^{n_1}(x_i-\bar{x}_1)^2+n_1(\bar{x}_1-\bar{x})^2+2(\bar{x}_1-\bar{x})\sum_{i=1}^{n_1}(x_i-\bar{x}_1)$$

But $\sum_{i=1}^{n_1}(x_i-\bar{x}_1)=0$ [$\because$ algebraic sum of the deviation of values of first series from their mean is zero]

Also, $$\sum_{i=1}^{n_1}(x_i-\bar{x})^2=n_1s_1^2+n_1(\bar{x}_1-\bar{x})^2=n_1s_1^2+n_1d_1^2$$ [from Eq. (i)]

Where, $d_1=(\bar{x}_1-\bar{x})$

Similarly, $$\sum_{j=1}^{n_2}(y_j-\bar{x})^2=\sum_{j=1}^{n_2}(y_j-\bar{x}_2+\bar{x}_2-\bar{x})^2$$

$$=n_2s_2^2+n_2d_2^2$$ [from Eq. (ii)]

Where, $d_2=\bar{x}_2-\bar{x}$

Combined SD, $$\sigma=\sqrt{\frac{[n_1(s_1^2+d_1^2)+n_2(s_2^2+d_2^2)]}{n_1+n_2}}$$

Where, $$d_1=\bar{x}_1-\bar{x}=\bar{x}_1-\left(\frac{n_1\bar{x}_1+n_2\bar{x}_2}{n_1+n_2}\right)=\frac{n_2(\bar{x}_1-\bar{x}_2)}{n_1+n_2}$$

And $$d_2=\bar{x}_2-\bar{x}=\bar{x}_2-\frac{n_1\bar{x}_1+n_2\bar{x}_2}{n_1+n_2}=\frac{n_1(\bar{x}_2-\bar{x}_1)}{n_1+n_2}$$

$\therefore$ $$\sigma^2=\frac{1}{n_1+n_2}\left[n_1s_1^2+n_2s_2^2+\frac{n_1n_2^2(\bar{x}_1-\bar{x}_2)^2}{(n_1+n_2)^2}+\frac{n_2n_1^2(\bar{x}_2-\bar{x}_1)^2}{(n_1+n_2)^2}\right]$$

Hence, $$\sigma=\sqrt{\frac{n_1s_1^2+n_2s_2^2}{n_1+n_2}+\frac{n_1n_2(\bar{x}_1-\bar{x}_2)^2}{(n_1+n_2)^2}}$$

Q.8 Two sets each of 20 observations, have the same standard deviation 5. The first set has a mean 17 and the second mean 22.

Determine the standard deviation of the set obtained by combining the given two sets.

Ans. Given, $n_1=20$, $\sigma_1=5$, $\bar{x}_1=17$ and $n_2=20$, $\sigma_2=5$, $\bar{x}_2=22$

As we know, $$\sigma=\sqrt{\frac{n_1s_1^2+n_2s_2^2}{n_1+n_2}+\frac{n_1n_2(\bar{x}_1-\bar{x}_2)^2}{(n_1+n_2)^2}}$$

$$=\sqrt{\frac{20\times(5)^2+20\times(5)^2}{20+20}+\frac{20\times20\,(17-22)^2}{(20+20)^2}}$$

$$=\sqrt{\frac{1000}{40}+\frac{400\times25}{1600}}$$

$$=\sqrt{25+\frac{25}{4}}=\sqrt{\frac{125}{4}}=\sqrt{31.25}=5.59$$

Q.9 The frequency distribution

x	A	$2A$	$3A$	$4A$	$5A$	$6A$
f	2	1	1	1	1	1

where, A is a positive integer, has a variance of 160. Determine the value of A.

Ans.

x_i	f_i	$f_i x_i$	$f_i x_i^2$
A	2	$2A$	$2A^2$
$2A$	1	$2A$	$4A^2$
$3A$	1	$3A$	$9A^2$
$4A$	1	$4A$	$16A^2$
$5A$	1	$5A$	$25A^2$
$6A$	1	$6A$	$36A^2$
Total	7	$22A$	$92A^2$
	$\Sigma f_i = 7$	$\Sigma f_i x_i = 22A$	$\Sigma f_i x_i^2 = 92A^2$

$$\therefore \quad \text{Variance}(\sigma^2) = \frac{\Sigma f_i x_i^2}{\Sigma f_i} - \left(\frac{\Sigma f_i x_i}{\Sigma f_i}\right)^2$$

$$\Rightarrow \quad 160 = \frac{92A^2}{7} - \left(\frac{22A}{7}\right)^2$$

$$\Rightarrow \quad 160 = \frac{92A^2}{7} - \frac{484A^2}{49}$$

$$\Rightarrow \quad 160 = (644 - 484)\frac{A^2}{49}$$

$$\Rightarrow \quad 160 = \frac{160A^2}{49} \Rightarrow A^2 = 49$$

$$\Rightarrow \quad A = 7 \qquad [\because A \text{ is a positive integer}]$$

Q.10 For the frequency diviation

x	2	3	4	5	6	7
f	4	9	16	14	11	6

Find the standard deviation.

Ans. Take assumed mean as 4, we construct the following table

x_i	f_i	$d_i = x_i - 4$	$f_i d_i$	$f_i d_i^2$
2	4	−2	−8	16
3	9	−1	−9	9
4	16	0	0	0
5	14	1	14	14
6	11	2	22	44
7	6	3	18	54
Total	$\Sigma f_i = 60$		$\Sigma f_i d_i = 37$	$\Sigma f_i d_i^2 = 137$

Now, $$\text{SD} = \sqrt{\frac{\Sigma f_i d_i^2}{\Sigma f_i} - \left(\frac{\Sigma f_i d_i}{\Sigma f_i}\right)^2} = \sqrt{\frac{137}{60} - \left(\frac{37}{60}\right)^2}$$

$$= \sqrt{2.2833 - (0.616)^2} = \sqrt{2.2833 - 0.3794}$$

$$= \sqrt{1.9039} = 1.38 \text{ (approx)}$$

Mistake Alert! *While using the formula for standard deviation in grouped data, students may forget to multiply each frequency (f_i) with its corresponding (d_i^2).*

Q.11 There are 60 students in a class. The following is the frequency distribution of the marks obtained by the students in a test :

Marks	0	1	2	3	4	5
Frequency	$x-2$	x	x^2	$(x+1)^2$	$2x$	$x+1$

where, x is positive integer. Determine the mean and standard deviation of the marks.

Ans. $\because$ Sum of frequencies = 60

$$x - 2 + x + x^2 + (x+1)^2 + 2x + x + 1 = 60$$

$$\Rightarrow \quad 2x^2 + 7x - 60 = 0$$

$$\Rightarrow \quad 2x^2 + 15x - 8x - 60 = 0$$

$$\Rightarrow \quad x(2x + 15) - 4(2x + 15) = 0$$

$$\Rightarrow \quad (2x + 15)(x - 4) = 0$$

$$\Rightarrow \quad x = -\frac{15}{2}, 4$$

But $$x \neq -\frac{15}{2} \quad [\because x \in I^+]$$

So, $$x = 4$$

Let the assumed mean be $A = 3$

Now, we construct the following table.

x_i	f_i	$d_i = x_i - 3$	$f_i d_i$	$f_i d_i^2$
0	2	−3	−6	18
1	4	−2	−8	16
2	16	−1	−16	16
$A = 3$	25	0	0	0
4	8	1	8	8
5	5	2	10	20
Total	$\Sigma f_i = 60$		$\Sigma f_i d_i = -12$	$\Sigma f_i d_i^2 = 78$

$$\text{Mean} = A + \frac{\Sigma f_i d_i}{\Sigma f_i} = 3 + \left(\frac{-12}{60}\right) = 2.8$$

$$\sigma = \sqrt{\frac{\Sigma f_i d_i^2}{\Sigma f_i} - \left(\frac{\Sigma f_i d_i}{\Sigma f_i}\right)^2} = \sqrt{\frac{78}{60} - \left(\frac{-12}{60}\right)^2}$$

$$= \sqrt{1.3 - 0.04} = \sqrt{1.26} = 1.12 \text{ (approx)}$$

Q.12 The mean life of a sample of 60 bulbs was 650 hours and the standard deviation was 8 hours. A second sample of 80 bulbs has a mean life of 660 hours and standard deviation 7 hours. Find the overall standard deviation.

Sol. Here, $n_1 = 60, \bar{x}_1 = 650, s_1 = 8$ and $n_2 = 80, \bar{x}_2 = 660, s_2 = 7$

$$\therefore \quad \sigma = \sqrt{\frac{n_1 s_1^2 + n_2 s_2^2}{n_1 + n_2} + \frac{n_1 n_2(\bar{x}_1 - \bar{x}_2)^2}{(n_1 + n_2)^2}}$$

$$= \sqrt{\frac{60 \times (8)^2 + 80 \times (7)^2}{60 + 80} + \frac{60 \times 80(650 - 660)^2}{(60 + 80)^2}}$$

$$= \sqrt{\frac{6 \times 64 + 8 \times 49}{14} + \frac{60 \times 80 \times 100}{140 \times 140}}$$

$$= \sqrt{\frac{192 + 196}{7} + \frac{1200}{49}}$$

$$= \sqrt{\frac{388}{7} + \frac{1200}{49}}$$

$$= \sqrt{\frac{2716 + 1200}{49}}$$

$$= \sqrt{\frac{3916}{49}} = \frac{62 \cdot 58}{7} = 8 \cdot 9 \text{ (approx)}$$

Q.13 Mean and standard deviation of 100 items are 50 and 4 respectively. Find the sum of all the items and the sum of the squares of items.

Ans. Here, $\bar{x} = 50, n = 100$ and $\sigma = 4$

$$\because \quad \text{Mean } (\bar{x}) = \frac{\Sigma x_i}{100} = 50$$

$$\Rightarrow \quad \Sigma x_i = 5000$$

And
$$\sigma^2 = \frac{\Sigma x_i^2}{n} - \left(\frac{\Sigma x_i}{n}\right)^2$$

$$\Rightarrow \quad (4)^2 = \frac{\Sigma x_i^2}{100} - (50)^2$$

$$\Rightarrow \quad 16 = \frac{\Sigma x_i^2}{100} - 2500$$

$$\Rightarrow \quad \frac{\Sigma x_i^2}{100} = 16 + 2500 = 2516$$

$$\therefore \quad \Sigma x_i^2 = 251600$$

Q.14 If for a distribution $\Sigma(x - 5) = 3$, $\Sigma(x - 5)^2 = 43$ and total number of item is 18, find the mean and standard deviation.

Ans. Given, $n = 18, \Sigma(x - 5) = 3$ and $\Sigma(x - 5)^2 = 43$

$$\therefore \quad \text{Mean} = A + \frac{\Sigma(x - 5)}{18}$$ [where, A = Assumed mean]

$$=5+\frac{3}{18}=5+0.1666=5.1666=5.17$$

And $$\text{SD}=\sqrt{\frac{\Sigma(x-5)^2}{n}-\left(\frac{\Sigma(x-5)}{n}\right)^2}$$

$$=\sqrt{\frac{43}{18}-\left(\frac{3}{18}\right)^2}$$

$$=\sqrt{2.39-0.0277}=\sqrt{2.3623}\approx 1.53$$

Q.15 Find the mean and variance of the frequency distribution given below

x	$1 \le x \le 3$	$3 \le x \le 5$	$5 \le x \le 7$	$7 \le x \le 10$
f	6	4	5	1

Ans.

x	f_i	x_i	$f_i x_i$	$f_i x_i^2$
1-3	6	2	12	24
3-5	4	4	16	64
5-7	5	6	30	180
7-10	1	8.5	8.5	72.25
Total	$\Sigma f_i = 16$		$\Sigma f_i x_i = 66.5$	$\Sigma f_i x_i^2 = 340.25$

$\therefore$ $$\text{Mean}=\frac{\Sigma f_i x_i}{\Sigma f_i}=\frac{66.5}{16}=4.15$$

And $$\text{variance}\,(\sigma^2)=\frac{\Sigma f_i x_i^2}{\Sigma f_i}-\left(\frac{\Sigma f_i x_i}{\Sigma f_i}\right)^2$$

$$=\frac{340.25}{16}-(4.15)^2=21.2656-17.2225=4.043$$

Long Answer Type Questions

Q.16 Calculate the mean deviation about the mean for the following frequency distribution.

Class interval	0-4	4-8	8-12	12-16	16-20
Frequency	4	6	8	5	2

Ans.

Class internal	f_i	x_i	$f_i x_i$	$d_i = \lvert x_i - \bar{x} \rvert$	$f_i d_i$
0-4	4	2	8	7.2	28.8
4-8	6	6	36	3.2	19.2
8-12	8	10	80	0.8	6.4
12-16	5	14	70	4.8	24.0
16-20	2	18	36	8.8	17.6
Total	$\Sigma f_i = 25$		$\Sigma f_i x_i = 230$		$\Sigma f_i d_i = 96$

$\therefore$ $$\text{Mean} = \frac{\Sigma f_i x_i}{\Sigma f_i} = \frac{230}{25} = 9.2$$

And mean deviation about mean $= \dfrac{\Sigma f_i d_i}{\Sigma f_i} = \dfrac{96}{25} = 3.84$

Q.17 Calculate the mean deviation from the median of the following data.

Class interval	0-6	6-12	12-18	18-24	24-30
Frequency	4	5	3	6	2

Thinking Process We are to find the mean deviation about the median. So, first of all, median is to be calculated. It is continuous data. So, median can be calculated by using the formula

$$\text{Median} = l + \left(\frac{\frac{N}{2} - cf}{f}\right) \times h$$

Ans.

Class interval	f_i	x_i	cf	$d_i = \lvert x_i - M \rvert$	$f_i d_i$
0-6	4	3	4	11	44
6-12	5	9	9	5	25
12-18	3	15	12	1	3
18-24	6	21	18	7	42
24-30	2	27	20	13	26
Total	$N = 20$				$\Sigma f_i d_i = 140$

$\because$ $$\frac{N}{2} = \frac{20}{2} = 10$$

So, the median class is 12-18.

$\because$ $$\text{Median}\,(M) = l + \left(\frac{\frac{N}{2} - cf}{f}\right) \times h$$

Here, l = lower limit of median class = 12

N = Total frequency = 20

cf = Cumulative frequency of pre-median class = 9

f = Frequency of median class = 3

h = Class size = 6

$\therefore$ $$M = 12 + \frac{\frac{20}{2} - 9}{3} \times 6$$

$$= 12 + \frac{1}{3} \times 6 = 12 + 2 = 14$$

$\therefore$ $$\text{MD about median} = \frac{\Sigma f_i d_i}{\Sigma f_i} = \frac{140}{20} = 7$$

Mistake Alert! *Students may mistakenly take the value of 'cf' of the median class instead of the value of 'cf' of the class preceding the median class.*

Q.18 Determine the mean and standard deviation for the following distribution

Marks	2	3	4	5	6	7	8	9	10	11	12	13	14	15	16
Frequency	1	6	6	8	8	2	2	3	0	2	1	0	0	0	1

Ans.

Marks x_i	f_i	$f_i x_i$	$d_i = x_i - \bar{x}$	$f_i d_i$	$f_i d_i^2$
2	1	2	$2-6=-4$	-4	16
3	6	18	$3-6=-3$	-18	54
4	6	24	$4-6=-2$	-12	24
5	8	40	$5-6=-1$	-8	8
6	8	48	$6-6=0$	0	0
7	2	14	$7-6=1$	2	2
8	2	16	$8-6=2$	4	8
9	3	27	$9-6=3$	9	27
10	0	0	$10-6=4$	0	0
11	2	22	$11-6=5$	10	50
12	1	12	$12-6=6$	6	36
13	0	0	$13-6=7$	0	0
14	0	0	$14-6=8$	0	0
15	0	0	$15-6=9$	0	0
16	1	16	$16-6=10$	10	100
Total	$\Sigma f_i = 40$	$\Sigma f_i x_i = 239$		$\Sigma f_i d_i = -1$	$\Sigma f_i d_i^2 = 325$

$$\therefore \quad \text{Mean } (\bar{x}) = \frac{\Sigma f_i x_i}{\Sigma f_i} = \frac{239}{40} = 5.975 \approx 6$$

$$\text{And S.D. } (\sigma) = \sqrt{\frac{\Sigma f_i d_i^2}{\Sigma f_i} - \left(\frac{\Sigma f_i d_i}{\Sigma f_i}\right)^2} = \sqrt{\frac{325}{40} - \left(\frac{-1}{40}\right)^2} = \sqrt{8.125 - 0.000625}$$

$$= \sqrt{8.124375} = 2 \cdot 85 \text{ (approx)}$$

Q.19 The weights of coffee in 70 jars is shown in the following table :

Weight (in grams)	Frequency
200-201	13
201-202	27
202-203	18
203-204	10
204-205	1
205-206	1

Determine variance and standard deviation of the above distribution.

Ans.

Class-interval	f_i	x_i	$d_i = x_i - 202\cdot5$	$f_i d_i$	$f_i d_i^2$
200-201	13	200.5	–2	–26	52
201-202	27	201.5	–1	–27	27
202-203	18	202.5	0	0	0
203-204	10	203.5	1	10	10
204-205	1	204.5	2	2	4
205-206	1	205.5	3	3	9
Total	$N = 70$			$\Sigma f_i\, d_i = -38$	$\Sigma f_i\, d_i^2 = 102$

$\therefore$ Variance,

$$\sigma^2 = \frac{1}{N}\sum f_i d_i^2 - \left(\frac{\sum f_i d_i}{N}\right)^2$$

$$= \left(\frac{1}{70}\times 102\right) - \left[\frac{1}{70}\times(-38)\right]^2$$

$$= 1.457 - 0.295 = 1.162 \text{ gm}$$

Standard derivation

$$\sigma = \sqrt{1.162} = 1\cdot08 \text{ gm}$$

Q.20 Determine mean and standard deviation of first n terms of an AP whose first term is a and common difference is d.

Ans.

x_i	$x_i - a$	$(x_i - a)^2$
a	0	0
$a + d$	d	d^2
$a + 2d$	$2d$	$4d^2$
.....	.....	$9d^2$
.....	.....	.....
.....	.....	.....
$a + (n-1)d$	$(n-1)d$	$(n-1)^2 d^2$
$\Sigma x_i = \frac{n}{2}[2a + (n-1)d]$		

$\because$ $$\text{Mean} = \frac{\Sigma x_i}{n} = \frac{1}{n}\left[\frac{n}{2}(2a + (n-1)\,d)\right] = a + \frac{(n-1)}{2}d$$

$\therefore$ $$\Sigma(x_i - a) = d[1 + 2 + 3 + \ldots + (n-1)]$$ [where, a is assumed mean]

$$= d\frac{(n-1)n}{2}$$

And $$\Sigma(x_i - a)^2 = d^2\,[1^2 + 2^2 + 3^2 + \ldots + (n-1)^2]$$

$$= \frac{d^2(n-1)n(2n-1)}{6}$$

$$\sigma = \sqrt{\frac{\Sigma(x_i - a)^2}{n} - \left(\frac{\Sigma(x_i - a)}{n}\right)^2}$$

$$= \sqrt{\frac{d^2(n-1)(n)(2n-1)}{6n} - \left[\frac{d(n-1)\,n}{2n}\right]^2}$$

$$= \sqrt{\frac{d^2(n-1)(2n-1)}{6} - \frac{d^2(n-1)^2}{4}}$$

$$= d\sqrt{\frac{(n-1)(2n-1)}{6} - \frac{(n-1)^2}{4}} = d\sqrt{\frac{(n-1)}{2}\left(\frac{2n-1}{3} - \frac{n-1}{2}\right)}$$

$$= d\sqrt{\frac{(n-1)}{2}\left[\frac{4n-2-3n+3}{6}\right]}$$

$$= d\sqrt{\frac{(n-1)(n+1)}{12}} = d\sqrt{\frac{n^2-1}{12}}$$

***Q.21** Following are the marks obtained, out of 100, by two students Ravi and Hashina in 10 tests.

Ravi	25	50	45	30	70	42	36	48	35	60
Hashina	10	70	50	20	95	55	42	60	48	80

Who is more intelligent and who is more consistent?

Ans. For Ravi, we construct the following table

x_i	$d_i = x_i - 45$	d_i^2
25	−20	400
50	5	25
45	0	0
30	−15	225
70	25	625
42	−3	9
36	−9	81
48	3	9
35	−10	100
60	15	225
Total	$\Sigma d_i = -9$	$\Sigma d^2{}_i = 1699$

Here, assumed mean, $A = 45$

$$\therefore \text{ Standard deviation } (\sigma) = \sqrt{\frac{\Sigma d^2{}_i}{n} - \left(\frac{\Sigma d_i}{n}\right)^2}$$

$$= \sqrt{\frac{1699}{10} - \left(\frac{-9}{10}\right)^2}$$

$$= \sqrt{169.9 - 0.81} = \sqrt{169.09} \approx 13$$

Now, $\quad \text{mean } (\bar{x}) = A + \frac{\Sigma d_i}{\Sigma f_i} = 45 - \frac{9}{10} = 44.1$

(✱) Topics related to these question have been removed from latest NCERT.

For Hashina, we construct the following table.

x_i	$d_i = x_i - 55$	d_i^2
10	–45	2025
70	15	225
50	–5	25
20	–35	1225
95	40	1600
55	0	0
42	–13	169
60	5	25
48	–7	49
80	25	625
Total	$\Sigma d_i = -20$	$\Sigma d_i^2 = 5968$

Here, we assumed mean $=55$

$\therefore$ Standard deviation $(\sigma) = \sqrt{\frac{5968}{10} - \left(\frac{-20}{10}\right)^2} = \sqrt{592.8} = 24.43$

And $\quad$ mean $(\bar{x}) = A + \frac{\sum di}{\sum fi}$

$$= 55 + \left(\frac{-20}{10}\right) = 53$$

For Ravi, coefficient of variation $(CV_1) = \frac{\sigma}{\bar{x}} \times 100 = \frac{13}{44.1} \times 100 = 29.48$

For Hashina, coefficient of variation $(CV_2) = \frac{\sigma}{\bar{x}} \times 100 = \frac{24.43}{55} \times 100 = 46.09$

Hence, Hashina is more consistent and intelligent.

Q.22 Mean and standard deviation of 100 observations were found to be 40 and 10, respectively. If at the time of calculation two observations were wrongly taken as 30 and 70 in place of 3 and 27 respectively, find the correct standard deviation.

Ans. Given, $n = 100$, incorrect standardar deviation $(\sigma) = 10$ and Incorrect mean $(\bar{x}) = 40$

$\therefore \quad \frac{\Sigma x_i}{n} = 40$

$\Rightarrow \quad \frac{\Sigma x_i}{100} = 40$

$\Rightarrow \quad$ Incorrect $\Sigma x_i = 4000$

Now, $\quad$ Correct $\Sigma x_i = 4000 - 30 - 70 + 3 + 27$

$\therefore \quad = 4030 - 100 = 3930$

Correct mean $= \frac{3930}{100} = 39.3$

Now, $\sigma^2 = \frac{\Sigma x_i^2}{n} - (40)^2$

$\Rightarrow$ $100 = \frac{\Sigma x_i^2}{100} - 1600$

$\Rightarrow$ Incorrect $\Sigma x_i^2 = 170000$

Now, Correct $\Sigma x_i^2 = 170000 - (30)^2 - (70)^2 + 3^2 + (27)^2$

$= 164938$

$\therefore$ Correct $\sigma = \sqrt{\frac{164938}{100} - (39.3)^2}$

$= \sqrt{1649.38 - 39.3 \times 39.3}$

$= \sqrt{1649.38 - 1544.49}$

$= \sqrt{104.89} = 10.24$

Q.23 **While calculating the mean and variance of 10 readings, a student wrongly used the reading 52 for the correct reading 25. He obtained the mean and variance as 45 and 16 respectively. Find the correct mean and the variance.**

Ans. Given, $n=10$, incorrect mean $(\bar{x}) = 45$ and incorrect variance $(\sigma^2) = 16$

$\because$ $\bar{x} = 45$

$\Rightarrow$ $\frac{\Sigma x_i}{n} = 45$

$\Rightarrow$ $\frac{\Sigma x_i}{10} = 45$

$\Rightarrow$ Incorrect $\Sigma x_i = 450$

Now, Correct $\Sigma x_i = 450 - 52 + 25 = 423$

$\therefore$ Correct mean $= \frac{423}{10} = 42\cdot 3$

Also, $\sigma^2 = \frac{\Sigma x_i^2}{n} - \left(\frac{\Sigma x_i}{n}\right)^2$

$\Rightarrow$ $16 = \frac{\Sigma x_i^2}{10} - (45)^2$

$\Rightarrow$ $\Sigma x_i^2 = 10\,(2025 + 16)$

$\Rightarrow$ Incorrect $\Sigma x_i^2 = 20410$

$\therefore$ Correct $\Sigma x_i^2 = 20410 - (52)^2 + (25)^2 = 18331$

$\therefore$ Correct $\sigma^2 = \frac{18331}{10} - (42\cdot 3)^2 = 43.81$

Objective Type Questions

Choose the correct answer out of the given four options in each of the exercises 24 to 39.

Q.24 The mean deviation of the data 3, 10, 10, 4, 7, 10, 5 from the mean is

(a) 2 (b) 2.57 (c) 3 (d) 3.75

Thinking process Mean deviation about mean can be calculated by the formula $= \frac{\Sigma|x_i - \overline{x}|}{n}$, where, $\overline{x}$ = mean of the given observations.

Ans. ***(b)*** Given, observations are 3, 10, 10, 4, 7, 10 and 5.

$$\therefore \quad \text{Mean}(\overline{x}) = \frac{3 + 10 + 10 + 4 + 7 + 10 + 5}{7} = \frac{49}{7} = 7$$

x_i	$d_i = \lvert x_i - \overline{x} \rvert$
3	4
10	3
10	3
4	3
7	0
10	3
5	2
Total	$\Sigma d_i = 18$

Now, mean deviation about mean (MD) $= \frac{\Sigma d_i}{N} = \frac{18}{7} = 2 \cdot 57$

Q.25 Mean deviation for n observations $x_1, x_2, \ldots, x_n$ from their mean $\overline{x}$ is given by

(a) $\sum_{i=1}^{n}(x_i - \overline{x})$ (b) $\frac{1}{n}\sum_{i=1}^{n}|x_i - \overline{x}|$ (c) $\sum_{i=1}^{n}(x_i - \overline{x})^2$ (d) $\frac{1}{n}\sum_{i=1}^{n}(x_i - \overline{x})^2$

Ans. ***(b)*** MD about mean $= \frac{1}{n}\sum_{i=1}^{n}|x_i - \overline{x}|$

Q.26 When tested, the lives (in hours) of 5 bulbs were noted as follows

1357, 1090, 1666, 1494, 1623

The mean deviations (in hours) from their mean is

(a) 178 (b) 179

(c) 220 (d) 356

Ans. ***(a)*** Since, the lives of 5 bulbs are 1357, 1090, 1666, 1494 and 1623.

$$\therefore \quad \text{Mean}(\overline{x}) = \frac{1357 + 1090 + 1666 + 1494 + 1623}{5}$$

$$= \frac{7230}{5} = 1446$$

x_i	$d_i = \lvert x_i - \bar{x} \rvert$
1357	89
1090	356
1666	220
1494	48
1623	177
Total	$\Sigma d_i = 890$

MD about mean $= \dfrac{\Sigma d_i}{N} = \dfrac{890}{5} = 178$

Q.27 Following are the marks obtained by 9 students in a mathematics test

50, 69, 20, 33, 53, 39, 40, 65, 59

The mean deviation from the median is

(a) 9
(b) 10.5
(c)12.67
(d) 14.76

- **Concept Insight** For ungrouped data, arrange the data in ascending or descending order. If n is odd, then median $= \left(\dfrac{n+1}{2}\right)$th observation.

Ans. *(c)* Since, marks obtained by 9 students in Mathematics are 50, 69, 20, 33, 53, 39, 40, 65 and 59.

Rewrite the given data in ascending order.

20,33, 39, 40, 50, 53, 59, 65, 69,

Here, $n = 9$ [odd]

$\therefore$ Median $(M) = \left(\dfrac{9+1}{2}\right)$ term $= 5$ th term

$\therefore$ $M = 50$

x_i	$\lvert x_i - M \rvert$
20	30
33	17
39	11
40	10
50	0
53	3
59	9
65	15
69	19
Total	$\Sigma \lvert x_i - M \rvert = 114$

$\therefore$ MD about median $\dfrac{\Sigma \lvert x_i - M \rvert}{n} = \dfrac{114}{9} = 12.67$

Q.28 The standard deviation of data 6, 5, 9, 13, 12, 8 and 10 is

(a) $\sqrt{\frac{52}{7}}$ (b) $\frac{52}{7}$ (c) $\sqrt{6}$ (d) 6

- **Concept Insight** Use the formula of standard deviation (S.D) = $\sqrt{\frac{\Sigma x_i^2}{N} - \left(\frac{\Sigma x_i}{N}\right)^2}$.

Ans. *(a)* Given, data are 6, 5, 9, 13, 12, 8, and 10.

x_i	x_i^2
6	36
5	25
9	81
13	169
12	144
8	64
10	100
$\Sigma x_i = 63$	$\Sigma x_i^2 = 619$

Now, $$\text{SD}(\sigma) = \sqrt{\frac{\Sigma x_i^2}{N} - \left(\frac{\Sigma x_i}{N}\right)^2} = \sqrt{\frac{619}{7} - \left(\frac{63}{7}\right)^2}$$

$$= \sqrt{\frac{7 \times 619 - 3969}{49}} = \sqrt{\frac{4333 - 3969}{49}}$$

$$= \sqrt{\frac{364}{49}} = \sqrt{\frac{52}{7}}$$

Q.29 Let $x_1, x_2, \ldots, x_n$ be n observations and $\bar{x}$ be their arithmetic mean. The formula for the standard deviation is given by

(a) $\Sigma(x_i - \bar{x})^2$ (b) $\frac{\Sigma(x_i - \bar{x})^2}{n}$ (c) $\sqrt{\frac{\Sigma(x_i - \bar{x})^2}{n}}$ (d) $\sqrt{\frac{\Sigma x^2{}_i}{n} + \bar{x}^2}$

Ans. *(c)* The formula for SD is given by $\sigma = \sqrt{\frac{\Sigma(x_i - \bar{x})^2}{n}}$

Q.30 The mean of 100 observations is 50 and their standard deviation is 5. The sum of all squares of all the observations is

(a) 50000 (b) 250000 (c) 252500 (d) 255000

Ans. *(c)* Given, $\bar{x} = 50$, $n = 100$ and $\sigma = 5$

Now, $$\sigma = \sqrt{\frac{\Sigma x_i^2}{n} - \left(\frac{\Sigma x_i}{n}\right)^2} \Rightarrow \sigma^2 = \frac{\Sigma x_i^2}{n} - (\bar{x})^2$$

$$\Rightarrow \quad 25 = \frac{\Sigma x_i^2}{100} - (50)^2 \Rightarrow 25 = \frac{\Sigma x_i^2}{100} - 2500$$

$$\Rightarrow \quad 2525 = \frac{\Sigma x_i^2}{100}$$

$$\therefore \quad \Sigma x_i^2 = 252500$$

Q.31 Let a, b, c, d, e be the observations with mean m and standard deviation s. The standard deviation of the observations $a+k, b+k, c+k, d+k$ and $e+k$ is

(a) s (b) ks (c) $s+k$ (d) $\frac{s}{k}$

Ans. **(a)** Given, observations are a, b, c, d and e.

$$\therefore \quad \text{Mean} = m = \frac{a+b+c+d+e}{5}$$

$$\Rightarrow \quad \Sigma x_i = a+b+c+d+e = 5m$$

And
$$\text{SD} = s = \sqrt{\frac{\sum x_1^2}{5} - m^2}$$

Now,
$$\text{Mean} = \frac{a+k+b+k+c+k+d+k+e+k}{5}$$

$$= \frac{(a+b+c+d+e)+5k}{5} = m+k$$

Now,
$$\text{SD} = \sqrt{\frac{\Sigma(x_i+k)^2}{5} - (m+k)^2}$$

$$= \sqrt{\frac{\Sigma(x_i^2+k^2+2k\,x_i)}{5} - (m^2+k^2+2mk)}$$

$$= \sqrt{\frac{\Sigma x_i^2}{5} - m^2 + \frac{2k\Sigma x_i}{5} - 2mk}$$

$$= \sqrt{\frac{\Sigma x_i^2}{5} - m^2 + 2km - 2mk} \qquad \left[\because \frac{\Sigma x_i}{5} = m\right]$$

$$= \sqrt{\frac{\Sigma x_i^2}{5} - m^2} = s$$

Q.32 Let x_1, x_2, x_3, x_4, x_5 be the observations with mean m and standard deviation s. The standard deviation of the observations kx_1, kx_2, kx_3, kx_4 and kx_5 is

(a) $k+s$ (b) $\frac{s}{k}$ (c) ks (d) s

Ans. **(c)** We have,
$$m = \frac{\Sigma x_i}{5},\ s = \sqrt{\frac{\Sigma x_i^2}{5} - \left(\frac{\Sigma x_i}{5}\right)^2}$$

Now,
$$\text{SD} = \sqrt{\frac{k^2\Sigma x_i^2}{5} - \left(\frac{k\Sigma x_i}{5}\right)^2}$$

$$= \sqrt{\frac{k^2\Sigma x_i^2}{5} - k^2\left(\frac{\Sigma x_i}{5}\right)^2}$$

$$= k\sqrt{\left(\frac{\Sigma x_i^2}{5}\right) - \left(\frac{\Sigma x_i}{5}\right)^2} = ks$$

Q.33 Let $x_1, x_2, \ldots x_n$ be n observations. Let $w_i = lx_i + k$ for $i = 1, 2, \ldots, n$, where l and k are constants. If the mean of x_i's is 48 and their standard deviation is 12, the mean of w_i's is 55 and standard deviation of w_i's is 15, then the value of l and k should be

(a) $l = 1.25, k = -5$ (b) $l = -1.25, k = 5$
(c) $l = 2.5, k = -5$ (d) $l = 2.5, k = 5$

Ans. (a) Given, $w_i = lx_i + k$, $\bar{x}_i = 48$, SD of $x_i = 12$, $\bar{w}_i = 55$ and SD of $w_i = 15$

Then, $\bar{w}_i = l\bar{x}_i + k$

[where, $\bar{w}_i$ is mean w_i's and $\bar{x}_i$ is mean of x_i's]

$\Rightarrow$ $55 = l \times 48 + k$ ...(i)

Now, SD of $w_i = l \times$ SD of x_i

$\Rightarrow$ $15 = 12l$

$\Rightarrow$ $l = \dfrac{15}{12}$

$= 1.25$ ...(ii)

From Eqs. (i) and (ii), we get $k = 55 - 1.25 \times 48$

$= -5$

Q.34 Standard deviations for first 10 natural numbers is

(a) 5.5 (b) 3.87 (c) 2.97 (d) 2.87

Ans. *(d)* We know that SD of first n natural number $= \sqrt{\dfrac{n^2 - 1}{12}}$

$\therefore$ SD of first 10 natural numbers $= \sqrt{\dfrac{(10)^2 - 1}{12}}$

$$= \sqrt{\frac{100 - 1}{12}} = \sqrt{\frac{99}{12}} = \sqrt{8.25} = 2.87$$

Q.35 Consider the numbers 1, 2, 3, 4, 5, 6, 7, 8, 9, 10. If 1 is added to each number the variance of the numbers, so obtained is

(a) 6.5 (b) 2.87 (c) 3.87 (d) 8.25

Ans. *(d)* Given, numbers are 1, 2, 3, 4, 5, 6, 7, 8, 9 and 10.

If 1 is added to each number, then observations will be 2, 3, 4, 5, 6, 7, 8, 9, 10 and 11.

$\therefore$ $\Sigma x_i = 2 + 3 + 4 + \ldots + 11$

$= \dfrac{10}{2}[2 \times 2 + 9 \times 1] = 5[4 + 9] = 65$ [Since, this is an A.P. series]

and $\Sigma x_i^2 = 2^2 + 3^2 + 4^2 + 5^2 + \ldots + 11^2$

$= (1^2 + 2^2 + 3^2 + \ldots + 11^2) - (1^2)$

$= \dfrac{11 \times 12 \times 23}{6} - 1$ $\left[\because 1^2 + 2^2 + 3^2 + \ldots + n^2 = \dfrac{n(n+1)(2n+1)}{6}\right]$

$= \dfrac{11 \times 12 \times 23 - 6}{6} = 505$

$$\therefore \quad \sigma^2 = \frac{\Sigma x_i^2}{n} - \left(\frac{\Sigma x_i}{n}\right)^2 = \frac{505}{10} - \left(\frac{65}{10}\right)^2$$

$$= 50.5 - (6.5)^2$$

$$= 50.5 - 42.25 = 8.25$$

Q.36 Consider the first 10 positive integers. If we multiply each number by −1 and then add 1 to each number, the variance of the numbers so obtained is

(a) 8.25 (b) 6.5 (c) 3.87 (d) 2.87

Ans. ***(a)*** We have, the first 10 positive integers are 1, 2, 3, 4, 5, 6, 7, 8, 9 and 10.

On multiplying each number by −1, we get

$$-1, -2, -3, -4, -5, -6, -7, -8, -9, -10$$

On adding 1 in each number, we get

$$0, -1, -2, -3, -4, -5, -6, -7, -8, -9$$

$$\therefore \quad \Sigma x_i = 0 - 1 - 2 - 3 - 4 - 5 - 6 - 7 - 8 - 9$$

$$-[1 + 2 + 3 + \dots + 9]$$

$$= -\frac{9 \times 10}{2}$$

$$= -45$$

And $$\Sigma x_i^2 = 0^2 + (-1)^2 + (-2)^2 + \dots + (-9)^2$$

$$= 1^2 + 2^2 + 3^2 + \dots + 9^2$$

$$= \frac{9 \times 10 \times 19}{6}$$

$$= 285$$

$$\therefore \quad \text{New variance} = \frac{285}{10} - \left(\frac{-45}{10}\right)^2 = \frac{285}{10} - \frac{2025}{100}$$

$$= \frac{2850 - 2025}{100} = 8.25$$

Q.37 The following information relates to a sample of size 60; $\Sigma x^2 = 18000$, and $\Sigma x = 960$. The variance is

(a) 6.63 (b) 16 (c) 22 (d) 44

Ans. ***(d)*** Given, $\Sigma x^2 = 18000$, $\Sigma x = 960$, $n = 60$

$$\text{Variance} = \frac{\Sigma x_i^2}{n} - \left(\frac{\Sigma x_i}{n}\right)^2$$

$$= \frac{18000}{60} - \left(\frac{960}{60}\right)^2 = 300 - 256 = 44$$

***Q.38** Coefficient of variation of two distributions are 50 and 60, and their arithmetic means are 30 and 25 respectively. Difference of their standard deviation is

(a) 0 (b) 1 (c) 1.5 (d) 2.5

(*) Topics related to these question have been removed from latest NCERT.

Ans. *(a)* We have, $CV_1 = 50,\ CV_2 = 60,\ \bar{x}_1 = 30$ and $\bar{x}_2 = 25$

$\therefore \quad CV_1 = \frac{\sigma_1}{\bar{x}_1} \times 100 \Rightarrow 50 = \frac{\sigma_1}{30} \times 100$

$\Rightarrow \quad \sigma_1 = \frac{30 \times 50}{100} = 15$

And $\quad CV_2 = \frac{\sigma_2}{\bar{x}_2} \times 100$

$\Rightarrow \quad 60 = \frac{\sigma_2}{25} \times 100$

$\Rightarrow \quad \sigma_2 = \frac{60 \times 25}{100} = 15$

Now, $\quad \sigma_1 - \sigma_2 = 15 - 15 = 0$

Q.39 The standard deviation of some temperature data in °C is 5. If the data were converted into °F, the variance would be

(a) 81 (b) 57 (c) 36 (d) 25

Ans. *(a)* Given, $\sigma_C = 5$

We know that $\frac{5}{9}(F - 32) = C$

$\Rightarrow \quad F = \frac{9C}{5} + 32$

$\Rightarrow \quad \sigma_F = \frac{9}{5}\sigma_C = \frac{9}{5} \times 5 = 9$

Hence, $\quad \sigma_F^2 = (9)^2 = 81$

Fill in the blanks in exercises from 40 to 46.

***Q.40** Coefficient of variation $= \frac{\dots}{\text{Mean}} \times 100$

Ans. $CV = \frac{SD}{\text{Mean}} \times 100$

Q.41 If $\bar{x}$ is the mean of n values of x, then $\sum_{i=1}^{n}(x_i - \bar{x})$ is always equal to .... If a has any value other than $\bar{x}$, then $\sum_{i=1}^{n}(x_i - \bar{x})^2$ is .... than $\Sigma(x_i - a)^2$.

Ans. If $\bar{x}$ is the mean of n values of x, then $\sum_{i=1}^{n}(x_i - \bar{x}) = 0$ and if a has any value other than $\bar{x}$, then $\sum_{i=1}^{n}(x_i - \bar{x})^2$ is less than $\Sigma(x_i - a)^2$.

(*) Topics related to these question have been removed from latest NCERT.

Q.42 If the variance of a data is 121, then the standard deviation of the data is ....

Ans. If the variance of a data is 121.

Then, $$SD = \sqrt{\text{Variance}}$$
$$= \sqrt{121} = 11$$

Q.43 The standard deviation of a data is ...... of any change in origin, but is .... of change of scale.

Ans. The standard deviation of a data is independent of any change in origin, but is dependent on change of scale.

Q.44 The sum of squares of the deviations of the values of the variable is .... when taken about their arithmetic mean.

Ans. The sum of the squares of the deviations of the values of the variable is minimum when taken about their arithmetic mean.

Q.45 The mean deviation of the data is .... when measured from the median.

Ans. The mean deviation of the data is least when measured from the median.

Q.46 The standard deviation is .... to the mean deviation taken from the arithmetic mean.

Ans. The SD is greater than or equal to the mean deviation taken from the arithmetic mean.

Chapter 16

Probability

Short Answer Type Questions

Q.1 If the letters of the word 'ALGORITHM' are arranged at random in a row what is the probability the letters 'GOR' must remain together as a unit?

Ans. Number of letters in the word 'ALGORITHM' = 9

If 'GOR' remain together, then consider it as 1 group.

$\therefore$ Number of letters = 6 + 1 = 7

Number of word, if 'GOR' remain together = 7!

Total number of words from the letters of the word 'ALGORITHM' = 9!

$\therefore$ Required probability $= \frac{7!}{9!} = \frac{7!}{9 \times 8 \times 7!} = \frac{1}{72}$

Q.2 Six new employees, two of whom are married to each other, are to be assigned six desks that are lined up in a row. If the assignment of employees to desks is made randomly, what is the probability that the married couple will have non-adjacent desks?

Thinking Process First, find the probability that couple has adjacent desk and then subtract it from 1.

Ans. Let the couple occupied adjacent desks, consider those two as 1.

There are (4 + 1) *i.e.*, 5 persons to be assigned.

$\therefore$ Number of ways of assigning these five persons = 5! × 2!

Total number of ways of assigning 6 persons = 6!

$\therefore$ Probability that the couple has adjacent desk

$$= \frac{5! \times 2!}{6!}$$

$$= \frac{5! \times 2 \times 1}{6 \times 5!} = \frac{2}{6} = \frac{1}{3}$$

Probability that the married couple will have non-adjacent desks

$$= 1 - \frac{1}{3} = \frac{2}{3}$$

Q.3 Suppose an integer from 1 through 1000 is chosen at random, find the probability that the integer is a multiple of 2 or a multiple of 9.

Ans. Multiples of 2 from 1 to 1000 are 2, 4, 6, 8, ..., 1000.

Let n be the number of terms of above A.P. series.

$\therefore$ nth term = 1000

$\Rightarrow$ $2 + (n-1)\,2 = 1000$ $[T_n = a + (n-1)d]$

$\Rightarrow$ $2 + 2n - 2 = 1000$

$\Rightarrow$ $2n = 1000$

$\therefore$ $n = 500$

So, the number of multiples of 2 is 500.

The multiples of 9 are 9, 18, 27, ..., 999.

Let m be the number of term in above A.P. series.

$\therefore$ mth term = 999

$\Rightarrow$ $9 + (m-1)\,9 = 999$ $[T_n = a + (n-1)d]$

$\Rightarrow$ $9 + 9m - 9 = 999$

$\Rightarrow$ $9m = 999$

$\therefore$ $m = 111$

So, the number of multiples of 9 is 111.

The multiples of 2 and 9 both are 18, 36, ..., 990.

Let p be the number of terms in above A.P. series.

$\therefore$ pth term = 990

$\Rightarrow$ $18 + (p-1)18 = 990$ $[T_n = a + (n-1)d]$

$\Rightarrow$ $18 + 18p - 18 = 990$

$\Rightarrow$ $18p = 990$

$\therefore$ $p = \dfrac{990}{18} = 55$

So, the number of multiples of 2 and 9 is 55.

$\therefore$ Number of multiples of 2 or 9 $= 500 + 111 - 55 = 556$

$[\because n(A \cup B) = n(A) + n(B) - n(A \cap B)]$

$\therefore$ Required probability $= \dfrac{556}{1000} = 0.556$

Q.4 An experiment consists of rolling a die until a 2 appears.

(i) How many elements of the sample space correspond to the event that the 2 appears on the kth roll of the die?

(ii) How many elements of the sample space correspond to the event that the 2 appears not later than the kth roll of the die?

Ans. In a throw of a die there is 6 sample points.

(i) If 2 appears on the kth roll of the die.

So, first $(k-1)$ roll have 5 outcomes each and kth roll results 2 *i.e.*, 1 outcome.

$\therefore$ Number of elements of sample space correspond to the event that 2 appears on the kth roll of the die $= 5 \times 5 \times 5 \times \ldots (k-1)$ times $= 5^{k-1}$

(ii) If we consider that 2 appears not later than kth roll of the die, then it is possible that 2 comes in first throw *i.e.,* 1 outcome.

If 2 does not appear in first throw, then outcomes will be 5 and 2 comes in second throw *i.e.,* 1 outcome.

Possible outcome $= 5 \times 1 = 5$

Similarly, if 2 does not appear in second throw and appears in third throw.

$\therefore$ Possible outcomes $= 5 \times 5 \times 1$

Given, series $= 1 + 5 + (5 \times 5) + (5 \times 5 \times 5) + \ldots + 5^{k-1}$

$$= 1 + 5 + 5^2 + 5^3 + \ldots + 5^{k-1}$$

$$= \frac{1(5^k - 1)}{5 - 1} = \frac{5^k - 1}{4} \qquad \left[S_n = \frac{a(r^n - 1)}{r - 1}, \text{when } r > 1\right]$$

Q.5 **A die is loaded in such a way that each odd number is twice as likely to occur as each even number. Find $P(G)$, where G is the event that a number greater than 3 occurs on a single roll of the die.**

Ans. Let $P(O)$ be the probability of an odd number and $P(E)$ be the probability of an even number.

It is given that 2 × Probability of even number = Probability of odd number

$$\Rightarrow \quad P(O) = 2P(E)$$

$$\Rightarrow \quad P(O) : P(E) = 2 : 1$$

$\therefore$ Probability of occurring an odd number, $P(O) = \frac{2}{2+1} = \frac{2}{3}$

and probability of occurring an even number, $P(E) = \frac{1}{2+1} = \frac{1}{3}$

Now, G be the event that a number greater than 3 occurs in a single roll of die.

So, the possible outcomes are 4, 5 and 6 out of which two are even and one odd.

$\therefore$ Required probability $= P(G) = 2 \times P(E) \times P(O)$

$$= 2 \times \frac{1}{3} \times \frac{2}{3} = \frac{4}{9}$$

Q.6 **In a large metropolitan area, the probabilities are 0.87, 0.36, 0.30 that a family (randomly chosen for a sample survey) owns a colour television set, a black and white television set or both kinds of sets. What is the probability that a family owns either anyone or both kinds of sets?**

Ans. Let E_1 be the event that family owns colour television set and E_2 be the event that family owns a black and white television set.

It is given that, $P(E_1) = 0.87$

$$P(E_2) = 0.36$$

and $P(E_1 \cap E_2) = 0.30$

We have to find probability that a family owns either anyone or both kinds of sets *i.e.,* $P(E_1 \cup E_2)$.

Now, $P(E_1 \cup E_2) = P(E_1) + P(E_2) - P(E_1 \cap E_2)$

$$= 0.87 + 0.36 - 0.30 = 0.93$$

Hence, the required probability is 0.93.

Q.7 If A and B are mutually exclusive events, $P(A)=0.35$ and $P(B)=0.45$, find

(a) $P(A')$ (b) $P(B')$

(c) $P(A\cup B)$ (d) $P(A\cap B)$

(e) $P(A\cap B')$ (f) $P(A'\cap B')$

● **Concept Insight** If A and B are mutually exclusive events, then $P(A\cap B)=0$

Ans. Since, it is given that, A and B are mutually exclusive events *i.e.*, $A\cap B=\phi$

$\therefore$ $P(A\cap B)=0$

and $P(A)=0.35,\ P(B)=0.45$

(a) $P(A')=1-P(A)=1-0.35=0.65$

(b) $P(B')=1-P(B)=1-0.45=0.55$

(c) $P(A\cup B)=P(A)+P(B)-P(A\cap B)=0.35+0.45-0=0.80$

(d) $P(A\cap B)=0$

(e) $P(A\cap B')=P(A)-P(A\cap B)=0.35-0=0.35$

(f) $P(A'\cap B')=P(A\cup B)'=1-P(A\cup B)=1-0.80=0.20$

Q.8 A team of medical students doing their internship have to assist during surgeries at a city hospital. The probabilities of surgeries rated as very complex, complex, routine, simple or very simple are respectively, 0.15, 0.20, 0.31, 0.26 and 0.08. Find the probabilities that a particular surgery will be rated

(a) complex or very complex.

(b) neither very complex nor very simple.

(c) routine or complex.

(d) routine or simple.

Ans. Let E_1, E_2, E_3, E_4 and E_5 be the events that surgeries are rated as very complex, complex, routine, simple or very simple, respectively.

$\therefore$ $P(E_1)=0.15,\ P(E_2)=0.20,\ P(E_3)=0.31,\ P(E_4)=0.26,\ P(E_5)=0.08$

(a) P(complex or very complex) $=P(E_1 \text{ or } E_2)$

$=P(E_1\cup E_2)=P(E_1)+P(E_2)-P(E_1\cap E_2)$

$=0.15+0.20-0$ $[\because P(E_1\cap E_2)=0]$

$=0.35$

(b) P(neither very complex nor very simple) $=(P(E_1'\cap E_5')=P(E_1\cup E_5)'$

$=1-P(E_1\cup E_5)$

$=1-[P(E_1)+P(E_5)]$ $[\because P(E_1\cap E_5)=0]$

$=1-(0.15+0.08)$

$=1-0.23$

$=0.77$

(c) $P(\text{routine or complex}) = P(E_3 \cup E_2) = P(E_3) + P(E_2)$ $[\because P(E_3 \cap E_2) = 0]$

$= 0.31 + 0.20 = 0.51$

(d) $P(\text{routine or simple}) = P(E_3 \cup E_4) = P(E_3) + P(E_4)$ $[\because P(E_3 \cap E_4) = 0]$

$= 0.31 + 0.26 = 0.57$

Q.9 Four candidates *A, B, C, D* have applied for the assignment to coach a school cricket team. If *A* is twice as likely to be selected as *B* and *B* and *C* are given about the same chance of being selected, while *C* is twice as likely to be selected as *D*, what are the probabilities that

(a) *C* will be selected? (b) *A* will not be selected?

Ans. It is given that *A* is twice as likely to be selected as *B*.

$\therefore \quad P(A) = 2P(B)$

$\Rightarrow \quad \frac{P(A)}{2} = P(B)$

$\because$ *B* and *C* are given about the same chance of being selected.

i.e., $\quad P(B) = P(C)$

While *C* is twice as likely to be selected as *D*.

$\therefore \quad P(C) = 2P(D) \Rightarrow \quad P(B) = 2P(D)$

$\Rightarrow \quad \frac{P(A)}{2} = 2P(D) \Rightarrow \quad P(D) = \frac{P(A)}{4}$

Now, sum of probabilities = 1

$$P(A) + P(B) + P(C) + P(D) = 1$$

$$P(A) + \frac{P(A)}{2} + \frac{P(A)}{2} + \frac{P(A)}{4} = 1$$

$$\Rightarrow \quad \frac{4P(A) + 2P(A) + 2P(A) + P(A)}{4} = 1$$

$$\Rightarrow \quad 9P(A) = 4 \Rightarrow P(A) = \frac{4}{9}$$

(a) $P(C \text{ will be selected}) = P(C) = P(B) = \frac{P(A)}{2}$

$= \frac{4}{9 \times 2}$ $\left[\because P(A) = \frac{9}{4}\right]$

$= \frac{2}{9}$

(b) $P(A \text{ will not be selected}) = P(A') = 1 - P(A) = 1 - \frac{4}{9} = \frac{5}{9}$

Q.10 One of the four persons John, Rita, Aslam or Gurpreet will be promoted next month. Consequently the sample space consists of four elementary outcomes S = {John promoted, Rita promoted, Aslam promoted, Gurpreet promoted}. You are told that the chances of John's promotion is same as that of Gurpreet, Rita's chances of promotion are twice as likely as John's. Aslam's chances are four times that of John.

(a) Determine

P (John promoted), P (Rita promoted),

P (Aslam promoted), P (Gurpreet promoted).

(b) If A = {John promoted or Gurpreet promoted}, find $P(A)$.

Ans. Let E_1 = John promoted

E_2 = Rita promoted

E_3 = Aslam promoted

E_4 = Gurpreet promoted

Given, sample space, S = { John promoted, Rita promoted, Aslam promoted, Gurpreet promoted}

i.e., $S = \{E_1, E_2, E_3, E_4\}$

It is given that, chances of John's promotion is same as that of Gurpreet.

$P(E_1) = P(E_4)$

Rita's chances of promotion are twice as likely as John.

$P(E_2) = 2P(E_1)$

And Aslam's chances of promotion are four times that of John.

$P(E_3) = 4P(E_1)$

Now, $P(E_1) + P(E_2) + P(E_3) + P(E_4) = 1$ [$\because$ sum of probabalities = 1]

$\Rightarrow P(E_1) + 2P(E_1) + 4P(E_1) + P(E_1) = 1$

$\Rightarrow 8P(E_1) = 1$

$\therefore P(E_1) = \frac{1}{8}$

(a) P(John promoted) $= P(E_1) = \frac{1}{8}$

P(Rita promoted) $= P(E_2) = 2P(E_1) = 2 \times \frac{1}{8} = \frac{1}{4}$

P(Aslam promoted) $= P(E_3) = 4P(E_1) = 4 \times \frac{1}{8} = \frac{1}{2}$

P(Gurpreet promoted) $= P(E_4) = P(E_1) = \frac{1}{8}$

(b) A = {John promoted or Gurpreet promoted}

$\Rightarrow A = E_1 \cup E_4$

$\therefore P(A) = P(E_1 \cup E_4) = P(E_1) + P(E_4) - P(E_1 \cap E_4)$

$= \frac{1}{8} + \frac{1}{8} - 0$ [$\because P(E_1 \cap E_4) = 0$]

$= \frac{2}{8} = \frac{1}{4}$

Q.11 The accompanying Venn diagram shows three events, A, B and C and also the probabilities of the various intersections [for instance, $P(A \cap B) = 0.07$]. Determine

(a) $P(A)$ (b) $P(B \cap \overline{C})$

(c) $P(A \cup B)$ (d) $P(A \cap \overline{B})$

(e) $P(B \cap C)$ (f) Probability of exactly one of the three occurs.

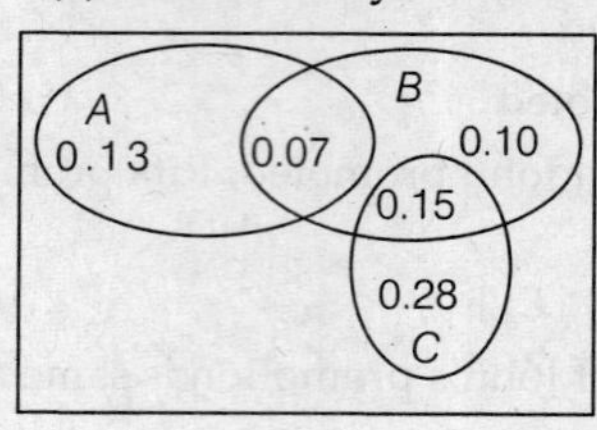

Ans. From the above Venn diagram,

(a) $P(A) = 0.13 + 0.07 = 0.20$

(b) $P(B \cap \overline{C}) = P(B) - P(B \cap C) = 0.07 + 0.10 + 0.15 - 0.15 = 0.07 + 0.10 = 0.17$

(c) $P(A \cup B) = P(A) + P(B) - P(A \cap B)$

$= 0.13 + 0.07 + 0.07 + 0.10 + 0.15 - 0.07$

$= 0.13 + 0.07 + 0.10 + 0.15 = 0.45$

(d) $P(A \cap \overline{B}) = P(A) - P(A \cap B) = 0.13 + 0.07 - 0.07 = 0.13$

(e) $P(B \cap C) = 0.15$

(f) P (exactly one of the three occurs)

$= P(A \cap \overline{B} \cap \overline{C}) + P(\overline{A} \cap \overline{B} \cap C) + P(\overline{A} \cap B \cap \overline{C})$

Now, $P(A \cap \overline{B} \cap \overline{C}) = P(A) - P(A \cap B) - P(A \cap C) = 0 \cdot 13 + 0 \cdot 07 - 0 \cdot 07 + 0 = 0.13$

$P(\overline{A} \cap \overline{B} \cap C) = P(C) - P(A \cap C) - P(B \cap C) = 0.28 + 0.15 - 0 - 0.15 = 0.28$

$P(\overline{A} \cap B \cap \overline{C}) = P(B) - P(A \cap B) - P(B \cap C) = 0.10 + 0.07 + 0.15 - 0.07 - 0.15 = 0.10$

$\therefore P(A \cap \overline{B} \cap \overline{C}) + P(\overline{A} \cap \overline{B} \cap C) + P(\overline{A} \cap B \cap \overline{C}) = 0.13 + 0.28 + 0.10 = 0.51$

Long Answer Type Questions

Q.12 One urn contains two black balls (labelled B_1 and B_2) and one white ball. A second urn contains one black ball and two white balls (labelled W_1 and W_2). Suppose the following experiment is performed. One of the two urns is chosen at random. Next a ball is randomly chosen from the urn. Then, a second ball is chosen at random from the same urn without replacing the first ball.

(a) Write the sample space showing all possible outcomes.

(b) What is the probability that two black balls are chosen?

(c) What is the probability that two balls of opposite colour are chosen?

Ans. It is given that one of the two urn is chosen, then a ball is randomly chosen from the urn, then a second ball is chosen at random from the same urn without replacing the first ball.

(a) $\therefore$ Sample space,

$S = \{B_1B_2, B_1W, B_2B_1, B_2W, WB_1, WB_2, BW_1, BW_2, W_1B, W_1W_2, W_2B, W_2W_1\}$

$\therefore$ Total sample points = 12

(b) If two black balls are chosen,

so, the favourable events are B_1B_2, B_2B_1 *i.e.*, 2 in number

$\therefore$ Required probability $= \frac{2}{12} = \frac{1}{6}$

(c) If two balls of opposite colour are chosen,

so, the favourable events are $B_1W, B_2W, WB_1, WB_2, BW_1, BW_2, W_1B, W_2B$ *i.e.*, 8 in number

$\therefore$ Required probability $= \frac{8}{12} = \frac{2}{3}$

Q.13 A bag contains 8 red and 5 white balls. Three balls are drawn at random. Find the probability that

(a) all the three balls are white.

(b) all the three balls are red.

(c) one ball is red and two balls are white.

Ans. $\because$ Number of red balls = 8

and number of white balls = 5

Total number of balls = 8 + 5 = 13

(a) $P(\text{all the three balls are white}) = \frac{^5C_3}{^{13}C_3} = \frac{\frac{5!}{3!2!}}{\frac{13!}{3!10!}} = \frac{5!}{3!2!} \times \frac{3!10!}{13!}$ $\left[\because {}^nC_r = \frac{n!}{r!(n-r)!}\right]$

$$= \frac{5 \times 4 \times 3 \times 2!}{2!} \times \frac{10!}{13 \times 12 \times 11 \times 10!} = \frac{5 \times 4 \times 3}{13 \times 12 \times 11}$$

$$= \frac{5}{13 \times 11} = \frac{5}{143}$$

(b) $P(\text{all the three balls are red})$

$$= \frac{^8C_3}{^{13}C_3} = \frac{\frac{8!}{3!5!}}{\frac{13!}{3!10!}} = \frac{8!}{3! \times 5!} \times \frac{3!10!}{13!}$$

$$= \frac{8 \times 7 \times 6 \times 5!}{5!} \times \frac{10!}{13 \times 12 \times 11 \times 10!}$$

$$= \frac{8 \times 7 \times 6}{13 \times 12 \times 11} = \frac{28}{143}$$

(c) P(one ball is red and two balls are white)

$$= \frac{{}^8C_1 \times {}^5C_2}{{}^{13}C_3} = \frac{\frac{8!}{7! \times 1!} \times \frac{5!}{2! \times 3!}}{\frac{13!}{3! \times 10!}}$$

$$= \frac{8 \times 7!}{7!} \times \frac{5 \times 4 \times 3 \times 2!}{2! \times 3!} \times \frac{3! \times 10!}{13 \times 12 \times 11 \times 10!}$$

$$= \frac{8 \times 5}{13 \times 11} = \frac{40}{143}$$

Q.14 If the letters of the word 'ASSASSINATION' are arranged at random. Find the probability that

(a) four S's come consecutively in the word.

(b) two I's and two N's come together.

(c) all A's are not coming together.

(d) no two A's are coming together.

Ans. Total number of letters in the word 'ASSASSINATION' is 13.

Out of which 3A's, 4S's, 2 I's, 2 N's, 1 T's and 1 O's.

(a) If four S's come consecutively in the word, then we considers these 4 S's as 1 group.

Now, the number of letters is 10.

S	S	S	S	A	A	A	I	I	N	N	T	O
1				9								

Number of words when all S's are together $= \frac{10!}{3!2!2!}$

Total number of words using letters of the word 'ASSASSINATION'

$$= \frac{13!}{3!4!2!2!}$$

$$\therefore \quad \text{Required probability} = \frac{\frac{10!}{3!2!2!}}{\frac{13!}{3!4!2!2!}}$$

$$= \frac{10! \times 4!}{13!} = \frac{4!}{13 \times 12 \times 11} = \frac{24}{1716} = \frac{2}{143}$$

(b) If 2 I's and 2 N's come together, then there are 10 alphabets.

Number of words when 2 I's and 2 N's come together

$$= \frac{10!}{3!4!} \times \frac{4!}{2!2!}$$

$$\therefore \quad \text{Required probability} = \frac{\frac{10!4!}{3!4!2!2!}}{\frac{13!}{3!4!2!2!}} = \frac{4!10!}{2!2!3!4!} \times \frac{3!4!2!2!}{13!}$$

$$= \frac{4!10!}{13!} = \frac{4! \times 10!}{13 \times 12 \times 11 \times 10!} = \frac{24}{13 \times 12 \times 11} = \frac{2}{143}$$

(c) If all A's are coming together, then there are 11 alphabets.
Number of words when all A's come together

$$= \frac{11!}{4!2!2!}$$

Probability when all A's come together

$$= \frac{\frac{11!}{4!2!2!}}{\frac{13!}{4!3!2!2!}} = \frac{11!}{4!2!2!} \times \frac{4!3!2!2!}{13!} = \frac{11! \times 3!}{13!}$$

$$= \frac{6}{13 \times 12} = \frac{1}{26}$$

Required probability when all A's does not come together

$$= 1 - \frac{1}{26} = \frac{25}{26}$$

(d) If no two A's are coming together, then first we arrange the alphabets except A's.

S	S	S	S	I	N	T	I	O	N

All the alphabets except A's are arranged in $\frac{10!}{4!2!2!}$ ways.

There are 11 vacant places between these alphabets.

So, 3 A's can be placed in 11 places in ${}^{11}C_3$ ways $= \frac{11!}{3!8!}$

$\therefore$ Total number of words when no two A's are coming together

$$= \frac{11!}{3!8!} \times \frac{10!}{4!2!2!}$$

$\therefore$ Required probability $= \frac{11! \times 10!}{3!8!4!2!2!} \times \frac{4!3!2!2!}{13!} = \frac{10!}{8! \times 13 \times 12}$

$$= \frac{10 \times 9}{13 \times 12} = \frac{90}{156} = \frac{15}{26}$$

Q.15 A card is drawn from a deck of 52 cards. Find the probability of getting a king or a heart or a red card.

Ans. $\because$ Total number of possible events of choosing cards = 52

and favourable events = 4 kings + 13 hearts + 26 reds − 13 − 2 = 28

$\therefore$ Required probability $= \frac{28}{52} = \frac{7}{13}$

Q.16 A sample space consists of 9 elementary outcomes $e_1, e_2, ..., e_9$ whose probabilities are

$$P(e_1) = P(e_2) = 0.08, P(e_3) = P(e_4) = P(e_5) = 0.1$$
$$P(e_6) = P(e_7) = 0.2, P(e_8) = P(e_9) = 0.07$$

Suppose $A = \{e_1, e_5, e_8\}$, $B = \{e_2, e_5, e_8, e_9\}$

(a) Calculate $P(A)$, $P(B)$ and $P(A \cap B)$.

(b) Using the addition law of probability, calculate $P(A \cup B)$.

(c) List the composition of the event $A \cup B$ and calculate $P(A \cup B)$ by adding the probabilities of the elementary outcomes.

(d) Calculate $P(\overline{B})$ from $P(B)$, also calculate $P(\overline{B})$ directly from the elementary outcomes of $\overline{B}$.

Ans. Given,

$$S = \{e_1, e_2, e_3, e_4, e_5, e_6, e_7, e_8, e_9\}$$
$$A = \{e_1, e_5, e_8\},\ B = \{e_2, e_5, e_8, e_9\}$$
$$P(e_1) = P(e_2) = 0.08$$
$$P(e_3) = P(e_4) = P(e_5) = 0.1$$
$$P(e_6) = P(e_7) = 0.2,\ P(e_8) = P(e_9) = 0.07$$

(a) $P(A) = P(e_1) + P(e_5) + P(e_8)$

$= 0.08 + 0.1 + 0.07 = 0.25$

Now, $P(B) = P(e_2) + P(e_5) + P(e_8) + P(e_9)$
$= 0.08 + 0.1 + 0.07 + 0.07 = 0.32$

$A \cap B = \{e_5, e_8\}$

$\therefore\ P(A \cap B) = P(e_5) + P(e_8) = 0.1 + 0.07 = 0.17$

(b) $P(A \cup B) = P(A) + P(B) - P(A \cap B) = 0.25 + 0.32 - 0.17 = 0.40$

(c) $A \cup B = \{e_1, e_2, e_5, e_8, e_9\}$

$\therefore\ P(A \cup B) = P(e_1) + P(e_2) + P(e_5) + P(e_8) + P(e_9)$
$= 0.08 + 0.08 + 0.1 + 0.07 + 0.07 = 0.40$

(d) $\because\ P(\overline{B}) = 1 - P(B) = 1 - 0.32 = 0.68$

and $\overline{B} = \{e_1, e_3, e_4, e_6, e_7\}$

$\therefore\ P(\overline{B}) = P(e_1) + P(e_3) + P(e_4) + P(e_6) + P(e_7)$
$= 0.08 + 0.1 + 0.1 + 0.2 + 0.2 = 0.68$

Q.17 Determine the probability p, for each of the following events.

(a) An odd number appears in a single toss of a fair die.

(b) At least one head appears in two tosses of a fair coin.

(c) A king, 9 of hearts or 3 of spades appears in drawing a single card from a well shuffled ordinary deck of 52 cards.

(d) The sum of 6 appears in a single toss of a pair of fair dice.

Ans. (a) When a die is throw, then possible outcomes are

$S = \{1, 2, 3, 4, 5, 6\}$ out of which 1, 3, 5 (i.e. 3 members) are odd,

$\therefore$ Required probability $= \frac{3}{6} = \frac{1}{2}$

(b) When a fair coin is tossed two times, then sample space is

$$S = \{HH, HT, TH, TT\}$$

For at least one head, favourable outcomes are HH, HT, TH

$\therefore$ Required probability $= \frac{3}{4}$

Mistake Alert ! *At least one heads means one or more heads, not just exactly one so always include all cases.*

(c) Total number of cards = 52

Number of favourable outcomes = 4 kings + 9 of hearts + 3 of spades

$= 4 + 1 + 1 = 6$

$\therefore$ Required probability $= \dfrac{6}{52} = \dfrac{3}{26}$

(d) When a pair of dice is rolled, then total sample point are 36. If sum is 6, then favourable outcomes are (1, 5), (5, 1), (2, 4), (4, 2) and (3, 3).

$\therefore$ Required probability $= \dfrac{5}{36}$

Objective Type Questions

Choose the correct answer out of four options in each of the exercises 18 to 29.

Q.18 In a non-leap year, the probability of having 53 Tuesday or 53 Wednesday is

(a) $\dfrac{1}{7}$ (b) $\dfrac{2}{7}$ (c) $\dfrac{3}{7}$ (d) None of these

Ans. ***(b)*** In a non-leap year, there are 365 days which means 52 weeks and 1 day. If this day is either a Tuesday or Wednesday, then the year will have 53 Tuesday or 53 Wednesday.

$\therefore$ Required probability $= \dfrac{2}{7}$

Mistake Alert ! *Students may get confused between the number of days in a leap year (366) and either a non-leap year (365).*

Q.19 Three numbers are chosen from 1 to 20. Find the probability that they are not consecutive

(a) $\dfrac{186}{190}$ (b) $\dfrac{187}{190}$ (c) $\dfrac{188}{190}$ (d) $\dfrac{18}{^{20}C_3}$

● **Concept Insight** The sum of the probability of an event occurring and the probability of the event not occurring is always 1.

Ans. ***(b)*** Since, the set of three consecutive numbers from 1 to 20 are 1,2,3; 2,3,4; 3,4,5; ....., 18, 19, 20 *i.e.*, 18 in numbers.

$$P\text{ (three numbers are consecutive)} = \frac{18}{^{20}C_3} = \frac{18}{\frac{20 \times 19 \times 18}{3 \times 2 \times 1}} = \frac{18}{1140} = \frac{3}{190}$$

$\therefore P$ (three numbers are not consecutive) $= 1 - \dfrac{3}{190} = \dfrac{187}{190}$

Q.20 While shuffling a pack of 52 playing cards, 2 are accidentally dropped. Find the probability that the missing cards to be of different colours.

(a) $\dfrac{29}{52}$ (b) $\dfrac{1}{2}$ (c) $\dfrac{26}{51}$ (d) $\dfrac{27}{51}$

Ans. ***(c)*** Since,in a pack of 52 cards, there are 26 red colour cards and 26 black colour cards.

$\therefore P(\text{both cards of different colours}) = \frac{26}{52} \times \frac{26}{51} + \frac{26}{52} \times \frac{26}{51}$

$= 2 \times \frac{26}{52} \times \frac{26}{51} = \frac{26}{51}$

Q.21 Seven persons are to be seated in a row. Then, the probability that two particular persons sit next to each other is

(a) $\frac{1}{3}$ (b) $\frac{1}{6}$ (c) $\frac{2}{7}$ (d) $\frac{1}{2}$

Ans. ***(c)*** If two persons sit next to each other, then consider these two persons as 1 group.

Now, we have to arrange 6 persons.

$\therefore$ Number of arrangements = $2! \times 6!$

Total number of arrangements of 7 persons = $7!$

$\therefore$ Required probability $= \frac{2!6!}{7!} = \frac{2}{7}$

Q.22 Without repetition of the numbers, four-digit numbers are formed with the numbers 0, 2, 3 and 5. The probability of such a number divisible by 5 is

(a) $\frac{1}{5}$ (b) $\frac{4}{5}$ (c) $\frac{1}{30}$ (d) $\frac{5}{9}$

● **Concept Insight** A number is divisible by 5, when unit place digit is zero or five.

Ans. ***(d)*** We have to form four-digit number using the digits 0, 2, 3 and 5 which are divisible by 5.

If 0 is fixed at unit place, then number of ways = $3 \times 2 \times 1 = 6$

If 5 is fixed at unit place, then number of ways = $2 \times 2 \times 1 = 4$

$\therefore$ Total four-digit numbers divisible by 5 $= 6 + 4 = 10$

Total number of four digit numbers = $3 \times 3 \times 2 \times 1 = 18$

$\therefore$ Required probability $= \frac{10}{18} = \frac{5}{9}$

Q.23 If A and B are mutually exclusive events, then

(a) $P(A) \le P(\overline{B})$ (b) $P(A) \ge P(\overline{B})$

(c) $P(A) < P(\overline{B})$ (d) None of these

Ans. ***(a)*** For mutually exclusive events,

$$P(A \cap B) = 0$$

$$P(A \cup B) = P(A) + P(B) - P(A \cap B)$$

$\Rightarrow$ $P(A \cup B) = P(A) + P(B)$

Now, $P(A) + P(B) \le 1$ $[\because P(A \cup B) \le 1]$

$\Rightarrow$ $P(A) + 1 - P(\overline{B}) \le 1$ $[\because P(B) = 1 - P(\overline{B})]$

$\therefore$ $P(A) \le P(\overline{B})$

Q.24 If $P(A \cup B) = P(A \cap B)$ for any two events A and B, then

(a) $P(A) = P(B)$ (b) $P(A) > P(B)$ (c) $P(A) < P(B)$ (d) None of these

● **Concept Insight** In this question, we will use the formula,
$P(A \cup B) = P(A) + P(B) - P(A \cap B)$

Ans. ***(a)*** Given, $P(A \cup B) = P(A \cap B)$

$\Rightarrow \quad P(A) + P(B) - P(A \cap B) = P(A \cap B)$

$\Rightarrow \quad [P(A) - P(A \cap B)] + [P(B) - P(A \cap B)] = 0$

But $\quad P(A) - P(A \cap B) \geq 0$

and $\quad P(B) - P(A \cap B) \geq 0 \quad [\because P(A \cap B) \leq P(A) \text{ or } P(B)]$

To satisfy (i), we must have

$\Rightarrow \quad P(A) - P(A \cap B) = 0$ and $P(B) - P(A \cap B) = 0$

[since, sum of two non-negative numbers can be zero only when these numbers are zero]

$\Rightarrow \quad P(A) = P(A \cap B)$

and $\quad P(B) = P(A \cap B)$

$\therefore \quad P(A) = P(B)$

Q.25 6 boys and 6 girls sit in a row at random. The probability that all the girls sit together is

(a) $\frac{1}{432}$ (b) $\frac{12}{431}$ (c) $\frac{1}{132}$ (d) None of these

Ans. ***(c)*** If all the girls sit together, then it is considered as 1 group.

$\therefore$ Arrangement of $6 + 1 = 7$ persons in a row is 7! and the girls interchanges their seats in 6! ways.

Total number of arrangements = 12!

$$\therefore \quad \text{Required probability} = \frac{6!7!}{12!} = \frac{6 \times 5 \times 4 \times 3 \times 2 \times 1 \times 7!}{12 \times 11 \times 10 \times 9 \times 8 \times 7!} = \frac{1}{132}$$

Q.26 A single letter is selected at random from the word 'PROBABILITY' The probability that it is a vowel is

(a) $\frac{1}{3}$ (b) $\frac{4}{11}$ (c) $\frac{2}{11}$ (d) $\frac{3}{11}$

Ans. ***(b)*** Total number of alphabets in the word PROBABILITY = 11

Number of vowels = 4

$\therefore$ Required probability, $P(\text{letter is a vowel}) = \frac{4}{11}$

Q.27 If the probabilities for A to fail in an examination is 0.2 and that for B is 0.3, then the probability that either A or B fails is

(a) > 0.5 (b) 0.5 (c) ≤ 0.5 (d) 0

Ans. ***(c)*** Given, $\quad P(A \text{ fails}) = 0.2$ and $P(B \text{ fails}) = 0.3$

$$\therefore \quad P(\text{either } A \text{ or } B \text{ fails}) \leq P(A \text{ fails}) + P(B \text{ fails})$$
$$\leq 0.2 + 0.3$$
$$\leq 0.5$$

Q.28 The probability that at least one of the events A and B occurs is 0.6. If A and B occur simultaneously with probability 0.2, then $P(\overline{A}) + P(\overline{B})$ is equal to

(a) 0.4 (b) 0.8 (c) 1.2 (d) 1.6

Thinking process First, find the value of $P(A) + P(B)$ by using the formula, $P(A \cup B) = P(A) + P(B) - P(A \cap B)$, then find $P(\overline{A}) + P(\overline{B})$ as $1 - P(A) + 1 - P(B)$ *i.e.*, $2 - [(P(A) + P(B)]$.

Ans. ***(c)*** Given, $P(A \cup B) = 0.6$ and $P(A \cap B) = 0.2$

$$\therefore \quad P(A \cup B) = P(A) + P(B) - P(A \cap B)$$

$$\Rightarrow \quad 0.6 = P(A) + P(B) - 0.2$$

$$\Rightarrow \quad P(A) + P(B) = 0.8 \quad \text{...(i)}$$

$$\therefore \quad P(\overline{A}) + P(\overline{B}) = 1 - P(A) + 1 - P(B)$$

$$= 2 - [P(A) + P(B)]$$

$$= 2 - 0.8 = 1.2 \quad \text{[from Eq. (i)]}$$

Q.29 If M and N are any two events, the probability that atleast one of them occurs is

(a) $P(M) + P(N) - 2P(M \cap N)$
(b) $P(M) + P(N) - P(M \cap N)$
(c) $P(M) + P(N) + P(M \cap N)$
(d) $P(M) + P(N) + 2P(M \cap N)$

Ans. ***(b)*** If M and N are any two events, then

$$P(M \cup N) = P(M) + P(N) - P(M \cap N)$$

State whether the statements are True or False in each of the exercises 30 to 36.

Q.30 The probability that a person visiting a zoo will see the giraffee is 0.72, the probability that he will see the bears is 0.84 and the probability that he will see both is 0.52.

Ans. *False*

Given, P (to see giraffee) = 0.72

P (to see bear) = 0.84

P (to see giraffee and bear) = 0.52

P (to see giraffee or bear) = P (to see giraffee) + P (to see bear) − P (to see giraffee and bear)

$$= 0.72 + 0.84 - 0.52 = 1.04$$

Which is not possible. Hence, statement is false.

Q.31 The probability that a student will pass his examination is 0.73, the probability of the student getting a compartment is 0.13 and the probability that the student will either pass or get compartment is 0.96.

Ans. *False*

Let A = Student will pass examination

and B = Student will get compartment

$$P(A) = 0.73,\ P(A \text{ or } B) = 0.96 \text{ and } P(B) = 0.13$$

$\therefore$ $P(A \text{ or } B) = P(A) + P(B) = 0.73 + 0.13 = 0.86$ $[\because P(A \cap B) = 0]$

But $P(A \text{ or } B) = 0.96$

Hence, it is a false statement.

Q.32 The probabilities that a typist will make 0, 1, 2, 3, 4, 5 or more mistakes in typing a report are respectively, 0.12, 0.25, 0.36, 0.14, 0.08, 0.11.

Ans. *False*

Sum of these probabilities must be equal to 1.

But $P(0) + P(1) + P(2) + P(3) + P(4) + P(5)$

$$= 0.12 + 0.25 + 0.36 + 0.14 + 0.08 + 0.11 = 1.06$$

which is greater than 1.

So, it is a false statement.

Q.33 If A and B are two candidates seeking admission in an engineering college. The probability that A is selected is 0.5 and the probability that both A and B are selected is at most 0.3. Is it possible that the probability of B getting selected is 0.7?

Ans. *False*

Here, $P(A) = 0.5$, $P(A \cap B) \leq 0.3$

Now, $P(A) \times P(B) \leq 0.3$ $[\because P(A \cap B) = P(A) \times P(B)$, for independent events$]$

$\Rightarrow$ $0.5 \times P(B) \leq 0.3$

$\Rightarrow$ $P(B) \leq 0.6$

$\therefore$ $P(B) \neq 0.7$

$\therefore$ It is a false statement.

Mistake Alert! *Do not confused between 'at most' and 'alteast'*

$\therefore$ *The probability that both A and B are selected is at most 0.3 i.e.,* $P(A \cap B) \leq 0.3$

Q.34 The probability of intersection of two events A and B is always less than or equal to those favourable to the event A.

Ans. *True*

We know that $P(A \cap B) \leq P(A)$

Hence, it is a true statement.

Q.35 The probability of an occurrence of event A is 0.7 and that of the occurrence of event B is 0.3 and the probability of occurence of both is 0.4.

Ans. *False*

Here, $P(A) = 0.7$

$P(B) = 0.3$

and $P(A \cap B) = 0.4$

$\because$ $P(A \cap B) \le P(A)$ and $P(A \cap B) \le P(B)$

Here, $0.4 \le 0.7 = P(A)$

But $0.4 \not\le 0.3 = P(B)$

Hence, it is a false statement.

Q.36 The sum of probabilities of two students getting distinction in their final examinations is 1.2.

Ans. *True*

Since, these two are events not related to the same sample space.

So, sum of probabilities of two students getting distinction in their final examination may be 1.2.

Hence, it is a true statement.

Fill in the blanks in the exercises 37 to 41.

Q.37 The probability that the home team will win an upcoming football game is 0.77, the probability that it will tie the game is 0.08 and the probability that it will lose the game is ....

Ans. P(lossing the game) $= 1 - (0.77 + 0.08) = 1 - 0.85 = 0.15$

Q.38 If e_1, e_2, e_3 and e_4 are the four elementary outcomes in a sample space and $P(e_1) = 0.1$, $P(e_2) = 0.5$ and $P(e_3) = 0.1$, then the probability of e_4 is ....

Ans. $\because$ e_1, e_2, e_3 and e_4 are outcomes of a sample space

$\therefore$ $P(e_1) + P(e_2) + P(e_3) + P(e_4) = 1$

$\Rightarrow$ $0.1 + 0.5 + 0.1 + P(e_4) = 1$

$\Rightarrow$ $0.7 + P(e_4) = 1$

$\therefore$ $P(e_4) = 1 - 0.7 = 0.3$

Q.39 Let $S = \{1, 2, 3, 4, 5, 6\}$ and $E = \{1, 3, 5\}$, then $\overline{E}$ is ....

Ans. Here, $S = \{1, 2, 3, 4, 5, 6\}$

and $E = \{1, 3, 5\}$

$\therefore$ $\overline{E} = S - E = \{2, 4, 6\}$

Q.40 If A and B are two events associated with a random experiment such that $P(A) = 0.3$, $P(B) = 0.2$ and $P(A \cap B) = 0.1$, then the value of $P(A \cap \overline{B})$ is ....

Thinking Process Use the formula, $P(A \cap \overline{B}) = P(A) - P(A \cap B)$ and simplify it.

Ans. $P(A \cap \overline{B}) = P(A) - P(A \cap B) = 0.3 - 0.1 = 0.2$

Q.41 The probability of happening of an event A is 0.5 and that of B is 0.3. If A and B are mutually exclusive events, then the probability of neither A nor B is ....

Ans. $P(\overline{A} \cap \overline{B}) = P(\overline{A \cup B}) = 1 - P(A \cup B)$ $[\because P(A \cup B)' = P(A' \cap B')]$

$= 1 - [P(A) + P(B)]$ [since, A and B are mutually exclusive events]

$= 1 - (0.5 + 0.3) = 1 - 0.8 = 0.2$

Q.42 Match the proposed probability under column C_1 with the appropriate written description under column C_2.

	Column C_1 (Probability)		Column C_2 (Written Description)
(a)	0.95	(i)	An incorrect assignment
(b)	0.02	(ii)	No chance of happening
(c)	− 0.3	(iii)	As much chance of happening as not
(d	0.5	(iv)	Very likely to happen
(e)	0	(v)	Very little chance of happening

Ans. (a) 0.95 is very likely to happen, as it is close to 1.

(b) 0.02 very little chance of happening because probability is very low.

(c) − 0.3 an incorrect assignment because probability of any event lie between 0 and 1.

(d) 0.5, as much chance of happening as not, because sum of chances of happening and not happening is one.

(e) 0 is no chance of happening.

$\therefore$ (a) → (iv), (b) → (v), (c) → (i), (d) → (iii), (e) → (ii)

Q.43 Match the following.

	Column I		Column II
(a)	If E_1 and E_2 are the two mutually exclusive events	(i)	$E_1 \cap E_2 = E_1$
(b)	If E_1 and E_2 are the mutually exclusive and exhaustive events	(ii)	$(E_1 - E_2) \cup (E_1 \cap E_2) = E_1$
(c)	If E_1 and E_2 have common outcomes, then	(iii)	$E_1 \cap E_2 = \phi, E_1 \cup E_2 = S$
(d)	If E_1 and E_2 are two events such that $E_1 \subset E_2$	(iv)	$E_1 \cap E_2 = \phi$

Ans. (a) If E_1 and E_2 are two mutually exclusive events, then $E_1 \cap E_2 = \phi$.

(b) If E_1 and E_2 are mutually exclusive and exhaustive events, then $E_1 \cap E_2 = \phi$ and $E_1 \cup E_2 = S$.

(c) If E_1 and E_2 have common outcomes, then $(E_1 - E_2) \cup (E_1 \cap E_2) = E_1$ (as show below)

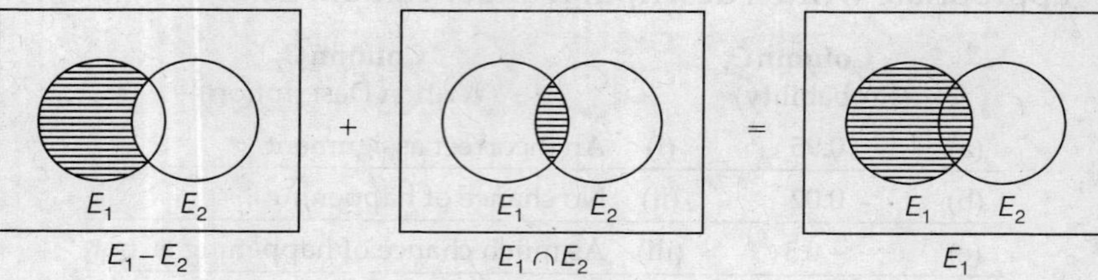

(d) If E_1 and E_2 are two events such that $E_1 \subset E_2 \Rightarrow E_1 \cap E_2 = E_1$ (as show below)

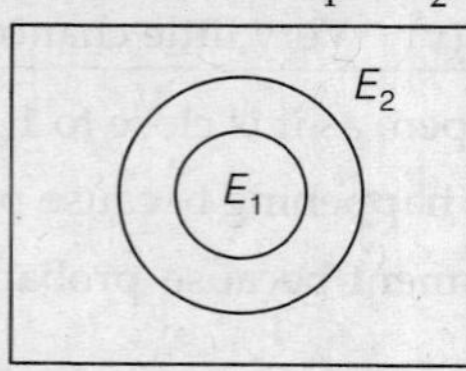

$\therefore$ (a) $\rightarrow$ (iv), (b) $\rightarrow$ (iii), (c) $\rightarrow$ (ii), (d) $\rightarrow$ (i)